UNITED STATES
ARMY

UNITED STATES
ARMY

THE DEFINITIVE ILLUSTRATED HISTORY

D. M. Giangreco

STERLING
New York

Dedication

For Ike Skelton, whose passion for professional
military education—and military history in
particular—has had a profound and lasting effect
on two generations of soldiers.

PAGE 1: Standard-bearers proudly display the colors of the 34th
New York Infantry, c. 1863. The regiment was mustered into Federal
service on June 15, 1861, and ultimately assigned to the Army of
the Potomac's II Corps. The 34th New York lost three officers and
ninety enlisted men killed and mortally wounded as well as another
officer and sixty-eight enlisted men to disease.

PAGE 2: World War I recruiting poster

PAGE 3: Members of the 3d Infantry Regiment (Old Guard) drill
team perform their precision movements at Fort Eustis, Virginia,
during Super Day festival in 2006.

OPPOSITE: Fort Myer, Virginia, commandant, Colonel Jonathan M.
Wainwright, gets generals' stars upon promotion to brigadier
general, November 1, 1938. The highest ranking non-commissioned
officers of the post, Sergeant Major Timothy Carragher (left) of
the 16th Field Artillery, and Sergeant Major Frank Benegas of the
3d Cavalry, were chosen to make the presentation.

PAGE 6–7: A 1943 poster created for the War Department by Brown
& Bigelow of St. Paul, Minnesota, honoring the courage of the United
States Infantry during World War II.

PAGE 8: World War I recruiting poster created by Harry S. Mueller,
an infantry major in the U.S. Army.

PAGE 9: A member of the Joint Ceremonial Honor Guard stands
at attention at the Lincoln Memorial on the National Mall in
Washington, D.C.

Contents

SCHLAIKJER 1943

Introduction

Freedom doesn't come easy. Ask the sergeant helping train an Iraqi infantry battalion who, four tours and ten long years ago, was a young private conducting weapons searches in Baghdad's slums. Perhaps a soldier struggling to keep the HMMWV trucks in his unit's motor pool running in spite of the choking dust of southern Afghanistan might have some thoughts on this, or a 2d Infantry Division trooper forward deployed near the Demilitarized Zone separating a vibrant South Korea from the misery that is North Korea. Ask a veteran of Vietnam, Korea, or World War II—whose numbers grow ever smaller.

From the earliest days of the republic through to the dawn of a new century, the number of young men, and in recent times, women, who have worn the uniform of the United States Army—be it blue-died wool, khaki cotton, or a modern "battle dress uniform"—has reached into the tens of millions. Yet even during the "big" wars, the army has always been a force stretched painfully thin. When not fighting the British and the Mexicans during the seven decades between the Revolution and the Civil War, the size of the army generally averaged about five to six thousand men before the numbers gradually floated up into the range of about nine thousand. After the Civil War and Reconstruction the number of soldiers spread from seacoast garrisons to isolated frontier forts hovered in the narrow range of twenty-six to twenty-eight thousand. And all of these totals are, frankly, on the high side as desertion and death—more often from sickness than combat—took their toll.

After the Spanish-American War, the size of the army fluctuated wildly but only once dipped below 65,000 as new possessions—stretching from the Caribbean and Panama Canal all the way across the Pacific to the Philippines—and growing storm clouds in Europe required a larger and more professional force. It was more than twice this size between the World Wars, but still considered small and ineffectual by the "Great Powers" of Europe and even the Asian littoral. After the next global war, the army quickly shed more than six million men, and though it would never again be required to raise and sustain such a massive force, its ranks would swell and deflate time and time again for wars along Asia's periphery. Throughout it all, the United States Army, a mixture

ABOVE: Sergeant John Mills of the 1st Infantry, c. 1861. Mills enlisted in the regiment in 1808 and the arm full of hash marks represent fifty-three years of his continual service. The sergeant is wearing his regulation full dress uniform, including a frock coat, sash, non-commissioned officers sword, and "Hardee" hat.

of both professional and citizen soldiers, never failed its fellow Americans.

The secret of the army's success is, in many ways, not a secret at all. Although its "body" is plain for all to see—personnel, weapons, bases—what makes it an army and not a well-armed mob ready to dissolve under the stress of combat, is its "soul"—an intangible flame called *esprit de corps*, the unity of purpose and will to win that is fundamental to victory. Leadership, training, and discipline instilled in America's soldiers is all undergirded by an institutional culture that is fundamentally historical in nature. The army cherishes its past, especially its combat history, and units preserve their histories, proudly displaying them in crests, patches, and regi-

mental mottoes. Ceremony and custom nourish the army's institutional memory, and its traditions reinforce this *esprit de corps* and the distinctiveness of the profession.

Yet even *esprit de corps* goes only so far. An army of both professional and citizen soldiers—a national army—is affected in fundamental and profound ways by the character of the nation and the will of its people to resist the forces that would destroy it. Since its founding, the army has often been severely tried by the indifference, and even hostility, of many of those it protects. But the army did, and does, persevere. As it always has, it salutes smartly and its soldiers do their duty, all while upholding the highest ideals of the nation's founders.

As each generation of soldiers came forth and then faded away, the exhilaration, the terror, the crushing boredom and frustrations of soldiering in war and peace passes inexorably from living memory as America rushes on to its destiny. Throughout it all, more men, and now women, have stepped up. At different times in our nation's history they have entered the army through the compulsion of a military draft. More often they have volunteered, as four generations of Americans have since U.S. forces left Vietnam in 1972 when volunteers alone supported a Cold War army averaging more than three-quarters of a million active duty soldiers for nearly two decades.

During the first battles of the twenty-first century, some supporters of the armed forces and the war against the trans-national Islamic extremists who attacked America warned that the nation's now shrunken army could break under the strain of a two-front war. Meanwhile, critics and pundits confidently predicted that enlistments would dry up and that National Guardsmen—who they imagined had "only joined for the benefits"—would flee the service when their terms were up now that they were actually being sent off to fight.

None of this happened. Young Americans stepped up yet again by the tens of thousands, year in and year out, to enlist and reenlist, into the Active Army, Guard, and Reserves, knowing full well what lay ahead. In the second longest war in our nation's history, victory was achieved in Iraq, and the fight still goes on to ensure that Afghanistan never again becomes a sanctuary for those who would attack America.

ABOVE: The original concept sketch created by the J.H. Wilson Company in 1880 for the seal of the Headquarters of the Army of the United States. The design was approved by General William T. Sherman, who signed the bottom right corner. The original sketch now resides in the Office of the Secretary of the Army.

Chapter One

Creating a Continental Army, 1607–1782

The birth of the U.S. Army can be traced back to the training bands the colonists formed to protect themselves in a new land. The training bands, or "trainbands," were principally made up of Englishmen who brought with them the tradition of an organized militia dating back to the time of Henry II. Many U.S. Army units can actually trace their lineage back to the Revolutionary or Civil Wars. Others within the National Guard trace their heritage to these early settlers, with some units currently serving at home and abroad extending back to the trainbands of the seventeenth century. The 181st Infantry Regiment's Company A, based in Worcester, Massachusetts, for example, originally was formed in 1632, and four years later became part of the Massachusetts Bay Colonial Militia when the trainbands—centered in Charlestown, New Town, Concord, Watertown, and Dedham—were organized into a single regiment, one of three raised to fight the Pequot Indian tribe. (It was mobilized into federal service, along with thousands of other guardsmen from the state, after the attacks on the United States on September 11, 2001.)

The constant danger presented by France, Spain, and the native tribes soon encouraged all of the other colonies but one, Pennsylvania, to organize their scattered forces into militias with formal organizations and regular training periods. All males of military age were obligated to serve when called and to provide their own weapons. From this large pool, which could include every farmer and townsman from sixteen to sixty years old, most colonial governments attempted to establish a core force similar to that of Massachusetts, where the legislature declared that a third of its militia "shall be ready at half an hour's warning." This was the birth of the "Minuteman" concept that would prove so effective nearly 150 years later at Lexington and Concord.

The various colonies organized and disbanded units as needed to face sudden emergencies, and they remained strictly local defense forces capable of operating for only short periods of time within their own county and colony. During King Philip's War, however, the militias of Massachusetts, Rhode Island, and Connecticut—plus the allied Pequot and Mohegan (Mohawk) tribes—acted in concert against the Wampanoag, Narragansett, Podunk, and Nipmuck peoples under Wampanoag leader Metacom. Derisively nicknamed "King Philip" after the Spanish monarch because of his open disdain of the English, Metacom was eventually hunted down and killed by a Ranger Company made up of colonists and Indians under Captain Benjamin Church. In all, more than six hundred colonists and three thousand Indians, both allied and enemy, died during raids on villages and towns along the New England frontier during 1675 and 1676. Though Connecticut towns largely escaped

ABOVE: George Washington's gorget (the symbol of an officer's commission) pointedly displaying Virginia's seal. Authorized by royal decree earlier that century, it pronounces Virginia a kingdom equal in rank to Great Britain, France (still claimed by the king), and Ireland.

OPPOSITE: Washington as colonel of the Virginia Regiment during the French and Indian War. Although fully trained and combat-experienced, the regiment was not recognized as part of the British Army, and Washington was subject to the orders of mere lieutenants of the regulars. When a new British commander was sent to Boston in 1756, Washington presented himself in a style calculated to reflect his rank and the prestige of Virginia, with both he and his aide wearing the gold-trimmed uniform he had designed. Though unsuccessful at first, it was decreed the following year that provincial officers would no longer be subject to regulars of lesser rank. In the 1758 British drive to take a key French fort at present-day Pittsburgh, Washington commanded the advance brigade with the temporary rank of brigadier general.

RIGHT: Much lighter than metal breastplates worn by the earliest colonists, "buff coats," with or without sleeves, as well as thickly padded quilt jackets, were the principal uniforms worn by American militiamen in the seventeenth and early eighteenth centuries. The thick leather of buff coats gave adequate protection against the cutting edge of swords and frequently stopped or slowed the penetration of arrows. The worn and carefully mended example here is probably of English origin.

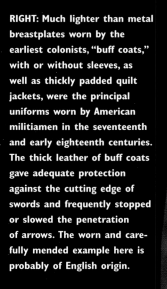

ENGLISH MATCHLOCK MUSKET, C. 1675

The effective range of this weapon was approximately thirty yards. A slow-burning matchcord of loosely braided cord depressed into a flashpan containing gun power when the trigger was pulled, firing the lead ball at the target. Its average rate of fire was two rounds a minute, and required great caution because the lighted matchcord was always in close proximity to the powder. Note the rest fork midway along the barrel. A musket of this type weighed roughly sixteen pounds and required a rest (also pictured above) to steady it for firing.

RIGHT: English sword, c. 1620. Well into the eighteenth century, virtually all weapons used in the colonies were manufactured in England.

ABOVE: On December 13, 1636, the General Court of the Massachusetts Bay Colony ordered the organization of militia companies in three formations: the North, South, and East regiments. Patterned on the English militia system, all males between ages sixteen and sixty were obligated to possess arms, drill once a week, and provide guard detail each evening to sound the alarm in case of attack. This was in response to the Pequot Indians' ongoing siege of Fort Saybrook in Connecticut, which ground on throughout that fall and winter. As spring arrived in 1637, the Pequots stepped up their raids, and the growing threat to the Massachusetts Bay Colony kept the militia in a high state of readiness. The first muster of the East Regiment, illustrated above, took place early in 1637, and their lineage today is carried on by the 101st Engineer Battalion, Massachusetts Army National Guard. The 101st Infantry Regiment continues the North Regiment's heritage.

unharmed, the colony allowed its militia to serve beyond its borders, and more than one hundred of its men were killed helping their fellow colonists.

Connecticut, Rhode Island, lower New York, and most of Massachusetts were now almost completely free of hostile Indians, and the Royal Navy protected their ports from invasion. Consequently, the militia units in these areas fell into disuse and all too frequently became little more than ceremonial artifacts. In Tidewater Virginia, the militia companies that existed as more than paper formations were usually manned by indentured servants. The muster rolls listed the names of plantation owners, bound by law to furnish their quota of men, with a figure for the number of servants provided. To the west and north, it was a different story. Indian raids, often including French colonists and even soldiers, continued to plague Maine, New Hampshire, New York, and northern Massachusetts, keeping outnumbered militia companies busy for nearly eighty years before the turmoil along the frontier erupted into full-scale war. These units, whether formally established or ad hoc, were made up of individuals who had lived all their lives in this dangerous setting. Their skills would serve their country well in the coming years.

FRENCH AND INDIAN WAR

France continued to encourage, finance, and play an active role in raids on English settlements and expanded their activities south into the strategic Ohio Valley, claimed by Virginia. In 1754, twenty-two-year-old Colonel George Washington led Virginia's militiamen—and, due to battlefield circumstances, British soldiers, or "regulars"—in fights against these marauders at the beginning of the French and Indian War. Large numbers of troops were sent from Britain and supplemented by colonial forces whose training, motivation, and leadership varied radically from one unit to the next. British regular officers came to heartily distrust the militias, who were just as apt to take flight as fight, and at first didn't recognize the value of the colonials' irregular tactics that were suited to fighting in the wilderness. For example, during the disastrous battle of Monongahela, when ranks of red-coated troops were mowed down by unseen foes shooting from the woods, the Virginia militia knew exactly what to do and did not need Colonel Washington, who was elsewhere on the battlefield, to issue them specific orders. According to British Army historian J.W. Fortescue:

> The Virginians alone, who were accustomed to such work, kept their presence of mind, and taking shelter behind the trees began to answer the Indian fire in Indian fashion. A few of the British strove to imitate them as well as their inexperience would permit; but [General Edward] Braddock would have none of such things. Such fighting was not prescribed in the drill-book nor familiar in the battlefields of Flanders, and he would tolerate no such disregard of order and discipline. Raging and cursing furiously, he drove British and Virginians alike back to their fellows with his sword.

ABOVE: George Washington and his troops, approximately three hundred Virginia volunteers and one hundred regulars, retreat from Fort Necessity in western Pennsylvania. The brief siege of Washington's hastily built fort (Indians allied to the British referred to it as "that little thing in the meadow") marked the beginning of the French and Indian War in July 1754.

General Braddock was killed and much of his force was destroyed before Washington, with great difficulty, extricated the survivors from the fight. The value of such techniques soon became so clear that, in spite of what Fortescue called a "bigotry in favour of European methods," other British commanders soon strove to adopt the more flexible tactics of the colonists, forming "light" units to support their more numerous European-styled regiments. They were particularly impressed with the colonial Ranger units. Some of which, like His Majesty's Independent Companies of Rangers ("Rogers' Rangers"), time and time again saved the scalps of the king's scarlet-coated soldiers during the confusion of wilderness warfare.

England defeated the French and in 1763 assumed control over the area east of the Mississippi that stretched from the southern tip of Florida (ceded to the British by Spain in

LEFT: A contingent of Ottawas, Potawatomis, and Chippewas led by Charles Michel de Langlade ambush British Major General Edward Braddock and his advance "detachment" of thirteen hundred troops as they prepare to march against Fort Duquesne in western Pennsylvania. Nearly all of the British and Provincial officers, including Braddock, fell in the July 9, 1755, Battle of Monongahela, but Colonel George Washington staved off a massacre of the force by forming an ad hoc rear guard of grenadiers, Virginia Rangers, and soldiers from some of the regular line companies. Other survivors of the ordeal included future generals who served on both sides during the American Revolution: Charles Lee, Daniel Morgan, Horatio Gates, and Thomas Gage.

exchange for Britain's newly acquired French Louisiana) up through the Great Lakes and beyond—a vast, untapped empire in itself. Also that year, King George III in London decreed that most of the newly acquired territory was off-limits to new colonization and reserved for the use of the American Indians. The colonies immediately saw this as a distant power's complete disregard of their right to use the Western Territories as they saw fit. The war also had been enormously expensive. Britain's attempts to expand imperial authority in the colonies and impose taxes to help cover these costs—even though the colonists, as Englishmen in America, had no representation in Parliament—was deeply resented. British authorities seldom referred to their citizens in the colonies as Englishmen, instead calling them "provincials," but more and more, they looked upon themselves as a separate people: Americans.

Patrick Henry and the Virginia legislature denounced the Stamp Act of 1765 as "taxation without representation." Americans broke into tax offices and burned the stamps that were to be affixed to certain items—like playing cards, marriage licenses, and sheet music—requiring the payment of a tax. The level of opposition astonished the British, who thought the Stamp Act was a fair way of producing the revenue needed to pay for the defense of the colonies. In the next few years, additional taxes imposed upon other goods, such as paper, paint, and glass, further angered Americans. Emotions ran high in Boston, where tax officials were occasionally mistreated. This caused the British to dissolve the Massachusetts legislature and station two regiments there. This agitated Americans even more, prompting widespread protests and a number of violent incidents, like the Boston

OPPOSITE BOTTOM: The halberd of a British Cold Stream Guards sergeant from the French and Indian War period. Halberds were carried in colonial militias and up through the American Revolution. They were used by noncommissioned officers to direct soldiers on the march and "dress" their ranks on parade or in firing lines, but sergeants in light units carried firearms instead.

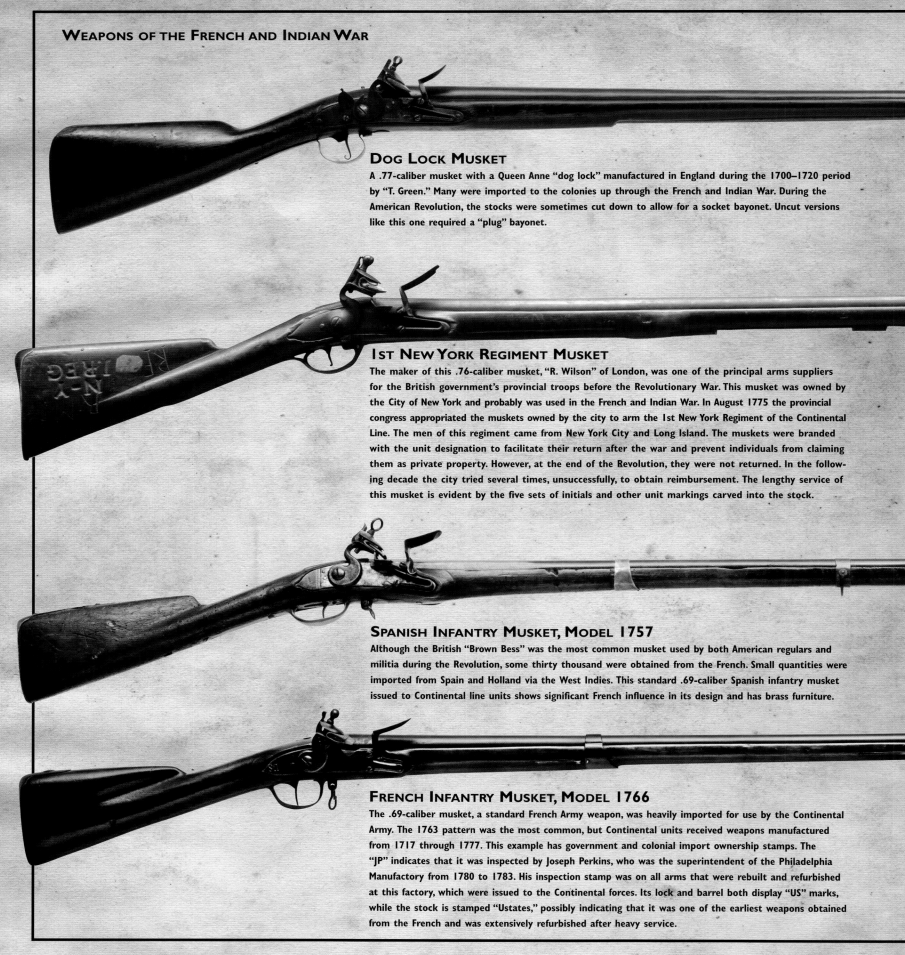

DOG LOCK MUSKET

A .77-caliber musket with a Queen Anne "dog lock" manufactured in England during the 1700–1720 period by "T. Green." Many were imported to the colonies up through the French and Indian War. During the American Revolution, the stocks were sometimes cut down to allow for a socket bayonet. Uncut versions like this one required a "plug" bayonet.

1ST NEW YORK REGIMENT MUSKET

The maker of this .76-caliber musket, "R. Wilson" of London, was one of the principal arms suppliers for the British government's provincial troops before the Revolutionary War. This musket was owned by the City of New York and probably was used in the French and Indian War. In August 1775 the provincial congress appropriated the muskets owned by the city to arm the 1st New York Regiment of the Continental Line. The men of this regiment came from New York City and Long Island. The muskets were branded with the unit designation to facilitate their return after the war and prevent individuals from claiming them as private property. However, at the end of the Revolution, they were not returned. In the following decade the city tried several times, unsuccessfully, to obtain reimbursement. The lengthy service of this musket is evident by the five sets of initials and other unit markings carved into the stock.

SPANISH INFANTRY MUSKET, MODEL 1757

Although the British "Brown Bess" was the most common musket used by both American regulars and militia during the Revolution, some thirty thousand were obtained from the French. Small quantities were imported from Spain and Holland via the West Indies. This standard .69-caliber Spanish infantry musket issued to Continental line units shows significant French influence in its design and has brass furniture.

FRENCH INFANTRY MUSKET, MODEL 1766

The .69-caliber musket, a standard French Army weapon, was heavily imported for use by the Continental Army. The 1763 pattern was the most common, but Continental units received weapons manufactured from 1717 through 1777. This example has government and colonial import ownership stamps. The "JP" indicates that it was inspected by Joseph Perkins, who was the superintendent of the Philadelphia Manufactory from 1780 to 1783. His inspection stamp was on all arms that were rebuilt and refurbished at this factory, which were issued to the Continental forces. Its lock and barrel both display "US" marks, while the stock is stamped "Ustates," possibly indicating that it was one of the earliest weapons obtained from the French and was extensively refurbished after heavy service.

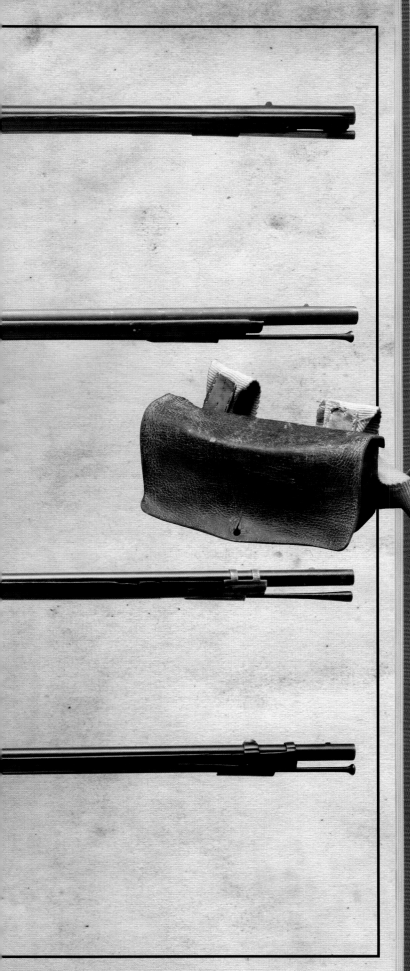

ROGERS' RANGERS

In the late 1750s, Major Robert Rogers of New Hampshire formalized certain standing orders for his men. Commonsense directives, such as marching spread out "so one shot can't go through two men," posting sentries when the men stopped to eat, and acting "the way you would if you was sneaking up on a deer" when on the march, were considered radical—even dangerous—by Rogers' British superiors. Yet they proved sound practices when confronting an enemy in the forests of New England, and they are just as relevant for Special Forces soldiers in the mountains of Afghanistan today. Because Rogers' men frequently fought as light-infantry shock troops in direct support of larger conventional forces (much as today's U.S. Army Rangers are trained to do) while also engaging in long-term, largely independent missions (which generally characterize current Special Forces operations), both modern-day organizations lay claim to Rogers' Rangers as predecessors.

LEFT: *A standard-issue ammunition box, or "cartouche," from the Revolutionary period with twenty-three holes (in rows of eight, seven, and eight) drilled into a wooden block to hold paper cartridges. A pick and small brush on a lightweight chain were usually attached to the linen sling to ease the breaking of the powder-filled cartridges.*

ABOVE: *Snowshoe-clad Rangers fight their French and Indian enemies during a winter battle.*

ABOVE: Americans fall on Lexington Green as ranks of redcoats fire on militiamen who already had started to disperse when the skirmish erupted. The British force continued on to Concord, where a small amount of military supplies were destroyed. The survivors of the Lexington Green fight, now joined by companies from nearby towns, fought the British again during the redcoats' costly retreat to Boston on April 19, 1775.

ABOVE RIGHT: The powder horn of 1st Lieutenant Reuben Hoar of the 1st Hampshire County Regiment, Massachusetts militia, was made in 1758 by Hoar's brother Leonard for Reuben to use in the French and Indian War.

Massacre of 1770 and the Boston Tea Party in 1773. The British response was to close the port of Boston in 1774. The colonies, in turn, sent members to a newly established Continental Congress in Philadelphia, whose delegates organized an economic boycott of Great Britain in protest, and petitioned the king for a redress of grievances.

LEXINGTON AND CONCORD

British policies finally pushed its American colonies into armed revolt in 1775 when, late on the night of April 18, a thousand British troops marched from Boston to seize supplies of gunpowder stored twenty miles away at Concord. Patriots learned of the impending operation and militiamen Paul Revere and William Dawes galloped through the night, taking separate roads, to warn the countryside that the British were on the march.

At Lexington the following morning, the king's troops found a company of seventy Minutemen drawn up on the village green. The British commander ordered the "rebels" to disperse. Some unknown soldier fired a shot, and then a British volley killed eight Americans in what was to begin eight years of war that ended with an independent nation.

The redcoats continued to Concord, where they found another contingent of Massachusetts militia that had learned of the bloody confrontation at Lexington and fired "the shot heard round the world." The British succeeded in seizing the powder, but as they retraced their long march along the hot, dusty road, Minutemen by the hundreds were arriving at the scene. Enraged at the British assault and the burning of houses by retreating troops, the Minutemen kept up a steady fire from behind trees and stone walls and refused to become engaged when contingents were sent to drive them away at the point of their bayonets. As soon as British skirmishers withdrew to the road, the Minutemen would simply follow in their wake and continue their deadly harassment. By the time the British reached the safety of their fortifications at Charlestown, across the river from Boston, they had lost nearly three hundred men.

News of Lexington and Concord electrified the colonies. Men left their accustomed tasks of keeping the store and plowing the field to take up arms and strike a blow for freedom. In Virginia, Patrick Henry, who the month before had made the speech in which he said "Give me liberty, or give me death!" assembled 350 men for drill at Culpeper Court House. As part of their rustic, homemade uniforms, Henry's men wore green hunting shirts with white letters spelling "Liberty or Death" sewn across the front. In the regiment formed at Charleston, South Carolina, the militia wore silver badges on their caps with the same motto. Meanwhile, across New England, farmers took down the muskets hanging over chimney places and hurried to join the militia surrounding Boston.

During the night of June 16, 1775, Americans occupied the high ground across the bay from Boston. Intending to fortify the larger and more defensible Bunker Hill, they mistakenly began their work on the smaller Breed's Hill. The next day, British warships bombarded them, and the colonials watched redcoats forming for an attack straight up the slope. Colonel Israel Putnam passed the word along: "Boys, don't shoot till you can see the whites of their eyes." Twice the British advanced with parade-ground precision up the hill. Twice the colonials held their fire until the last second and then poured it on. The British fell back and formed for a third assault, but the Americans had run out of ammunition and were forced to give up the hill after losing 450 men. The redcoats had taken the hill, but in doing so they lost 1,054 men out of twenty-five hundred. The British were stunned by the losses, and General Henry Clinton remarked in his diary that "...another such victory and we are utterly undone."

BELOW LEFT: This powder horn was carried by Peter Vanorder in 1780 while he served in the Second Regiment of the Orange County militia, which garrisoned Fort Stanwix in New York's hotly contested Mohawk Valley. The outline of the fort is engraved on the horn and shows a bird's-eye view of the fortification.

BELOW: Colonel William Smallwood's 1st Maryland Battalion of the Continental line leaves Annapolis in July 1776 to meet up with George Washington's army on Long Island, New York. Smallwood proved to be an effective leader and rose to the rank of major general.

BUNKER HILL/BREED'S HILL

After the Battle of Lexington and Concord, militia forces from throughout the New England colonies poured into the Boston area and stiffened the siege of the city begun by the Massachusetts militia. The British garrison also was reinforced by sea and rose to some sixty-five hundred men. With more troops now on hand, they decided to occupy some of the high ground on either side of the surrounding bay. Learning of British plans, the New Englanders immediately countered by dispatching a force under Colonel William Prescott on the night of June 16, 1775, to the Charlestown peninsula where Bunker and Breed's hills overlooked Boston from the north.

Against orders, Prescott, Colonel Israel Putnam, and chief engineer Captain Richard Gridley decided to build the redoubt on Breed's Hill, closer to Boston—but the morning light showed why Bunker Hill originally had been picked. Located on a wider part of the peninsula, Breed's Hill could be outflanked easily, and this is precisely what the British force of more than three thousand men planned to do. After rowing across the bay, they formed ranks to the east, in front of the hill, and northeast along the Mystic River, then attacked the redoubt and the open ground to its north, intending to sweep around behind the defenders.

The New Englanders, however, moved quickly to minimize the danger created by their earlier mistake. The slow buildup of British regulars gave them time to fortify the area between the redoubt and the wide Mystic River as Connecticut, then New Hampshire, then Massachusetts units were fed into the left (northern) flank as quickly as they arrived. British soldiers ran into a storm of shot from the farmers and townsmen, leaving great numbers of dead and wounded on the field. A second assault against the redoubt and flank ended with the same result.

Despite its success against the British regulars, the colonial rear was mired in confusion, and Colonel Putnam had great difficulty moving the diverse assortment of units where they were needed. The British massed for one last, desperate attempt, this time straight up the hill. Though suffering terrible losses, the British managed to reach the redoubt and adjoining breastworks, where defenders were running out of ammunition and had few reinforcements. Redcoats and a contingent of Royal Marines swarmed over the fortifications, and widespread hand-to-hand combat erupted across the crest of the hill. Yet, the decimated British were unable to take full advantage of the situation, and the militias were able to remove their wounded, withdrawing to the west. Further efforts to surround the colonials by pressing forward again along the Mystic River flank were frustrated by the steady fighting withdrawal along that front led by Colonel John Stark (1st New Hampshire

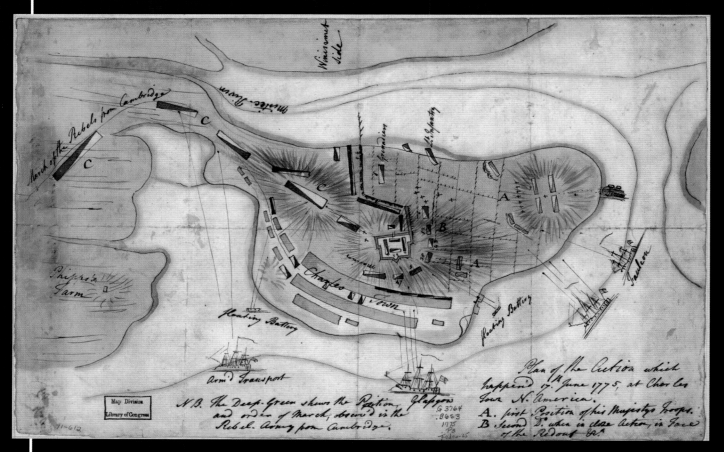

ABOVE: *This 1775 map represents the "Plan of the Action which happen'd 17th. June 1775, at Charles Town, N. America." The pink bands on the southern side of the peninsula represent the village. A failed British attempt to outflank the redoubt along the open ground to the north precipitated a series of disastrous frontal attacks up the eastern slope of Breed's Hill.*

Regiment) and Captain Thomas Knowlton (commanding a Connecticut battalion). A surprised British general, John Burgoyne, later described the militias' retreat as "no flight; it was even covered with bravery and military skill."

The flag of King George now flew over the Charlestown peninsula, but the new Army of New England was firmly entrenched in Cambridge Heights, dominating any movement inland. The British, twice within sixty days, precipitated battles in which their already-outnumbered forces lost far more soldiers—particularly among officers and sergeants—than the "armed rabble" that they fought. Other than some minor forays, no more offensive operations were launched from the city in the bay.

ABOVE: British troops pour into the redoubt atop Breed's Hill. Most of the New Englanders' losses occurred in the later stages of the battle, including the president of the Massachusetts provincial congress, Dr. Joseph Warren, who was shot dead by a British officer.

2ND MODEL SHORT PATTERN BROWN BESS MUSKET

This .75-caliber Brown Bess was made in Dublin, Ireland. The barrel shows signs of regimental markings and the escutcheon has all the markings of the 5th Regiment, Light Company. The Light Company was involved in the assault of Breed's or "Bunker Hill," where they were heavily engaged. This musket shows signs of very heavy use.

As news of the battle spread, the realization struck home that all the colonies, not just Massachusetts, faced a war with the most powerful country in the world. The Continental Congress provided for a "Continental Army"—the beginning of a regular force serving the nation rather than individual states. It accomplished this by adopting the New England Army at Boston as an American Army on June 14, 1775, and passed a resolution that "a general be appointed to command all the continental forces, raised, or to be raised, for the defence of American liberty." This resolution established the beginnings of the United States Army, and the next day Congress chose George Washington to be its commander in chief.

On July 2, now-General Washington arrived in Cambridge, Massachusetts, to assume command of the seventeen thousand poorly trained New England troops besieging Boston. He tightened the siege, blocking all roads, while the British garrison simply held on, awaiting reinforcements from England. Though appalled by his own troops' lack of discipline, the civilian-soldiers had proved that they could stand up to British regulars, and Washington endeavored to have them engaged only in defensive battles until their training could be improved. Washington could neither attack the city, nor could he force a British withdrawal until its defense became hopeless. He was desperately short of both powder and cannons to accomplish this, but understood that unless he did so prior to the arrival of British troops, the margin for victory would be extremely slim.

To obtain powder and cannons, Washington sent Colonel Henry Knox westward to the well-stocked fortress of Fort Ticonderoga in upper New York, seized by Colonel Ethan Allen's Green Mountain Boys the previous May, to haul its many cannons to Boston. Through the bitter winter weather, Knox's men used oxen and sleds to drag the huge guns, disassembled into pieces to lighten their weight, through the snowbound countryside.

In all, fifty-one cannons, including five great 24-pounders, and eight heavy mortars and howitzers suitable for siege warfare, were safely delivered into Washington's hands and reassembled. On March 4, 1776, a force of American infantry and artillery took Dorchester Heights, from which their cannons could dominate Boston and its sea approaches. Recognizing that the situation was hopeless, the British evacuated the city on St. Patrick's Day. Driving the enemy from Boston was a satisfying conclusion to the city's decade of troubles, but long, dark days lay ahead before final victory would be won.

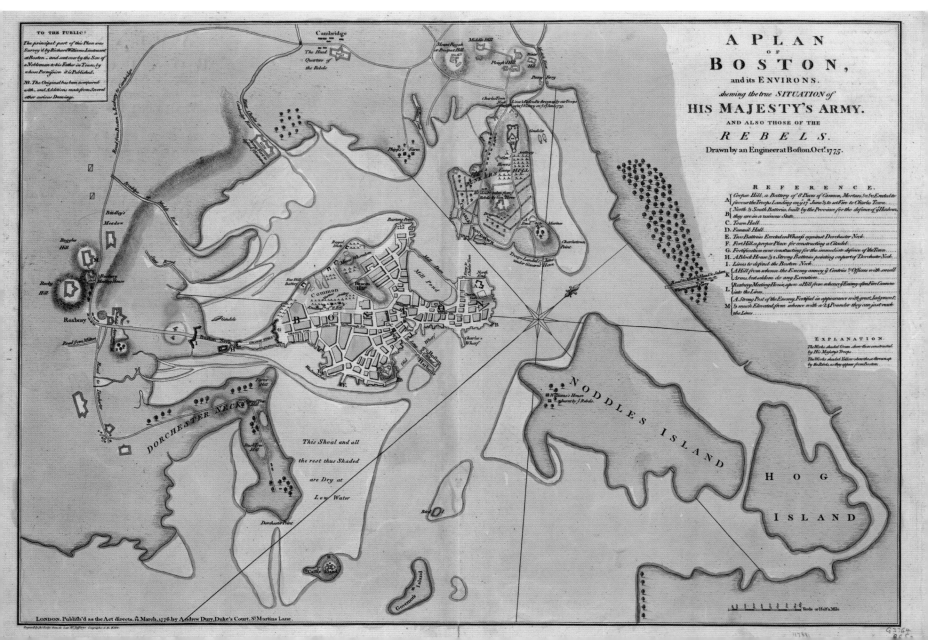

BACKGROUND: The seizure of British forts at Crown Point by Colonel Benedict Arnold and Ticonderoga by Captain Ethan Allen in May 1775 brought a windfall of 197 pieces of artillery to the Continental Army. George Washington's chief of artillery Colonel Henry Knox selected fifty-nine weapons from among its eighty-six pieces for the hard, overland journey to Boston. Disassembled, they weighed nearly sixty tons. Heavy barges were used to float the weapons whenever possible, but during most of the first two hundred miles, the "noble train of artillery" was loaded upon stout sleds and dragged through the snow by oxen.

Upon reaching Springfield, the artillery was pulled in wagons by teams of horses to Framingham for reassembly and to await specially made ammunition from New York. Smaller cannons immediately were incorporated into Washington's field forces, but the fourteen mortars, two howitzers, twelve 18-pounder plus single 24-pounder cannons were held for the coming seizure of Dorchester Heights, which commanded Boston and its harbor. Because of the speed required to build and set up the battery of heavy weapons, more than two thousand men and four hundred oxen were gathered for the March 4, 1776, operation, which rendered the British occupation of the city untenable.

OPPOSITE BACKGROUND: On August 22, 1776, a force of twenty thousand British and Hessian troops landed on the southwestern tip of Long Island. Five days later, a surprise attack up the Jamaica-Bedford road against the American left flank crumpled the entire defense line. Continental troops panicked in the face of enemy bayonet charges, but a determined stand by the 1st Maryland Regiment under Colonel William Alexander (Lord Stirling) prevented most of the soldiers from being captured. The largely disorganized mass of men fled to the fortifications on Brooklyn Heights, but instead of the British pressing the assault and perhaps capturing much of the Continental Army, they dug in for a siege, wary of a repeat of the bloody battle at Breed's Hill. For George Washington, with the East River to his back, there could be no withdrawal to a next line of defense on high ground. So, on the night of August 29, he skillfully evacuated his nine-thousand-man force and all its equipment to Manhattan before the Royal Navy could block his retreat.

LONG ISLAND TO PRINCETON

Washington knew that his army was in for a difficult struggle that could last for many years. With Boston's fine port denied to the British, the new Continental Army marched toward New York because it was obvious that the city's harbor, a much more difficult site to defend, would be Britain's next target. Meanwhile, the Continental Congress made the decision that turned the rebellion into a war for independence. It issued a declaration that summed up the grievances and closed with this pledge: "And for the support of this declaration, with firm reliance on the protection of Divine Providence, we mutually pledge to each other our lives, our fortunes, and our sacred honor." Now it was up to the army to make that Declaration of Independence stick.

LEFT: This regimental drum of a Massachusetts unit is embellished with a pine tree symbol used throughout the Revolutionary period. The Latin text on the scrollwork means "It's sweet and distinguished to die for one's country."

RIGHT: After defeats at White Plains and Fort Washington in New York, General Washington and his remaining forty-four hundred men retreat through New Jersey in November 1776. The Continentals were pursued by an advance guard of ten thousand British and Hessian troops until they crossed the Delaware River into Pennsylvania.

Some two and a half months after Washington had reached New York, the British Army, including a large Hessian German contingent whom George III had hired to assist in the invasion, arrived on nearby Staten Island with a force approximately three times that of the Continentals. Confronted with such an overwhelming force of highly trained troops, Washington realized the futility of trying to hold New York and requested authority from Congress to abandon the city. When this request was refused, he set about establishing the best defense within his capabilities. With the British encamped only a few miles away on Staten Island, the possibility existed for an attack either on New York proper or on Long Island.

The southern end of Long Island was crowned by Brooklyn Heights; by the emplacement of a few cannons there, whoever held the Heights could dominate New York City. Washington believed that a strong enough force here, particularly if it fought a defensive battle from well-prepared fortification, could force the British into as costly a fight as at Breed's Hill, from which they might withdraw. However, denying this strategic location from the British while also protecting New York proper compelled Washington to divide his forces.

The British chose to attack Brooklyn Heights, and there, at the Battle of Long Island, Washington suffered a thumping defeat on August 27, 1776. His army lost 2,905 men—almost eight times the number of British casualties—with more than a thousand captured. Washington's army, in fact, might have been forced to surrender en mass had it not been for Colonel John Glover and his 14th Continental Regiment from Marblehead, Massachusetts, who used their skill as boatmen to successfully evacuate more than nine thousand troops across the East River during the night of August 29.

LONG ISLAND 1776

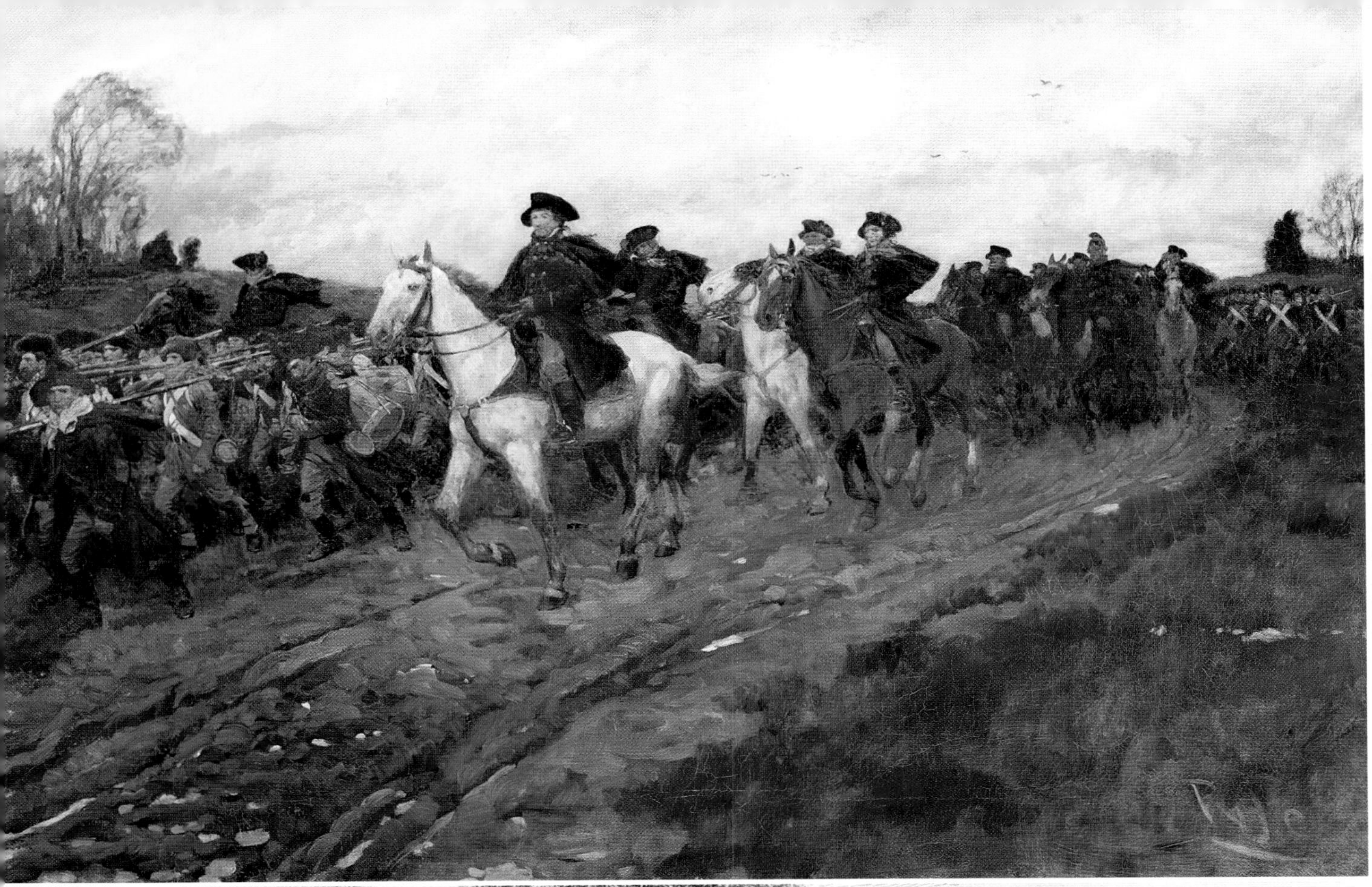

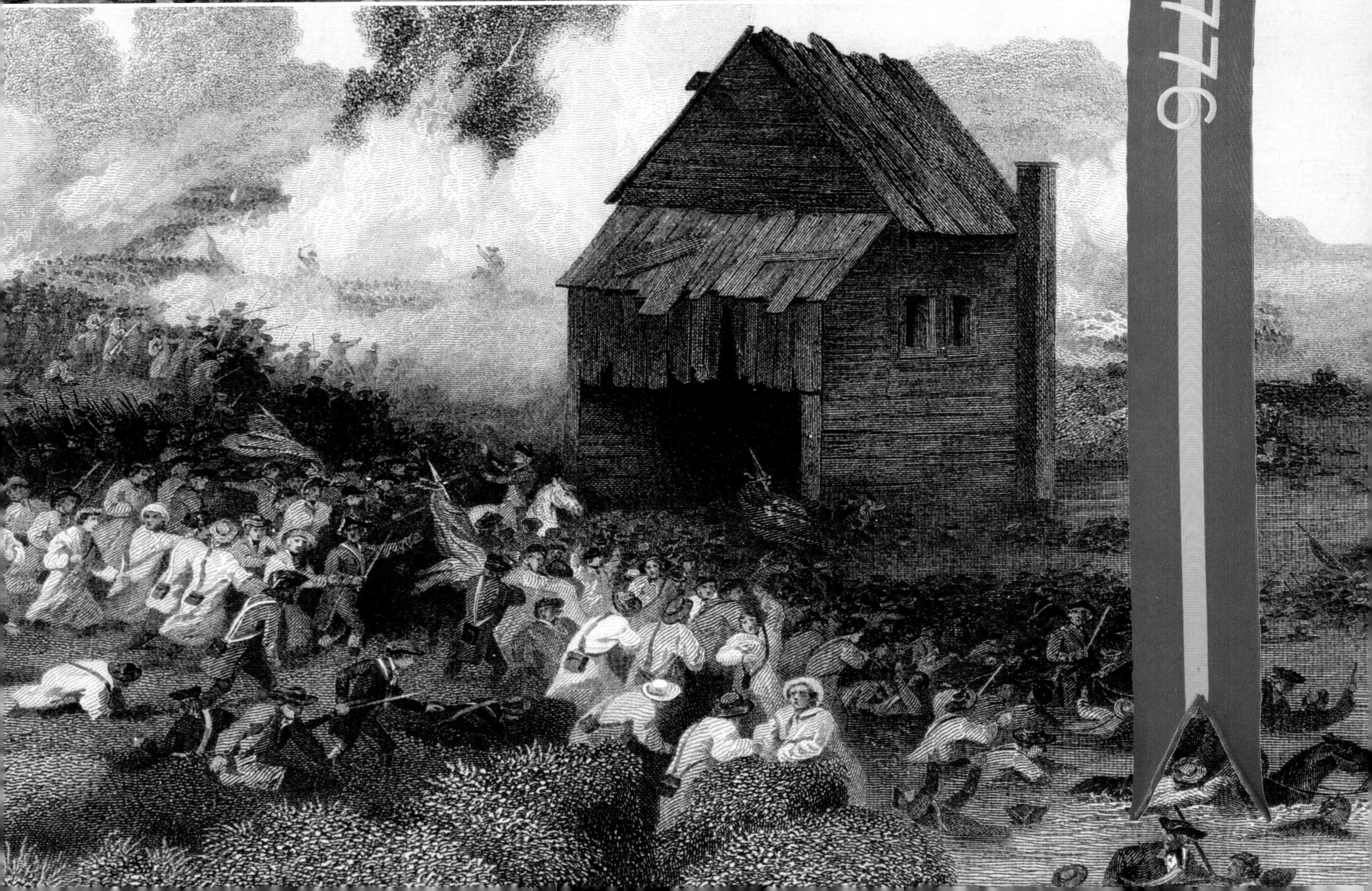

Now Washington needed a spy to gather as much information as possible on British intentions. Captain Nathan Hale volunteered for the mission but was captured with incriminating notes and was ordered to be hanged. Hale went bravely to his death, knowing he would be an example to his fellow patriots. His last words were: "I only regret that I have but one life to lose for my country."

The Continentals were compelled to retreat first to New York, and then, through bitter winter weather, across New Jersey, just ahead of the British, who were led by General Charles Cornwallis. When they came to the Delaware River near Trenton, New Jersey, Washington ordered all the boats along the Delaware seized, and in December, rowed across to Pennsylvania before the British arrived. Upon reaching the other bank, they could finally rest and gather supplies because there were no longer any boats available to the British. Outrunning the British, though, was hardly a victory, and Washington knew that the nation needed a win to keep up its spirits. Plus, with many soldiers near the end of their one-year enlistments, such a victory needed to come sooner rather than later as an encouragement to sign up for another year. But with little to show except a record of defeat and retreat, even Washington was in despair: "If every nerve is not strained to recruit a new army, I think the game is pretty nearly up."

Then Washington hit upon a bold idea. The British had left a number of Hessian regiments to establish winter outposts between the British Army and the Continentals. Washington judged that their thirteen-hundred-man garrison at Trenton was vulnerable to attack, particularly after a raucous night of Christmas celebrations. Christmas Eve 1776 was a miserable day. It rained and hailed and sleeted. By evening, a cold wind sprang up and it began to snow. Cakes of ice filled the river. These were the conditions when Washington attacked the garrison. Late Christmas night, Glover's fishermen-turned-soldiers ferried the little force of twenty-four hundred men across the icy Delaware in relays. After marching nine miles through a blinding snowfall as the Hessians celebrated before their fireplaces in Trenton, the men reached their destination.

At 8 A.M. the ragged, half-frozen Americans arrived at the edge of the town, and the Germans awoke to the sound of gunfire, yelling, and a charging infantry. Hitting the town from both the west and north, American muskets and rifles drove Hessian sentries to cover, and kept up a hot fire against Hessian lines struggling to form in the streets. Lieutenant James Monroe, eighteen years old and a future president of the United States, charged into the town at the head of a company of Virginia infantry. He fell wounded, but now Americans were sweeping through the streets. At the head of King Street, Captain Alexander Hamilton's artillery battery went into action. A pair of Hessian cannons went off. Hamilton spotted them. A counterattack was forming. His brass 3-pounders roared, then others joined. The fire at the head of King Street broke up the counterattack. After forty-five minutes of this, the Hessians had had enough. The whole garrison surrendered. (Today, Hamilton's battery is D Battery of the 5th Field Artillery Regiment. The only unit in the active army showing battle credit for the Revolutionary War, it has deployed to Iraq in 2003.)

Leaving three regiments to guard his base at Princeton, New Jersey, Cornwallis marched the rest of his troops toward Trenton. The Continentals dug in behind a small creek, and Cornwallis waited till the next morning to attack. Posting a few men to keep campfires going all night to deceive the British, Washington gathered his army and slipped out, marched around the British, and headed for Princeton. Nearing the redcoat base, the Americans met two of the regiments that had been left behind but were then on their way to join Cornwallis at Trenton. The British opened fire, and at first the Americans fell back, but Washington rode up to rally them until veteran New England and Pennsylvania troops arrived, and the entire body pressed forward.

One badly mauled British regiment fled south toward safety with the main British force, while the Continentals drove the other regiment ahead of them into Princeton. There still was another British regiment in the town, but that was not enough to stop the Americans, who fought their way through. With the British in New Jersey now scattered and apprehensive, Washington led his exhausted men to the Morristown area, where they camped for the rest of the winter while embarrassed British commanders and politicians bickered over why the Continental Army had not been destroyed.

ABOVE: A pair of silver-mounted officer's pistols belonging to George Washington (likely presented to him as a gift). Washington subsequently gave them to his nephew, Bartholomew Dandridge Jr., who served as a private secretary during Washington's presidency.

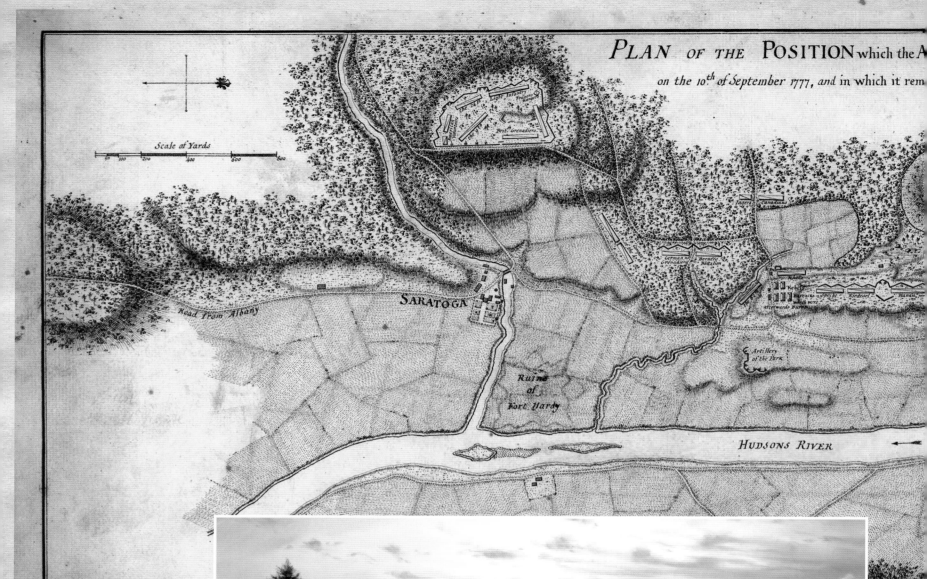

PLAN OF THE POSITION which the A[...]
on the 10th of September 1777, and in which it rem[...]

SARATOGA

Road from Albany

Ruins of Fort Hardy

Artillery of the Park

HUDSONS RIVER

71-659

RIGHT: Morgan's Rifles and Massachusetts Continentals turn the flank of the Brunswick Grenadiers at the Breymann Redoubt. This October 7, 1777, action was the turning point of the second battle at Saratoga and the nearly month-long effort to contain and defeat Lieutenant General John Burgoyne's campaign to divide New England from the other colonies. Colonel Daniel Morgan's newly formed Provisional Rifle Corps was comprised of about five hundred specially selected marksmen from Pennsylvania, Maryland, and Virginia.

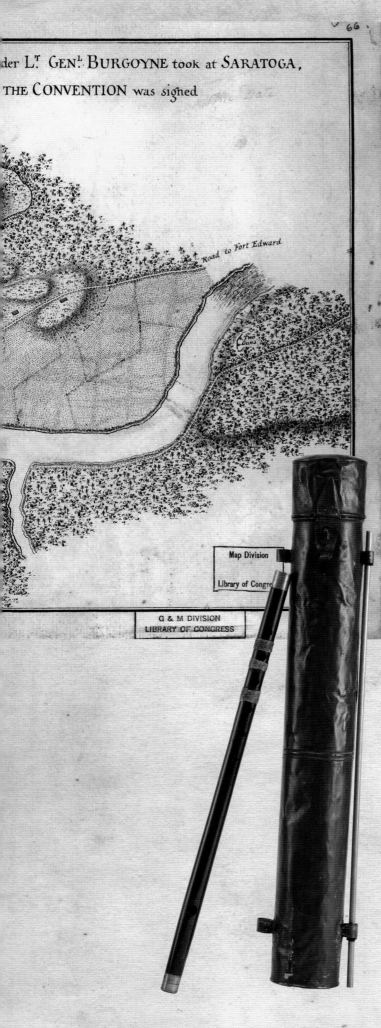

der Lt. Genl. BURGOYNE took at SARATOGA,

THE CONVENTION was signed

Road to Fort Edward

Map Division

Library of Congre

G & M DIVISION
LIBRARY OF CONGRESS

SARATOGA

Having survived the winter, the Continental Army was threatened by a new danger in the summer of 1777. In order to divide the colonies along the vital Hudson River, the British intended to seize Albany, New York, by simultaneous advances from Canada and New York City. A smaller British force under Colonel Barrimore Matthew St. Leger was marching eastward down the Mohawk Valley with the intent of meeting General John Burgoyne near Albany. The British attack from New York never materialized, instead becoming pointlessly diverted toward Philadelphia, but General Burgoyne marched according to plan with a strong British force from Canada to the Hudson River Valley. Americans checked St. Leger's column in the Mohawk Valley, but Burgoyne was certain that his force alone could reach Albany and then march down the Hudson to cut the colonies in two. As the threat from Canada grew, more New England volunteers arrived to join the growing number of New Yorkers with General Horatio Gates' Continental Army in the northern part of the state.

Although many American units contained at least a few riflemen within their ranks, most were made up principally of soldiers armed with far less accurate muskets. Washington had organized the army's first all-rifle regiment under Colonel Daniel Morgan, and now he told the commander that he was sending him and his riflemen to join Gates. Morgan's riflemen hurried northward, but his first concern was to make sure that every man's weapon was in perfect shape. The rifle was a distinctive American weapon. Its grooved barrel gave the bullet a spinning motion, which made it travel farther and much straighter than the round ball fired by musketeers. Morgan stopped at Bethlehem, Pennsylvania, where master gunsmith Daniel Kleist personally examined each man's rifle and made whatever adjustments were necessary.

A few miles from Saratoga, the Americans dug in on Bemis Heights along the Hudson River. The British arrived on September 19, and as they approached, Morgan's riflemen advanced on the left in a long, broken line through the woods on Freeman's Farm. Imitating wild turkey calls to signal their positions, these sharpshooters took cover behind trees and fences and fired down the British ranks. During the next four hours, the marksmen kept the British confused, and only the arrival of British cannons saved them from a rout. The Americans returned to their lines that night, while the British began digging in around Freeman's Farm.

The opposing forces jockeyed for position during the following weeks, but the American strength was growing. Burgoyne saw that his British Army was being hemmed in, and decided to send out fifteen hundred men with General Simon Fraser on October 7, to test the American defenses on the heights. Gates then sent a message: "Order on Morgan to begin the game." Morgan's riflemen fanned out again to hit the British on the left— over almost the same ground where they had fought the previous Battle of Freeman's Farm. Once more, wild turkey calls echoed through the woods as sharpshooters took up positions as skirmishers. Morgan called several of his best marksmen around him, and pointing to the British general he said, "That officer

LEFT: A map of the defenses thrown up by British and contract German forces on October 10, 1777. Lieutenant General John Burgoyne's retreat to this spot came after his defeat at the Second Battle of Saratoga (often referred to as the Battle of Bemis Heights). Surrounded by constantly increasing Continental forces and militia, he was forced to surrender his surviving 6,222 troops a week later on October 17. A few officers were exchanged for captured Americans. But during the next few years, most of the British troops, as well as many of the Germans who passed into American captivity, were paroled or allowed to "escape" and remain in the former colonies. Some joined the Continental Army in the closing stages of the war.

LEFT INSET: A military fife used during the Revolutionary War by a soldier named M. Mumbler, and carried during the War of 1812 by Cambridge musician Nathaniel Munro, who fought with Lieutenant Colonel Joseph Valentine's Regiment of Massachusetts militia. The fife has a crack, which was repaired at some point with glue and string.

RIGHT TOP: During the Saratoga Campaign, British Colonel Barry St. Leger moved his force of seven hundred regulars plus one thousand loyalists and native allies across New York from Lake Ontario with the objective of joining forces with John Burgoyne at Albany. St. Leger laid siege to Fort Stanwix in the Mohawk Valley, and two days later the Tryon County militia under Brigadier General Nicholas Herkimer set out to relieve the fort. They were ambushed in a wooded ravine near Oriskany, where the militia, under the direction of a mortally wounded Herkimer, scattered in the woods and fought a bloody afternoon's battle in a summer thunderstorm. Both sides suffered heavy losses. Although the militia was unable to relieve Stanwix, the losses and raids from the fort discouraged St. Leger's Indians, who already were restless. They abandoned the effort, forcing the British and loyalists to give up the siege and turn back.

RIGHT BOTTOM: A kettle drum from the band of the British 9th Regiment of Foot (later, the Royal Norfolk Regiment), which surrendered to American forces after the Battle of Saratoga in 1777. Drums played an important part in military discipline, recruiting, and in the pomp and ceremony of armies well into the twentieth century.

is General Fraser; I admire him, but he must die; our victory depends on it. Take your stations in that clump of bushes, and do your duty." Within five minutes, Fraser fell mortally wounded.

The British fell back, and sensing that a sudden strike might collapse their line, General Benedict Arnold, Gates' second in command, ordered a general attack on the British entrenchments. The first assault on the line's center was repulsed with heavy losses, but Arnold then struck the right flank, which gave way completely. The British were forced to withdraw hastily, abandoning some five hundred sick and wounded in their camp. Now far outnumbering the British, the Continentals followed closely when they retreated to Saratoga. The British were nearly surrounded, and Burgoyne, seeing that he was in a tight spot, sent a message asking for help from British forces at New York. American soldiers captured the messenger. Nevertheless, a British force did start up the Hudson, but it was too late. Burgoyne surrendered his entire army, and after the surrender met Morgan. Extending his hand, the British general said, "My dear sir, you command the finest regiment in the world."

The American victory at Saratoga in September and October 1777 had brought America its first major victory over a British field army, and it led directly to an alliance with France, greatly complicating the war for the British. Although it was truly a turning point in the war, and one of the decisive battles of world history, it was important that Americans had such a victory to look upon, for during the next two years there was little else to brighten the dismal picture. Darkest of all was the miserable winter of 1777–1778, which Washington's little Continental Army spent at Valley Forge, Pennsylvania. Yet, it was in those cold, dark days that the United States Army had its real beginning.

ABOVE: General John Burgoyne reportedly surrendered this sword after the Battle of Saratoga as depicted in this engraving. It is a "British Officer's small sword," c. 1768, with the arms of the Georgian period bearing the initials "G.R." (*Georgius Rex*, Latin for George the King) under a crown. However, the blade of this sword is engraved "C.R." for "Charlotte Regina," the wife of George III and the Queen of England. Thus, the original owner of this sword was a member of a "Queens" regiment.

ABOVE: Assault on the Chew House during the October 4, 1777, Battle of Germantown. Some fifty-seven Continental soldiers—more than a third of all the Americans killed in the battle—died in a series of ill-considered assaults on six British companies that were cut off behind American lines. George Washington's failure to deal a telling blow to a detached portion of the British Army at Germantown prolonged the occupation of Philadelphia, and it remained under British control until the following summer.

VALLEY FORGE AND STONY POINT

Washington's men went into Valley Forge in December 1777 as a battered, sick, and hungry lot. During that month, more than two thousand men were unfit for duty for lack of shoes and clothing. By February this number was four thousand. The Marquis de Lafayette, a young Frenchman who had offered his services to Washington, commanded a division at Valley Forge. He reported, "Their feet and legs froze until they grew black, and it was often necessary to amputate them." Food was as scarce as clothing. Time after time, Washington ordered provisions but they failed to arrive. The soldiers' diet was likely to contain little more than water and doughy bread called "firecake" that was baked in cooking pots, a gravy of boiled flour and water called "bleary," or a sort of hash stew that they called "lobscouse." Bad food kept many soldiers weakened with diarrhea, or "quickstep" as they called it.

Of all the foreign soldiers who volunteered their services to the American cause, it's doubtful that anyone gave more valuable service than Friedrich Wilhelm von Steuben at Valley Forge. Steuben portrayed himself as a baron in order to gain credibility and enter a position of authority among Washington's

officers—and it was a good thing for the colonial army that he did. The crusty, overweight soldier was a veteran of Frederick the Great's Prussian Army, and he brought his skill as a drill-master to Washington's Continentals. When he found no uniform drill regulations, he wrote a simplified but effective version of the drill formations and movements of European armies, then organized squads and companies and personally drilled a select group of sergeants so they could instruct others. And as newly appointed inspector general of the army, Steuben insisted on strict camp discipline and sanitation.

Many American soldiers had learned to use a musket or rifle during life on the frontier, while others had received military experience in earlier colonial wars in the service of the British. Yet nearly all of them needed lots of training in fighting as members of a team, and it took practice to learn to reload a musket in a hurry. Americans were not very fond of the bayonet, but Steuben insisted that they learn how to use it. The bayonet gave some protection for a man when the enemy came upon him before he could get his gun reloaded, and it was a valuable weapon when facing an enemy during an attack.

In a parsimonious effort to save money, early Continental uniforms had been designed to be tight-fitting and consequently tore easily. Although some colonies' regiments started out with individual uniforms, soldiers who weren't officers quickly took on a rag-tag appearance since replacement clothing was scarce. Though few uniforms were to be found at Valley Forge, Steuben demanded that men be as neat as possible. Blue coats were prized items among the soldiers, and the Corps of Artillery—the oldest element of the regular Continental Army—had the first prescribed uniforms: blue coats with red linings. Washington also knew the "morale effect" of riflemen against the British, and he liked to have ordinary musketeers dye their clothes butternut brown so they would look like the feared riflemen. Men who had served more than three years in the army "with bravery, fidelity, and good conduct" could wear a "Badge of Military Distinction," a simple strip of white cloth on the left sleeve, while a six-year veteran could add a second stripe—forerunners of present-day service stripes or "hash marks" and good conduct medals.

Much of what Steuben taught those soldiers is still in use today, but his knowledge and experience would have been of little benefit to the army and the cause if he had not possessed such a clear appreciation of the difference between the European professional soldiers and the American citizen-soldiers. Steuben understood that these men performed best when they were told why things had to be done a certain way instead of simply

BELOW: This wood, canvas, and iron camp bed from the New York Historical Society is said to have been used by George Washington at Valley Forge.

BOTTOM: George Washington reviews his ragged army at Valley Forge during the winter of 1777–1778.

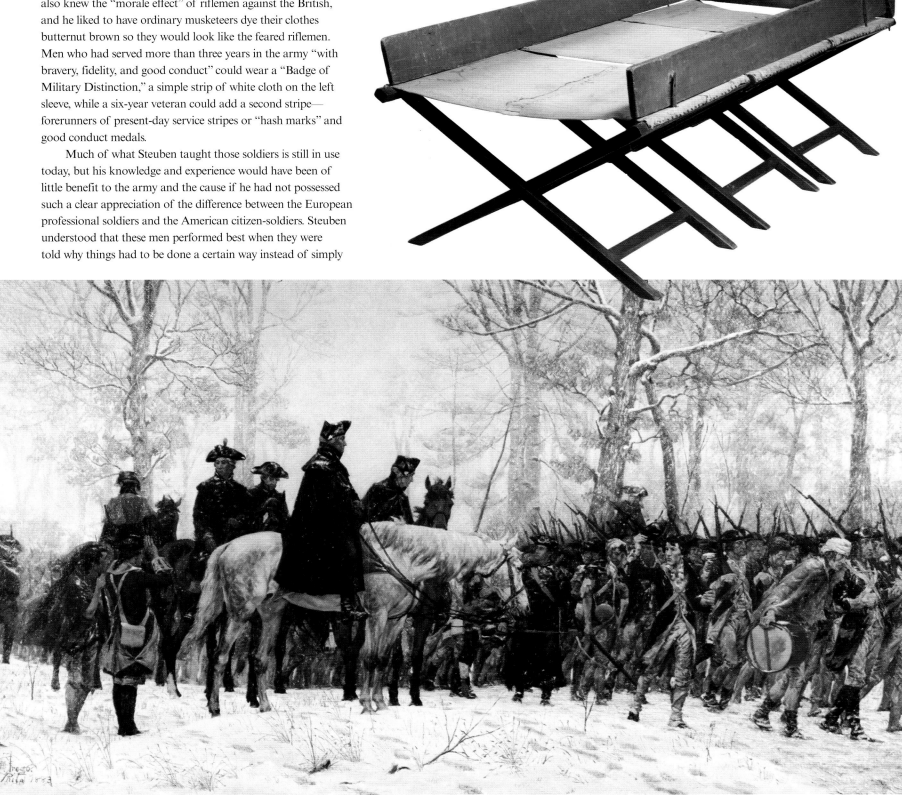

UNIFORMS OF THE REVOLUTION

The Continental Congress in November 1775 designated brown for the army's uniform, with different colors used in certain combinations on collars, cuffs, and lapels to distinguish the regiments. This was not universally adopted because many units already had been outfitted locally in a wide variety of patterns and colors. A large French shipment of blue and brown coats in the spring of 1778—on the heels of the extensive training conducted at Valley Forge—resulted in more uniformity among line units. Western troops, however, still wore more efficient patterns derived from Indian clothing and principally of unbleached, homespun fabric or deerskin. General orders issued by George Washington in October 1779 formed the basis of the army's dress regulations: dark blue coats with different facings and distinctions to codify units by region and type. Still, he was not completely happy with the basic design: "If it was left to my own inclination, I would not only order the men to adopt the Indian dress, but cause the officers to do it also, and be the first to set the example myself."

ARTILLERY 1777–1783

ABOVE TOP: A generic leather folding cap was worn principally by light troops and artillery units in both American and British forces during the last quarter of the eighteenth century. The hackle feather on this example is a modern replacement.

ABOVE BOTTOM: Epaulets worn by Noah A. Phelps when he was a colonel in the Connecticut militia during the American Revolution. These decorations often were stored in cardboard boxes.

COMMANDER-IN-CHIEF, AIDE-DE-CAMP, LINE OFFICERS 1779–1783

LIGHT INFANTRY 1782

INFANTRY CONTINENTAL ARMY 1779–1785

INDEPENDENT COMPANY ORGANIZATIONS 1774–1775

MISCELLANEOUS ORGANIZATIONS CONTINENTAL ARMY 1776–1779

RIGHT: The compass of Dr. Bodo Otto, senior surgeon of the Continental Army at Valley Forge.

TOP: Baron Friedrich Wilhelm von Steuben drills troops at Valley Forge, Pennsylvania. To carry out von Steuben's idea to form a corps of drill instructors, George Washington directed that his hand-picked headquarters guard of fifty Virginians be augmented by "one hundred draughts...taken from the troops of the other States." Beginning in March 1778, at least one hundred men were always made available for training. Steuben worked closely with individual squads before drilling them in company-size maneuvers. These men in turn were sent back to drill their regiments, a task at which they—as events later proved—excelled.

receiving orders of unknown purpose or objective. His men set the tradition for the United States Army and were the men who stood fast through the misery of Valley Forge and came out trained soldiers and the equal of the British forces.

The Americans had no cavalry arm until they reached Valley Forge, where Captain Allan McLane organized troops of Delaware horsemen. For their daring raids on British supply columns, they became known as "market shoppers." Later, the mounted legions of Colonel "Light Horse Harry" Lee from Virginia and Colonel William Washington of South Carolina distinguished themselves during campaigns in the southern colonies. The cavalry legion of Polish-born Brigadier General Casimir Pulaski joined the Revolution at the request of Benjamin Franklin and was instrumental in preventing the British from seizing Charleston, South Carolina in May 1779.

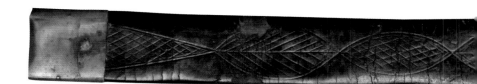

ABOVE: The Marquis de Lafayette

LEFT: George Washington and Lafayette ride among the soldiers encamped at Valley Forge, Pennsylvania. Of the twelve thousand Continental soldiers in camp during the winter of 1777, a "hard core" of six thousand remained in the spring. Poorly clothed and living in crowded, damp conditions, as many as two thousand had died of typhoid, dysentery, pneumonia, and other sicknesses. At the peak of the suffering, nearly four thousand soldiers were listed as unfit for duty. Both General Washington and British Superintendent General in occupied Philadelphia, Joseph Galloway, agreed that thirteen hundred men deserted to the British lines outside the city. Others either left at the end of their enlistments or simply trudged away in the dead of night. The "hard core" who remained throughout the bitter winter became the Revolution's symbol of courage and perseverance.

On the heels of the army's struggles to build itself into a highly trained professional force at Valley Forge, the Continental Congress in 1778 established an engineering department of three companies, and Brigadier General Louis Lebèque Duportail, a Frenchman who became the army's first chief engineer, gave it the motto that it still carries: *Essayons*, which means "We'll try." Under the leadership of Duportail and the skillful Polish-Lithuanian patriot Colonel Andrzej Tadeusz Kosciusko, the engineers established their headquarters in the Hudson River fortress of West Point, New York.

Down the Hudson a few miles from West Point was Stony Point, another strategic location that in 1780 remained in British hands. Washington sent General "Mad Anthony" Wayne with twelve hundred men to take it. A marsh separated the point from the mainland, and the British had dug defensive works and set up pointed poles against possible attack. Wayne decided to make the attack at night on July 16 and gave orders that no one should fire a shot. They would rely on the bayonet alone. Wayne divided the force into two columns, and after midnight they stole across the marsh. His own column made straight for the main defenses, while the other column followed down the bank of the river and hit the fort from the rear. An alarm brought heavy

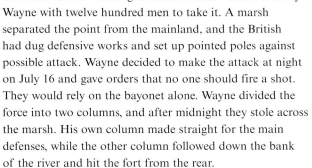

LEFT: This saber was likely used by a member of the cavalry detachment assigned to supplement Washington's headquarters guard in May 1778. It is typical of American cavalry sabers used by both officers and other ranks during the war.

ABOVE: Major General Nathanael Greene arrives at Charlotte, North Carolina, to take over as commander of the army from Horatio Gates after his August 1880 defeat at Camden. Although the Continental Army benefited greatly from Gates' previous experience as an officer in His Majesty's army when he served as George Washington's adjutant general, he proved to be a timid—but politically well connected—field commander who conspired to replace Washington. Gates also was involved in intrigues against other general officers, notably Greene and Benedict Arnold. Although Greene never won a major battle against the British, he emerged the victor during the southern campaign by skillfully husbanding his forces and bleeding the British in both conventional operations and those where he used well-organized guerrilla contingents.

cannon and musket fire, but the two columns charged and killed or captured the entire garrison. Americans had learned well Steuben's bayonet lessons.

THE WAR MOVES SOUTH

Large battles such as Monmouth in 1778 and countless smaller actions demonstrated the growing competence and professionalism of the Continental Army. The British Army was forced to admit that the situation had degenerated into an unending war that could not be maintained in the face of growing parliamentary opposition. To break the stalemate, the British turned their eyes to the south, where large segments of the population remained loyal to the Crown.

Already, bands of fast-riding patriots had harassed the British in the south to no end. But much of the fighting thus far actually had occurred between the patriots and loyalist Tories—Americans who still saw themselves as Englishmen and were recruited to fight the rebels. As such, it was largely a civil war during the early stages of the

conflict, in which neighbors and brothers fought each other in engagements that became increasingly vicious and merciless. Even when the British introduced large numbers of troops into the south, the essential character of the fighting changed little because the vastness of the region almost immediately forced them to disperse their forces to assist the loyalists.

The British, led by General Charles Cornwallis, easily captured Charleston, and their enterprise looked like a complete success until a trio of large guerrilla bands coalesced under Thomas Sumter, Andrew Pickens, and Francis "The Swamp Fox" Marion. Although Marion would become the best known of the commanders—it helps to have a catchy nickname—all three greatly disrupted British operations and worked in varying degrees of cooperation with the Continental Army of the south under General Nathanael Greene. Unlike most commanders who disdained irregular forces of any kind, Greene was eager to work with the guerrillas, and he pioneered techniques for the effective coordination of such groups with conventional forces.

LEFT: Maryland and Virginia Continentals surge into the 7th Regiment of Foot, also known as the Royal Fusiliers. During the January 17, 1781, Battle of Cowpens, they seized both of the unit's colors in hand-to-hand combat. The near-total loss of the 1,150-man British and loyalist force greatly constrained British operations and ultimately led to their abandonment of the South.

BELOW: Pommel holsters (c. 1780–1820) were draped across horses in front of the saddle and were issued to both officers and enlisted personnel. This example shows a heavy fabric with red upholstery fringe and the remains of a lightweight linen fabric with simulated leopard skin.

RIGHT: An eighty-two-man detachment of the 1st and 3d Continental Light Dragoons under Lieutenant Colonel William Washington clashes with the 17th Light Dragoons during the January 17, 1781, Battle of Cowpens. When the battle was lost, British commander Lieutenant Colonel Banastre Tarleton fled the scene with the mounted troops of the green-coated Loyalist Legion. During his retreat, Tarleton saw Washington in close pursuit, and he turned and engaged again in combat. Washington struck Tarleton's right hand with a saber blow, while Tarleton creased Washington's knee when he wounded Washington's horse, sending both animal and man crashing to the ground.

INSETS RIGHT: (*top*) British infantry sword and scabbard, c. 1750–1780 and (*bottom*) Continental enlisted dragoon sword and shoulder harness manufactured by sword cutler Jeremiah Snow of Springfield, Connecticut. Most scabbards and shoulder harnesses from this period did not survive because the leather deteriorated.

The British never succeeded in establishing a solid base of operations in the southern colonies because they had far too few troops to control the countryside. The loyalist strongholds fell one by one. The British Army's situation became increasingly untenable, and Cornwallis decided to evacuate the Carolinas. As they plodded north toward their final defeat at Yorktown, Virginia, they were closely beset by even more guerrilla bands under William Davie and William Lee Davidson while passing through North Carolina. But despite the activities of Sumter (who later had a fort in Charleston Harbor named after him) and the other guerrilla leaders, Marion is generally acknowledged as a father of the modern-day Green Berets.

During the southern campaign, Greene, by far Washington's most skilled subordinate commander, led Cornwallis on a merry chase through the Carolinas. Greene sent Colonel Morgan with a detachment to cooperate with Sumter in harassing the British forces. In early January 1781, Cornwallis sent out Colonel Banastre Tarleton with a contingent of infantry and cavalry to find and destroy Morgan's force. Tarleton set a trap, but Morgan avoided it and then prepared his own surprise for Tarleton on a rolling meadow half cleared of trees, called the Cowpens.

The American force included both militiamen and regulars. Knowing that the poorly trained militia could not stand long, Morgan put them into a line on the brow of a low hill with instructions to fire at least two volleys at "killing distance," and then to run from their position as if retreating to a new position in back of a second hill. There they were to reorganize behind the main line made up of his Continentals and the dependable Virginia militia. Behind that second hill, Morgan also hid Colonel William Washington's small but potent force of light dragoons.

The British had to march most of the night to reach Morgan's force, but in eager-beaver fashion Tarleton attacked at sunrise. As instructed, the militia opened a killing fire and then ran for cover. The British thought they had the whole army on the run. Spreading out, the redcoats hit the second line that bent back but did not break. At just the right moment, Colonel Washington's dragoons hit the unguarded British right flank. Morgan, meanwhile, had hurried back to reorganize the militiamen and, within ten minutes, they swooped around to the British left. Now the Continental line charged. At the Cowpens, it was Tarleton's force that was destroyed, losing nearly every soldier of his eleven-hundred-man force in a battle that has become legendary. Morgan's men had twelve killed and sixty-one wounded.

Victory at the Cowpens, however, did not relieve Greene's army from its dance with Cornwallis. Greene's persistence had won back nearly all of the south as the British forces Cornwallis left behind abandoned their outposts and returned to the seacoast, even as Greene's main army marched into North Carolina and fought Cornwallis on even terms. However, they could not defeat him at Guilford Courthouse. In fact, throughout the entire southern campaign, General Greene never won a major battle—but neither did he lose any—and his constant, well-coordinated pressure on the enemy won the day. "We fight, get beaten, rise, and fight again," he said.

GUILFORD COURT HOUSE 1781

YORKTOWN 1781

YORKTOWN

Having lost thousands of men and many irreplaceable officers, Cornwallis' exhausted army moved into Virginia to join forces with the British contingent already there. They were raiding aggressively into the colony's interior; almost capturing the author of the Declaration of Independence, Thomas Jefferson, in the process. General Benedict Arnold, who had switched sides and joined the British after failing in his treacherous attempt to betray General Washington and the West Point stronghold, was the leader of these operations.

As Cornwallis overran Virginia, the baby-faced General Marie Joseph Paul Yves Roch Gilbert du Motier, better known as Lafayette, led a force to meet him but dared not risk his badly outnumbered "army" in an open battle. At the same time, General George Washington had the main Continental Army positioned near New York, and because of his threat to British forces there, the superior British commander in New York ordered Cornwallis to further deplete his southern army by sending reinforcements to New York. Then Cornwallis received new orders. He was to fortify a naval base in the lower Chesapeake Bay and await developments. He chose Yorktown as the site for the base and in August 1781 transferred his whole army there.

Beholding the opportunity this presented, Washington decided to catch Cornwallis. A French fleet arrived in the Chesapeake, defeated the Royal Navy's attempt to reach Yorktown, and blocked British escape by sea. Leaving a detachment to watch New York, Washington's army hurried south, together with a French army under Rochambeau. The allied force of 15,000 men surrounded the town and on the

BELOW: A 1782 map of the route the Comte de Rochambeau's French Army took from Providence, Rhode Island, to Yorktown, Virginia, and the return march to Boston. Leaving fifteen hundred troops to guard the Providence-Newport area, four thousand had temporarily joined the Continentals besieging British-occupied New York. In the siege at Yorktown, the British did not discover the withdrawal of those men or the three thousand Continental soldiers from the lines above New York until it was too late to respond effectively.

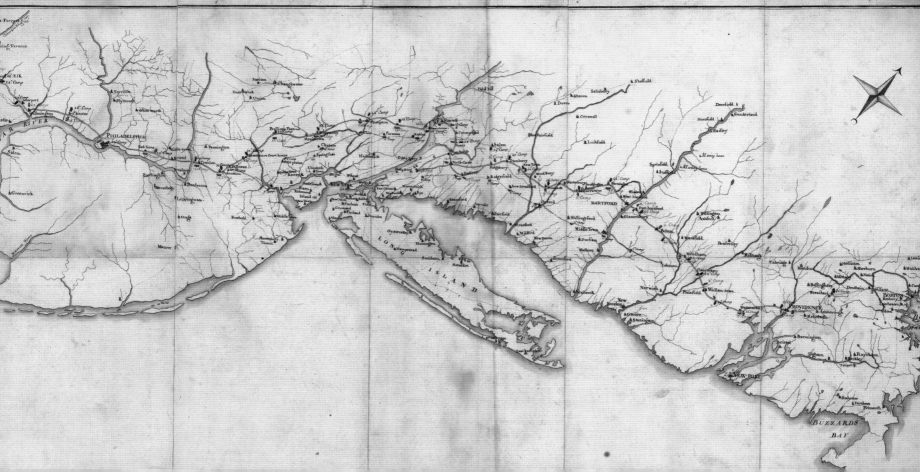

BATTLE OF YORKTOWN

Major General Charles Cornwallis' troops joined British forces in northeast Virginia, where he assumed command in May 1781. Once there, however, Cornwallis' own hesitation—plus a continual stream of conflicting messages and orders between him, theater commander General Sir Henry Clinton in New York, and Britain's cabinet secretary for the America department—largely immobilized his army even before it was cut off by the French fleet at sea and the combined forces of George Washington and the Comte de Rochambeau on land.

Before the main Continental and French armies arrived in Virginia, Major General Lafayette's little force of twelve hundred men menaced any movement inland by Cornwallis. The one effort to catch him at Richmond simply saw the young general retire quickly to avoid battle. As one British Army historian noted, Lafayette turned and "hung continually on Cornwallis' flanks and rear." Clinton, meanwhile, perceiving great risk to his garrison from the combined Franco-American army on his doorstep, ordered Cornwallis to establish a defensive post on the coast and prepare to send nearly half of his men to New York.

Cornwallis withdrew to Yorktown on the lower Chesapeake Bay in August 1781. No men were transferred north, however, because of the unexpected arrival of the entire French West Indies fleet under Rear Admiral François Joseph Paul de Grasse. Although reinforced by the Virginia militia as well as the Continentals under generals Friedrich Wilhelm Baron von Steuben and Anthony Wayne, Lafayette was still outnumbered and remained so with little more than five thousand men to Cornwallis' seven thousand. Even the arrival of three thousand French troops from the fleet didn't help. (The latter were a generally lethargic contingent; unlike Rochambeau's soldiers, many were sick with disease.)

In New York Clinton could plainly see that the Continentals were aggressively probing his defenses, but the French were more interested in eliminating the sizable, yet more vulnerable, Yorktown garrison first. In mid-August they forced the issue. Washington was informed that the French fleet was bypassing New York for the Chesapeake, where they would remain as late as October 14. It was immediately clear that a superior concentration of force on the land side, plus de Grasse holding the bay, would destroy the British army in Virginia before Clinton had a chance to relieve it.

Yet what if de Grasse failed to appear or was defeated by the Royal Navy after the bulk of the Franco-American army had moved itself far to the south? Despite the risks, Washington could not ignore this priceless opportunity. Within days, the combined army began its long, forced march. The soldiers masked their purpose by creating numerous ruses to make Clinton believe that Washington and Rochambeau planned to attack from the New Jersey shore to Staten Island—a perfectly credible threat, since the Continentals' victory there would deny easy access to New York's harbor. In the meantime, de Grasse's fleet arrived off Yorktown as promised and sent French regulars to reinforce Lafayette. On September 5, they fought a naval engagement off the Virginia Capes with an inferior British fleet under Rear Admiral Sir Thomas Graves.

Though indecisive, the action nevertheless forced Graves to retire temporarily to New York for repairs, leaving de Grasse in complete control of Yorktown's sea approaches. This also allowed a smaller French fleet carrying siege cannon from Newport to unload the heavy artillery a scant ten miles from the garrison. It also let French ships quickly ferry American and French troops down Chesapeake Bay from Annapolis and Head of Elk near the Delaware border, eliminating time-consuming road marches of nearly two hundred miles.

Not perceiving the rapidly approaching disaster, and believing that the Royal Navy would ultimately

drive de Grasse away, Cornwallis strengthened his fortifications instead of pushing his army inland. His reward was to find his garrison invested by a vastly superior force of roughly eighteen thousand Continentals, French, and Virginia militia that seemingly appeared out of nowhere on September 28. The British now were trapped against the York River where it joined the bay. Though their defensive works had been expertly designed and constructed, Rochambeau, who had taken part in some fourteen sieges in Europe, quipped to Washington that the British defeat was now just a matter of engineering and the sequence of movement dictated by military science.

Much to the Continentals' surprise, Cornwallis inexplicably abandoned his outer defenses, thus allowing them to build, perhaps as much as a week earlier than otherwise would have been the case, a series of artillery revetments within a parallel trench line (called the first parallel) barely six hundred yards from his inner fortifications. A punishing bombardment began on October 9. Sappers dug a zig-zagging trench another three hundred yards closer to the British, began construction of a second parallel with more artillery positions, and then seized a pair of key outerworks on October 14. These redoubts were incorporated into the second parallel, sealing the fate of the garrison. On the night of October 16, an attempt to evacuate across the York River in the longboats of the twenty-four British transports that were trapped in Yorktown was foiled by a sudden squall, and Cornwallis signaled his intention to begin surrender negotiations the following morning.

Two days later, Cornwallis surrendered 7,241 officers and men—fully a quarter of all the British troops in North America—plus 840 seamen, 244 pieces of land and naval artillery, and thousands of muskets. That same morning, October 19, 1781, a powerful relief force sailed from New York only to find that they were too late. If Cornwallis had not left his outer defenses to the delighted French and Continentals, the battle certainly would still have been raging when the relief arrived.

SOLDIER MORALE AND THE BADGE OF MILITARY MERIT

The winter of 1780–1781 at the Continental Army's Morristown, New Jersey, camp was, if anything, even worse than at Valley Forge. Soldiers were cut back to half rations and clothed in the tattered remnants of uniforms and civilian clothes. The men could not even purchase their own food and clothing because they had not been paid in many months. Not that the pay would have helped much; the paper currency issued by the Continental Congress had sunk to roughly a quarter of its face value, prompting the expression "not worth a Continental" by the troops.

Soldier mutinies increased in number and severity and were dealt with by a combination of careful diplomacy and the judicious hanging of several ringleaders. Spring, and the beginning of the campaign season, brought some relief. A German officer with the French at Yorktown wrote: "It is incredible that soldiers composed of men of every age, even of children of fifteen, whites and blacks, almost naked, unpaid, and rather poorly fed, can march so well and stand fire so steadfastly."

The army was better provisioned and uniformed in 1782, but was largely idle and vulnerable to morale problems. With an eye to the coming winter encampment, George Washington instituted the Army's first awards on August 7, 1782, to help promote "virtuous ambition in his soldiers, as well as to foster and encourage every species of Military merit."

The Badge of Military Merit (above) was awarded to at least three soldiers for their "singularly meritorious action" and "extraordinary fidelity and essential service." In addition—and in a profound break from European tradition—the Honorary Badges of Distinction were conferred upon lowly noncommissioned officers and common soldiers. For men who had served more than three years, "a narrow piece of white cloath [sic] of an angular form is to be fixed to the left arm on the uniform Coat," while those having served more than six were "to be distinguished by two pieces of cloth set in parellel [sic] to each other."

The ceremonial presentation of the honorary badges, still awarded today and commonly referred to as hash marks, occurred in virtually every regiment and was considered a highly prized mark of honor by their recipients. The far more prestigious and rare Badge of Military Merit fell into disuse after the war, and although its award criteria was closer to that of today's Medal of Honor, the Purple Heart, authorized in 1932, is its official "successor decoration."

LEFT: Badge of Military Merit awarded to Sergeant Elijah Churchill of the 2d Continental Light Dragoons on May 3, 1783, for service in the American Revolutionary War.

BELOW: A company officer of a mid-Atlantic state's Continental line infantry regiment, c. 1780–1783, with spontoon polearm signifying his commission.

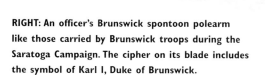

RIGHT: An officer's Brunswick spontoon polearm like those carried by Brunswick troops during the Saratoga Campaign. The cipher on its blade includes the symbol of Karl I, Duke of Brunswick.

night of October 1, began preparations to construct trenches around the British position. On the tenth of the month, the artillery opened fire at a range of eight hundred yards.

The next day, Americans opened a second siege line, or parallel, three hundred yards from the British. Now they had to take a pair of key enemy redoubts, and—as had Wayne's men at Stony Point—they were to rely only on the bayonet. The most dangerous assignment in this kind of attack was that of the volunteers who led the way, and this advance party was called a "forlorn hope": a term from the Dutch meaning "lost troop." Sergeant Daniel Brown of Connecticut led this forlorn hope across the field under the light of bursting shells, quickly covering the two hundred yards to the redoubt. Without pause they went down into the outer ditch and climbed up the other bank, over the sharpened poles. The British opened fire, but they had little effect as the Americans swarmed upon them with bayonets and clubbed rifles. In less than five minutes, the Americans had seized the redoubt at the loss of only forty-four men. A French force took the other redoubt, but they used less stealth, and it cost them one hundred casualties. The next night, Cornwallis tried to ferry his army across the York River, but a storm swamped his boats. The game was up.

On October 19, 1781, Cornwallis surrendered. American and French columns drew up along each side of the road, and the British marched out while the Yankee band played the popular tune "The World Turned Upside Down." The defeat of Cornwallis at Yorktown broke the will of the British and ended major fighting in the Revolution, but the war dragged on for more than a year. As sporadic fighting continued from Maine to the Carolinas, Washington—at his Newburgh, New York, headquarters—issued his August 7, 1782, general order establishing the Purple Heart award for military merit. It was the first military decoration in history to be open to all soldiers, regardless of rank. Today, the Purple Heart is awarded to those who are wounded in action against the enemy, but in the beginning it was equivalent to the Medal of Honor. One of the first winners of the Purple Heart was Sergeant Daniel Brown for his bravery in leading the "forlorn hope" at Yorktown.

ABOVE: George Washington signed this conditional discharge for Christopher Shultz, fife player of the 2d Continental Artillery from New York. Over the course of several months, Washington personally signed more than eight thousand discharge papers for troops with the Northern Command in Newburgh, New York.

LEFT: A fife player in the U.S. 2d Artillery, c. 1783.

CANADA 1812-1815

Chapter Two
The Army and the Young Republic, 1794–1848

The Americans had achieved a remarkable—and improbable—victory. When it became clear that peace was at hand, General Washington wrote General Greene in February 1783 that "Posterity" would see in stories of the Revolution "marks of fiction; for it will not be believed that such a force as Great Britain has employed for eight years in this Country could be baffled" by a such a small army "composed of men oftentimes half starved, always in rags, without pay, and experiencing, at times, every species of distress which human nature is capable of undergoing." The end finally came seven months later with the 1783 Treaty of Paris recognizing American independence. Even so, significant forces were kept outside New York until the last British troops evacuated the city on November 25, 1783.

The general disbandment of the Continental Army, however, did not wait for these events. Following the pattern of the militias, the Continental Army was dissolved piecemeal throughout the year as units furled their colors and furloughed their men, who simply faded back into civilian life. A weak Confederation Congress replaced the Continental Congress, appointed Colonel Knox its secretary of war, and retained only a single unit under Colonel Josiah Harmar. This was the First American Regiment (currently the 3d Infantry) to garrison West Point and a handful of outposts scattered across the frontier. Meanwhile, the state militias were responsible for safeguarding both the state and confederation armories. The state governments, suspicious of standing armies, would have been just as happy if there were no army at all, but the settlers streaming across the Appalachian Mountains into the Ohio Valley could hardly depend on militias called up for thirty- or ninety-day

enlistments far to the east for their protection. Besides, the western outposts were beyond the states' responsibilities and had to be continually garrisoned by someone.

Originally the highly decentralized government believed that a small, permanent force would be sufficient for all the nation's needs. Said Washington: "A *large* standing Army in time of Peace hath ever been considered dangerous to the liberties of the Country, yet a few Troops, under certain circumstances, are not only safe, but indispensably necessary. Fortunately for us our relative situation requires but few." It soon became apparent, however, that a few were not enough. Britain would not abide by the terms of the just-signed Treaty of Paris. They refused to evacuate their troops from the huge area called the Northwest Territory that had been ceded to the new nation, and encouraged Indians throughout the region to resist the settlers.

Domestic strife also pointed to the need for adequate funds, more independent authority, and a clear chain of command. The growing unrest among poor Massachusetts farmers—angered over state taxes and the seizure of property to repay debts—spurred efforts by Secretary Knox to fill out the already small army's thin ranks. An armed uprising eventually broke out and, in February 1787, rebels led by Daniel Shays marched on the confederation armory at Springfield to seize its munitions. The Massachusetts militia moved immediately to its defense, and Knox found himself in the position of having to refuse their request for additional arms. With Congress not in session, he could not obtain permission to supply the armory stores to its defenders.

The militia helped itself to the armory's ordnance anyway, and the first militia round from a federal cannon killed numerous rebels, prompting the others to flee.

OPPOSITE: Major General Winfield Scott shortly after commanding U.S. forces in an 1847 drive from the Gulf Coast to Mexico City, during which several major battles were won. Scott also fought in both the War of 1812 and the Second Seminole War. Though a strict disciplinarian, he also was well known for taking extremely good care of his soldiers and was repeatedly criticized for enacting and enforcing humanitarian measures during the Indian removal from the southern states. Scott settled territorial disputes with the British in Maine and the Pacific Northwest, became the first officer to rise to the rank of lieutenant general since George Washington, and developed the strategy that defeated the South during the Civil War.

THE NORTHWEST INDIAN WAR AND WAYNE'S LEGION

Long before the U.S. Constitution was approved and Washington was inaugurated as the nation's first president on April 30, 1789, continual strife west of the Appalachians had forced the Confederation Congress to increase the size of the army from one under-strength regiment to two under-strength regiments. Harmar, meanwhile, had made brigadier general. In 1790 he marched from Fort Washington (present-day Cincinnati) with three hundred twenty regulars and roughly eleven hundred mostly untrained militiamen from Pennsylvania and Kentucky. Defeated in a pair of battles by a British-supported coalition of Indian tribes called the Western Confederacy, Harmar lost 129 men, with nearly as many wounded. The following year, some 623 men under General Arthur St. Clair, as well as an unknown number of women and children, were killed when their camp was overrun during the disastrous Battle of the Wabash.

The ever-larger defeats of 1790 and 1791 made it clear that dependence on forces drawn principally from state militias would not secure the Northwest Territory. Knox proposed that a highly professional army be organized and trained. Thus, in 1792, Congress authorized the Legion of the United States, made up of four sub-legions, each with its own attached artillery and cavalry, plus both light and heavy infantry. President Washington put one of his former

generals, Stony Point hero Anthony Wayne, in charge of the Legion. Major General Wayne trained his soldiers to fight independently in small units, as well as in large formations. Their basic method of attack was to move quickly on the Indians with bayonets after the first volley. Just as during the Revolution, Wayne was known among his own troops as "Mad Anthony," but the Indians called him "Chief Who Never Sleeps."

It took a year of intensive training, but by the spring of 1793, Wayne was confident that he now had twenty-five hundred men "worthy of being trusted in campaign." When he started to move into the Indian Territory from Pennsylvania, his army—his legion—numbered 2,643, after some Kentucky sharpshooters joined him along the way. With this small American Army, Wayne was to meet a greatly superior force of Indians well armed and egged on by the British. He built Fort Defiance at the junction of the Maumee and Anglaise rivers in Ohio as a base of operations, and Wayne, who'd first earned his appreciation of the bayonet at the hands of Inspector General Steuben, went looking for a fight.

It was August 20, 1794, when the Legion came face to face with a large force composed of numerous tribes and some Canadian militia set up for battle in a strong position on the banks of the Maumee. A tornado had left a wide path of fallen trees through the woods; hence the engagement's name, Battle of Fallen Timbers. The uprooted trees and tangled branches made an excellent cover for the tribesmen, who were well hidden even though their faces were bright with war paint. These same Indians had fought with soldiers before and were confident that, as always, they would mow down the Americans. But these were different soldiers— ones that kept on coming when they should have melted away under the storm of bullets from unseen riflemen. As they'd been trained, the troops of "Mad Anthony" Wayne fired once and then drove the Indians from cover with their fixed bayonets, or "the sharp ends of guns," as the Indians called them. Dragoons rode down the exposed defenders, slashing with sabers, or "long knives."

Fleeing to the nearby British post Fort Miami near present-day Toledo, the Indians and Canadians were denied entry because its commander feared that if he offered His Majesty's protection, he could well be responsible for starting a second war with the Americans. The Indians' defeat led to the Treaty of Greenville in 1795, ceding much of present-day Ohio to the United States. One young Shawnee war leader at Fallen Timbers, named Tecumseh, did not sign the Greenville treaty. The U.S. Army would meet him again.

THE WHISKEY REBELLION

Shortly after the Articles of Confederation were replaced by the U.S. Constitution in 1789, creating a much stronger federal government, discontent began to brew in western Pennsylvania over the Federal tax imposed on whiskey. By 1794 it had grown into an insurrection centered principally in the Monongahela Valley, where Washington had fought some four long decades before. Tax collectors were assaulted, court proceedings stopped, the mail robbed, and threats were made of an assault against Pittsburgh.

The memory of Shays' Rebellion was still fresh in the minds of Washington and Treasury Secretary Alexander Hamilton, who saw the Whiskey Rebellion as a test of federal authority. Washington ordered federal marshals to serve court orders requiring the tax protesters to appear in federal district court. With virtually the entire fledgling army of General Wayne far to the west and in the midst of operations against the Indians, Washington declared martial law by invoking the Militia Act of 1792 to summon the citizen soldiers of Pennsylvania, New Jersey, Maryland, and Virginia. A force of 12,950 men—roughly the size of the Continental Army at its peak strength—was quickly mustered in August and September, then marched in October, with Washington at its head. Arriving in western Pennsylvania in October, the army found that the rebels had speedily dispersed. Federal authority had been upheld, and this demonstrated for interested parties in Europe how quickly a strong American military force could be gathered.

OPPOSITE BOTTOM: "Mad Anthony" Wayne's dragoons crash into the Indians' left flank during the Battle of Fallen Timbers on August 20, 1794.

BELOW: A Model 1800 U.S. Army officer's hat, c. 1810. The half-moon-shaped *chapeau de bras* (from the French "hat under the arm," as it was popularly carried) remained a part of full dress regulations for officers until just prior to World War II. (*See also the illustrations on page 72.*)

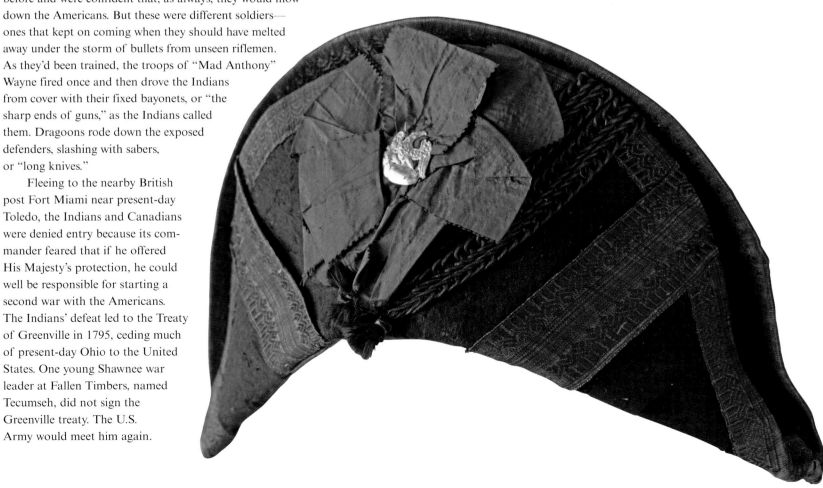

EXPLORING THE WEST

While the army safeguarded the country east of the Mississippi, the young nation more than doubled in size in 1803 when it acquired a huge expanse of territory from France in what became known as the Louisiana Purchase.

Army explorers traveled from the Mississippi to the Pacific and far to the southwest, mapping the Great Plains; surveying the towering Rockies; and reporting on Indians, animals, and the resources of this vast inland empire. Early in 1803—and *before* the Louisiana Purchase—President Thomas Jefferson authorized an expedition up the Missouri River to gather detailed knowledge of the territory and establish "the most friendly & conciliatory manner which their own conduct will admit." Army captains Meriwether Lewis and William Clark, with little more than two dozen men in their Corps of Discovery, accomplished far more than that. Pushing beyond the Rocky Mountains and all the way to the Pacific Ocean, they took accurate surveys, plotted maps, and made friends—and a few enemies—with Indians that had never seen white men, while bringing all but one of their men back alive.

From 1805 to 1806 another army explorer, Lieutenant Zebulon Pike, took twenty men to explore the far reaches of the upper Mississippi. Upon returning to St. Louis, he almost immediately embarked on a journey to the headwaters of the Arkansas River deep in Colorado, then south into Spanish territory where he was briefly held while they contemplated whether or not he was a spy. It was on this latter exploration through the Indian and buffalo country that he gave his name to a great mountain, Pikes Peak in the Rockies, which long beckoned to adventurous spirits back east who vowed to make "Pikes Peak or bust."

The feats of these explorers captured the admiration and imagination of the American people. Although an 1820 expedition to the Rockies by Major Stephen H. Long would temporarily lead to the belief that the Great Plains were unfit for settlement because of the lack of trees and water—a "Great American Desert"—an eager public was anxious to learn all it could about the explorations. Americans became better acquainted with the vast lands beyond the Mississippi and their undeveloped riches. The settlers owed the trailblazing of the West to the suffering and daring of these soldier-explorers.

ABOVE: The Corps of Discovery under captains Meriwether Lewis and William Clark begins its journey up the Missouri River in the spring of 1804. A bronze swivel cannon capable of firing a 1-pound ball or a canister of sixteen musket balls is mounted on the bow of their flat-bottomed keelboat, while two smaller swivel guns are mounted high on the stern. Storage lockers line the length of the outer deck areas. In case of attack, both their contents and upraised heavy lids provided a degree of protection for the soldiers who used the narrow space between the lids as fire slits. The soldiers in this well-trained and highly disciplined unit were largely recruited from frontier posts and principally armed with the Model 1795 musket and bayonet. Fifteen Model 1792 rifles specially refurbished for the mission at the Harpers Ferry Arsenal also were acquired, and an undetermined number of personally owned Pennsylvania and Kentucky long rifles were brought by the men.

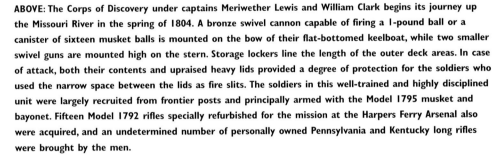

GIRANDONI SYSTEM AUSTRIAN REPEATING AIR RIFLE, C. 1795

This Girandoni System Austrian Repeating Air Rifle is believed to have been carried by Lewis on the expedition. The air reservoir in the butt of the weapon could be pumped up to nine hundred pounds per square inch, allowing the twenty-two .463-caliber balls held in a tubular magazine to be fired in succession on a single charge of air. Although its accuracy was not dependable beyond fifty yards, the primary purpose of the air rifle was to impress the Indians during the shooting demonstrations that are mentioned twenty-six times in the expedition's journals. Because the rifle had an unusually loud discharge, the weapon often was used as a signal to guide hunters into camp at night.

ARTILLERY 1783–1796

ARTILLERY 1796–1799

U.S. FLINTLOCK PISTOL, MODEL 1806

Manufacture of the .54-caliber pistol was authorized on November 13, 1805, and a total of 4,096 were produced at the Harpers Ferry Arsenal in Virginia from 1806 to 1808. Originally it did not have the brass front sight. Although well balanced and accurate, the pistol was found to be too weakly constructed for military service, so production was discontinued.

ARTILLERY 1799–1802

ARTILLERY 1799–1802

FLINTLOCK MUSKET OR "CONTRACT MUSKET," MODEL 1794

In 1794, national armories were established at Springfield, Massachusetts, and Harpers Ferry, Virginia, to make weapons for the U.S. Army. Congress adopted the workhorse of America's War of Independence, the Model 1763 French flintlock musket, as a pattern for the United States' first standardized weapon. The possibility of war with France prompted the government to greatly expand production of the .69-caliber musket through the addition of nineteen private firms. This example was made by John Miles of Bordertown, New Jersey, for the Pennsylvania militia. Marked "CP" (Commonwealth of Pennsylvania) on the lock and barrel, it was sent to the 28th Regiment, Philadelphia County, during the War of 1812 and issued to soldier number "123."

SHORT LAND PATTERN BROWN BESS, MODEL 1769

Regimentally marked on the barrel with "RHR" (Royal Highland Regiment, 42 Regiment of Foot or "Black Watch"), this .75-caliber musket is stamped as "[Company] B" and number "69." A nineteenth-century paper found in the barrel documents that the weapon was carried by John Wilson and later by his son, Sergeant Jeremiah Wilson, who served with the 61st New York Infantry during the War of 1812. The .75-caliber weapon apparently was captured during the fighting on Long Island, where the Black Watch and John Wilson's Dutchess County militia company were heavily engaged in 1776.

BELOW: (*left*) A U.S. artillery officer's cloak and cape issued between 1812 and 1821, and (*right*) enlisted uniform jacket of a pattern adopted two years before the War of 1812 and worn as late as 1818. Made of wool, its once-white metal buttons indicate infantry use. It is believed to have been worn by a New Hampshire soldier.

THE WAR OF 1812—ACTION IN THE NORTH

Violations of America's rights on the high seas led Congress in 1812 to declare a second war against Great Britain. A series of spectacular naval duels between the U.S. and Royal navies enhanced the young nation's prestige, but they played no part in deciding the war. The decision rested upon the army and cooperating naval fleets on the Great Lakes. In a sense, the conflict in this northern theater had been going on ever since the British had refused to abide by the Treaty of Paris that ceded the vast territory to the United States at the close of the Revolution. British forts such as Niagara and Detroit held key positions in New York, Ohio, and Michigan, until defeat of their Indian allies at the Battle of Fallen Timbers made them untenable. A treaty negotiated in 1795 resulted in their transfer to the United States, but it wasn't long before the British were up to their old tricks.

BELOW: The British 103d Regiment of Foot, jammed into a narrow front between an embankment and the lake, suffered extremely heavy casualties during the Fort Erie redoubt on August 15, 1814. This sword, found forty yards in front of the American position, belonged to one of the ten British officers killed or wounded when attacking the redoubt, and was presented to David Bates Douglass, who was promoted to captain one month later.

LEFT: A detachment of infantry and artillery under 2d Lieutenant David Bates Douglass, an engineer officer who recently had graduated from West Point, repulsed repeated attacks against its Fort Erie redoubt.

American forces had invaded Lower Canada (Ontario) in July 1814 and captured Fort Erie. Following the battles of Chippawa and Lundy's Lane—which left both sides exhausted and badly mauled—they withdrew to the lake and greatly strengthened the old British fort. Anxious to expel the U.S. forces under Major General Jacob Jennings Brown from the Canadian soil, the British launched their four-pronged assault on the redoubt and the original fort. It cost them 905 killed, wounded, or missing.

One month later, a successful American sortie against two of the three siege batteries caused the loss of another six hundred men and a third of their cannons, forcing the British to withdraw. However, resupply of the outpost was difficult. In November, after setting off a series of explosions to destroy the fortifications, the Americans withdrew to winter quarters near Buffalo.

The continual agitation of British agents and the British army among the Indians, whom they supplied with arms and promises of support, encouraged Chief Tecumseh to renew Indian resistance to American settlement. By 1811 he had succeeded in organizing many Northwest tribes into a new confederation, and he prepared an uprising to eject the white settlers and set up an Indian empire. When Tecumseh left the region on a mission to enlist the support of the southern tribes, Indiana Territorial Governor William Henry Harrison, who later became president of the United States, moved against Tecumseh's villages with a force of 250 regulars from the 4th U.S. Infantry Regiment, 100 Kentucky volunteers, and nearly 600 Indiana militia to keep his followers in check. On November 6, 1811, Harrison's force camped for the night on a rise of ground where Tippecanoe Creek flows into the Wabash River. Indian braves attacked the camp later that night, and they were driven off after a sharp fight. Harrison then proceeded to Tecumseh's village and ordered it be burned. With Harrison's victory at Tippecanoe, Indian resistance in the Northwest was temporarily broken.

The opening of hostilities with the British the following year saw all of the former British forts, as well as new American outposts such as Fort Dearborn (Chicago), seized early in the fighting by the British and their Indian allies. After the American loss of Detroit, Harrison, who was named a general at the beginning of the War of 1812, assembled a force to strike back into Canada, and his men beat back two major assaults by the British and Indians. Then, Commodore Oliver Hazard Perry cleared the way with a brilliant naval victory against a British fleet on Lake Erie, and sent a message to Harrison: "We have met the enemy, and they are ours." Harrison, called "Old Tip" by the troops, recaptured Detroit, marched his men onto boats, and ferried them across to the Canadian shores where they attacked a force of British and Indians on October 5, 1813, at the Thames River. Tecumseh was killed and his forces scattered, leaving the British unable to mount any counterstrike.

After a series of poor showings on the part of green recruits in the Niagara area more than two hundred miles to the east, Winfield Scott, then a twenty-eight-year-old brigadier general, set up a rigorous training schedule for his troops near Buffalo, New York. Like Inspector General Steuben at Valley Forge and General Wayne at Pittsburgh, Scott spent long hours drilling his men. After two months of intensive training, they were ready for action, and he was anxious to have them in crisp new uniforms for their date with the British. The uniform, with swallow-tailed coat, long trousers, and "tar bucket" hat was supposed to be dark blue, but there was a shortage of blue material, so Scott put his men in gray—the color that state militia usually wore.

On the night of July 3, 1814, Scott's brigade crossed the Niagara River into Canada and approached the British near the Chippewa River. The 11th Infantry, ancestor regiment of the present-day 6th Infantry, advanced on the left, and predecessors of the 2d Infantry and 5th Infantry advanced in the center. A battery of artillery supported on the right. Scott arranged his units into a "V" formation with its point to the rear, which had an effect like that of Colonel Morgan at the Cowpens when the Americans came up on both ends of the enemy line. The British commander noticed the gray

uniforms and expected an easy victory. "Why, those are nothing but Buffalo militia," he said. But when a British cannon tore a gap through the line and the gray-clad soldiers kept up their steady advance, he changed his tune. "Those are regulars, by God!"

When he was seventy yards from the British, Scott galloped to the front of the 11th Infantry and called out: "They say that Americans cannot stand the cold iron. I call on you instantly to give the lie to that slander! Charge!" A cheer went up as the men lowered their bayonets and charged. The British lines, as Scott reported it, "mouldered away like a rope of sand." The present-day dress uniform of the West Point cadet corps was adopted in tribute to these gray-clad victors at Chippawa.

Three weeks later, a force of two thousand Americans met a British force of three thousand in another battle along the Niagara, Lundy's Lane, and American soldiers again proved their ability to stand up against a superior force. British artillery was holding up the American advance when Lieutenant Colonel James Miller brought up the 21st Infantry, his reserve regiment. Major General Jacob

Brown pointed out the British main battery and asked Miller if his regiment could take it. "I'll try, Sir," he said. While the British were distracted by an attack on their right, he moved his men in quickly and seized the guns in a short, vicious engagement. Miller's reply, "I'll try, Sir," is still the motto of the formation that has evolved into today's 5th Infantry, and is the oldest regimental motto in the Regular Army.

LEFT: Bearing the initials "SNY" for "State of New York," this backpack follows the basic pattern of those manufactured in the late eighteenth to the early nineteenth century. The bag, with waterproof outer flap, along with the canteen, was issued to units raised in New York during the War of 1812. Leather straps on the inside can hold either a soldier's blanket or overcoat, but the canteen's strap is missing. The canteen is made of wood with metal bands on the outer edges.

ABOVE: Alexander Macomb entered the U.S. Army in 1799 as a cornet (2d lieutenant) of light dragoons and by 1814 had risen to the rank of brigadier general. He defeated the British at the battle of Plattsburg, New York, on September 11, 1814, and received a brevet rank of major general and a gold medal. In 1828 he received the permanent rank of major general and was named commander-in-chief of the army.

RIGHT: The 5th Regiment of the Maryland militia holds the right flank of the American line outside Baltimore, Maryland, to buy time to complete entrenchments around the city. A British force of four thousand had landed earlier that day, September 12, 1814, with the intent of seizing Baltimore. Despite a two-hour artillery and rocket bombardment, followed by determined assaults carried out by British veterans of the Napoleonic wars, the 5th Maryland in Godly Wood stood its ground. After inflicting some three hundred casualties, the 5th was ordered to fall back, and the British Army, exhausted by the fighting and surprised by the militia's stubborn defense, withdrew. In the bay, the Royal Navy failed to silence the guns of Fort McHenry that guarded the Baltimore harbor, and the British force was withdrawn. Today's 1st Battalion, 175th Infantry, Maryland Army National Guard carries on the gallant traditions of the 5th Maryland.

THE BURNING OF WASHINGTON AND VICTORY AT NEW ORLEANS

The darkest point in the War of 1812 came in August 1814, when a British force landed in Maryland, crossed the upper Potomac at Bladensburg, and struck toward Washington. A large force of militia gathered to meet the invaders, but when the British crossed the river (on a bridge that should have been destroyed or at least covered by the Baltimore militia's artillery) and fired a few rockets, the six-thousand-man—but virtually untrained—force turned and ran. Only a small group of less than five hundred regulars, sailors and Marines in a unified effort, stood their ground. But they were poorly positioned and could not hold back the British, who marched on to the capital.

In retaliation for the burning of Upper Canada's parliament buildings and Government House at York by American forces the previous year, the victorious British now burned the White House, as well as the Capitol, Treasury, and War Office, before returning to their ships and setting off for the real prize of the campaign: the port city of Baltimore, from which the vital Chesapeake Bay could be controlled. Fortunately, when the British turned toward Baltimore, they found its land approaches effectively defended. Their commander was killed in the attack, and a heavy, sustained bombardment of Fort McHenry, guarding Baltimore's harbor, during the night of September 13 proved futile. It was during this bombardment that American emissary Francis Scott Key, detained for the night on a British ship, wrote the words for "The Star-Spangled Banner."

After the failed attempt to take Baltimore, the British combined naval and land force was sent to capture New Orleans. Meanwhile, General Andrew Jackson had moved his headquarters and tiny contingent of sixty regulars to that very city after defeating a deadly band of Creek Indians who, incited by Chief Tecumseh, had massacred more than four hundred settlers and militia at Fort Mims, Alabama. His victory over the renegade Creeks at Horseshoe Bend had been accomplished by a polyglot force of regulars, militia, volunteers, and allied Indian tribes, but

INSET: Cartridge boxes like this U.S. Army M1808 model were probably the most important accoutrement of the nineteenth-century soldier. Cartridge boxes had to be both sturdy and waterproof to protect the fragile paper cartridges that held the powder and ball used to load a musket. The M1808 box shown here was capable of holding twenty-six cartridges and included implement pockets to hold musket tools and spare flints.

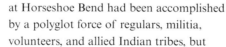

determined regulars at Fort McHenry, and an aroused citizenry.

Ably led by Major General Samuel Smith of the Maryland Militia (who replaced a major general of the regulars), the citizen soldiers began constructing a line of stout defensive works covered by the fort. Meanwhile, Smith sent the 3d Maryland Division's three-thousand-man 3d Brigade under Brigadier General John Stricker to hold a mile-wide bottleneck across the peninsula, where the British had landed, to delay them while the line was strengthened. British commander Major-General Robert Ross, the victor at Bladensburg, was warned that close to twenty thousand militiamen were preparing to defend the Baltimore approaches. Ross, unimpressed, stated, "I don't care if it rains militia." Within a few hours, he would lay dying in front of the Maryland ranks.

Stricker, a veteran of Princeton, Brandywine, and Monmouth, had formed his brigade's five regiments in depth. The 5th and 27th Maryland regiments that were arrayed to the front bore the brunt of the attacks, even as the two formations in support and one in reserve left the field when the fire got hot. These Marylanders would not be moved and delayed the British regulars for two critical hours, fighting toe to toe and only withdrawing when it became apparent that they were being flanked. The exhausted and much bloodied redcoats, finally able to observe up close the well-manned fortifications along and crowning Hampstead Hill, immediately recognized that they could go no farther without the direct support of the Royal Navy's cannons, and the fleet would have to subdue Fort McHenry first.

Cochrane's attempt to force the fort's surrender that night failed. The city's merchants had sunk their own ships to block the entrance to Baltimore's harbor. Though the naval commanders had airily dismissed the submerged ships' effectiveness to their army colleagues, the distance at which the cargo ships were sunk rendered the fleet's fire against Fort McHenry less effective and accurate. With no ability to reduce Smith's defenses, Cochrane's amphibious force withdrew, and then conducted a number of minor raids along the Virginia and Maryland coasts before sailing to Jamaica, where it received reinforcements. Some 590 British soldiers had been killed or wounded during the Chesapeake Campaign, with only the burning of the unfinished capital to show for it.

Cochrane now set his sights on capturing yet another rich prize: the port city of New Orleans on the Mississippi River. Intent on avoiding a potentially costly battle between his fleet and the American forts at the mouth of the Mississippi, he directed troops to the Lake Borgne shore in late December—above

Despite the sterling quality of the U.S. Navy's ships and seamen, the Chesapeake Bay had become a rich hunting ground for the Royal Navy by the war's second year. Shockingly, the government in Washington was unperturbed at the enemy's freedom of movement on its very doorstep and made no effort whatsoever to fortify either the capital or Baltimore beyond maintaining the forts guarding their sea approaches. The reckoning came when Napoleon Bonaparte's defeat and exile to the island of Elba in April 1814 freed thousands of seasoned British troops in Europe for the fighting in North America. Command of all British forces operating along the Atlantic and Gulf of Mexico was given to Vice Admiral Alexander Cochrane, who eagerly began a series of large-scale amphibious operations.

By mid-August, more than four thousand British had landed and begun their lunge toward Washington as frantic calls went out for militia to oppose them. Assembling as if arriving at a country fair, the militia companies formed a defense along the British line of march toward Bladensburg, northeast of the capital, and were promptly put to flight by the redcoats' first shots. Some militia did put up a stout, if brief, fight, but they were very poorly led. More than six thousand Americans were routed by a vanguard of British that was just one-third their numbers. Only a force of four hundred fifty U.S. Marines, land-bound sailors manning their cannons, and a handful of regulars stood their ground until finally overwhelmed. Late that afternoon, August 24, 1814, British forces

entered the city—their general and senior officers dining on a meal hastily left behind at the White House—and all the public buildings were set afire before the British evacuated back to their ships.

Washington was, in truth, an insignificant town at this time. It had only been attacked and its federal buildings burned in retaliation for the Americans' burning and looting of Upper Canada's parliament buildings and private residences in York (Toronto) two years earlier. The real objective, as far as the British admiral that controlled the Chesapeake Campaign was concerned, was Baltimore with its fabulous wealth of shipping and merchandise—"and consequently of prize money," as a semi-official British Army history delicately put it, adding "the naval commanders [were] always eager for operations ashore."

The British seized Fort Washington several days later, then conducted a successful raid into Virginia, where they accepted the surrender of Alexandria. After more reinforcements arrived in November, they briefly considered seizing Rhode Island as a base for a strike against New York—even as the Americans, fearing just such a move, began to hastily fortify Brooklyn and Manhattan. Baltimore, however, was close at hand and looked to be ripe for the picking since, judging by recent experience, the local militia was utterly ineffective and since even the regulars holding Fort Washington on the Potomac had fled their posts. What the British found on September 12 was a well led and generally better trained militia,

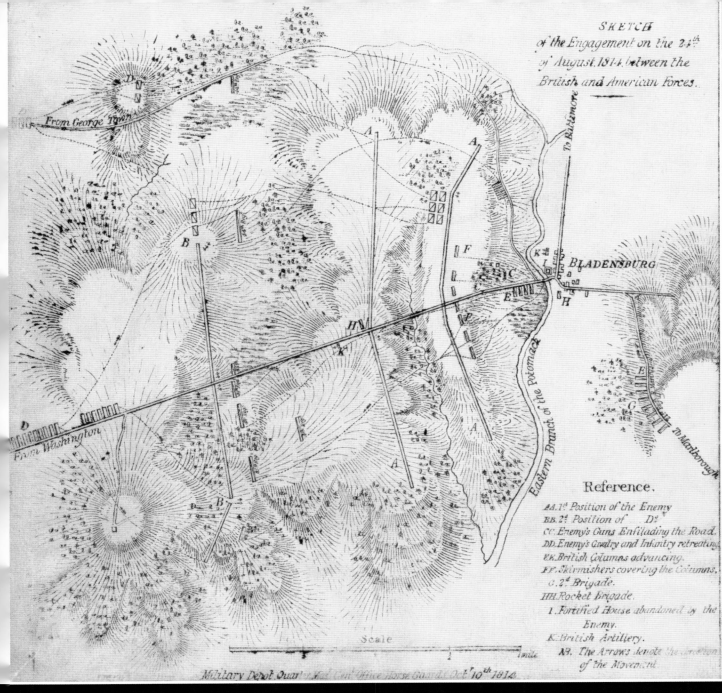

SKETCH of the Engagement on the 24th of August 1814 between the British and American Forces.

From George Town

To Baltimore

BLADENSBURG

To Marlborough

Eastern Branch of the Potomack

From Washington

Reference.
A.A. 1st Position of the Enemy
B.B. 2d Position of Do
C.C. Enemy's Guns Enfilading the Road.
D.D. Enemy's Cavalry and Infantry retreating
E.E. British Columns advancing.
F.F. Skirmishers covering the Columns.
G. 2d Brigade.
H.H. Rocket Brigade.
I. Fortified House abandoned by the Enemy.
K. British Artillery.
X.X. The Arrows denote the direction of the Movement.

Scale _____ 1 mile

Military Depot Quarter Mas. Genl. Office Horse Guards Octr. 10th 1814.

the forts and "only" five miles east of the river, but across boggy ground that made it almost impossible to keep the men supplied.

The new British Army commander, Sir Edward Pakenham, found himself confined to the relatively thin stretch of farmland that extended along the Mississippi, and he had few options other than to launch a frontal assault. Confronting him was Major General Andrew Jackson's mixed force of two infantry regiments; three "companies" of pirate cannoneers; locally raised (largely Creole) militia; Tennessee riflemen; and a completely useless gaggle of Kentuckians, many of whom, surprisingly, were poorly armed. The inevitable battle on January 8, 1815, in which Parkenham was killed, added two thousand British casualties to the more than three hundred others since they had arrived outside New Orleans.

The February 11 surrender of Fort Bowyer, which defended the port of Mobile, was an inadequate consolation after the disaster at New Orleans. Three days later, word arrived that a peace had been concluded between the United States and Britain on December 23, the very day that Cochrane had put troops ashore in Louisiana. So ended six months of British amphibious operations along the Atlantic. Looking back at the ill-fated operations, historian J.W. Fortescue maintained that they provided "perhaps the most striking warning upon record . . . against conducting operations ashore on the sole advise of naval officers," and to never use "combined forces upon the sole advise either of a naval or a military officer." Sound advice that would be followed by the Americans themselves nearly a half century later.

OPPOSITE: "Capture of the City of Washington," engraving in 1815 for The History of England.

ABOVE: "Sketch of the Engagement on the 24th of August 1814 between the British and American Forces" depicting troop movements during the Battle of Bladensburg.

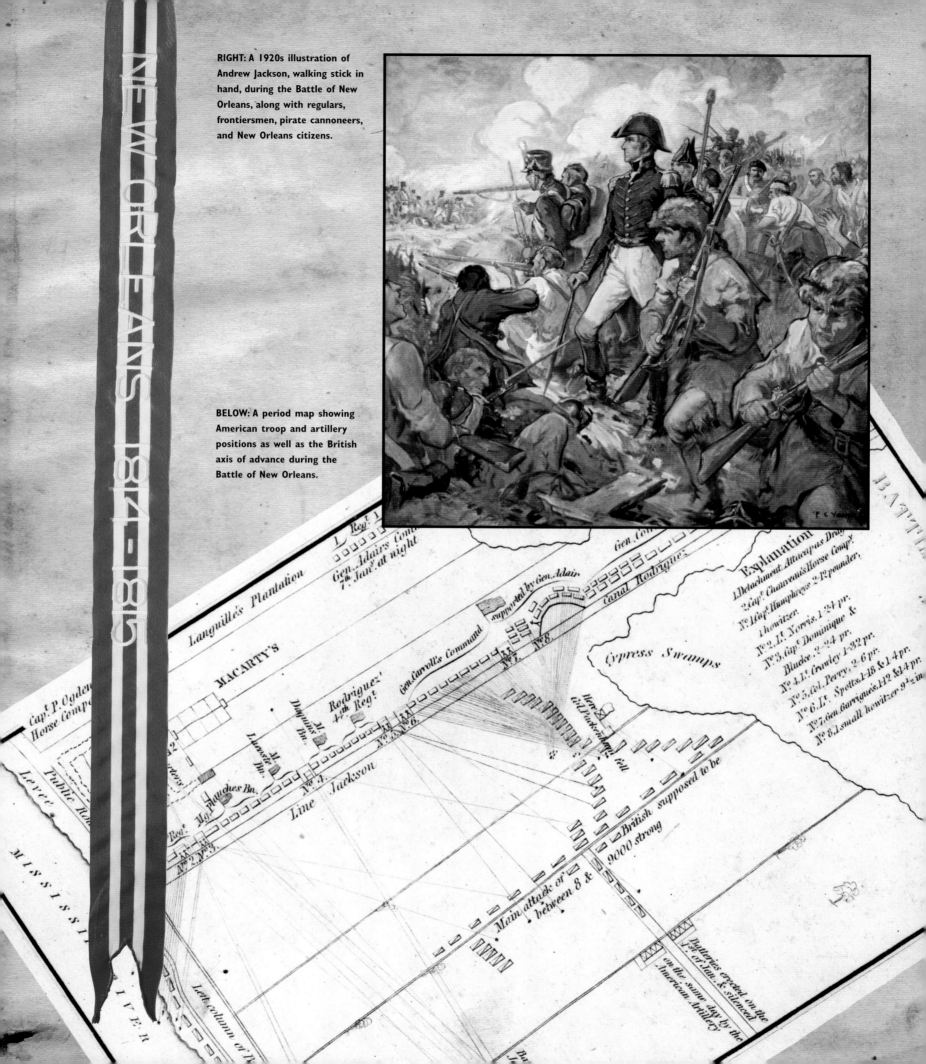

NEW ORLEANS 1814–1815

RIGHT: A 1920s illustration of Andrew Jackson, walking stick in hand, during the Battle of New Orleans, along with regulars, frontiersmen, pirate cannoneers, and New Orleans citizens.

BELOW: A period map showing American troop and artillery positions as well as the British axis of advance during the Battle of New Orleans.

at New Orleans a similar force would face the cream of the British Army.

Ironically, the battle occurred after peace already had been sighted. General Jackson, "Old Hickory," gathered together his few regulars and a much larger number of militiamen and local recruits, including a contingent of pirates handling some of his artillery. A defense was set up along both banks of the Mississippi. Jackson expected the British to come up the river along the north bank, so he organized his main position there. The lines stretched from the levee along the river to an impassable swamp on the right, and the men dug trenches and set up barricades of cotton bales. On January 8, 1815, the British, in precise formation, attacked the works, but Jackson's force was far stronger than it appeared. Jackson put his best sharpshooters in front, and the others kept them supplied with ready-loaded rifles, and at three-hundred-yards range, they fired with an accuracy that these British veterans had never seen in Europe. The red-coated soldiers were mowed down by the hundreds before they withdrew, leaving two thousand killed, wounded, or prisoners out of a total of fifty-three hundred men in the assault. American losses were fewer than one hundred. In honor of their part in the Battle of New Orleans, the 7th Infantry now wears an insignia showing a cotton bale and a pair of crossed rifles.

RIGHT TOP: United States Army dragoon shako of the style worn during the American Revolution through the War of 1812. This example shows the bearskin crest, leather cockade, and pompom. The bearskin roach, which stretches from brim to brim across the top of the headgear, originally would have been taller but has shrunk with age.

ABOVE: Bearskin-covered pommel holster of the pattern issued to enlisted personnel from 1790 to 1820.

RIGHT BOTTOM: United States Army light dragoon helmet used in the War of 1812. Contracts were made in 1812 and 1814 to create these helmets, and this particular example was manufactured by H. Cressman of Philadelphia. The helmet is made of thick leather with metal banding (incorporated to ward off saber blows) and a white horsehair plume.

RIGHT: Shako worn by the Montgomery Guards, an Irish Catholic militia company in Boston.

During a September 1837 muster of the city's ten independent companies of the Boston Brigade of Militia, the enlisted men of six companies left the field when the Guards arrived. The drilling continued without them, but anti-Irish rioting broke out along their line of march back to their armory. Early the next year the governor of Massachusetts disbanded the six companies that refused to take orders, and within months, the Guards were disbanded as well because of fears that their very existence would provoke more violence. When the city's militia was subsequently reorganized, the Irish Catholics were not allowed to form a unit.

The Guards were named after Daniel Montgomery, an Irish-born general who fought for the United States in the Revolutionary War, and "shako" is derived from the Hungarian *csákós süveg* for "peaked cap."

THE INDIAN REMOVAL AND SEMINOLE WARS

Black Hawk of the Sauk and Fox tribes was the last Indian war chief to resist the advance of the settlers and the Indian Removal Act of 1830, which decreed that all tribes east of the Mississippi should be relocated to the west. Like Tecumseh, he tried to organize his people in 1832, and with his defeat in the Battle of Bad Axe River in Wisconsin, the last uprising in the Old Northwest was over. This same year, however, saw the eruption of violence at the opposite corner of the United States, among the Seminoles far to the southeast in Florida.

The army under Jackson had fought a series of engagements with mixed forces of Seminole Indians and runaway slaves armed by the British in the aftermath of the War of 1812, then went on to capture Spanish forts and attack their settlements. Later called the First Seminole War, Jackson's incursion convinced the Spanish in 1819 that it would be best if they simply sold Florida, which then stretched all along the Gulf of Mexico coast to Louisiana, to the Americans before it was seized outright.

American settlers poured into the region around Tallahassee, a Seminole settlement, and frequently clashed with the tribe. The Seminoles, themselves Creek Indians that only recently had migrated to the area, agreed to move to a large reservation south of present-day Ocala and stop providing sanctuary to runaway slaves. Tensions mounted after passage of the Indian Removal Act and nearly every soldier in a 110-man column under Major Francis L. Dade was killed by Seminoles on December 28, 1835, while moving from Fort Brooke (Tampa) to relieve Fort King (Ocala). During the following years, more and more of the small American Army was sent to central Florida in an effort to quell the Indian resistance, reaching a peak of more than nine thousand regulars and militia in 1837. Roughly fifteen hundred of the soldiers died, most of disease rather than the Indians' guerrilla-styled attacks.

General Scott was placed in command but found it extremely difficult to come to grips with an enemy that raided plantations and settlements at will. It was nearly impossible to provision large bodies of troops in an area where the swampy terrain prevented the building of roads for supply wagons. The Seminoles were slowly pushed farther south, and the fighting began to taper off after Chief Osceola was captured in 1837. Portions of the tribe were also captured or agreed to move west.

WAR OF 1812 YEOMAN PATTERN SHAKO
This simple, easily manufactured shako lacks the leather front extension of other patterns of the period, and was issued to a variety of infantry regiments.

1813 PATTERN SHAKO
This 1813 pattern leather shako continued in general use long after the war. Diamond-shaped front plates were popular in the 1816–1825 period.

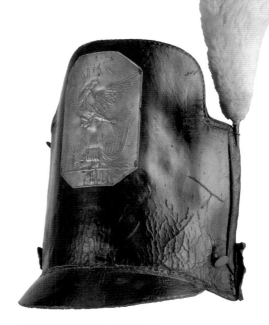

REGULATION 1813 LEATHER INFANTRY SHAKO
This "Tombstone" shako has its original helmet plate and period pom-pom but lacks the white worsted helmet cord that went with it.

1814 U.S. INFANTRY OFFICER'S CAP

Officers were expected to purchase their own uniforms and there was little uniformity to the cap insignias they put on their headgear. The example above has scalloped edges and is of better quality than the pewter plates worn by soldiers in the ranks.

MODEL 1821 BELL CROWN SHAKO

Issued to all enlisted personnel by the middle of the 1820s. Its trimming indicates that it was worn by a militia infantryman.

U.S. PISTOL, MODEL 1842

This .54-caliber pistol contained design features similar to the Model 1842 musket, the most important of which was the new percussion cap system—a vast improvement over flintlocks, which were prone to misfire in wet weather. The pistol also incorporated a swivel-headed ramrod, which prevented the ramrod from being dropped while reloading in the saddle. Mounted officers carried two pistols in saddle-mounted holsters, while dragoons and mounted riflemen carried one.

SERGEANT'S SWORD, C. 1812

Manufactured by William Rose of Philadelphia, this sword was used in the War of 1812. Rose had a contract to make sergeants' swords with wooden handles for the army. Its scabbard is made of leather.

OFFICER'S SWORD, C. 1812

Sword worn by Cornelius R. Van Wyck, a militia captain of light infantry raised in Dutchess County, New York, during the Revolution. He retired as a major shortly before hostilities reopened with Great Britain.

Nevertheless, the war dragged on and was not officially over until an uneasy peace was declared in 1842. Even then, a third war broke out between 1855 and 1858, and the remaining Seminoles withdrew to the Everglades.

Some 130 years later, even as a war began to brew a world away in Vietnam, an astute student of the army and its history, Russell Weigley, wrote of the army's performance during the Seminole Wars:

A historical pattern was beginning to work itself out; occasionally the American Army has had to wage a guerrilla war, but guerrilla warfare is so incongruous to the natural methods and habits of a stable and well-to-do society that the American Army has tended to regard it as abnormal and to forget about it whenever possible. Each new experience with irregular warfare has required, then, that appropriate techniques be learned all over again. So it was in the Seminole War, for even more than forest Indians farther north, the Seminoles refused to stake their future upon showdown battles but preferred instead to wear out their adversaries by means of raids and terror, and by turning their forbidding homeland itself into a weapon against their foes.

Coming in the midst of the Second Seminole War was the 1838 forced removal of the Cherokee Nation to the Indian Territory west of the new state of Arkansas. Because most of the Regular Army was tied down in Florida, Georgia's militia largely carried out the rounding up and confinement of the Cherokees. Scott was so appalled by the conditions he found in the temporary forts where Indians were held before the migration that he issued meticulous instructions on the handling of their property, personal weapons, and provisioning, as well as a stern warning that the order "will be carefully read at the head of every company in the Army." The order directed:

Every possible kindness, compatible with the necessity of removal, must therefore, be shown by the troops, and, if, in the ranks, a despicable individual should be found, capable of inflicting a wanton injury or insult on any Cherokee man, woman or child, it is hereby made the special duty of the nearest good officer or man, instantly to interpose, and to seize and consign the guilty wrench to the severest penalty of the laws.

As historians have noted, however, Scott's orders "were ignored by most troops that were not directly under his control."

RIGHT: James Bankhead served as a brigade major in the War of 1812, a lieutenant colonel of the 3d Artillery in 1832, and brevet colonel for meritorious conduct in the Florida campaign in 1838. He distinguished himself at the siege of Vera Cruz while commanding the 2d Artillery and was brevetted brigadier-general in March 1847. The following year, he was made commander of the Department of Orizaba, Mexico. At the time of his death in 1856, he commanded the Military Department of the East.

BELOW: Presentation Regimental Color is believed to be the oldest known flag used by the United States Corps of Cadets. On July 25, 1821, the entire Corps of Cadets from West Point began a summer march to Boston, after first traveling via steamship to Albany, New York. In Boston, the corps visited former President John Adams and received a stand of colors as a gift from the citizens of Boston. One of these colors was adopted as the "peculiar standard of the battalion" and shows Minerva presenting a wreath to Mars under the view of the Goddess of Liberty. The motto of the Corps of Engineers, *Essayons* (French for "Let us try"), appears under the figures, reflecting the long association between the United States Military Academy and the Corps of Engineers.

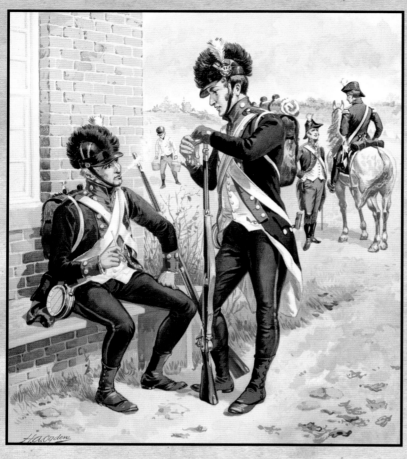

INFANTRY & ARTILLERY 1802–1810

GENERAL STAFF & LINE OFFICERS, LIGHT ARTILLERY 1813–1821

ARTILLERY, INFANTRY, CADET, DRAGOON 1813–1821

MAJOR GENERAL, STAFF & LINE OFFICERS, CADETS 1832–1835

RIGHT: This 1812 militia coatee was worn by James Hayward, who was in an Acton, Massachusetts, militia company of dragoons.

ARTILLERY, INFANTRY & DRAGOON (FULL DRESS) 1835–1850

BELOW: Militia coatee, c. 1808, believed to have been worn by a member of a Connecticut artillery company. The 1808 Militia Act placed the burden of national defense upon the states with federal support, and these coats are loosely based on U.S. Army uniform regulations of the period. The use of red coats was common for American militia in the early nineteenth century and understandably caused problems in the field when trying to identify mounted units at a distance, as occurred with the New York dragoon companies.

RIGHT: Mexican War-era U.S. dragoon coatee, issued from 1833 to 1847. This rare uniform example, which carries corporal's stripes, was used as a template for manufacturing firms holding government contracts. Its pristine condition is partially due to spending most of its time in storage.

ENGINEERS, FOOTRIFLES, DRAGOON, LIGHT ARTILLERY, INFANTRY 1851–1854

VOLTIGEUR, INFANTRY, DRAGOON, ARTILLERY (CAMPAIGN UNIFORM) 1844–1851

MAJOR GENERAL, STAFF, LINE OFFICERS UNDRESS UNIFORM 1841–1850

CAVALRY, DRAGOONS 1855–1858

ABOVE: Regular Army artillery drum made by Thomas Bringhurst of Germantown (Philadelphia), Pennsylvania. The style of the painted eagle on the "artillery red" drum dates it from the 1820–1830s. It is the earliest known artillery branch drum marked for the Regular Army. The scroll's painted "REGU.S.ARTLL.Y" indicates that branch of service.

BELOW: Drum used by Company A of the City Battalion of Newark, New Jersey. Organized as part of Essex Brigade of 1855, Company A was reorganized as the 8th New Jersey volunteers and today is an element of the 113th Infantry New Jersey National Guard. The drum was manufactured by William Hall & Sons of New York and has the state seal of New Jersey painted on its shell.

GENERAL-IN-CHIEF, ENGINEERS, ARTILLERY, CADETS 1858–1861

THE WAR WITH MEXICO

As Americans moved west in search of land and opportunity, not all of that expansion fell within the boundaries of the United States. Another new nation to the southwest, Mexico, was at first eager to have American immigrants develop its sparsely settled northern province called Texas. Between 1821 and 1830, large numbers of Americans moved there at the invitation of the Mexicans. But as their numbers quickly grew, the Mexican government became uneasy and ordered a halt to all immigration. Reassertion of its authority in the area spurred a revolt by Texans of both English and Spanish heritage, and volunteers from across the United States went to Texas to lend their support. Battles—which failed to subdue the revolt—were fought at the Alamo and San Jacinto that weakened and ultimately destroyed the Mexican Army under General Antonio López de Santa Anna.

Soon after winning its independence, the Republic of Texas—which was not recognized by Mexico in spite of having beaten its army—tried to become part of the United States, but objections from the northern states over its joining as a slave state delayed admittance to the Union until March 1845. Mexico, which harbored hopes of regaining its lost province, promptly broke off diplomatic relations with the United States, and both countries prepared for war.

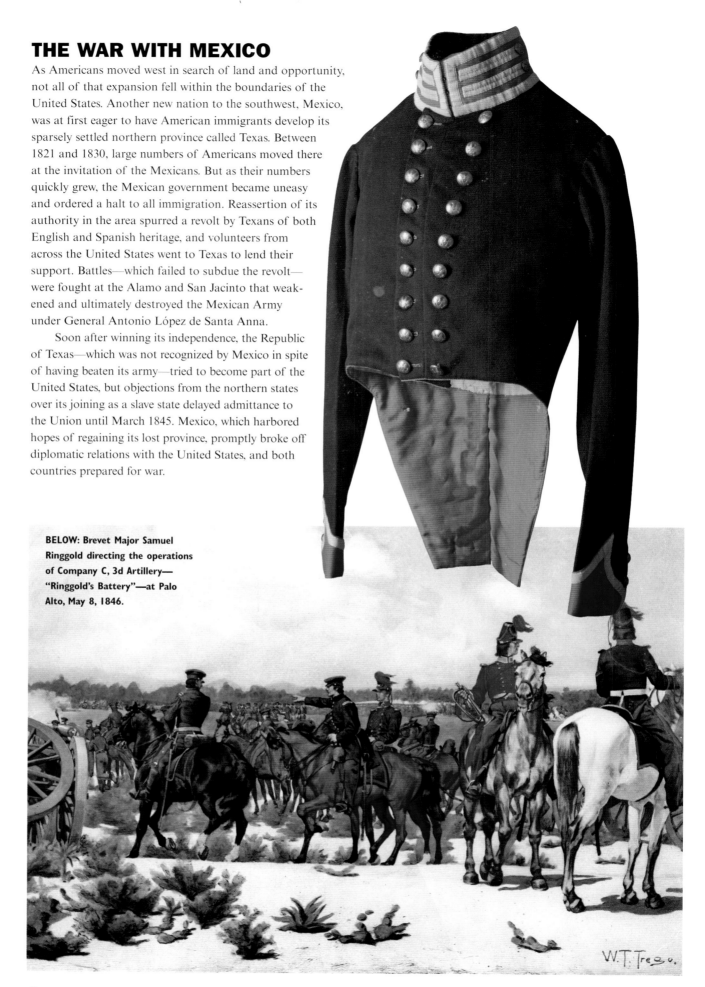

BELOW: Brevet Major Samuel Ringgold directing the operations of Company C, 3d Artillery— "Ringgold's Battery"—at Palo Alto, May 8, 1846.

PALO ALTO AND MONTEREY

Fighting began April 25, 1846, near Matamoros and was inevitably followed by full-scale battles. Mexican forces had ventured north of the Rio Grande, and Americans under General Zachary Taylor met them on May 8, 1846, at a watering hole known as Palo Alto. After an hour's artillery duel, the Americans attacked and drove the Mexicans back. Another battle the next day at Resaca de la Palma put the Mexicans to flight, and they scrambled back across the Rio Grande by ferry, by fords, and by swimming. As soon as news of those first victories reached home, people everywhere began taking up the slogan of the soldiers: "On to the Halls of the Montezumas!"

But the army was far too weak for such a task and wisely stayed on the defensive for the time being. In the weeks of waiting, the men on the Rio Grande were beginning to fear that they would see no action. But as autumn approached, it became clear that the Mexicans were preparing for a decisive confrontation. Their country had been torn by revolution, but the revolution had also developed skilled fighters, and now the war united all parties in complete confidence of victory. Able to outnumber the American troops almost everywhere and at any time of their choosing, Mexican leaders had little respect for their foe, and they welcomed battle.

Organizing his army of six thousand men into four divisions, Taylor took the offensive in September, heading toward Monterey and the Sierra Madre Mountains. Monterey guarded the pass through the mountains, and the Mexican force outnumbered the Americans by one thousand. Approaching the fortified hills of the city from the north, Taylor, affectionately called "Old Rough and Ready" by his men, planned to attack from two sides on September 24. The night before, American soldiers had silently neared Independence Hill and waited in a pouring rain. Early in the morning they began the

OPPOSITE TOP: Uniform coat of a private of "Ringgold's Battery," c. 1846. This full dress coatee is the pattern worn by enlisted men of Company C, 3d U.S. Artillery in the 1840s. Commanded by Brevet Major Samuel Ringgold, it was one of four companies designated as light artillery. With their field guns pulled by horse, the light artillery's maneuverability and firepower was crucial to the U.S. Army's ultimate success during the Mexican War. Ringgold's battery was called "horse" or "flyer" artillery because each man had his own mount, unlike the other light batteries in which most enlisted men walked or rode on the limbers or caissons of the battery. Therefore, Ringgold's men were given these mounted uniforms similar to those of the dragoons but trimmed distinctly as artillery.

ABOVE: Major General Zachary Taylor, c. 1848

BELOW: A U.S. Army supply train under attack by Mexican cavalry in 1847.

THE FIRST MILITARY PHOTOGRAPHY

Louis-Jacques-Mandé Daguerre's invention in the late 1830s of the first practical photographic process was an immediate sensation. A growing legion of photographers produced "daguerreotype" images but were limited to portraits and still-life subjects because of the length of time it took for images to be exposed on the photographic plates of silver-coated copper. Capturing any kind of action was utterly impossible, as even the slightest, slowest motion would produce a blur or fuzzy streak. If, for example, an arm movement was made fast enough, the appendage could completely disappear in the final print.

Newspaper accounts and other contemporary sources show that a handful of photographers followed the American armies that fought their way into Mexico. At least one of these intrepid businessmen, whose name is unknown today, set up a studio near the American headquarters in Saltillo. But instead of confining himself to portraits of soldiers, Mexican notables, and local architecture, he made it a point to capture events in progress and thus produced the first photographs of an army at war.

Within a decade after these images were recorded, the highly labor-intensive daguerreotype process was almost completely abandoned in favor of cameras using glass plate negatives. A simpler and much less expensive photographic process, glass plate negatives would capture some of the most memorable images of the coming war between the states.

BELOW: *The troops of the American volunteer infantry on a street in Saltillo, Mexico, in 1847 are lined up approximately fifteen abreast in about ten ranks. Two mounted American officers and about thirteen members of what is probably a regimental band appear in the foreground. The soldiers belong to either the 1st Virginia, 2d Mississippi, or 1st North Carolina volunteers.*

OPPOSITE TOP: *Major General John Ellis Wool daguerreotype portrait taken between 1844 and 1860. Wool served as General Taylor's deputy and later commander of the army of occupation in Mexico.*

RIGHT: *The Exeter New Hampshire volunteers march on parade in 1846 before beginning their long trip south.*

BELOW: *Mounted soldiers in Saltillo, Mexico, near the Buena Vista battlefield, c. 1847–1848. Notations of unknown provenance with another photo of this group identify this as Wool and his staff, but the senior officer wearing a greatcoat at center right is more likely the heavily mustachioed commander of the 1st Virginia volunteers, Colonel John Francis Hamtramck. He may be riding with a large party due to Wool's constant warning to volunteers against "the indulgence of a fancied security" and insistence that they maintain a strong vigilance in an enemy's country.*

almost vertical climb. Suddenly Mexican guards spotted them while they were still sixty feet from the top and opened fire. With a yell the Americans rushed up, and soon they had taken the western approach to Monterey. Meanwhile other fighting had been going on across the city as the troops had succeeded in breaking in from both directions. Though they had no special training in street fighting, almost instinctively the soldiers began scrambling to the roofs, breaking holes through house walls to move from one building to the next. On September 24, the Mexican flag came down, and American soldiers marched into the streets to the strains of "Yankee Doodle."

ABOVE: Major John M. Washington, pictured here in an early daguerreotype, was lost with 183 officers and men of the 4th Artillery when the steamer *San Francisco* was battered by two storms off the eastern seaboard. At least 150 passengers, mostly civilians, were rescued by other ships before the steamer went down. Washington had been washed overboard before the *San Francisco* sank on or about January 3, 1854. The major had been brevetted lieutenant colonel on February 23, 1847, for gallant and meritorious conduct in the Battle of Buena Vista when serving with the 3d Artillery. He was a relative of George Washington.

BUENA VISTA AND ACTION IN THE WEST

Early in 1847, Taylor continued his operations in northern Mexico where, at Buena Vista, American forces faced a much larger Mexican Army under General Santa Anna himself— the self-styled "Napoleon of the West." Many gullies and a deep-channeled stream broke up the old flood plain in the bottom of the pass, where the soldiers took up their positions. American forces prepared to meet an attack, which might come straight down the middle. But Santa Anna marched his troops around the edge of the plain, over rough ground, and came up on their left flank. The Indiana and Illinois volunteers were hard pressed, but conducted a fighting withdrawal in the face of a relentless Mexican attack.

At this moment, General Taylor came riding up. Waving an old, worn-out straw hat over his head, he called out, "Give them a little more grape, Captain [Braxton] Bragg." (The insignia of the 1st Field Artillery now

HALL CARBINE, MODEL 1843

In 1833 dragoon units received Hall breech-loading carbines with the percussion ignition system. This was the first military percussion arm adopted by any army in the world, and the 1st and 2d Regiments of Dragoons carried it during the Mexican War. This example was manufactured around 1849 in Middletown, Connecticut, under the Simon North contract.

BELOW: American Volunteer Infantry stand along a street in Saltillo, Mexico. Although the image was originally labeled "View in Parras, Mexico," the street is identical to that on the previous pages, and is possibly the only existing daguerreotype that clearly illustrates the common soldier of the Mexican War. Wearing federally issued, sky blue, woolen roundabout jackets and trousers with dark blue woolen forage caps, the volunteers are uniformed according to regulations for the U.S. Regular Army. The officer leaning on his sword at center-right wears a dark blue frock coat and pants with a wide white stripe on the uniform pant leg.

ABOVE INSET: The U.S. Model 1839 officer's forage cap was conceived as a universal fatigue headgear for all branches and was issued until the Civil War. This cap, c. 1845, has an infantry officer's insignia of a French hunting horn, which designated an infantry branch from 1833 to 1875.

shows a round of grapeshot.) Then Taylor saw the Kentuckians coming, and he rose in his stirrups shouting, "Hurrah for old Kentuck! That's the way to do it. Give 'em hell, damn 'em." Also coming up at a run were Colonel Jefferson Davis and his Mississippi Rifles, plus the 3d Indiana with a battery of cannons (now the 1st Battalion, 6th Field Artillery Regiment) that blasted other enemy formations with such a storm of grapeshot as to break them up completely. What had been nearly a defeat turned into a great triumph. That night the Mexican Army retreated, leaving the road strewn with debris and wounded men.

While Taylor's men were fighting in northern Mexico, General Stephen Kearny was marching with a force of one thousand men from Fort Leavenworth in the summer of 1846 to lay claim to the great Southwest. Kearney then left Santa Fe in September for the Pacific coast. Along the way he met Kit Carson with news that Commodore Robert Field Stockton of the U.S. Navy and Captain John C. Frémont, "The Pathfinder" of the U.S. Army Corps of Topographical Engineers, had already won control of California. On arriving there, however, Kearney found California's population less friendly than had been expected. Frémont seemed to have the area around San Francisco Bay and the Sacramento Valley pretty much in

hand, but the situation was not as good in the south, where a detachment of sailors and Marines under Stockton had won and then lost Los Angeles and Santa Barbara, and where a small garrison lay besieged in San Diego. Stockton was finally able to relieve that garrison, and Kearney's men fought their way in to join forces. Together they marched northward to Los Angeles and restored American control.

VERA CRUZ TO MEXICO CITY

Many years had passed since General Scott had fought in the War of 1812, but he was just as determined a fighter as ever. "Old Fuss and Feathers" intended to bring the war to a close by a seaborne expedition to the gulf city of Vera Cruz, and then striking directly at Mexico City. His army arrived on that foreign shore without accident or the loss of a man, and by midnight on March 9, 1847, ten thousand men surrounded Vera Cruz, which surrendered after a bombardment and siege.

At Cerro Gordo, American forces faced Mexican forces that, outnumbering them by nearly four thousand men, were entrenched in a mountain pass. But Captain Robert E. Lee, the engineer on Scott's staff, found a route where they could get through to attack the Mexicans from the rear. Key to the position was a steep hill known as El Telégrafo because there was a semaphore flag signal tower—or "telegraph"—on the hill. Men of the 2d, 3d, and 7th Infantry regiments stormed

LEFT: The storming of the Citadel of Chapultepec in Mexico City by U.S. soldiers and marines was illustrated by British artist James Walker, who witnessed the war's climactic September 13, 1847, battle. One hundred years later, U.S. President Harry S. Truman paid an unannounced visit to the monument that honors the young Mexican cadets who fought to the death defending the citadel. He placed a wreath and stood for a few moments in silent reverence. When asked by American reporters why he had gone to the monument, Truman said, "Brave men don't belong to any one country. I respect bravery wherever I see it."

ABOVE: Pre-Civil War military bugle, c. 1845–1855. The bugle is made of copper with brass floating rim and seams and has its original mounted cavalry cord.

BELOW: The attack on Mexico City as drawn by Joseph Goldsborough Bruff, a U.S. Military Academy graduate then working for the United States Bureau of Topographical Engineers. The Citadel of Chapultepec is at center left.

FUTURE CIVIL WAR GENERALS GAIN VALUABLE EXPERIENCE

On paper, the U.S. Army entered the Mexican-American War with a strength of more than nine thousand soldiers in fourteen regiments: eight of infantry, two of dragoons, and four of artillery. The sad reality, however, was that the army numbered barely fifty-three hundred in more than one hundred forts, stations, and posts scattered from Maine to Florida and west to a chain of forts stretching from Minnesota through Kansas and Oklahoma to the Gulf Coast of Texas. More than fifty thousand volunteers—not militia—rushed to the colors (less than a third of whom would reach Mexico before the shooting stopped). Trained to army standards, they were well led by their own officers and, for the first time in large numbers, professional soldiers who had graduated from the U.S. Military Academy (USMA) at West Point.

The West Pointers could always be found in the thick of the fighting, and both generals Scott and Taylor made excellent use of them on their staffs. Said Scott:

But for our graduated cadets the war between the United States and Mexico might, and probably would, have lasted some four or five years, with, in its first half, more defeats than victories falling to our share, whereas in less than two campaigns we conquered a great country and a peace without the loss of a single battle or skirmish.

Unlike the volunteer officers and men, the West Pointers and other regulars soldiered on. Some resigned their commissions only after many long years on the frontier and tedious garrison duty, while others remained in army blue until the division of the nation forced them to make hard choices as to where their loyalties lay.

Braxton Bragg (USMA class of '37) resigned to become a sugar planter, while classmate Joseph Hooker became a land developer. Jubal Anderson Early (also class of '37) left the army after the Second Seminole War to become a successful trial lawyer, then returned long enough to fight in Mexico. George B. McClellan (class of '46) made a small fortune as a railroad executive, and the popular William Tecumseh Sherman (class of '40) turned to banking. However, Sherman's roommate,

George Henry Thomas stayed in the army and, while teaching at West Point, recommended a promising young student, J.E.B. Stuart (class of '54), to the cavalry. The year before the Civil War, Thomas received an arrow in the chest during Indian fighting along the Brazos River in Texas.

Young Stuart stuck with military service as did John F. Reynolds (class of '41), James Longstreet (class of '42), and Winfield Scott Hancock (class of '44). Ulysses S. "Sam" Grant (class of '43), despite his assignment as a quartermaster during the war with Mexico, nevertheless participated in some of its fiercest battles and was twice brevetted for bravery in action. He resigned in 1855 under mysterious circumstances (rumored at the time to drink but with his official record completely clean) and was unable to keep any job for long. Grant's closest friend at West Point, John Bell "Sam" Hood, stayed in uniform, receiving a Comanche arrow through his left hand during action at Devil's River, Texas, in 1857.

Robert E. Lee (class of '29), whom many of these officers had served under at one time or another, was offered the rank of major general and command of the Union Army gathering around Washington. He regretfully refused, resigned his commission, and offered his services to his beloved state of Virginia.

Captain Ulysses S. Grant (USMA class of '43), shortly before he shipped out with the 4th Infantry in 1852, via Panama, to Fort Vancouver in the Washington Territory.

Brevet Major George S. Thomas (class of '40), during the period when he returned to West Point as an instructor of artillery and cavalry. Photo taken between early 1853 and May 1854.

Joseph Hooker (class of '37), possibly during his service as the assistant adjutant general of the Pacific Division, c. 1848, and after taking part in the Mexican-American War.

Major Robert E. Lee (class of '29), around the time of his 1855 transfer to the Indian Wars in Texas.

ABOVE: *Thomas J. Jackson (class of '46) as an instructor at the Virginia Military Institute, c. 1851. He had previously served in the Mexican-American War, and various garrisons. He later became General Lee's most trusted commander during the Civil War.*

OPPOSITE CENTER: *Brevet Second Lieutenant George Crook, 4th Infantry; Cadet Philip H. Sheridan; and Brevet Second Lieutenant John Nugen, 2d Infantry, taken when Crook and Nugen graduated from the U.S. Military Academy in 1852. Sheridan was originally part of the same class, but a one-year suspension due to his menacing a superior cadet from the South with a bayonet during a drill session delayed his graduation. Indian fighter Nugen died of consumption in 1857, and Crook served under Sheridan in the Civil War and again later against the Indians.*

First Lieutenant James Ewell Brown "J.E.B." Stuart (class of '54) was assigned to the U.S. Mounted Rifles in Texas after graduation, and promoted after transfer to the 1st Cavalry the following year.

the hill and successfully fought their way to the top, dislocating the Mexican defense and capturing three thousand troops and much of the Mexican Army's supplies.

By September, Scott's men were marching through the Valley of Mexico, approaching the capital city. Only one obstacle—Chapultepec—remained before them. Chapultepec was a hill rising nearly two hundred feet above the plain with a massive castle near its summit that housed the Mexican military academy. Cliffs and crags guarded its sides, and young cadets joined with the soldiers to defend their hill. All day long on September 12, American artillery battered the great stone walls of the fortress. After more bombardment the next day, American infantrymen advanced with columns, first attacking from the west and from the south. The first ladders were set up, and men began climbing, but the Mexicans hurled them to the ground. Other regiments were coming up. Soon there were enough ladders in place for men to scramble up fifty abreast. Though some of the cadets fought to the death rather than give up, this commanding hill was now in American hands, and Mexico City, two miles away, was at their mercy. The 6th Infantry later added scaling ladders to its regimental insignia to indicate its part in the taking of Chapultepec.

At dawn on September 14, General John Quitman, commanding the army's 4th Division, marched with his soldiers and Marines into Mexico City, covered in dust and minus one shoe that he had lost in battle. The 3d Cavalry, then the Regiment of Mounted Riflemen, led the way into the capital. Its men rushed up to raise the Stars and Stripes over the National Palace and flew their regimental colors from the balcony. When General Scott rode in and saw what had happened, he said, "Brave Rifles: You have been baptized in fire and blood and come out steel!" The inscription "Brave Rifles" is still displayed on the 3d Cavalry's regimental insignia. Other American troops continued to march into the city, but Scott left it to other generals to review them. Instead, Scott slowly climbed the stairway of the "Halls of the Montezumas" to write his dispatch announcing the victory that had effectively doubled the size of the United States.

ABOVE TOP: As regimental quartermaster and commissary officer of the 1st Cavalry at Fort Leavenworth, Kansas Territory, Lieutenant J.E.B. Stuart was responsible for acquiring local meat and produce, a task that required everything from personal inspections to running advertisements in area newspapers.

ABOVE BOTTOM: The model 1851–1858 uniform cap of a staff officer. This particular one belonged to George Archibald McCall who graduated the U.S. Military Academy in 1822 and was a colonel and Inspector General of the Army when he wore it. He reentered the army as a brigadier general at the outbreak of the war, was captured in 1863, and exchanged for Confederate Brigadier General Simon Bolivar Buckner (class of '25).

Victory over Mexico brought the United States an enormous amount of territory—more than 525,000 square miles—stretching from northern California to Texas. The trickle of American settlers pushing into the bleak, inhospitable lands soon grew to a torrent, and it fell to the tiny U.S. Army to keep the peace between them and the roughly 100,000 Indians sprinkled throughout the region. But unlike the Indians who could move great distances on almost no supplies, each troop movement had to be planned from water hole to creek to water hole, with anything further requiring the addition of slow-moving wagons carrying casks of water and grains for the animals.

As early as 1837, Major George Crossman proposed the use of camels as pack animals and, after the hard wartime experience of the southwest, Major Henry C. Wayne and Colonel Jefferson Davis, now a senator from Mississippi, pressed for the establishment of a Camel Corps in spite of considerable derision from their peers. The appointment of Davis as secretary of war in 1852, plus a $30,000 appropriation, finally pushed matters forward and Ward was sent to the Middle East to secure animals for testing. Camels of both one- and two-humped breeds were purchased from a variety of countries to find which types were most adaptable to the southwest's climate and food sources. Some 34 beasts and a small group of experienced handlers reached Texas in May 1856.

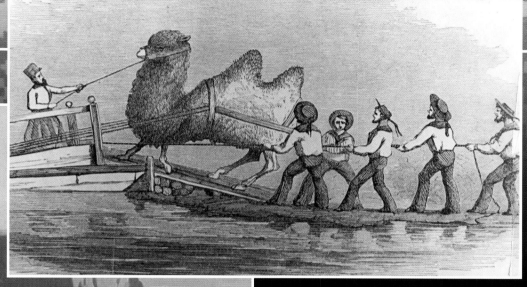

LEFT: *A detachment of the army's Camel Corps makes its epic 1857–1858 march of nearly 3,400 miles from Camp Verde, Texas, to Fort Tejon, California—and back.*

The U.S. Army Camel Corps was established at Camp Verde, Texas, sixty miles northwest of San Antonio, and forty-one more camels arrived in June 1857. Horses and mules initially were frightened by the shaggy monsters, and soldiers found that a normally docile camel, if not handled properly, could be just as troublesome as the most stubborn Missouri mule and could deliver a vicious bite. They also discovered that camels were unsuited to cavalry operations because the troops "almost to a man, complained of motion sickness after riding the animals for any distance or at a gallop." However, as pack animals they exceeded all expectations.

An average one-humped dromedary camel could carry five-hundred-fifty-pound loads—just over two mule loads—while the largest dromedaries could easily handle seven hundred to eight hundred pounds. Loads of more than twelve hundred pounds were not uncommon among the even more powerful, two-humped creatures. Wayne reported on a carefully timed and measured supply run from San Antonio to Camp Verde in September 1856: "From this trial it will be seen that the six camels transported over the same ground and distance, the weight of two six-mule wagons, and gained on them 42 hours in time."

The camels' ability to support far-flung military operations in even the most severe terrain and weather was manifest, and the War Department enthusiastically requested an appropriation for one thousand more in 1858. But Congress, heavily embroiled in the growing turmoil between the North and South, did not follow up. When war broke out, the Camel Corps, which had grown on its own to 111 animals (eighty at Camp Verde and thirty-one at Fort Tejon, California), was divided between the antagonists and fell into almost total disuse. Despite their superb performance and continued fighting with the Indians, support for anything having to do with Jefferson Davis, now the president of the Confederacy, was anathema to the Union.

Most of the camels were sold to circuses at public auctions. A number of them that were purchased by prospectors and freight haulers ultimately escaped. Others were released into the desert when no longer of any use. These animals and their descendants continued to haunt the southwest, some say as late as the 1920s. In 1885 or 1886 one wandered out of the waterless tract known as the Jornada del Muerto in the New Mexico Territory to pay a visit to Company K at Fort Selden. A sentinel and two small boys were flabbergasted to see the strange beast moving unconcernedly through the post's sheep herd, which scattered in a noisy panic.

The boys rode off to tell their father, garrison commander Captain Arthur MacArthur, who immediately recognized what it was and how it came to be there. The youngest of the wide-eyed pair was future U.S. Army General Douglas MacArthur.

SUMTER 1861

Chapter Three

Regulars, Volunteers, and Civil War, 1861–1865

The fifty thousand Americans who volunteered for the Mexican War returned to their civilian lives. The regulars, meanwhile, soldiered on with an authorized force of only ten thousand men to garrison the coastal fortifications and provide security to a western frontier that had ballooned by more than a million square miles. Yet while the number of regulars had grown only slightly from before the war, the expansion came from a very important addition to the force: the Regiment of Mounted Riflemen, generally known as the U.S. Mounted Rifles. Authorized by Congress in 1845 to establish "military stations on the route to Oregon," and outfitted specifically for extended, long-distance operation, it was thrust into the fighting with Mexico and did not begin the mission for which it was intended for several years.

In 1851, the U.S. Mounted Rifles began a decade-long struggle with the Indian tribes of west Texas, New Mexico, and Arizona. The other two conventional cavalry regiments, originally designated the 1st and 2d Dragoons, as well as all or part of eight Infantry regiments, fought a remarkable 208 engagements during this period, along with four more formations that were begrudgingly authorized by Congress in 1855. Ominously, one of these new units was given not one, but two, missions. The 4th Cavalry's detachment at Fort Riley in the Kansas Territory was principally involved in defending settlers and movement along the western trails from Cheyenne Indians, while its soldiers at Fort Leavenworth to the east were given the futile task of bringing order along the Missouri-Kansas border region as pro- and anti-slavery factions jockeyed for control of the territory's legislature during its bloody path to statehood.

During this same period, nearly one-third of the army was painstakingly gathered together in 1857 and 1858 for a mission that no one anticipated. Sent west into Utah, it was to remove Mormon leader Brigham Young from his position of territorial governor and reimpose federal authority in the face of attacks on immigrant wagon trains and the eviction of federal judges. The need to keep a lid on the unrest stretching all the way from Fort Leavenworth south to the Arkansas River resulted in a piecemeal deployment that Mormon guerrillas effectively countered for a time by using scorched-earth tactics and burning army supply columns. Federal forces continued to grow, however, and a negotiated settlement eventually defused the situation before the Mormon militia and U.S. Army came to blows. While the standoff in the Utah Territory came and went before most Americans even learned much about it, the deep divide over slavery and states' rights only worsened.

THE FIRST BLOWS

In 1859 the Harpers Ferry Arsenal in Virginia was briefly seized by raiders led by abolitionist John Brown, who was wanted for murder in Kansas. Brown's plans to spark a slave rebellion were thwarted by local militia and a company of Marines led by Robert E. Lee, now an army lieutenant colonel. But his attack and subsequent execution of Brown inflamed passions on both sides of the issue. The sixteen-thousand-man U.S. Army, and especially its officer corps, was not immune to these currents.

The grim situation reached the point of no return when southern states began to secede from the Union after the election of Abraham Lincoln in 1860. More joined the new Confederate States of America when the Union garrison at Fort Sumter was fired on and surrendered to South Carolinian forces. Rank-and-file soldiers under fixed enlistments stayed almost to a man with the Union, but officers had the option of resigning their commissions, and many agonized over the question of whether or not they should stay true to the oath they swore to

ABOVE: Canteen carried by G. Brandon, Company K, 30th Pennsylvania Infantry Regiment.

OPPOSITE: Abner Doubleday, here as a brigadier general, began the war as a captain of artillery firing the first shot in defense of Fort Sumter, and ended it as a brevet major general.

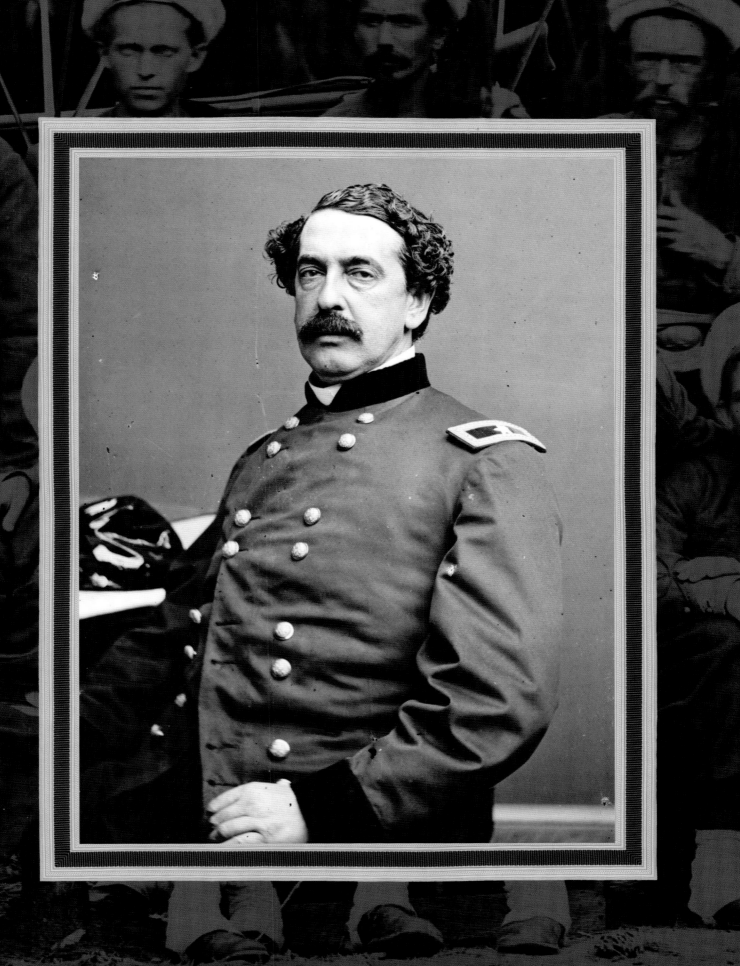

the United States. For Lee of Virginia, duty lay with the home state. For Winfield Scott, also of Virginia and now a lieutenant general, duty lay in support of the federal government. Of the army's 460 officers from secessionist states, 297—plus nineteen from the North—sided with the new Confederacy.

The resource-poor South's much smaller population and dependence on imported supplies from European nations put the Confederacy at a marked disadvantage for a lengthy war in comparison to the northern Union states. Scott proposed to take advantage of this disparity by establishing "a complete blockade of the Atlantic and Gulf ports" and "a powerful movement down the Mississippi to the ocean," which together would "envelop the insurgent States and bring them to terms with less bloodshed than by any other plan." Adequate ships and river craft for such campaigns, however, did not yet exist, and fire-brands in the North saw this strategy of strangulation—dubbed the "Anaconda Plan"—as too timid and time consuming.

Although the Navy would begin carrying out its part of the strategy immediately with the few ships available—as would Ulysses S. Grant when he assumed command in the west—the Confederate capital of Richmond, Virginia, lay tantalizingly close to Washington, D.C. Critics of Scott's strategy were convinced that if the Union forces could seize Richmond, the South would simply give up. Years of indecisive battle would consume the blood and treasure of the nation in this relatively small area as Union and Confederate armies attempted to win a decisive victory that would decide the war.

BULL RUN AND THE PENINSULA CAMPAIGN

As the politicians and newspapers cried out "On to Richmond," Union troops under Brigadier General Irvin A. McDowell marched out from Washington in July 1861 and into Virginia. The "Grand Army" was in high spirits and escorted by congressmen, federal officials, and untold numbers of sightseers who went along to watch "the rebellion crushed by a single blow." The Confederates under Brigadier General Pierre G.T. Beauregard met them near Manassas Junction, along Bull Run Creek, on July 21, 1861, and the result was confusion piled upon confusion as two ill-trained, ill-disciplined armies locked in fierce combat. Defeat would come to whichever side ran first.

At first it seemed that Federal troops had the upper hand. The main body of McDowell's force crossed Bull Run and succeeded in rolling back Beauregard's left flank. But the retreating Confederates rallied on a low ridge behind a brigade led by Brigadier General Thomas J. Jackson, who that day

ABOVE: Brigadier General Irvin A. McDowell

FAR RIGHT: Detail of a telegram sent by the commander of Fort Sumter, Major Robert Anderson, describing the events of the attack on his command in 1861. The island fort, defended by two companies of the 1st Artillery (only eighty-five officers and men, or less than an eighth of its designated strength), stood no chance of holding out for long against the much more numerous shore batteries manned by South Carolina militia and cadets from the Citadel military academy.

The brief dispatch mentions the garrison's final salute to the Stars and Stripes on April 13, 1861. It was only later that Northerners learned that the flagpole had been severed during the bombardment and that Lieutenant Norman J. Hall had raced through a raging fire—sustaining serious burn injuries to his face—and hoisted the flag on a makeshift pole with the help of other gunners. The 1st Artillery's Captain Abner Doubleday fired the first Union shot of the war in response to the bombardment.

RIGHT: This model 1850 staff and field officer's sword was carried by then-serving Captain Abner Doubleday, who, as second-in-command at Fort Sumter, used the sword to signal the firing of the first federal shot of the Civil War.

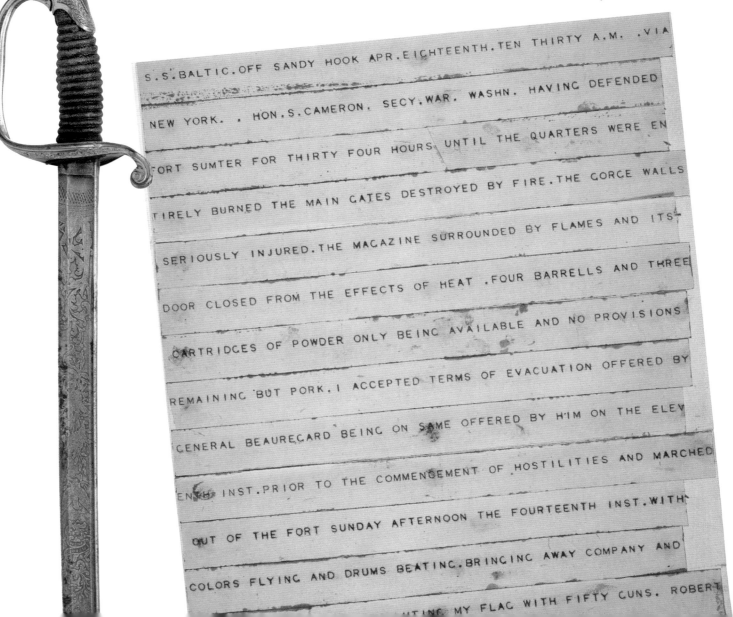

earned the name "Stonewall." After these troops' exhausting ten hours of fighting, Southern reinforcements arrived to turn the decision, and Beauregard staged a counterattack that drove the Federals from the field. Only a battalion of Regular Army— made up of detachments from the 2d, 3d, and 8th Infantry regiments—stood its ground and protected the retreat.

The rout sobered the North, but in the South success at Bull Run added to their confidence, and Confederate leaders felt sure they could whip the Yankees without any training. Military men knew better. Brigadier General Joseph E. Johnston, and then Lee, now a major general, were placed in command of the Confederacy's Army of Northern Virginia, while Major General George B. McClellan now commanded the Union's Army of the Potomac. All were determined to build their forces into effective professional armies. The ambitious McClellan, nicknamed "The Young Napoleon" and later "Little Mac," also lobbied success-fully to become general in chief of the Union armies—which by now had swelled to five hundred thousand men—when the aging Scott was edged into retirement late in 1861.

In the spring of 1862 the Union Army was ferried down the Potomac and Chesapeake to the end of the peninsula between the York and James rivers and began a cautious movement toward Richmond. The operation, commanded by McClellan, was an amphibious turning movement intended to capture the

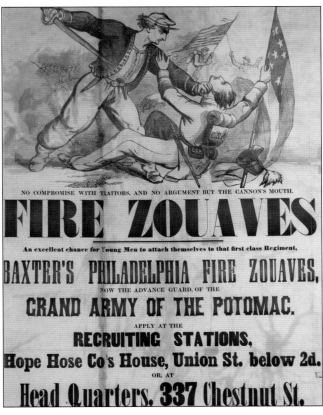

NO COMPROMISE WITH TRAITORS, AND NO ARGUMENT BUT THE CANNON'S MOUTH.

FIRE ZOUAVES

An excellent chance for Young Men to attach themselves to that first class Regiment,

BAXTER'S PHILADELPHIA FIRE ZOUAVES,

NOW THE ADVANCE GUARD, OF THE

GRAND ARMY OF THE POTOMAC.

APPLY AT THE

RECRUITING STATIONS,

Hope Hose Co's House, Union St. below 2d.

OR, AT

Head Quarters, 337 Chestnut St.

LEFT: The national colors of the 5th New York were made by "some admiring ladies of New York" in July 1861. After the unit's survivors were mustered out in May 1863, the extensive damage suffered in combat was cut away. The flag is preserved as part of the New York State Battle Flags Collection at the New York State Military Museum in Saratoga. The legend at the top reads: "Above Us, or Around Us."

RIGHT: Serving as part of V Corps' 2d Division, the 5th New York (Duryee's Zouaves) in full regalia attacks into the face of concentrated rebel fire during the Seven Days' Battle at Gaines' Mill. This June 27, 1862, action cost the unit fifty-five men killed, thirty-seven wounded, and fifteen unaccounted for. By the time the 5th fought at the Second Bull Run on August 30, the regiment was down to four hundred ninety men, and 117 more were killed or mortally wounded that day—the greatest single-day loss of life of any regiment during the war.

BELOW: Union soldiers gaze down upon the great Union supply base established at Cumberland Landing on the Pamunkey River to support General George B. McClellan's methodical advance toward Richmond. Like many panoramic scenes from the war, this image from the Peninsula Campaign is a composite of several photos.

Confederate capital by circumventing the Confederate Army in northern Virginia. The maneuver eventually involved more than one hundred fifty thousand Union troops, although no more than one-third of the force was in combat at any one time.

McClellan initially was successful against the equally cautious Johnston. But the character of the campaign changed after Johnston was badly wounded and Lee, now a brigadier general, emerged. Confederate forces under Lee—including Brigadier General J.E.B. Stuart's aggressively handled cavalry—stopped the Union Army within sight of Richmond in a complex series of hard-fought engagements known as the Seven Days' Battles, and in July it withdrew to the James River. McClellan had done a superb job of organizing and equipping the confused assortment of volunteer units sent forward by the Northern states but had performed poorly as a field commander. Though popular with the troops, would he learn from his mistakes and lead them to victory?

WAR IN THE WEST

Meanwhile, the first true signs of victory for the Union appeared in the west. "When in doubt, fight" was the motto of Major General Grant, who commanded forces in the Department of the Missouri and was determined to open the way to Tennessee. To protect a lateral railroad that was vital to their communications, the Confederates had built two forts ten miles apart— Fort Henry on the Tennessee River and Fort Donelson on the Cumberland—along the northern border of Tennessee. Finding a weak spot in the enemy's line, Grant moved boats up the Tennessee River to a point near Fort Henry, landed, and marched overland to seize the fort on February 6, 1862. His force then moved swiftly across the dozen miles to the stronger Fort Donelson on the Cumberland. He attacked with the support of naval gunboats in the river, but the fort's big guns drove them back. Unable to successfully storm the stronghold, his men hemmed in the defenders and prepared for a lengthy siege. Finally the Confederate commander, Brigadier General Simon B. Buckner, asked for terms. Grant's answer went back: "No terms except unconditional surrender can be accepted. I propose to move immediately on your works." The fort, along with some eleven thousand five hundred Confederate soldiers, surrendered on February 16.

In an attempt to recoup the situation after the losses of Fort Henry and Fort Donelson, Confederate forces under Beauregard and General Albert Sidney Johnston launched a surprise attack against Grant and very nearly defeated him. Grant's Army of the Tennessee, which was camped in peacetime fashion around the small log church named Shiloh, was caught completely off guard by the appearance of rebel troops on April 6, 1862. Although Confederate battle lines became confused and Johnston was killed during the first day's fighting, things had gone well for the Confederates. Union reinforcements from Major General Don Carlos Buell arrived in the evening and turned the tide the next morning when he and Grant launched a counterattack along the entire line. Beauregard's men were forced to retreat from the bloodiest battle in United States history up to that time— almost thirty-five hundred dead and sixteen thousand four hundred wounded, with the losses almost equally divided

ENLISTED DRESS HARDEE PATTERN HAT
Company G of a 6th Infantry Regiment
This style was made famous by the Iron Brigade
but also was worn by many other units.

OFFICER'S KEPI
143d New York Infantry Regiment
1st Division, XII Corps

OFFICER'S "PLUG" HAT
5th Infantry Regiment

ENLISTED BUMMER HAT
Company G, 24th Massachusetts Infantry Regiment
1st Division, XXIV Corps

ABOVE: Quartermaster Sergeant Henry E. Hayes of the 10th New York Cavalry before his promotion to second lieutenant. The fighting at Gettysburg, as well as battles and skirmishes throughout Virginia, wore away at the 10th—on one occasion driving its strength down to seventy-five men—but periodic surges of replacements from Syracuse, New York, helped keep it an effective fighting force. Excluding many losses to sickness and disease, the 10th New York Cavalry saw 537 of its ranks killed, captured or wounded before the South surrendered.

between the soldiers of the North and the South.

Later that month and far to the south, a powerful Union naval force under Captain David G. Farragut ran a gauntlet of fire from Confederate shore batteries that were guarding the approaches of New Orleans on April 24. His force arrived at the port three days later to find that it had been abandoned by the enemy. Although New Orleans was now denied to Southern blockade runners, men and supplies from states west of the Mississippi still flowed to the Confederate armies in the east.

Vicksburg, Mississippi, was the key to control of the river, and it was strongly fortified with cannons placed so high along its bluffs that guns on the Union's ships could not bombard them. Early in 1863 Grant, now commanding the Army and Department of the Tennessee, developed a bold plan for the conduct of the campaign. In late March, a corps under Major General William Tecumseh Sherman conducted a demonstration north of Vicksburg in an area where Union forces had earlier failed to reach the city. Grant's other two corps made a wide swing southward on the west side of the Mississippi, and then back to the river about thirty miles below the city. Sherman's corps followed the same route and, beginning on April 30, Admiral David D. Porter's river fleet ferried Grant's troops across to the Vicksburg side of the river.

Grant fought his way northeast and interposed his army between the garrison in Vicksburg and a large Confederate force under Brigadier General Joseph E. Johnston concentrated in the vicinity of Jackson, Mississippi, forty miles to the east. Assaults on May 18 and 22 failed to breach Vicksburg's defenses, and the Federals settled down to a siege. This meant weeks of keeping the Confederates penned in, improving trenches and digging them closer and closer to the defenders, and almost constant exchanges of cannon and rifle fire whenever an enemy showed his head. Inside Vicksburg the situation was becoming desperate as weeks went by without food and supplies. Lieutenant General John C. Pemberton, a Pennsylvanian in Confederate gray who commanded the Vicksburg garrison, saw that there was no way out. He met with Grant (they had served together in the same division in the Mexican War) and agreed to surrender on July 4, 1963. The 13th Infantry was the only Union regiment to plant its colors on the Confederate positions and today carries the motto "First at Vicksburg" on its insignia.

LEFT: A Federal artillery sergeant's frock coat. Though seldom worn by enlisted personnel in the field during the summer, the garment was much admired, and every soldier in the photo below is wearing it. To ease identification in the confusion of battle, everyone from private to captain (with officers wearing a grade device on each shoulder instead of chevrons on their arms) wore a single-breasted coat, while those of field-grade officers (majors through colonels) wore double-breasted. The buttons were arranged by twos on the double-breasted coats of brigadier generals and by threes on those of major generals and above, as in the photo on page 103.

BELOW: The 29th Connecticut Infantry Regiment (Colored) shortly after its arrival at Beaufort, South Carolina, in April 1864. Deployed to Virginia in August, the regiment counted 198 men dead during operations in the Richmond area and was the first formation to enter the Confederate capital after the surrender.

LEFT: At age seventeen in September 1861, Dominick Connolly enlisted in the Irish Brigade's 63d New York Infantry as a musician. Having survived the carnage at Antietam, where the regiment suffered 202 casualties (nearly a third of its losses during the war), he was captured at Gettysburg on July 2, 1863.

OPPOSITE: North of Sharpsburg, Maryland, Brigadier General William Edwin Starke's 2d Louisiana Brigade attempts to hold the Hagerstown Turnpike during the September 17, 1862, Battle of Antietam, but is on the verge of being overwhelmed by the Iron Brigade of Major General Joseph Hooker's I Corps. Led by Brigadier General John Gibbon, the unit was the 4th Brigade of Brigadier General Abner Doubleday's 1st Division and was then composed of one Indiana and three Wisconsin regiments. Three bullets mortally wounded Starke, and his Louisianans suffered grievous losses along this fence line, yet the hard-won Union advantage was not followed up.

BACKGROUND: Union soldiers and horses lie dead in a part of the Antietam battlefield where elements of Major General Edwin V. Sumner's II Corps came under fire from three sides during a disastrous mid-morning attack that followed Hooker's assault. The battle flared up again in the afternoon when Major General Ambrose Burnside's IX Corps attempted to turn the Confederate right flank south of Sharpsburg.

THRUST AND COUNTER-THRUST IN THE EAST

Shortly before McClellan's campaign on the peninsula, a small Confederate force in western Virginia's Shenandoah Valley, superbly handled by Stonewall Jackson, now a major general, had nearly defeated a much larger Union force in March 1862. While Jackson's force had been beaten, it nevertheless remained a significant threat to Washington, D.C., forcing Union troops that would have gone to McClellan's operation to remain behind and guard the capital. At the height of the fighting on the peninsula, more troops were added to Union forces in the region with orders to advance south down the Shenandoah Valley and then east against Richmond to relieve McClellan. Though outnumbered three to one, Jackson maneuvered with great skill, making two and a half round-trips up and down the valley and through mountain passes over a six-week period, and defeating the superior—but uncoordinated—Union commands during five battles against three Union armies. By June 9, 1862, Union troops were forced to withdraw almost completely from the area, having failed to develop either a threat against Richmond or provide reinforcements to McClellan.

After the stinging defeat to Jackson in the Valley, the separate Union commands in western Virginia were gathered into a single army under Major General John Pope. Lee hoped to draw Pope into a battle on his own terms and to destroy the Union

force before it could join with McClellan's Army of the Potomac. To this end, Jackson struck northwest from Richmond in late July and captured the Union supply depot at Manassas Junction, threatening Pope's line of communications with Washington, D.C. Going on the attack to destroy the apparently outnumbered Jackson, Pope's army was soundly defeated when additional Confederate forces under the command of Lieutenant General James Longstreet, fresh from the fighting on the peninsula, arrived almost unseen on his flank. A massive assault by Longstreet's five divisions on September 2 crushed the Union left and Pope's army was thrown into retreat in what became known as the Second Battle of Bull Run.

Lee immediately followed his victory at Manassas Junction with an invasion of the North in order to gather supplies, relieve pressure on Virginia, and perhaps force the Union to sue for peace. By September 4, Lee's Army of Northern Virginia had reached Frederick, Maryland, with roughly fifty-five thousand men, but was forced to detach Jackson's divisions to guard against interference from the large Union garrison at Harpers Ferry. While Lee moved with the remainder of his command across the Blue Ridge Mountains to Hagerstown, McClellan approached from the southeast with ninety thousand men, arriving at Frederick on September 12. Learning of Lee's plans, he set off in pursuit, hoping to defeat the Confederate units in detail as they passed through mountain gaps. However, Lee was able to concentrate his army, including Jackson's corps, at Sharpsburg on Antietam Creek. McClellan

SPRINGFIELD RIFLE-MUSKET, MODEL 1855
The stamp on the butt of this .58-caliber rifle says "11 CV," indicating its use by the 11th Connecticut Volunteers, and was the type used by the regiment at Antietam. This rifle is also stamped 1858 on the lock plate and uses the Maynard percussion priming system.

ABOVE: Major General Ambrose Burnside

RIGHT TOP: Viewed from the Federal side of Antietam Creek, the 51st Pennsylvania makes its first assault over the Rohrbach Bridge on the Confederate right flank. Their brigade commander Brigadier General Edward Ferrero had galloped up to the regiment with the fateful command, "General Burnside orders the Fifty-first Pennsylvania to storm the bridge," and the instant his men came into the open ground in the valley they received a withering fire from Confederate infantry on the high ground. A fence skirting the road proved a serious impediment, and in crossing it, the men were badly exposed even before funneling onto the narrow structure.

RIGHT BOTTOM: A Confederate rifleman's view of the Rohrbach Bridge. The heights above the bridge were defended by troops of the 2d and 20th Georgia regiments. The successful assault cost the Union forces dearly, with more than five hundred casualties, almost half in the last attempt alone.

ABOVE: Colonel Edward Ferrero, pictured here after his promotion to major general two years later in 1864. At Antietam, during the first fight for the bridge, Ferrero commanded the 2d Brigade of Brigadier General Samuel Sturgis' division, as well as the 51st New York and the similarly designated 51st Pennsylvania. Ferrero recently had taken the unruly Pennsylvanians' whiskey rations away and promised to give it back if they were able to carry the bridge. True to his word, the soldiers got their whiskey. The subsequent drive by Ambrose Burnside's IX Corps was blunted by the timely arrival of Confederate Major General A.P. Hill's division from Harpers Ferry.

On this bloodiest day in American history, September 17, 1862, the Union and Confederate armies lost approximately twenty-three thousand men, including more than thirty-six hundred dead. In a pattern that would repeat itself over and over again, the North's 12,401 casualties exceeded the South's 10,318. While this amounted to a quarter of the Union force, it represented nearly a third of the smaller Confederate Army.

LEFT: The Rohrbach Bridge (also called the "lower bridge") from the Union-held west bank.

BELOW: The 93d New York
Infantry camp at Antietam,
Maryland, September 1862. Like
nearly twenty-five thousand
other soldiers in Major General
McClellan's ninety-thousand-
man Army of the Potomac,
the regiment was not actively
engaged. They had been detailed
to perform provost guard
duty at headquarters, a post
occupied by the 93d for two
years. Then, at the beginning
of the Battle of the Wilderness
in May 1864, the regiment (a
large proportion of which had
reenlisted) was assigned to the
2d Brigade of II Corps' 3d
Division and showed its fighting
mettle, resulting in 258 killed or
wounded out of 433 engaged.

launched attack after attack on September 17, but was unable to break the Confederate line.

Lee's much smaller army suffered more than 10,300 casualties and shrank even more when it reached the safety of Virginia as another 3,400 men simply left for home. Antietam also provided President Lincoln with the victory he needed to announce the abolition of slavery in the South—a move that would have looked like an act of desperation if it were announced after a string of Union defeats. With the Emancipation Proclamation, Lincoln was able to broaden the base of the war, and prevented England and France from lending stronger support to a country that engaged in human bondage.

Lincoln and his senior military and civilian advisors were disappointed that McClellan's much larger force had not destroyed Lee's Army of Northern Virginia, and became outraged when McClellan refused to pursue the beaten Lee even though fully one-third of his force was completely fresh, having never entered the battle. McClellan was replaced by Major General Ambrose Burnside, who decided to make a drive across the Rappahannock River at Fredericksburg to get between Lee and Richmond. Success depended on speed, but Burnside's ponderous, poorly coordinated advance allowed Lee plenty of time to gather his forces along Marye's Heights, against which the Union commander obligingly conducted a series of massive, exceedingly costly assaults. Repulsed with dreadful casualties, the Army of the Potomac withdrew across the river on the night of December 15, and Major General Joseph Hooker replaced Burnside as winter brought an end to the terrible carnage of 1862.

*My Dear McClellan:
If you are not using the
army, I should like to
borrow it for a short while.*

*Yours respectfully,
Abraham Lincoln*

LINCOLN'S QUEST FOR AN AGGRESSIVE GENERAL

The crushing Confederate losses at Antietam and the large number of fresh Union formations placed General Robert E. Lee's Army of Northern Virginia in a dangerous situation. Lee was fortunate, however, that his opponent was "Little Mac" George B. McClellan.

Under Irvin McDowell, the Union forces had been outgeneraled by Southern commanders at Bull Run and again under John Pope at the Second Battle of Bull Run. McClellan, for a time, had been put in charge of all Federal forces on the confident promise that he would build the Union Army into a fighting machine of unrivaled power. He was true to his word, yet it soon became apparent that McClellan did not handle his formations as adroitly as Lee, and he became increasingly cautious over time. McClellan was placed in charge solely of the Army of the Potomac—ostensibly so that he could better focus his attention on destroying Lee's forces—but his unending stream of excuses for not pursuing the battered Confederates after Antietam finally resulted in his relief in November 1862.

IX Corps' Ambrose Burnside assumed the Army of the Potomac's command but was sent back to IX Corps after his defeat at Fredericksburg. Burnside generally handled his divisions well, but IX Corps literally became lost in the woods at a critical time during the Battle of the Wilderness. Worse still, the afternoon before he attacked across a massive crater that was blown in the enemy lines outside Petersburg, the Negro division that he had trained for two weeks in the intricate and swift maneuvers to exploit the blast was replaced by an inexperienced white division with disastrous results—yet it was Burnside who was relieved in disgrace. After the South's surrender, Ulysses S. Grant admitted that replacing the specially trained troops was a mistake, and Burnside was exonerated by a joint committee of Congress.

Next to command the Army of the Potomac was Joseph Hooker, who had led a Grand Division of two corps under Burnside. After his defeat at Chancellorsville, Hooker was transferred to Tennessee. There he successfully commanded a succession of corps under Grant, and then William Tecumseh Sherman, with victories at Lookout Mountain, Chattanooga, and the drive to Atlanta. Although Burnside and Hooker saw considerable action as corps commanders after their brief stints in higher command, their predecessors, Pope and McDowell, were far less fortunate. Both generals found themselves banished to postings in the west, where Pope almost immediately became involved in a major conflict with the Sioux, while McDowell sat out the war in California.

As for McClellan, he ran for president on the Democratic ticket in 1864 and was beaten handily by incumbent Abraham Lincoln. Moreover, the results of the "soldier vote" came as a bitter disappointment to "Little Mac," as nearly one hundred twenty thousand of their one hundred fifty-four thousand ballots were cast for Lincoln. Although the dashing young general was immensely popular with the troops, particularly those outside Washington, by late 1864 these same men all agreed that if a less cautious commander had been in charge early in the war, they'd have all been home by now. As it was, though, Lincoln struggled for almost a year after Antietam to find the right man to lead the Army of the Potomac.

ABOVE INSET: *General George B. McClellan and his staff meet with President Abraham Lincoln after the Battle of Antietam. Lincoln removed McClellan from command shortly after the meeting and replaced him with Major General Ambrose Burnside, who he believed would be more aggressive.*

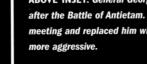

ENLISTED DRESS HARDEE PATTERN HAT
Army Engineer, Company B

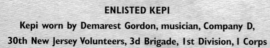

ENLISTED KEPI
Kepi worn by Demarest Gordon, musician, Company D,
30th New Jersey Volunteers, 3d Brigade, 1st Division, I Corps

OFFICER'S KEPI
16th New York Infantry Regiment

FOUR-BUTTON BLOUSE OR SACK COAT

The regulation fatigue coat, commonly called a four-button blouse or sack coat, was the standard outer garment of Union enlisted troops and was frequently worn by cavalry officers in the latter years of the war. The fatigue coat contained an interior pocket and muslin lining that was frequently ripped out by soldiers in the heat of the summer and also used to make bandages in an emergency. Displayed with this coat: a standard infantry cross belt, a bayonet attached to the belt by a bayonet frog, and a leather cap pouch for the storage of copper percussion caps needed to fire a rifle.

ENLISTED ZOUAVE CAP
Regiment unknown

ENLISTED KEPI
Company A, 122d New York Infantry Regiment

OFFICERS'S KEPI
14th New York Infantry Regiment

SHELL JACKET

Originally adopted by the U.S. Army in 1833, waist-length shell jackets were worn principally by enlisted soldiers of the artillery and cavalry with piping (trim) and chevrons of, respectively, red and yellow. This pattern was still used among the artillery and cavalry for a time after the South's surrender, but even during the war numerous units began to switch to the tougher and more comfortable four-button blouse—a process that occurred much more quickly and fully among the infantry and engineer units that began the war with the jacket.

LEFT: *An infantry overcoat with a cape. Frequently referred to as a cape or great coat, this garment's owner modified it in the field with chest pockets that helped keep his hands warm during cold weather. Although some soldiers found the detachable cape alternately unwieldy or restrictive (and top buttons were known to be pulled off during frequent wear), it was warm, looked sharp, and was popular with the troops.*

RIGHT: *Unknown soldier outfitted with his full field equipment, including his overcoat.*

CIVIL WAR ERA ARMY CAMP LIFE

In the field, every soldier would carry a "shelter half" which, combined with a second piece carried by another soldier, made a two-man pup tent. When bivouacking at a location for more than a few days or at a large encampment, troops could expect that better shelter would be made available, usually ten-man Sibley tents like those at left, which were almost invariably warmed by . . . Sibley stoves. Conically shaped like the tents, the stoves were admired for their fuel efficiency and remained standard issue within the Army all the way up to World War II, although the unwieldy tents were largely discarded after the Civil War. In the painting at left, the enterprising occupants of the second tent have removed its unique adjustable vent and run a chimney pipe through the top. The photo below shows a mix of Sibley and four-man wedge tents (the officers were quartered in the row of cabins at left). Ironically, Henry Hopkins Sibley, who designed the equipment, which bore his name, threw in his lot with the South and became a brigadier general in the Confederate Army.

A small force of perhaps 10,000 to 15,000 men could generally live off the land while on the march—and columns of up 30,000 regularly did do so in abundant counties—but quartering in "permanent" camps and large troop move-ments required Army quartermasters to make extensive arrangements for provisioning. Even if a corps of roughly 20,000 men was camped close to a railhead or river base, provisioning commonly required the use of at least 500 wagons to make the ponderously slow round trips. The raw quantity of needed wagons, horses, and mules (which themselves required many of the wagons to be filled with forage) could easily double depending on distance and circumstances. If the corps was ordered to move out, the number could double again. Wagons moved at a pace no faster than a marching soldier on their round-trip supply runs, each carrying about a ton of cargo, which, in terms of food, equaled roughly 1,000 rations.

Despite wide-scale graft and profiteering among civil-ian contractors, food and war supplies were considered plentiful—at least for Union soldiers. Sickness was the principal scourge of camp life, and in fact, twice as many men died from smallpox, dysentery, typhoid, measles, and other diseases than to bullets and cannon fire. The war would ultimately see 244,771 Union men succumb to illness and accidental deaths, and an undocumented—but certainly nearly as high—number of Confederate men losing their lives to nonbattle causes as well.

OPPOSITE TOP: *Soldiers emerge from their Sibley tents for reveille on a cold, cold winter morning.*

BELOW: *The 150th Pennsylvania Infantry parading in winter camp near Belle Plain, Virginia, during March 1863, three weeks before the battle of Chancellorsville. Later that summer, two members of the regiment would be awarded the Medal of Honor for their deeds at Gettysburg. Before they were mustered out in June 1865, the regiment would lose 112 men to the enemy and 94 to disease.*

Let us cross over the river and rest under the shade of the trees.

—General Thomas "Stonewall" Jackson
His last words.

GETTYSBURG

The Army of the Potomac, this time under Hooker, crossed the Rappahannock River on the morning of April 27, 1863. Commanding a force roughly twice as large as anything the Confederacy could put into the field, the Union leadership was confident of victory as Hooker's planned double envelopment involving two corps under Major General John Sedgwick, and five under Hooker himself, should have had little trouble overpowering Lee. However, Lee took the risk of dividing his army in the presence of the much larger Union force—timidly handled by Hooker—and succeeded in keeping him off balance through a series of skillful maneuvers near Chancellorsville. Heavy fighting raged for nearly a week, particularly near the village of Spotsylvania Court House, before Hooker withdrew across the Rappahannock on May 6. The magnificent Confederate victory was tempered, however, when in the smoke and confusion Jackson was mortally wounded by his own troops, a loss that shook Lee and prompted him to declare, "I have lost my right arm!" The loss would soon be keenly felt.

Encouraged by the victory at Chancellorsville, and perhaps anxious for a victory to counter the imminent, disastrous loss of Vicksburg in the west, Lee pushed on to make an all-out effort for complete victory by an invasion of the North. In June 1863, Lee led his splendid Army of Northern Virginia—nearly eighty thousand strong—across the Potomac, through Maryland, and into Pennsylvania with the hope of drawing the Union forces into a decisive battle. Because his force was sadly lacking in supplies, Lee dispersed it across a broad front so that individual columns could live off the rich stores of food and materials it would certainly find in the North.

Hooker, meanwhile, had become aware of Lee's movement and promptly started north, crossing the Potomac with the intention of keeping his men between the Confederates and Washington. But as Hooker moved to shield the capital, he became embroiled in an argument with Lincoln's army chief of staff, Lieutenant General Henry W. "Old Brains" Halleck, and was replaced by Major General George G. Meade, a methodical, but not overly cautious, officer who would command the Army of the Potomac for the rest of the war. Although Lee wouldn't

ABOVE: Major General George G. Meade. An aggressive officer, Meade rose from brigade to division to I Corps commander in the space of three weeks in September 1862. Unexpectedly thrust into command of the Army of the Potomac immediately before the July 1863 Battle of Gettysburg, he led the army for the duration of the war.

BELOW: Federal soldiers removing wounded across the Rappahannock River under a flag of truce after the Battle of Chancellorsville. Of the ninety thousand Union men who bore the brunt of the fighting, more than seventeen thousand fell in battle from April 30 through May 6, 1863. The Union was shocked by the defeat, and President Abraham Lincoln was quoted as saying, "My God! My God! What will the country say?"

RIGHT: An enlisted man's belt with cap pouch, bayonet, and scabbard. The volume and accuracy of rifle fire significantly reduced the number of casualties generated by man-to-man combat—unlike the result of earlier wars—as assaults were frequently forced to a halt before reaching their objectives. But if a strong body of bayonet-wielding soldiers looked like it might reach the defenders, it was sometimes enough to make even veteran soldiers turn and run. In either case, most bayonets never tasted an enemy's blood, but the rounded or three-sided weapons—they were sharpened only at the tip—did make excellent tent pegs or candle holders. The bayonet's greatest utility, however, came when both Blue and Gray infantrymen combined it with a pair of cupped hands or tin plate to create their principal entrenching tool.

ABOVE: Brigadier General John Buford

learn of the command change until it was reported in the newspapers, he was aware that Union troops were coming after him and ordered his Army of Northern Virginia to immediately concentrate at a Pennsylvania crossroads town called Gettysburg.

On June 29, elements of Lee's army were camped along the roads converging on Gettysburg from the north. Marching toward the town the next morning, Southern brigades ran into some Federal cavalry. "That's all right," said Brigadier General Henry Heth, the ranking Confederate officer at the little skirmish. "[It's] only some of that Pennsylvania militia." What they had actually run into was the 1st Cavalry Division of Brigadier General John Buford. Armed with rapid-firing carbines, the troopers held off the increasingly large Confederate attacks, buying time for more Federal units to reach the town. Finally the troopers began to give way, but as the Confederates reached the edge of the woods, intense firing broke out, and a line of men, with bayonets low, came at their flank. It was Brigadier General Solomon Meredith's "Iron Brigade."

After the first repulse, Confederate reinforcements began arriving from the north and west, while the Federals were streaming up from the south. Soon, Lee arrived on the scene, and the Confederates were able to push back the forces in front of the town. Neither side had planned to fight here, but now the Battle of Gettysburg was on as Meade directed his units—some as far south as Washington—to meet the threat. Commanding the Union defenders in front of Gettysburg was I Corps commander Major General John F. Reynolds, who promptly ascended a ridge that ran between the fighting and the town to observe the developing battle. To the north and west he could see more and more columns of gray coming toward him. Turning to the rear, he could see the town and, beyond it to the south, the ground that seemed to dominate the area. The key feature appeared to be a big hill up near the old cemetery.

The hills south of Gettysburg followed the shape of a giant fishhook. Cemetery Hill formed the bent part of the hook closest to the town. The hook's barb, to the north and east, was a low

SPENCER REPEATING RIFLE

A soldier was considered a fast shooter if he could get off three rounds per minute from a muzzle-loading rifle, but the Spencer repeating rifle used rimfire cartridges stored in a seven-round tube magazine, enabling the rounds to be fired one after another. When empty, the tube could be reloaded rapidly with fresh cartridges. To fire the Spencer, a soldier used a lever to extract the used shell and feed a new cartridge from the tube while almost simultaneously cocking the hammer manually.

LEFT: The Lutheran Theological Seminary at Gettysburg, Pennsylvania. From the cupola at the top of the building, Federal commanders watched the steadily growing battle and the advance of rebel forces on July 1, 1863.

BELOW: The fanciful *Gettysburg: the First Day*, painted for Confederate cavalry officer Fitzhugh Lee after the war, depicts soldiers fighting hand to hand on the Harrisburg Road as Southern forces close in on the seminary. Further in the distance is the "fishhook" of high ground that bedeviled the Confederates on the battle's second and third days.

GETTYSBURG, DAY 2

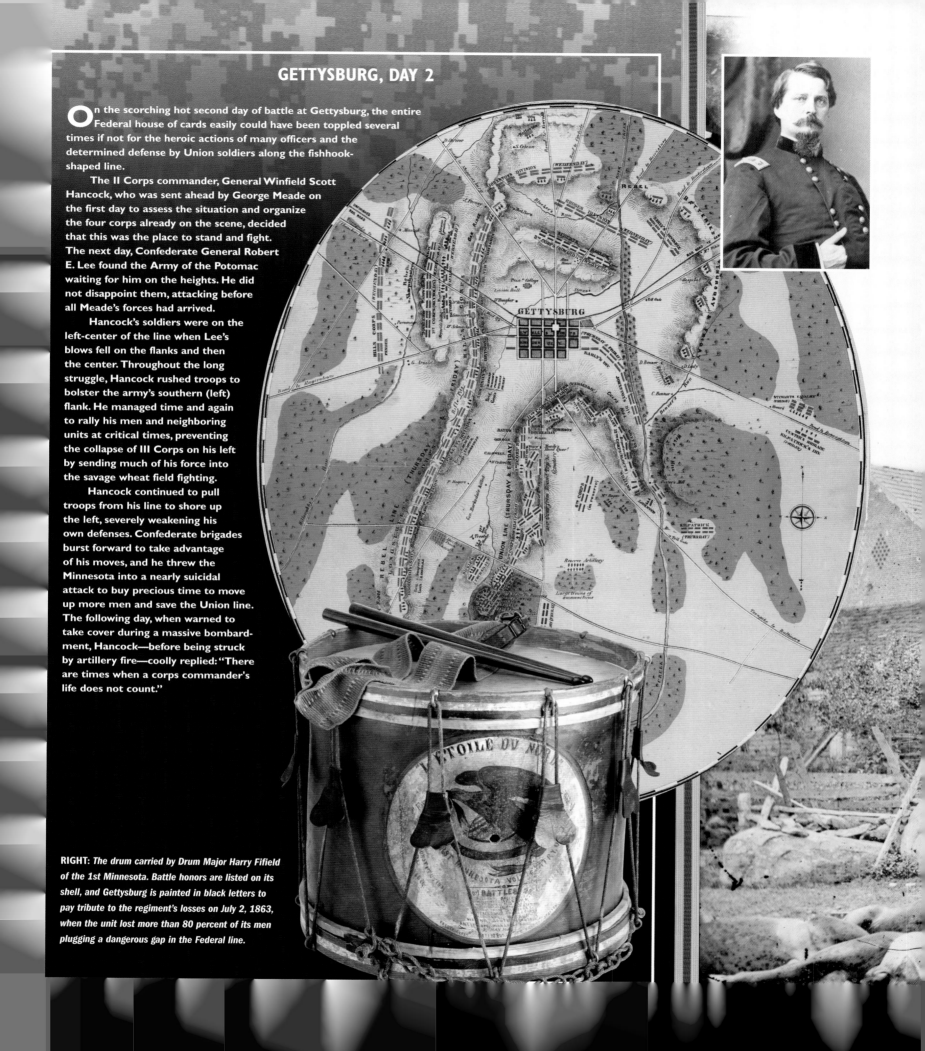

On the scorching hot second day of battle at Gettysburg, the entire Federal house of cards easily could have been toppled several times if not for the heroic actions of many officers and the determined defense by Union soldiers along the fishhook-shaped line.

The II Corps commander, General Winfield Scott Hancock, who was sent ahead by George Meade on the first day to assess the situation and organize the four corps already on the scene, decided that this was the place to stand and fight. The next day, Confederate General Robert E. Lee found the Army of the Potomac waiting for him on the heights. He did not disappoint them, attacking before all Meade's forces had arrived.

Hancock's soldiers were on the left-center of the line when Lee's blows fell on the flanks and then the center. Throughout the long struggle, Hancock rushed troops to bolster the army's southern (left) flank. He managed time and again to rally his men and neighboring units at critical times, preventing the collapse of III Corps on his left by sending much of his force into the savage wheat field fighting.

Hancock continued to pull troops from his line to shore up the left, severely weakening his own defenses. Confederate brigades burst forward to take advantage of his moves, and he threw the Minnesota into a nearly suicidal attack to buy precious time to move up more men and save the Union line. The following day, when warned to take cover during a massive bombard-ment, Hancock—before being struck by artillery fire—coolly replied: "There are times when a corps commander's life does not count."

RIGHT: *The drum carried by Drum Major Harry Fifield of the 1st Minnesota. Battle honors are listed on its shell, and Gettysburg is painted in black letters to pay tribute to the regiment's losses on July 2, 1863, when the unit lost more than 80 percent of its men plugging a dangerous gap in the Federal line.*

LEFT: On the second day at Gettysburg, Major General Winfield S. Hancock ordered the 1st Minnesota Volunteer Infantry forward to help stop the Confederate surge, knowing full well that they would take horrific casualties. His actions arguably saved the day for the Union forces and helped preserve their lines.

LEFT: Captain John Bigelow, commander of the 9th Massachusetts Light Battery. On July 2, 1863, under heavy artillery fire, he reinforced the hard-pressed lines of the III Corps near the Peach Orchard at Gettysburg.

BELOW: The field outside of Trostle's barn where Captain Bigelow's battery was badly mauled by Confederate fire. His artillerymen delayed the rebels long enough for the Union line to be reformed, leaving twenty-eight killed and wounded (including Bigelow, who was wounded by a shot in the side), sixty of its eighty-eight horses dead, and twenty more horses wounded. Four of the battery's six guns were captured, but all were recovered that evening during a Union counterattack. On the following day the battery, now under the command of Junior Second Lieutenant John S. Milton and consisting of but two guns, was engaged at Zeigler's Grove near Cemetery Hill, where it helped to stem Major General George E. Pickett's charge.

LEFT: Gouverneur K. Warren after his promotion to major general. During the brutal fighting below the heights, Warren discovered that the crest of Little Round Top was not occupied. Although as George Meade's chief engineer he had no command authority, he immediately rushed forces into the area on his own initiative to defend the Federals' left flank and ward off what could have been complete disaster for the Army of the Potomac.

BELOW: Little Round Top from the vantage point of Colonel Strong Vincent's brigade. The Emmitsburg Road passes through the center of the image, and Devil's Den is below the line of sight at the foot of the hill.

knoll called Culp's Hill, and the point was a lower knob six hundred yards south of the hill. The shank of the hook was Cemetery Ridge, which had long, cleared slopes that ran southward from Cemetery Hill to two other hills at the southern end of the formation—the eye of the fishhook. The two hills, called Round Top and Little Round Top, looked like big piles of boulders covered with scrubby bushes and trees. Across a small valley to the northwest of Round Top was another hill, not as high, but broken and wild. It was called Devil's Den because of its deep, treacherous chasms.

Reynolds saw that the ground around Cemetery Hill would be best used for defense, so he sent a note to Meade with a recommendation that this was the place to stand and fight. Reynolds went back down to join his troops and was killed almost immediately by a Confederate bullet through his head.

During the afternoon the outnumbered Union troops gave way, retreating back through Gettysburg and up Cemetery Hill. That night was one of feverish activity on both sides. Meade ordered II Corps commander Major General Winfield Scott Hancock to take command on the ground. Lee arrived and set up headquarters on Seminary Ridge across a wide open field from Cemetery Ridge. Longstreet brought up other troops on the Confederate side right behind Seminary Ridge. Meade, on the opposite side of Cemetery Ridge, worked through the night

ABOVE: Joshua L. Chamberlain, whose badly undermanned 20th Main defended the extreme left of the Federal left flank on Little Round Top. A colonel during the action and pictured here as a brigadier general, he rose to the rank of major general before the war's end.

LEFT: Colonel Strong Vincent directs his brigade's right flank in the defense of Little Round Top. He was killed in the fighting.

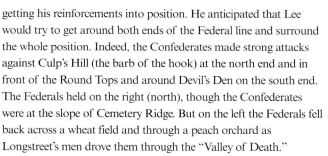

getting his reinforcements into position. He anticipated that Lee would try to get around both ends of the Federal line and surround the whole position. Indeed, the Confederates made strong attacks against Culp's Hill (the barb of the hook) at the north end and in front of the Round Tops and around Devil's Den on the south end. The Federals held on the right (north), though the Confederates were at the slope of Cemetery Ridge. But on the left the Federals fell back across a wheat field and through a peach orchard as Longstreet's men drove them through the "Valley of Death."

Brigadier General Gouverneur K. Warren, Meade's chief engineer, rode up to the fighting at the southern end of the Union line, and to his shock, found that the Round Tops had been left unguarded. He could see that the Confederates were preparing to assault Little Round Top, and he knew if they took it, they would be able to sweep the entire Federal line with fire. Warren gathered up what men he could find and raced for that knoll. He barely beat the Confederates to it, and his men held it with bitter hand-to-hand fighting amongst the boulders and thickets. Darkness closed on the second day of the battle, and both sides braced for the final decision.

Lee was outnumbered at Gettysburg, but in this situation he knew he could win only by going on the attack. After trying the ends of the line again with no success, he decided on July 3 to regroup his forces and make an all-out assault straight for the Federal center on Cemetery Hill. Lee had Longstreet assemble fifteen thousand men to make the charge, and all morning the divisions moved up around Seminary Ridge to get into position; the Confederate assault would be nearly one mile wide. Major General George E. Pickett's Virginia Division, which had arrived

LEFT INSET: The field glasses used by Warren at Gettysburg. It was through these field glasses that he viewed the on-rushing Confederates from the crest of Little Round Top.

the night before, would lead the charge as the center formation of three divisions. The Confederate Infantry would have to storm through the Peach Orchard and across nearly a mile of open ground to reach the Federal positions, all the while in the face of the Union artillery and, during their last desperate lunge, the massed fire from thousands of Yankee rifles and muskets.

At one o'clock, 159 Confederate guns in front of Seminary Ridge opened fire, concentrating primarily on the clump of trees on Cemetery Hill that marked the center of the Union position. Not all the Federal artillery could fire on Seminary Ridge, but seventy-seven guns replied, and during the next hour the batteries kept up fire in the greatest artillery duel ever to take place on the American continent. (The 18th Field Artillery today shows a fishhook on both its regimental insignia and its coat of arms signifying its participation at Gettysburg.) In order to save ammunition, replace damaged cannons, and cool the gun barrels, the Union artillery chief ordered a cease-fire. The Confederates, whose own ammunition was short, thought this meant that Union artillery had been knocked out. At three o'clock Longstreet's men started moving forward.

RIGHT: Brigadier General Lewis Armistead thrusts his decimated brigade into the II Corps line along Cemetery Ridge at Gettysburg. His men were quickly overwhelmed after two thirds of them were killed during the attack and with no other units of Major General George Picket's Virginia Division following in support. Because Armistead's brigade got farther than any others, the event during Picket's Charge is often called the "high water mark of the Confederacy." Shortly after three bullets struck Armistead, he heard that his close friend, General Winfield Scott Hancock of the Union II Corps, also had been cut down. He cried out, "Not both of us on the same day!" Armistead later died of his wounds.

RIGHT: Lieutenant Rolandes F. Fisher of Company K, 5th Ohio Volunteer Infantry Regiment, along with his Colt Root pistol, his watch, and the bullet that struck it. On the morning of July 3, 1863, Fisher, who had survived five major battles, including Antietam and Chancellorsville, was checking the position of his company at Gettysburg when a rebel sharpshooter shot him. The round ripped through his left arm at the elbow, then cut through his uniform coat, striking the pocket watch that saved his life.

In perfect formation, the long, gray lines of soldiers moved across the fields. Fifteen minutes later, Pickett's division disappeared briefly as it moved across a slight hollow. Then it came to view again and, with a wild rebel yell, became a mass of charging infantry. Cannons and muskets opened fire in deadly fury. The gray ranks thinned but kept coming; Brigadier General Lewis A. Armistead led one of Pickett's brigades right into the gun positions, where he fell, mortally wounded. Armistead's advance was the "high water mark" of the Confederacy. Pennsylvanians and New Englanders counterattacked and cut down or drove back the surging Confederates.

In three days at Gettysburg, Union forces suffered 23,055 casualties, including more than 3,155 killed, and the Confederates had 18,523 injured plus 4,708 killed. Losses throughout the entire campaign reached a forbidding 57,225 and effectively ended major fighting in the eastern theater for the rest of the year. In dedicating the cemetery at Gettysburg, President Lincoln paid tribute to those who gave "the last full measure of devotion."

Sixty-three of the heroes of Gettysburg received a new decoration: the Medal of Honor. This award had been established for the army in 1862; in 1863 it was made permanent and extended to all who should "most distinguish themselves." It remains the country's highest military award.

We have come to dedicate a portion of that field, as a final resting place for those who here gave their lives that that nation might live. It is altogether fitting and proper that we should do this. But, in a larger sense, we can not dedicate… we can not consecrate…we can not hallow…this ground. The brave men, living and dead, who struggled here, have consecrated it, far above our poor power to add or detract. The world will little note, nor long remember what we say here, but it can never forget what they did here.

—President Abraham Lincoln

BELOW: President Abraham Lincoln seated on the platform at Gettysburg around noon on November 19, 1863, roughly three hours before giving his address. Bodyguard Ward Hill Lamon is to the right.

GETTYSBURG'S MEDAL OF HONOR RECIPIENTS

The Medal of Honor was born out of the need to recognize the valor exhibited by soldiers in the Civil War, and nowhere were actions of bravery and courage in the war recognized more than at the Battle of Gettysburg. In all, sixty-three medals were awarded to soldiers for their actions on the battlefield in southern Pennsylvania. Below is a list of those sixty-three men along with the complete citation that accompanied the award.

ALLEN, NATHANIEL M.
Corporal, Company B, 1st Massachusetts Infantry

BACON, ELIJAH W.
Private, Company F, 14th Connecticut Infantry

BENEDICT, GEORGE G.
Second Lieutenant, Company C, 12th Vermont Infantry

BROWN, MORRIS, JR.
Captain, Company A, 126th New York Infantry

CAREY, HUGH
Sergeant, Company E, 82d New York Infantry

CARLISLE, CASPER R.
Private, Company F, Independent Pennsylvania Light Artillery

CHAMBERLAIN, JOSHUA L.
Colonel, 20th Maine Infantry

CLARK, HARRISON
Corporal, Company E, 125th New York Infantry

CLOPP, JOHN E.
Private, Company F, 71st Pennsylvania Infantry

COATES, JEFFERSON
Sergeant, Company H, 7th Wisconsin Infantry

DE CASTRO, JOSEPH H.
Corporal, Company I, 19th Massachusetts Infantry

DORE, GEORGE H.
Sergeant, Company D, 126th New York Infantry

ENDERLIN, RICHARD
Musician, Company B, 73d Ohio Infantry

FALLS, BENJAMIN F.
Color Sergeant, Company A, 19th Massachusetts Infantry

FASSETT, JOHN B.
Captain, Company F, 23d Pennsylvania Infantry

FLYNN, CHRISTOPHER
Corporal, Company K, 14th Connecticut Infantry

FUGER, FREDERICK
Sergeant, Battery A, 4th Artillery

FURMAN, CHESTER S.
Corporal, Company A, 6th Pennsylvania Reserves

GILLIGAN, EDWARD L.
First Sergeant, Company E, 88th Pennsylvania Infantry

HART, JOHN W.
Sergeant, Company D, 6th Pennsylvania Reserves

HINCKS, WILLIAM B.
Sergeant Major, 14th Connecticut Infantry

HORAN, THOMAS
Sergeant, Company E, 72d New York Infantry

HUIDEKOPER, HENRY S.
Lieutenant Colonel, 150th Pennsylvania Infantry

IRSCH, FRANCIS
Captain, Company D, 45th New York Infantry

JELLISON, BENJAMIN H.
Sergeant, Company C, 19th Massachusetts Infantry

JOHNSON, WALLACE W.
Sergeant, Company G, 6th Pennsylvania Reserves

KNOX, EDWARD M.
Second Lieutenant, 15th New York Battery

LONERGAN, JOHN
Captain, Company A, 13th Vermont Infantry

MAYBERRY, JOHN B.
Private, Company F, 1st Delaware Infantry

MCCARREN, BERNARD
Private, Company C, 1st Delaware Infantry

MEARS, GEORGE W.
Sergeant, Company A, 6th Pennsylvania Reserves

MILLER, JOHN
Corporal, Company G, 8th Ohio Infantry

MILLER, WILLIAM E.
Captain, Company H, 3d Pennsylvania Cavalry

MUNSELL, HARVEY M.
Sergeant, Company A, 99th Pennsylvania Infantry

O'BRIEN, HENRY D.
Corporal, Company E, 1st Minnesota Infantry

PIPES, JAMES
Captain, Company A, 140th Pennsylvania Infantry

PLATT, GEORGE C.
Private, Company H, 6th United States Cavalry

POSTLES, JAMES PARKE
Captain, Company A, 1st Delaware Infantry

PURMAN, JAMES J.
Lieutenant, Company A, 140th Pennsylvania Infantry

RAYMOND, WILLIAM H.
Corporal, Company A, 108th New York Infantry

REED, CHARLES W.
Bugler, 9th Independent Battery, Massachusetts Light Artillery

REISINGER, J. MONROE
Corporal, Company H, 150th Pennsylvania Infantry

RICE, EDMUND
Major, 19th Massachusetts Infantry

RICHMOND, JAMES
Private, Company F, 8th Ohio Infantry

ROBINSON, JOHN H.
Private, Company I, 19th Massachusetts Infantry

ROOD, OLIVER P.
Private, Company B, 20th Indiana Infantry

LEFT: Medal of Honor recipient Marshall Sherman, Company C, 1st Minnesota Infantry. Sherman was awarded the decoration for capturing the flag of the 28th Virginia Infantry on the battle's third day at the climax of Pickett's Charge. The flag never was returned to the state of Virginia, as was common practice at the turn of the century, and is still in the possession of the Minnesota Historical Society.

CHICKAMAUGA AND CHATTANOOGA

The western theater's front stretched several hundred miles from northeastern Mississippi through Tennessee and Kentucky. Opposing armies had been sparring here in the closing months of 1862 as separate Confederate attempts to seize Corinth, Mississippi—and the whole state of Kentucky in October—both failed. These were followed by a Union campaign in Tennessee under Brigadier General William S. Rosecrans that ran from late December through early January and culminated in a costly battle at Murfreesboro that ended the Confederate threat to central Tennessee posed by General Braxton Bragg. With the exception of numerous small engagements, this front remained relatively quiet throughout the spring and summer as the antagonists gathered and trained their forces. But after Gettysburg and Vicksburg, the center of strategic interest shifted here. Preliminary moves to take Chattanooga, Tennessee, an important rail center almost on the Georgia border, developed into the Chickamauga Campaign.

The Chattanooga area was defended by Bragg's Army of the Tennessee reinforced by Longstreet's corps. In July 1863, Rosecrans moved his Army of the Cumberland southeast out of Murfreesboro, intending to swing south of Chattanooga, cut off Bragg's southern escape route, and then attack. Rosecrans made contact sooner than expected, however, and had difficulty concentrating his troops in the mountainous terrain of northwest Georgia. Bragg launched an attack across Chickamauga Creek on September 18 and, after two days of fighting, pierced the Union line and threw about one-third of Rosecrans' force into a retreat north toward Chattanooga. Major General George H. Thomas, commanding XIV Corps, gathered together the remaining force and stood fast under repeated attacks, preventing a rout of the entire army. He withdrew his force from the field in good order that night, and the next day he joined Rosecrans in Chattanooga.

Now, instead of Bragg bottled up in Chattanooga, the Federals were surrounded without any supplies. Grant, as newly appointed commander of the Military Division of the Mississippi, took overall charge of the operation, appointing Sherman to take over the Army of the Tennessee and Thomas to replace Rosecrans in Chattanooga. The Army of the Potomac under Hooker also supplied twenty thousand men in two corps to bolster Grant's burgeoning force. Grant telegraphed Thomas to hold his position at all costs, and Thomas wired back: "I will hold the town till we starve." Finally supplies got through from Bridgeport, Tennessee, by steamboat and wagon train on a supply route that soon became known as the "Cracker Line." In the November 23–25 battle at Missionary Ridge and Lookout Mountain—the "Battle above the Clouds"—the Union forces made their position secure.

It was during a lull on Lookout Mountain that a Yankee from the East, proudly wearing his red star badge of the XII Corps, met a soldier of the XV Corps. "What is your badge?" he asked. The man just tapped his cartridge case and said, "Forty rounds." This became the badge of the XV Corps—a shield picturing a cartridge case and the motto, "Forty Rounds." (The 13th Infantry preserves this emblem on both its regimental

ABOVE: Major General William S. Rosecrans. A mediocre commander of the Army of the Cumberland from October 1862 through October 1863, he battled Braxton Bragg (a Confederate general of equal abilities) in Kentucky, Tennessee, and northern Georgia. The able George H. Thomas succeeded him in command.

SUPPLYING AN ARMY: THE U.S. MILITARY RAILROAD

The South's network of railroads not only was far less developed than the North's, but many lines were built to different standards, preventing each line's locomotives and cars from being used elsewhere. The Union armies needed massive quantities of supplies and munitions as they fought their way into the Confederacy, and wagon transport clearly was insufficient to the task. Secretary of War Edwin Stanton established the U.S. Military Rail Road (USMRR) to build and maintain the railroads that supplied Federal armies throughout the South.

Herman Haupt, who literally wrote the book on bridge building, was picked as the USMRR's superintendent, serving as a civilian major general. Immense resources were poured into the construction and movement of railroad engines, cars, rails, and other equipment, but the wood for ties and trestles invariably came from southern forests, where they were cut down by army units "loaned" to his construction corps. Haupt and his engineers were interested not only in techniques for quickly building rail lines and their infrastructure—but also in the most expeditious ways to destroy them.

A "laboratory" was established at the maintenance yard of the shops of the Orange and Alexandria Railroad in Alexandria, Virginia, where he and his engineers experimented with techniques for how to render the maximum number of wrought iron rails completely unusable in the least amount of time. The simplest and most effective method was to build a big fire under the middle of rails removed from a roadbed, then twist the red-hot iron sections around a tree into a bow-like shape. During General William Sherman's operations in Georgia, these were called "Sherman's bow ties."

Much to the frustration of rebel raiders, Haupt's engineers also developed faster ways to lay and repair track, as well as build bridges using pre-assembled trestle components. Said one amazed observer: "The Yankees can build bridges quicker than the rebs can burn 'em down."

LEFT: *Rail cars and Federal army wagons belonging to William Sherman's army group at the railroad depot in Atlanta, Georgia, during the fall of 1864.*

BELOW: *Forced to abandon Knoxville by Major General Burnside's Army of the Ohio in September 1863, Confederates burned the 1,800-foot London Bridge over the Holston River to cover their retreat. Union engineers, however, speedily built this new trestle on the piers of the original structure, then strengthened it to handle heavier traffic.*

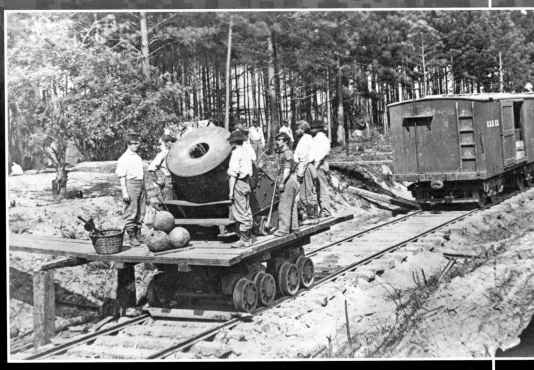

ABOVE LEFT: *Laborers repair single-track railroad near Murfreesboro, Tennessee, after the Battle of Stones River.*

ABOVE RIGHT: *A rail-mounted, 13-inch mortar nicknamed "Dictator" was used to pound the Confederate trench defending Petersburg, Virginia.*

RIGHT: *The City Point, Virginia, railroad yard and supply ship that supported Union forces during George McClellan's Peninsula Campaign.*

RIGHT TOP: General Ulysses S. Grant examines a map, perhaps brought to him by one of the unidentified soldiers in the photo, a field grade officer (standing) or the officer holding the rank of lieutenant or captain seated next to him.

RIGHT BOTTOM: General Grant's last uniform coat with the unique four-button arrangement of a full general.

OPPOSITE: Council of war at Massaponax Church, Virginia, on May 21, 1864. After two weeks of fighting at Spotsylvania, the Army of the Potomac left its trenches and began moving east and south, hoping to lure the Confederates into the open. At noon, General Grant called together his and George Meade's staffs and the corps commanders for a brief conference. Soldiers brought the church pews outside for a more functional arrangement, and three photos were taken from a small second-floor window.

In a different, likely earlier photo, General Grant sits in front of the foremost tree flanked by his chief of staff, Brigadier General John A. Rawlins, and Charles Dana, a deputy secretary of war, while Meade and an unidentified major general examine a map at center left. In this photo, a curious Grant gets up and bends over (obscuring Meade) to see what the generals are looking at. Rawlins moves over to Dana, taking Grant's seat, and more officers have arrived at the conference. One bends down to examine the map in front of Meade, another moves behind Grant, and a pipe-smoking third takes a seat in the pew at center right, where he looks up at the photographer in the second-story window.

insignia and coat of arms.) Hooker's troops eventually attacked Confederate forces southwest of Chattanooga, thereby opening up the rail supply line to the city late in October, enabling it to become a giant Union supply base for a drive into the heart of the South.

TIGHTENING THE NOOSE

Early in 1864, Grant was made the commander-in-chief of all the Federal armies, becoming the first man in modern history to lead an army of a million men. Grant made his headquarters with Meade's Army of the Potomac, now one of the finest armies in the world. It was well-equipped, had an efficient supply and transport service—its wagon trains would have reached sixty-five miles in a single line—had a highly developed signal corps that laid telegraph wire to brigades by reels mounted on mules, and had developed an experienced body of leaders and trained men. Its soldiers were known as the "thinking bayonets."

Grant sent the Army of the Potomac south of the Rapidan River and met Lee's army on May 5, beginning a series of intense battles that would last almost nonstop for seven full weeks. First came the close-in fighting across the forests of Virginia in the ominously named Battle of the Wilderness. As the Federals halted briefly near Chancellorsville, Lee struck hard at Meade's right, or western, flank. Grant and Meade swung the troops into line and fought back in terrain that frequently allowed them to see no farther than ten yards. The battle raged during May 5 and 6 without decisive result, but Grant had been foiled in his initial attempt to envelop Lee. In one sector, Private James Young, with two other soldiers, volunteered to go forward through the thicket to determine the layout of the Confederate lines. Moving in close to the trenches, they hit the ground as musket balls cracked through the brush. One of the men was hit, but Young lifted him onto his back and, with shot still whistling all around him, carried the soldier back to the Union lines and made his report. He won a Medal of Honor.

The battle continued around Spotsylvania Court House when the Federals, during major attacks on May 10 and 12, hit both sides and the nose of a wedge, which formed part of the Confederate lines. In some of the bloodiest fighting of the war, men fought across this corner that came to be known as the "Bloody Angle," or "Hell's Half-Acre." The Army of the Potomac and Burnside's corps struck repeatedly at these positions at Spotsylvania but were repulsed with heavy losses. Then, on May 20, Grant side-slipped south in another effort to surround his opponent. Lee skillfully avoided the trap and retired to the North Anna River. There he established a defensive position that Grant considered too strong to attack.

It was a costly, nasty business, but it was here that Grant said he had "put his foot down," and wrote in a dispatch, "I propose to fight it out on this line if it takes all summer." It did take all summer, and winter too, as Grant's men fought on and Lee's men contested every foot through the thickets around the North Anna, down to Cold Harbor from May 22 through June 3, and on to Petersburg as Lee fell back to the well-developed defenses around Richmond. Rather than attack Lee directly, Grant decided to

ABOVE: Sergeant Thomas Plunkett of the 21st Massachusetts Infantry poses with the flag he carried at the Battle of Fredericksburg. The flag is stained with his blood after a shell took his arms.

LEFT AND BOTTOM: The V Corps
flag with tears made by flying
shrapnel during the siege of
Petersburg. The holes are clearly
visible in the group photo of
Major General Gouverneur K.
Warren and his staff in late 1864.

BELOW INSET: The flag of the 2d
Brigade in II Corps' 1st Division.

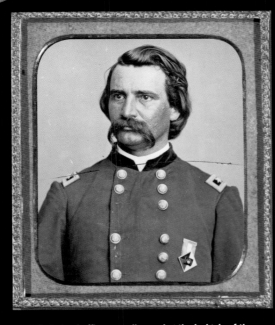

ESPRIT DE CORPS

With straggling along the roads and identification in combat a perpetual problem, accusations and recriminations as to whose men were responsible for what became an increasing problem among the Federal commanders. To help rectify the problem, General Joseph Hooker issued orders to the seven corps that each was to have a distinctive badge "for the purpose of ready recognition of corps and divisions of this army [in order] to prevent injustice by reports of straggling and misconduct through mistake as to their organizations." The Army of the Potomac immediately adopted corps badges, which most commonly were worn on soldiers' hats. Other armies soon followed its example.

Hooker's designated patterns for his formations were: I Corps—a sphere (still used today), II Corps—trefoil, III Corps—lozenge, V Corps—Maltese Cross,

VI Corps—cross, XI Corps—crescent, and XII Corps—star. The first three divisions within each corps carried the badges in the national colors: 1st Division—red, 2d Division—white, and 3d Division—blue. The two formations that contained a fourth division used green. Some regiments and even companies added their designations at the center.

While Southern units generally maintained strong regional bonds throughout the war, this was almost impossible in the much larger Union Army, where the organizational system encouraged locally raised regiments to be whittled down by disease and combat until they became nearly unrecognizable as such. Though not originally issued to improve morale and cohesion, corps badges helped extend unit pride beyond the men's steadily diminishing regiments.

II CORPS
1st Division
Army of the Potomac
Adopted: March 21, 1863

5TH CORPS
3d Div., 129th Pennsylvania
Company K
Army of the Potomac
Adopted: March 21, 1863

14TH CORPS
2d Div., 78th Pennsylvania
Company H
Army of the Cumberland
Adopted: April 26, 1864

ABOVE: *Federal officer proudly wearing the insignia of the XV Corps on his chest. Its badge incorporates a cartridge pouch with their motto, "Forty Rounds," in the insignia design.*

BATTLE FLAGS

The regimental colors represented the identity and fighting spirit of a unit, and fierce brawls often raged around the flags as enemy soldiers strove to seize them and their own men came to their defense. Even if the colors were not in imminent danger of capture, they served as a "bullet magnet." The flag bearers—and every soldier close by—knew they had a better chance of being shot than anyone else in the regiment, including their colonel. Even before the Civil War, the British Army had decided to refrain from carrying colors into battle because of the appalling mortality rate of its highly visible standard-bearers during the Crimean War of 1853–1856. Yet it was this visibility that gave the colors their value.

Whether an engagement was large or small, the only things that usually could be seen above the smoke and confusion were the flags. A scattered regiment could use theirs as a rallying point, commanders could gain a sense of how the battle was progressing by observing the shifting positions, and both officers and men alike could gauge the size of an approaching enemy force by simply counting the banners fluttering in the distance. This, naturally, worked both ways, and except for cavalry units whose fast-moving troops still needed their colors for organization, the U.S. Army followed the British practice after the war.

RIGHT TOP: *Like all Union regiments, the 34th New York Infantry had two banners. The bearer on the left holds the regimental colors while the one on the right has the national colors as an almost square battle flag. Both usually measured six feet six inches by six feet.*

RIGHT BOTTOM: *Saving the Flag at Gettysburg. As fighting swirls around him in the wheatfield at Gettysburg, Colonel Harrison H. Jeffords of the 4th Michigan tries to retake his unit's flag but is both shot and bayoneted. Other soldiers from the 4th succeeded in reclaiming it, but Colonel Jeffords died the next day of his wounds.*

OPPOSITE: *Detail of the regimental flag from the 5th U.S. Heavy Artillery. The 5th was a colored regiment, and the colored citizens from Natchez, Mississippi, donated the flag to the unit. It's now in the collection of the West Point Museum.*

THE FALL OF ATLANTA AND SHERMAN'S MARCH THROUGH GEORGIA

Confederate General Joseph E. Johnston had done all that could reasonably be asked of him. Though outnumbered roughly two to one and facing a trio of armies under Lieutenant General William Tecumseh Sherman, he had slowed the Yankees to a crawl by forcing them to lever his soldiers out of one strong defensive position after another while suffering few losses and managing to keep the much larger force from cutting off his army and destroying it. This was not good enough for the Confederacy's leaders in Richmond.

Corps commander John B. Hood, who had led a gallant but extremely costly assault against Sherman the previous month, assumed command from the methodical Johnston in late July 1864. He immediately initiated a series of aggressive attacks that badly depleted his already small army and was forced to abandon Atlanta to Sherman on September 1. The Northern army group had lost more than thirty-one thousand men but still retained eighty-one thousand for Sherman's destructive march through Georgia to the sea. Hood, who had expended most of the South's thirty-five thousand losses in little more than a month, had but thirty thousand troops and could do little to stop the blue-clad tide.

Detaching the Army of the Cumberland under Major General George H. Thomas to protect Union gains in Tennessee, Sherman left his supply lines behind as his remaining two armies cut a wide swath of destruction through the Confederate heartland to Savannah, Georgia. Not finished with his campaign "to make the South howl," he then repeated the process in a march through northern Georgia, then the Carolinas, in the spring of 1865.

BELOW: *Confederate defenses outside of Atlanta, Georgia. Although formidable, they could not stop the advance of the Union Army, as there were far too few troops to man them.*

starve him into the open by taking Petersburg to the south, through which ran all the railways and main roads connecting Richmond with the rest of the Confederacy. In a move that took Lee by surprise, Grant suddenly crossed the James River below Richmond on June 14. The next day his leading elements reached Petersburg, which was lightly held, but the Federals unaccountably delayed their attack, and Lee was able to move a large number of troops into the city. A Federal assault on June 18 failed to pierce the Confederate defenses, and Grant thereupon undertook siege operations, which lasted until April 1865.

MARCHING THROUGH GEORGIA

While the armies of Grant and Lee bled each other in Virginia (and an ailing Winfield Scott watched with great interest from his forced retirement at West Point), Sherman was carrying out the other part of the North's strategic plan, which called for a drive southeast from Chattanooga, through Georgia to Atlanta, and from Atlanta to the Atlantic.

As the commander of the Military Division of the Mississippi, Sherman moved out of Chattanooga on May 4, 1864, at the head of three armies. Opposing him was Johnston's Army of the Tennessee, which cleverly fought a series of delaying actions and constantly forced Sherman to halt, deploy, and maneuver. On June 27 Sherman attempted a direct assault against prepared positions at Kennesaw Mountain but was bloodily repulsed and compelled to return to a war of maneuver, forcing Johnston back to positions in front of Atlanta. The Confederacy's president, Jefferson Davis, was dissatisfied with Johnston's delaying tactics, even though they had resulted in Sherman's massive force advancing little more than seventy miles in a month and a half. Johnston was replaced by Major General John B. Hood, a more aggressive commander who so weakened his army through useless attacks that Sherman was able to march his army unopposed into the Georgia capital on the evening of September 1, 1864.

USELESS DISTRACTIONS

Confederate efforts to distract and draw away Union forces from their death grip on the South occurred from Virginia's Shenandoah Valley to Missouri far to the west. After Lee had firmly established his position at Petersburg, he sent Major General Jubal A. Early with one corps on a raiding expedition up the Shenandoah

ABOVE: Major General George H. Thomas. A graduate of the Virginia Military Institute whom fellow Virginian J.E.B. Stuart wanted to hang because he fought on the side of the Union, Thomas played a key role in the western fighting, first leading a corps, then the Army of the Tennessee. He commanded the Army of the Cumberland during the battles around Chattanooga, William Sherman's drive to Atlanta, and the Franklin-Nashville Campaign, which destroyed the southern army of Lieutenant General John B. Hood.

LEFT TOP: The 5th, 7th, 9th, and 10th Minnesota regiments charge across a muddy cornfield during the Battle of Nashville. The December 16, 1864, battle cost them three hundred casualties.

LEFT BOTTOM: Walter G. Jones was a private in Company C, 8th New York Cavalry, whose life was saved twice by this Bible carried in his blouse pocket. The strike in the upper corner occurred at Cedar Creek, Virginia, on October 19, 1864, and the body-armor Bible stopped the center bullet during the Battle of Appomattox, April 8–9, 1865—likely saving him from being one of the last men killed in the war.

CIVIL WAR ARTILLERY

Most of the artillery used by both North and South during the war was smoothbore cannons made of bronze: simple point-and-shoot weapons that were easy to operate by any soldier with minimal (and in some cases, no) training. Smoothbores firing a 6-pound ball, called "shot," could be used effectively at targets up to approximately one thousand yards, while the larger "12-pounder" Napoleons could engage targets with a reasonable degree of accuracy up to fifteen hundred or eighteen hundred yards and at less range when used with explosive shells filled with musket balls. Well-handled rifled cannons, commonly called "guns," could hit targets at roughly twice these distances, but the constricted nature of the terrain in which most battles were fought—plus the rapid buildup of smoke from their own firing—usually limited a gun battery to ranges little different than those of the smoothbores.

Cannons were principally defensive weapons that, in fact, accounted for less than one in ten combat casualties because of their extremely slow rate of fire—a maximum of two aimed rounds per minute. That said, they always served as an important morale builder, and their sheer presence often encouraged nervous soldiers to hold a line instead of skedaddling to the rear. Their most telling effect came when smoothbores were used like giant shotguns against an enemy charge. As soon as the massed infantry approached to within a few hundred yards, gunners would switch to firing canisters containing cast iron balls of one inch or more that would rip through whole ranks of men. Thinner-barreled rifled guns, which fired shells containing similar .96-caliber balls, were found to be less effective during the final moments of an enemy assault.

Throughout the war the much less industrialized South continually struggled to equip its armies with cannons, adequate ammunition, and a wide assortment of captured Union weapons. It was not unusual to see Confederate batteries equipped with two and even three different kinds of artillery, which further complicated the precarious supply situation.

INSET: *Mortars often were used as siege artillery. Rather than battering fortification walls with cannon fire, mortars were developed to project shells high enough to clear the walls so they could explode within a fortress.*

BELOW: *A Union battery of either 3-inch ordnance rifles or smoothbore 12-pounder Napoleons behind Union breastworks during the siege of Petersburg in late 1864.*

OPPOSITE BOTTOM: *The 1st Connecticut Artillery drills with 24-pounder cannons mounted on siege carriages at Fort Richardson on the Virginia side of the District of Columbia. Fort Richardson, which had fifteen embrasures for such behemoths, was one of the 161 forts and artillery redoubts that made up the thirty-seven-mile circle of fortifications around Washington. It guarded the Columbia Pike, which ran to Washington through the area near where the Pentagon now stands.*

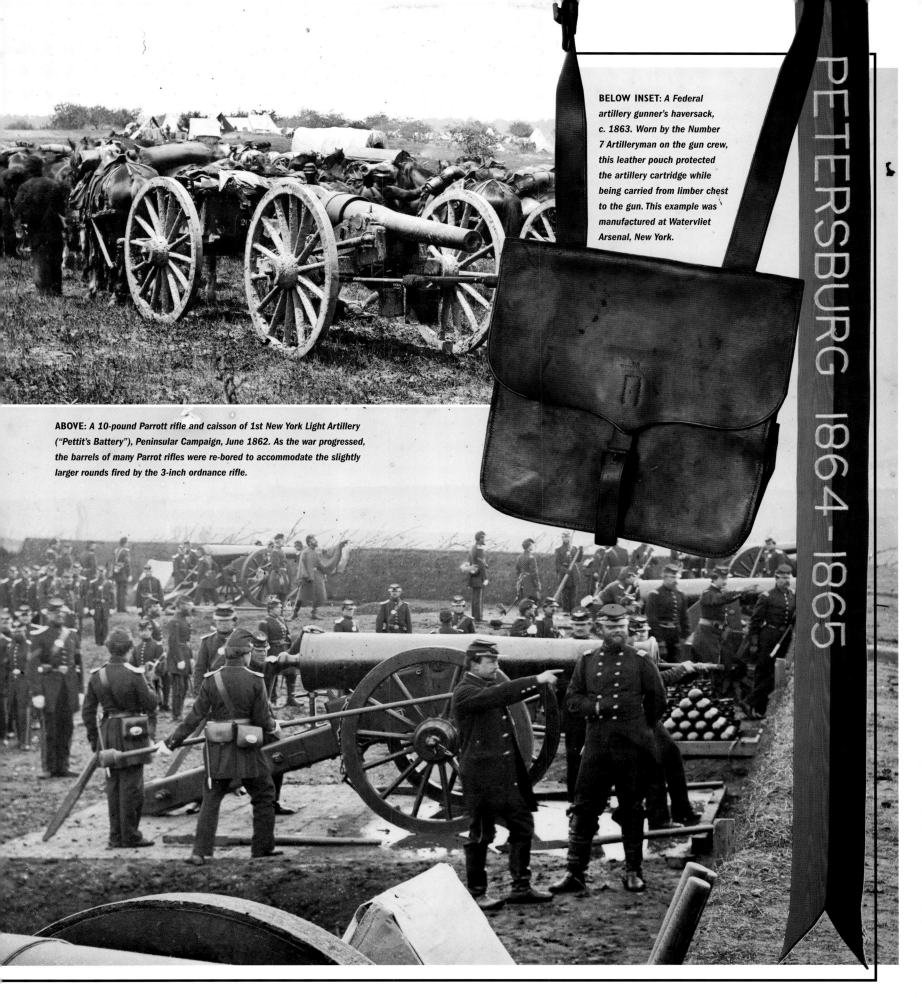

BELOW INSET: *A Federal artillery gunner's haversack, c. 1863. Worn by the Number 7 Artilleryman on the gun crew, this leather pouch protected the artillery cartridge while being carried from limber chest to the gun. This example was manufactured at Watervliet Arsenal, New York.*

ABOVE: *A 10-pound Parrott rifle and caisson of 1st New York Light Artillery ("Pettit's Battery"), Peninsular Campaign, June 1862. As the war progressed, the barrels of many Parrot rifles were re-bored to accommodate the slightly larger rounds fired by the 3-inch ordnance rifle.*

RIGHT TOP: The bugle of Nathaniel Sisson, trumpeter in the 3d Division, Cavalry Corps, Army of the Potomac, then commanded by Major General Armstrong Custer. The bugle was blown at the April 8, 1865, engagement that led to the surrender of General Robert E. Lee at Appomattox, Virginia, the following day. As General George Custer's cavalry scattered Lee's supply train, trumpeter Sisson was called on to sound the charge, and the Union cavalry moved forward to engage a portion of the main Confederate body. As Custer's horsemen galloped forward, Colonel Robert M. Sims from General James Longstreet's staff approached the Union force with a flag of truce fashioned from a white towel. Sisson was ordered to sound "assembly," which halted the charge and, as it turned out, signaled the end of the war.

RIGHT: A quick pencil sketch of the event by Alfred Waud, who covered the Army of the Potomac for *Harper's Weekly.*

Valley to ease pressure that had been exerted from that direction. Although Early skillfully eluded Federal opposition in a rapid drive north and then east that carried him to the northern outskirts of Washington on July 11, he prudently retreated. Major General Philip H. Sheridan then spent the next four months in the valley, defeating Early in late September and finally shattering his forces at Cedar Creek on October 19. Sheridan then laid waste to the rich Shenandoah Valley in order to prevent it from being used as a base for raids against the North and to destroy sources of food for Lee's army.

Anticipating that General Hood would attempt to invade Tennessee in order to hamper further operations in Georgia, Sherman sent reinforcements under Major General John M. Schofield to Major General George H. Thomas at Nashville. Hood struck this force on November 30 at Franklin, Tennessee, but was beaten back in a short, furious engagement. The next day, Schofield moved on to Nashville where his arrival brought the Federal force under Thomas to a strength of about fifty thousand men. Thomas made careful preparations to attack Hood and, in a two-day battle beginning December 15, struck hard, shattering Hood's Army of the Tennessee, which was never again an offensive threat.

Across the Mississippi, Major General Sterling Price conducted a three-division force on a raid into Missouri in

September and October. Striking north from Arkansas, he suffered a stinging defeat near Fort Davidson, then swung west away from St. Louis looking for easy victories. Finding the state capital, Jefferson City, too heavily defended, he continued toward Kansas, but delaying actions by Brigadier General James G. Blunt slowed his advance and allowed significant Union forces under Major General Samuel R. Curtis, commander of the Federal Department of Kansas, to gather at Westport, Missouri, on the Kansas border. Price was defeated in the Battle of Westport on October 23, 1864, and was pursued almost all the way back to Arkansas.

APPOMATTOX

It was clear by early 1865 that the Confederacy was nearing the end. Sherman's army was grinding its way north from Georgia to join Grant after burning a sixty-mile-wide path of destruction from Atlanta to Savannah on the Atlantic coast while, at Petersburg and Richmond, the Army of Northern Virginia grimly manned their trenches. On March 29, Grant began an encircling movement with part of his force around Lee's right, or southern, flank, while his main body of troops positioned itself to strike the flank directly. Though the movement was stopped by Confederate forces under Pickett and General

Richard S. Ewell in battles around White Oak Road and at Five Forks, Grant mounted an assault that broke the Confederate line on April 2. Lee was forced to pull Longstreet's corps away from Richmond to help hold the line as other Confederates withdrew toward Petersburg, then further west, abandoning the defenses that they had manned since June 1864.

Hoping to break loose and eventually join forces with Johnston to the south, Lee hastened west along the Appomattox River, but Grant pursued relentlessly, and a four-day running fight ensued during which the Army of Northern Virginia began to disintegrate. Finally, a Union force under Sheridan raced ahead and took a position squarely across Lee's line of retreat at Appomattox Court House, ending the army's flight. On April 9, 1865, Lee met Grant in Appomattox and surrendered. Johnston continued to resist Sherman's unstoppable advance for more than two additional weeks, but finally surrendered near Raleigh, North Carolina, on April 26, 1865. By the end of May, other Confederate forces had given up. The long struggle was over.

ABOVE: Southern soldiers carefully furl a Confederate battle flag after the surrender of General Robert E. Lee's army on April 9, 1865. During the final parade of the defeated army three days later, Joshua Chamberlain, now a major general in V Corps, presided over the ceremony. On his own initiative, the hero of Little Round Top at Gettysburg ordered his men to come to attention and carry arms as a mark of respect when the Southerners marched passed.

LEFT: The gold officer's sash worn by Robert E. Lee at the surrender of Confederate forces at the Appomattox Court House.

Chapter Four
War on the Plains and Domestic Strife, 1865–1878

The cost of the Civil War had been enormous, with more than six hundred thousand dead on both sides. Few at the beginning of the conflict had even the remotest inkling of what was to come when firebrands on both sides cried for battle. Major General Sherman was one of those few who did. Writing to his brother shortly after the 1862 blood-letting at Shiloh, Sherman marveled at the commonly held belief that the fighting would soon be over. He wrote, "The people should know that this war will consume three hundred thousand men per year [North and South] for a long time." Two years later, in April 1864, he lamented that although the South was running out of manpower:

Full three hundred thousand of the bravest men of this world must be killed or banished [captured] in the South before they will think of peace, and in killing them we must lose an equal or greater number, for we must be the attacking party. Still, we as a nation have no alternative or choice.

The increased tempo of the fighting, beginning the following month, as Grant, now a lieutenant general, began his drive on Richmond, took a terrible toll on both sides. The following is a brief compilation of Union casualties from Grant's opening moves and does not include those from Sherman's imminent march through Georgia and the Carolinas, or the fighting to the west:

The Wilderness, May 5–7	17,666
Spotsylvania, May 10–12	14,267
Drewry's Bluff, May 12–16	4,160
Cold Harbor, June 1–3	13,078
Petersburg, June 15–30	16,569

This totals 65,740 Union combat casualties with an incomplete tally of the missing. Those who fell sick are not factored in. North Anna, Bermuda Hundred, New Market, and other lesser fights cost an additional eleven thousand men—an average of fourteen hundred casualties every day for seven weeks. Until General Lee's surrender on April 9, 1865, Union losses in this theater of operations would subsequently average more than three thousand per month, but they spurted past twelve thousand during a bloody series of failed assaults from the end of July through late August 1864. The final ten days of the Appomattox Campaign cost an additional 11,200 men.

Except for a significant number of its commissioned officers, most of the U.S. Army's 14,663 men had remained with the Union and were joined by an additional 2,672,341 recruits throughout the conflict. The Army's strength at the war's close stood at 1,000,516, with many of the missing men having left at the end of their initial enlistments or been invalided out (frequently with amputations) because of the severity of their wounds. Those who were killed in action or died of wounds made up 114,757 of this disparity, but more than twice this many—233,789—died of disease, with an additional 10,982 non-battle deaths due to other causes. These and other grim statistics have been frequently quoted, but less well known is that while Union medical officers examined literally hundreds of thousands of wounds, they also treated more than seven *million* cases of disease. The average soldier became ill on multiple occasions during his enlistment, with dysentery replacing the deadly Revolutionary War scourge, smallpox, as a far greater threat to an American soldier's life than a bullet or a bayonet.

Although the war would sputter on feebly for almost two more months, the capitulation of the most dangerous

OPPOSITE: Colonel Eugene A. Carr, before his promotion to brigadier general in 1892. Carr took part in many of the major battles and campaigns of the Indian Wars and was awarded the Medal of Honor during the Civil War for actions at the Battle of Pea Ridge. When commanding the 6th Cavalry in August 1881, Carr was denied reinforcements ahead of his mission to arrest a "notorious and mischief-making" medicine man in a village of more than six hundred. He had to set out with only two troops totaling seventy-nine men plus twenty-three Indian scouts. During their return to Fort Apache after apprehending the medicine man, the Indian scouts treacherously turned on the soldiers while several hundred hostiles attacked their evening encampment at Cibicu Creek in the Arizona Territory. Quick action by Carr and his disciplined troops prevented a massacre. Only nine soldiers, including a captain, were killed. However, two small detachments away from the fort were wiped out, and many settlers in the region were killed before the Indians fled to Mexico. Later, five of the scouts were apprehended and courts-martialed—three were hanged, and two received prison sentences.

SPRINGFIELD RIFLE MUSKET, MODEL 1855

This .58-caliber rifled musket has the impression of a cannon-ball near the center of the barrel. The buttstock may have broken off at the time of impact. The weapon is loaded. The rifle reportedly was found at Gettysburg.

ON THE MEXICAN BORDER

Knowing that the United States was powerless to enforce the Monroe Doctrine while it was divided against itself in a civil war, Napoleon III of France, a supporter of the Confederacy and desirous of a colonial empire in the former Spanish Territory, sent an invading army across the Atlantic in December 1861, ostensibly to recover Mexican debts. Although initially defeated, the French Army succeeded in capturing Mexico City in 1863, and Napoleon III installed Archduke Maximilian of Austria as emperor of Mexico the following year. Grant believed that the invasion of Mexico was so closely related to the Southern rebellion as to be essentially a part of it and this was only reinforced by Maximilian's willingness to shelter Confederate diehards who crossed into Mexico to avoid surrender.

The military division of the Gulf of Mexico was quickly established under Major General Sheridan. In a massive show of force, Sheridan set fifty thousand men in two corps and two separate cavalry divisions along the Mexican border— IV Corps, formerly with the Army of the Cumberland, at San Antonio, and the all-black XXV Corps from Virginia, which landed at Brownsville at the mouth of the Rio Grande. A military railroad was built to help support the corps at Brownsville, and from here Sheridan provided support to the Mexican President Benito Juárez, who had been forced to move his government north.

Confederate Army at Appomattox allowed Grant to dissolve most of his million-man force, and he was determined to do so as expeditiously as possible after Lee put his name to the surrender. Captain Horace Porter on the general's small staff wrote:

> [Grant] surprised us by announcing his intention of starting for Washington early the next morning. We were disappointed at this, for we wished to see something of the opposing army…and to meet some of the officers who had been acquaintances in former years. The general, however, had no desire to look at the conquered—indeed, he had little curiosity in his nature—and he was anxious above all things to begin the reduction of the military establishment, and diminish the enormous expense attending it, which at this time amounted to nearly four millions of dollars a day.

A large force was required to remain in the South for an unknown length of time, yet by November 1865, the army had been reduced to 183,000 men and would have been smaller but for unfinished business along the Rio Grande.

BELOW: In 1864, the remains of eighteen hundred war dead who fell at the Battle of Bull Run were buried on the grounds of Arlington House across the Potomac River from Washington, D.C. The house and its property were the family home of Mary Anna Custis Lee and her husband, Robert E. Lee, who served as its custodian. U.S. troops occupied the area after Virginia's secession, and the property subsequently was seized for nonpayment of federal taxes.

Grant wrote that the United States should be no less neutral toward the legally constituted government of Mexico than France had been toward the Confederacy. He countermanded earlier orders to the U.S. commanders along the California border, made while the Civil War was in progress, that had blocked the flow of arms south. In the east, Sheridan coordinated his activities with President Juárez and his "liberals," and ensured that their foes, the "imperialists," saw much of the U.S. Army's preparations so that they might be intimidated into withdrawing from the area. For example, arrangements were made to purchase—in Mexico—forage for the army's horses if it moved south, and no effort was made to hide the arrival of components for a pontoon bridge across the Rio Grande.

Meanwhile, supplies—including thirty thousand muskets direct from the Baton Rouge arsenal—were "left at convenient places on our side of the river," according to Sheridan, "to fall into [the liberals'] hands." In all, U.S. troops managed to "lose" some sixty thousand muskets near the Rio Grande and Baja California. By the middle of the following year, the liberals—also known as Juáristas—were in control along the entire border. Grant also picked Major General John M. Schofield, who had returned from a seven-month diplomatic mission to France on the Mexican issue, for another special assignment. If it became necessary, Schofield would be granted a leave of absence to lead volunteers against the French and imperialists while lending advice and support to Juárez's army.

Napoleon III, as was intended, was well aware of much of this and could ill afford to lose an army in Mexico, especially since storm clouds were gathering between France and Prussia. In the spring of 1866 he ordered a three-stage withdrawal of French troops over the next year, which would give Maximilian time to either succeed or fail in solidifying his hold on Mexico, independent of French arms. Maximilian, unable to garner enough support, was left to his tragic end (he was executed by Juárez's forces) as French troops left the capital in February 1867 and sailed from Vera Cruz the following month. The Monroe Doctrine had been enforced without the U.S. Army firing a shot.

RECONSTRUCTION

Throughout the Civil War, military governments had been established in the wake of the advancing Union armies in order to administer newly seized Southern areas. Operated by the army's provost marshals (who were normally concerned with policing the troops), it became the responsibility of these organizations to ensure that the needs of the civilian populations were taken care of so that the fighting forces would not be distracted by the disturbances behind the lines that were caused by famine, disease, or unrest.

Generally, as little responsibility as possible was taken on, and in areas where a significant portion of the population bore pro-Union sentiments, little action was necessary after the most overt Confederate sympathizers were removed from positions of authority. In other areas, a considerably heavier hand was required, and for a time some military authorities would find themselves managing everything from a city's sanitation to its brothels, or, as in the case of Vicksburg, making sure that its inhabitants did not starve to death.

ABOVE: Major General John M. Schofield

BELOW: An army band, c. 1868. Musicians were kept extremely busy. In camp they performed during parades, reviews, guard mount ceremonies, funerals, executions, and even serenaded soldiers as they went about their everyday duties. They also played for troops marching into battle, actually performing in forward positions during the fighting. At Dinwiddie Court House in 1865, Sheridan massed all his musicians on the firing line with the order to "play the gayest tunes in their books. . . . Play them loud and keep on playing them, and never mind if a bullet goes through a trombone, or even a trombonist, now and then." Sheridan later remarked "Music has done its share, and more than its share, in winning this war," and a soldier of the 24th Massachusetts wrote, "I don't know what we should have done without our band."

Chief Trumpeter Artillery

Sergeant Hospital Steward

First Sergeant, Infantry

Commissary Sergeant

Regimental Color Sergeant, Cavalry

Regimental Color Sergeant, Infantry

Sergeant, Infantry

Hospital Steward

This role continued after the collapse of the Confederacy when Congress adopted a tough "Reconstruction" policy to restore the Southern states to the Union. Congress had already established, near the end of the war, a Bureau of Refugees, Freedmen, and Abandoned Lands—the Freedmen's Bureau—within the War Department. Administered by army officers, its main purpose was to protect and help the former slaves, and in late 1865 most of the civilian-related functions of the provost marshals were also transferred to this bureau. In a more basic sense, the soldiers' thankless job was to demonstrate to Southerners that slavery was, in fact, at an end. The Bureau established schools funded by private benevolent organizations, and, backed by the bayonets of the closest garrison, they adjudicated disputes between landless former slaves and local property owners.

Though the questions of slavery and of state sovereignty seemed to be settled once and for all, the Reconstruction was a massive undertaking for which the army had not been trained, and it was made all the more complex by the battles in Washington over the nature of the policies themselves. Initially, most former Confederates only had to swear an oath of allegiance to the United States before they were permitted to reestablish their civil governments. But in 1867 Congress undid Lincoln's policy of reconciliation that President Andrew Johnson was attempting to carry out and put the South under military control. The occupation forces unconstitutionally removed presidential authority but Johnson, fully embroiled in a battle with Congress that eventually led to impeachment, did not challenge the First and Third Reconstruction Acts that dictated this.

The South was divided into five military districts, and the army, which had been cut down to fifty-seven thousand men when it became clear that the French would be withdrawing from Mexico, was ordered to insert itself into a dizzying array of decidedly unmilitary functions. The roughly twenty thousand officers and men spread throughout the South found themselves, in addition to the maintenance of basic law and order, also deeply involved in registering voters, holding elections, removing public officials, ferreting out voter fraud, regulating commercial law, overseeing public education, suppressing anti-black riots, monitoring civil court proceedings, and approving or disapproving new state constitutions.

Army manpower was destined to fall even further. It was readjusted by an act of Congress to 39,275 soldiers in March 1869 after the dismantling of all Freedmen's Bureau operations, other than education, in January of that year. Other duties in the South shrank, too. Seven former Confederate states—Arkansas, Florida, North Carolina, South Carolina, Georgia, Alabama, and Louisiana—had been readmitted to the Union the previous year. There was also a realistic expectation that the last rebel states—Virginia, Mississippi, and Texas—would be readmitted early in 1870, further reducing the need for troops. It would not be long, however, before the residual forces in the South would find themselves confronting a new enemy: the Ku Klux Klan.

OPPOSITE: Noncommissioned officers from the 13th New York Cavalry gather for a portrait near the end of the Civil War. The variations of sleeve insignia include the regiment's sergeant major, quartermaster sergeant, color sergeant, first sergeant, hospital steward, and bugler. The 13th clashed repeatedly with the cavalry of Confederate Brigadier General John S. Mosby, engaging in particularly hot—and costly—skirmishes in July and October 1864. In the midst of a sudden action in December 1864, Mosby departed so quickly that he left his hat behind at a house in Rectorstown (also called Rector's Cross Roads), Virginia. Forty years later, Sarah Halstead, the daughter of one of the 13th's officers, returned the hat to Mosby. All told, the 13th lost 131 officers and men to combat and disease during its service.

THE INDIAN WARS

While the army in the South struggled with the unfamiliar terrain of governing a sullen—if not hostile—population, the forces in the West immediately returned to their traditional role of Indian fighting. It hadn't been long before the withdrawal of regulars to battle against the Confederacy precipitated an increase in violence against settlers and among the tribes. In Minnesota, a bloody uprising by the Sioux resulted in no less than five hundred dead among the settlers. Although Sioux casualties were far smaller, what they lost was title to their Minnesota reservations, and they were forced into the Dakotas and Nebraska. In Texas, the frontier was pushed back as much as 150 miles by the depredations of the Comanches, while further north, Kiowa and Comanche warriors had brought the movement along the Santa Fe Trail almost to a complete halt by 1863. An attack the next year led by Colonel Christopher "Kit" Carson's New Mexico militia against hostiles in Texas failed to achieve decisive results, while Colorado militia massacred a village of Arapahos and southern Cheyennes who had nothing to do with the bloodshed along the trail.

The work of the army in the first half of the century was almost undone, so far as the safety of the great West was concerned. But the army, with a heavier emphasis on cavalry, reorganized its regular units as rapidly as possible for service against the Indians, and most of the men were hard-bitten campaigners of Civil War battles (but unfamiliar with Indian fighting). The final result was a foregone conclusion. From 1865 to 1898 the U.S. Army fought 943 engagements against the Western tribes that ran the gamut from skirmishes to pitched battles. From 1866 to 1892 there was hardly a three-month period in which there was not an expedition against the Indians. Roughly two hundred of the most deadly fights occurred from 1866 to 1875, with the army heavily outnumbered in most of them, and many a skirmish meant death to all. A faint taste of the depth of the warfare can be gained from the eligibility list of the Indian Campaign Medal that Congress belatedly authorized in 1907 for veterans of the western fighting:

1865–1868	operations in southern Oregon, Idaho, northern California, and Nevada
1867–1875	against the Kiowas, Comanches, Arapahos, and other tribes in Kansas, Colorado, Texas, New Mexico, and Indian Territory

RIGHT: Of the two thousand Dakota Sioux taken into custody by the army in the days following the September 23, 1862, Battle of Wood Lake, Minnesota, some 393 warriors were tried, and 303 convicted, by military tribunals for "murder and other outrages." President Abraham Lincoln personally reviewed the trial transcripts and commuted the sentences of those not proven to have committed rape or the murder of women or children. Of the thirty-nine whose death sentences stood, one Indian brave was removed from the execution list when new evidence cast doubt upon his guilt. The remaining captives were hung on December 26, 1862, as more than three thousand people looked on. At one point after the trials, several Dakota prisoners were killed by an angry mob. Later, when a group of several hundred civilians armed with hatchets, clubs, and knives prepared to attack the condemned men, they were surrounded and disarmed by the troops. Private Peter Morgan of the 7th Minnesota Volunteers was one of the guards at the execution. He would later be wounded at the Battle of Nashville (see page 129) and his great, great, great grandson, Staff Sergeant Robert J. Miller, received a posthumous Medal of Honor for saving the lives of the American and Afghani soldiers under his command (see page 498).

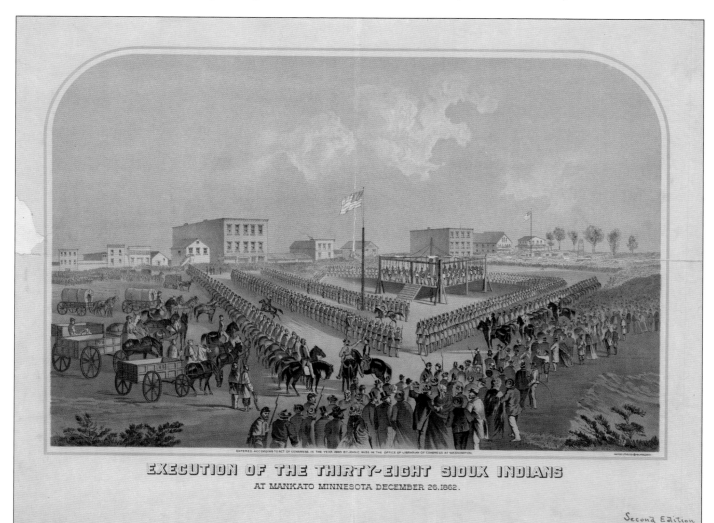

EXECUTION OF THE THIRTY-EIGHT SIOUX INDIANS
AT MANKATO MINNESOTA DECEMBER 26.1862.

Second Edition

1872–1873	Modoc War in California
1873	against the Apaches in Arizona
1876–1877	against the Northern Cheyennes and Sioux in Montana and Wyoming
1877	Nez Perce War across Oregon, Idaho, Wyoming, and Montana
1878	Bannock War (including Northern Shoshone) in Idaho and Oregon
1878–1879	against the Northern Cheyennes in Kansas and Nebraska
1879	against the Sheep Eaters (Western Shoshones), Paiutes, and Bannocks in Idaho and Oregon
1879–1880	against the Utes in Colorado and Utah
1885–1886	against the Apaches in Arizona and New Mexico
1890–1891	against the Sioux in South Dakota

Protecting the construction of the transcontinental railroad and freeing the existing overland routes from attack was the army's first order of business once units were available for service in the West. In characteristic fashion, Sherman, now a lieutenant general and commander of the vast Military Division of the Missouri, wrote Grant: "We are not going to let a few thieving, ragged Indians check and stop the progress of the railroads… I regard the railroad as the most important element now in progress to facilitate the military interests of our Frontier." However, the lack of progress in subduing the Comanches, Kiowas, and Arapahos along the Santa Fe Trail, as well as the Sioux and Northern Cheyennes along the Bozeman Trail, which ran through the Powder River country to the Montana gold fields, were significant setbacks.

Continued costly skirmishing, including the annihilation of eighty-one infantry and cavalry under Captain William J.

BELOW: Major General Philip H. Sheridan and his staff during the Civil War. (*Left to right*) Sheridan, chief of staff Brevet Brigadier General James William Forsythe, Brevet Major General Wesley Merritt, Brevet Brigadier General Thomas C. Devin, and Brevet Major General George Armstrong Custer. All five officers would play major roles during the Indian Wars.

ABOVE: A depiction of the battle near Fort Philip Kearny, Dakota Territory, which resulted in Sioux Chief Crazy Horse's annihilation of a relief force under Captain William J. Fetterman in December 1866. The post commander, Colonel Henry B. Carrington, concerned over the propensity of his officers to chase Sioux horsemen acting as decoys, ordered that no unsupported troops should be sent beyond a certain ridge near the fort. During attacks on a party of woodcutters, Fetterman disobeyed orders, leaving the party to withdraw on its own and blindly charging far beyond the ridge. In the resultant massacre, Fetterman—along with seventy-eight soldiers of the 2d Cavalry and 18th Infantry, as well as two civilians—were killed.

Fetterman at Fort Kearny by Sioux Chief Crazy Horse in December 1866, led to Sherman personally negotiating the Treaty of Fort Laramie with Sioux Chief Red Cloud in May 1868—a humiliating turn of events, as he had earlier written to Grant, "We must act with vindictive earnestness against the Sioux, even to their extermination, men, women and children." In return for the United States abandoning the Bozeman Trail, withdrawing from the three forts guarding it, agreeing to bar settlers from the Powder River country and above the North Platte River (nearly all of northwestern Nebraska), and recognizing most of present-day South Dakota as Sioux land, Sherman received Red Cloud's promise that he would "withdraw all opposition to the construction of the railroad" being built along the North Platte. The new railroad also provided access to an overland route to the gold fields that bypassed the Sioux.

Sherman had seen the writing on the wall and, in fact, had gained approval almost a year and a half earlier from Grant and Secretary of War Edwin M. Stanton to withdraw to the North Platte. In January 1867 he told Grant that he was confident that the army could protect a corridor to the Rockies running between the North Platte and Arkansas Rivers, but a withdrawal could not be done on the heels of a defeat. Victories by small contingents of soldiers and contract workers over vastly superior Indian forces in the Wagon Box Fight and Hayfield Fight in August of that year provided what Sherman needed, and the peace conference was called at which Red Cloud and his allies received everything they wanted.

The "strategic withdrawal" in July 1868 from forts C.F. Smith, Phil Kearny, and Reno after a three-year campaign to keep open the Bozeman Trail deeply wounded the army's pride and left its senior commanders in the West itching for revenge. Called alternately Red Cloud's War or the Powder River War, it was also a campaign that the army of that time did its best to downplay and, as an institution, this continued well into the next century. It inadvertently continues today.

Institutional memory dies hard, and despite the campaign's length, the depth of the army's commitment along the Bozeman Trail, and the fact that it was the scene of some of the most famous battles in the West—the Fetterman Massacre and the Wagon Box Fight—the 1865–1868 campaign against the Sioux and Northern Cheyenne remained missing from the orders creating the Indian Campaign Medal forty years later. What made this even more odd was that included among the only eleven soldiers to receive a Silver Citation Star with the medal was Private Samuel Gibson of the 27th Infantry. Gibson, who later rose to the rank of sergeant, received the medal for his actions during the Wagon Box Fight under the catch-all criteria, "against hostile Indians in any other action in which United States troops were killed or wounded between 1865 and 1891."

Today, the 9th Infantry Regiment, whose 4th Battalion is the descendant of the old 27th, carries no Campaign Participation Credit for the fighting in the Powder River area among its honors, or a campaign ribbon on its flag, because the embarrassment of the senior commanders involved led to the campaign becoming all but invisible to posterity. Although the Little Bighorn

LEFT: Soldiers from Brigadier General George Crook's September–October 1876 pursuit of a large band of Indians involved in the Custer massacre. Known alternately as the Starvation March, the Horsemeat March, and the Mud March, Crook's force ultimately included elements of four cavalry and three infantry regiments. After a lengthy period on half rations, the command was forced to slaughter any animal that had gone lame or was very weak. Here, a soldier prepares to sever a pack mule's tongue while others remove large slabs of meat. Later, on November 25, cavalry troops and a contingent of Pawnee and Sioux scouts under Colonel Mackenzie forced the Cheyenne to abandon a large village containing their food and clothing stocks for the coming harsh winter.

BELOW: 5th Infantry officers near their advance cantonment on the Tongue River, Montana Territory, in January 1877. Colonel Nelson A. Miles (in broad-brimmed hat) conducted a relentless campaign against the Sioux and Cheyenne throughout the winter months. Unable to obtain proper clothing from army stores, he arranged for the garrison at nearby Fort Buford to manufacture buffalo hide overcoats and extra-heavy underclothing from blankets. The winter campaign of 1876–1877 spurred the army to design and adopt specialized clothing for extreme temperatures, and the 5th Infantry advance base grew to become Fort Keogh.

ABOVE: Major George A. Forsyth as a brevet brigadier general in 1865.

BELOW INSET: Soldiers were in such short supply in the shrunken, post-Civil War Army that in 1868 General Philip H. Sheridan instructed Forsyth to hire a company of "fifty first-class, hardy frontiersmen" to serve as an independent unit. "Forsyth's Scouts" operated in support of the 10th Cavalry, a regiment composed of freed slaves from the southern states and some Civil War veterans, in the area of the Republican and Smoky Hill rivers (northwest Kansas, southeast Nebraska, and extending to the Rockies). On September 17, the major and his men, all armed with deadly Spencer repeating rifles, were attacked by a large war party of roughly six hundred Cheyennes and Arapahos. Taking refuge on a sandbar in the middle of the shallow Arikaree River, the little force was nearly overrun but managed to hold out because of Forsyth's superb leadership—plus their superior fire-power and ample ammunition. Unable to escape, the scouts settled in for a siege, subsisting on muddy water and the deteriorating meat from their dead horses, while receiving steady fire from the nearby bluffs, as well as periodic attacks. Two men who were sent for help succeeded in reaching Fort Wallace, more than sixty miles away, and on September 25 the scouts were relieved by two troops of "Buffalo Soldiers," as the 10th's troopers were called. Six of the scouts were killed and fifteen wounded, including the thrice-wounded Forsyth.

Campaign a decade hence is duly noted in the 9th's lineage, few in or out of the unit know that its predecessors in the beleaguered 27th Infantry had fought bitterly to keep open the Bozeman Trail until they were pulled from the thankless task after three long years. When the men marched out on July 31, 1868, the column hadn't gone far before the men saw smoke rising from Fort Kearny—the Sioux burned it to the ground before the soldiers were even out of sight.

SEARCH AND DESTROY

The secret for success against the Plains Indians was, in many ways, not a secret at all. Frontiersman-turned-army-colonel Kit Carson had understood through his deep associations with the Indians (he had twice married into tribes as a young fur trapper in the Rockies) that the warrior bands were most vulnerable in the winter when their horses' ability to graze became extremely difficult. In retaliation for repeated attacks up and down the Santa Fe Trail, Carson launched a winter campaign in November 1864. Attacking a Kiowa village through the snow with a force of

©History Colorado

335 troopers of the First Cavalry, New Mexico Volunteers (militia), plus seventy-five Apache and Ute scouts, he discovered that his target was only the first in a string of villages and found that he was outnumbered by ten or fifteen to one.

Skillful use of his two mountain howitzers to break up gathering concentrations of warriors succeeded in keeping his opponents off balance. This was followed by the timely maneuvering of his men to more defensible ground, the setting of his own backfire to thwart Indian efforts to block his retreat by burning the dry brush, and a night counterattack that killed a chief and burned down the first village. Unlike a later commander who, when facing a similar situation, died along with much of his command, Carson's force was able to escape with a loss of only six men, demonstrating to the Indians that despite the regulars' withdrawal to the Civil War, the army in the West was still a force to be reckoned with.

Carson's short winter expedition was considered a success, but even though the army found itself faced with a stalemate in the West, Sherman and Grant were reluctant to emulate Carson's tactic on the larger scale necessary to ensure that columns would not be overwhelmed. Not only would an operation on the frozen plains entail the utmost endurance by the troops, but it would require lots of them and even more men to support the combat elements by keeping the horses fed and the men supplied in the dead of winter while fighting hundreds of miles from their supply bases. The deteriorating situation in western Kansas finally forced the issue.

While the Sioux and their allies maintained a truce with the army for almost a decade along the North Platte after the Treaty of Fort Laramie, it quickly became apparent that a large number of Cheyenne, Kiowa, and Comanche braves were dissatisfied with a similar agreement fashioned at Medicine Lodge near Fort Larned, Kansas. Bloody raiding by several bands began as soon as the hunting and grazing season opened in 1868, and army detachments were seldom able to catch up with the elusive renegades. During one remarkable fight in September 1868, a forty-eight-man company of army scouts under Major George A. Forsyth fought off Chief Roman Nose's six-hundred-man band of mostly Arapahos and Northern Cheyennes at tiny Beecher Island on Colorado's Arikaree River for nine days.

ABOVE: Major George A. Forsyth's second in command, Lieutenant Frederick Beecher, a nephew of prominent abolitionist clergyman Henry Ward Beecher, was killed on the first day of the fight. He was replaced by First Sergeant William H.H. McCall, who had commanded the 200th Pennsylvania Infantry as a brevet brigadier general and fought through most of the nine-day siege with a bullet wound in his neck. He later performed the dangerous job of courier at Fort Whipple in the Arizona Territory and became a deputy U.S. marshal in nearby Prescott.

BACKGROUND: The site of the September 1868 Beecher Island action, shown here, around 1899, after the south channel had been closed off.

Captain Louis H. Carpenter
10th United States Cavalry

On October 14, 1868, two weeks after Captain Louis H. Carpenter had returned to Fort Wallace with the survivors of Forsyth's command, he was ordered out once again. Troops H and I of the 10th Cavalry sallied forth to escort Major Carr of the 5th Cavalry to his new command with supplies to Beaver Creek. Near there Carpenter's supply train and command was attacked by a force of about five-hundred Indians with no sign of the 5th Cavalry present.

Carpenter, seeking a more defensive posture closer to Beaver Creek, advanced for a short period then circled the supply wagons in a defendable area. This was possible because his mounted troopers fought a mobile delaying action. On his command, Carpenter's men rushed inside at the gallop. They dismounted and took up a defensive firing line at the gap between the wagons they had just entered.

On Carpenter's command, several massive volleys of aimed Spencer repeating rifles hit the front waves of the mounted Indians. The volleys decimated them as if hit by cannon filled with musket balls. A number of warriors dismounted, and using their ponies as bullet breaks, returned fire. Nearly all of these warriors died along with their ponies. Only three warriors made it to within fifty yards of the wagons before their demise. The Indians were so traumatized and demoralized by Carpenter's defense that they did not renew their attack.

Carpenter's troopers then accomplished their primary task by sending out scouts to find the location of the 5th Cavalry. This was done without further incident and they arrived back to Fort Wallace on October 21.

Carpenter's command had traveled some 230 miles in a week, routed some five-hundred mounted Indians, delivered the needed supplies with the new commander of the 5th Cavalry, and completed all as effectively and professionally as any other command could do.

For their gallantry in this fight on Beaver Creek, the officers and men of the "Buffalo Soldiers" were thanked by General Sheridan in a general field order and in official dispatches to the War Department in Washington. Captain Carpenter was brevetted Colonel. In 1898, for his efforts in September and October 1868, Carpenter became one of seven 10th Cavalry soldiers to be awarded the Medal of Honor during its service on the frontier.

RIGHT TOP: Lieutenant Colonel George Armstrong Custer's 7th Cavalry attacks Cheyenne Chief Black Kettle's winter camp on the Washita River. The camp was wiped out, with every teepee burned, 103 braves killed, and fifty-three women and children captured. The cavalry also took possession of eleven hundred buffalo robes, five hundred pounds of powder, one thousand pounds of lead, four thousand arrows, and approximately 875 horses. What couldn't be quickly removed was destroyed, including 675 horses.

RIGHT BOTTOM: Custer demands that Kiowa chiefs Santana, Lone Wolf, Kicking Bird, and Lone Heart return to their reservation in the Indian Territory. General Philip H. Sheridan and his cavalry watch at a distance. Also pictured at the December 17, 1868, meeting is Custer's brother, Lieutenant Tom Custer, interpreter Amos Grover (who, in fact, wasn't present), and Sheridan's aide-de-camp, Lieutenant Colonel John Schuyler Crosby.

Nearly one hundred braves were killed versus six of the scouts, but engagements like these were fought on the Indians' terms and did little to protect the settlers. Sheridan, now a lieutenant general, devised plans for a six-month winter campaign that met with the approval of Sherman and Grant, and an arduous series of operations began. At one point an entire regiment, the 19th Kansas Volunteer Cavalry, floundered in deep snow, and while its men managed to subsist on buffalo meat, roughly seven hundred horses died from lack of forage.

A force under Lieutenant Colonel George Armstrong Custer located a great encampment along the Washita River. By luck he had come across the most destructive group of marauders under Chief Black Kettle and, in a dawn attack on November 27, the 7th Cavalry killed or scattered the entire group, burned its dwellings, and killed the ponies it seized when it became clear that the escalating Indian counterattacks from nearby villages might result in their recapture. During the fighting, Black Kettle was killed, as was an entire detachment of cavalry that had pursued a group of fleeing Cheyennes and was unable to fight its way back to the regiment. The campaign continued throughout the winter and succeeded in weakening the hostile bands before their raids resumed in the spring. On July 11, 1869, Colonel Eugene A. Carr's 5th Cavalry and a group of scouts caught up with Chief Tall Bull's hostile Cheyennes and defeated them in the Battle of Summit Springs near Sterling, Colorado.

ABOVE: Emil Adams of the 5th U.S. Cavalry was brevetted major on September 25, 1872, for gallant conduct in engagement with Apache-Mojave Indians at Muchos Cañons.

BELOW: Colonel Christopher "Kit" Carson of the New Mexico Volunteers, c. 1864. After the Battle of Valverde against Confederate forces, campaigns against the Mescalero Apaches and Navajos in 1862–1863, and the 1864 Southern Plains Campaign against a combined force of Kiowa, Comanche, and Cheyenne, Carson received the brevet rank of brigadier general and was appointed commandant of Fort Garland, Colorado.

ABOVE: Eugene A. Carr as a brigadier general during the Civil War. Compare this photo to the one on page 135, taken after many years of arduous service on the frontier.

LEFT: Behind a barrier of lava rocks, along northern California's Tule Lake east of Mount Shasta, some Warm Spring Indians served as scouts for Colonel Alvan Cullem Gillem during the Modoc uprising of 1873. They kept a sharp watch as correspondent McKay of the *San Francisco Bulletin* leisurely writes a dispatch. The Modocs' effective defense of these well-fortified positions stymied militia and army operations from December 1872 through early May 1873.

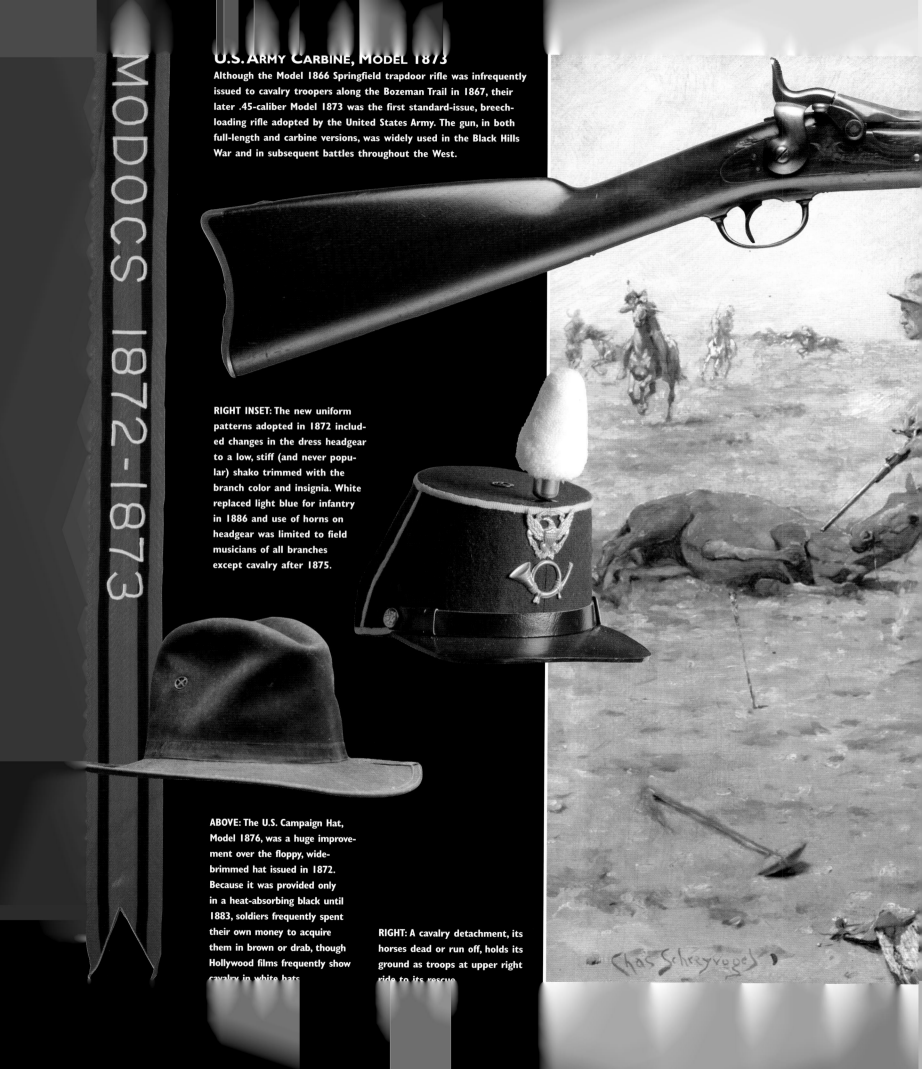

U.S. ARMY CARBINE, MODEL 1873

Although the Model 1866 Springfield trapdoor rifle was infrequently issued to cavalry troopers along the Bozeman Trail in 1867, their later .45-caliber Model 1873 was the first standard-issue, breech-loading rifle adopted by the United States Army. The gun, in both full-length and carbine versions, was widely used in the Black Hills War and in subsequent battles throughout the West.

RIGHT INSET: The new uniform patterns adopted in 1872 included changes in the dress headgear to a low, stiff (and never popular) shako trimmed with the branch color and insignia. White replaced light blue for infantry in 1886 and use of horns on headgear was limited to field musicians of all branches except cavalry after 1875.

ABOVE: The U.S. Campaign Hat, Model 1876, was a huge improvement over the floppy, wide-brimmed hat issued in 1872. Because it was provided only in a heat-absorbing black until 1883, soldiers frequently spent their own money to acquire them in brown or drab, though Hollywood films frequently show cavalry in white hats.

RIGHT: A cavalry detachment, its horses dead or run off, holds its ground as troops at upper right ride to its rescue.

BATTLES ACROSS A CONTINENT

Fighting temporarily tapered off in this region, but flare-ups continued across the West. Beginning in 1871, Brigadier General George Crook conducted a series of winter campaigns against hostile Apaches, including the band of Chief Cochise, in the Department of Arizona. Operating from his stronghold in the Dragoon Mountains, he conducted raids on both sides of the Mexican-American border. Cochise was captured, escaped, and was captured again after he returned to raiding, until U.S. representatives relented to a number of his terms and he retired to a reservation. Meanwhile, Crook's small, highly mobile detachments and extensive use of Apache scouts had by 1874 convinced the other bands to also return to the reservation, and Crook began to develop a reputation among the Apaches as being uncharacteristically honest for a white man. (In one example of how white men treated Indians, an Apache chief, Mangas Coloradas, had been lured to negotiations by California militia soldiers and then taken into custody and executed.) Due to Crook's success, Arizona remained pacified for more than a decade before trouble again broke out among the Apaches under chiefs Victorio, Chato, and Geronimo.

In northern California, a 1st Cavalry detachment skirmished with Modocs during a November 1872 mission to disarm the braves and return the tribe to its reservation. In the subsequent fighting, elements of the 1st Cavalry and 21st Infantry were unable to make any headway against a band of one hundred twenty warriors under Chief Kintpuash, better known as Captain Jack. The Indians were well stocked and strongly fortified in the impassable terrain of the Lava Beds east of Mount Shasta. A peace delegation headed by Brigadier General Edward R.S. Canby, commander of the Department of the Pacific, was attacked on April 11, 1873, during negotiations. Canby was shot twice before his throat was slashed. Three columns made up of the 1st Cavalry, 12th and 21st Infantry, and 4th Artillery were then pushed deep into the Lava Beds. The Modocs held out against the U.S. forces and the near-constant mortaring of their positions through May—killing eighty-three soldiers and scouts—only to be forced into the open and captured on June 1 after their water was cut off. The tribe subsequently was sent to the Indian Territory and Captain Jack was hanged for murder.

On the other side of the Rockies, the Comanches, Kiowas, Arapahos, and Southern Cheyennes went to war over the destruction of the buffalo herds that were crucial to their nomadic way of life. The fighting continued as the army moved to enforce the tribes' relocation from the southern plains to reservations in Indian Territory. The Red River War opened on June 27, 1874, with an attack by roughly three hundred Comanches on an encampment of buffalo hunters—a particularly hated group of white men who had been slaughtering buffalo by the thousands for their skins and leaving the carcasses to rot. The small group at Adobe Walls—only twenty-eight hunters—were well armed with long-range rifles and successfully defended themselves. The close proximity of army posts allowed five columns to converge on the area, and, though the bands were as nimble as always, fewer hostiles were involved in the raids than in previous wars, and the large number of army units chasing them resulted in more than twenty engagements.

The hostiles' numbers and will to fight were steadily eroded by battles such as the September 27, 1874, attack by Colonel Ranald S. Mackenzie's 4th Cavalry on the Kiowa-Comanche camp in Palo Duro Canyon, and the scattering of Cheyenne Chief Greybeard's large encampment in the Texas Panhandle on November 8 by a 6th Cavalry detachment under 1st Lieutenant Frank D. Baldwin, which was spearheaded by infantry loaded in mule wagons. With little chance to graze their livestock because of the constant pressure, and faced with the disappearance of the great buffalo herds, the bands eventually surrendered. Although serious fighting would again flare up in 1878 and 1879, the Red River War officially ended in June 1875 when the last free band of southwestern Indians, Chief Quanah Parker's Comanches, surrendered at Fort Sill in the Indian Territory.

That same summer, a precipitous event seven hundred miles to the north led inexorably to one of the most famous battles in American history. Custer's announcement that he had discovered gold in the Black Hills while on a scouting mission prompted an

ABOVE: Nelson A. Miles, pictured here as a brevet major general during the Civil War, took part in nearly every campaign against the tribes of the Great Plains.

BOTTOM LEFT: Second Lieutenant (later Colonel) Hugh T. Reed of the 1st Infantry donated this buckskin jacket to the U.S. Military Academy in 1873 while serving as a quartermaster in Michigan. He subsequently served as the commander of several frontier posts and led troops in actions against the Sioux and Nez Perces.

BOTTOM RIGHT: Lieutenant Colonel George Armstrong Custer used this footlocker during the campaign in which he and much of his command were killed.

SOLDIER ATTIRE

Soldiers dressed for comfort on the trail, and officers had even more leeway in what they wore. Captain Charles King of the 5th Cavalry described the varied attire of the different commands during the ill-fated 1876 campaign against the Sioux:

General Terry, as became a brigadier, was attired in the handsome uniform of his rank; his staff and his line officers, though looking eminently serviceable, were all in neat regimentals, so that shoulder-straps were to be seen in every direction. General Crook, as became an old campaigner and frontiersman, was in a rough hunting rig, and in all his staff and line there was not a complete suit of uniform. Left to our fancy in the matter, we had fallen back upon our comfortable old Arizona scouting-suits, and were attired in deerskin, buckskin, flannels, and corduroy; but in the 5th Cavalry, you could not have told officer from private.

Here, Brigadier General George Crook sports a sun hat, light canvas jacket, and shotgun across his lap as he sets off on a mule—which he usually preferred over horses—during his 1882–1886 campaign against the Chiricahua Apaches under Geronimo. To Crook's left is Scout Sergeant William Alchesay, a White Mountain Apache, who had earlier won a Medal of Honor during the winter campaign of 1872–1873 against the Chiricahua Apaches lead by Cochise.

ABOVE: Brigadier General George Crook, a fierce and clever Indian fighter, used his senior positions in the West to speak out against the unjust treatment of both native allies and his former enemies.

ABOVE: Alfred H. Terry as a brevet major general during the closing days of the Civil War. He served as a brigadier general during his two decades as an Indian fighter.

ABOVE: Colonel Ranald S. MacKenzie was wounded seven times while leading the 41st Infantry (Buffalo Soldiers), then the 4th Cavalry, against hostile Apaches, Oglala Sioux, Comanches, and Cheyennes.

I consider the services of the 5th Cavalry in Arizona as unequalled by that of any cavalry regiment during the late civil war.

—General W. T. Sherman

LITTLE BIGHORN

In the summer of 1876, three expeditionary forces under Major General George Crook, Brigadier General Alfred H. Terry, and Colonel John Gibbon were to converge on the Indians' principal hunting grounds in the southeastern portion of the Montana Territory.

Crook moved north from Fort Fetterman in the Wyoming Territory with about one thousand men (elements of the 2d and 3d cavalries and 4th and 9th infantries). At the same time, two columns under Terry set out to meet Crook. One column of more than one thousand men (7th Cavalry and elements or the 6th, 17th, and 20th infantries) under Terry's direct command moved from Fort Abraham Lincoln in the Dakota Territory to the mouth of Powder River, then southwest along the Yellowstone River Valley. Meanwhile, the second of Terry's columns, numbering about four hundred fifty men (elements of the 2d Cavalry and 7th Infantry) under Gibbon, moved east down the Yellowstone River from Fort Ellis to meet him.

On June 17, 1876, Crook's troops fought an indecisive engagement with a large band of Sioux and Cheyennes under Crazy Horse, Sitting Bull, and other chiefs on the Rosebud River. They withdrew from the area, then waited nearly two months for reinforcements. Meanwhile, Terry had discovered the trail of the same Indian band and sent Custer with the 7th Cavalry up the Rosebud to locate the war party. Custer was to position his men south of the Indians and engage them if it seemed necessary. Terry intended to continue, with the rest of his command, up the Yellowstone to meet Gibbon and then close on the Indians from the north, catching them between his force and Custer's.

The 7th Cavalry proceeded south along the Rosebud. In the early morning hours of June 25, a large village of Lakota Sioux and Cheyennes was observed from a high promontory in the Wolf Mountains. A distant fourteen miles to the west in the valley of the Little Bighorn, the village, from all indications, was de-camping and scattering. Fearful that the Indians would escape, Custer ordered his command to advance. In the rush to engage the Indians, he divided the 7th Cavalry into four units to

Captain Frederick W. Benteen

Captain Frederick W. Benteen became part of the 7th Cavalry upon its organization in 1866, together with Lieutenant Colonel George Armstrong Custer. In 1876, after Major Marcus Reno retreated from the valley of Little Bighorn, it was Benteen, as senior captain, who reinforced Reno's besieged troops and inspired the survivors to resist the Sioux throughout the days of June 25 and 26.

Captain Thomas W. Custer

Captain Thomas W. Custer was the recipient of two Congressional Medals of Honor during the Civil War and commanded Company C at the famed "Last Stand" at Little Bighorn. He was killed on Custer Ridge along with his brother, George, and brother-in-law, James Calhoun.

First Lieutenant James Calhoun

First Lieutenant James Calhoun was the Custers' brother-in-law and commander of Company L at the Battle of Little Bighorn. Warriors overran his position on the southern end of Battle Ridge, nearly a mile from where Custer fell.

First Lieutenant Edward S. Godfrey

First Lieutenant Edward S. Godfrey commanded Company G at Little Bighorn and was with Reno's battalion when Custer and his men were being wiped out. Godfrey remained with the 7th Cavalry as captain of K Company. Though severely wounded during the 1877 Battle of Bear Paw Mountain, he continued to lead his men and was awarded the Medal of Honor for valor.

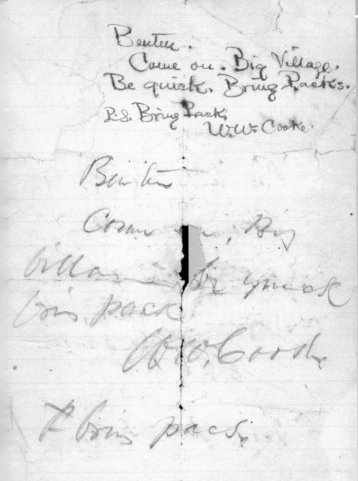

ABOVE: *Custer's last order to Captain Frederick W. Benteen on June 25, 1876, was written out by his adjutant, Lieutenant William W. Cooke. Upon sighting the Indian village on the Little Bighorn, Custer called his bugler, Private John Martini, to carry an order to Benteen, whose column included the pack train of mules hauling the ammunition. Fearing Martini might garble the message, he hastily had it written down before the bugler rode off. Martini was the last white man to see Custer and his force that day and live to tell about it. The message was simply: "Benteen: Come on. Big Village. Be quick. Bring packs. W. W. Cooke. P.S. Bring pacs." The smaller, more carefully penned text at upper right was added after the battle. Custer's last message is housed at the West Point Museum at the U.S. Military Academy.*

RIGHT: *Lieutenant Colonel George Armstrong Custer*

OPPOSITE TOP: *This drawing by Amos Bad Heart Buffalo likely depicts the last action of the battle, when twenty-eight troopers attempted to escape but became cornered in an area called "Deep Ravine."*

cover possible contingencies. The regiment went into battle piecemeal before it became apparent that the early morning assumption—that the village was escaping—was incorrect.

The massive encampment—really a series of villages stretching for miles along the Little Bighorn—contained four thousand to five thousand Indians, including roughly twenty-five hundred warriors. Though surprised by the approaching cavalry, the warriors were able to concentrate overwhelming numbers against a now divided 7th Cavalry and defeat it in detail. First, Major Marcus Reno's battalion of three companies was repulsed, suffering severe losses, when they attacked the southernmost village. Three miles to the northwest and on the other side of the river, Custer's force of 211 men in five companies was surrounded and completely destroyed. Reno's soldiers soon would have met the same fate, but they were joined by four companies, including a pack train, under Captain Frederick Benteen.

The combined force was able to withstand heavy attacks that finally ceased when the Indians withdrew late the following day as Gibbon approached. Approximately 380 members of the 7th Cavalry, including fifty wounded, survived the battle.

ABOVE: *Period illustrations of the action on "Last Stand Hill" usually depict a swirling tide of Indians around a small band of troopers. This later painting is more in line with Sioux and Cheyenne accounts, which generally describe the force being overrun.*

RIGHT: *The only survivor from the companies in General George Armstrong Custer's immediate command was this horse named Comanche, ridden by Captain Myles Keogh. Shot at least seven times, the soldiers who found him two days later were going to put him out of his misery but recognized that his wounds, though serious, were not life threatening if properly tended. Also pictured is Private (later Sergeant) Gustave Korn, who had been a member of Keogh's Company I but fought the battle with Captain Marcus A. Reno's battalion. Until his death at the Battle of Wounded Knee in 1890, Korn cared for Comanche, who survived for another year.*

LEFT: *Guidon (a military standard, or flag) used by Company G, 7th Cavalry at the Battle of Little Bighorn. Company G was commanded by First Lieutenant Edward S. Godfrey and was with Reno's battalion.*

ABOVE: *The last man to depart Custer's column once the fighting had begun was Curly, a young Crow scout. One of the many scouts assigned to the Custer column, he was sent to the rear perhaps because of his youth, or as a last attempt to get a message to Captain Frederick W. Benteen. Curly described riding upward a short distance from the command, then stopping, turning around and actually seeing Custer's men engaged in the opening moments of the battle.*

BELOW: *July 6, 1876, newspaper from Bismarck in the Dakota Territory.*

BELOW: *Lakota Sioux arrows recovered from the Battle of Little Bighorn battlefield.*

FIRST ACCOUNT OF THE CUSTER MASSACR

TRIBUNE EXTRA.

BISMARCK, D. T., JULY 6, 1876.

Price 25 Cents.

MASSACRED

GEN. CUSTER AND 261 MEN THE VICTIMS.

NO OFFICER OR MAN OF 5 COMPANIES LEFT TO TELL THE TALE.

3 Days Desperate Fighting

Full Details of the Battle.

LIST OF KILLED AND WOUNDED.

THE BISMARCK TRIBUNE'S SPECIAL CORRESPONDENT SLAIN.

Squaws Mutilate and Rob the Dead

Victims Captured Alive Tortured in a Most Fiendish Manner.

What Will Congress Do About It?

Sioux, emptying several cham his revolver, each time brin red-skin before he was down—shot through the h was here Bloody Knife sur his spirit to the one who gav ing the natural and heredito his tribe, as well as the fo whites.

The Sioux dashed up bes diers in some instances them at their pleasure. T case with Lt. McIntosh. armed except with a sab pulled from his horse, finally murdered at the the red devils. It was fi Girard was separated mand and lay all nig screeching fiends dea destruction to his co a few feet of him, and not permit us to re through some means saving his fine black he took so much prid crossed and the sum having, Col. Smith h sides that he ever horse or mule; reach cent was made un

The companies fair were those French and McIn gone ahead with obedience to the fighting most g repeatedly the in their front. bluff being so movement her signals were with the fou came up in the fate wit time met time repulse

BELOW: An army camp on French Creek in the Montana Territory after the arrival of a supply column during Major General George Crook's unsuccessful 1876 expedition against Sitting Bull. Gold had been discovered near French Creek, and it became a booming mining town that was soon renamed Custer City.

BELOW RIGHT: Human and horse skeletons litter the ground atop "Last Stand Hill" on the Little Bighorn battlefield. The remains of at least two cavalry boots are clearly visible. With very little time, many wounded to be cared for, and few shovels available, the initial burials of enlisted troops amounted to little more than shovelfuls of dirt thrown over the mutilated and bloated bodies. All were unmarked except identifiable officers, whose names were written on a piece of paper, slipped inside a spent cartridge, then pounded into the head of a stake for later identification. A shallow grave was dug for the 7th's commander. Later burial parties found thousands of gleaming bones scattered by predators.

influx of whites into the sacred Sioux lands, which the army was utterly unable to prevent. Some ten thousand miners and traders had surged into the Black Hills by 1876, and the Sioux were on the warpath.

Orders to return to the reservation in the Dakotas were ignored, and Sheridan, now commander of the Division of the Missouri, conceived of a plan to converge several columns simultaneously on the Yellowstone River area to trap the Sioux in the Montana Territory and force their return to the reservation. On June 17, 1876, a column under Crook, approaching the area from the south, fought an indecisive engagement with a large band of Sioux and Cheyennes under Crazy Horse, Sitting Bull, and other chiefs on the Rosebud River and then withdrew to await reinforcements. Brigadier General Alfred H. Terry, converging from the east, came across the trail of the same band that fought Crook and sent the 7th Cavalry up the Rosebud on a wide left hook to a point south of where the Indians were believed to be. From the Rosebud, Custer could then cut over to the Little Big Horn valley and turn north to approach the Indians from behind, while Terry, with the rest of his command, closed in on the Indians from the opposite direction.

In a disastrous confrontation, Custer divided his regiment into four elements before discovering that he had stumbled upon a string of villages stretching for several miles up Little Bighorn River. In a series of actions on June 25 and 26, 268 of the approximately 650-man force, including Custer, were killed. The Indians under Crazy Horse and the other chiefs suffered far fewer casualties. The bands split up after this victory and eluded Terry's subsequent efforts to corner them. Crook, however, captured Chief American Horse's Sioux village on September 9, and Chief Dull Knife's Cheyenne village on November 26, while Colonel Nelson A. Miles attacked Crazy Horse's mountain camp in the dead of winter on January 8, 1877.

By the summer, Sitting Bull and a small band of Sioux escaped to Canada, and nearly all of the other tribes had returned to their reservations. Crazy Horse turned himself in at Fort Robinson, Nebraska, on May 7, 1877, flanked by chiefs He Dog and Little Big Man, and at the head of a two-mile-long column of fully armed braves, their bodies and horses painted for war; women, children, and the elderly followed in their finest clothes. As the column approached, the chiefs began to sing, then the braves joined in. The thousands of agency Indians who lined

the route through the White River Valley joined in, and an astonished army officer remarked, "By God, this is a triumphal march, not a surrender." Four months later, fearing that Crazy Horse was preparing to lead a revolt, authorities moved to take him into custody, and he was killed while resisting arrest.

Vicious and bloody fighting continued to erupt with little or no warning for nearly fifteen more years, then sputtered on into the twentieth century, but the Indians were no longer a threat to the settlement of the West. Looking back on the battles he had fought against the Sioux, the Cheyennes, and a dozen other tribes, General Sheridan wrote in 1878:

We took away their country and their means of support, broke up their mode of living, introduced disease and decay among them. And it was for this and against this that they made war. Could anyone expect less?

SMITH AND WESSON ARMY REVOLVER, MODEL NO. 3

Armed with only his .44-caliber Smith and Wesson American stuffed into his belt, Second Lieutenant (later Colonel) Hobart Kemper Bailey calmly walked up to Sitting Bull and one thousand Sioux warriors drawn up in a line of battle near the Cedar Creek in the Montana Territory to arrange a parlay with Colonel Nelson A. Miles. The October 20, 1876, negotiations were futile, and skirmishing continued for nearly a week before the 5th Infantry gained the upper hand. Out of the one thousand revolvers that Smith and Wesson delivered to the army in the spring of 1871, only two hundred received a nickel-plated finish. This revolver carries serial number 2106 from shipping crate number 47. Though refinished at some point in its past, it retains traces of its original nickel finish.

STAR PISTOL, MODEL 1856

This .44-caliber revolver was carried by Medal of Honor recipient Robert G. Carter, who earned it fighting a Comanche raiding party on the Brazos River in Texas in 1877. Carter carried this pistol even though it was an old cap-and-ball-style weapon.

BELOW: Third Cavalry troops from Fort Robinson in a close-quarter battle with the Cheyennes on January 9, 1879. The desperate band under Dull Knife was made up of proud men, women, and children who had not eaten in more than a week and decided to die fighting rather than starve. The soldier climbing over the embankment is Corporal Carter P. Johnson, who crawled up a ledge and fired into the rifle pits a mere nine feet away. Johnson, one of the few soldiers during this period to rise from the ranks to become an officer, retired as a major in 1909 and, ironically, moved to a ranch near the old post.

Bear Paw Battle Official Report
To Col. Samuel D. Sturgis

On the morning of September 30th, 1877, the battalion of the Seventh Cavalry, Company A Captain Moylan; Company D Captain Godfrey, and the 1st Lieutenant E.P. Eckerson; Company K Captain Hale, and 2d Lieutenant J.W. Biddle, all under command of Captain Owen Hale, Seventh Cavalry, and constituting a part of the force under command Colonel Nelson A. Miles, Fifth Infantry, moved from its camp near the northeast end of Bear Paw Mountain, M.T. at 2:30 o'clock, a.m. The column moved as follows: battalion of the Second Cavalry in advance, Seventh Cavalry center, Fifth Infantry rear. The march was continued until about 8 a.m., as near as I can recollect, when the trail of the Nez Perce Indians was discovered pointing in a northerly direction, it was pronounced by the Cheyenne Indian scouts who accompanied the command, to be two days old.

After a short halt on the trail the march was resumed in the same order as above mentioned. The command had marched about five or six miles from the point where the halt was made on the trail when information was received from the Cheyenne scouts that the Nez Perce village was located on a creek about seven miles in front.

The command was immediately given for the column to take the trot, and subsequently the gallop was taken up. About this time an order was brought to me from Captain Hale, commanding battalion, that the Seventh Cavalry would, by order of Colonel Miles, charge the village, mounted, with pistols. After passing over the divide which separated us from the Indian village, the battalion was formed in line about 1-1/2 miles from the village, Company "K" on the right, Company "D" in the center, Company "A" on the left.

The line being formed, the battalion moved forward at the trot, then the gallop and the charge. During the movement to the front in line, Company "K" under Captain Hale, diverged to the right and struck at the Indians almost at right angles to the direction the companies "A" and "D" charged. Company "K" struck the Indians first and was repulsed with some loss. The Company retired to a distance of about 250 or 300 yards, dismounted and deployed as skirmishers. After repulsing Company "K" the Indians turned their attention to the other two Companies, ("A" and "D"), which charged them in front.

These two Companies charged a high bank which overlooked their village (the village being situated in a deep ravine through which Snake Creek ran), and owing to the fact that this bank was at the point charged by the Companies almost perpendicular, they could not dislodge the Indians, neither could they charge through them owing to the nature of the ground.

Taking in the situation, at once and seeing the hopelessness of being able to do anything at this point mounted, I gave the order for the Companies to fall back, the movement was executed by "fours left about." In the execution of this movement confusion occurred for the very good reason that the men were under a heavy fire from the Indians and that the large majority of them had never been under fire before, being mostly all recruits.

The loss of the companies in the action thus far was not as great as might have been expected for the reason that a heavy depression in the ground between them and the Indians protected them somewhat, the Indians overshooting them. The movement was executed, however, and the companies reformed on the right of the line occupied by the Infantry, some 200 or 300 yards to the rear.

The loss thus far in Companies "A" and "D" was three men killed and four wounded. During the movement to the rear, Captain Godfrey, who was riding in rear of his company and watching the Indians, had his horse killed under him. The fall of the horse was so sudden that Godfrey was thrown heavily to the ground, falling upon his shoulder and partially stunned for the moment. Captain Godfrey would certainly have lost his life at this time, as the Indians were advancing in his direction, but for the gallant conduct of Trumpeter Thomas Herwood, Company "D," Seventh Cavalry, who seeing Captain Godfrey's danger, separated himself from his Company and between where Captain Godfrey was lying and the Indians, thereby drawing the attention of the Indians to himself till Captain Godfrey was sufficiently recovered from the effects of his fall to get him upon his feet and join his company. In his gallant attempt to save his officer, Trumpeter Herwood was wounded through the body, and, I believe, since discharged the service on Surgeon's certificate of Disability.

An order was at this time received from Colonel Miles to dismount the Companies and that they be deployed to the right and make connections with Company "K," that Company being at this time severely handled by the Indians. The Indians, not being particularly engaged at any other point, concentrated most of their force upon it and succeeded in driving back its skirmish, also in driving the horse-holders who were dismounted, from their lead-horses.

Having thus far been unsuccessful in driving the men away from their horses the Indians attempted to lead into their village several horses of Company "K," and were only prevented from accomplishing their purpose by the rapid advance of Companies "A" and "D" on foot at the double-time. It was during this movement that Companies "A" and "D" suffered their heaviest losses. The Indians poured a heavy cross-fire into them as they advanced, killing and wounding a great many of the men. It was in this advance that Captain Godfrey was wounded, he, having mounted another horse, was gallantly cheering on his men to the assistance of their comrades in Company "K."

Being mounted, he was a conspicuous mark for the Indians to shoot at.

It is proper that I should here mention the gallantry and coolness of Captain Godfrey throughout the action up to the time of his being wounded and taken from the field. His conduct was brave, cool and soldierly throughout and added very materially to the success of the movement of the Companies to the assistance of Captain Hale's Company. The connection with Company "K" was made with considerable loss. Having established my line, I reported to Captain Hale for further instructions and was in the act of receiving orders from him when I was shot through the upper part of my right thigh and had to be taken from the field. Farther than this I have no personal knowledge of the part taken by the Companies of the Seventh Cavalry in action.

The conduct of the officers and men up to the time of my being taken from the field was superb. I am unable to mention any particular men for individual acts of gallantry when all did so well, except in the case of 1st Sergeant Charles R. Miller, Company "A," Seventh Cavalry, who has already been recommended for Certificate of Merit, and Trumpeter Thomas Herwood, Company "D," Seventh Cavalry, who I believe is now out of the service.

I am unable to give the loss the battalion sustained at the time I was wounded. From what I was able to observe of Captain Hale in the action, his conduct was such as might be expected of him—cool and gallant. When I reported to him after connecting my line with his, I found him in the skirmish line encouraging his men by words and acts. The line of all three Companies of the Seventh Cavalry was at this time no more than 100 yards from the enemy. I would further state that, to the best of my recollection, the whole time I was engaged in the action, from its opening to the time I was wounded, was not more than forty-five minutes. I may be somewhat in error as to time and distance, but what I have stated on these points is my best recollection of them.

Below is the loss sustained by the battalion in the action:

Company "A," 5 men killed; 1 officer (Captain Moylan), 8 men wounded.
Company "D," 4 men killed; (Captain Godfrey) 11 men wounded.
Company "K," 3 officers (Captain Hale, Lt. Biddle) and 9 men killed, 12 men wounded.
Making a total of 53 officers and men killed and wounded out of 115 officers and men engaged. All of which occurred during the first day's fight.

(Signed) M. Moylan,
Captain, Seventh Cavalry

OPPOSITE INSET: Captain Edward S. Godfrey, commanding D Company, 7th Cavalry, and his Medal of Honor, awarded for his leadership at Bear Paw Mountain while severely wounded.

BELOW: Two of Colonel Wesley Merritt's ten 5th Cavalry companies move in a column outside of Custer City in the Black Hills of the Dakota Territory as dust from additional companies rises in the distant town. After the disaster at Little Bighorn, the 2d, 3d, and 7th cavalries, plus elements of the 4th, 6th, 7th, 9th, 17th, and 20th infantries, were swelled by the addition of all or part of the 4th and 5th cavalries; the 5th, 14th, 22d, and 23d infantries; and the 4th Artillery. By the summer of 1877 most of the Sioux were back on the reservations, but a small band under Sitting Bull escaped to Canada.

Captain Owen Hale, commanding K Company, 7th Cavalry, was killed in action at Bear Paw Mountain on September 30, 1877.

ABOVE: The Indian Campaign Medal of 1907 was authorized for veterans of the many campaigns conducted against hostile Indians from 1865 through 1891. It also was awarded for any individual action during this period in which troops were killed or wounded. The medal on the left has the original issued red ribbon, and the example on the right has the 1917 revised ribbon design with two vertical black stripes. With U.S. involvement in World War I, the ribbon was changed in order to avoid confusion with the French Legion of Honor.

OUTPOST LIFE

Some forts like Leavenworth, which was part of the original chain of posts defending the frontier from Jesup in Louisiana to Snelling in Minnesota, were maintained to a very high standard, but the rapid expansion and poor funding during the Indian Wars resulted in a decidedly uneven collection of forts throughout the West. Whether garrisoned by a few hundred men or a few thousand, life in these far outposts of civilization was nearly identical—a never-ending round of drills, hard work, and more drills. Battling boredom far more than "hostiles," and civil disturbances, the men could at least depend on being fed. Yet even units with conscientious officers and quartermasters often found that food was delivered infested with insects and mice, with beef already spoiled and turning green. As always, Army chow was the target of derision, and a standard joke of the day was that the cooks killed more troopers than the Indians.

By 1880, nearly all permanent posts had barracks that, while still overcrowded, were spacious enough that sergeants could now have a private, if diminutive, room, and enlisted men no longer had to bed down nose-to-toe with a "bunky" whose feet were always inches from his face. The actual directive for individual beds had been issued nearly a decade before, but it could only be carried out where practical. Similarly, War Department orders mandated that each soldier bathe at least once a week but almost no posts had bath houses. "The regulations," quipped one officer, "say the men must be made to bathe frequently; the doctors say it should be done; the men want to do it; the company officers wish them to do so; the Quartermasters' Department says it's important. Yet we have no bathrooms."

Still, even if the pace was uneven and accomplished in fits and starts, visible improvements were being made. The rude dwellings where officers often quartered on the more remote posts, with walls of adobe in the southwest and logs in the north, had largely been replaced by conventional housing that improved according to rank. On posts with enough room, even enlisted men were able to make arrangements for their families to live, but all—including officers—understood that rank had its privileges. The arrival of a new officer or sergeant could, and usually would, start a process of "ranking out" down the line as he was ordered to occupy quarters appropriate to his stature, thus displacing a quarter's current tenants who would immediately continue the unpleasantness by displacing anyone of inferior rank whose abode met their fancy. An army wife at Camp Supply described a typical "ranking out" where "one junior second lieutenant, six or more captains and first lieutenants had to move. It was great fun the next day to see the moving up and down the officers' line of all sorts of household goods."

ABOVE: *Officers' quarters at Fort Grant, Arizona Territory. After the Apache wars, the post received a new lease on life as a staging point for soldiers being sent to the Philippines. It was abandoned in 1905 when all remaining troops were transferred to Fort Huachuca.*

BELOW: *Fort Thomas on the Gila River, Arizona Territory, in 1885. Widely regarded as "the worst fort in the army" because of its rotting buildings and ever-present problems with malaria, it was abandoned to the termites and the elements when the last of its garrison departed in 1891.*

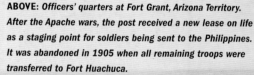

ABOVE: *Although the center structure disappeared nearly a century ago, these other pre-Civil War buildings at Fort Leavenworth, Kansas, are still in use. At left is the extreme west end of Stotsenburg Hall, part of the Ordnance Arsenal built in 1859. It later served as the post's finance department, then Foreign Military Studies Office, and currently the Center For Army Lessons Learned. The building at right was the Arsenal Headquarters, then a bachelor officers quarters, or BOQ, which "other than for the bats, was a nice place to live." The edge of a Civil War revetment encompassing artillery batteries and the main storehouse (today named Sherman Hall) can be seen at left. Seizure of the arsenal was one of the objectives of a large—and unsuccessful—Confederate raid from Arkansas in 1864. Because of its location adjacent to the principal trails west, Leavenworth remained a key supply point and source of reinforcements during the Indian Wars even as other old forts were sold off.*

BELOW: *Troops in formation on the parade ground of Fort Yates in the Dakota Territory. In order to help ensure that its garrison would not develop a defensive mentality, Yates, like most forts in the West, contained no walled stockade. The post was decommissioned in 1905 because it was clear that the Sioux were no longer a threat.*

Chapter Five

Beyond the Borders: The Far East, Caribbean, and Mexico, 1877–1917

A compromise between the political parties in the angrily disputed presidential election of 1876 placed Republican Rutherford B. Hayes in office and ended the last vestiges of Reconstruction in the South. The already depleted army units attempting to counter an ascendant Ku Klux Klan were transferred to duties elsewhere as the army braced itself for a round of personnel cuts now that the mission in the South was at an end. What happened next caught even some of the most pessimistic soldiers by surprise.

The winding down of Reconstruction had seen a corresponding reduction in the army to roughly thirty-nine thousand men in 1869, thirty thousand the following year, and twenty-five thousand in 1874. In 1877, the House of Representatives, now under the control of southern Democrats, moved to cut the army—"the unholy instrument of repression" during Reconstruction—to seventeen thousand, then fifteen thousand, lest the federal government be tempted to use it again domestically. Proposed amendments and legislative maneuvering also resulted in the Fifty-fourth Congress adjourning in March before they had passed an appropriations bill for the coming fiscal year and, for the sake of political expediency, the president did not call Congress back into session to rectify the matter. As of June 30, neither officers nor enlisted men—be they soldier, sailor, or marine—was able to draw even a dime of pay.

The delegation from Texas, however, broke ranks and made it clear that they wanted even more troops because of the on-going problems with the Apaches along the Mexican border and the continued raiding by the Cheyennes. Congressman and future president James A. Garfield of Ohio became the army's fiercest advocate on Capitol Hill. Garfield, who had fought as a brigade commander at Shiloh, then rose to major general, and had helped negotiate the compromise that brought Hayes to the presidency, was incensed at the treatment of the soldiers and told the House that they "might as well take command of the pickets; say where the guards are to be posted." Coming close on the heels of the Little Big Horn disaster and winter campaign against the Sioux, Garfield spoke for most Americans when he berated his colleagues:

> It is not enough that our poor, unpaid, starving army shall, by the delay of the House, be doomed to many days of starvations while their numbers are reduced by sickness and Indian warfare only to learn that a merciful Congress proposes still further to reduce them? That at last the commander-in-chief shall be shackled and the army itself shackled and finally that the House of Representatives shall itself take command of the army and post its Cavalry regiments where they choose?

Enlisted men received a degree of protection because the army could continue to contract for food, clothing, and other basic needs, but the lack of funding prevented them from having money for other "essentials" such as beer and female companionship. Officers had it even worse. Whether unmarried or the head of a household, they had been responsible since 1870 for covering the cost of all personal necessities, including their uniforms, out of their own meager salaries. Many, unable to live on their savings, were forced to borrow money at usurious rates against their future pay or live off the charity of relatives and friends. A lucky few received the assistance of the Louisiana National Bank, which offered loans without interest to army officers, and Americans pitched in to help in whatever way they could. For example, some hotels like the Occidental in San Francisco let it be known that they would present no bills to officers in transit.

The situation finally was rectified in November 1877 when House members, under mounting pressure from constituents,

OPPOSITE: Captain Richmond Smith, commanding the 6th Infantry's Company B at Sierra Boca Grande, gives an order to the sergeant of the guard during the army's punitive expedition into Mexico in late March 1916. Nearly forty years earlier in 1877, the mountainous mass twenty-eight miles south of Columbus, New Mexico, had served as a staging area for raids into the United States and had been the site of a skirmish between the 9th Cavalry's C Troop and an Apache band.

RIGHT: Noncommissioned officers of the 9th Cavalry, 1889. *Standing left to right*: Sergeant James Wilson, I Troop; First Sergeant David Badir, B Troop; First Sergeant Thomas Shaw, K Troop; and First Sergeant Nathan Fletcher, F Troop. *Seated left to right*: Chief Trumpeter Stephen Taylor; Sergeant Edmund McKenzie, I Troop; Sergeant Robert Burley, D Troop; and Sergeant Jekiel Sykes, B Troop. Shaw received a Medal of Honor in 1890 for his actions during the August 12, 1881, skirmish at Carrizo Canyon in New Mexico. Although in a dangerously exposed position, the sergeant stubbornly held his ground against attacking Apaches and prevented their superior numbers from surrounding his command.

including those from the South, produced an appropriations bill and authorized a force of twenty-five thousand men—a troop strength that remained largely unchanged for the next two decades.

DOMESTIC UNREST

Ironically, the shenanigans on Capitol Hill occurred at the same time that the army was experiencing its most active period since the Civil War. Large forces stayed on alert in the Central Plains in case the still-dangerous Sioux, Cheyennes, or Kiowas left their reservations in significant numbers. Warfare continued with the elusive Apaches, and a sizable chunk of the U.S. Army—elements of the 1st, 2d, 5th, and 7th Cavalry; the 5th Infantry; and the 4th Artillery—spent four months chasing the Nez Perce across the rugged terrain of Oregon, Idaho, and Montana until they were finally cornered by Colonel Miles. But while the Indian wars became the stuff of legend, the domestic unrest that accompanied the growing pains of an increasingly industrial society now are largely forgotten.

Until passage of the Posse Comitatus Act of 1878—a "Never Again!" measure by the Southern Democrats—restricting the use of Federal forces without authorization by either "the Constitution or . . . Congress," they had frequently been called to action by governors, federal marshals, and even local authorities (the most famous example of this being Lieutenant Colonel Lee and a Marine detachment during the seizure of the Harpers Ferry Arsenal in 1859). This became so widely abused, with individual soldiers and units being dragooned into assisting in such things as county revenue collections, that Secretary of War Edwin M. Stanton issued an 1868 directive that such requests "must be held subordinate to [the soldiers'] paramount duty as members of the permanent military body."

Stanton ordered that "troops can act only in their proper organized capacity, under their own officers, and in obedience to the immediate orders of those officers." Commanders could decide for themselves if a request was proper and of a sufficiently imperative nature to justify the immediate use of their men but were told that if time allowed, they were to request guidance from the president (really their next higher headquarters) first, "whether it be for the execution of civil process or to suppress insurrection."

During the Great Railroad Strike of 1877, the threat of national anarchy and disruption of mail service prompted the army to rush soldiers from three states and two territories to occupy rail yards in Chicago and St. Louis. Troops from seventeen other states were directed to move immediately to riot-torn areas of West Virginia, Kentucky, Maryland, and Pennsylvania, virtually emptying every post in Major General Winfield Scott

SPRINGFIELD RIFLE, MODEL 1888

The Model 1888 round-rod bayonet rifle was Springfield's last attempt at producing a trapdoor weapon with a working and reliable bayonet retention mechanism. More than sixty thousand were produced between 1890 and 1893, when trapdoor production came to an end. Along with the Model 1884, it saw service in the Spanish-American War with the National Guard and most of the volunteer regiments in Cuba while the Regular Army was issued the new Krag-Jorgensen rifles.

U.S. CAVALRY ENLISTED MAN'S HELMET, MODEL OF 1881

When redesigning its uniforms in 1872, the army adopted a distinctive, plumed helmet for all mounted troops. That design, however, proved to be too cumbersome for soldiers to wear comfortably. In 1881 a new, lighter and generally smaller helmet was introduced, this time for all soldiers and officers. Those worn by mounted troops (*left*) were still trimmed with cords and plumes, while foot soldiers (*right*) had only spikes on the tops of their helmets. Originally issued in lemon yellow, which proved to be highly susceptible to fading (*see facings on the uniform coat below*), the cavalry helmet's plume and cords now had a deeper shade, which proved more resistant to sunlight.

U.S. CAVALRY ENLISTED MAN'S UNIFORM COAT, MODEL OF 1872

For several years after the end of the American Civil War, the U.S. Army continued to wear uniforms that were made during the war and left as surplus after large wartime armies disbanded. By 1872, however, the army decided to adopt newer styles rather than remanufacture the old patterns. Nevertheless, great quantities of serviceable surplus uniforms continued to be issued and frequently resulted in an odd mix of patterns within units until the stocks were officially declared expended in 1880.

RIGHT: Rounds fired by Apache warriors in Mexico's Pinto Mountains kick up dust around Second Lieutenant Powhattan H. Clarke of K Troop in the 10th Cavalry, as he rescues Corporal Edward Scott on May 3, 1886. Scott's leg wound proved to be severe, and the limb had to be amputated. Buffalo Soldiers provided effective cover fire during the action, but an additional trooper was added for dramatic purposes to this illustration, which was done for a period magazine.

BELOW: Inspection of Company B, West Point Cadet Battalion, at Camp Rendrick, c. 1890. Regular Army officers, *left to right*: unidentified artilleryman; Lieutenant Colonel Hamilton S. Hawkins, 23d Infantry; First Lieutenant Samuel W. Dunning, 16th Infantry; Second Lieutenant T. Bentley Mott, 1st Artillery; and First Lieutenant George W. McIver, 7th Infantry. Mott and McIver had long and distinguished careers in the army, both serving in France during World War I and rising to the rank of brigadier general. Hawkins later became a major general; he had served as a young officer during the Civil War. He received a severe chest wound during the final stages of the charge up San Juan Hill in 1898 while leading the 1st Brigade of V Corps' 1st Division as a brigadier general.

In letters that he wrote home during the fighting against Geronimo in Arizona and Mexico, Lieutenant Powhattan H. Clarke described the action in which he saved the life of Corporal Edward Scott and earned a Medal of Honor. Clarke casually referred to the Buffalo Soldiers as "nigs" and "darkies," but his letters demonstrate his deep respect for their ability, dedication, and toughness, and he called them *chasseurs d'Afrique* after the elite French cavalry corps raised in North Africa.

Nogales, May 4, 1886:
My dear Father. . . . The day before yesterday evening followed an awful trail 27 miles in mountains, Yesterday broke camp at 6 a.m., struck remains of a large camp. Walked all day over the worse trail I ever want to see. Spotted Indians in a saddle of very high mountains, drove them off the saddle but caught flank fire from inaccessible rocks on our left at 200 yds while the Indians from the same place let our horses have it and stampeded the whole of them. One man was killed and a Corporal shot through both legs. I had some close calls while I was trying to pull the Corporal from under fire and succeeded in getting him behind a bush and you can be sure it was a very new sensation to hear bullets whiz and strike within six inches of me and not be able to see anything.

My dear Mother . . . . Do not tell me about the colored troops. There is not a troop in the U.S. Army that I would trust my life to as quickly as this K troop of ours. . . The firing was at 200 yards from rocks nearly over our heads. No men could have been more determined and cooler than these same darkies were and as for their officers they like them and will risk themselves for them. The wounded Corporal has had to have his leg cut off, the ball that shattered it lodging in the other instep. This man rode seven miles without a groan, remarking to the Captain that he had seen forty men in one fight in a worse fix than he was. Such have I found the colored soldier.

Seven years later, Clarke drowned when trying to save another Buffalo Soldier caught in a raging river.

ABOVE: An Apache sergeant and other scouts with the 6th Cavalry at Fort Wingate in the New Mexico Territory. Some Indian scouts were hired for specific missions or campaigns, but others—never exceeding an authorized ceiling of one thousand—enlisted and "received the pay and allowances of cavalry soldiers." Until 1902, when new regulations were introduced, scouts were allowed wide latitude in what they wore, and they remained active along the Mexican border until deactivated at Fort Huachuca in 1947.

BELOW: The M1881 dress helmet for Indian Scouts had a crossed-arrows insignia on the helmet shield.

Hancock's Military Division of the Atlantic in the process. Some sixty thousand regulars and militia ultimately were called out, and the army found that simply providing a restrained but strong show of force—with bayonets glistening—was enough to bring order to the chaos, as Hancock reported, "by their presence alone."

Although Hayes subsequently established a policy of using troops only to protect federal property or upon the request of a governor or federal judge, civil disturbances such as the Lincoln County War in New Mexico required the presence of troops. Here, in 1878 and 1879, a large, well-armed gang in the employ of wealthy ranchers was pitted against a large and well-armed gang organized by the equally wealthy owners of a monopolistic general store, and it was the job of the 10th Cavalry's Buffalo Soldiers to separate the two factions and impose order.

Over the following years, increasingly troubled economic times for many workers led to calls for the army to maintain law and order or ensure the movement of the U.S. mail. However, during the Pullman Strike of 1894, which brought all rail traffic between Chicago and the west coast to a screeching halt, the Illinois governor strenuously objected to the use of Federal troops to oust the strikers from Chicago's rail yards. President Grover Cleveland, unimpressed, warned, "If it takes the army and the navy to deliver a postcard in Chicago, that postcard will be delivered," and ordered in Miles, now a major general, and two thousand regulars to seize the yards and break up the strike without the governor's consent. By the time the last spasms of labor unrest had petered out the following year, the army had deployed units a remarkable 328 times between 1886 and 1895 to quell unrest or enforce federal laws.

RIGHT: Brassards, the sleeve insignia used to differentiate specialists from line troops, were placed midway between the elbow and top of the shoulder. Authorizations varied in the late nineteenth century, but they generally were worn by first-class privates and corporals, often appeared to have been made locally by military wives, and measured from four to five inches tall. During World War I, all aspects of this insignia were standardized.

Pioneer, Cavalry

Saddler, Cavalry

Mechanic Artificer, Artillery

Farrier, Cavalry

Cook, Infantry

BELOW: Battery E of the 1st Artillery was attached to the 7th Cavalry at Wounded Knee in December 1890. The breech-loaded Hotchkiss 1.65-inch (42-mm) light mountain guns replaced the 12-pound mountain howitzer and were later used at the Battle of San Juan Hill. The gun, its disassembled carriage, and some ammunition could be carried easily on two mules.

BACKGROUND: First lieutenants, second lieutenants, and a sprinkling of captains at an 1890 rifle competition. Virtually all of these men would become field grade officers (majors through colonels) and general officers, with several attaining the rank of major general. Their commands would include regiments, brigades, divisions, posts, districts, and schools, with combat in the West, Mexico, Cuba, the Philippines, China, and France. The tall gentleman in the rear row, Captain George D. Wallace of the 7th Cavalry, survived the Little Bighorn battle but was killed at Wounded Knee not long after this photograph was taken. To his left is Captain Frazier A. Boutelle, whose service extended from 1861 to 1919. The fourth man in the top row is First Lieutenant George H. Morgan of the 3d Cavalry. Eight years earlier as a boyish second lieutenant, he "gallantly held his ground at a critical moment and fired upon the advancing enemy [Apaches] until he was disabled by a shot," for which he later received a Medal of Honor. The bullet was too close to his heart to be taken out safely, and he carried it from the action at the Big Dry Fork in Arizona until his death in 1948 at the age of 93. Forward Operating Base Morgan in Bosnia is named after him.

BELOW: Major General Fitzhugh
Lee, shown with his VII Corps
staff at Camp Columbia near
Havana, Cuba, served as the
military governor of the western
provinces. Lee was an 1855
graduate of West Point and
one of three former Confederate
officers who were made major
generals of United States
Volunteers during the Spanish-
American War. Due to the swift
end of the war, Lee did not
take part in combat operations.
However, as consul-general at
Havana under both Democratic
and Republican administrations
during the run-up to the war,
he had delicately performed
diplomatic and military-related
duties in addition to the
regular consular functions. Lee
subsequently commanded the
Department of the Missouri and
retired in 1901 as a brigadier
general in the Regular Army.

RIGHT: A Spanish-American
War U.S. Army infantry officer's
cotton coat with wool facings of
dark blue.

FAR RIGHT: This Spanish-American
War uniform coat was worn by a
Lieutenant Bauer of the 3d
Missouri Cavalry.

SPANISH-AMERICAN WAR

The spark that touched off the Spanish-American War was the battleship USS *Maine*. It was anchored in the harbor at Havana, Cuba, when it mysteriously exploded on the night of February 15, 1898, killing 266 American sailors. Public opinion—already hostile toward Spain—clamored for war, which Congress declared on April 25, 1898. Although the greatest battles were naval, such as Commodore George Dewey's victory at Manila Bay, success on the sea had to be followed up quickly by the seizure of Cuba and the Philippines, even though the army still had only twenty-five thousand men. Spain, on the other hand, had an army more than eight times as large on Cuba alone. Once again, the U.S. Army struggled to organize, equip, instruct, and care for raw

recruits flooding into its training camps where, not unlike what General Washington found outside Boston in 1775 or President Lincoln beheld at the capital in 1861, total chaos reigned.

On May 8, the War Department ordered seventy thousand men to Cuba, but there was only enough ammunition in the whole country to supply a force of that size for a single battle. Unlike the navy, which had a clear idea for how it wanted to carry out its campaigns, the army and War Department had not even considered the possibility that an expeditionary force would have to be organized and equipped. Everything was lacking: food, transportation, horses, guns, and ammunition. The regulars and a few volunteer regiments had modern Krag-Jorgensen rifles that were the equal of the German-made Mausers of the Spanish, but the militias—now called the

National Guard by most states—and the rest of the volunteers had to be equipped with the single-shot Springfields, which belched out highly visible clouds of smoke when their black powder cartridges were fired. Cotton khaki was first issued for uniforms in this war, but with both the supply and the time short, most soldiers wore the old blue wool serge uniforms as they fought in the steaming Caribbean and Asian jungles.

A dangerous lack of intelligence existed on the Spanish Army's dispositions and what degree of assistance, if any, could be expected from the well-organized guerrilla forces on Cuba as well as nearby Puerto Rico. Two regulars were sent with minimal guidance as scouts: Lieutenant Henry F. Whitney to Puerto Rico and, to Cuba, Lieutenant Andrew Summers Rowan, whose mission to rebel General Calixto Garcia was

LEFT TOP: The steamship *Yucatan* carries Rough Riders of the 1,250-man 1st Volunteer Cavalry Regiment to Cuba in June 1898. A lack of shipping prevented the enlisted mens' horses from being brought to the island, too. Although one of Lieutenant Colonel Theodore Roosevelt's horses, Texas, survived the trip, the other, Rain-In-The-Face, drowned while trying to make it to shore, prompting its owner to "split the air with one blasphemy after another."

FAR LEFT BOTTOM: This 1895 undress coat was worn by a 1st Volunteer Cavalry officer.

LEFT BOTTOM: This wool uniform shirt belonged to a 1st Volunteer Cavalry trooper.

KRAG-JORGENSEN RIFLE, MODEL 1892

The Krag's smaller round—.30-caliber versus .45-caliber—had less stopping power than the army's standard Model 1873 Springfield trapdoor rifle, but its smokeless powder cartridges allowed its shooter to hide better and not have to wait for the smoke to clear before acquiring another target. Although a 5-pound magazine enhanced the rate of fire, the army officially discouraged its use, preferring instead for troops to load each round individually and not "waste" ammunition. The original 1892 models were upgraded to conform to the 1896 design Krags used in Cuba. The rear sight also was improved, and the cleaning rod below the barrel was moved to a butt trap bored into the stock.

RIGHT: The 71st Infantry, on the march during the campaign in Cuba, suffered from poor leadership and malaria. The New York regiment was nearly "combat ineffective" during the July 1, 1898, battle of San Juan Hill—only a week after its arrival on the island. More soldiers were struck down as a wave of yellow fever, then dysentery, surged through their ranks. By the time it returned to New York on August 22, the formation could muster barely three hundred fifty men.

immortalized as "A Message to Garcia." By the middle of June, the embarkation of V Corps' seventeen thousand soldiers had begun, and units, including the 1st Volunteer Cavalry—nicknamed the Rough Riders—under Colonel Leonard Wood and Lieutenant Colonel Theodore Roosevelt, came ashore at Siboney and Daiquiri to the west of Santiago Bay on June 22. Remarkably, the landing was without incident, except for the drowning of many horses, and was even without opposition in spite of the Spanish having some thirty-six thousand troops in the immediate vicinity. But soon the great heat, the swamps, the rugged country, and the onset of malaria and yellow fever began to take their toll on V Corps.

Led by two columns, one of regulars and one of volunteers, V Corps advanced over muddy trails through a dense, mosquito-filled jungle while hidden snipers took a bloody toll. The "yellow canaries," as the Spaniards were dubbed, were first encountered in force when the Rough Riders of Brigadier General Joseph W. Wheeler's dismounted cavalry division caught up with the rear guard of a retiring Spanish force at Las Guasimas. The rear guard quickly retreated after a short, sharp fight, but from then on, the Americans had to fight hard all the way to Santiago. The road to the city followed a valley covered with jungle and crossed by a long, broken ridge with a feature called San Juan Hill at its southern end. Here, the Spaniards had dug in and fortified the top, and two miles farther along the ridge had built a blockhouse, trenches, and barbed-wire traps at El Caney.

The advance toward El Caney was slow and painful, and the attack on the position was made without artillery support, as bad roads made it impossible to bring the guns up. Losses

were heavy on both sides as the infantry under fierce fire took the enemy position in a charge. As the soldiers stormed El Caney, another fierce battle was raging at San Juan. Thousands of men slogged forward on the narrow jungle trails on the morning of the attack, raked by Spanish Mausers, and it wasn't until noon that they reached the open spaces before the Spanish entrenchments on the hill. The blue-shirted infantrymen fought their way up the slope under withering fire from the Spaniards on top. It was here that Lieutenant Jules G. Ord called to his men, "All who are brave, follow me," and charged up the hill at their head, to be shot dead at the summit.

Meanwhile, at Kettle Hill on the north side of the San Juan position, the dismounted cavalry were advancing. The Rough Rider 1st Volunteers under Roosevelt and the black troopers of the 9th and 10th cavalries, including Lieutenant John J. "Black Jack" Pershing, fought their way up the slopes and finally took the fortifications in a short but costly fight. Seeing that the infantry was beginning to stall as it battled for San Juan Hill nearby, Roosevelt led his men in as well. During the height of battle, division commander Wheeler, a former Confederate cavalryman suffering from a malarial fever and now overcome with emotion, cried out, "We have got the damn Yankees on the run!" and "Give those Yankees hell, boys!" for which he later was teased unmercifully by brother officers, but always took with good humor.

With the Spanish driven from the San Juan and El Caney heights overlooking Santiago on July 1, 1898, the Spanish ships

ABOVE INSET: U.S. canvas looped .45-70 cartridge belt, Model 1887.

ABOVE TOP: Rough Riders fill cartridge belts. The trooper at left checks one of the Krag carbines that were issued to the 1st Volunteer Cavalry along with the standard Krag rifle.

BELOW: U.S Artillery during the July 1, 1898, fighting at El Caney. The fire support on the well-prepared Spanish positions consisted of this single battery. American losses totaled at least four hundred thirty, including eighty-one killed.

LIEUTENANT COLONEL THEODORE ROOSEVELT ON THE CREATION OF THE 1ST UNITED STATES VOLUNTEER CAVALRY, HIS "ROUGH RIDERS"

The mustering places for the regiment were appointed in New Mexico, Arizona, Oklahoma, and Indian Territory. The difficulty in organizing was not in selecting, but in rejecting men. Within a day or two after it was announced that we were to raise the regiment, we were literally deluged with applications....Without the slight trouble, so far as men went, we could have raised a brigade or even a division.

The difficulty lay in arming, equipping, mounting, and disciplining the men selected. Hundreds of regiments were being called into existence and each was sure to have innumerable wants to be satisfied. To a man who knew the ground as [Colonel Leonard] Wood did, and who was entirely aware of our national unpreparedness, it was evident that the ordnance and quartermaster's bureaus could not meet, for some time to come, one-tenth of the demands that would be made upon them; [so] it was all-important to get in first with our demands...

Harvard being my own college, I had such a swarm of applications from it that I could not take one in ten. What particularly pleased me, not only in the Harvard but the Yale and Princeton men, and, indeed, in these recruits from the older states generally, was that they did not ask for commissions....These men formed but a small fraction of the whole. They went down to San Antonio where the regiment was to gather and where Wood preceded me, while I spent a week in Washington hurrying up the different bureaus and telegraphing my various railroad friends as to ensure our getting the carbines, saddles, and uniforms, we needed.

I found the men from New Mexico, Arizona, and Oklahoma already gathered while those from the Indian Territory came in soon after my arrival.... In all the world there could be no better material for soldiers than those afforded by these grim hunters of the mountains; these wild rough riders of the plains.... The captains and lieutenants were sometimes men who had campaigned against the Apache, Ute, and Cheyenne.

We were notified that our horses were to be left behind, and that only eight troops of seventy men each taken....No outsider can appreciate the bitterness of the disappointment....Captain Maximilian Luna commanded F Troop from New Mexico. The captain's people had been on the banks of the Rio Grande before my forefathers came to the mouth of the Hudson or Wood's landed at Plymouth; and he made the plea that it was his right to go as a representative of his race, for he was the only man of pure Spanish blood who bore a commission in the Army and he demanded the privilege of proving that his people were precisely as loyal Americans as any others. I was glad when it was decided to take him."

When we reached Tampa, we had 24 hours of utter and absolute confusion. There was no one to show us where we were to camp. The railroad system

ABOUT: "Rough Riders" detrain at Tampa, Florida, on May 30, 1918. Roosevelt found that his regiment and two others had been assigned to a ship that couldn't carry even one, so eight of the Rough Riders 12 troops essentially commandeered the ship for their movement to Cuba.

was in a state of absolute congestion...I had to take matters into my own hands so as to get my horses watered and fed, and get provision for my troops. On arrival at Port Tampa there was the same state of confusion. There were ten thousand men swarming over the quay. Transports were pulling in from midstream, but nobody could tell what transports the troops were to get on.

RIGHT: This revolver was recovered from the captain's cabin of the sunken battleship *Maine* by divers from the gunboat USS *Fern*. The *Fern*'s captain, Commander William S. Cowles, presented it to his brother-in-law, Assistant Secretary of the Navy Theodore Roosevelt, who subsequently used it during combat operations in Cuba.

BELOW: 10th Cavalry Buffalo Soldiers, with their own colors at right, watch the proceedings, as Lieutenant Colonel Theodore Roosevelt (*center, without hat*) poses with his men at the top of San Juan Hill.

ABOVE: Trenches hastily prepared by the 9th Infantry just north of the captured Spanish blockhouse atop San Juan Hill. The 9th Infantry occupied this area during the July 1898 siege of Santiago, Cuba, and similar defenses were constructed by the 1st Volunteer Cavalry on their right. Said Roosevelt: "An engineer officer stated that he did not think our work had been scientific; and I assured him that I did not doubt that he was right, for I had never before seen a trench, excepting those we captured from the Spaniards, or heard of a traverse, save as I vaguely remembered reading about them in books."

Second Lieutenant Ira Clinton Welborn
9th United States Infantry

Only weeks after his graduation from the U.S. Military Academy, Second Lieutenant Ira C. Welborn shipped off to Cuba with the regulars of the 9th Infantry. Taking part in the Battle of San Juan Hill, his regiment settled into the captured Spanish trenches south of the Rough Riders. Throughout the following day, July 2, 1898, fire rained on the American positions from the Spaniards' second line of defense, greatly increased in tempo, then, with little warning, abruptly died down. Sometimes this was accompanied by local counterattacks described by Lieutenant Colonel Theodore Roosevelt as "raging fitfully at intervals."

During one attack at 10 A.M., an infantryman from the 9th was shot in the chest. Reacting to his agonizing wound, he jerked up and then toppled forward over the embankment. The soldier rolled part way down the hill and was fully exposed to Spanish fire. Heedless of the Mauser bullets whipping through the air and striking all along the embankment, Welborn jumped from cover and followed him down. While his men watched in amazement, the young lieutenant quickly carried the wounded private to safety. For his selfless action that day, Welborn received the Medal of Honor.

Two years later he and the 9th took part in numerous engagements during the Boxer Rebellion, including the heavy fighting at Tientsin, China. Combat against guerillas in the Philippines followed, and Welborn was appointed the tactical officer at the Military Academy from 1904 to 1906. During World War I, now-Colonel Welborn was named the first director of the Tank Corps when it became a separate branch in March 1918, commanding an organization of 914 officers and 14,746 men.

Welborn supervised all activities of the fledgling Tank Corps, including procuring its personnel and establishing and maintaining training camps in the United States, for which he received the Distinguished Service Medal. He retired in 1932 and lived long enough to see his son, John C. Welborn, also attend West Point and command the 33d Armored Regiment of the 3d Armored Division, during World War II.

BELOW: Battery B of the 4th Light Artillery fires its 3.2-inch bag guns on a Spanish blockhouse during the August 9, 1898, assault on Coamo, Puerto Rico. After twenty-five minutes' firing, the blockhouse was set on fire. The Spanish delaying action west of the resort town collapsed under the weight of the artillery and the advance of the 2d and 3d Wisconsin Volunteer regiments, the 16th Pennsylvania, and a cavalry troop from Brooklyn, New York.

in the port were forced to flee into the waiting guns of the United States Navy, which destroyed all of them in a running battle along the coast. The stiff but incremental fighting around the city's outer defenses came to an end with the surrender of Spanish forces on July 17. Within a month, Puerto Rico was also under American control after quickly being overrun by a three-thousand-man force personally led by Miles, now the army's commanding general.

Meanwhile, twelve thousand miles away on the other side of the world, another American Army was testing the might of the Spanish Empire in the Philippines. A convoy carrying VIII Corps' two thousand regular and thirteen thousand volunteer troops under Major General Wesley Merritt sailed from the United States and, after stopping mid-Pacific to raise the flag over Wake Island on the Fourth of July, besieged the Philippine capital of Manila on the island of Luzon before the end of the month. Rain came down without end. In trenches half filled with water and sweating in blue wool serge like their comrades in Cuba, Merritt's soldiers fought the mud, mosquitoes, heat, and tropical diseases that killed more men than bullets.

KRAG-JORGENSEN CARBINE, MODEL 1892

At twenty-two-inches long, the Krag carbine was a full eight inches shorter than the rifle and had a lighter stock. During the Spanish-American War, a small number of the carbines were issued to the 1st Volunteer Cavalry, raised at Camp Wood at San Antonio, Texas, and the 2d Volunteer Cavalry, raised at Fort Russell (today Warren Air Force Base), Wyoming. But the 2d's Rough Riders were able to get no further than Jacksonville, Florida, before the war ended. Additional carbines soon were issued. Later, on May 5, 1905, First Lieutenant Horace P. Hobbs used this weapon during close action at Pala's Cotta, on the southern Philippine island of Jolo—for which he was awarded a Distinguished Service Cross for extraordinary heroism.

After a few night skirmishes, they prepared for a general attack on Manila. Filipino rebels were already harassing the Spanish who held the city, and the defenders—who had no heart in fighting—were anxious to turn themselves over to the Americans, fearing a massacre of the garrison if the ill-disciplined rebels took control. The Spanish commander agreed to surrender to Merritt after only a token show of resistance and, as they had at Wake Island weeks earlier, the army raised the Stars and Stripes from its new headquarters in the city of Manila on August 14, 1898.

The war with Spain saw 345 men killed in action or dead from wounds, but more than seven times that number in squalid camps in the southern United States and Cuba fell to disease, an occurrence which could have had a disastrous impact on the army's ability to carry out its missions if it had found itself faced with a more skillful and tenacious foe. Still, when the shooting stopped, Puerto Rico, the Philippines, and the Pacific stepping-stones of Guam and Wake Island were ours, while a new nation, Cuba, had been given its freedom by the American soldier.

INSURRECTION IN THE PHILIPPINES

Defeat of the Spanish did not end the fighting in the Philippines. Emilio Aguinaldo, leader of the Philippine rebels, who had at first helped the Americans drive out the Spanish, lost little time in launching bloody guerrilla warfare against the army. Moreover, the savage Moros (Muslim Filipinos) started a small war of their own against the new government. They eventually were conquered by Pershing, later to lead the U.S. Army in World War I. This was the hardest kind of combat, marked by treachery and stealth, as the army lived and fought among a large, half-civilized, hostile population.

On one occasion on the island of Samar, most of a seventy-four-man company of the 9th Infantry Regiment's Company C garrisoning Balangiga were eating breakfast in their mess hall when they were set upon by the local villagers who, on the prearranged signal of the church bells, attacked the soldiers with axes, picks, shovels, and large bolo knives. In the stabbing, slashing fight, the troops used kitchen knives and chairs to defend themselves, and some were able to obtain rifles. Forty-eight soldiers were killed, many horribly dismembered, and another twenty-two wounded during the August 11, 1901, attack with, depending on the account, anywhere from twenty to two hundred fifty of the attackers killed. Survivors managed to escape to a nearby garrison where a gunboat was immediately dispatched. In a reprisal typical of the war, they mowed down twenty villagers with Gatling guns when troops seized and burned the town.

Although Aguinaldo had been unsuccessful in his efforts to oust the Spanish during a 1896–1897 insurrection, he nevertheless succeeded in organizing a native army and securing control of several islands, including much of Luzon beyond the capital. Spain's ceding of the Philippines to the United States in the December 1898 Treaty of Paris greatly disappointed many Filipinos, and on February 4, 1899, Aguinaldo's followers clashed with American troops outside Manila. Major General Elwell S. Otis, commanding more than twelve thousand troops, defeated Aguinaldo's army of some forty thousand men and suppressed an attempted uprising in Manila. The army's principal military objective after beating back Aguinaldo's initial efforts was to seize the initiative by aggressively moving to establish American control across all of Luzon. To accomplish this, U.S. forces embarked upon an arduous series of counter-guerrilla campaigns to suppress the Filipino *insurrectos* who still fought for independence.

American columns pushed north, east, and south from Manila to split the insurgent forces, seize key towns, and cut the five-hundred-mile-long island in half, thereby permanently interrupting communications between *insurrectos* in northern and southern Luzon. From March 1899 to February 1900, strong columns led by Brigadier General Lloyd Wheaton, and major generals Henry W. Lawton and

Arthur MacArthur (father of Douglas MacArthur), conducted raids, captured key territory, and dispersed or killed the opposition until the summer rainy season called a halt to further operations. It was during this pause that the first Philippine Scout units were organized. Large numbers of additional troops began to arrive, bringing the strength of the U.S. force, VIII Corps, to more than forty-seven thousand five hundred men by the end of 1899, and seventy-five thousand a year later.

Operations resumed in October, and Otis launched a three-pronged offensive in northern Luzon directed at Aguinaldo's remaining forces that included a large-scale amphibious operation under Wheaton. After these campaigns, only scattered insurrectionist elements remained active in the north and south, but in one of the final battles, a Filipino sharpshooter shot down Lawton on December 18, 1899. Ironically, the former 4th Cavalry commander who had fought Apache Chief Geronimo for many years—on both sides of the Mexican border—was confronting an *insurrectos* general named Licerio Geronimo in this final action.

Aguinaldo remained at large for more than a year, and the story of his capture is stranger than fiction. Brigadier General Frederick Funston, who had earlier won the Congressional Medal of Honor for gallantry in the Philippines, discovered the location of Aguinaldo's secret hideout in the wilds of Luzon. Funston knew that the guerrilla chief would simply vanish in the jungle if troops in large numbers went after him, so he hatched a daring plan. On the night of March 4, 1901, a small party of men—guided by a former Philippine rebel who had just pledged his loyalty to the United States—was quietly set ashore on northern Luzon from the USS *Vicksburg*. Funston pretended to be a prisoner of this rebel and his men, who had also joined the United States forces, and supposedly were taking him and several other "captured" soldiers to Aguinaldo.

The group made their way through dense jungles and unfriendly villages where one slip might have meant death, and it gained access to Aguinaldo's camp. Aguinaldo and his men were caught completely off guard on March 23, 1901. The successful raiders rendezvoused with the *Vicksburg* eleven days later; their mission accomplished. Funston had his man, and Aguinaldo's capture took the heart out of the insurrection.

RIGHT: Brigadier General Frederick Funston captured the rebel General Emilio Famy Aguinaldo in March 1901 with the aid of the army's newly raised "Macabebe Scouts," which were made up of former guerrillas.

LEFT: These Barong swords belonged to Aguinaldo, who was captured by Funston during the daring mission behind enemy lines.

Till my Regiment is mustered out.

—Funston's reply when asked how long he could hold a captured trench

LEFT: Theodore Roosevelt, now a colonel, chats with a sorefooted Colonel Henry L. Turner, commander of the 1st Illinois Regiment (National Guard), during the siege of Santiago. Though recommended for a Medal of Honor for his assaults on Kettle and San Juan hills, the award was denied because of a letter Roosevelt had written to the commanding general in Cuba detailing the debilitating losses to the troops from tropical diseases and urging their evacuation. (Roosevelt himself caught malaria, and Turner's feet possibly suffered from a tropical infection.) Roosevelt's letter was released to the press by V Corps' commander, Major General William Rufus Shafter, in the hope that its publication would pressure the War Department to withdraw the troops to the United States. The effort was successful, but the incensed secretary of war subsequently blocked Roosevelt's award. His medal was awarded posthumously in 2001.

BELOW: Previous Medal of Honor winners gather in the East Room of the White House on November 7, 1910, for the presentation of the medal to a young protégé of Roosevelt, Lieutenant Gordon Johnston. *Left to right*: Major General Charles F. Humphrey, Brigadier General John M. Wilson, Colonel Charles H. Heyl, Brigadier General Theodore Schwan, Colonel Frederick Fuger, Major General William H. Carter, Brigadier General Albert L. Mills, and Johnston. During the fighting against the Moros in March 1906, Johnston, while serving as a signaler, "voluntarily took part in and was dangerously wounded during an assault on the enemy's works" at Mount Bud Dajo on the Philippine island of Jolo.

BELOW: 1904 version of the Medal of Honor.

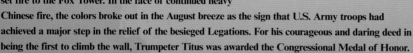

Citation: During the fiercely opposed relief expedition to Peking in the Boxer Rebellion in 1900, when two companies of the U.S. Army's 14th Infantry Regiment were pinned by heavy fire from the east wall of the Tartar City and the Fox Tower between abutments of the Chinese City Wall near Tung Pien Gate, volunteers were called for to attempt the first perilous ascent of the wall. Trumpeter Calvin P. Titus of E Company immediately stepped forward saying, "I'll try, sir!" Using jagged holes in the stone wall, he succeeded in reaching the top. He was followed by the rest of his company, who climbed unarmed, and hauled up their rifles and ammunition belts by a rope made of rifle slings. As the troops ascended the wall artillery fire from Reilly's battery set fire to the Fox Tower. In the face of continued heavy Chinese fire, the colors broke out in the August breeze as the sign that U.S. Army troops had achieved a major step in the relief of the besieged Legations. For his courageous and daring deed in being the first to climb the wall, Trumpeter Titus was awarded the Congressional Medal of Honor.

The 14th Infantry's commander, Colonel Aaron Simon Daggett, later wrote:

With what interest did the officers and men watch every step as he placed his feet carefully in the cavities and clung with his fingers to the projecting bricks! The first fifteen feet were passed over without serious difficulty, but there was a space of fifteen feet above him. Slowly he reaches the twenty-foot point. Still more carefully does he try his hold on those bricks to see if they are firm. His feet are now twenty-five feet from the ground. His head is near the bottom of the embrasure. All below is breathless silence. The strain is intense. Will that embrasure blaze with fire as he attempts to enter it? Or will the butts of rifles crush his skull? Cautiously he looks through, and sees and hears nothing. He enters, and as good fortune would have it, no Chinese soldiers are there.

Titus subsequently received a presidential appointment to the U.S. Military Academy, and served into the 1930s in a variety of staff and instructor positions (including on General Pershing's 1916 Mexican Expedition), as well as in France and Germany as a lieutenant colonel. Some sixty years later Titus described his feat:

I took off all my equipment: haversack, canteen, pistol, and belt, and hat, and started up. I recall that the wall was made of brick of some kind—some 18 inches long and 4 inches thick. The mortar had fallen out in places making it possible for me to get finger- and toe-holds in the cracks. About halfway up, a convenient bush grew out of the bricks and that also helped some.

At last I got to a point where I could look through one of the notches or firing ports at the top of the wall. It was empty. I slid over the top and onto the floor behind. To my surprise I saw no one.

President McKinley, just before his death, granted Titus a West Point appointment. In 1902, the first-year plebe attended with all cadets a ceremony marking the Academy's centennial and received a shock when he was called front and center before the entire assembly. The commandant and McKinley's successor, President Theodore Roosevelt, walked over, and pinned the Medal of Honor on the surprised plebe's coat. Roosevelt then said "Now don't let this give you the big head!" After the group was dismissed, a second-year classman named Douglas MacArthur approached Titus, looked at his medal, and said "Mister, that's something!"

ABOVE: This bugle belonged to Calvin P. Titus, musician, Company E, 14th Infantry.

THE BOXER REBELLION

In the summer of 1900, news flashed over the wires that some Chinese known as "The Fists of Righteous Harmony," or "Boxers," who wished to drive "foreign devils" out of China, had suddenly begun the mass killing of foreign Christian missionaries and of Chinese church members, including women and children. Americans and other foreign nationals living in the Forbidden City of Peking (now Beijing) also were attacked; some were killed and the rest besieged in the international section of the Chinese capital. The gallant American Legation Guard—along with those of Britain, France, Germany, Italy, Spain, Belgium, Austria-Hungary, the Netherlands, Russia, and Japan—held out against the attackers for weeks while the world held its breath.

The winding down of the Philippine Insurrection resulted in a large number of American units being available to take part in relief efforts, and the 9th Infantry under Colonel Emerson H. Liscum, though delayed by a typhoon, rushed from Manila to the rescue. It was the first outfit to arrive in China, with the 14th Infantry, 15th Infantry, and the 6th Cavalry soon under way. At Tientsin, they carried out a murderous, fifteen-hour attack in conjunction with other foreign contingents against the Boxers, who were now joined by Chinese imperial forces. Liscum was mortally wounded. As he fell dying, his last words to his men, "Keep up the fire," became the motto that soldiers of the 9th still wear on their regimental crest. They kept up the fire, and the city finally was captured on July 13 at the cost of ninety-five American casualties.

Joined by the 14th Infantry and the 6th Cavalry, the 9th marched toward Peking as part of an international army, engaging the enemy along the way. Peking was a completely enclosed city with the walls from thirty to fifty feet high and twenty to forty feet wide on top. Chinese rifles and "jingals," or two-man guns (large muskets fired from a nest or carriage), raked the approaches to the city with fire, but directly under the walls were dead spaces where the Chinese could not fire. The Americans, with the 14th Infantry leading, scaled the wall at a partially sheltered angle. The first men scrambled up the bare face of the wall by climbing on spaces where bricks had fallen or been blown out. They pulled rifles and ammunition up after them and, once on top, guarded the wall as more soldiers climbed up behind them.

The 14th had penetrated the city and planted the regimental colors on the wall—the first foreign flag to fly there—and opened the way for British units to relieve the legation compound. Many more troops were needed to fight the Boxers and imperial forces.

On the following day, "Reilly's Battery" (Captain Henry J. Reilly's Light Battery F, 5th Artillery) blasted open the gates on the American front in the assault on the inner city after Lieutenant Charles P. Summerall nonchalantly used a piece of chalk to mark the spot on the gate where the guns should aim. Most of the American troops left China that winter, but the 15th Infantry remained for many years. Its regimental insignia bears the motto "Can Do," a phrase of pidgin English picked up from the Chinese.

The 6th U.S. Cavalry assaulting the South gate of the city of Pekin.
C Fred A. Ackerman

ABOVE: M Troop of the 6th Cavalry head for the south gate of Peking's inner Forbidden City on August 15, 1900. The gate's heavy doors were blown in by close-range cannon fire, and the 14th Infantry suppressed Chinese fire in house-to-house fighting.

RIGHT: U.S. signalmen heliographing from the top of the Tartar Wall near where the 14th Infantry breached the defenses on August 14 and relieved a Russian contingent that was cut off the previous day.

BELOW: Battery F of the 5th Artillery in action during the drive from Tientsin to Peking. Its commander, Captain Henry J. Reilly, was killed by a sniper on August 15, 1900.

RIGHT TOP: Colonel Frank T.D. Baldwin, commander of the 27th Infantry, led a successful campaign against the Moros on the Philippine island of Mindanao.

RIGHT BOTTOM: Captain Frank R. McCoy killed the outlaw chieftain Dato Ali in hand-to-hand combat on Mindanao.

FAR RIGHT: Major Case Wheately of the 29th Infantry with his company commanders and staff during the securing of the Philippine island of Masbate.

BELOW: A firing line of Kansas volunteer infantry pour lead into insurgent entrenchments just across a river at Bigaa (today Balagtas), north of Manila in March 1899.

FIGHTING THE MOROS

Although the capture of Aguinaldo in the Philippines had dealt the final blow to the insurgent cause, and although Roosevelt, now the president, had announced the official conclusion of the Philippine Insurrection on July 4, 1902, the fighting was not actually over. Enough resources were available that the army could now move to assert American authority in the southern islands. This turn of events was not at all to the liking of the Moros, the Muslim people in Mindanao and the Sulu Archipelago, who had never been completely subjugated by the Spanish. When the army occupied former Spanish garrisons in the south, which had lain abandoned for nearly two years, the Moros began to raid Christian villages, attack soldiers, and otherwise resist American jurisdiction.

Beginning in July 1902 and extending through December 1904, then again in late 1905, the army dispatched a series of expeditions into the interior of Mindanao to destroy Moro strongholds. Colonel Frank D. Baldwin and some one thousand troops, including elements of his own 27th Infantry and a battery of mountain guns, invaded the territory of the Sultan of Bayan, near Lake Lanao and defeated the Sultan's forces in a hotly contested battle on May 2, 1902. Pershing, now a captain, had studied Moro dialects and culture, read the Koran, and formed close relationships with Moro chieftains. He headed a similar expedition into the Lanao country in 1903, and Captain Frank R. McCoy finally killed the notorious Moro outlaw, Chief Dato Ali, in the Cotabato district in October 1905.

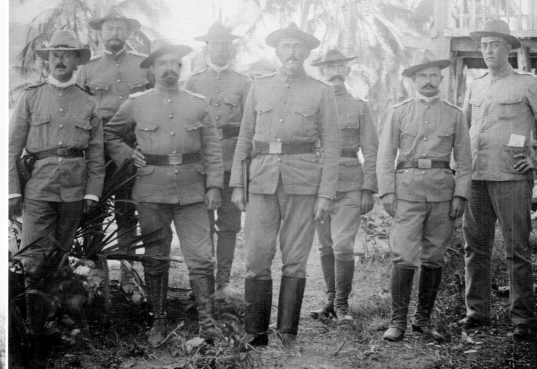

Meanwhile on the island of Jolo, a Moro stronghold, the army found itself dealing with one uprising after another, with serious fighting occurring in 1905, 1906, and 1913. Disorders were far too extensive to be handled by the local constabulary and Philippine Scouts, so U.S. troops were regularly forced to subdue lawless elements. During May 1905, the pirate slave trader Datu Pala and some of his followers were killed; the remainder, gathered in a volcanic crater, surrendered to American forces. On March 6–8, 1906, regulars fought the first battle of Bud Dajo to a successful conclusion, and in mid-June 1913 other Moros at Bagsac were beaten.

RIGHT INSET: This "Jippe Joppa," c. 1899, belonged to then-Captain Matthew Batson. Batson organized a special force called the Macabebe Scouts for operations against insurgent Philippine guerrillas. The unit is credited with capturing the famous Philippine Insurrection leader Emilio Aguinaldo. Batson adopted the Spanish military straw hat called a Jippe Joppa and added a blue silk hat band, gold hat cord, and embroidered Federal eagle hat badge.

RIGHT: Batson organized and led the Macabebe Scouts.

MEDAL OF HONOR
First Lieutenant Matthew Batson
4th United States Cavalry

Citation: The Medal of Honor citations for First Lieutenant Matthew Batson and Captain Hugh J. McGrath stated only the bare fact that the two 4th Cavalry officers "swam the San Juan River in the face of the enemy's fire and drove him from his entrenchments" during the July 26, 1899, attack against Calamba, a major town south of Manila on the lake Laguna de Bay. College professor Dean C. Worcester was sent to the Philippines to help in their administration, and he was close enough to the action to provide the details.

"It was at Calamba," said Worcester, "an important town that was taken by [Major General Henry] Lawton. While the [1st Division] troops were in front of this town and in the face of a hot and furious fire from the Filipinos, it was found necessary to cross a stream that was swelled with recent rains until it was most difficult to get over. There were neither boats nor rafts, but on the opposite side and directly under the rifles of the Filipinos were two canoes."

Not waiting for orders or asking for volunteers, the officers "stripped and plunged into the whirling stream and came back in half an hour with two canoes." Although "there were some bullet holes in the canoes," they were in good enough shape "to serve the purpose of transporting a storming party across the stream." Some thirty-five troopers were gathered for the assault, which took the Filipinos by surprise, and the position was taken. Worcester said, "It was the most daring thing I ever witnessed, and I believe the most daring action that has come to my attention."

McGrath died later that year on November 7 from wounds suffered in an action at Noveleta. Lawton, who won a Medal of Honor during the Atlanta Campaign of 1864, was cut down the following month by a sniper in the midst of a December 19 ambush that killed thirteen other soldiers near San Mateo.

Batson, meanwhile, would very nearly lose his leg after being shot through the foot while leading a special unit on a raid deep in rebel-held northern Luzon on November 19. Batson had proposed that the Macabebes, a Philippine tribal community that originally had been loyal to Spain, put together a company of infantry to fight the insurgents. While some senior officers thought this a "crazy idea," Lawton, who had seen firsthand the value of the Apache Scouts in the southwest, approved. The first hundred-man company of Macabebe Scouts was formed in September 1899 and quickly gained a reputation as rugged, loyal fighters. They achieved numerous victories through the "banco" raids along Luzon island's numerous rivers, including the one where Batson was shot. Two more companies were authorized. When Batson recovered from his wounds in April 1890, he immediately was put in command of the battalion and promoted to Major of Volunteers.

Ordinance Sergeant

First Sergeant, Cavalry
1884 Dress Uniform

Quartermaster Sergeant

BELOW: The 17th Infantry goes to the front on Spanish rail cars in the Manila area during the Philippine Insurrection. The 17th fought principally on the island of Luzon in 1899 and 1900, but also saw action on Mindanao and at San Isidro on Leyte.

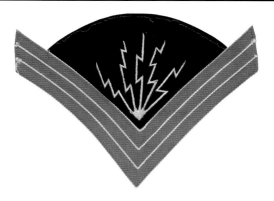

Sergeant Electrician, Corps of Engineers

Drum Major Sergeant, Infantry

Corporal, Signal Corps

ABOVE: U.S. signalmen worked with Allied colleagues, principally British and French, in China, c. 1900. The American sergeant on the far right wears the chevrons with the Signal Corps insignia.

RIGHT: The 1902 uniform dress coat of Colonel Hobart Kemper Bailey, who served in the Indian Wars, Spanish-American War, and Philippine Insurrection. Sometime after his retirement as commander of the 29th Infantry Regiment (Buffalo Soldiers), his coat survived a fire. The missing gold-knot shoulder boards likely indicate that Bailey later presented them as a gift to another officer at his promotion to colonel.

1902 UNIFORM CHANGES

Before the invention of smokeless powder, the immense amount of smoke generated by black powder cartridges necessitated that chevrons of noncommissioned officers be large and bright so they would more readily be seen through the haze. By the turn of the century, however, the less murky environment on the battlefield, coupled with the increasing accuracy of firearms, made it imperative that the identifying insignia remain visible to friendly troops who were near at hand yet not so large as to make the men an easy target for enemy sharpshooters. Chevrons, which once filled the width of a uniform's upper sleeve, shrank to three inches wide.

Advances in technology also led to the expansion of specialist categories within the army, and this was reflected in the increased number of authorized patterns. Though the regulations of 1902 called for field uniforms of khaki for summer and olive drab for winter, it originally was decreed that the chevrons on field uniforms be in branch colors. The ongoing problem of the dyes holding up to the rigors of harsh sunlight and lye soap, however, finally prompted the army to surrender on the matter. Within two years olive drab was adopted for the stars and arcs of the chevron, with various combinations of khaki, tan, olive, and brown predominating on special markings and other cloth insignia.

ABOVE: *U.S. Army Maxim machine gun and crew during 1911 maneuvers in Texas. Though inventor Hiram Maxim was American, he developed and patented the self-powered machine gun in Britain. Manufactured as a .45-caliber weapon, most of the original barrels of the MK I model were converted by the British to .303-inch. This is likely the original caliber. Note the gunner's seat on the rear leg of the tripod.*

**Ordinance Sergeant
Ordinance Corps**

**Sergeant Second Class Electrician
Coast Artillery Corps**

Quartermaster Sergeant

Sergeant First Class Signal Corps

First Sergeant Infantry

Fireman Coast Artillery Corps

Corporal Hospital Corps

Corporal Ordinance Corps

BELOW: *The army barracks at Plattsburgh, New York, c. 1905. Ten years later, Plattsburgh would become the site of monthlong military training camps, which produced officers for a prospective volunteer army that was intended to augment the Regular Army. The camps were organized by leaders of the preparedness movement, a group of career officers and politicians, including former President Theodore Roosevelt and Army Chief of Staff Major General Leonard Wood, who sought to mobilize American society for what they expected to be the imminent entry of the United States into World War I.*

SPRINGFIELD RIFLE, MODEL 1903

The M1903 Springfield, formally the United States Rifle, Caliber .30, Model 1903, is a magazine-fed, bolt-action rifle. Though officially replaced as the standard infantry rifle by the faster-firing, semi-automatic M1 Garand in 1936, the Springfield remained in service as a sniper rifle and as a standard issue training rifle during World War II. The weapon's legendary range and accuracy also led to its use as a sniper rifle during the Korean War and the early stages of the Vietnam War. It remains in use by the Army in ceremonies and the ROTC as a drill rifle.

BACKGROUND PHOTOS: Soldiers of the 18th Infantry Regiment training at Fort Devens, Massachusetts, before sailing to France as part of the 1st Expeditionary Division (later redesignated as the 1st Infantry Division) in June 1917. The commander of the American Expeditionary Forces, General John J. Pershing, hand-picked the 18th Infantry for inclusion in the first U.S. combat division to join the Allies because it performed well during the 1916–1917 Punitive Expedition into Mexico and contained many experienced soldiers, including veterans of the Philippine Insurrection. However, like most American regiments, the 18th was significantly undermanned, and had to be brought up to strength and trained as a unit before it was ready for operations in France.

BELOW INSET: The Model 1917 cartridge belt with an ammunition clip for the Springfield.

PANCHO VILLA AND THE MEXICAN EXPEDITION

Mexico had been wracked by revolution for a half-dozen years when the anarchy in the northern provinces finally spilled across the border into the United States in 1916. An increasing number of border incidents early that year had raised tensions to the boiling point and finally culminated in an invasion of American territory on March 8, when Francisco "Pancho" Villa and his band of five hundred to one thousand men raided Columbus, New Mexico. Part of the 13th Cavalry was stationed near the town. They drove off Villa and hastily pursued, killing about one hundred "Villistas" before returning to Columbus, but twenty-four Americans were dead, including ten civilians.

In an attempt to bring Villa to justice or destroy his ability to raid the United States, immediate steps were taken to organize a punitive expedition of about ten thousand men under Pershing, who was recently promoted to brigadier general. On the orders of President Woodrow Wilson, most of the Regular Army in the continental United States—the 7th, 10th, 11th, and 13th Cavalry regiments; 6th and 16th Infantry regiments; part of the 6th Field Artillery; plus supporting elements—crossed the border into Mexico in mid-March, followed later by the 5th Cavalry, 17th and 24th Infantry regiments, as well as engineer and other units.

Pershing was subject to orders that required him to respect the sovereignty of Mexico, and was further hindered by the fact that the Mexican government and people resented the incursion. Advanced elements of the expedition penetrated as far as Parral, some four hundred miles south of the border, but Villa was never captured. The campaign consisted primarily of dozens of minor skirmishes with small bands of insurgents. There were even clashes with Mexican Army units; the most serious was on June 21, 1916, at Carrizal, where a detachment of the Buffalo Soldiers of the 10th Cavalry was nearly destroyed. War would probably have been declared but for the critical situation in Europe. Even so, virtually the entire Regular Army

was involved, and some one hundred twelve thousand National Guardsmen had been federalized, with even more concentrated on the border before the end of the affair.

Normal relations with Mexico eventually were restored by diplomatic negotiation, and the troops were withdrawn from Mexico in February 1917, but minor clashes with Mexican irregulars continued to disturb the border from 1917 to 1919. Engagements took place near Buena Vista, Mexico, and in San Bernardino Canyon, Mexico, in December 1917; near La Grulla, Texas, in January 1918; at Pilares, Mexico, in late March 1918; at Nogales, Arizona, on August 1918; and near El Paso, Texas, in June 1919.

ABOVE: At a brigade head-quarters near Casas Grande, Mexico, Pershing surveys newly arrived terrain maps, 1916.

BACKGROUND: Brigadier General John J. Pershing and his staff cross the Santa Maria River at El Valle, Mexico on August 29, 1916 (note the wagon, piled high with forage, at right). Pershing was only a month away from earning his second star when this photo was taken. Eleven years earlier, the army establishment was stunned by the news that the highly experienced but low-ranking Captain Pershing had been promoted to brigadier general by President Theodore Roosevelt ahead of 835 other officers of higher seniority.

WHEELS IN MEXICO: THE MECHANIZATION OF THE ARMY

Although motor vehicle production in the United States was already strong at the turn of the century, the army was very slow to acquire its own. By 1905, the Artillery Branch had a Long Distance Automobile Company "battery repair wagon and forge" at Fort Myer, Virginia; the Medical Bureau had a steam-powered White Motor Company ambulance in Washington; and Ordnance operated a Winton "automobile telegraph car" at Fort Omaha, plus a Cadillac "automobile repair car" at Fort Leavenworth.

Vehicle purchases remained tentative and ad hoc for nearly another decade, but the advent of war in Europe prompted a surge of uncoordinated purchases. For example, the thirty-five trucks operated by the Quartermaster Department in the United States in June 1914 increased to sixty-one trucks plus twenty-one cars from seventeen manufacturers by the end of the year. Some progress had been made at producing a guide

to acquiring vehicles, but no production specification standards were developed beyond those required by the vehicle-hungry European militaries. The punitive expedition changed all that. General John Pershing demanded trucks, insisting that mule-drawn wagons were far too slow for the "flying columns" he planned to thrust deep into Mexico.

The resulting scramble to acquire vehicles from eight different manufacturers resulted in many unsuitable models. However, this did serve the purpose of finally focusing the army's attention on the matter, and thirteen different truck types were settled on, from tankers to mobile machine shops. The army also gained

a clear understanding of what it would take to maintain a force that would increasingly travel on wheels instead of hooves. While it would find itself deficient in virtually every category of modern weapons when war was declared on Germany in 1917, the factory expansions plus mobilization lessons garnered from the border crisis would greatly benefit the soldiers who fought in France just two years later.

RIGHT: *An early model of the fifteen-ton Holt Caterpillar tractor is used by troops to flatten the bumps on roadbeds in Mexico on July 21, 1916. Although commonly described as a fifteen-ton machine, the model actually weighed just short of fourteen tons.*

BELOW: *A convoy of the White Motor Company's rugged one-ton trucks, with their distinctive hard-rubber tires, arrives at Boca Grande, Mexico.*

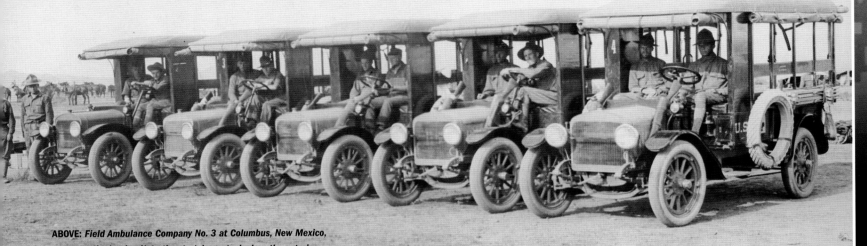

ABOVE: *Field Ambulance Company No. 3 at Columbus, New Mexico, or across the border. Note the stretchers stacked on the exterior brackets of the vehicle at right. The next version of this General Motors Corporation ambulance, heavily used in France, had an all-wooden compartment for the wounded.*

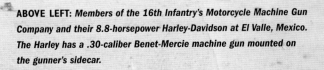

ABOVE LEFT: *Members of the 16th Infantry's Motorcycle Machine Gun Company and their 8.8-horsepower Harley-Davidson at El Valle, Mexico. The Harley has a .30-caliber Benet-Mercie machine gun mounted on the gunner's sidecar.*

THE HORSE IS MAN'S NOBLEST COMPANION

JOIN THE
CAVALRY
and have a courageous friend
U.S. ARMY RECRUITING OFFICE:

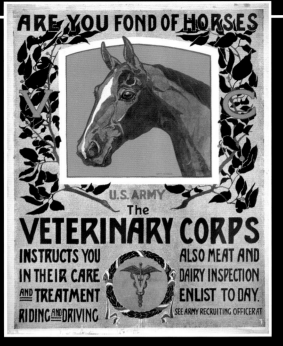

ARE YOU FOND OF HORSES

U.S. ARMY
The
VETERINARY CORPS
INSTRUCTS YOU IN THEIR CARE AND TREATMENT RIDING AND DRIVING

ALSO MEAT AND DAIRY INSPECTION ENLIST TO DAY.
SEE ARMY RECRUITING OFFICER AT

Say! Young Fellow
Do you want to be a Mechanic?
The MOTOR TRANSPORT CORPS WILL TRAIN YOU
EARN WHILE YOU LEARN
APPLY

PFC, Farrier

PFC, Tank Corps

PFC, Ordinance

PFC, Air Service

RIGHT: Artillerymen in Mexico set up a German-designed Goerz range finder, a highly regarded piece of equipment.

FAR RIGHT: Signal corpsmen hold wig-wag flags (*right*) and the semaphore flags (*left*) that replaced them in 1912. The red flag with white spot was used in bright daylight, and the opposite pattern was used during lower-visibility conditions. The semaphore system uses both flags simultaneously.

OPPOSITE BOTTOM: Soldiers from Company A of the 16th Infantry sit around a campfire near San Geronimo, Mexico, on the evening of May 27, 1916.

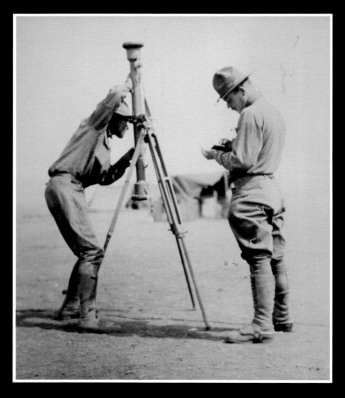

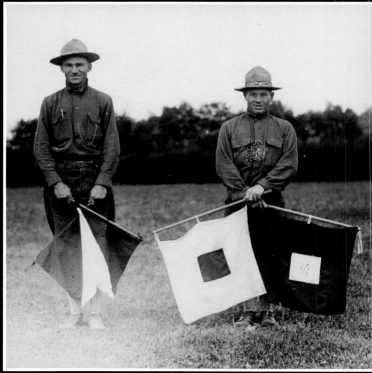

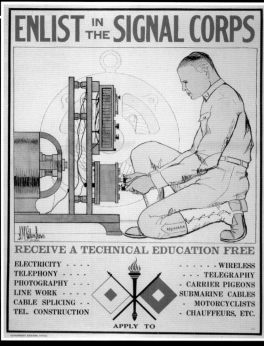

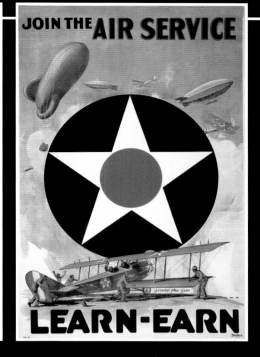

PFC, Coxain   PFC, Cavalry   PFC, Artillery   PFC, Infantry

Chevron PFC, Signal Corps

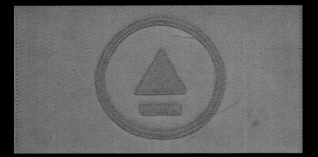

Chevron PFC, Observer First Class

Chevron Master Gunner, Coastal Artillery

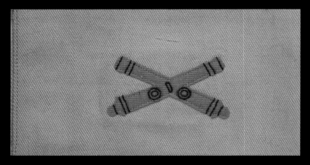

Chevron Gun Commander, Artillery

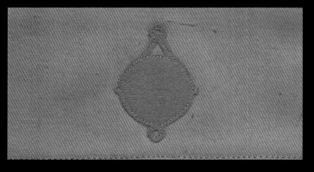

Chevron Second Class Mine Company, Coast Artillery

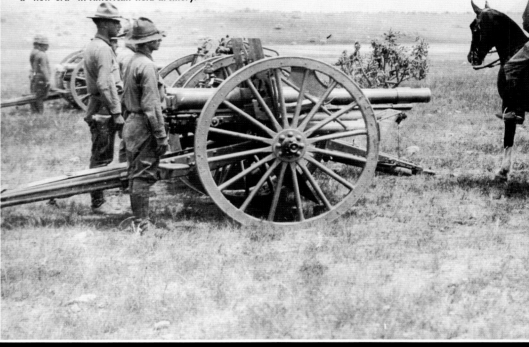

BELOW: Officers inspecting the 6th Field Artillery (Light), a 3-inch gun outfit. The weapon was looked upon as something of an antique in 1916, but when first introduced fourteen years earlier—with its panoramic sights, hydrospring recoil system, and ability to rapid-fire either shrapnel or high-explosive shells out to a range of nearly three and a half miles—the M1902 had been widely proclaimed as marking a "new era" in American field artillery.

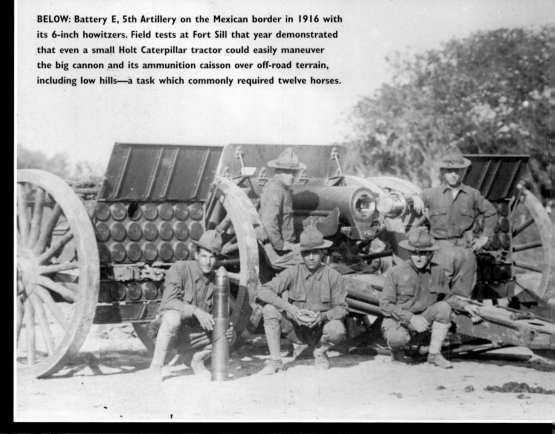

BELOW: Battery E, 5th Artillery on the Mexican border in 1916 with its 6-inch howitzers. Field tests at Fort Sill that year demonstrated that even a small Holt Caterpillar tractor could easily maneuver the big cannon and its ammunition caisson over off-road terrain, including low hills—a task which commonly required twelve horses.

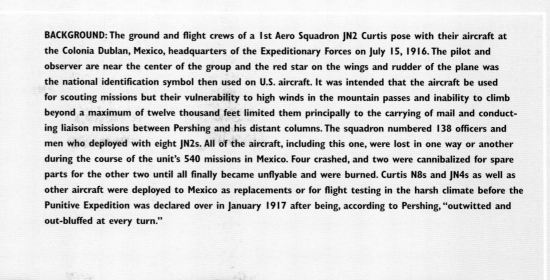

BACKGROUND: The ground and flight crews of a 1st Aero Squadron JN2 Curtis pose with their aircraft at the Colonia Dublan, Mexico, headquarters of the Expeditionary Forces on July 15, 1916. The pilot and observer are near the center of the group and the red star on the wings and rudder of the plane was the national identification symbol then used on U.S. aircraft. It was intended that the aircraft be used for scouting missions but their vulnerability to high winds in the mountain passes and inability to climb beyond a maximum of twelve thousand feet limited them principally to the carrying of mail and conducting liaison missions between Pershing and his distant columns. The squadron numbered 138 officers and men who deployed with eight JN2s. All of the aircraft, including this one, were lost in one way or another during the course of the unit's 540 missions in Mexico. Four crashed, and two were cannibalized for spare parts for the other two until all finally became unflyable and were burned. Curtis N8s and JN4s as well as other aircraft were deployed to Mexico as replacements or for flight testing in the harsh climate before the Punitive Expedition was declared over in January 1917 after being, according to Pershing, "outwitted and out-bluffed at every turn."

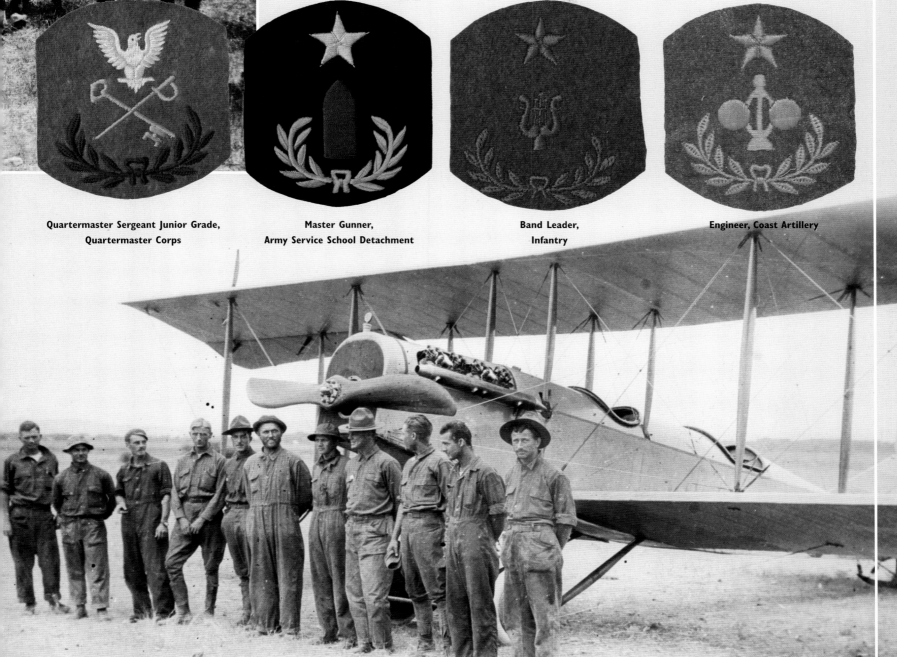

Quartermaster Sergeant Junior Grade, Quartermaster Corps

Master Gunner, Army Service School Detachment

Band Leader, Infantry

Engineer, Coast Artillery

ABOVE: American soldiers at Colonia Dublan, Mexico, unload supplies from a Mexican train that has just arrived from Juarez on the border. The headquarters area of the expeditionary force is at upper right.

BELOW: A supply train of fifty-two wagons carrying hay and oats heads south to rendezvous with one of General Pershing's far-flung columns. Pershing was only partially successful in his effort to quickly mechanize the army along the border.

LEFT: Members of a 16th Infantry machine gun platoon fire their M1909 .30-caliber Benet-Mercie during an inspection near Casas Grande. A lighter version of the French Hotchkiss, some 1,070 of the weapons were manufactured by the Springfield Armory and Colt's Manufacturing Company. Complaints arose over its awkward, inverted feeding system, which took rounds from stiff, 30-round metal strips and belts of 3-round metal striplets. Though it saw service during the Mexican expedition as well as subsequent operations along the border and some in France, the Benet-Mercie principally was used to train machine-gun crews before they left the United States.

BELOW: Pancho Villa's anger at the new U.S. administration's support for the national government of Venustiano Carranza during Mexico's ongoing civil war prompted a costly series of cross-border raids and attacks against American interests. Here, American and Carranzista soldiers pose for a picture at the 6th Infantry's camp near San Antonio, Mexico, on April 27, 1916.

Chapter Six
Over There, 1917–1921

It seems odd at first but, among themselves, many officers in 1917 offered a tip of the hat to Pancho Villa for the blessing in disguise that his depredations along the U.S.-Mexico border had provided the army. The need to defend America's outlying possessions—Alaska, Hawaii, the Panama Canal Zone, and Puerto Rico—while suppressing insurrection in the Philippines had prompted Congress to willingly provide for the largest "peacetime" strength since the early days of Reconstruction. But the approximately sixty-five thousand regulars and thirty-five thousand volunteers were spread from San Juan to Manila and, in world terms, were still a paltry force. The outbreak of general war in Europe, involving armies of millions of men, threatened to one day involve the United States as well, but every example of rapid mobilization that Americans could look back on, including that of the recent war with Spain, had only reinforced the belief that little preparation—and even less thinking—had gone into such a basic matter.

Villa's attacks on Columbus, New Mexico, then Glen Springs, Texas, and the skirmishing between the regulars initially deployed by General Pershing and the Mexican Army prompted passage of legislation in 1916 that allowed the National Guard to be mustered into federal service not as state militias, but as organized units of citizen soldiers. Nearly one hundred sixty thousand Guardsmen were called to the colors in formations that ran the gamut from disorganized and woefully unprepared to well disciplined and more heavily armed than the Regular units of the same size. Resembling in some instances more a migration than a mobilization, they gathered on the border, exposing a whole raft of deficiencies to be rectified. Once on the border, they received a valuable degree of hardening, discipline, and field training on the very eve of America's entry into the European war. In short, the threat of war with Mexico had provided a priceless dry run for what was to come just one year later.

Some within the officer corps already had begun to prepare themselves for such an eventuality. America's sudden and unexpected inclusion among the select club of colonial powers, and its construction of the Panama Canal, had done a marvelous job of focusing various military and civilian leaders' attention on the nation's glaring deficiencies. However, most officers, be they West Point graduate, regular, volunteer, or National Guard, still couldn't see the divisional and corps "forest" for the platoon and company "trees." President Theodore Roosevelt's War Department, under the energetic direction of Secretary of War Elihu Root, moved to break the paralysis within the officer corps caused by its rigid seniority system. The inquisitive Root was made aware of a decades-old, uncompleted manuscript buried within what General Douglas MacArthur aptly described as "the dusty pigeon holes of the War Department." Its contents had long been discussed in certain army circles. With Root as war secretary, the time seemed ripe for a new look at the document, which contained a prophetic notation scrawled in pencil across the top:

I doubt if you will convince the powers that be, but the facts stated, the references from authority, and the military conclusions are most valuable and should be printed and made accessible. The time may not be now, but will come when these will be appreciated, and may bear some fruit even in our day.

—W.T. Sherman

In the proposals of Emory Upton, long since deceased, the major general had outlined why and how a general staff should be formed. Here, Root found a blueprint for

OPPOSITE: Lieutenant Colonel William Donovan wears the ribbons of a Distinguished Service Medal and French Croix de Guerre that he was awarded for his valor while leading a battalion of the 165th Infantry, 42d Division, at Château-Thierry in July 1918. Uncharacteristically, the citation for his medal spells out his full middle name instead of using an initial and even presents his nickname: "William Joseph 'Wild Bill' Donovan." Within just a few months, as commander of the 165th, he "personally led the [regiment's] assaulting wave in an attack upon a very strongly organized position, and when our troops were suffering heavy casualties he encouraged all near him by his example, moving among his men in exposed positions, reorganizing decimated platoons, and accompanying them forward in attacks. When he was wounded in the leg by machine-gun bullets, he refused to be evacuated and continued with his unit until it withdrew to a less exposed position." In October 1918, Donovan was awarded a Medal of Honor for those actions. Donovan organized and led the Office of Strategic Services (OSS) during World War II and later played a key role in the establishment of the Central Intelligence Agency (CIA).

ABOVE: Emory Upton was a brevet major general during the Civil War. Taking part in nearly every major battle in the East, Upton personally commanded an artillery battery, then brigade; an infantry regiment, then brigade; and finally both infantry cavalry divisions. After the war he served as the commandant of cadets at West Point; went to Europe to closely observe the conduct of the Franco-Prussian War; conducted detailed, on-site examinations of European and Asian armies; wrote the analysis of American military preparedness mentioned at right; and, as the superintendent of theoretical instruction at the Artillery School of Practice, Fort Monroe, Virginia, promoted the close coordination of infantry and artillery elements. Suffering grievously from an apparent brain tumor, he took his own life at age forty-one in 1881 while commanding the 4th Artillery at the Presidio in San Francisco.

RIGHT: Recruiting poster, c. 1918

OPPOSITE BOTTOM INSET: Men of the 6th Field Artillery, 1st Division, at Exermont, France, on October 4, 1918, months after the United States declared war on the Central Powers and joined WWI.

what he wanted—a flexible general staff kept fresh and vibrant by a continual rotation of members from line units and back again, and whose chief would bridge the gap between the paramount civilian authorities and the military command. Upton's proposals also included a robust system of military education.

Root seized upon these ideas. The Army War College, tasked with training senior staff officers, was established at Carlisle Barracks, Pennsylvania. Likewise, the Command and General Staff School was created at Fort Leavenworth, Kansas, with the mission of educating and training intermediate-level officers. In addition, West Point was expanded, schools were opened for the army's different branches such as infantry and artillery, and an embryonic general staff itself was created. In 1904, twenty years after Upton's death and forty years after General Sherman prophesied that his proposals would one day be appreciated for their value and insight, the manuscript was released under the title *Military Policy of the United States* and made mandatory reading for army officers.

Although the number of graduates of the Command and General Staff School and War College were comparatively small—only a tiny fraction of the army's less than ten thousand officers—they played a critical role in organizing the force for the coming conflagration, which was of a scope and size far exceeding that of even the Civil War. This was accomplished in spite of obstacles large and small. In one instance, Woodrow Wilson, elected to the presidency on a pledge to maintain neutrality between the Allies and the Central Powers, threw what the soldiers of the day referred to as a "childish tantrum" and "hissy fit" upon reading in a newspaper that officers at Fort Leavenworth had engaged in an academic study of how a war against Germany might be fought. President Wilson, who did not understand the function of contingency planning, threatened "to relieve at once every officer" found to be involved, but nothing ever came of the matter.

Members of the Kaiser's general staff in Berlin would have found such an outburst laughable, yet it is equally likely that many Americans would have agreed with Wilson's sentiments if they had been made public. An interesting aspect of this incident also had to do with the maps used in the Fort Leavenworth study.

Terrain maps were scarce during the early days of the school, and tactical problems were examined on old German-made maps of the Franco-German border at the time of their 1870–71 war. Thus, when war finally did come with Germany, and army planners found themselves working out real problems for real battles, it was over terrain already familiar to many of them from maps that had been acquired by either Major General Sheridan, or Upton himself, since both officers had been sent to examine the Prussian military during and after the Franco-Prussian War.

THE AEF

In the nearly two decades leading up to America's involvement in the First World War, the army had revamped its educational system. It also had made increasing strides toward both integrating the National Guard into the federal military system and bringing its training up to the standards of the Regular Army. It had kept abreast of rapidly changing combat technologies even if it had not been able to fully equip itself with all of the modern marvels at a uniform or even adequate pace. Motorized supply and aviation units had been formed; field telephones and primitive radios distributed; artillery and rifles modernized; and, of immense importance to the battle about to be joined, an appreciation developed of how to field, maintain, and operate large formations. Yet despite the mobilization for possible war with Mexico, this "appreciation" did not extend beyond the theoretical. Colonel William A. Ganoe, former history instructor of Dwight D. Eisenhower, Omar Bradley, and

OUR REGULAR DIVISIONS

Honored and Respected by All
Enlist for the Infantry—
or in one of the other 12 branches.

BACKGROUND: An AEF situation map produced during the Meuse-Argonne offensive, c. October 7–9, 1918.

WORLD WAR I DIVISIONS

The army that fought during World War I was made up of three components: the Regular, or permanent, divisions manned principally by professional soldiers; National Guard divisions of state troops (numbered 26–41); and National Army divisions made up of draftees (numbered 76–91), with the area supporting a Guard division generally coinciding with a National Army divisional area. Seven divisions were not intended to fight, but instead acted as "depot divisions," training and supplying replacements to those in combat. The War Department also soon found that far more regulars were required to properly train the new units than had been anticipated, and that large numbers of draftees had to be assigned to the Guard and Regular formations if they were to be brought up to strength quickly.

Many states had wanted the honor of having their soldiers become the first in France and pressed for that assignment. To stop the clamor, the 43d Division was formed from a "rainbow" of surplus units from twenty-six states. The 92d Division was formed for the fielding of regiments of black troops with the 93d Division (Provisional), acting as an eighth depot formation. Much to the disappointment of Pershing, the new 15th Cavalry Division was never sent to France. Because of continuing strife along the Mexican border, its brigades operated in the southwestern states, and it was reorganized into the 1st Cavalry Division in 1920.

Some forty-four divisions deployed to France with seven Regular Army, eleven National Guard, and eleven National Army divisions serving in combat. Of the others, one arrived after the armistice, and five (as well as two of the eight depot formations) were stripped of their personnel for replacements in fighting units, rear area laborers, or as expeditionary forces sent to northern Russia or Italy.

1st Division   2d Division   3d Division   4th Division   5th Division

26th Division   28th Division   42d Division   77th Division   78th Division

82d Division   91st Division

many others at the U.S. Military Academy, as well as adjutant at "The Point," later wrote:

When April 6, 1917, tossed the American spectators onto the European gridiron, they had not even a high school squad to meet the professionals. The 1916 Defense Act had been merely the promise of a team for which only a few freshmen had reported. The army had no large tactical units in a modern sense, few weapons, a dearth of officers, no experience with trench warfare, little training and less strength. It had 9,750 officers of all grades and experience, while 180,000 of the utmost efficiency were immediately necessary.

Germany's new, unlimited submarine warfare, and its offer to support Mexico's reacquisition of Texas, Arizona, and New Mexico if it should join the war on the side of the Central Powers, finally ended American neutrality in April 1917. It was clear to the Wilson administration and Congress that the French and British armies, whose morale and manpower were weakened by the prolonged slaughter, would need a massive influx of American fighting men if the western democracies were to emerge victorious. The United States immediately took steps to form a massive American Expeditionary Force (AEF), which would eventually number more than two million men. This was accomplished in May 1918 by federalizing the National Guard upon the declaration of war and establishing conscription for the first time since the Civil War.

To ensure that U.S. troops would reach the battlefield before the Allied armies gave out, American units would not wait for their own artillery, machine guns, and countless other implements of war to be produced, but would be rushed overseas and largely armed by the British and French.

CHAUCHAT MACHINE RIFLE, MODEL 1915

The cheaply manufactured Chauchat was fed by a twenty-round, open-box magazine that performed poorly even under controlled conditions, and frequently jammed at least once when firing each magazine. Although issued by the army as the standard personal machine gun, many soldiers refused to use it or "lost" it in combat as soon as officers were not present. Numerous efforts to fix its many problems—including the substitution of a short, box-type magazine—met with no success, and the remaining Chauchat guns were scrapped soon after the war.

OPPOSITE TOP: Near Varennes, France, soldiers of the 28th Division's Battery A, 180th Field Artillery, fire their French-made 155-mm howitzer during the opening days of the Meuse-Argonne Offensive. The gas masks worn by the men at center and left are the French Tissot type favored by artillery-men because the tanks' place-ment on the men's backs kept them out of the way when handling ammunition. The soldier at right wears a British-pattern small box respirator, or SBR. Because Quakers were exempt from the draft due to their religious convictions, a cheeky artilleryman has added the words "Quaker Mers" (in frac-tured French, "Quaker town") to the back of his 155's gun shield.

LEFT: Behind a roughly impro-vised barricade at Camp Dix in New Jersey, infantrymen train for war on the Colt M1917 machine gun, an improved version of the M1895 weapon that had been used since the Spanish-American War.

One principle, however, was to remain inviolate. The commander of the AEF, General John Joseph Pershing, was given firm instructions that no matter what the pressure or clever maneuvering of the Allies—who desperately wanted American soldiers to be fed immediately into their depleted units—the United States Army was to enter battle as an independent command.

It took a strong and stubborn personality like Pershing's to fend off the heated and persistent demands of the Allies. Occasionally he would relent and loan formations that were large, homogenous, and easily recognized as all-American during emergencies and special situations, but the AEF remained the independent, growing—and ultimately deci-sive—force that American military and political leaders intended it to be.

THE DRAFT AND TRAINING

The slow pace of recruiting after America's entry into World War I prompted Congress on May 18, 1917, to pass a Selective Service Act giving the president the power to draft men for military service. All males aged twenty-one to thirty, then eighteen to forty-five, were required to register for military service. Many men continued to enlist in the Regular Army—and especially its specialist branches—as well as the Navy and Marines. But of the more than four million eight hundred thousand Americans who served in the armed forces during the war, far more than half, some two million eight hundred thousand soldiers, were draftees.

Regular and Guard units lacked adequate heavy weapons and modern equipment in 1917 but at least had strong organizational structures and cadres of commissioned and non-commissioned officers that could be depended on. The men who were inducted and sent to the new National Army formations faced a far different situation. Severe shortages of weapons, equipment, and supplies retarded training. The quartermaster general maintained that hats and cotton undershirts were the only items of clothing he expected to be initially available to outfit the masses of soldiers swelling the army's freshly built camps. Worse yet, the newly authorized Reserve Officers' Training Corps had yet to produce many potential officers and, except for a handful of regulars, the National Army divisions had to make do with newly minted officers fresh from twelve weeks of training.

BOTTOM AND OPPOSITE TOP: *Hat cords were worn by officers on their 1911 "Montana Peaked" service hats. A wide variety of color combinations were authorized for enlisted personnel (see pages 208–211), organizations, and civilians attached to the army, such as newspaper correspondents. Branch colors were the most common, but certain personnel could be further delineated. For example, the "acorn" tips would be blood red at the end of an infantry machine gunner's light blue cord or a cavalryman's yellow cord.*

BELOW: *Members of Reserve Officers' Training Corps, Squad 15, Company 8, conduct rifle practice at Fort Niagara in upstate New York, around August through December 1917. Bucknell University student Dwite H. Schaffner, who would later earn a Medal of Honor in France, was a member of Squad 15 when this photo was taken.*

Sq 15 Co 8 Shooting the bull 514 F.N.

GENERAL OFFICER

OFFICER

INFANTRY

ROTC

FIELD CLERK

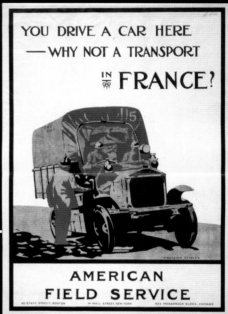

ABOVE: *Recruiting posters for the Regular Army and some of its branches.*

RIGHT: *Ranks of California ROTC students stand ready for inspection at the University of California's Berkeley campus in 1917–1918. In the face of looming American involvement in World War I, the National Defense Act of 1916 included a provision that set up the Reserve Officers' Training Corps, but the Corps' inception occurred too late to produce large numbers of officers for World War I.*

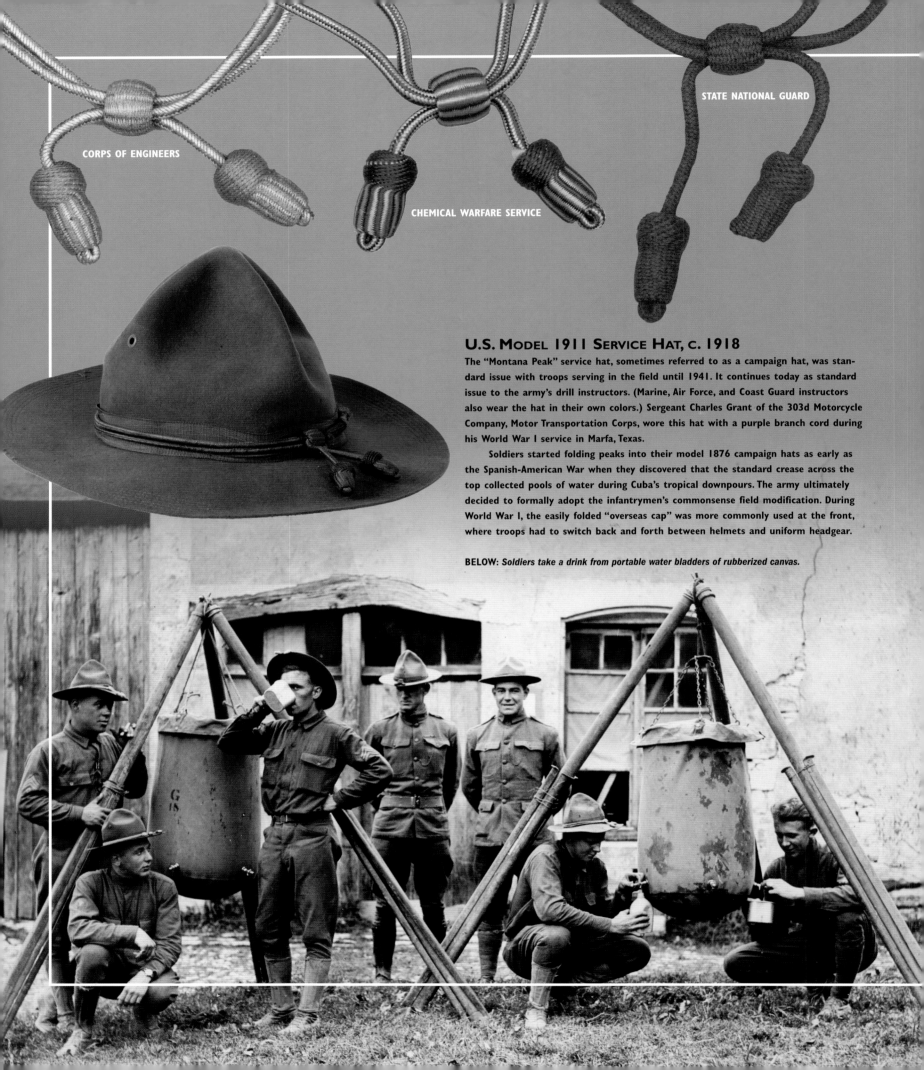

CORPS OF ENGINEERS

CHEMICAL WARFARE SERVICE

STATE NATIONAL GUARD

U.S. MODEL 1911 SERVICE HAT, c. 1918

The "Montana Peak" service hat, sometimes referred to as a campaign hat, was standard issue with troops serving in the field until 1941. It continues today as standard issue to the army's drill instructors. (Marine, Air Force, and Coast Guard instructors also wear the hat in their own colors.) Sergeant Charles Grant of the 303d Motorcycle Company, Motor Transportation Corps, wore this hat with a purple branch cord during his World War I service in Marfa, Texas.

Soldiers started folding peaks into their model 1876 campaign hats as early as the Spanish-American War when they discovered that the standard crease across the top collected pools of water during Cuba's tropical downpours. The army ultimately decided to formally adopt the infantrymen's commonsense field modification. During World War I, the easily folded "overseas cap" was more commonly used at the front, where troops had to switch back and forth between helmets and uniform headgear.

BELOW: *Soldiers take a drink from portable water bladders of rubberized canvas.*

MEDICAL DEPARTMENT

RIGHT: *Members of the Hospital Corps at Camp Wadsworth near Spartanburg, South Carolina, practice how to remove wounded soldiers from the trenches. Roughly 136,000 troops passed through the mobilization center from September 1917 through December 1918, including the 27th Division from New York, which trained there.*

BELOW: *A detachment of the 3d Motor Mechanics Regiment at the 1st Air Depot, Colombey-les-Belles, France, in 1918.*

AIR CORPS

ABOVE INSET: *At first glance, the U.S. Army's 1917 helmet appears to be identical to the British Mark I, which initially was issued to American troops. The American helmet, however, is made of a stronger steel alloy than the Mark I, has a better interior liner, and has a rougher finish than its British counterpart in order to cut down on its surface sheen.*

LEFT INSET: *This hat cord was worn by Herbert H. Price, U.S. Army Air Service, 1918–1919. This was the first type of cord used when the Air Service was organized. After 1922 or 1923, the cords were blue and gold.*

INFANTRY MACHINE GUN BATTALION

TANK CORPS

MOTOR TRANSPORT CORPS

CALIBER .30 BAYONET, MODEL 1903

This numbered bayonet was made in November 1909 at the Springfield Armory in Massachusetts.

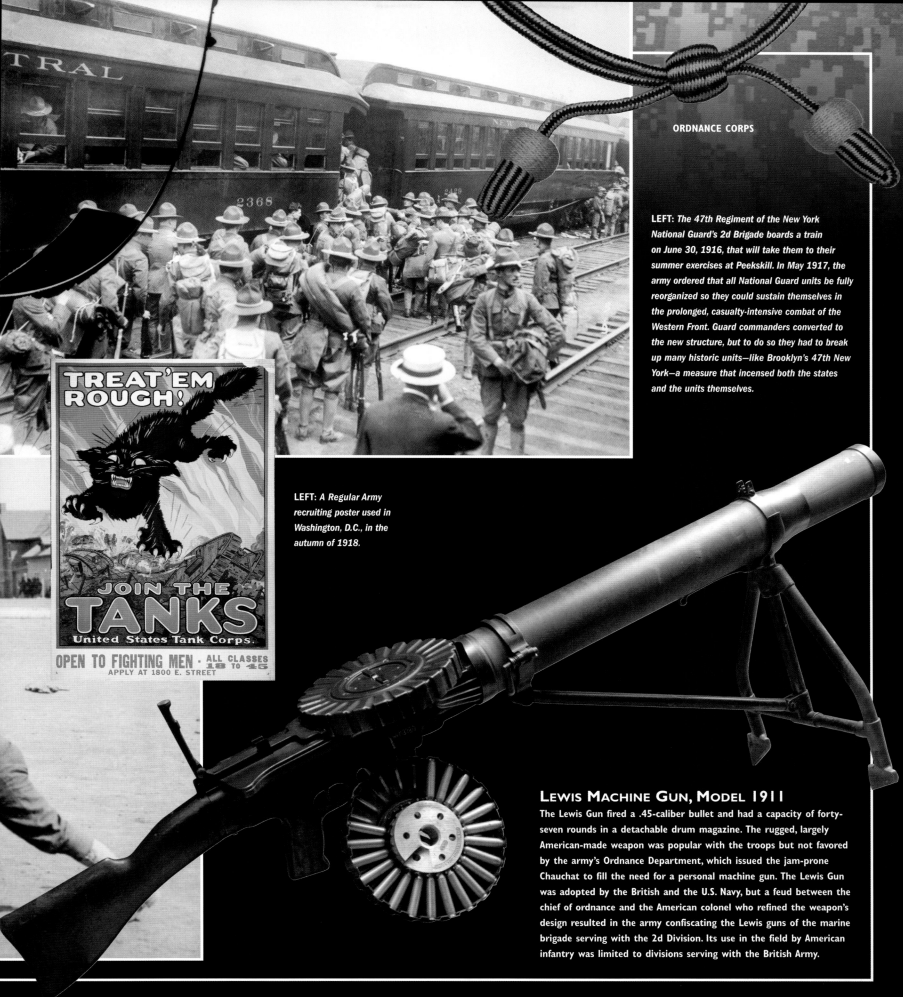

LEFT: *The 47th Regiment of the New York National Guard's 2d Brigade boards a train on June 30, 1916, that will take them to their summer exercises at Peekskill. In May 1917, the army ordered that all National Guard units be fully reorganized so they could sustain themselves in the prolonged, casualty-intensive combat of the Western Front. Guard commanders converted to the new structure, but to do so they had to break up many historic units—like Brooklyn's 47th New York—a measure that incensed both the states and the units themselves.*

LEFT: *A Regular Army recruiting poster used in Washington, D.C., in the autumn of 1918.*

TREAT'EM ROUGH!

JOIN THE TANKS

United States Tank Corps.

OPEN TO FIGHTING MEN · ALL CLASSES 18 to 45
APPLY AT 1800 E. STREET

LEWIS MACHINE GUN, MODEL 1911

The Lewis Gun fired a .45-caliber bullet and had a capacity of forty-seven rounds in a detachable drum magazine. The rugged, largely American-made weapon was popular with the troops but not favored by the army's Ordnance Department, which issued the jam-prone Chauchat to fill the need for a personal machine gun. The Lewis Gun was adopted by the British and the U.S. Navy, but a feud between the chief of ordnance and the American colonel who refined the weapon's design resulted in the army confiscating the Lewis guns of the marine brigade serving with the 2d Division. Its use in the field by American infantry was limited to divisions serving with the British Army.

BELOW: General John Joseph Pershing steps ashore at Boulogne, France, on June 13, 1917. More than 2,056,000 Americans would follow him.

"LAFAYETTE, WE ARE HERE!"

The lead elements of the AEF arrived at St. Nazaire in the Bay of Biscay on June 26, 1917. In honor of its new ally, France declared the Fourth of July a holiday, and these first American soldiers—a battalion of the 1st Division's 16th Infantry, together with a large miscellany of other units and even YMCA personnel—marched through the streets of Paris to cheers and shouts of "*Vive L'Amerique!*" The parade culminated at the tomb of the Marquis de Lafayette, a gallant Frenchman who had come to aid the hard-pressed army of George Washington one hundred forty years before. As the massed Americans and throngs of Parisians watched, General Pershing laid a wreath at the foot of the tomb, and a member of the general's staff, Captain Charles E. Stanton, gave a short speech that touched the hearts of Americans and French alike:

> *I regret I cannot speak to the good people of France in the beautiful language of their own fair country.*
> *The fact cannot be forgotten that your nation was our friend when America was struggling for existence, when a handful of brave and patriotic people were determined to uphold the rights their Creator gave them—that France in the person of Lafayette came to our aid in words and deed.*
> *It would be ingratitude not to remember this and America defaults no obligations...*
> *Therefore it is with loving pride we drape the colors in tribute of respect to this citizen of your great Republic, and here and now in the shadow of the illustrious dead we pledge our hearts and our honor in carrying this war to successful issue.*
> *Lafayette, we are here!*

The transit of American units across the Atlantic proceeded slowly at first, but gradually the AEF's strength was built up behind the Western Front. American and Allied leaders agreed that all combat divisions, even the Regulars, required a lengthy period of retraining on their new equipment and had to become thoroughly familiar with French methods before being committed to combat. It was planned that after each division reached a certain level of proficiency, it would be placed into a "quiet" sector along the line where

LEFT: During the effort to push the Germans back across the Vesle River, a regimental staff of the 4th Division plans its next moves during an August 9, 1918, conference.

BOTTOM: A French Saint Chamond heavy tank, bereft of its 75-mm gun, maneuvers menacingly as men of the 26th Infantry, U.S. 1st Division, practice anti-tank techniques near Breteuil, France, on May 11, 1918.

SPRINGFIELD RIFLE WITH FRENCH VB RIFLE GRENADE, MODEL 1903

Use of rifle grenades allowed the infantry to apply explosive force at a greater distance than even the best throwing arm could. Since such weapons were not manufactured in the United States, the French provided them. Some American units even received the launchers with French rifles and special launching racks that incorporated an adjustable elevation system calibrated to the propellant charge of French bullets, which, in effect, turned them into mortars.

the formation could obtain some seasoning before being thrust into more challenging situations. On the night of October 20, 1917, the 1st Division, formed from units in service on the U.S.–Mexico border and at various army posts, took its place along the line with French units, and under French command. It would see no fighting until the following spring, and the unexpected employment of the 11th, 12th, and 14th engineer regiments to assist the British in the Cambrai sector led them to be the first American units in action.

By March 1918, an average of one thousand men per day were landing in France—a daily figure that would eventually grow to ten times that number. This greatly bolstered the morale of the British and French soldiers and had a correspondingly negative effect on the Germans. Russia, wracked by the Bolshevik Revolution, had withdrawn from the war after the communists took over the government, allowing thousands of German soldiers to be transferred to the Western Front. The Kaiser's generals believed that with these additional forces at its disposal, they could smash the Allied armies in one final titanic blow before the American soldiers streaming across the Atlantic had arrived in such strength that the balance of power had irretrievably slipped into the Allies' favor.

The opening strike fell on March 21, 1918, when three German armies comprising more than sixty divisions smashed through British defense lines in the Somme area. Within two weeks, the Germans had advanced forty miles to the town of Cantigny, inflicting two hundred thousand casualties and taking another seventy thousand prisoner, yet failed to either

destroy the British or cut their army off from the French. At the height of the German drive, Pershing had reluctantly offered the four American divisions that were the most combat-ready, but only engineer and aviation units saw action. The Germans attacked the British again with forty-six divisions beginning on April 9. American engineer and air elements again lent their support before the attack began to falter. The next phase of the Germans' series of spring offensives opened on May 27 and was so dangerous that the AEF's 2d and 3d Divisions were thrown into the battle.

TOP LEFT: Georgia Guardsmen of the 122d Infantry, 31st Division at the 1st Corps School in Gondrecourt, France, train to repel enemy infantry during a gas attack. Not long after this photo was taken on August 15, 1918, the division was "skeletonized" for replacement to fill divisions that had already suffered severe losses at the front.

BACKGROUND: French dragoons pass American infantrymen as German gas shells fall nearby.

RIGHT: An American battery with French-made 75-mm guns uses a tree line to help mask their position. The artilleryman with the megaphone appears to be listening to the signalman at right and is likely the battery's executive officer.

BELOW: Gunners of either the 1st or 42d Division fire on Montsec from the Beaumont area on the opening day of the St. Mihiel Offensive on September 12, 1918.

Just before these forces were committed, however, the 1st Infantry Division, known as the "Big Red One" for its distinctive shoulder patch, conducted a long-planned assault to dislodge the Germans entrenched on the key, high ground at Cantigny, the site of their deepest penetration in March. This first American attack of the war opened on May 28, and it was crucial that the operation be a success, because the British and French would be watching closely to see how Americans stood up in battle. To this end, the division planned its attack far in advance and in the most minute detail, leaving nothing to chance and even rehearsing the assault itself behind the lines and far from the enemies, on ground similar to that of the coming battle.

The day before the attack, the Germans, sensing that something was up, raided the whole front line and drenched it with fifteen thousand deadly gas shells. But they managed to capture only one prisoner, and he refused to talk. That night, the Big Red One moved up and readied for the push-off. From 5:45 to 6 A.M., American and French artillerymen shelled Cantigny in a deceptively short bombardment. Then, at zero hour, the doughboys went over the top of their trenches and advanced across shell-torn fields, staying close behind a curtain of their own artillery fire—the famous "rolling barrage." Heavy guns shelled the German rear areas to prevent them from bringing up supplies or more soldiers, while French tanks and flamethrowers supported the American Infantry.

Within eighty-eight minutes the 1st Division had killed, captured, or wounded every German within its zone of advance. The 28th Infantry, supported by the 18th Infantry, 1st Engineers, and divisional artillery, dug in and beat off bitter counterattacks—six of them over a three-day period— before the Germans finally gave up. Taking and holding Cantigny had cost the 1st Division 199 dead and more than 1,400 gassed or wounded. While these losses were not much different than a thousand other local operations conducted during the war, it showed the Allies, and the Americans themselves, what the Yanks could do, and was a bitter omen for the German Army.

LEFT: On the Verdun front, Second Lieutenant Val A. Browning of the 79th Division examines an M1917 .30-caliber heavy machine gun designed by his father. Note the use of wooden boards to provide stability on the muddy ground.

INSET: American Expeditionary Forces general headquarters unit patch. The design was later used by U.S. Army Ground Forces and today by U.S. Army Forces Command.

BELOW: A French-designed M1916 37-mm gun—a "one-pounder"—rests on a second-line trench parapet. Capable of firing twenty-eight rounds per minute with great accuracy, the gun was extremely popular with troops, but only small numbers of the gun reached the front by the time the Armistice was signed.

WINCHESTER TRENCH SHOTGUN, MODEL 1897

Although their paper cartridges did not hold up well during the very rainy weather of September 1918, the doughboys loved their "trench sweepers," and there were never enough to fill unit requests. The Germans (who previously introduced the flame thrower, poison gas, aerial bombing of civilian targets, and unrestricted submarine warfare) hated and feared the weapon. A diplomatic protest over its use was filed through the Swiss government after its highly effective use in combat by soldiers in the 5th Division's 6th Infantry and 77th Division's 307th Infantry. The Germans claimed that the shotgun violated article 23(e) of the Hague Convention and threatened to execute any American prisoner "found to have in his possession such guns or ammunition." Acting Judge Advocate General Brigadier General Samuel T. Ansell immediately wrote the American response delivered by Secretary of State Robert Lansing: that the shotgun "cannot be the subject of legitimate or reasonable protest" and that "if the German government should carry out its threat in a single instance, it will be the right and duty of the...United States to make such reprisals as will best protect the American forces." The military-issue pump shotguns carried six rounds and were issued with a perforated heat shield along the barrel, as well as a bayonet adapter.

SPRINGFIELD .30-CALIBER SNIPER RIFLE, MODEL 1903

After experimenting with various rifles in 1917, the army settled on the standard-issue Springfield with a Warner & Swasey M1913 scope as its sniper rifle. A large rubber eyepiece that fit up against the shooter's head is not attached to this example. The Springfield continued as an Army sniper rifle into the early stages of the Vietnam War.

BELOW: A soldier from the 30th Infantry Division snipes in Belgium on July 9, 1918.

BACKGROUND: Doughboys move quickly down a sodden trench as German shells rain down.

RIGHT: An aerial observer goes over the maps he will use before his balloon is sent aloft near Mentreuil in July 1918. He and the surrounding ground crewmen belong to the Signal Corps' 2d Balloon Company. The observer uses a field telephone to report German activity and, when necessary, calls in artillery fire. If he comes under attack by German aircraft before the crew has reeled his balloon back to earth, he may be forced to parachute from the basket before the giant bag of highly flammable hydrogen gas above him explodes into flames.

BACKGROUND: Atop the roof of Crown Prince Wilhelm's Montfaucon observatory on October 17, 1918, American troops take turns peering through observation instruments that the Germans left behind in their hasty retreat.

LEFT: The Signal Corps' 117th Field Battalion, formerly the 1st Battalion, Missouri Signal Corps, companies B and C, install telephone lines to the frontline trenches by way of an old culvert near Montigny, France, on March 12, 1918.

FAR LEFT: Second Lieutenant Edward E. French of the 52d Telegraph Battalion acts as a switchboard operator for the 32d Division headquarters during the Meuse-Argonne Offensive. This board was a key spot for communications in this portion of the front because the lines that connected the infantry and artillery regiments and division and two brigade head-quarters all met at this point. The young officer became a switchboard operator when a series of emergencies on October 2 left virtually every other signaler in the unit out "shooting trouble" along the phone lines.

LEFT: A soldier at the 2d Corps Signal School at Chatillon sur Seine, Cote D'Or, France, carries a two-bird assault basket on November 10, 1918.

"ROCK OF THE MARNE"

While the 1st Division was winning the Americans' first victory of the war roughly sixty miles north of Paris at Cantigny, the great German drive that had thrust across the Aisne River barely thirty miles to the southeast was grinding inexorably forward. They advanced rapidly toward the Marne River and, meeting little resistance, started to drive toward Paris. Reserves, including the U.S. 2d and 3d Divisions, rushed from all sections of the front to the danger sector to help hold the line. On May 31, the 3d went into action at Château-Thierry amid cheers from the French, who at last saw some relief in sight. The very presence of Americans raised the morale of the Allies, who now had been fighting for years. Here, American machine gunners on the south bank held off the Germans who tried to cross the Marne at Château-Thierry, just where the French had blown up a bridge.

As the 3d lent its strong arm to the French at Château-Thierry, the 2d Division met a German advance, which threatened Paris itself. The 2d had been hurrying north to aid the 1st Division when it turned aside in the nick of time to meet the Germans advancing along the Paris road, threatening to reach the capital. They had been moving forward for days, but the French, worn out from battle, had been unable to stop their advance. The 2d succeeded in beating back the attacks and stopped the drive on Paris.

With these victories and the hard-won capture of Belleau Wood by the 2d Division's marine brigade, the reputation of the Americans increased, and the Germans realized that they had taken on more than they had expected. When the

COLT .45-CALIBER AUTOMATIC PISTOL, MODEL 1911

The M1911 had a capacity of seven rounds in a detachable magazine. Considered among the best handguns of its type, it was one of the few arms designed before World War I that was recommended by the U.S. Ordnance Department to remain unchanged in postwar service. Though replaced by the Beretta M9 in the 1990s, the hundred-year-old weapon is still issued to certain army Special Forces units because of the acknowledged "stopping power" of its large round. It's also used by Special Operations personnel in Iraq and Afghanistan.

BELOW: A French-built Renault FT-17 light tank, followed by a light GMC truck and a pair of heavy Mack trucks, trundles across the Boureuilles bridge over the Aire River south of Varennes on September 28, 1918. Two days earlier at the start of the Meuse-Argonne Offensive, the freshly blown structure had blocked the advance of the 35th Division's 129th Field Artillery, forcing the horse-drawn regiment—including Captain Harry S. Truman's Battery D—to pull its guns across the shredded ground of "no man's land" and the German trench system.

LEFT: The 369th Infantry, 93d Division, trains near Maffrecourt on May 4, 1918. These black troops wear French Adrian helmets plus brown leather belts and pouches with their otherwise American uniforms because their unit had been seconded to the French Army. Just days after this photo was taken, they were incorporated into the French 16th Division, then later the 161st Division, where the Germans they fought nicknamed them the "Hellfighters."

RIGHT INSET: The standard-issue American trench knife and sheath, c. 1917. Knives were held so that the triangle-shape spikes could be used like brass knuckles during man-to-man combat in the narrow confines of a trench.

ABOVE: Soldiers of the 1st Division's 28th Infantry rest during a road movement near Soissons on July 16, 1918. The "Big Red One" had seized the town and its key road and rail junction at the cost of more than seven hundred dead and wounded.

Citation: General Freddie Stowers distinguished himself with exceptional heroism on September 28, 1918, while serving as a squad leader in Company C, 371st Infantry Regiment, 93d Division. His company led the attack on Hill 188, Champagne-Marne Sector, France, during World War I.

A few minutes after the attack began, the enemy ceased firing and began climbing up onto the parapets of the trenches, holding up their arms as if surrendering. The enemy's actions caused the American forces to cease fire and come out into the open. As the company started forward and got within about one hundred meters of the trench line, the enemy jumped back into their trenches and greeted Stowers' company with interlocking bands of machine gun fire and mortar fire, killing well over 50 percent. Faced with incredible enemy resistance, Stowers took charge, setting such an example of personal bravery and leadership that he inspired his men to follow him in the attack. With extraordinary heroism and complete disregard of personal danger under devastating fire, he crawled forward, leading his squad toward an enemy machine gun nest that was causing heavy casualties to his company. After fierce fighting, the machine-gun position was destroyed, and the enemy soldiers were killed. Displaying great courage and intrepidity, Stowers continued to press the attack against a determined enemy. While urging his men to continue crawling forward with him to attack a second trench line, he was gravely hit by machine-gun fire. Although Stowers was mortally wounded, he pressed forward, advancing the members of his squad until he died. Inspired by Stowers' efforts, his company continued the attack against incredible odds, contributing to the capture of Hill 188 and causing heavy enemy casualties. Stowers' conspicuous gallantry, extraordinary heroism, and supreme devotion to his men went well above and beyond the call of duty, following the finest traditions of military service and reflecting the utmost credit on him and the United States Army.

"Ammunition!"

And remember –
Bonds buy Bullets!

ABOVE: Standard issue American trench knife, 1918

Germans learned that U.S. soldiers were entering the line, orders were issued that "American units appearing on the front should be hit particularly hard" in order to quickly establish their dominance over the green Yankees. They soon found, however, that American attacks "were carried out smartly and ruthlessly," and that "the moral effect of our fire did not materially check the advance of the infantry." American losses during the offensive exceeded 25,800.

The Germans made one last desperate bid to strike across the Marne toward Paris and, at the same time, take the important French city of Rheims with a second prong of the attack further to the east. The French stopped this eastern effort with little difficulty and the AEF, whose units included the 26th, 28th, and 42d divisions, the 369th Infantry, and supporting elements (in all, about eighty-five thousand Americans when the 3d Division was added). The western prong was principally a renewed assault on the 3d Division. Beginning with a great barrage of artillery on July 15, the Germans attempted to cross the river under a cover of fog and a smoke screen. Throwing in everything they had, the Germans proved to be unstoppable in their initial, overwhelming rush, although the 3d Division inflicted heavy casualties on the

BELOW LEFT: This campaign service coat, c. 1914, belonged to Jonas P. Peterman, Company B, 305th Infantry.

BELOW RIGHT: An Illinois National Guard first sergeant in the 33d Division wore this musician's coat during World War I. However, it's made in the 1912 pattern, so the insignia color should have been bronze to match the buttons. This gilt example demonstrates that uniform insignia was not completely standardized yet.

BOTTOM: Company A, 9th Machine Gun Battalion, sets up this machine gun in a railroad shop at Château-Thierry on June 7, 1918. The M1914 Hotchkiss pictured here and in the poster on the opposite page was the machine gun most widely used by U.S. forces during the war.

ABOVE: Major General Joseph Theodore Dickman, commander of the 3d Division

RIGHT: The skipper and gunner sit in a Renault FT17 tank with its hatches open, northwest of Verdun.

BELOW: Armored Tank Corps patch

BACKGROUND: Tank 2367, a Renault FT, was ditched near the Moselle River when it ran out of gas after eight hours of action on September 12, 1918—the opening day of the St. Mihiel operation.

attackers. The division's 38th Infantry was assailed across its front and flanks, but the resolute doughboys held on. When asked by a French commander if his division could hold, Major General Joseph Dickman replied, "*Nous resterons la*"—"We shall remain there."

To the right of the 3d Division, deployed along the south bank of the Marne River, was a French division. Attached to the French was a battalion of the U.S. 28th Division, National Guardsmen from Pennsylvania. As the German attack reached and began crossing the Marne River, the French units were forced to withdraw but did not inform the guardsmen. The Keystone soldiers fought against a force many times their own number, delaying and inflicting heavy losses on the Germans, but ultimately most of the Pennsylvanians were killed or captured. Nonetheless, their bravery and sacrifice helped make the remarkable stand of the 3d Division possible. Down river of the Pennsylvanians, Company E men of the division's 38th Infantry, who had survived the hours of shelling, met every German attempt with rifle and automatic-weapon fire. Scores of boats were shattered and sunk or else disabled and sent drifting harmlessly down the river. Hundreds of the enemy jumped into the water and were drowned, while those who reached the American-held shore by swimming were either killed or captured.

However, the Germans made a successful crossing further up river from Château-Thierry. Dickman, the 3d's commander, prepared to counterattack. Although his French corps commander advised him to wait, the 3d struck anyway and threw the enemy back across the river. From this action, the 3d Division is known as the "Marne" or the "Rock of the Marne." The 38th Infantry, which gets the lion's share of the credit for the victory, wears the phrase "Rock of the Marne" on its regimental badge. The badge also shows a chevron broken in the center, which indicates that the 38th broke the point of the German drive on the Marne. The crest of the badge shows a boulder to signify the 38th's strength as the "Rock of the Marne," while the 10th Field Artillery, which supported the 38th Infantry, has a crossed cannon supporting a rock on its unit badge to indicate its part in the action. Said Pershing:

A single regiment of the 3d Division wrote one of the most brilliant pages in our military annals. It prevented the crossing at certain points on its front, while on either flank, the Germans who had gained a footing pressed forward. Our men, firing in three directions, met the German attacks with counterattacks at critical points and succeeded in throwing two German divisions into complete confusion, capturing six hundred prisoners.

LEFT: During Germany's Champagne-Marne Offensive in July 1818, the 109th Infantry Regiment's L and M companies were attached to a French division on the front line when, in the early hours of July 15, the German 36th Division crossed the Marne River and attacked the Allied front. The adjacent French units fell back, leaving L and M companies surrounded. Wave after wave of Germans attacked the Pennsylvanians, but despite the overwhelming odds, the two companies stubbornly held their position and inflicted heavy casualties before fighting their way back to the front line, which was now five kilometers to the rear. Of the five hundred assigned officers and men, only one hundred fifty remained.

Citation: For conspicuous gallantry and intrepidity above and beyond the call of duty. During the attack, the 2d and 3d battalions of the 28th Infantry merged, and after several hours of severe fighting, they successfully established a front-line position. In so doing, a gap was left between the right flank of the French 153d Division on their left and the left flank of the 28th Infantry, exposing their own left flank to a terrific enfilade from several enemy machine guns in a rock quarry on high ground. Parker, observing this serious situation, ordered his depleted platoon to follow him in an attack upon the strong point. Meeting a disorganized group of French colonials wandering about without a leader, he persuaded them to join his platoon. This consolidated group followed Parker through direct enemy rifle and machine-gun fire to the crest of the hill. Rushing forward, they took the quarry by storm, capturing six machine guns and about forty prisoners. When the assault continued the next day, Parker supported the 1st Battalion. Although painfully wounded in the foot, he refused to be evacuated and continued to lead his command until they reached their objective. Noting the gap between the assault battalion and the French, Parker led his men through this heavy fire to the left of the 1st Battalion, thereby closing the gap. He remained in command of his battalion until the newly established lines of the 28th Infantry were thoroughly consolidated. While supervising the consolidation of the new position, Parker's painful wound compels him to crawl about on his hands and knees. His conspicuous gallantry and spirit of self-sacrifice were a source of great inspiration to the members of the entire command.

BELOW: The legendary Signal Corps Pigeon "President Wilson" was bred in France and known for his speed. In early 1918 he performed a valuable service for the American Tank Corps. After the St. Mihiel operation, he was assigned to a unit headed for the Meuse-Argonne Offensive. In the midst of an intense firefight at Grand Pre on the morning of November 5, 1918, "President Wilson" was dispatched with an important message for his home base at Rampont, forty kilometers away. Despite having a leg shot away and being wounded in the breast, he reached his destination in the remarkable time of twenty-five minutes. After the Armistice, the heroic pigeon was returned to the Signal Corps Breeding and Training Center at Fort Monmouth, New Jersey, where he died on June 8, 1929, and subsequently was "preserved" for posterity.

ST. MIHIEL

By July 17, the last great offensive had petered out, and the initiative passed to the Allies. The Germans had gained considerable ground since March, but failed to achieve a decisive advantage at any point along the front. Furthermore, what successes they could claim had been bought at an enormous price in manpower and matériel. Their more than six hundred thousand casualties were irreplaceable, while the Allied loss of some eight hundred thousand men was more than compensated for by the deluge of new American units. These units had been arriving at the Western Front in such numbers that the Allies now solidly outnumbered the Germans. The German people had also built up great hopes for the success of this *Friedensturm* (peace offensive); its failure was a tremendous psychological blow to the whole nation. Other factors also contributed to the decline of German morale, notably the pinch of the British blockade and the effectiveness of Allied propaganda—and the Allies took this opportunity to move to the offensive.

A French-American offensive to eliminate the Marne salient that the Germans had punched toward Paris was conducted from mid-July through the first week of August. Eight AEF divisions—more than a quarter million men—spearheaded much of the advance, demonstrating offensive capabilities that helped to inspire new confidence in the war-weary Allied armies. This was immediately followed by a British drive in the Somme in which two American divisions took part. Even more divisions were in action intermittently as part of the French armies after the Marne salient was eliminated, gaining valuable combat experience as the Germans were driven steadily back toward the Belgian border. These later British and French operations had involved another quarter million U.S. troops, and the AEF was now ready to test its own field army against the Germans. With the elimination of the Marne and Amiens salients, only one major threat remained to lateral rail communications behind the Allied lines—the deep gouge that the Germans had driven to St. Mihiel on the Meuse River that stretched almost to the Paris-Nancy line.

General Pershing's first great American offensive was to be a nine-division assault into the base of this giant bulge, with three more divisions in reserve. A success here would not only free the main rail link between Paris and Nancy from German interdiction, but also remove the Germans blocking the line running north to yet another, and much larger, American thrust north toward the vital communications center at Sedan. These twin drives were scheduled to take place literally back to back and were to be launched by a single formation, the new U.S. First Army, which would also have significant French forces under its command during the St. Mihiel operation. If successful, the First Army's launching of a double offensive would be a feat that no French or British

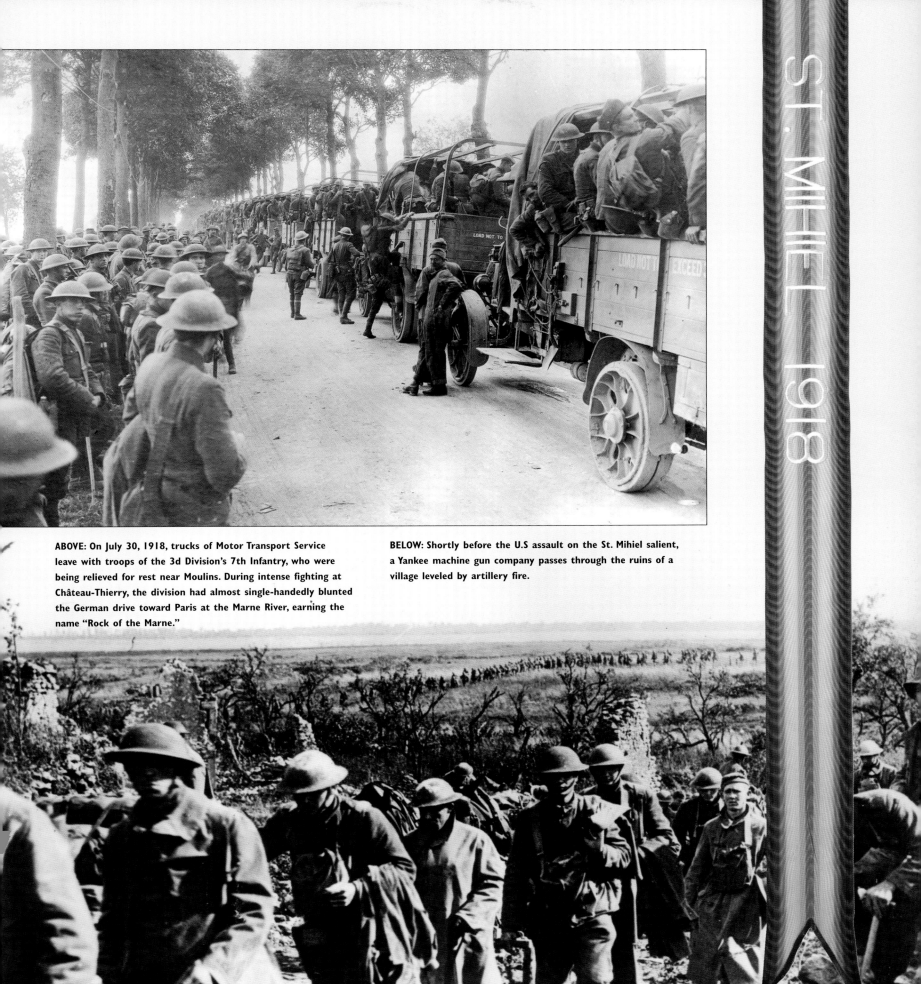

ABOVE: On July 30, 1918, trucks of Motor Transport Service leave with troops of the 3d Division's 7th Infantry, who were being relieved for rest near Moulins. During intense fighting at Château-Thierry, the division had almost single-handedly blunted the German drive toward Paris at the Marne River, earning the name "Rock of the Marne."

BELOW: Shortly before the U.S assault on the St. Mihiel salient, a Yankee machine gun company passes through the ruins of a village leveled by artillery fire.

ABOVE: Brigadier General Palmer E. Pierce, commander of the 54th Infantry Brigade, 27th Infantry Division.

BELOW INSET: This map case was used by Pierce during the war.

RIGHT: Lieutenant Colonel Ruby D. Garrett, chief signal officer of the 42d Division, tests a field telephone left behind by the Germans during their hasty retreat from the St. Mihiel salient in Essey, France, on September 19, 1918.

BOTTOM: On September 13, 1918, soldiers of the 107th Infantry, 27th Division, hurriedly advance along a path that a tank has just cleared through barbed-wire entanglements near Beauquesne in the Somme area of France. One man has tripped over the wire or has been shot.

army had been able to pull off during the war and would pave the way for an American-French drive into traditionally German territory in mid-November—the carrying of the war into Germany itself.

AEF units scattered from Flanders on the western end of the front to Switzerland hundreds of miles to the southeast and were put into motion in a complex series of night movements designed to secretly position them for the operations. Although the American divisions contained ample infantry and machine-gun units for the attack, the earlier priority given to shipment of infantry meant that little heavy equipment or weaponry was on hand. The French made up this deficiency by assigning enough artillery and aviation units to ensure that the First Army would be a well-balanced force, with the result that roughly half the aircraft, tanks, and artillery units commanded by Pershing at St. Mihiel were made and manned by Frenchmen.

The offensive began on September 12 with a threefold assault on the salient. The main attack was made against the south face by the AEF's I Corps with, left to right, the 2d, 5th, 90th, and 82d divisions along the line, plus the 78th in reserve, then IV Corps composed of the 1st, 42d, and 89th divisions in line with the 3d in reserve. A secondary thrust was carried out against the west face along the Heights of the Meuse by V Corps made up of the 4th and 26th divisions, 8th Brigade, and the French 15th Colonial Division, while other French units of the French II Colonial Corps conducted holding attacks across the north. In all, more than six hundred fifty thousand troops, some five hundred fifty thousand of them American, stormed the salient supported by four hundred tanks, three thousand guns, and, in what was the largest single air operation of the war thus far, six hundred aircraft.

The attack went so well that Pershing ordered the offensive speeded up, and the following morning saw the 1st Division, advancing from the east, link up with the 26th Division, moving in from the west. By evening, all objectives were captured. The Americans' task had been immeasurably eased by the Germans, who were now desperately short of manpower, having wisely begun a step-by-step withdrawal from the salient only the day before the offensive began. Nevertheless, many soldiers died and sixteen thousand were taken prisoner. The total Allied casualties came to seven thousand men. With the threat to the rear of the coming Meuse-Argonne offensive removed, Pershing quickly began to redeploy most of his victorious forces so that they could join those still forming to the north, and he looked forward to St. Mihiel as an important staging area for his planned invasion of Germany.

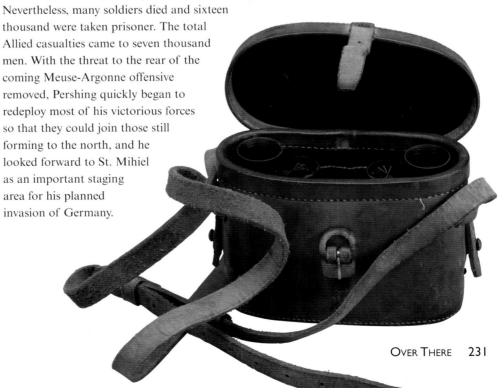

RIGHT: Stubborn German resistance on Montrefagne just north of Exermont forced 1st Division troops to dig in during the assault on the hill in October 1918.

BELOW INSET: This Mark II fragmentation grenade has gray paint on the body and red paint near the pin, and is from the World War I era.

BOTTOM: Soldiers of the 332d Infantry, attached to the Italian 31st Division, hurl hand grenades at an Austrian trench near Varage, Italy, during fighting on the Piave front on September 16, 1918.

THE "BIG PUSH"

Just two weeks after St. Mihiel, the Allied armies under Marshal Ferdinand Foch of France began the great attack, which shattered the German Army and led to its surrender. Foch assigned the Meuse-Argonne sector to the AEF, which prepared for its part in the offensive with a far greater degree of stealth than was required of the French and British to the west. All men and weapons moved entirely under cover of darkness; during daylight they stopped all activity and concealed themselves in the forests and wooded areas that covered most of the region. At night, roads leading into the area were jammed with men and guns, and along the front (which in this area had barely moved since the beginning of the war), French soldiers stayed in outpost positions until the last minute to keep the Germans from seeing any Americans or capturing any who might indicate an attack was coming. Only during the very last stages of the gigantic six-hundred-thousand-man movement did the Germans get even the slightest hint of what was to come.

Pershing decided to strike his heaviest blow in a zone about twenty miles wide between the Heights of the Meuse on the east and the western edge of the high, rough, and densely wooded Argonne Forest. This was difficult terrain, broken by a central north-south ridge that dominates the valleys of the Meuse and Aire rivers. Three heavily fortified areas—Montfaucon, Cunel, and Barricourt—as well as numerous strong points, prevented penetration of the elaborate German defenses that extended behind the entire front. This fortified system consisted of three main defense lines backed up by a fourth line that was not as well-constructed. Pershing hoped to launch an attack with enough momentum to drive through these lines into the open area beyond, where his troops could then strike at the exposed German flanks and, in a coordinated drive with the French Fourth Army coming up on the left, cut the Sedan-Mézières railroad.

Many untried divisions had to be placed in the vanguard of the attacking forces. On the twenty-mile Meuse-Argonne front, where the main American attack was to be made, Pershing disposed three corps side by side, each with three divisions in line and one in reserve. In the center opposite Montfaucon was the V Corps commanding, from left to right, the 91st, 37th, and 79th divisions, with the 32d in reserve. On the right was the III Corps, from left to right, the 4th, 80th, and 33d divisions, with the 3d in reserve. I Corps was on the left, fielding the 77th, 28th, and 35th divisions, from left to right, with the 92d in reserve and the French Fourth Army on its western flank.

Finally, on the night of September 25, the First Army stood on its new front, ready for the battle that was to begin at dawn. By the following evening, the strong German first

ABOVE: This French V-B rifle grenade was manufactured for use with Springfield rifles.

Citation: For conspicuous gallantry and intrepidity above and beyond the call of duty in action with the enemy. On the morning of September 26, 1918, during the advance of the 364th Infantry, Bronson was struck by an exploding enemy hand grenade, receiving deep cuts on his face and the back of his head. He nevertheless participated in the action, which resulted in the capture of an enemy dugout and a great number of prisoners. This attack was difficult and extremely hazardous because they had to advance without cover and, from an exposed position, throw hand grenades and phosphorous bombs to compel the enemy to surrender.

On the afternoon of the same day, Bronson was painfully wounded in the left arm by an enemy rifle bullet. After receiving first aid treatment, he was directed to the rear. Disregarding this instruction, Bronson remained on duty with his company through the night, despite suffering from severe pain and shock. On the morning of September 27, his regiment resumed its attack on the village of Eclisfontaine. Bronson's Company H was left supporting the attacking line, Company E. He gallantly joined that company in spite of his wounds and helped capture the village.

After that, he remained with Company E and assisted in the capture of an enemy machine gun, killing the enemy gunner himself. Shortly after this encounter, the company was compelled to retire due to the heavy enemy artillery barrage. During this retirement Bronson, who was the last man to leave the advanced position, was wounded again in both arms by an enemy high-explosive shell. Another officer helped him take cover and applied first aid. Although faint from the profuse loss of blood, Bronson remained with the survivors of the company throughout the night of the second day, refusing to go to the rear for treatment. His conspicuous gallantry and spirit of self-sacrifice were a source of great inspiration to the members of the entire command.

ABOVE: *On September 29, 1918, the fourth day of the Meuse-Argonne Offensive, the wounded are treated at the 137th Field Hospital by the 110th Sanitary Train, 35th Division, which set up operations in a shattered church in Neuvilly. An empty stretcher has been placed between the wounded and the DOWs (died of wounds) to provide the living with a degree of psychological separation.*

THE AEF'S BLOODIEST GROUND

During the opening phase of the Meuse-Argonne Offensive, the long line of American divisions that stretched from the center of the attack east to the Meuse River all advanced more or less abreast. This was not true, however, on the left flank, where the dense Argonne Forest extended all the way up to the bluffs along the Aire River Valley. Here, the 28th Division's lines were bent far back to the rear, beyond the left of its hard-charging 110th Infantry, because its other regiments couldn't make much progress in the forest.

The situation was even worse on the 28th's left, where the 77th Division made no gains at all for a time. As a result, the western end of the American Expeditionary Forces' line resembled a descending staircase with the 110th as the top step. From

September 26 through 29, this "staircase" on the left generally moved apace with the Pennsylvania Guardsmen of the 110th Infantry and the Missouri-Kansas Guardsmen of the 35th Division to their right across the Aire.

In and of itself, this came as no surprise to any of the senior commanders at brigade level and higher since the campaign plan did not call for a strong effort against the forest defenses. The mission of the 28th and 35th divisions was to plunge ahead as far and as fast as possible to the right of the obstacle so that the Germans in the Argonne would be compelled to withdraw on their own or be cut off. But as the Romans had learned in the time

of Caesar (and the Allies would learn in the Ardennes two decades hence), the Germans were not shy about pushing forces into such terrain and fighting it out.

Road congestion that hampered the movement of the 28th's artillery—and restrictions imposed to prevent the accidental killing of U.S. troops by their own guns—resulted in almost no American and French shells falling into the wide expanse of forest on the 35th Division's ever-lengthening left flank until the fourth day of the assault. This flank, despite the presence of the 110th Infantry, was completely open to German observation and directed fire. The Germans did not withdraw for fear of encirclement and capture, according to German XVI Corps chief of staff Major Herman von Giehrl. Instead, they poured significant light artillery into the area ensuring that "the enemy infantry suffered

LEFT: *This British-issue helmet was used by an American soldier. A bullet, which tore through the helmet, entered the rear and left this gaping exit hole in the front. The helmet liner, which has been torn loose, is visible in the exit hole.*

BELOW: *18th Infantry soldiers of the 1st Division scurry for cover as a German barrage begins to fall on Exermont on October 7, 1918. Both the 1st and 35th divisions suffered very heavy casualties in the town and its environs.*

First Lieutenant Dwite H. Schaffner
306th Infantry Regiment, 77th Division

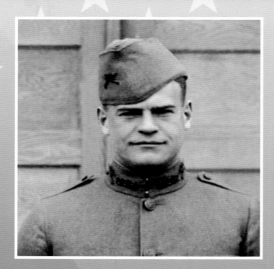

Citation: Schaffner led his men in an attack on St. Hubert's Pavilion through terrific enemy machine gun, rifle, and artillery fire and drove the enemy from a strongly held entrenched position after hand-to-hand fighting. His bravery and contempt for danger inspired his men, enabling them to hold fast in the face of three determined enemy counterattacks. With his company's position exposed to enemy fire from both flanks, he made three efforts to locate an enemy machine gun that had caused heavy casualties. On his third reconnaissance he discovered the gun position and personally silenced the gun, killing or wounding the crew.

The third counterattack made by the enemy was initiated by the appearance of a small detachment in advance of the enemy attacking wave. When almost within reach of the American front line, the enemy appeared behind them, attacking vigorously with pistols, rifles, and hand grenades, causing heavy casualties in the American platoon. Schaffner mounted the parapet of the trench and used his pistol and grenades to kill a number of enemy soldiers. When he finally reached the enemy captain leading the attacking forces, he shot and mortally wounded him with his pistol. He dragged the captured officer back to the company's trench, coaxing him to reveal valuable information about the enemy's strength and position. The information enabled Schaffner to maintain for hours the advanced position of his company, despite the fact that strong enemy forces bordered it on three sides. The undaunted bravery, gallant soldierly conduct, and leadership displayed by Schaffner undoubtedly saved the survivors of the company from death or capture.

particularly from the flanking fire of thirteen field batteries, which, from their position on the eastern edge of the Argonne, constantly held up the advance."

The battlefield typography tended to mask the Pennsylvanians from enemy artillery observers, and the dastardly "Huns," displaying no respect for American divisional boundaries, directed a murderous fire over their heads and into the 35th. These infantry regiments frequently complained of being shelled by their own units because much of this German fire was coming not just from their flank but literally from behind them, too. Several days later, the Pennsylvanians of the 110th Infantry and the rest of

RIGHT: *This type of first aid packet was regularly carried by U.S. troops.*

BELOW: *Near Varennes, a soldier of Company E, 110th Infantry (formerly the 3d and 10th infantry regiments of the Pennsylvania National Guard), receives first aid from a comrade after receiving a bullet wound to the face on September 26, 1918.*

the 28th Division started to receive their full share of Teutonic abuse.

The 35th Division's four-day average of two thousand casualties every twenty-four hours represents one of the highest daily loss rates of any U.S. division during the war. By contrast, the loss rate of formations on its flanks was fewer than four hundred men per day. The 28th Division suffered 2,916 casualties in eight days of combat (September 26–October 3), and the 91st on the 35th's right experienced 4,735 over twelve days (September 26–October 7). The German army's firm determination to block the drive up the Aire Valley was made painfully evident by their shifting of more and more forces, including elite Guard divisions, to its defense.

The same artillery that wracked the 35th Division was still active when the 1st Division took over its sector. The nearly unimpeded use of these guns on the Big Red One's left flank inflicted most of its dead and wounded. The 1st Division initially reported 9,186 men lost before being pulled out on October 12. Although this number was later adjusted down to 6,629, the 1st and 35th's 14,600 to 17,000 casualties— roughly one of every eight soldiers who fell in the battle—turned the few miles from the Varennes-Cheppy area through Exermont and Hill 240 into the American Expeditionary Forces' bloodiest ground of the war.

LEFT: *III Corps commander Major General John L. Hines (left) and 90th Division commander Major General Henry T. Allen just south of Stenay, France, in the valley of the Meuse River on November 16, 1918.*

BELOW: *Road congestion during the Meuse-Argonne Offensive was so great that the streams of vehicles were not able to move faster than an average of two miles an hour. This scene in the ruins of Esnes during the first day of the attack is typical.*

BELOW: Black National Guardsmen of the 369th Infantry (formerly the 15th New York Regiment) storm the fortified town of Sechault during the final offensive in the Champagne region. The September 29, 1918, seizure of Sechault earned the Croix de Guerre, or "War Cross," for the entire regiment from a grateful French government. Its sister units, the 371st and 372d infantries, fought immediately to their west in a different French division. During this action, Lieutenant George S. Robb of the 369th earned a Medal of Honor for his actions when, as the sole surviving (though severely wounded) officer in his company, he successfully led his men in fierce, costly fighting. As the only officer in his battalion to advance beyond the town, he organized its defense before being wounded again. The 369th lost nearly a third of its soldiers during the two days of fighting but kept intact its proud record as "the regiment that never lost a man captured, a trench, or a foot of ground." Today's 369th Corps Support Battalion, New York Army National Guard, carries on the traditions of the "Harlem Hellfighters."

ABOVE: On October 8, 1918, Corporal Alvin C. York of the 328th Infantry, 82d Division, assumed command near Chatel-Chéhéry after his platoon had suffered heavy casualties, including losing three other noncommissioned officers. Leading seven men, he charged a machine-gun nest that was pouring deadly, incessant fire upon his platoon. He took control of the machine-gun nest, along with 132 German prisoners and several more machine guns.

position was in American hands. As the American front advanced in the middle, on its left side, just as Grant plunged into the wilderness in 1864, so Pershing's men plunged into the deadly Argonne Forest in 1918. The forest was a mass of barbed wire strung from tree to tree; death was everywhere. Carefully hidden machine gun nests spouted fire into advancing Americans. Two notable incidents of this phase of the campaign were the fight of the "Lost Battalion" of the 77th Division (October 2–7), and the feat of Corporal (later Sergeant) Alvin C. York, who single-handedly killed fifteen Germans and captured 132 on October 8.

Before the third and final phase of the campaign, which extended from November 1 until the war ended eleven days later, many of the First Army's exhausted divisions were replaced, roads were built or repaired, and supply was improved. When the final assault began, penetration was rapid and spectacular. Despite the Germans' strenuous efforts to strengthen their fourth line of defense, V Corps in the center advanced about six miles the first day, compelling the German units west of the Meuse to hurriedly withdraw. On November 4, III Corps forced a crossing of the Meuse and advanced northeast toward Montmédy, and elements of V Corps occupied the heights opposite Sedan on November 7. This accomplished the First Army's chief mission: denial of the Sedan-Mézières railroad to the Germans, and the

THE "LOST BATTALION"

On October 2, 1918, elements of the 77th Division that were advancing through the dense Argonne Forest were cut off by Germans who erected barbed wire entanglements and a fighting position behind them. Made up principally of men from six companies of the 308th Infantry, plus two more from the 306th Machine Gun Battalion and one from the 307th Infantry, the "Lost Battalion" originally was thought to have been destroyed, but its soldiers were holding out in the face of unrelenting attacks.

Carrier pigeons released by the unit to tell of its plight failed to get through, and finally they were down to their last bird, "Cher Ami." A note with the men's location was attached to the pigeon's leg, and she flew into the smoke of the battle. Despite losing a leg and most of a wing, Cher Ami made it to headquarters, allowing the 77th to launch costly, but ultimately successful, attempts to rescue the battalion. Only 252 of the 700 men who had made the first attack survived the five days of fighting. And just 191 were able to walk out on their own feet by the time the new attacks forced the Germans back.

A Medal of Honor citation was given to Major Charles W. Whittlesey; second-in-command Major George G. McMurtry; and Captain Nelson M. Holderman, whose Company K, 307th Infantry, managed to reach and reinforce Whittlesey's battered command. The citations read in part:

Major Charles W. Whittlesey

Major George G. McMurtry

Captain Nelson M. Holderman

"Although cut off for 5 days from the remainder of his division, Maj. Whittlesey maintained his position and held his command... together in the face of superior numbers of the enemy....No rations or other supplies reached him, in spite of determined efforts, which were made by his division. On the 4th day Maj. Whittlesey received from the enemy a written proposition to surrender, which he treated with contempt, although he was at the time out of rations and had suffered a loss of about 50 percent in killed and wounded."

"Although wounded in the knee by shrapnel on 4 October and suffering great pain, he continued throughout the entire period to encourage his officers and men with a restless optimism that contributed largely toward preventing panic and disorder among the troops, who were without food, cut off from communication with our lines.... During a heavy barrage, he personally directed and supervised the moving of the wounded to shelter before himself seeking shelter. On 6 October he was again wounded in the shoulder by a German grenade, but continued personally to organize and direct the defense."

"...was wounded on 4, 5, and 7 October, but throughout the entire period, suffering great pain and subjected to fire of every character, he continued personally to lead and encourage the officers and men under his command with unflinching courage and with distinguished success. On 6 October, in a wounded condition, he rushed through enemy machine gun and shell fire and carried two wounded men to a place of safety."

BELOW: The unwounded survivors of the "Lost Battalion" rest near Binarville after their relief.

Citation: On the afternoon of October 16, 1918, when the Cote-de-Chatillion had just been gained after bitter fighting and the summit of that strong bulwark in the Kriemhilde Stellung was being organized, Private Neibaur was sent out on patrol with his automatic rifle squad to enfilade enemy machine-gun nests.

As he gained the ridge he set up his automatic rifle and was directly thereafter wounded in both legs by fire from a hostile machine-gun on his flank. The advance wave of the enemy troops, counterattacking, had about gained the ridge, and although practically cut off and surrounded, the remainder of his detachment being killed or wounded, this gallant soldier kept his automatic rifle in operation to such effect that by his own efforts and by fire from the skirmish line of his company, at least 100 yards in his rear, the attack was checked. The enemy wave being halted and lying prone, 4 of the enemy attacked Neibaur at close quarters. These he killed.

He then moved alone among the enemy lying on the ground about him, in the midst of the fire from his own lines, and by coolness and gallantry captured 11 prisoners at the point of his pistol and, although painfully wounded, brought them back to our lines. The counterattack in full force was arrested to a large extent by the single efforts of this soldier, whose heroic exploits took place against the skyline in full view of his entire battalion.

ABOVE: A World War I Victory Medal. Note that the medal's ribbon design matches the battle streamers on page 234.

AEF's boundary was shifted eastward so that the French Fourth Army would have the honor of capturing Sedan, which had fallen to the Prussians in 1870.

In this largest campaign in American history up to that time, the First Army suffered a loss of about 117,000 killed and wounded. It captured 26,000 prisoners, 847 cannons, 3,000 machine guns, and huge quantities of matériel. More than 1,200,000 American troops had taken part in the forty-seven-day campaign. In his *Final Report* on the Meuse-Argonne Campaign, General Pershing noted with pride that:

Between September 26 and November 11, twenty-two American and four French divisions, on the front extending from southeast of Verdun to the Argonne Forest, had engaged and decisively beaten forty-seven different German divisions, representing 25 percent of the enemy's entire divisional strength on the Western Front.

ABOVE: General of the Armies John J. Pershing. He wears just three of his many decorations, a Distinguished Service Medal and Croix de Guerre (War Cross) with Palm flanking a rare Médaille Militaire (Military Medal), one of the very few awarded for service in the 1st World War. Originally established in 1852 to recognize acts of bravery by enlisted men and noncommissioned officers, it was later approved as the supreme award for leadership to generals and admirals who had served as commanders in chief. Its franchise has since been greatly expanded.

ABOVE: The Distinguished Service Medal, established in 1918, was awarded for exceptionally meritorious service in a position of great responsibility.

FAR LEFT: The service coat worn by General Pershing during the war. It is adorned by the service ribbon of the decoration he most prized, the Distinguished Service Medal.

ABOVE: New York Guardsmen from the 369th Infantry proudly wear the Croix de Guerre awarded to them by the French Army. *Front row left to right*: Private Ed Williams, Private Herbert Taylor, Private Leon Fraitor, and Private Ralph Hawkins. *Back row left to right*: Sergeant H.D. Prinas, Sergeant Dan Storms, Private Joe Williams, Private Alfred Hanley, and Corporal T.W. Taylor.

RIGHT: Pershing awards medals to officers in France. Nearly all of the officers—including Pershing—wear spurs on their boots. The Distinguished Service Medal, established in 1918, was awarded for exceptionally meritorious service in a position of great responsibility.

Chapter Seven

Between Two Wars, 1919–1941

The Germans had long seen the writing on the wall: Their inability to defeat the French and British even when massively reinforced with whole armies from the Eastern Front, the impossibility of keeping pace with the relentless influx of aggressive American troops, and the rapidly deteriorating situation on the home front all prompted its military leaders to quickly conclude an armistice while they still had at least some ability to influence events. For the two million doughboys in France, however, the armistice meant only one thing—that they could go home!

Almost as soon as the guns fell silent on the eleventh hour of the eleventh day of the eleventh month in 1918, units began to be cycled back to the very ports where they had arrived, in some cases, only a few short months before. But not all the soldiers would be leaving any time soon. The armistice required Germany to evacuate all invaded and occupied territory in Belgium, Luxembourg, and France (including the long-disputed Alsace-Lorraine territory), and to withdraw her armies across the Rhine River. It also provided that the Allied forces, Americans in particular, be permitted to occupy bridgeheads, eighteen miles in radius, east of the Rhine at Cologne, Mayence, and Coblenz. A neutral zone in which neither the Allies nor Germany could maintain troops would extend another six miles from these bridgeheads.

Throughout the liberated districts of France and Luxembourg, the doughboys were received with wild demonstrations of joy. However, upon entering Germany they were met with the same mixture of curiosity and suspicion that had greeted American units in Alsace-Lorraine during the war. In the end, the fine conduct of the men—plus the firmness and justice of the American commanders—quickly quieted

4th Division shoulder patch with Army of Occupation symbol, 1919

any apprehensions that the civil population may have had, and no incidents of hostility took place. The new American Second Army, which had been slated to strike toward Fortress Metz, took temporary possession of a large swath of French territory southwest of Luxembourg that was still under German control, most of Luxembourg itself, and enough of Belgium and the German Moselle on either side of the French-Lux territory to create a corridor to the Rhine River. Beyond Luxembourg, through the German Rhineland, the even newer Third Army occupied the rest of the corridor through to Coblenz.

The leading elements of the Third Army, wearing shoulder patches containing a large, white "A" within a red "O" for "Army of Occupation," reached the Rhine on December 9, 1918, and along with the British and French on its flanks, crossed the river four days later. In the meantime, the transfer of troops to the United States had been progressing rapidly, and the army did not intend to keep its forces in Germany any longer than it had to. Marshal Foch wished to retain a large American force of at least fifteen divisions in Europe but was told that the army would be withdrawn as soon as possible. President Wilson finally agreed that American representation in the occupied territory would be only a regimental-size organization, to be known as the "American Forces in Germany," which would serve, as the French said, merely to keep the American flag on the Rhine.

By May 19, 1919, all American combat divisions, except five in occupied German territory, had received their embarkation orders to sail for home. The units of the Army of Occupation were relieved as fast as practicable during the summer of 1919, and the Third Army was officially dissolved on July 2, 1919. The 1st Division—the first large body of combat troops sent to France and the last occupying German

LEFT: The cavalry's M1913 saber was designed by Lieutenant George S. Patton Jr., Master of the Sword at the Mounted Service School, Fort Riley, Kansas, in 1912.

OPPOSITE: Patton, now a colonel, commanding the 5th Cavalry at Fort Clark, Texas, in 1938. He replaced the 5th Cav's leisurely routine with a demanding training schedule, and the aging officer greatly enjoyed his all-too-brief time at the desolate post.

G S Patton Jr
Col. 5th Cav.

WORLD WAR I AND THE EVOLUTION OF DIVISIONAL INSIGNIA

General John Pershing originally strove to minimize the distinctive state and regional character of the National Guard and National Army formations. However, as casualties mounted in the latter months of 1918, he began to look for ways to increase the men's patriotism, morale, and fighting spirit. Earlier that year an effort to simplify and speed the recognition of each deploying division's baggage and freight had led to orders for each formation to come up with a unique symbol and issue stencils for the insignia. Clever ways to further identify property by division components also were devised. For example, the 35th Division used the Santa Fe Cross in a circle and had a different background color for each brigade, with other colors filling one or two quadrants to identify regiments. Special sections carried their own colors.

This proved to be highly popular—with some divisions even running contests for the best design—and soldiers eagerly applied them, especially to the vehicles they were issued in France. Some commanders, on their own authority, had shoulder patches of these designs made for headquarters personnel and, in the case of the 81st Division, for the entire formation because they helped control units during combat. Pershing approved the use of shoulder patches based on the property control symbols, but did not issue orders for their use until after the armistice.

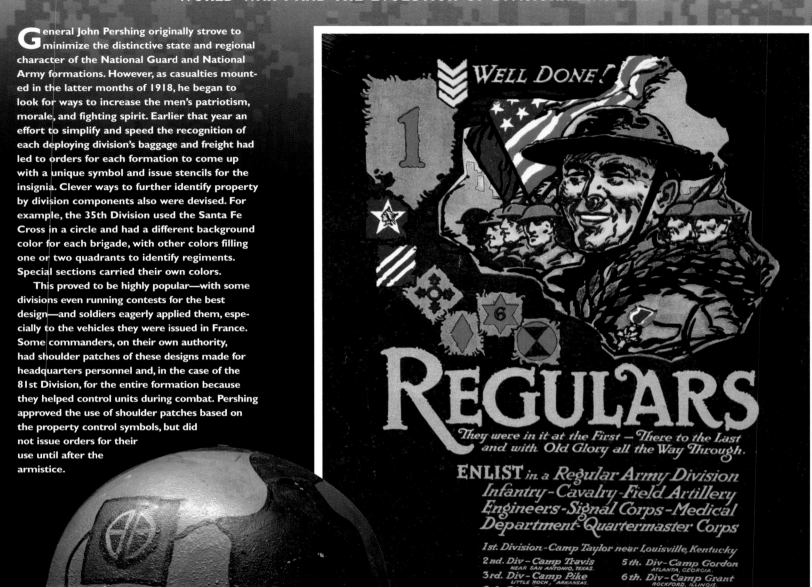

ABOVE: This 82d Division emblem painted on an M1917 helmet is from the immediate post-war period.

ABOVE: Recruiting poster from 1919

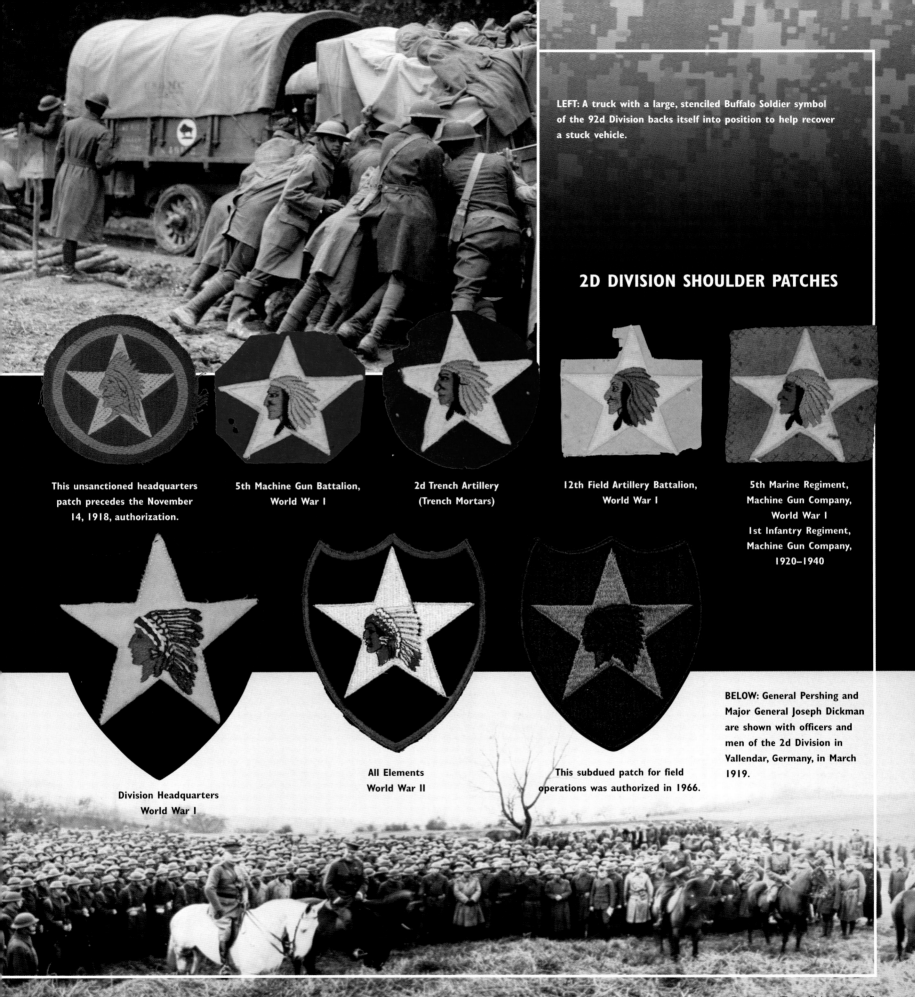

LEFT: A truck with a large, stenciled Buffalo Soldier symbol of the 92d Division backs itself into position to help recover a stuck vehicle.

2D DIVISION SHOULDER PATCHES

This unsanctioned headquarters patch precedes the November 14, 1918, authorization.

5th Machine Gun Battalion, World War I

2d Trench Artillery (Trench Mortars)

12th Field Artillery Battalion, World War I

5th Marine Regiment, Machine Gun Company, World War I
1st Infantry Regiment, Machine Gun Company, 1920–1940

Division Headquarters World War I

All Elements World War II

This subdued patch for field operations was authorized in 1966.

BELOW: General Pershing and Major General Joseph Dickman are shown with officers and men of the 2d Division in Vallendar, Germany, in March 1919.

ABOVE: Major General William S. Graves, commander, American Expeditionary Forces, Siberia.

RIGHT: Graves and Japanese General Kikuzo Otani, the senior Allied commander in Siberia (*seated third and fourth from left*) pose with their senior staff members and officers of other nations involved in the intervention, c. 1918–1919.

soil—began their movement out on August 15, and the sixty-eight-hundred-man American Forces in Germany remained on the Rhine for more than three years. The American flag on Fort Ehrenbreitstein was finally lowered on January 24, 1923, when the final thousand-man contingent of American troops boarded a train heading west. The American zone was formally turned over to the French three days later, and the French themselves later withdrew, leaving the Rhineland, under the Treaty of Versailles, a wide demilitarized zone between France and the German interior.

YANKS IN RUSSIA

Vast quantities of supplies had been sent from the western Allies to czarist Russia when that country battled their common enemies: Germany, the Austro-Hungarian Empire, and Turkey. Russia's descent into chaos and withdrawal from the war put the stockpiles at the ports of Murmansk and Archangel in northwestern Russia and Vladivostok, thousands of miles to the east on the Sea of Japan, at risk of capture by the Bolshevik revolutionaries that had seized control of the government. With great reluctance, President Wilson acquiesced to persistent Allied requests to provide American troops to help guard these supplies and support the "White Russian" counter revolutionaries against the new "Red" Army.

The American force landing at Vladivostok also had additional missions. First, it was to provide a counterweight to the Japanese contingent that ostensibly was part of the same operation, but was rightly suspected of being part of an effort to incorporate the area into Japan's empire as had already been done in Korea. Second, the American force was to assist in the withdrawal of the fifty-thousand-man Czech Legion so that it could be redeployed on the Western Front, a task that ultimately involved guarding the Trans-Siberian Railroad that ran thousands of miles into the Asian interior. These missions were to be carried out while engaged in a strict neutrality between the multiple warring factions (including factions within factions) and despite the pressure likely to be applied by the British and Japanese, who had their own agendas. Secretary of War Newton D. Baker did not envy the task awaiting 8th Division commander Major General William S. Graves, who would lead the effort, and told him: "You will be walking on eggs loaded with dynamite."

RIGHT: A long column of U.S. supply wagons near Vladivostok, Siberia, c. 1918–1919. The army's horses had an even more difficult time adjusting to the cold than the troops from the Philippines. The men spent considerable time and effort keeping the horses performing properly. The operations in Siberia buttressed the arguments of those in the army who advocated that, other than the cavalry units, the force should become completely mechanized.

LEFT: Company A soldiers of the 31st Infantry plop down in the snow and sample the food from their new rolling kitchens during a break in a December 3, 1918, practice march near Vladivostok, Siberia.

U.S. ARMY IN SIBERIA

Unlike at Archangel, the commitment of American forces to Siberia, more than eight thousand men, required a base organization at the Russian port of Vladivostok, which even included a YMCA. Alphia W. Goreham, a young private with the 31st Infantry's Company D, wrote this letter after several days of fighting that temporarily cleared the Ugolnaya-Shkotova sector. Its rail spur to nearby coal mines was key to the railroad's operation. Goreham earlier recalled that when the 31st arrived in Russia, his group had been taken to a low field and told to pitch pup tents. "We had two blankets and thin clothing," he said, "and we about froze for we had been in the Philippine Islands where it was hot. A lot of the boys caught cold and some even died of exposure so we were pretty disgusted." Later, Wilber, as Goreham was known in the unit, slipped and fell into an icy river and was fished out by his squad. He afterwards found that the $300 in bills that he had carried in his wallet had become stuck together.

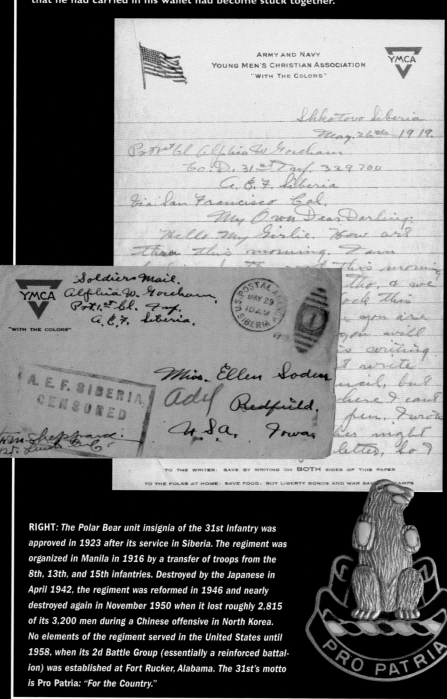

RIGHT: *The Polar Bear unit insignia of the 31st Infantry was approved in 1923 after its service in Siberia. The regiment was organized in Manila in 1916 by a transfer of troops from the 8th, 13th, and 15th infantries. Destroyed by the Japanese in April 1942, the regiment was reformed in 1946 and nearly destroyed again in November 1950 when it lost roughly 2,815 of its 3,200 men during a Chinese offensive in North Korea. No elements of the regiment served in the United States until 1958, when its 2d Battle Group (essentially a reinforced battalion) was established at Fort Rucker, Alabama. The 31st's motto is Pro Patria: "For the Country."*

BELOW: An advanced outpost of the Vologda Railway Front at Verst 455 (a marker for a Russian linear measurement, similar to kilometers), outside Archangel, Russia, on February 21, 1919. Private Art Peglow of Company I, 339th Infantry, 85th Division, watches the edge of the clearing for any indication of Bolshevik activities. The other soldiers are, *left to right*, Corporal Stanley Pigut, and privates Arnold Busberger, Eddie Egher, and George Johnston. The entrance to the log blockhouse where the men live is pictured on the right. The men are armed with the Mosin-Nagant M1891 rifle, manufactured for the Russian Army by both the Remington Arms Company and the New England Westinghouse Company. Confiscated in large numbers by the British who controlled the North Russian Theater, the rifles were supplied to the 339th Infantry along with ample American- and Russian-made 7.62-mm ammunition. The Lewis gun with Pigut—a highly prized weapon in Russia's cold weather, since water-cooled machine guns quickly froze—also was supplied by the British. The temperature at this location had plummeted to fifty degrees below zero just five days earlier. Some five thousand U.S. combat and support troops were sent to the North Russian Theater. The 339th Infantry, like its parent division, originally was composed of troops from Michigan and Wisconsin.

LEFT: Colonel George E. Stewart, commander of the 339th Infantry, appears with his regimental staff shortly after their September 4, 1918, arrival at Archangel, Russia. American Ambassador David R. Francis instructed Stewart to cooperate fully with the British effort to overthrow the Bolshevik regime. But the colonel was unaware that the ambassador was receiving repeated instructions from Secretary of State Robert Lansing only "to establish lines of operation and defense from Siberia to Archangel" even as details for their involvement in an offensive were being finalized.

Graves sailed from San Francisco with five thousand support troops and left behind his infantry regiments because his American Expeditionary Forces in Siberia (AEF Siberia) would absorb the units already being rushed to Vladivostok from the Philippines. The 27th Infantry landed on August 16, 1918, followed by the 31st Infantry five days later and 8th Division elements on September 1. Arriving well ahead of Graves and unaware that they were to attempt to be as neutral as possible under the circumstances, the 27th Infantry joined up with a Japanese division moving against a combined force of Bolsheviks and freed German prisoners in the Ussuri River Valley whom the Japanese maintained were a threat to Vladivostok. In spite of the frigid temperatures and difficult terrain, the regiment marched more than one thousand miles in pursuit of the retreating communists, resulting in the capture of their headquarters at Blagoveschensk. The White Russians, impressed with America's drive and determination, nicknamed the 27th Infantry the "Wolfhounds," and the Russian wolfhound was adopted as the unit insignia. The 31st Infantry adopted a sitting polar bear as its symbol, and it still serves as the unit's insignia, appearing on its coat of arms.

Despite a bloody flare-up in the summer of 1919 and numerous skirmishes with both communists and Cossacks, the roughly nine thousands Americans of AEF Siberia were able to maintain a truce of sorts with the multitude of warring groups. Americans occupied portions of the Trans-Siberian Railroad as much as two thousand miles down the line when U.S. forces began their gradual withdrawal from

the area in December 1919, and the last troops shipped out on April 1, 1920, as a Japanese military band played "Hard Times Come Again No More."

Meanwhile at Archangel, almost on the other side of the world, AEF North Russia, centered around the 339th Infantry, had come and gone, landing on September 4, 1918, and departing on June 27, 1919. Roughly five hundred died or were wounded—more than three times the number in the Siberian operation. In all, casualties in Russia approximated those during the campaign in Cuba two decades earlier, but, unlike that "splendid little war" (as Ambassador John Hay dubbed it in a letter to then-Colonel Teddy Roosevelt), most Americans then and now know little or nothing of the Yanks in Russia.

DEMOBILIZATION

Continuing unrest in Mexico had necessitated that the army maintain a significant presence along the U.S.-Mexico border during and after the war, with skirmishes occurring in both countries' territory until the Mexican government was able to establish firmer control in the region. Beyond this and the temporary stationing of troops in Russia and Germany, America's overseas and continental territories also required that a large number of troops be dispersed across the globe just as before the war. The only army unit stationed on foreign soil after the withdrawal from the Rhineland was the 15th Infantry Regiment, assigned to

Arrival at Commonwealth Pier, Boston, Mass. Troops "Formerly

Agamemnon, with 26th (Yankee) Division boys, April 7th 1919
ex-German Liner "Kaiser Wilhelm II."

© Commercial Photo Shop.
Geo H. Russell Mgr.,
Lowell, Mass.
4-7-19.

FUTURE LEADERS

Many of America's best leaders in World War II came close to shedding their uniforms during the two decades of peace following The Great War. In more than a few cases, the change would not have been voluntary, as some ran seriously afoul of their commanders. One of their number, Dwight D. Eisenhower, even faced jail time over financial improprieties when he ignorantly filed for financial compensation for two abodes for his family instead of the authorized one. The army's acting inspector general, desiring a scalp on his belt, intended to prosecute young Captain Eisenhower for fraud, even though Ike was the one who discovered and reported the error. Thankfully for the nation, the direct intervention in 1921 of General John J. Pershing and his former chief of staff, Major General Fox Conner, resulted only in a reprimand going into Eisenhower's file.

This wasn't Eisenhower's sole problem. The previous year, in league with his good friend George Patton, Ike's firm—and public—advocacy of officers placing increased emphasis on tanks earned him a warning from the chief of the Infantry branch, who said his views were "incompatible with established Infantry doctrine." Because of this, some officers, as late as 1925, tried to keep Eisenhower from attending the Command and General Staff School (CGSS) at Fort Leavenworth. Patton, meanwhile, also was finding his career at risk; his abrasive manner and decision to set training standards higher than his commander thought desirable (he was judged "a disturbing element in a peace-time army") led to his removal as the Hawaiian Division's operations officer.

Many National Guard officers during World War I continued to soldier on well into the 1930s as members of the Officers' Reserve Corps. Most Americans know that Harry S. Truman served as the captain of an artillery battery in France, but

few are aware that, after a brief time as a civilian, he rejoined the army as a major in the Reserves.

In the spring of 1919, Truman received multiple recommendations that he become a major in the organization of his choosing—either the Reserves or the Regular Army itself. He ultimately achieved the rank of colonel, commanding an exceptionally well-trained National Guard artillery regiment long before his election to the U.S. Senate in 1934, and he was offered command of another regiment in 1936. Truman was a founder of the Reserve Officers Association (ROA) immediately after the war, attended classes at CGSS, organized regular lectures for Reserve and Guard officers in Kansas City (his first lecturer was a bright young captain named Omar Bradley), and was a familiar figure at the Fort Riley artillery range.

During his time as a Reserve officer and as the junior senator from Missouri, Truman came to know an extremely large number of the officers who would lead the army in World War II. On one occasion, he humorously wrote home to his wife, Bess, that he'd just left a promotion party for Patton early because "it was too rough for me." (Patton had reverted to his "permanent rank" of captain after the war.) Three decades after his return from the battlefields of France, Truman wrote that if fate had played out differently, he might have ended his career as a two-star general in the Regular Army.

Douglas MacArthur, at the top of the chain of command as the army chief of staff, narrowly missed being at the center of a headline-grabbing scandal when his affair with a Philippine movie actress nearly became public. Though President Franklin D. Roosevelt appointed the general to a second term, many in the administration openly disdained MacArthur. The two leviathans also squared off

behind closed doors when the general fought tooth and nail to delay actions against New Deal proposals that would gut the army. At one such meeting MacArthur said, "When we lose the next war and an American boy is writhing in pain in the mud with a Japanese bayonet in his belly, I want the last words that he spits out in the form of a curse to be not against Douglas MacArthur but against Franklin Roosevelt." Roosevelt was enraged and commanded: "Never speak to the president of the United States that way!"

The general offered to resign, but Roosevelt successfully defused the situation and said, "No, no, Douglas, we must get together on this." MacArthur later wrote that his agitation was so great upon leaving the president that he vomited on the White House steps.

OPPOSITE TOP: *Officers of the 129th Field Artillery at Regimental Headquarters, March 1919. Nearly a quarter of these men would continue their association with the army into the mid-1920s, but the short fellow in the second row, Captain Harry S. Truman, would remain an active member of the Reserves into the late 1930s. L. Curtis Tiernan, fourth from right at top, became the European Theater senior chaplain in 1944.*

Major Omar N. Bradley
19th Division, c. 1921

Major James A. Van Fleet
c. 1938

Lieutenant Colonel Dwight D. Eisenhower
Camp Colt, Gettysburg, Pennsylvania

Brigadier General Douglas MacArthur
42d Division, 1918

Lieutenant Colonel George C. Marshall
c. 1919

Lieutenant Colonel George S. Patton Jr.
1918

Lieutenant Colonel Harry S. Truman
Fort Riley, July 1926

BELOW: Officers and men at Fort Mead in 1919. George Patton, who reverted to his permanent rank of captain after the war, and Captain Dwight Eisenhower are in the second row. Both men were firm, some might even say strident, advocates of armored warfare. Eisenhower learned to temper his words, however, after getting into deep trouble for publishing criticisms such as "the clumsy, awkward and snail-like progress of the old tanks," which were designed to match the walking pace of the infantry, "must be forgotten, and in their place the army must picture a more steady, reliable engine of destruction."

garrison duties in Tientsin, China, near Peking. This formation, whose crest and coat of arms feature a large Chinese dragon, took over the former German barracks and served in the city until 1938. (A regiment of marines was stationed in Shanghai.)

At home, the nation began at once to take its army apart—as fast as the flood of troop ships reached port. But that's not to say that the doughboys weren't given a hero's welcome. Captain Harry S. Truman describes the 35th Division's arrival at Hoboken, New Jersey, in New York Harbor on Easter Sunday, 1919, after fighting in the Vosges Mountains, the Meuse-Argonne Campaign, and along the Verdun front:

> I've never seen anything that looked so good as the Liberty Lady in New York Harbor and the mayor's welcoming boat, which came down the river to meet us. You know the men have seen so much and been in so many hard places that it takes something real to give them a thrill, but when the band on that boat played "Home Sweet Home" there were not very many dry eyes. The hardest of hard-boiled cookies even had to blow his nose a time or two. Every welfare organization in America met us and gave us something.

> The Jews gave us handkerchiefs; the Y.M.C.A. chocolate; the Knights of Columbus, cigarettes; the Red Cross, real homemade cake; and the Salvation Army, God bless 'em, sent telegrams free and gave us Easter eggs made of chocolate. They took us off the boat at Pier No.1 in Hoboken, fed us till we wouldn't hold any more, put us on a ferry, and sent us to Camp Mills, where they gave us a bath and lots of new clothes, the first some of the men have had since they joined. Then we made a raid on the canteens and free shows. I'll bet ten barrels wouldn't hold the ice cream consumed that first evening.

The four-million-man U.S. Army shed nearly 3,250,000 of its soldiers within nine months of the Armistice, and the force was down to barely two hundred thousand by the summer of 1920. After additional "fine tuning" by Congress in January 1921, its authorized strength was reduced to 175,000, and in June, pushed down to 150,000. A year later Congress limited the army to 12,000 commissioned officers and 125,000 enlisted men, plus 7,000 Philippine Scouts. The Regular Army strength remained at about this level for the next fifteen years.

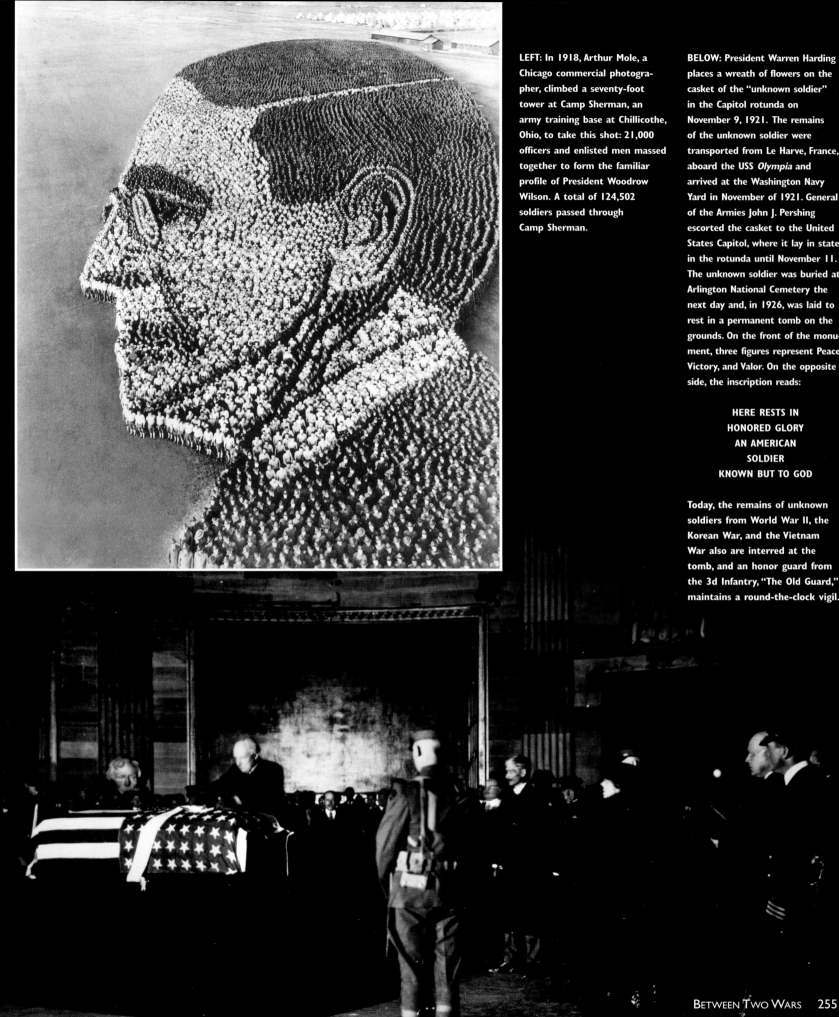

LEFT: In 1918, Arthur Mole, a Chicago commercial photographer, climbed a seventy-foot tower at Camp Sherman, an army training base at Chillicothe, Ohio, to take this shot: 21,000 officers and enlisted men massed together to form the familiar profile of President Woodrow Wilson. A total of 124,502 soldiers passed through Camp Sherman.

BELOW: President Warren Harding places a wreath of flowers on the casket of the "unknown soldier" in the Capitol rotunda on November 9, 1921. The remains of the unknown soldier were transported from Le Harve, France, aboard the USS *Olympia* and arrived at the Washington Navy Yard in November of 1921. General of the Armies John J. Pershing escorted the casket to the United States Capitol, where it lay in state in the rotunda until November 11. The unknown soldier was buried at Arlington National Cemetery the next day and, in 1926, was laid to rest in a permanent tomb on the grounds. On the front of the monument, three figures represent Peace, Victory, and Valor. On the opposite side, the inscription reads:

> **HERE RESTS IN
> HONORED GLORY
> AN AMERICAN
> SOLDIER
> KNOWN BUT TO GOD**

Today, the remains of unknown soldiers from World War II, the Korean War, and the Vietnam War also are interred at the tomb, and an honor guard from the 3d Infantry, "The Old Guard," maintains a round-the-clock vigil.

REORGANIZATION

In the midst of these reductions—which every soldier knew was coming as sure as night follows day—came one of the most constructive pieces of military legislation ever adopted in the United States: the National Defense Act of 1920, which governed the organization and regulation of the army until 1950, when the aforementioned Captain Truman was in the White House as the country's thirty-third president.

On a personal level, the act brought a much-needed across-the-board pay increase of 20 percent, and made a reality the dream of a National Army organization complete with Regular and civilian components: the professional Regular Army, the National Guard, and the Organized Reserves (Officers' and Enlisted Reserve Corps). In effect, the act acknowledged the folly of the United States through-

out its history of maintaining a standing peacetime force too small to meet the needs of a major war and, therefore, being continually dependent on raising new legions of untrained civilian soldiers through large, chaotic mobilizations. Now, each component would be maintained in readiness to contribute its appropriate share of troops in a war emergency.

The training of reserve components became a major peacetime task of the Regular Army. To accomplish this, the army was authorized a maximum officer strength more than three times that before World War I, which at first sounds adequate to the officer corps' increased tasks, but as a practical reality still left its members hard pressed to fulfill their many duties. The act also directed that officer promotions, except for doctors and chaplains, be made from a single list, a reform that equalized opportunity for advancement throughout most of the service. Changes relating to the civilian soldiers were equally important.

Browning Automatic Rifle (BAR), Model 1918

Designed by John Browning in 1917 for the American Expeditionary Forces in France as a replacement for the substandard French Chauchat and Benet-Mercie machine guns, this weapon arrived too late for U.S. units to employ it in combat. The BAR used the same .30-06 cartridge as the Springfield rifle and was appreciated for its robust construction, resistance to jamming, and accuracy when fired in short bursts by a standing soldier. Indeed, the weapon was designed for "walking fire" from the hip, but because of its twenty-pound weight was most commonly used with a bipod. The principal complaint of gunners from World War I through the early stages of the Vietnam War was the limited capacity of its standard twenty-round magazine.

The new National Defense Act contemplated a National Guard of 436,000, but its actual peacetime strength became stabilized at about 180,000. With one exception—evicting the "Bonus Marchers" from their Washington, D.C., encampment—this force relieved the Regular Army of any duty to curb domestic disturbances within the states from 1921 until 1941, and it stood ready for immediate induction into the active army whenever necessary. The War Department, in addition to supplying large quantities of surplus World War I material for equipment, applied about one-tenth of its military budget directly to the support of the National Guard in the years between wars, and Guardsmen engaged in regular armory drills and fifteen days of field training each year. This increasingly federalized Guard was far better trained in 1939 than it had been when mobilized for Mexican border duty in 1916 and was the largest component of the army between 1922 and 1939.

The Act of 1920 specifically charged the War Department with mobilization planning and preparation for the event of war, assigning the military aspects of this responsibility to the chief of staff and the general staff and the planning and supervision of industrial procurement to the assistant secretary of war. It also authorized the army to continue all of its armed and service branches established before 1917, and added three new branches, the Air Service, the Chemical Warfare Service, and a finance department—the first two reflecting new combat techniques developed during the war. However, the Tank Corps, representing another new technique, was absorbed by the infantry branch (and a young major named Dwight David Eisenhower was called on the carpet by his superiors for publicly advocating a more independent role for the army's fledgling armored force).

LEFT: General Douglas MacArthur as army chief of staff, July 1932.

BOTTOM: The Hawaiian Division's 11th Field Artillery Brigade during June 24, 1921, maneuvers on Oahu. In addition to French-made 75-mm guns and caissons, other equipment readily visible in this photo includes five-ton armored tractors, manufactured by Holt and Army Ordnance, pulling the 75-mm guns and caissons; a motorcycle with sidecar from Hendee Manufacturing Company; numerous "Car, Passenger, Light, Open" staff cars manufactured by Studebaker and Ford; as well as several "Car, Passenger, Medium, Open" vehicles manufactured by Dodge. The brigade was built around the 8th and 13th field artilleries (75-mm guns) and the 11th Field Artillery (155-mm howitzers).

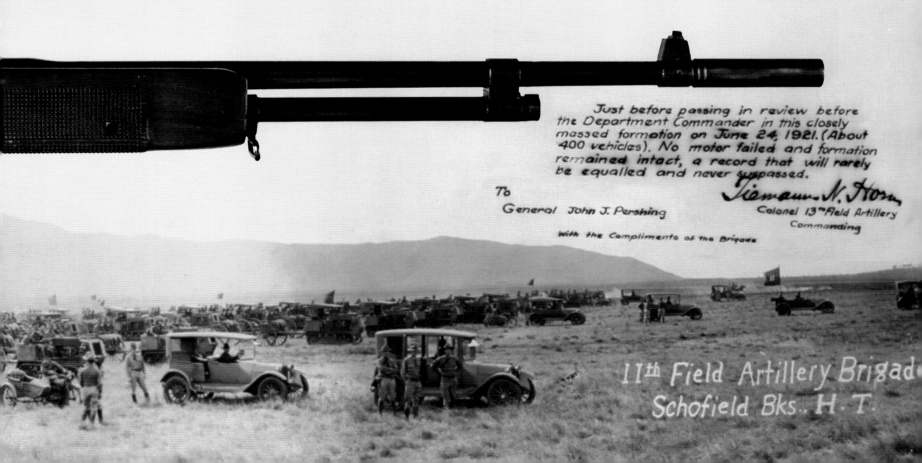

Just before passing in review before the Department Commander in this closely massed formation on June 24, 1921. (About 400 vehicles). No motor failed and formation remained intact, a record that will rarely be equaled and never surpassed.

To
General John J. Pershing

Tiemann N. Horn
Colonel 13th Field Artillery
Commanding

With the Compliments of the Brigade

11th Field Artillery Brigade
Schofield Bks., H.T.

MODERNIZATION

Technology provided new, more lethal weapons, which the army sought to use effectively. Under Army Chief of Staff Lieutenant General Douglas MacArthur, a continuous effort at modernization ensued, and the clank of tank treads slowly but steadily replaced the clatter of horses' hooves. The army began to put intellectual effort into determining the best ways to use existing technologies (such as armor and aircraft) and to defend against current or future threats, realizing that warfare, tactics, weapons, and priorities would also be used by the country's enemies and would evolve over time.

During the 1920s and 1930s, the army took advantage of the long period of respite from major conflicts by conducting war games, simulations, and in-depth studies. While industry proceeded to develop better radios, tanks, planes, and other tools of war, the army continued to think through the complex problems of integrating the new technologies, training soldiers, mobilizing, and supporting mechanized forces. But the army had a serious drawback in its inability to conduct large-scale exercises to confirm theory. Officers could visualize how new techniques *might* work, but could not prove their value nor incorporate lessons learned from actual application.

One thing the army could and did do during this period was spend a great deal of its scarce resources on educating officers so they could be adaptive and versatile leaders. The Command and General Staff School at Fort Leavenworth and the Infantry School at Fort Benning were two of the most important centers, not only in the educational processes but also in the development of doctrine and concepts. Meanwhile, a doctrine of air-ground operations was evolving at the service schools and was further elaborated on over the inter-war years as air and ground elements thrashed out whether it was better for air units to directly support ground troops or act more independently to achieve strategic objective while continuing to cooperate tactically.

Most important of all, in 1932 the framework of a national mass army had been set up with nine corps areas comprising territorial compartments in an overall concept of four field armies with Regular, National Guard, and Organized Reserve elements allotted a critical role in each. The skeleton of a command and staff organization was now complete and, for the first time, the army had a mobilization plan to deal with a national emergency.

ABOVE: Major General George Patton spots through his field compass during an exercise at the Desert Training Center he set up in the Mojave Desert at Camp Young, stretching from Pomona, California, almost to Phoenix, Arizona. Nearly one million men used the center's twelve camps for training during World War II. In the background, Patton's M1A1 light tank has the marking of his I Armored Corps.

RIGHT: This Model 15 experimental tanker's helmet was produced by the Army Ordnance Department in 1917 and sent to American tank battalions in France for testing. The helmet included quilted panels, which could be closed tight over the nose with a draw string and were intended to prevent neck and facial wounds from lead splash. This example was worn by Sergeant David Pyle, 301st Tank Battalion (Heavy), Tank Corps.

RIGHT: Into the mechanized age: an M2A4 light tank of the 7th Cavalry Brigade (Mechanized) overtakes a horsed squadron in the summer of 1940. The M2A4 was the first U.S. tank to be built in quantity in 1940–1945.

BOTTOM: 5th Cavalry troopers with their colors, 1940.

Unit Insignia for the 5th Cavalry Regiment

5TH CAVALRY COLORS. 1940

OPPOSITE TOP LEFT: President Calvin Coolidge's son, John Coolidge (*with armband*), after his enlistment in 1925. Because of experience gained at the Citizens' Military Training Camp at Ayer, Massachusetts, two years earlier, Coolidge was made acting corporal of his training squad at Camp Devens.

OPPOSITE TOP RIGHT: Recruiting poster for the Pennsylvania Guard, c. 1919

OPPOSITE BOTTOM: Preparing for review at a Citizen's Military Training Camp, a regular officer dresses the ranks of a rather disinterested squad (note the hands in the pockets of the recruit next to him), while a second squad behind him attempts to straighten itself up. The officer at center, emerging between the units, does not look amused.

RIGHT INSET: Shoulder patch for the Reserve Officers Training Corps

"OTHER DUTIES"

As noted earlier, the Regular officers' training of the nation's civilian soldiers proceeded apace with their required command, educational, and staff duties, but there were only so many officers. Try as it might, the army could not stretch a day beyond twenty-four hours. Obligations to the civilian components—a robust National Guard now a fully federal element, an Officers' Reserve Corps seventy-thousand strong, a Reserve Officers' Training Corps of 223 units, and the increased attendance at the service schools—all served to bleed the Regular troop units dry of leaders. What was left of the Regular Army's commissioned officers was still further burdened by the Guard's summer camps—and especially the Citizens' Military Training Camps (CMTC).

The proposal immediately after World War I to establish a system of universal military training had gone absolutely nowhere, but the CMTC program proved to be a modest, yet effective, alternative that for more than a decade provided about thirty thousand fine young volunteers with four weeks of military training in annual summer camps. Those who completed four years of CMTC training became eligible for Reserve commissions; thus the CMTC provided a small but dependable source for the rolls of the Officers' Reserve Corps and the National Guard. This was all well and good, as it would pay off handsomely during the Second World War; but as one officer who struggled through the period recalled, it left "the Regular scratching his head as he tried to make a twenty-four-hour day contain a forty-eight-hour schedule."

And then, another new problem was dumped into the army officer's lap: the famed Civilian Conservation Corps (CCC), formed as one of many Depression-era projects during the administration of President Franklin Delano Roosevelt. Colonel R. Ernest Dupuy recalled an unpleasant situation that was repeated countless times during the 1930s—and on the heels of a steep, army-wide pay cut:

> The Regular officer assigned to this duty had an interesting problem while smarting over his own pay cut, to explain to the Regular private soldier also detailed to CCC duty just why that private's pay had been cut to seventeen dollars and eighty-five cents a month while the pampered pet of the CCC for whom he was caring got thirty dollars plus complete immunity from military discipline!

The hastily conceived CCC had been dumped into the army's lap for the most practical of all bureaucratic reasons—there simply was no other element of the government capable of the task. After Congress passed the 1933 act that put these large numbers of jobless young men into reforestation and

other reclamation work, Roosevelt directed the army to mobilize them and thereafter to run their work camps. Surprisingly, there turned out to be a bright side to the army's management of the program, and it had a beneficial effect upon practically all officers involved. It was a job to be done and a tremendous challenge to personal leadership to be met. These CCC men were not the malleable, willing youth of the CMTC; they were a mix of irresponsible veterans and youth in the raw, with more than a dash of "Dead End Kids" added. In handling this tough conglomeration successfully, Regular and reserve officers learned much that would stand them in good stead when, beginning in 1940 and 1941, the Selective Service System began to funnel men (with varying degrees of willingness) by the hundreds of thousands into the great draft armies that would soon battle Germany and Japan.

In the short run, however, this distinctly nonmilitary duty was extremely disruptive. The army was also to ensure that the program—both in appearance and in fact—was not a military project in disguise. The Regular Army, seldom a popular entity in American society except when that society was immediately in need of it, was at its lowest ebb of popular esteem since Reconstruction and the labor troubles of the previous century. The reasons for this, aside from Americans' traditional distrust of standing armies, was a growing sense among many people that perhaps America had not needed to be involved in the previous "European" war, as well as the recent spectacle of U.S. Army tanks and bayonet-wielding infantry being called out to disperse the Bonus Marchers in Washington, D.C. The army swallowed hard, saluted the commander in chief, and, within just seven weeks, organized 310,000 men into 1,315 camps. The practical result was that the army had accomplished a mobilization more rapid and orderly than any in its history.

The army knew only too well, however, that this success and the continued operations of the camps were coming at a tremendous cost to the basic readiness and its ability of its small force to defend the nation. For more than a year the War Department had to keep about 3,000 Regular officers and many noncommissioned officers assigned to this task, and in order to do so, the army had to strip tactical units of their leadership, literally bringing unit training to a standstill. In the second half of 1934, the War Department called a large number of Reserve officers to active duty to replace the regulars, and, by August 1935, some 9,300 Reserve officers were managing the CCC. Many continued in this service until 1941 and, as with the regulars, gained not only valuable experience for themselves but also provided nonmilitary but disciplined training to many hundreds of thousands of young men who were to become soldiers and sailors in a few short years.

"Come On, Boys!"

Give the Guard a Fighting Chance

Fight alongside Your Friends
Fill up the National Guard

ALL BRANCHES OF ARMY SERVICE ARE OPEN TO YOU.

COMMITTEE OF PUBLIC SAFETY, DEPARTMENT OF MILITARY SERVICE, SOUTH PENN SQUARE, PHILADELPHIA.

THE CIVILIAN CONSERVATION CORPS (CCC)

By March 1933, 13.6 million people were unemployed in the United States. Only two days after his inauguration, President Franklin Roosevelt called a meeting to create a Civilian Conservation Corps. The CCC would put more than three million young men to work improving public lands. Rather than create a new bureaucracy, the president used existing governmental departments. The army's primary function was to organize and administer the **CCC** camps. This was a major logistical undertaking. Each state normally had as many as several dozen camps in operation at any one time—and the numbers frequently shifted over very short periods. For example, enrollment peaked at 505,782 at about 2,900 camps in August 1935, followed by a reduction to 350,000 enrollees at 2,019 camps the following summer.

A typical camp consisted of a dozen or more barracks, a post exchange, recreational building, mess hall, classroom, dispensary, officers' quarters, blacksmith shop, garage, bathhouse, supply room, greenhouse, and storage buildings. Many regular and reserve officers, who otherwise would not have had an opportunity to construct and administer an installation or supervise large numbers of men

during the interwar years, benefited significantly from this experience.

As America drew closer to involvement in World War II, the CCC was carefully refocused to support national defense and develop infrastructure for military training facilities as well as forest protection. To make this change less apparent to the general public, the Roosevelt administration distributed the CCC's programs

among various civilian agencies, such as the National Youth Administration and Works Progress Administration. By July 1940, roughly five thousand reservists who were running the camps no longer wore their uniforms, were now paid by the Civil Service Administration, and were not addressed by rank. As far as most Americans were concerned, the camps no longer had any obvious military leadership.

OPPOSITE INSET: *Lester Dankin, a "civilian" in the employ of the Civil Service Administration, instructs CCC vocational students during a code class at the Cache National Forest, Utah National Defense Radio School in 1940.*

RIGHT: *Youths, most of whom soon will be inducted into the army, gather around a campfire at the Huntsville CCC camp on March 10, 1941.*

BELOW INSET: *CCC Garrison Cap, c. 1940. This forest-green, overseas-type cap was manufactured to army specifications with a round patch depicting an outdoor forest and lake scene below the initials of the corps.*

BOTTOM: *Lunchtime in the field at Lassen National Forest, California.*

A YOUNG MAN'S OPPORTUNITY

CCC

FOR WORK PLAY STUDY & HEALTH

APPLICATIONS TAKEN BY
ILLINOIS EMERGENCY RELIEF COMMISSION
ILLINOIS SELECTING AGENCY

COASTAL ARTILLERY

The acquisition of new territories at the turn of the century prompted an upsurge in coast defense requirements, and Army Engineers heavily fortified the Panama Canal as well as key points on Hawaii, Cuba, the Philippines, and U.S. harbors. Defenses centered around Army Coastal Artillery batteries with "disappearing guns" that were held erect by counterweights or hydraulics, then rotated backwards and down below ground level by their own recoil when fired. Upon reaching the point where they were fully retracted, they automatically locked into place where they could be easily reloaded and aimed while remaining unseen. When ready, the guns would be released and glide back up into firing position.

   Though effective against ships, the open gun pits were highly vulnerable to the burgeoning air forces of potential enemies and the army turned increasingly to mobile guns towed by full or partially tracked vehicles or mounted on rail cars so that they could be moved in and out of heavy shelters. During the Japanese invasion of Luzon, mobile artillery operated by the Philippine Army and U.S. Army Philippine Scouts was most effective in long range and counter battery fire during the months of fighting on the Bataan Peninsula in 1942, and subsequent siege of Corregidor.

LEARN TO MAKE AND TEST THE BIG GUNS BETTER YOURSELF—ENLIST AND LEARN A TRADE *in the* ORDNANCE DEPARTMENT *U·S·A·*

ABERDEEN PROVING GROUND
DAILY PEACE TIME FIRING

ABOVE: A recruiting poster showing 6-inch and 8-inch rail-mounted cannons enticed young men who wanted to "learn a trade"—or simply liked things that go "bang!"—to the artillery.

LEFT: The soldiers of either the 91st or 92d Coast Artillery (Philippine Scouts) train on a mobile 155-mm gun before the Japanese invasion of Luzon.

BELOW: A 14-inch gun on a Buffington-Crozier "disappearing" gun mount hurls its massive round toward the horizon during a training exercise.

EXPANSION OF THE ARMY

Though the World War—the Roman numeral "I" wasn't yet needed to distinguish it—was romantically touted as "The War to End All Wars," not even a generation had passed before the hunger for land and power led to myriad confrontations and bloody wars in Asia, Africa, and Europe, with the League of Nations unwilling and unable to do anything to stop the aggressors. The former Allied countries were equally unwilling to do anything on their own when Adolf Hitler, who came to power in Germany in 1933 as the head of the Nazi Party, denounced the Treaty of Versailles, began rearming, and reoccupied the demilitarized Rhineland in 1936.

The Nazi invasion of Poland, precipitating a war with France and Britain, forced an immediate reappraisal of America's defense policies. President Roosevelt proclaimed a limited national emergency and authorized increases in Regular Army and National Guard enlisted strengths to 227,000 and 235,000, respectively, in order to protect the United States and the rest of the Western Hemisphere against any hostile forces. At his urging Congress soon gave indirect support to the besieged Western democracies by ending the prohibition on sales of munitions to nations at war. Simultaneously, the gearing up of American industry to fulfill British and French munitions orders helped to prepare America to become the "arsenal of democracy" that would supply the insatiable needs of its own army and those of its allies.

To fill the ranks of the newly expanding army, Congress approved induction of the National Guard into federal service and the call-up of the Organized Reserves. After the Nazis defeated the French and British armies in the summer of 1940, knocking France out of the war and occupying most of the country, Congress approved the first *peacetime* draft of untrained civilian manpower in America's history with the Selective Service and Training Act of September 1940. Units of the National Guard, draftees, and the Reserve officers to train them, entered service as rapidly as the army could build camps to house them. During the last six months of 1940 the active army more than doubled its manpower. By mid-1941 it achieved its planned strength of one-and-a-half million officers and men and laid the foundation for even larger expansion when war came the following year.

It was at this point that the Nazis invaded the Soviet Union on June 22, 1941. Three days later U.S. Army troops

LEFT: A mortar team is put through its paces with the best training tools that the rapidly expanding army could muster: three wooden slats arranged as a bipod and mortar tube. The least that one of the other crewmen could do would be to carry the "60MM MORTAR" yard sign for his buddy lugging the weapon.

ABOVE: Take a bent pipe, a board, some old farm implement wheels, and—presto! You now have a 37-mm anti-tank gun suitable for training.

ABOVE: Lieutenant Franklin O. Anders, H Company, 57th Infantry (Philippine Scouts), was stationed at Fort William McKinley on July 22, 1941. He headed up a bamboo raft development project and construction of rafts for a river crossing demonstration on the Pasig River, which bordered the post. Captured on Luzon by the Japanese and held at the Cabanatuan prison camp in the Philippines, he was liberated by a combined force of Army Rangers, Alamo Scouts, and Filipino guerrillas on January 30, 1945.

BELOW: Philippine Scouts of the 57th Infantry take part in an October 1941 field exercise. Members of this unit were U.S. Regular Army soldiers and not the Philippines' own national army, which also was under American command.

ABOVE: (Left to right) Captains Richard F. Hill, William P. Baldwin, and John C. Goldtrap of the 57th Infantry (Philippine Scouts). All three men were later detached from the Scouts and assigned to Philippine Army units. Hill and Baldwin were captured on Bataan by the Japanese, and Goldtrap, by then a lieutenant colonel, was captured on Mindanao. All three were killed when the transports bringing them to Japan in 1944 were sunk by U.S. submarines.

LEFT: Draftees train with wooden rifles on Governors Island, New York, during America's effort to rearm from scratch in 1941.

BELOW: M2A3 light tanks burst from a smoke screen during pre-war maneuvers. Approximately one hundred seventy M1A1 light tanks (earlier designated M1 combat cars) and M2A3 light tanks were built before production was switched fully to the M2A4—a tank that was further refined and standardized as the M3 Stuart.

landed in Greenland to protect it against a German attack, to build bases for the air route across the North Atlantic to Britain, and to act as patrol bases to scout for German submarines. Roosevelt also decided that Americans should relieve British troops guarding Iceland, and the initial contingent of Marines and Army Air Corps units arrived in early July. The whole of the 5th Infantry Division arrived in September. Meanwhile, in August, Roosevelt and British Prime Minister Winston Churchill met in Newfoundland and drafted the Atlantic Charter, which defined the general terms of a future just peace for the world.

These overt American moves in 1941 toward involvement in the war against Nazi Germany had solid backing in American public opinion, but the nation was still not in favor of a declaration of war. As for the army itself, instead of what Colonel Ganoe had characterized in 1917 as "not even a high school squad to meet the professionals," a competent professional officer corps was leading the core of a well trained—if still not well supplied—army.

BELOW: Men of Company C, 11th Field Artillery, 24th Infantry Division, pose for a group photo outside their quarters at Schofield Barracks in Hawaii days before Japan's December 7, 1941, attack on Pearl Harbor.

RIGHT: 24th Infantry Division insignia patch

1920–1942 RANK INSIGNIA

The number of insignia was reduced from eight to seven, and six pay grades were established. War Department Circular No. 303, dated August 5, 1920, stated that the chevrons would be worn on the left sleeve, point up, and were to be made of olive drab material on a background of dark blue.

Master Sergeant

First Sergeant

Technical Sergeant	Staff Sergeant	Sergeant	Corporal	Private First Class

ABOVE: The 57th Infantry (Philippine Scouts) conducts a reconnaissance of the Lingayen Gulf area on Luzon Island—where Japanese forces would invade in December 1941 and the United States would follow in 1945. Third from the right is Captain Harold K. Johnson, who would survive his imprisonment by the Japanese to become the army chief of staff during the Vietnam War. At far left is Lieutenant J. Edwin McColm, who would be killed in action. His brother George, a naval officer, would later become one of the principal planners for the invasion and occupation of Japan. George McColm deeply regretted that he had no pictures of his brother in the Philippines and did not know of this photo's existence. It was discovered several months after he passed away in 2007.

Chapter Eight
Victory in the Pacific, 1941–1945

Even as Germany and the United States moved closer to war, America prepared for another conflict in the Pacific. Imperial Japan had signed the Tripartite Pact, a military alliance with Nazi Germany and Fascist Italy, and after the defeat of France, moved large forces into that country's southeast Asian colonies (including present-day Vietnam) in July 1941. President Roosevelt responded by freezing Japanese assets and cutting off the oil and steel shipments critically needed by the Japanese military. The United States demanded Japan's withdrawal from the occupied French colonies, but the Japanese were unwilling to give up their newly acquired bases, which put them in reach of the rich oil- and rubber-producing regions farther south in what is today Indonesia and Malaysia.

Since the Japanese military, and especially its navy, could no longer maintain operations without oil, U.S. military and political leaders believed that Imperial Japan was likely to strike the Philippines and Britain's bastion at Singapore in order to protect the flanks of any strike to the south. The United States wanted to avoid a two-front war, but it would not do so by surrendering vital areas or interests to the Japanese as the price for peace. The Philippines had to be strengthened as quickly as possible, and the first elements of a steady stream of army ground and air units soon began to arrive in Manila Bay with the expectation that the islands' build-up would largely be completed by the spring of 1942. The forces of Imperial Japan, however, were already on the move.

PEARL HARBOR AND THE PHILIPPINES

While Japanese diplomats pretended to make peace negotiations in Washington, their planes struck without warning at Pearl Harbor, on the Hawaiian island of Oahu. The Japanese were confident that before the United States could recover from a crushing blow against its Pacific Fleet, they would be able to seize all their objectives in the Far East and that they would have ample time to make their new empire invulnerable to attack. By September 1941 the Japanese had largely completed their secret plans for a huge assault against Malaya, the Philippines, and the Netherlands East Indies. It all depended on their ability to inflict such a shocking series of victories that the United States and its allies would sue for peace and let them keep their ill-gotten gains.

Even before the smoke cleared on December 7, 1941, Americans grimly faced the fact that the Japanese had sunk or very heavily damaged virtually all of the Pacific Fleet's battleships that were moored at the naval base and had destroyed most of the army's planes in Hawaii. But while ships and planes could be replaced, those two thousand lives lost in action during the first two hours of the sneak attack could not. The first shock at seeing aircraft with blood-red suns on their wings attacking the fleet and strafing the planes at Wheeler Field quickly gave way to action as soldiers and sailors jumped to their posts. Men grabbed rifles and machine guns and hit out against the Japanese planes. They fought to put out fires. Some pilots even managed to get their outnumbered fighters off the ground to battle against the attackers. At home "Remember Pearl Harbor" became the war cry of a determined people.

OPPOSITE: Lieutenant General Douglas MacArthur *(right)* confers with his senior field commander in the Philippines, Major General Jonathan M. "Skinny" Wainwright, on October 10, 1941. MacArthur was promoted to full general when the Japanese invaded in late December, and Wainwright received his third star when MacArthur was evacuated to Australia in March 1942.

ABOVE: Wainwright's first-generation single-action army pistol, nicknamed the "Peacemaker" because of the Colt's extensive use in the Old West, was hidden from the Japanese before his surrender. Wrapped in an oilcloth and placed in the hollow of a tree, it was recovered after the war.

ABOVE: Private Joseph L. Lockard. Early on the Sunday morning of December 7, 1941, Signal Corps privates Joseph L. Lockard and George Elliot detected approaching aircraft while practicing with their radar equipment. The men reported their findings to the information center at Fort Shafter in Honolulu, where most of the staff was at breakfast. The duty officer who received the report reasoned that the activity was simply a flight of army B-17 bombers scheduled to arrive that morning. Although the radar crew was told not to worry about it, they followed the incoming formation until it disappeared from the screen. Lockard ended the war as a first lieutenant.

RIGHT: Soldiers set up a water-cooled, .50-caliber, antiaircraft machine gun on the runway at Wheeler Field near Pearl Harbor as others receive instructions. Several days before the Japanese attack, all U.S. troops were returned to their stations from field maneuvers to guard against what was expected to be attempts by Japanese saboteurs against army aircraft and facilities.

Four hours after Japan struck Pearl Harbor, Clark Field in the Philippines was bombed, catching much of the U.S. airpower on the ground as the Japanese began the process of softening the islands for a land invasion. Strafing and bombing had gone on for three days when a scout car crew of the 26th Cavalry in northern Luzon flashed an urgent radio message that Japanese troops were landing. A large invasion fleet with thousands of men stood out at sea waiting to come in at Aparri and Vigan, but there were no American units close enough to oppose the Japanese landings. The main body of the invasion force began landing at Lingayen Gulf on December 22, and Japanese infantry, artillery, and tanks soon were sweeping south along jungle roads toward Manila, the capital city of the Philippines. As General MacArthur planned his defense against the invaders, someone remarked, "General, the American flag flying from your headquarters makes a swell target for bombers." MacArthur looked up from his maps and said quietly, "Take every normal precaution, sir, but we'll keep the flag flying."

The fate of the Philippines had been sealed weeks earlier when American naval and air power in the Pacific was knocked out. MacArthur's ground forces consisted of the partly trained and equipped Philippine Army, a ten-division force totaling about one hundred thousand, as well as a Regular Army contingent of just over twenty-five thousand soldiers. Within the American force, the largest unit was the Philippine Division, consisting of the 31st Infantry, and the 45th and 57th Philippine Scouts regiments. Unable to stop the enemy at the Luzon shoreline, MacArthur withdrew his forces into the mountains and mosquito-filled jungles of the Bataan Peninsula in a complex, retrograde movement. To their rear and blocking Japanese access to Manila Bay was the island bastion of Corregidor and three smaller, fortified Manila Bay islands. Although this was a strong position, the American and Filipino troops had lost most of their equipment and supplies during their hurried withdrawal, and a Japanese blockade prevented any possibility of either withdrawal to fight again or reinforcements getting through. Meanwhile, on January 2, the Japanese occupied Manila, which had been declared on open city on Christmas Eve.

American forces successfully repulsed Japanese offensives in early January and February, destroying a

...we here highly resolve that these dead shall not have died in vain...

REMEMBER DEC. 7th!

LEFT: These are the remains of an army P-40 Warhawk pursuit plane at Wheeler Field, Oahu, after the Japanese air raid.

BACKGROUND: A Japanese bomber flies over aircraft and installations aflame at Wheeler Field during the December 7, 1941, attack.

Hawaiian Department Patch

BATTLING BASTARDS OF BATAAN

In many respects, the Philippine campaign was the U.S. Army's last battle of World War I. Fought with antique weapons like the Enfield rifle, Stokes mortar, 2.95-inch mountain gun, French-made 75mm and 155mm artillery, light tanks, and no close air support, it saw the army's last mounted charge when G troop, 26th Cavalry, attacked a Japanese force of tanks and infantry on January 16, 1942. The regiment's horses were subsequently eaten by the starving American and Filipino troops.

Approximately 60,000 of the 78,000 troops who surrendered on Bataan by April 10 were Philippine nationals. Roughly 45,000 survived the "Death March" to their prison camps. Between mid-April and July 10, another 22,000 would perish. American POWs in the Philippines experienced a mortality rate of 40 percent, with approximately 11,107 deaths out of the 27,465 soldiers interned in the Philippines.

The bulk of the U.S. ground forces during the Philippine Campaign were Filipino. Poorly trained and wretchedly supplied, they fought well until the bitter end under both Philippine and American officers. After the islands' surrender in May 1942, they made up the core of the guerrilla bands that formed around leaders of both nationalities. They coalesced into an increasingly effective underground force that operated, according to local circumstances, independently and in conjunction with MacArthur's headquarters.

1st Lieutenant Willibald C. Bianchi,
Medal of Honor Recipient

The wounded lieutenant led his 45th Infantry, Philippine Scouts platoon against enemy machine-gun nests, personally silencing one with grenades when he ran out of ammunition. Wounded a second time by two bullets in the chest, he climbed to the top of a tank, manned its antiaircraft machine gun, and fired into the enemy position until knocked to the ground by a third wound.

2d Lieutenant Alexander R. Nininger Jr.,
Medal of Honor Recipient

In hand-to-hand combat to recover positions lost by the 57th Infantry, Philippine Scouts, Nininger fought his way forward. Although wounded three times, he continued to attack with rifle and hand grenades. He destroyed several enemy groups in foxholes, as well as snipers positioned in trees. His body was found with three enemies, including an officer, that he had killed.

ABOVE: *Captain Arthur William Wermuth Jr. (left) and an unidentified Philippine Scout officer. After the Japanese invaded Luzon, Wermuth organized a 185-strong sniper/counter-sniper group within the Filipino 57th Infantry, a highly effective force in the regiment's defense zone. In a precursor to the guerrilla activities that would steadily mount during the Japanese occupation of the islands, the group began to conduct their own raids behind enemy lines, destroying a bridge and burning a Japanese encampment.*

RIGHT: *American or Philippine Scout machine gunners retreat after the Japanese invasion of Luzon at Lingayen Gulf in December 1941.*

RIGHT: *Brigadier General Edward P. King, at left, is with his chief medical officer, Captain (later Colonel) Achille C. Tisdale, on March 10, 1942, the day King was given command of all American and Filipino troops on Bataan. Tisdale later maintained that "ours was a logistics, not a military defeat."*

BELOW: *General Jonathan M. Wainwright carried a leather case and personal service saber. The case was used by Wainwright throughout his captivity, while the saber had been stolen early in the Battle of the Philippines. It was found in 1945 with the body of a Japanese officer.*

Japanese regiment in the latter operation. In March 1942, the president ordered MacArthur to leave for Australia, and a submarine slipped through the blockade to take him away, leaving newly promoted Lieutenant General Jonathan M. Wainwright in command of the U.S. Forces in the Philippines. Exhausted soldiers on Bataan held back the enemy while living on monkey and water buffalo— and finally their own horses and mules. Hunger, disease, and casualties finally reduced them to the point of military ineffectiveness. In the April offensive, American and Filipino units were overwhelmed in fierce, hand-to-hand fighting, and on April 9, the last units holding out on Bataan surrendered. A month later, the Japanese swarmed across the channel to Corregidor, and Wainwright ordered the remainder of the American forces there and throughout the Philippines to lay down their arms on May 6, 1942.

The army had fought until it could fight no more. Other battles and campaigns during the next three years would be far more costly in terms of casualties, but the Philippine Campaign of '41 and '42 was America's greatest military disaster of the war. The "Battling Bastards of Bataan" were left with nothing but MacArthur's promise: "I will return." The Japanese took 78,000 Americans and Filipinos prisoner on Bataan and another 11,574 on Corregidor. The infamous "March of Death" began at daylight on April 10, when the prisoners were marched for long hours under a broiling, tropical sun to reach their prison camps. Many were sick, and food was scarce. Hundreds died during the eighty-five-mile march, including those who fell by the wayside and were bayoneted by guards. Of those who survived this terrible ordeal, thousands more died in prison camps before their liberation at the end of the war.

ABOVE: Throughout the Japanese invasion of the Philippines, the U.S. Army's headquarters was set up in the bomb-proof tunnel complex deep within Malinta Hill on Corregidor Island. During the final siege of Bataan and Corregidor, the Army Finance Office shared Malinta Tunnel's lateral No. 12 with the Signal Corps. In this April 24, 1942, photo, code machines and telegraph operators of the Signal Corps Message Center are enclosed behind the partition (*rear right*), and members of the Finance Office staff appear in the foreground. Seated on the left hand side of the tunnel (*left to right*): Staff Sergeant Wehrner, Staff Sergeant Aaron A. Pressman, Staff Sergeant Ira William Salyer, and Major Dwight E. Gard. Standing in the rear (*left to right*): Technical Sergeant Roy Howard Davis, Colonel John. R. Vance and an unidentified man. Seated on the right hand side of the tunnel from the rear forward: Colonel Royal J. Jenks (*with message center equipment directly behind his desk*), Lieutenant Colonel Roy. E. McElfish, Private First Class True, Staff Sergeant Paul L. Long, (*left*) Master Sergeant Russell Harvey Walker, (*right*) Private First Class William Gene "Bill" Ballou, Private First Class Arthur Greenwell Kuykendall, Staff Sergeant Huff. This photo was taken by Major Paul R. Wing of the Signal Corps.

When Jenks and other key personnel were evacuated from Corregidor by the last submarine out on May 3, he took this picture and the army's finance records with him. Three days later Vance and his men destroyed all classified papers and spent several hours cutting up currency amounting to more than two million United States of America–Commonwealth of the Philippines pesos.

LEFT: The 93d Infantry Division, reactivated on May 15, 1942, was the first all-Negro division to be formed during World War II. The white officer at center, Second Lieutenant Arthur Bates, waits for zero hour before giving the command to attack during training at Fort Huachuca, Arizona. The division would serve on Guadalcanal, Bougainville, and in the Philippines.

BELOW: These nine-inch canvas leggings are date-stamped November 17, 1943. The soldiers below wear the standard twelve-inch pattern leggings that were introduced in 1938 and used throughout the war. The bright khaki color soon gave way to muted tan, brown, and olive shades.

BOTTOM: Company A soldiers of the 26th Infantry Regiment, 1st Infantry Division, pass in review after their arrival at Camp Blanding, Florida, from Fort Devens, Massachusetts, in February 1942. The 26th Infantry would fight in North Africa, Sicily, France, Belgium, and Germany.

WAR GAME EXERCISES

As fighting raged across Europe and China before the Japanese attack on Pearl Harbor, another full scale "war"—the Lousiana Maneuvers—involving more than four hundred thousand ground troops broke out between the fictitious nations of Kotmk (Kansas-Oklahoma-Texas-Missouri-Kentucky) and Almat (Arkansas-Louisiana-Mississippi-Alabama-Tennessee) over navigation rights on the Mississippi River.

The army needed to train its rapidly expanding forces for operations on a massive scale, and the Louisiana Maneuvers of August–September 1941 filled the bill. Some nineteen combat divisions engaged in mock battles that were spread throughout a combat zone of thirty-four hundred square miles. Maneuver planners began by teaming division against division, then expanded to have corps fight against corps. The grand finale of the war games pitted the U.S. Third (Blue) Army against Second (Red) Army, with the Blue Army as the "aggressor" force and with each army supported by an air force of four hundred planes.

The 2d Armored Division under Major General George S. Patton faired badly in early fighting as a Red Army formation—losing 20 percent of its tanks. But after its transfer to the Blue Army, it successfully conducted a large-scale crossing of the Sabine River.

The Red force stiffened its defenses, and a battle erupted at Mansfield, Louisiana. Meanwhile, the Blue Army's 1st Cavalry Division crossed the Sabine at Logansport, Louisiana, and Carthage, Texas, then attacked Shreveport, Louisiana, from the south as Patton's forces drove in from the north.

The maneuvers enabled commanders to successfully simulate and test a variety of offensive and defensive techniques. Similar but smaller exercises were conducted in 1942 and 1943.

LEFT: *Lieutenant General Walter Krueger looks over the situation at Hadden's Ferry at Camp Polk on August 29, 1942. The rising Sabine River has complicated a crossing. Krueger commanded the U.S. Third Army during the 1941 and 1942 Louisiana Maneuvers, then the Sixth Army in its Southwest Pacific battles, including those on New Guinea and the Philippines. Krueger's Sixth Army was chosen to spearhead the planned invasion of Japan in late November 1945.*

BELOW: *A column of M3 Grant and M4 Sherman medium tanks (in both welded and cast hulls) await orders during a 1942 field exercise at Fort Knox, Kentucky. Further down the line is a company of the M2A4 predecessor to the M3 Stuart light tank as well as M2/M3-type half-tracks. The Sherman and Grant tanks utilized identical engines, chassis, and similar 75-mm main guns (the M3s with limited traverse on the side). Consequently, training units frequently employed them side by side until the M3s were withdrawn for conversion to tank recovery vehicles and prime movers.*

TOP LEFT: *Lieutenant General Lesley J. McNair (right) discusses ongoing training operations with 82d Infantry (later Airborne) Division commander Major General Omar N. Bradley during the Louisiana Maneuvers. McNair, who organized the massive, complex event, had previously served as the General Headquarters Chief of Staff in Washington and recently concluded his assignment as Commandant of the Command and General Staff School at Fort Leavenworth, Kansas.*

TOP RIGHT: *2d Infantry Division soldiers load a 37-mm antitank gun into a transport plane at Fort Sam Houston, Texas, as they prepare for field exercises in the southwestern United States.*

LEFT: *The crew of an M1917, .30-caliber, water-cooled, machine gun provides cover for troops maneuvering during infantry training at McClellan Field, near Sacramento, California, in 1942.*

NEW GUINEA AND GUADALCANAL

After the Japanese attack on Pearl Harbor, the army's major task was to prevent disaster and preserve American morale while building strength for the eventual counteroffensive. For the first time in its history, the country had entered a war with a large army—nearly 1,650,000 men—and an industrial system already partially retooled for war. Of far greater importance, the Japanese attacks on Pearl Harbor and the Philippines immediately led to an unprecedented, and equally historical, degree of popular support for going to war. But while the army was certainly capable of defending the Western Hemisphere against invasion, a vast expansion in both manpower and its corresponding training and support structure were needed if the fight was to be taken to America's enemies.

The U.S. Army was not ready to engage in lengthy, large-scale operations across the oceans, and many months would pass before it could launch even limited offensives. The enemy, however, was not waiting for the United States to build up its forces. During the early months of 1942, the Japanese were on the loose everywhere in the Southwest Pacific. Their forces were riding high, and after seizing the mineral-rich islands of the East Indies between Indochina and Australia, they made a determined effort to cut off Australia itself by attacking New Guinea and, to the east, Guadalcanal in the Solomon Islands.

The Japanese were thwarted in their attempts to take Port Moresby in southeastern New Guinea by the U.S. Navy in the May 1942 Battle of the Coral Sea, and again in August by the Australian Army at Milne Bay. From the Buna-Gona area in southeastern New Guinea, they pushed over the inhospitable Owen Stanley Mountains toward their objective, but Australian reinforcements pushed the Japanese back across the mountains. The U.S. 32d "Red Arrow" Division— composed of National Guard units from Michigan and

Wisconsin, as well as other American troops—joined the Australians. The combined force fought the Japanese in a series of battles conducted in steaming jungles and putrid swamps that stretched from December through January 1943. Though the Japanese received fresh troops from their nearby stronghold of Rabaul, they were soundly defeated in battles at Gona, Buna, and Sanananda.

Guadalcanal, meanwhile, was mainly a Marine show until Japanese reinforcements threatened to push them off the island. From the time the Marines landed on August 7, 1942, through the end of October, six major naval engagements were fought off the island—usually to provide cover for the arrival of additional Japanese troops—and air battles raged almost daily until 1943. The army's 25th "Tropic Lightning" Division from Hawaii and newly formed Americal Division relieved the Marines and, by February 1943, had turned the tide. Unable to defeat the Marines or hold back the army, the Japanese had no recourse but to begin a fighting withdrawal up the island chain. Together with New Guinea, Guadalcanal marked the end of their offensive operations in the Pacific.

LEFT: New England Guardsmen of the 43d Infantry Division's 172d Infantry Regiment and 103d Field Artillery Battalion conduct an orderly evacuation of the SS *Coolidge*, which struck two harbor defense mines when approaching the U.S. base at Espiritu Santo in the Southwest Pacific. Only two of the 5,340 men aboard died in the October 26, 1942, mishap, but the number would have been far higher if not for Captain Elwood J. Euart of the 103d. The captain was safely off the ship when he learned that men were trapped in the infirmary. He reentered the *Coolidge* through one of the sea doors and successfully rescued the men, but then was unable to escape himself and went down with the ship. Awarded the Distinguished Service Cross for his heroism, his citation states that Euart had "exhausted himself assisting many others, whose lives were thus undoubtedly spared at the expense of his own."

OPPOSITE: Officers inspect crewmen of the attack transport USS *McCawley* as it prepares to carry troops from New Caledonia to reinforce the marines on Guadalcanal, c. October 1942. Front to rear: Vice Admiral Robert Ghormley, who was then in command of the South Pacific Area; Captain Charles Paul McFeaters (wearing helmet), commander of the transport; and Major General Millard F. Harmon (wearing service cap), commander of the Army Forces in the South Pacific Area. Mistaking the *McCawley* for a large Japanese transport, U.S. Navy torpedo boats accidentally sunk it on the night of June 30, 1943.

32d Infantry Division insignia

FIRST SERGEANT	MASTER SERGEANT	TECHNICAL SERGEANT	STAFF SERGEANT	TECHNICIAN THIRD GRADE

Antiaircraft Command Patch

ABOVE: Antiaircraft troops at an army airbase in New Hebrides man a water-cooled, .50-caliber machine gun. *Left to right*: Private First Class Elliott Moore of Trenton, New Jersey; Corporal Raymond Elliott from Jaspar, Alabama; Corporal Johnny Jackson of Augusta, Georgia; and Private First Class Shade Mackee Jr. from Ashland, Alabama. Unlike black troops in the European and Mediterranean theaters, those in the Pacific were assigned principally to rear areas and had few opportunities to distinguish themselves in combat.

LEFT: Corporal Raymond Elliott prepares to load a 10-round feeder clip of 37-mm shells into an antiaircraft gun in New Hebrides.

SERGEANT   **TECHNICIAN FOURTH GRADE**   **CORPORAL**   **TECHNICIAN FIFTH GRADE**   **PRIVATE FIRST CLASS**

1942 RANK INSIGNIA

In January 1942, increased mechanization of the army and massive expansion of the technical requirements prompted the addition of technician third, fourth, and fifth grades. In September, the letter "T" was added to the formerly prescribed chevrons for grades three, four, and five, and the first sergeant was moved from second grade to first grade. This change described the first sergeant's patch as three chevrons and arc of three bars, with the upper bar of the arc forming a tie to the lower chevron. A hollow lozenge sits in the angle between lower chevrons and upper bar. This change also included the material as khaki chevrons, arcs, T, and lozenge on dark blue cotton background or olive-drab wool chevrons, arcs, T, and lozenge on dark blue wool backgrounds.

BELOW: Members of Battery B, 742d Antiaircraft Gun Battalion (Colored), set up a pair of 90-mm gun positions west of Borgen Bay, New Britain, on June 2, 1944. The unit, part of the 6th Antiaircraft Artillery Group, had transferred in from Espiritu Santo in the New Hebrides a week earlier and later served in New Guinea and the Philippines.

Citation: For conspicuous gallantry and intrepidity at the risk of his life above and beyond the call of duty near Munda Airstrip, New Georgia, Solomon Islands, on July 29, 1943. After twenty-seven days of bitter fighting, the enemy held a hilltop salient that commanded the approach to Munda Airstrip. Our troops were exhausted from prolonged battle and heavy casualties, but Scott advanced with the leading platoon of his company to attack the enemy position, urging his men forward in the face of enemy rifle and machine-gun fire. He had pushed forward alone to a point midway across the barren hilltop within seventy-five yards of the enemy when the enemy launched a desperate counterattack, which, if successful, would have gained undisputed possession of the hill. Enemy riflemen charged out on the plateau, firing and throwing grenades as they moved to engage our troops. The company withdrew, but Scott, with only a blasted tree stump for cover, stood his ground against the wild enemy assault. By firing his carbine and throwing the grenades in his possession, he momentarily stopped the enemy advance using the brief respite to obtain more grenades. Disregarding small-arms fire and exploding grenades aimed at him, and suffering a bullet wound in the left hand and a painful shrapnel wound in the head after his carbine had been shot from his hand, he threw grenade after grenade with devastating accuracy until the beaten enemy withdrew. Our troops, inspired to renewed effort by Scott's intrepid stand and incomparable courage, swept across the plateau to capture the hill. Four days later, from this strategic position, they captured Munda Airstrip.

RIGHT: As the intensity of the fighting increased in both Europe and the Pacific, the Medal of Honor was redesigned in 1944 to be worn around the neck and displayed above all other decorations.

BELOW: Soldiers clearing the Munda airstrip (*silhouetted by tail at right and at extreme left*) take cover beneath a derelict Ki-21-II "Sally" medium bomber at the end of the runway. Note the M-1 Garand rifle and entrenching tools at center bottom. The primary target of the 43d Infantry Division that invaded Munda on July 9, 1943, was the seizure of the Japanese airfield that had been used during the Guadalcanal campaign to bomb Henderson Field.

RIGHT: Soldiers use a portable LCV conveyor of aluminum rollers to speed the unloading of cased artillery shells on April 22, 1944, the opening day of the Hollandia, New Guinea, invasion. The operation bypassed and isolated the more than forty thousand Japanese troops that had strongly fortified Wewak—a predicament that the Japanese would repeatedly find themselves in during the war.

TWIN DRIVES

The nature of the war against Japan was such that much of its brutal combat erupted in a giant arc across the globe—in the frozen Aleutians near the Arctic Circle, to the jungles of Burma nearly five thousand miles away. The main drives, however, were right up the center in operational theaters separated by roughly a thousand miles. In the Southwest Pacific, forces under MacArthur took aim at the great Japanese base at Rabaul, located north of New Guinea on the island of New Britain, while in the Central Pacific area of Admiral Chester A. Nimitz, soldiers and Marines fought their way toward the Mariana Islands, where long-range B-29 bombers could begin their aerial campaign against the Japanese home islands. Although MacArthur had originally intended to wrest control of Rabaul from the Japanese in a frontal assault, it became evident that the same result would be achieved if the well-fortified base was cut off and its garrison allowed to wither on the vine. In both drives, U.S. forces ultimately were able to isolate and bypass the most dangerous Japanese defenses through control of the sea and air, saving countless American lives.

Operations against Rabaul began to heat up in June 1943. MacArthur intended to capture the remainder of the Solomons and clear the Japanese from the northern coast of New Guinea beginning with the villages of Lae and Salamaua. His forces landed on islands off eastern New Guinea and on the New Guinea coast northwest of Buna where they were to make contact with an Australian division that was already fighting near Salamaua. By this time, the ground combat elements of MacArthur's command were largely assigned to the U.S. Sixth Army, which began operations in the Southwest Pacific area in February 1943 under command of Lieutenant General Walter Krueger.

About the same time the Sixth Army troops began their June offensive, Admiral William "Bull" Halsey's South Pacific forces, operating under MacArthur's strategic direction, landed the 43d, then 25th Infantry divisions on the island of New Georgia in the central Solomons. The Japanese airstrip at Munda was Halsey's principal objective, and it fell on August 5, 1943, after six weeks of heavy fighting. There also was considerable air and naval action, and the Japanese lost heavily in ships and planes as they first reinforced and then evacuated their island positions.

The next major operation was an invasion of the island of Bougainville at Empress Augusta Bay in November by the 3d Marine Division. The Marines were followed within the month by the army's Americal Division, and the Japanese on the island expended much of their strength in useless attacks against these units. It was late November before the beachhead at Empress Augusta Bay was secure, and this beachhead was all that was needed to accomplish the mission. No attempt was made to capture the entire island. Allied planes neutralized enemy airfields in the northern part of the island. The Allied command made use of its naval and air superiority to contain the Japanese garrison on Bougainville and other Japanese-held islands in the area.

During the campaign in the northern Solomons, MacArthur moved ahead with the other

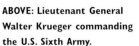

ABOVE: Lieutenant General Walter Krueger commanding the U.S. Sixth Army.

NEW GUINEA: 1942–1944

The Japanese established themselves along the northern shores of eastern New Guinea at Buna and Gona in late July 1942 and immediately pushed into the rugged Owen Stanley Mountains to attack America's Australian allies. Advancing along a mere path—the Kokoda Trail—that the Australians believed was unable to support a large-scale operation, their objective was Port Moresby on the southern coast. The Japanese also supported their offensive with an amphibious assault at Milne Bay, but this was defeated in a hard fight by a small force of Australians and U.S. Army combat engineers.

The same sort of desperate jungle fighting that occurred on Guadalcanal hundreds of miles to the east erupted along the Kokoda Trail, and the Japanese offensive ran out of steam as both sides battled the rain and sodden terrain as much as each other. A mostly Australian counteroffensive operated under the very same severe conditions that plagued the earlier fighting, but by November the Australians had secured the trail and now concentrated on capturing the three key Japanese bases on the northern coast: Buna, Gona, and Salamaua.

The Australian advance was aided by the U.S. 32d Division, which established bases to the south of Buna while the Australians pushed on down the trail. Gona was taken on December 9, Buna on January 2, 1943, and Sanananda, much further up the coast, was captured ten days later. With a firm footing on the north shore of New Guinea, General Douglas MacArthur opened a campaign to neutralize or capture the key Japanese base at Rabaul on the nearby island of New Britain. The pattern established here, as in the Solomon Islands to the east, was that American and Australian troops secured the ground, and the air forces then moved in to establish local control of the air and seas by providing an umbrella for further offensive operations.

The Japanese, anticipating another round of Allied offensives, began moving two fresh divisions from China and Korea to New Guinea. In early March 1943, the U.S. Army Air Force in the Southwest Pacific area located and massacred a convoy carrying most of the Imperial 51st Division through the Bismarck Sea to New Guinea. Navy PT boats moved in to mop up many of the survivors. The Japanese overreacted to this battle by never attempting another major convoy again and directing most of their reinforcements that had already reached New Guinea to undertake a costly attack against Allied airfields on the island. The result was even more strain on Japan's ground forces' already inadequate maritime logistic efforts. U.S. attacks relieved the pressure of a Japanese assault on the Australian airfield at Wau and bypassed imperial troops, many of whom would suffer a slow, starving death—unsupported in isolated jungles and unable to seize or neutralize the all-important Allied airfields.

MacArthur pushed Allied forces on toward the Huon Peninsula that poked like a finger toward Rabaul from New Guinea. Using a secretly built airstrip, U.S. airpower destroyed the preponderance of Japanese aircraft in the area, then an Australian division landed near the key villages of Lae and Salamaua on September 4, 1943. The U.S. 503d Parachute Infantry Regiment and a detachment of hastily trained Australian artillerymen conducted the first operational parachute assault in the Pacific, seizing a nearby airbase so that more Australian troops could be airlifted in. By mid-September 1943, both Lae and Salamaua were in Allied hands. MacArthur, advancing his timetable, then pre-empted a Japanese move to beef up its garrison at Finschafen, New Guinea, by landing an Australian brigade first. After some hard fighting, the town was captured. All subsequent attempts to recapture it, including one of the last Japanese amphibious attacks of the war, were defeated.

Subsequent amphibious operations established U.S. forces on New Britain and allowed the construction of airbases within easy reach of Rabaul, whose own airfields quickly were rendered unusable. The Allies, secure in their defensive positions on New Guinea and New Britain, simply left the Japanese ground forces to their own devices. Rabaul was no longer of any importance, and the bypassed Japanese Eighteenth Army on New Guinea battered itself uselessly against the U.S. 32d Infantry Division and 112th Cavalry Regiment along the Driniumor River in July and August of 1944.

LEFT: *Troops from the 41st Infantry Division push inland from their beachhead during the invasion of Wakde Island, New Guinea, on May 15, 1944. The Japanese airfield seized during three days of fighting was speedily converted to a U.S. base to support operations against the island of Biak.*

OPPOSITE: *George Strock photographed dead Americans on Buna Beach in February 1943 for Life magazine. The picture was not published until September 20, 1943. President Franklin D. Roosevelt authorized the release of this image, the first to depict American soldiers dead on the battlefield, because he was concerned that the American public was growing complacent about the human cost of the war.*

RIGHT: *Sergeant Carl Weinke and Private Ernest Marjoram, Signal Corps cameramen attached to the 24th Infantry Division, wade through a stream while covering the drive inland from Tanahmerah Bay, New Guinea, on April 22, 1944.*

prong of the offensive in New Guinea and western New Britain. At the same time, U.S. Army paratroopers, conducting the first American airborne operation in the Pacific, took the Japanese airstrip at Nadzab, and Australian forces—with American assistance—took Salamaua and Lae in September. Allied forces next moved to take Finschhafen in October 1943 in an unsuccessful effort to trap the Japanese survivors of Lae and Salamaua. Further U.S. and Allied operations in the area tightened the noose around Rabaul, and the capture of the Admiralty Islands by the 1st Cavalry Division in February enabled the navy to establish a major naval base for continued operations against Japan. More operations were conducted the following month, and the 100,000-man Japanese garrison at Rabaul was effectively isolated and out of the war.

Further north, as part of the navy's Central Pacific drive, the New York Guardsmen of the 27th Infantry Division struck at Makin Atoll in the Gilbert Islands, where fanatic Japanese—when not defending from deep underground bunkers—were hidden overhead, strapped into palm trees. After Makin and "Bloody Tarawa" fell in late November 1943, U.S. forces skirted the fringe of the Marshall Islands and struck at the heart. The 4th Marine and 7th Infantry "Hourglass" divisions penetrated Japan's outer defense zone at Kwajalein Atoll in January 1944, and the establishment of a major base of operations there was a nail in the coffin for the Imperial Navy's continued use of the region's islands as an effective barrier against the Americans. Soon, what had been the key Japanese bastion at Truk Atoll became, in effect, a giant prison camp and convenient target for U.S. Navy and Army Air Force practice bombing runs. The Japanese were learning the hard way that their outer defenses were highly vulnerable to the leap-frog and island-hopping tactics of MacArthur and Nimitz, but as American forces drove deeper and deeper toward Tokyo, it became harder to bypass Japanese defenses.

ABOVE INSET: Cattaraugus Cutlery produced a large quantity of 10⅜-inch fighting knives with heavy-duty blades and leather hand grips for both the army and navy during the war.

LEFT: Exhausted 32d Infantry Division soldiers await orders in a frontline slit trench during the two-month campaign to oust Japanese forces from Buna, New Guinea.

LEFT: A 7th Infantry Division soldier uses a flamethrower to burn out a Japanese bunker on Kwajalein Island on February 4, 1944, while others wait with rifles, ready to fire on any Imperial marines who try to escape.

BELOW: A Japanese fuel dump blazes as American forces thread their way up Pancake Hill during the invasion of Hollandia, New Guinea, on April 22, 1944. The 41st Infantry Division soldiers are supported by M4AI Shermans as they mop up snipers near Humbolt Bay beachhead, where they landed the previous day.

BURMA AND THE ALEUTIANS

As American forces fought and maneuvered their way west, other campaigns played themselves out on the peripheries. The 7th Infantry Division, which expertly took apart the Japanese defenses at Kwajalein, only recently had completed operations in the Aleutians, where it lost nearly as many men to frostbite as to Japanese bullets. Several frozen lumps of land located far to the west in this Alaskan island chain had been easily occupied by imperial forces as a sideshow to Japan's attempted invasion of Midway Island in 1942. Though of no particular strategic importance, these Japanese outposts were on

American territory and lay uncomfortably close to U.S. Lend Lease supply routes to the Soviet Union. If left alone, they had the potential to become dangerous bases for raiding Alaska and restricting air and sea operations in the North Pacific.

The United States did not have ships, planes, and troops to spare for the islands' immediate recapture, but advanced airfields were established in August 1942 on Adak and Amchitka, from which American bombers attacked the principal enemy concentrations on Kiska and Attu. When it became clear in the spring of 1943 that the U.S. strategic situation in the Pacific had stabilized, plans were made to evict the Japanese, and the "Hourglass" Division launched its assault on Attu in

M2 60-MM MORTAR ROUNDS

The mortar is the infantry's own artillery, ready to fire at a moment's notice. The most portable and easily employed of the U.S. mortars was the lightweight, 60-mm (2.36-inch) weapon that could be carried easily by a single soldier. It was designed to provide indirect fire support of platoons and companies, with each infantry company containing a mortar section in its heavy weapons platoon. When on the march and with no vehicles in support, some of the infantrymen often carried individual rounds for the mortar teams so that additional ammunition would be available in case of a sudden, prolonged fight.

BELOW: A 7th Infantry Division mortar team on Attu lobs 81-mm shells over a frozen ridge in support of a June 4 assault.

TRAINING PRACTICE SHELL   HIGH EXPLOSIVE SHELL   WHITE PHOSPHORUS SMOKE SHELL   ILLUMINATION SHELL

RIGHT: U.S. 7th Infantry Division troops maneuver under fire during the battle for the Aleutian island of Attu. The Japanese had decided not to oppose the May 11, 1943, landing in the face of U.S. naval guns, so they organized defenses inland instead. Subduing the roughly three-thousand-man Japanese garrison cost U.S. forces 3,929 casualties, including 1,481 dead. More than half of the casualties were a result of the cold, wet environment, as well as friendly fire incidents on the mist-shrouded terrain.

May 1943. The Japanese put up a desperate defense, but they were destroyed almost to a man in fighting that lasted three weeks. In August, a combined Canadian-7th Division force assaulted Kiska, where the Japanese had developed their largest base, and the combined force was surprised to find that the island had been secretly evacuated under the cover of heavy summer fogs.

Far across the Barents and Okhotsk seas, the coastal regions of Siberia, and vast expanse of China, another fight was brewing in terrain and weather that couldn't have been more different than that of the Aleutians. To help the British recover northern Burma and clear the way for construction of the Ledo Road from the northeast corner of India to China, the army called for volunteers to perform "a dangerous and hazardous mission" behind Japanese lines, cutting supply routes and communications. The soldiers who stepped forward were all veterans of the New Guinea and Solomons' fighting or of the intensive jungle training conducted in Panama. They arrived in India in November 1943 and began hard training under British Major General Orde Wingate of "Wingate's Raiders" fame. Formed as the three-battalion 5307th Composite Unit (Provisional), they quickly became known as "Merrill's Marauders" after their commander, Brigadier General Frank D. Merrill.

ABOVE: Lieutenant General Joseph "Vinegar Joe" Stilwell had been fighting Japanese field armies—and an inept, duplicitous, Chinese leadership—from 1942 to late 1944 in the China-Burma-India Theater. Placed in command of Army Ground Forces, he brought his experience to bear in training troops for the upcoming invasion of Japan. He subsequently was picked to lead the U.S. 10th Army during planned operations on Tokyo in 1946.

LEFT INSET: Lieutenant General Joseph Stilwell (*right*) marches his staff out of Burma ahead of advancing Japanese forces at a cadence that his men described as the "Stilwell stride"—105 paces per minute whether going uphill or downhill. Stilwell arrived at his command in the China-Burma-India Theater on March 11, 1943—just as Allied defenses were collapsing—and later told reporters: "We got run out of Burma, and it is humiliating as hell. I think we ought to find out what caused it, go back, and retake it." After the retreat, Stilwell famously placed on his desk a placard containing the motto "*illegitimi non carborundum*," which in fractured Latin translates as "don't let the bastards grind you down."

BELOW INSET: The M1943 field cap worn by Lieutenant Colonel McPherson LeMoyne in the China-Burma-India Theater of World War II. LeMoyne, who was promoted to colonel in 1945, was part of the joint Chinese-American 1st Provisional Tank Group (1st PTG) originally activated at Ramgarh, India, on October 1, 1943. U.S. Army Colonel Rothwell H. Brown commanded this group of six provisional tank battalions. The 1st PTG fought in Burma, supporting Merrill's Marauders and the Mars Task Force in 1944–1945.

Entering the wild country of northern Burma, they found that the jungle was even thicker than the Solomons. Clothes were damp all the time, even in the driest part of the year; weapons rusted if not taken apart and oiled every day. The mountains, forests, and rivers of Burma were imposing and beautiful, but they were deadly obstacles, and the land swarmed with enemies—animals, bugs, snakes, disease, and, of course, Japanese. In just over five months of combat, the Marauders and their trusty pack mules advanced seven hundred fifty miles through some of the harshest jungle terrain in the world, while fighting five major engagements and thirty-two separate actions.

Much to the disgust of the British who were successfully conducting wide-ranging special operations throughout Burma, senior American commanders didn't know exactly how to use the superbly trained, but very lightly armed, Ranger regiment—so the regiment was given conventional missions, such as maintaining positional road blocks against large enemy forces. Despite its excellent performance time and time again, missions for which the 5307th was not suited resulted in excessively high casualties for which there were no replacements. Disease and malnutrition also took a terrible toll, as the unit essentially expended itself. After its final mission against the Japanese air base at Myitkyina in August 1944, the Marauders were down to just one hundred thirty combat-effective soldiers out of its 2,997-man force.

The survivors were consolidated with the 475th Infantry Regiment (Special) of the division-sized Mars Task Force, which included the 1st Chinese Regiment and the Texas National Guardsmen of the 124th Cavalry Regiment (Special). Learning from the mistakes of the past, the Mars Task Force successfully conducted operations deep into the jungle and cut the Japanese-held Burma Road in January 1945. Today, the successor of the 5307th Composite Unit (Provisional) and 475th is the 75th Ranger Regiment, which bears the Nationalist Chinese sun symbol of the China-Burma-India theater in the upper-left quadrant of its crest.

BELOW: Second Lieutenant Philip H. Dunbar and Private Samuel P. Campbell, attached to the Chinese 112th Regiment, 38th Infantry Division, are among the first American combat men to cross from Burma into China as they ford the fast Namran River leading supply laden mules on December 29, 1944.

RIGHT: Brigadier General Frank Merrill (*left*), commander of the 5307th Composite Unit (Provisional), and some of his staff discuss new methods to hamper Japanese operations on June 16, 1944. Popularly known as "Merrill's Marauders," the regimental-size force battled the Japanese, hunger, and disease, as they traversed more jungle on their long-range missions than any other U.S. Army unit of the war.

BELOW: The perilous Ledo Road was built in sections from 1942 through early 1945 in order to reopen a land route to China after a portion of the original Burma Road was captured by the Japanese. Even before the road reached China, it was important to the logistical support of the Allied forces battling the Japanese. Black and white army engineer battalions totaling more than fifteen thousand men worked on the route along with thirty-seven thousand laborers.

more Firepower to 'em!

Your *METAL* is on the attack KEEP IT COMING!

U.S. ARMY

"THE GIRL HE LEFT BEHIND" IS STILL BEHIND HIM She's a **WOW** WOMAN ORDNANCE WORKER

OPPOSITE BOTTOM: The troops of the 148th Infantry, 37th Infantry Division, follow in the tracks of tanks advancing into Japanese territory along Bougainville's Numa Numa Trail on April 1, 1944. The Sherman tank belongs to the 754th Tank Battalion.

BREAKING THE RING

The Marianas, lying some fifteen hundred miles from Japan, were perfectly suited to serve as a base of operation for the new, long-range B-29 Superfortress—especially the islands of Saipan and Tinian. They also represented a new type of Pacific fighting. These were not flat, palm-fringed atolls where the tricky enemy fell back or fell dead. They were large islands where tanks could achieve at least some degree of maneuver and where massed artillery could be used with greater effect. The Marianas also presented high-level army planners with a convincing model for future combat against Japanese field armies on Formosa, the Philippines, and Japan itself. One hundred twenty-five thousand troops of a joint U.S. Army-Marine force conducted both an opposed landing and ground offensive on a corps (multidivision) frontage against sizeable enemy forces, defending terrain similar to that on Japan—all on an island that contained large numbers of enemy civilians.

Amphibious assaults were made against Saipan on June 15, Guam on July 20, and Tinian on July 23, 1944. All three islands were strongly garrisoned by Japanese troops that contested every yard of ground. The opening battle on Saipan pitted a U.S. corps containing the 27th Infantry Division, with the 2d and 4th Marine divisions on its flanks, against roughly twenty-nine thousand imperial troops, and it took nearly a month of vicious fighting before the island was secured. In an ominous precursor of what U.S. forces might expect when invading Okinawa and Japan's Home Islands, several hundred frightened Japanese civilians committed suicide by leaping to their deaths from the heights above

Marpi Point at the island's extreme northern tip. Marines, powerless to stop the carnage, even witnessed instances of armed Japanese soldiers forcing people over the edge to the jagged rocks below.

While fighting raged on Saipan, the Imperial Navy hastily reassembled their fleet from Biak and the Philippines and sailed north to defend the Marianas area and defeat the U.S. carrier task forces operating under Admiral Raymond A. Spruance. A massive air battle, soon dubbed the "The Great Marianas Turkey Shoot," erupted four days after the Saipan landings in which hundreds of Japanese aircraft were shot down. Stripped of carrier planes, the Japanese fleet fled westward but lost more ships and planes before reaching safety beyond the range of the U.S. Navy's aircraft. In all, the Japanese lost roughly four hundred fifty carrier aircraft, one hundred fifty land-based planes, and three aircraft carriers to submarine and air attack. The navy lost 123 aircraft but rescued most of its pilots.

With the Imperial Navy removed from the equation, the 77th Infantry and 3d Marine divisions retook Guam by the end of July, and Tinian was secured on August 1 by a pair of Marine divisions. Meanwhile, far to the southwest, the 41st Infantry Division (made up of Guardsmen from Oregon, Washington, Idaho, and Montana) succeeded in taking Biak after a lengthy struggle. Then, in mid-September, the 31st Infantry Division (Alabama, Florida, Louisiana, and Mississippi Guardsmen) landed at Morotai Island, on the veritable doorstep of the Philippines. With these moves in the Central and Southwest Pacific, the forces of Nimitz and MacArthur were poised for the reconquest of the Philippines.

DO IT RIGHT
MAKE IT BITE

The M-1 does MY talking!
Are you CAREFUL
what YOU say or write?

MINE EYES HAVE SEEN THE GLORY
WOMEN'S ARMY CORPS
ARMY OF THE UNITED STATES

ABOVE: Observing the pre-invasion bombardment and maneuver of assault craft from the bridge of the attack transport USS *Fremont* are Major General Paul J. Mueller, commander of the 81st Infantry Division (*center*); Rear Admiral William H.P. Blandy, commander of the navy amphibious unit (*left*); and an unidentified officer.

LEFT: 81st "Wildcat" Infantry Division troops descend cargo nets into landing craft headed for the beaches during the invasion of Angaur in the Palau Islands on September 17, 1944.

M1 GARAND

The M1 Garand (*above*) is a .30-06-caliber semi-automatic rifle. More than 4 million Garands were manufactured during the war and General George S. Patton Jr. firmly maintained that "the M1 rifle is the greatest battle implement ever devised." An additional 2.25 million were produced through 1957 with 25th Infantry and 101st Airborne division soldiers still carrying them as late as 1963.

ABOVE: Intelligence personnel attached to the 81st Infantry Division examine papers and other items captured from the Japanese during operations on Angaur, September 1944. Training large numbers of Americans and Japanese-Americans at Military Intelligence Service Language Schools began to pay big intelligence dividends for the army when combat operations began to ramp up in the summer of 1944 with the invasion of the Mariana Islands.

BELOW: M1 Garand bayonet and twelve-clip bandolier with pockets for carrying forty-eight rounds in eight-round clips. Beginning in 1942 the army cut the M1910 bayonet from the then-standard sixteen-inch blade down to ten inches for the Garand.

Citation: Captain Ben L. Salomon was serving at Saipan, in the Marianas Islands on July 7, 1944, as the surgeon for the 2d Battalion, 105th Infantry Regiment, 27th Infantry Division. The regiment's 1st and 2d battalions were attacked by an overwhelming force estimated between three thousand and five thousand Japanese soldiers. It was one of the largest attacks attempted in the Pacific Theater during World War II.

Although both units fought furiously, the enemy soon penetrated the battalions' combined perimeter and inflicted overwhelming casualties. In the first minutes of the attack, approximately thirty wounded soldiers walked, crawled, or were carried into Salomon's aid station, and the small tent soon filled with wounded men.

As the perimeter began to be overrun, it became increasingly difficult for Salomon to work on the wounded. He then saw a Japanese soldier bayoneting one of the wounded soldiers lying near the tent. Firing from a squatting position, Salomon quickly killed the enemy soldier. Then, as he turned his attention back to the wounded, two more Japanese soldiers appeared in the front entrance of the tent. As these enemy soldiers were killed, four more crawled under the tent walls. Rushing them, Salomon kicked the knife out of the hand of one, shot another, and bayoneted a third. He butted the fourth enemy soldier in the stomach, and a wounded comrade then shot and killed the enemy soldier.

Realizing the gravity of the situation, Salomon ordered the wounded to make their way as best they could back to the regimental aid station, while he attempted to hold off the enemy until they were clear. He then grabbed a rifle from one of the wounded and rushed out of the tent. After four men were killed while manning a machine gun, Salomon took control of it. When his body was later found, ninety-eight dead enemy soldiers were piled in front of his position. Salomon's extraordinary heroism and devotion to duty are in keeping with the highest traditions of military service and reflect great credit upon himself, his unit, and the United States Army.

LEFT: Two M4 Shermans of Company A, 710th Tank Battalion, guard the heavily fortified Bloody Nose Ridge used by the Japanese during the battle on Peleliu. The tanks were part of the 321st Regimental Combat Team, 81st Infantry Division, sent to the island on September 24, 1944, to reinforce the badly battered 1st Marine Division, which had landed little more than a week earlier. By mid-October, the 81st's 323d Infantry and other combat elements had arrived, and the division took over the reduction of the Japanese defenses.

BELOW: LSTs (landing ship, tanks) moored to hastily built jetties disgorge thousands of tons of vehicles and supplies onto a Leyte invasion beach to support the U.S. Sixth Army division's fight for the island, c. October 20, 1944. Army engineers expanded the Tacloban airfield (*center-left*) by constructing a twenty-five-hundred-foot runway of steel matting in just two days. It started receiving aircraft shortly after this photo was taken.

RETURN TO THE PHILIPPINES

Strategists on both sides of the Pacific believed that, as during the American invasion in 1898 and the Japanese invasion of 1941, the battle for the Philippines would be decided on the northernmost island of Luzon. U.S. intelligence confirmed as expected that the Japanese had massed their principal ground, air, and naval strength in Luzon, so American strategists planned to first gain a foothold close to Morotai and New Guinea by establishing a huge staging area on the large, weakly held island of Mindanao. Then, U.S. forces would leap north to Leyte and finally to Luzon after they had gained air supremacy over that area.

When naval reconnaissance and a series of raids in September 1944 revealed little apparent Japanese activity in the Philippines, Admiral Halsey proposed striking directly at Leyte. The U.S. Chiefs of Staff quickly approved this change of strategy, as it would split the Japanese forces in the Philippines, shorten the campaign for the islands, and practically force the Japanese Fleet to come out in the open to meet the threat. MacArthur's forces landed at Leyte on October 20, 1944, fulfilling his promise to return to the Philippines, and the campaign appeared to be off to a fine start. The U.S. Sixth Army invaded with four divisions abreast, and initial opposition was light. This was not to last.

BELOW: South of Tacloban off Highway #1 on the Philippine island of Leyte, the crew of No. 2 Gun, A Battery, 465th Field Artillery Battalion, stands poised to ram home a 214-pound projectile into the breech of their 8-inch howitzer.

BELOW: After breaking into Manila's Rizal Stadium, 1st Cavalry Division troops move cautiously across right field. An important Japanese supply dump was located under the bleachers, and a deep, fifteen-foot-wide drainage ditch on the other side of the facility limited tank access to the area. These soldiers are attempting to attack the "back door" of the fortified ballpark, but Imperial Marines had fortified the infield and waited until troops had entered the enclosed space before firing from the dugouts-turned-bunkers and concrete-lined stairwells in the bleachers. The 1st Cavalry used tanks, satchel charges, and flamethrowers to reduce the defenses on February 16, 1945.

RIGHT: General Douglas MacArthur passes wrecked enemy planes on Clark Field on Luzon after its recapture from the Japanese in January 1945. Three years earlier, Japanese generals were doing the same thing—only the planes were American.

LEFT: MacArthur visits the remains of Camp O'Donnell on Luzon, where the Death March of the captured Americans and Filipinos from Bataan ended, January 29, 1945. The general reads dog tags on the eight-foot cement cross built by American POWs. Japanese authorities had turned over a supply of concrete to the men for camp construction in June 1944, and a portion was used to cast a memorial to those who had died during the march and were continuing to succumb to malnutrition and disease.

BELOW: MacArthur and staff wade ashore in the Philippines on October 20, 1944.

The Japanese at first were reluctant to pull forces from the defense of Luzon, but buoyed by pilot reports of both real and imagined losses to the U.S. Fleet from the new kamikaze tactics—where suicidal pilots dove their aircraft directly into ships—the Japanese decided to commit a large portion of their forces and put up a hard fight for the island. The Japanese shifted their remaining air and naval might against the American forces in and around Leyte, and were successful for a time in sending large numbers of ground reinforcements to the island. The U.S. Navy was involved in a far-flung battle lasting several days, and then suffered from the steady attrition of kamikaze attacks against everything from transports to aircraft carriers.

As had been anticipated, the attack on Leyte had presented the Imperial Navy with a challenge it could not ignore. Gathering together its remaining strength, the Japanese Fleet converged on Leyte Gulf in three columns and seriously threatened the success of the whole operation. In the end, Japan's fleet was almost completely destroyed, and for the rest of the war Allied naval forces were in virtual control of the surface of the Pacific but still vulnerable to the suicidal kamikazes.

In the short run, however, Japanese soldiers poured into Leyte, and the Sixth Army found itself engaged in a major struggle. Two months of heavy ground fighting took place before American troops had secured the parts of the island necessary for air and logistical bases. It had taken equally long for the Army Air Force and naval elements to gain air superiority and began to seriously interdict the reinforcements. The campaign was decided in a last-ditch fight in the mountains, and an attempt by the Japanese to knock out a major air base ended in failure. The conquest of Leyte ultimately involved more than one hundred thousand additional ground troops than anticipated. It took the United States so long to accomplish that the island couldn't be used to significantly support the subsequent invasion of Luzon, but it did become the springboard from which the central and southern Philippines were liberated.

On January 9, 1945, Krueger's Sixth Army made a massive amphibious assault on Luzon along the shores of the Lingayen Gulf, and the 1st Cavalry Division spearheaded the assault, following the same invasion route that the Japanese had used in 1941 and 1942. The Japanese commander in the Philippines did not intend to defend the Central Plains and Manila Bay area; he sought only to pin down major elements of MacArthur's forces in order to delay Allied progress to Japan. Nevertheless, strong Japanese forces, primarily naval, disregarded his plan and held out in Manila.

The powerful American force that drove down the central valley was forced to battle for the capital during a month of bitter

BELOW: Close-in fighting forced this mortar team of the 129th Infantry, 37th Infantry Division, to dig in among the tombstones at the Baguio cemetery on Luzon on April 24, 1945.

Citation: Rudolph (then Tech Sergeant) was acting as platoon leader at Munoz, Luzon, Philippine Islands. While administering first aid on the battlefield, he observed enemy fire issuing from a nearby culvert. Crawling to the culvert with rifle and grenades, he killed three of the enemy concealed there. He then worked his way across open terrain toward a line of enemy pillboxes that had immobilized his company.

Nearing the first pillbox, he hurled a grenade through its embrasure and charged the position. With his bare hands, he tore away the wood and tin covering, then dropped a grenade through the opening, killing the enemy gunners and destroying their machine gun. Ordering several riflemen to cover his further advance, Rudolph seized a pick mattock and made his way to the second pillbox. Piercing its top with the mattock, he dropped a grenade through the hole, fired several rounds from his rifle into it, and smothered any surviving enemy by sealing the hole and the embrasure with earth. In quick succession he attacked and neutralized sixmore pillboxes. Later, when his platoon was attacked by an enemy tank, he advanced under covering fire, climbed to the top of the tank and dropped a white phosphorus grenade through the turret, destroying the crew. Through his outstanding heroism, superb courage, and leadership, and complete disregard for his own safety, Rudolph cleared a path for an advance that culminated in one of the most decisive victories of the Philippine campaign.

RIGHT: U.S. Army master sergeant's Eisenhower field jacket worn by Medal of Honor recipient Donald E. Rudolph during his service with the U.S. Fifth Army in the last days of World War II and before his promotion to second lieutenant.

BOTTOM RIGHT: A standard U.S. Army service coat was issued to enlisted personnel. This example was worn by Staff Sergeant Ross Shuler, 19th Infantry Regiment, 24th Infantry Division. The 24th was stationed at Schofield Barracks in Hawaii before the war, and the star on the American Defense Service ribbon (*bottom row, center*) indicates that Shuler was present during the attack on Pearl Harbor. The Purple Heart ribbon (*top row, center*) tells us that Shuler was wounded during one of the two operations in the Pacific in which he fought, which are indicated by the two stars on the Asiatic-Pacific service ribbon (*bottom row, right*).

fighting, but opening Manila's harbor couldn't wait for the city to be taken. As before, Corregidor guarded the sea approach, only now "The Rock," as it had long been known, was manned by six thousand Japanese marines. In a daring operation, the 503d Parachute Infantry Regiment was dropped onto the old American garrison's tiny, nine-hole golf course and parade ground in the midst of the great fortress. The February 16 assaults on these pinpoint drop areas took the Japanese completely by surprise, and an infantry regiment landed on a cleared beach the next day to join them in taking Corregidor. Bataan was now avenged, and the 503d earned its nickname, "The Rock," which today appears in its unit insignia.

While the Japanese in Manila were blasted and burned out yard by yard, the main Japanese forces concentrated in three mountainous strongholds where they could conduct a protracted defense, one just east of the capital that had to be reduced in a costly series of engagements. Except for the strong pocket in the mountains of north-central Luzon, where the Japanese were still fighting when the war ended, organized Japanese resistance in Luzon was overcome by the end of May 1945. Meanwhile, the new U.S. Eighth Army had completed the operation on Leyte, subdued the Japanese in the southern Philippines in a series of amphibious attacks, and conducted the mop-up phase of operations on Luzon. The Leyte and Luzon campaigns had cost the U.S. Army sixty-two thousand five hundred combat casualties, and the Philippines were liberated in fighting that did not end until the surrender of Japan.

LEFT: Paratroopers of the 503d Parachute Infantry Regiment land on a precariously small drop zone on Corregidor Island on February 16, 1945. Expecting a conventional seaborne assault like the one that captured the fortress in 1942, the jump caught the sixty-five-hundred-man Japanese garrison completely by surprise, severely disrupting its defenses.

BELOW INSET: U.S. Model 1941 helmet, c. 1944. Resembling football helmets of the period, these were made under contract by various sporting goods companies, including Rawlings and Spalding. Developed during an armored vehicle crew test in 1938, the tanker helmet was made of composite leather and vulcanized construction, and it contained a headset for crew communication.

BELOW: In preparation for the invasion of Japan, elements of the 81st "Wildcat" Infantry Division's 710th Tank Battalion and 2d Battalion, 321st Infantry, maneuver during an August 1945 field exercise near Valencia in Leyte.

Battalion (Armored Flamethrower)
were in constant demand during
the Okinawa Campaign. By the
time the fighting finally sputtered
to an end on June 30, 1945, an
estimated 4,788 enemy were killed
by the deadly machines
or infantry operating in direct support. Here, a 713th Sherman
torches a Japanese bunker built
into a coral escarpment midway
through the nearly three months
of fighting.

OKINAWA

When American soldiers landed on Okinawa on Easter
morning, April 1, 1945, they penetrated the inner defenses
of the Japanese Empire. Lying barely three hundred fifty
miles from the Japanese Home Islands, the Imperial Army
was determined to hold the island at all costs. Nearly one
hundred twenty thousand troops manned the extensive
fortifications dug into the rugged hills of southern Okinawa.
Against these elaborate enemy positions built around caves,
ancient tombs, the stone rubble of ruined villages, and tunnel
networks built from one side of its hills and ridges to the
other, the Americans fought a slow, tedious campaign of
continuous assault, hill by hill, cave by cave.

The campaign, conducted by the new U.S. Tenth Army,
actually had begun several days earlier with the seizure of
small but important islands near Okinawa, where forward
naval bases were established. The first few days after the main
assault saw little fighting, as the Japanese had decided not
to contest the invasion beaches—which they reasoned were far
too vulnerable to the direct fire of U.S. Navy warships
off shore. This soon ended when the 7th, 27th, and 96th
Infantry Divisions ran into the Shuri line. The defense was
fanatic in the extreme. American troops suffered heavy casualties, as did even more army and marine divisions that entered
the battle. And the navy, too, experienced heavy losses. The
kamikazes killed five thousand sailors and sank some twenty-
five American ships, plus damaged 165 others, during their

M3 SUBMACHINE GUN

Firing a heavy, man-stopping, .45-caliber bullet from a 30-round
magazine, the weapon had a rate of fire so slow that individual shots
could be squeezed off. The M3 was often described as a pleasant gun
to shoot and was fondly nicknamed the "grease gun" because of its
resemblance to a common auto mechanic's tool. Early models had a
distressing tendency to discharge when accidentally dropped on a
hard surface.

desperate attempt to stave off defeat. Among the nearly thirty-five thousand American ground force battle casualties (including seven thousand dead) was Lieutenant General Simon B. Buckner Jr., killed by Japanese artillery on June 18 in the final stages of the fighting.

When the Tenth Army's soldiers and marines completed the campaign on Okinawa in June, they had closed the ring around Japan, effectively isolating it from its conquered territories in Asia. Continued bombing by Army Air Force B-29s had by now nearly crippled its industry, but the Japanese government continued to ignore Allied demands for surrender. Twenty-one army and six marine divisions, along with a vast array of supporting units, had thrown the Japanese for a loss from New Guinea and Guadalcanal to Okinawa. Preparations now began for the invasion of Japan, and the Pacific forces were going to receive some greatly appreciated help from an unexpected quarter—the U.S. First Army, which had pummeled its way from Normandy to the heart of Germany, as well as the U.S. Eighth Air Force from its English bases.

LEFT: Tenth Army commander Lieutenant General Simon B. Buckner Jr. (*right*) observes the fighting along the final Japanese defense line above the southern tip of Okinawa. Moments after the photo was taken on June 18, 1945, the general was killed by a Japanese artillery round that struck near the officers.

BELOW: Members of a heavy weapons platoon on Okinawa lob a stream of mortar bombs into Japanese positions.

RYUKYUS 1945

BLOODBATH ON OKINAWA

The invasion of Okinawa, the main island in the Ryukyu Island chain, was in many ways like the savage battle just fought by the marines on Iwo Jima, but on a much larger scale. The Japanese objective was not simply to bleed and delay the Americans, but to defeat them and even throw them back into the sea. Having failed to achieve a decisive battle in the Philippines, the Japanese Army decided to make the defense of Okinawa the "decisive battle" that would bring the Americans to their senses as well as set the stage for favorable diplomatic efforts. Perhaps a repeat of the slaughter at Iwo Jima on a more massive scale would keep the barbarians from their sacred shores and leave their emperor on the throne and their imperial colonies intact.

Lieutenant General Simon B. Buckner Jr. (who had commanded in the Aleutians) was chosen to lead the U.S. Tenth Army, augmented by the III Marine Amphibious Corps under Major General Roy S. Geiger—eventually over half a million men—for this campaign, codenamed Operation Iceberg. Admiral Raymond Spruance would command overall, but would essentially be limited to naval support once the troops were ashore. Buckner had no idea what was in store for his men.

The Japanese 32d Army on Okinawa was ably commanded by Lieutenant General Mitsuru Ushijima who decided not to contest the beaches, but rather to withdraw into a series of heavily fortified lines along the perpendicular coral mountain ridges that formed natural barriers across the southern part of the island. As at Iwo Jima and Peleliu, the goal was to force the Americans into a World War I-style battle of attrition against defensive belts well supported by artillery. Despite losing his best combat division, taken away from him

to reinforce Formosa (Taiwan), Ushijima still had about 120,000 Imperial soldiers and auxiliaries plus more than one thousand kamikaze aircraft poised for action on Kyushu, the southernmost island of Japan, and Formosa.

The Americans' ground, air, and naval forces at Okinawa exceeded even those for Leyte Gulf and would go down in history as the greatest seaborne invasion, perhaps, of all time. More than 180,000 men were landed in the first twenty-four hours. However, first blood went to the Japanese as the American carrier forces attempted their now-predictable practice of neutralizing Japanese air power prior to the landing beginning as early as March 1945. By the time Buckner's forces landed on D-Day April 1, 1945, Spruance already had four large carriers damaged by the new Japanese aerial suicide tactics and the aircraft carrier USS *Franklin* was so badly pummeled that she almost

sank. Nevertheless, the landing forces—embarked on over 1,200 ships and craft—swarmed ashore and quickly overran the lightly defended northern three-quarters of the island.

When Buckner's army forces turned south they ran into fierce resistance along the first of the Japanese defense lines. The struggle now turned into an all-out battle of attrition on land and on sea. Ashore it was "cave warfare" against the Kakuza Ridge and then the even more formidable Shuri line. Fortunately for the Americans, the Japanese had planned a counteroffensive for the second week of April and damaged their defense in trying to execute it, frittering away critical manpower in needless assaults against the dug-in army and marine divisions with their superior firepower.

The withdrawal of Japanese forces from the Shuri line fortifications in late May did not conclude the fighting on Okinawa. Nearly ten

RIGHT: *A formidable task force carves out a beachhead on Okinawa, just 350 miles from the Japanese mainland on April 13, 1945. Landing craft of all kinds blacken the sea out to the horizon, where the fleet's battlewagons, transports, cruisers, and destroyers stand by.*

RIGHT: *The 193-page* Soldier's Guide to the Japanese Army *was released by the War Department in November 1944 and sent to the Pacific in time for the invasions of Luzon and Okinawa. Some copies also went to the marines. Meant to be distributed down to platoon level, many of the booklets were distributed to squad leaders, with additional copies circulated among the enlisted men. The guide described everything from the characteristics and training of Japanese soldiers to their personal and heavy weapons; organization from platoon to division; tactics in various combat settings; as well as mines, booby traps, and defense techniques. Unfortunately, the intelligence officers who wrote it occasionally became a little too enthusiastic about their subject and produced text like: "Japanese artillery weapons exhibit the outstanding characteristic of lightness, in some cases without the sacrifice of range"—pleasant reading, indeed, for a grunt or jarhead hitting the beach on Okinawa.*

BELOW: *7th Infantry Division soldiers carefully fight their way up an enemy ridge on Okinawa.*

Private First Class Desmond T. Doss
Medical Detachment, 307th Infantry Regiment, 77th Infantry Division

Citation: Doss was a company aid man when the 1st Battalion assaulted a jagged escarpment four hundred feet high. As our troops gained the summit, a heavy concentration of artillery, mortar, and machine gun fire crashed into them, inflicting approximately seventy-five casualties and driving the others back. Doss refused to seek cover and remained in the fire-swept area with many of the stricken, carrying them one by one to the edge of the escarpment and lowering them on a rope-supported litter down the face of a cliff to friendly hands.

On May 2, he exposed himself to heavy rifle and mortar fire while rescuing a wounded man two hundred yards forward of the lines on the same escarpment. Two days later, he treated four men who had been cut down while assaulting a strongly defended cave, advancing through a shower of grenades to within eight yards of enemy forces in a cave's mouth, where he dressed his comrades' wounds before making four separate trips under fire to evacuate them to safety. On May 5, he unhesitatingly braved enemy shelling and small arms fire to assist an artillery officer. He applied bandages, moved his patient to a spot that offered protection from small arms fire, and, while artillery and mortar shells fell close by, painstakingly administered plasma. Later that day, when an American was severely wounded by fire from a cave, Doss crawled to him where he had fallen—twenty-five feet from the enemy position—rendered aid, and carried him one hundred yards to safety while continually exposed to enemy fire.

On May 21, in a night attack on high ground near Shuri, he remained in exposed territory while the rest of his company took cover, fearlessly risking the chance that he would be mistaken for an infiltrating Japanese, and giving aid to the injured until he was himself seriously wounded in the legs by the explosion of a grenade. Rather than call another aid man from cover, he cared for his own injuries and waited five hours before litter bearers reached him and started carrying him to cover. The trio was caught in an enemy tank attack, and Doss, seeing a more critically wounded man nearby, crawled off the litter and directed the bearers to give their first attention to the other man. Awaiting the litter bearers' return, he was again struck, this time suffering a compound fracture of one arm. With magnificent fortitude he bound a rifle stock to his shattered arm as a splint and then crawled three hundred yards over rough terrain to the aid station.

Through his outstanding bravery and unflinching determination in the face of desperately dangerous conditions, Doss saved the lives of many soldiers. His name became a symbol throughout the 77th Infantry Division for outstanding gallantry far above and beyond the call of duty.

LEFT: Doss is presented the Medal of Honor in a White House ceremony on November 1, 1945.

BELOW: *Carbines at hand, members of the 7th Infantry Division take a break during a lull in the fighting, c. late May 1945.*

OPPOSITE TOP: *Lieutenant Richard K. Jones of Hollywood, California, feeds Japanese children found hiding in a tomb fifty yards from the front line on April 23, 1945. Jones was the commanding officer of the 3235 Signal Corps Photo Detachment.*

inches of rain fell on Okinawa during the last ten days of the month, slowing American progress and giving the Japanese 32d Army a chance to escape. Each retreating defender carried with him no more than a twenty-day ration and as much equipment and supplies as he could carry. The new Japanese defensive line now lay roughly east to west athwart the Yaeju-Dake Escarpment, the largest coral outcropping on the Okinawa battlefield. There, in the southeast corner of the island, the Japanese defenders burrowed in for a final stand.

Meanwhile, at sea the Japanese unleashed the full fury of their kamikaze strikes (including a futile suicide sortie by the super battleship *Yamato*), against the fleet, straining the nerves and defenses of the U.S. Navy to the breaking point. During the course of the two-month campaign, twenty-one ships were lost, sixty-six seriously damaged, and more than 10,000 sailors killed and wounded—the highest losses ever suffered throughout the navy's long history.

Ashore the butcher bill was no less sobering, and a reflection of the horrors of total war. In addition to the annihilation of the 120,000-man Japanese garrison, the civilian population lost at least 80,000 killed. Army and Marine ground-force casualties were the greatest of the Pacific War, numbering roughly 70,000 dead, wounded, and missing, including General Buckner who was killed during the last days of the fighting.

BELOW: *Field glasses in hand, the commander of an M18 tank destroyer directs the fire of its 76-mm gun in support of the 306th Infantry's May 11, 1945, attack against Chocolate Drop Hill on the Japanese Suri Defense Line. Imperial forces on Chocolate Drop and the nearby Flattop held out for more than a week against the 306th and the 307th, another 77th Infantry Division regiment.*

Chapter Nine
Defeating Nazi Germany, 1942–1945

In October 1942 Major General Mark W. Clark, deputy to the supreme Allied commander in England, made a dangerous trip by submarine to an isolated villa on Algeria's Mediterranean coast. Meeting in secret with several senior French generals, he successfully negotiated the cooperation of French forces in Morocco and Algeria ahead of Operation Torch, the American expedition to North Africa. Although Torch, on November 8, 1942, would be dwarfed by later American and Anglo-American amphibious operations, the simultaneous landing of more than one hundred thousand men at eight sites spread along nine hundred miles of coastline was by far the largest such operation ever conducted by any country up to this time. It was a bold, imaginative move that in many ways fell far short of its objectives.

After Germany's invasion of France, the French government, which had fled Paris, was allowed to set up a new capital at Vichy from where it would administer southeast France and its colonies in collaboration with the Nazis, but without German occupation. The chance visit by a senior Vichy minister to Algeria on the eve of the Allied landings suddenly made it impossible for the French commanders to abide by their agreement with General Clark. Instead of coming ashore unopposed and quickly surging east to occupy Tunisia's ports to cut off the German Army in North Africa with the help of the French, American and British troops were forced to briefly fight the French Army. The time lost allowed the Germans several days of unhindered access to Tunisian airfields, and they were able to rush in enough troops to form a defensive perimeter west of the ports of Tunis and Bizerte. Instead of a smooth, quick victory requiring relatively few divisions, the Allies were forced to battle for Tunisia throughout the winter and spring.

The American landing at the Moroccan port of Casablanca consisted of the three-division I Armored Corps under Major General George S. Patton Jr. This formation was shipped battle-ready directly from the United States; it was the only instance during the war when a force larger than division size was combat-loaded in United States ports for landing directly on a hostile shore. The forces landing near Oran and Algiers included the II Corps with elements of three divisions. During this operation, a battalion of paratroopers made the U.S. Army's first combat jump. Roughly four hundred miles to the west of Algiers, the lead elements of more than one hundred fifty thousand German and Italian troops were funneled into the Tunisian perimeter through Sicily. They were soon joined by an additional one hundred thousand men under Field Marshal Erwin Rommel, who had been engaged in a fighting withdrawal all the way across Libya after losing the Battle of El Alamein in Egypt to Lieutenant General Bernard L. Montgomery's British Eighth Army. Rommel's troops made contact with the German reinforcements and, by early February 1943, had established themselves behind the Mareth Line in southeastern Tunisia.

Having consolidated a giant, well-supplied lodgment, and with the Eighth Army stretched thin after its long pursuit, Rommel assumed the offensive on February 14. Powerful German armored units moved against the U.S. II Corps from passes in south-central Tunisia in an attempt to turn the south flank of the British First Army and capture an Allied base of operations around Tébessa. The Germans defeated the Allies in a series of sharp armored actions, forced a withdrawal of American troops through the Kasserine Pass and the valley beyond, and made a spectacular advance of almost a hundred

ABOVE: The shoulder patch of the Persian Gulf Command, which organized the rail lines and shipment of Lend-Lease supplies from Basra, Iraq, through Iran, to the Soviet Union. The red scimitar, from the flag of Iran, represents the warlike spirit of the ancient Persians; the white seven-pointed star was taken from the flag of the Kingdom of Iraq; and the shield's green color represents the Islamic faith of both countries.

OPPOSITE: Fresh from the Fort Dix reception center and wearing only helmet liners on their heads, soldiers from No. 2 Gun, Battery C, 115th Anti-Aircraft Artillery Battalion at Camp Davis, North Carolina, pose with the prized Thompson sub-machine guns issued to their section for close-in defense. The 90-mm gun battalion usually was attached to the 4th Armored Division as it fought its way across France and Germany.

miles before determined countermeasures by the Allies brought them to a halt, still short of their objectives, on February 22. Failing this attack, the Germans withdrew to their original positions. The Germans attempted two smaller offensives—one against the British First Army and the other against the British Eighth Army—during early March, but these also failed.

By this point the Allies were able to resume the attack. The II Corps, now under Patton, attacked toward the flank and rear of the Mareth Line, while elements of the British Eighth Army outflanked the Axis position and broke through into the eastern coastal region of central Tunisia. Within a month, all Axis troops had been compressed into a small bridgehead covering the Cape Bon Peninsula. In the final phase of the operation, Major General Omar N. Bradley assumed command of the II Corps so Patton, who'd been

promoted to lieutenant general, could prepare for the invasion of Sicily as the head of the new U.S. Seventh Army. In late April 1943, Bradley pushed from the west toward Mateur and Bizerte in northern Tunisia, while the British continued toward Tunis from the south and east.

The Germans had organized a whole series of positions protecting the valley to Mateur, and the area's key fortress was Djebel Tahent, or Hill 609, a flat-topped hill with wall-like cliffs at several points that dominated open country on all sides. American troops overran Hill 609 and other key heights as II Corps' 1st Armored Division tanks roared eastward. After nightfall on May 1 the Germans again withdrew, this time into Mateur. But two days later, the 1st Armored's tankers drove the enemy out of the town. The Americans had won an important urban center only twenty miles from their ultimate objective, Bizerte.

BELOW: Wary of running into an ambush by German antitank guns, Captain G.W. Meade of the 13th Armored Regiment (formerly 13th Cavalry), 1st Armored Division, cautiously advances on the heels of a German withdrawal through the Kasserine Pass, Tunisia, February 24, 1943. German Field Marshal Erwin Rommel later described the 13th's defense of the Sbeitla area during the German offensive as "clever and well fought." The tank is a newly fielded M4A1 Sherman.

RIGHT: The M1 "steel pot" worn by Captain (later Lieutenant Colonel) Robert E. Van Zant of the 13th Armored Regiment in North Africa and Italy.

In the final attack that began on May 6, the 1st Infantry Division faced strong opposition but maintained pressure to prevent the enemy from reinforcing other areas, and the 34th Infantry Division—Guardsmen from Minnesota, Iowa, and the Dakotas—took a key pass on the road to Tunis. In the northern half of II Corps' sector, the 1st Armored and 9th Infantry Divisions enveloped Bizerte and, the next day, pushed a retreating enemy into and through the city while the British entered Tunis. Troops of the II Corps moved through Bizerte on May 7, and the British cut off all escape from Cape Bon Peninsula. The last of some two hundred seventy-five thousand Germans and Italians surrendered to the Allied Armies on May 12, 1943.

RIGHT: 45th Infantry Division soldiers read letters and guidebooks on an eastbound troop ship, June 15, 1943. These Guardsmen would soon find that the climate in North Africa and their target, Sicily, was not much different than that of the southwestern states they were drawn from. The rifles hanging from their bunk frames are World War I-era bolt-action Springfields with leather straps. The Springfields were swapped out for semi-automatic M1 Garands after the Sicilian Campaign, but some of the soldiers preferred the older strap and held onto it until ordered to switch to the new fabric strap.

BELOW: The crew of an M15 halftrack awaits orders to commence firing on approaching German or Italian bombers during the Kasserine Pass fighting in February 1943. The early M15s sported a pair of water-cooled .50-caliber machine guns firing in combination with an automatic 37-mm gun fed by 8-round clips. The German Luftwaffe remained a threat to ground operations in the central Mediterranean region until well into 1944, and the M15 proved itself to be highly effective against low-flying attackers.

SICILY

After weeks of air bombardment on the island of Sicily, the U.S. Seventh and the British Eighth armies, staging from ports all along the Mediterranean's southern coast, converged on the island's shores in July. High winds sprang up the night before the assault was launched. More than one hundred sixty thousand men of Patton's Seventh Army and Montgomery's Eighth gathered on the southern invasion beaches, and a heavy sea was running when the landing craft shoved off. The winds also made the 82d Airborne Division's advance parachute drop far more dangerous. Paratroopers were scattered as far as thirty-five miles away from their intended drop zones, but even when separated from their units, small groups—and sometimes individual soldiers—ambushed supply trucks, cut telephone lines, and generally raised havoc. The U.S. 1st, 45th, and 3d Infantry and 2d Armored divisions hit the beaches. They initially went into action against light opposition because the high winds had put the enemy off guard.

The day after the landings, the Hermann Goering Panzer (Armored) Division struck the 1st Infantry Division hard. Enemy tanks broke through the front lines and headed for the beaches, but warships off the coast "joined the army," and their big guns poured fire into attacking tanks. The "Big Red One" launched its own attack and knocked the German panzers back from the shore. With the beachhead secure, the Allies pushed north toward the dominant ground in the east-central part of the island. From there, they intended to take Messina on the strait between Sicily and Italy. The Germans, however, quickly recovered from that initial surprise and succeeded in blocking the most direct route to Messina by concentrating against the British Eighth Army in the vicinity of Catania. Patton, meanwhile, sent a mobile provisional corps northwest toward Palermo on the far side of the island. The 2d Armored ("Hell on Wheels") and 3d Infantry ("Rock of the Marne") divisions covered seventy-two miles in two days. They captured Palermo on July 22, cutting Sicily in half and precipitating the surrender of many Italian units.

The Seventh Army was now in a position to break the deadlock opposite the British by attacking from the west. Realizing that they were in danger of being cut off, as had just happened several months earlier in Tunisia, the Germans began to withdraw across the Strait of Messina to Italy as soon as Patton began to strike eastward along the northern coast. First the 45th, then the 3d Division, spearheaded the drive, which was aided by repeated amphibious landings to outflank the German rear guards. Nevertheless, the Seventh Army could not catch the rapidly fleeing enemy, who was able to evacuate some sixty thousand troops despite attacks by Allied aircraft. Patrols of the 3d Infantry Division pushed into Messina on August 17, 1943, and discovered that the German and remaining Italian units were gone, having left behind some one hundred sixty-seven thousand killed, wounded, and captured—more than five times the Allies' losses.

RIGHT TOP: Lieutenant Colonel Lyle W. Bernard (*right*), commander of the 30th Infantry Regiment, discusses operations with his boss, Lieutenant General George S. Patton, at Brolo, Sicily, during the U.S. Seventh Army's drive toward Messina, August 12, 1943. Twice that month, Bernard led amphibious end runs along the northern coast of the island as part of Patton's effort to cut off the retreating Germans, but he was only able to bag just over a thousand prisoners.

RIGHT BOTTOM: U.S. Army mules support the Fifth Army advance in Italy as a cargo truck that failed to negotiate the same mountainous track lies helplessly on its back alongside a vineyard. Mules shipped in from the American southwest were sturdier than local animals, and regularly carried up to 20 percent of their body weight (150–300 pounds) for fifteen to twenty miles per day in the Apennines.

SICILY 1943

MESSINA

Citation: For conspicuous gallantry and intrepidity at risk of life above and beyond the call of duty in action on September 22, 1943, at Oliveto, Italy. Although Childers previously had just suffered a fractured instep he, with eight enlisted men, advanced up a hill toward enemy machine-gun nests. The group advanced to a rock wall overlooking a cornfield, and Childers ordered a base of fire laid across the field so that he could advance. When two enemy snipers from a nearby house fired upon him, he killed them both. He moved behind the machine-gun nests and killed all occupants of the nearer one. He continued toward the second one and threw rocks into it. When the two occupants of the nest raised up, he shot one. The other was killed by one of the eight enlisted men. Childers continued his advance toward a house farther up the hill and single-handedly captured an enemy mortar observer. The exceptional leadership, initiative, calmness under fire, and conspicuous gallantry displayed by Childers were an inspiration to his men.

BELOW: A truck-mounted anti-aircraft gun and ammunition trailer pull out from an LCVP landing craft onto Paestum beach near Salerno, Italy, on September 9, 1943. German artillery harassed unloading operations for nearly a week, and an MP assisting incoming troops in the foreground instinctively ducks for cover as a piece of shrapnel zings past. Many American units expected a largely "administrative" landing against little opposition, and their drive inland was slow at first, hampering the buildup in the beachhead until more ground was taken.

THE INVASION OF ITALY

Sicily had been conquered in thirty-eight days, and the Allies had high hopes that Italy itself could be quickly knocked out of the war. But even though the Allied victory in Sicily had prompted the overthrow of Benito Mussolini's Fascist government, and although the new government had entered into armistice negotiations with the Allies, the Germans had no intention of surrendering the country and allowing its enemies to advance unhindered all the way to Germany's southern border. Likewise, the Allies were going to fight the Germans in Italy no matter what the flailing Italian ministers did—and, indeed, the Italians capitulated as soon as a massive invasion fleet gathered off the coast. The announcement of the Italian surrender came on the eve of this invasion, and, at one minute past midnight on September 9, 1943, loudspeakers on the troop transports called the first boat teams to their stations.

Within moments, Texas Guardsmen of the 36th Infantry Division were clambering down nets into landing craft, and the dark sea came alive with snub-nosed craft circling to reach their designated positions. Given a signal, the landing craft turned east into a line behind the guide boats, six thousand yards from the targeted beaches in the Gulf of Salerno. Just to the north, on the other side of the port town of Salerno, the British were firing a furious bombardment on their beaches, but the American soldiers, aiming for surprise, were going in without naval gunfire support. Ahead, the

RIGHT: With her shoes slung around her neck and her coveralls rolled up, an American nurse wades ashore from an LCI (landing craft) at Naples as soldiers pass their gear to the beach along a human chain. By the time this photo was taken on November 4, 1943, all of the U.S. Fifth Army's combat divisions had arrived on the Italian peninsula and, with the British Eighth Army on its right, was fighting its way up the country's mountainous spine.

beaches were dark and still. When the boats finally ground to a halt in the surf, these descendants of the men who fought at San Jacinto and against the Comanche jumped into the shallow water and waded ashore. The Italian Campaign had begun.

Now-Lieutenant General Clark's Fifth Army, which initially included Britain's X Corps, was almost immediately embroiled in heavy fighting, and German counterattacks—centering around four panzer divisions—jeopardized the entire Allied beachhead. It was nearly a week before the Fifth Army was able to stabilize the situation and fully secure its position. The British Eighth Army had also made multiple landings far to the south at the great naval base of Taranto and opposite Messina, then moved in force on the east side of Italy's boot-shaped peninsula. On September 16, the Fifth and Eighth armies linked up southeast of Salerno, and on October 7, Clark's British corps seized Naples with its excellent port, then chased the Germans back to the strong position they had created along the Volturno River, twenty miles to the north.

ANZIO AND CASSINO

The Germans were dug in for a fight, and the 3d Infantry Division gave it to them. On the night of October 12, while massed artillery, machine guns, and mortars joined in a diversionary attack down the river, the 7th Infantry "Cotton Balers"—which had fought with Jackson at New Orleans—spearheaded its successful attack at a hairpin loop of the river. Yet as soon as the Allies broke through one barrier in Italy, the Germans had another ready. Each mountain had to be taken, each valley cleared, and then there were more mountains ahead and still another main defense line to be broken. Their next position, the Winter Line (also known as the Gustav Line), about seventy-five miles south of Rome, was a succession of interlocking defenses anchored on Monte Cassino.

The Fifth Army fought toward Cassino and the Liri Valley—the gateway to Rome—but it came to be known as Purple Heart Valley. Rain fell steadily, and the only shelters were a few caves in the mountainside. In the relatively flat areas, jeeps and trucks could churn through the mud. However, only mules could carry the ammunition and food

ABOVE: Major General Clarence R. Huebner (*left*) assumes command of the 1st Infantry Division in Sicily from Terry de la Mesa Allen on August 8, 1943. Allen had led the division in two arduous campaigns but allowed the 1st's discipline to slip badly and was relieved by Omar Bradley. "While the 1st might be the best division in the U.S. Army," said Bradley, "it nevertheless was a *part* of the army, a fact the division sometimes forgot." Although an initial announcement said that Allen had retired from the service, General George C. Marshall put him in command of the new 104th Infantry Division, which he trained and led successfully in combat in France and Germany.

RIGHT: American artillerymen take on German tanks in the Anzio area with their 57-mm gun in February 1944.

across the miles of rough, muddy trails that were impassable to vehicles. Beasts of burden were rushed across the Atlantic as quickly as possible. At the beginning of November, the 45th Division had thirty-two animals; by the end of December it had more than five hundred. Still, this was only a fraction of what was needed, and soon the few available were worn out or worked to death. Where the mules couldn't go, men did. Soldiers brought up all the ammunition they could carry during assaults, a few mortars, and no food other than "D" ration chocolate bars. On the worst slopes, men climbed upward only a few inches at a time and then hauled their packs up by rope, all while under constant enemy fire.

In December, Clark made a nearly simultaneous attempt to both break through the Gustav Line and envelop its western flank through an amphibious assault. The American VI Corps, made up of the 3d Infantry Division, a British division, Rangers, and British Commandos, landed fifty miles behind the line at Anzio, roughly thirty miles south of Rome, on January 22, 1944. The operation initially was successful, and additional forces arrived while the lead elements pushed inland against growing enemy resistance. After the first week, the Germans reacted with a strong series of counterattacks that reached a crescendo in mid-February and threatened to wipe out the beachhead. The dogged defense of the perimeter by Major General Lucian K.

Truscott's VI Corps brought the German effort to a halt on March 2. The promising end run had become a costly stalemate, and both sides settled into a siege that would not be broken for several months.

Shortly after the first landings at Anzio, the 34th and 36th divisions opened the battle for Cassino itself. The mountain defenses were practically impregnable, but in May 1944, the Allied forces made a carefully planned assault on the Winter Line, synchronizing their thrusts with a fresh attack from the Anzio beachhead. The U.S. Fifth and British Eighth armies took Cassino and joined up with troops breaking out of the Anzio beachhead, in a drive carried all the way to Rome. On June 4, Allied forces marched into the Eternal City two days before the D-Day invasion of France.

THE GOTHIC LINE

Taking advantage of the dry summer weather, the Allied armies chased the Germans fifty miles north of Rome, then ran into more mud, mountains, and mule warfare. The pursuit slowed as German demolitions of bridges and mountainside roads, plus extended supply lines and stiffening enemy resistance, hampered the movement of the American, British, and Free French troops, whose advance were frequently confined to narrow roads. This breather for the Germans

ABOVE: American infantrymen pick their way through the rubble of Castleforte, which had served as a key stronghold in the German's Gustav Line. The town fell to U.S. and French forces on May 13, 1944, the second day of the Fifth Army offensive that would capture the gutted Benedictine Abbey at Cassino then liberate Rome early the following month. The Sherman tank at left had been knocked out during the fighting.

Second Lieutenant Charles W. Shea
350th Infantry Regiment

Citation: For conspicuous gallantry and intrepidity at risk of life above and beyond the call of duty, on May 12, 1944, near Mount Damiano, Italy. As Shea and his company were advancing toward a hill occupied by the enemy, three enemy machine guns suddenly opened fire, inflicting heavy casualties upon the company and halting its advance. Shea immediately moved forward to eliminate these machine-gun nests in order to enable his company to continue its attack. The deadly hail of machine-gun fire at first pinned him down, but, boldly continuing his advance, Shea crept up to the first nest. Throwing several hand grenades, he forced the four enemy soldiers manning this position to surrender, and disarming them, he sent them to the rear. He then crawled to the second machine-gun position and after a short firefight forced two more German soldiers to surrender. At this time, the third machine gun fired at him, and while deadly small arms fire pitted the earth around him, Shea crawled toward the nest. Suddenly he stood up and rushed the emplacement and with well-directed fire from his rifle, he killed all three of the enemy machine gunners. Shea's display of personal valor was an inspiration to the officers and men of his company.

OPPOSITE BACKGROUND: These men are from the 115th AAA Gun Battalion, which fought with the Third Army in France and Germany.

BELOW: Troops of the 88th Infantry Division's 3d Battalion, 351st Infantry, prepare to board an LVT-4 Alligator amphibious tractor for an assault crossing of the Po River at Ostiglia, Italy, on April 24, 1945. The 88th was an extremely effective formation but remains little known to even American historians because it fought in the Italian front. Characterized as "shock troops" by the German Command, it became a magnet that attracted enemy reserves (to no avail) wherever it was placed in the line.

made the last fifty miles of the Allied advance to the Arno River a grim struggle, studded with hard-fought engagements.

By mid-August, the Pisa-Rimini Line had been reached at most points, and the enemy still had behind him the Gothic Line—a series of fixed defenses in the rugged Apennine Mountains even stronger than the Gustav Line. By the end of September, some of the Gothic Line positions had been penetrated. Clark hoped to break through to the important industrial city of Bologna beyond the Apennines before winter set in, but this was simply beyond the strength of the Fifth and Eighth armies. Allied troops dug in for the difficult winter after two months of struggling from mountain to mountain in a campaign that, for intensity and sustained action, matched any fought by an Allied army.

In April, as the ground dried and hardened, the last offensive was launched. Within a week the Allied forces broke into the Po Valley, and resistance began to crumble. A spectacular drive spearheaded by the U.S. 10th Mountain Division reached the foothills of the Alps and ended with the surrender of the German forces in Italy on May 2, 1945. The conquest of Italy had been completed, but it was of far greater strategic importance than was readily apparent. The Allies, although never having committed a large amount of resources and manpower to the campaign, had forced the Germans to maintain an average of twenty divisions in an effort to keep the Allies from the Brenner Pass and southern Germany—forces that might have upset the military balance in the main theater of operations to the northwest if they had been available for the initial battles in Normandy, France.

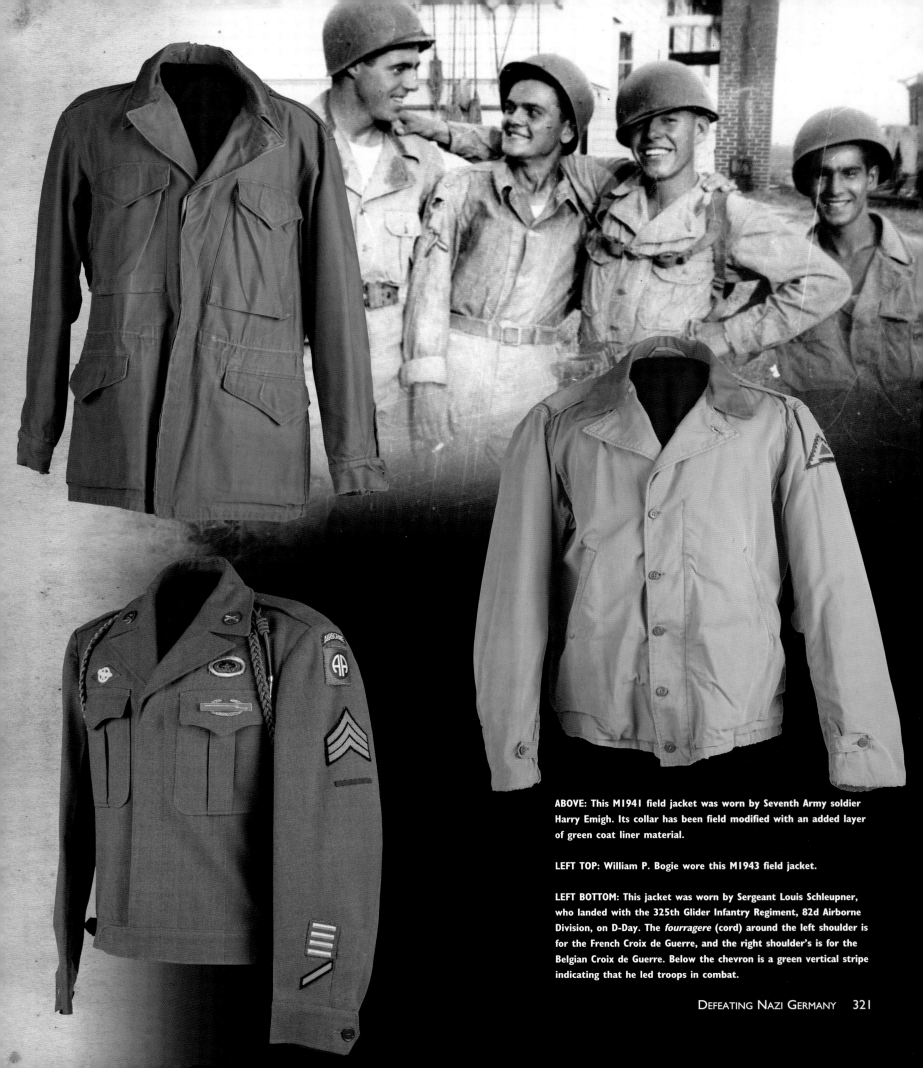

ABOVE: This M1941 field jacket was worn by Seventh Army soldier Harry Emigh. Its collar has been field modified with an added layer of green coat liner material.

LEFT TOP: William P. Bogie wore this M1943 field jacket.

LEFT BOTTOM: This jacket was worn by Sergeant Louis Schleupner, who landed with the 325th Glider Infantry Regiment, 82d Airborne Division, on D-Day. The *fourragere* (cord) around the left shoulder is for the French Croix de Guerre, and the right shoulder's is for the Belgian Croix de Guerre. Below the chevron is a green vertical stripe indicating that he led troops in combat.

RIGHT INSET: The army's quartermaster department procured more than ten thousand toy "crickets" from the ACME Thunderer Whistle Co. of England for use as an individual identification signaling device for paratroopers. The 101st Airborne Division used them extensively on D-Day.

BELOW: Flooded fields reflect the gleam of D-Day night's full moon; the fields were as much a danger to the paratroopers as the German defenders. The wide black and white bands painted around the aircraft's fuselage are a highly visible identification marking applied to all Allied aircraft immediately before the invasion. Any aircraft spotted without the stripes was assumed to be the enemy—and fair game for antiaircraft gunners and prowling Allied fighters.

M1 .30-CALIBER CARBINE

At half the weight of the infantry's basic weapon (the 10-pound M1 Garand rifle), the M1 Winchester carbine was ideal for any soldier who had to carry such items as ammunition or a radio. It also was regulation issue for sergeants, all officers up to the rank of major, and most vehicle personnel. At one point the army thought that paratroopers might find the weapon particularly useful, but airborne units considered the carbine to be principally a defensive weapon because of its limited range of only three hundred yards. Navy Lieutenant Raymond A. Havrilla, an assistant surgeon on tank landing ship LST-508, reportedly recovered this carbine from Utah Beach on D-Day+2, June 8, 1944.

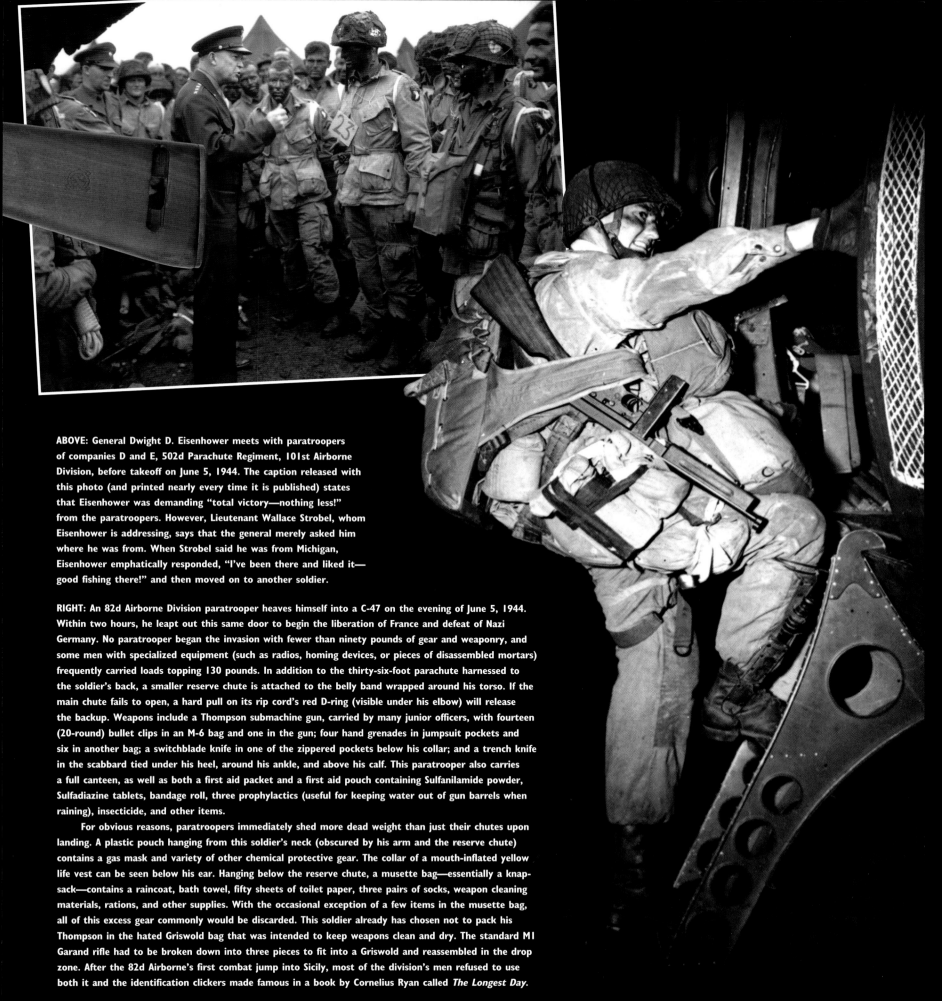

ABOVE: General Dwight D. Eisenhower meets with paratroopers of companies D and E, 502d Parachute Regiment, 101st Airborne Division, before takeoff on June 5, 1944. The caption released with this photo (and printed nearly every time it is published) states that Eisenhower was demanding "total victory—nothing less!" from the paratroopers. However, Lieutenant Wallace Strobel, whom Eisenhower is addressing, says that the general merely asked him where he was from. When Strobel said he was from Michigan, Eisenhower emphatically responded, "I've been there and liked it— good fishing there!" and then moved on to another soldier.

RIGHT: An 82d Airborne Division paratrooper heaves himself into a C-47 on the evening of June 5, 1944. Within two hours, he leapt out this same door to begin the liberation of France and defeat of Nazi Germany. No paratrooper began the invasion with fewer than ninety pounds of gear and weaponry, and some men with specialized equipment (such as radios, homing devices, or pieces of disassembled mortars) frequently carried loads topping 130 pounds. In addition to the thirty-six-foot parachute harnessed to the soldier's back, a smaller reserve chute is attached to the belly band wrapped around his torso. If the main chute fails to open, a hard pull on its rip cord's red D-ring (visible under his elbow) will release the backup. Weapons include a Thompson submachine gun, carried by many junior officers, with fourteen (20-round) bullet clips in an M-6 bag and one in the gun; four hand grenades in jumpsuit pockets and six in another bag; a switchblade knife in one of the zippered pockets below his collar; and a trench knife in the scabbard tied under his heel, around his ankle, and above his calf. This paratrooper also carries a full canteen, as well as both a first aid packet and a first aid pouch containing Sulfanilamide powder, Sulfadiazine tablets, bandage roll, three prophylactics (useful for keeping water out of gun barrels when raining), insecticide, and other items.

For obvious reasons, paratroopers immediately shed more dead weight than just their chutes upon landing. A plastic pouch hanging from this soldier's neck (obscured by his arm and the reserve chute) contains a gas mask and variety of other chemical protective gear. The collar of a mouth-inflated yellow life vest can be seen below his ear. Hanging below the reserve chute, a musette bag—essentially a knap-sack—contains a raincoat, bath towel, fifty sheets of toilet paper, three pairs of socks, weapon cleaning materials, rations, and other supplies. With the occasional exception of a few items in the musette bag, all of this excess gear commonly would be discarded. This soldier already has chosen not to pack his Thompson in the hated Griswold bag that was intended to keep weapons clean and dry. The standard M1 Garand rifle had to be broken down into three pieces to fit into a Griswold and reassembled in the drop zone. After the 82d Airborne's first combat jump into Sicily, most of the division's men refused to use both it and the identification clickers made famous in a book by Cornelius Ryan called *The Longest Day*.

BELOW: Soldiers aboard an LCI headed for Utah Beach are lost in their own private thoughts as they prepare to land on French soil. The silhouette of an M1 Garand rifle can be seen clearly in the waterproof pliofilm bag of the soldier in the background. Oddly, although the troops are wearing standard, olive-drab gas detectors on their left arms, they have no gas mask bags on their chests. The fiber storage tube hanging around the neck of the man in the foreground contains either a rifle grenade that can be affixed to his Garand or an individual 60-mm mortar round to supplement the stock of his company's heavy-weapons platoon.

OVERLORD: THE INVASION OF FRANCE

On D-Day, June 6, 1944, some 170,000 Allied troops penetrated the German defenses at Normandy, in the greatest amphibious invasion ever mounted. Five combat divisions—two American, two British, and one Canadian—were landing abreast on as many beaches after a trio of American and British airborne divisions landed on both flanks to protect and speed the expansion of the Allied lodgment. Behind them were some three million four hundred thousand more Allied soldiers, sailors, and airmen who had been assembled in England for the sole purpose of destroying the Nazi tyranny of Adolf Hitler that had engulfed nearly all of Europe.

Despite the depredations of German U-boats, a nonstop flow of Yanks and all the implements of war had flowed across the Atlantic for more than two years from the "arsenal of democracy," until it seemed the British Isles would certainly sink under their weight. Defending Hitler's "Atlantic Wall" were eight hundred fifty thousand German troops, including nine of the dreaded panzer divisions. Sequestered in the ports, staging areas, and airfields of Britain during the final days before the invasion, the men pondered what awaited them. General Dwight D. Eisenhower, the supreme Allied commander, described the Allied invasion force as "a great human spring, coiled for the moment when its energy would be released and it would vault the English Channel."

The day before the invasion, "pathfinders" of the 82d and 101st Airborne divisions climbed aboard their planes to parachute into Normandy and mark the drop zones for the thousands of paratroopers and glider troops coming in behind them. Below, as they winged their way toward France were the men on more than five thousand vessels moving across the channel and forming up for the most massive amphibious assault in history. Troop carrier planes ran into clouds as they approached the French coast, and then flak

began bursting all around them. Many planes veered off course, scattering their human cargoes miles from the intended drop zones. But, just as in Sicily, the troopers fought where they landed.

As the Germans rushed in patrols to search for these Allies in one area, others would come down in the opposite direction. Men gathered as best they could to do their jobs. Paratroopers and Germans frequently bumped into each other in the dark, and survival often depended on who got off the first shot. A small group from the 101st Airborne Division was walking a country road when something caught Private Bill True's eye.

I glanced out into the field, and a German soldier was just aiming his pistol at one of the guys up the line. That was the first time I had a really clear picture of what I was shooting at. There was the enemy. Thinking about it later, I was impressed with how

ABOVE: Inflatable flotation devices were issued to troops for the D-Day landings.

M1A1 .30-CALIBER CARBINE

The folding stock of the M1A1 carbine allowed the weapon's length to be reduced to a mere 25½ inches—ten inches shorter than the basic carbine and fully eighteen inches shorter than the M1 Garand rifle. Not surprisingly, the weapon was a favorite of tank personnel.

Citation: DeGlopper was a member of Company C, 325th Glider Infantry, on June 9, 1944, advancing with the forward platoon to secure a bridgehead across the Merderet River at La Fiere, France. At dawn the platoon had penetrated an outer line of machine guns and riflemen, but in so doing had become cut off from the rest of the company. Vastly superior forces began to decimate the stricken unit and put in motion a flanking maneuver that would have completely exposed the American platoon in the shallow roadside ditch where it had taken cover. Detecting this danger, DeGlopper volunteered to support his comrades by fire from his automatic rifle while they attempted a withdrawal through a break in a hedgerow forty yards to the rear. Scorning a concentration of enemy automatic weapons and rifle fire, he walked from the ditch onto the road in full view of the Germans and sprayed the hostile positions with assault fire. He was wounded, but he continued firing. Struck again, he started to fall—but his grim determination and valiant fighting spirit could not be broken. Kneeling in the roadway, weakened by his grievous wounds, he leveled his heavy weapon against the enemy and fired burst after burst until he was killed outright. He was successful in drawing the enemy action away from his fellow soldiers, who continued the fight from a more advantageous position and established the first bridgehead over the Merderet. In the area where DeGlopper made his intrepid stand, his comrades later found the ground strewn with dead Germans and many machine guns and automatic weapons that he had knocked out of action. DeGlopper's gallant sacrifice and unflinching heroism while facing unsurmountable odds were in great measure responsible for a highly important tactical victory in the Normandy Campaign.

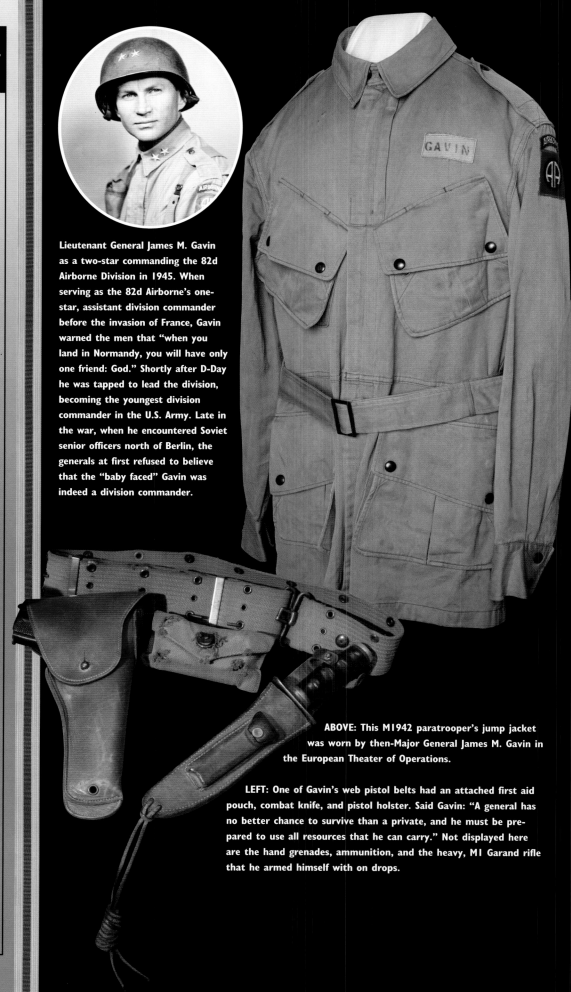

Lieutenant General James M. Gavin as a two-star commanding the 82d Airborne Division in 1945. When serving as the 82d Airborne's one-star, assistant division commander before the invasion of France, Gavin warned the men that "when you land in Normandy, you will have only one friend: God." Shortly after D-Day he was tapped to lead the division, becoming the youngest division commander in the U.S. Army. Late in the war, when he encountered Soviet senior officers north of Berlin, the generals at first refused to believe that the "baby faced" Gavin was indeed a division commander.

ABOVE: This M1942 paratrooper's jump jacket was worn by then-Major General James M. Gavin in the European Theater of Operations.

LEFT: One of Gavin's web pistol belts had an attached first aid pouch, combat knife, and pistol holster. Said Gavin: "A general has no better chance to survive than a private, and he must be prepared to use all resources that he can carry." Not displayed here are the hand grenades, ammunition, and the heavy, M1 Garand rifle that he armed himself with on drops.

Sergeant Marvin H. Karchner
A Company, 115th Infantry
29th Infantry Division

Sergeant John Ray
A Company, 505th Parachute Infantry,
82d Airborne Division

1st Sergeant Leonard G. Lomell
D Company, 2d Ranger Battalion

Private First Class Harold Baumgarten
B Company, 116th Infantry Regiment,
29th Infantry Division

Karchner landed with the third wave of troops on Omaha Beach and made it ashore, only to be wounded in the leg by machine-gun fire on the night of June 6. He was sent to England to recover from his wound, and returned to his unit in July. While fighting in the hedgerows outside of Saint-Lô on July 14, Karchner was seriously wounded when an 88-mm shell exploded nearby and blew off both of his hands above the wrist.

Ray landed in the church square of Sainte-Mére-Église and, although mortally wounded, he killed a German soldier who was aiming at two paratroopers. Private John Steele's chute was snagged on the bell tower, and Private Ken Russell came down hard on the slate roof of the nave. Steele and Russell, both helpless targets, survived the Normandy Invasion because of Ray's efforts.

Lomell scaled the six-story cliff of Pointe du Hoc while under German rifle and machine-gun fire. The Ranger battalion's mission was to knock out six French, 155-mm, long-range guns that were focused on the main American landing areas. Finding no artillery in the cliff-top revetments, patrols went inland. Lomell found the guns and personally destroyed two of them with thermite grenades.

A Company of the 116th Infantry landed with 164 officers and men in front of the D1 Exit of Omaha Beach. They were virtually annihilated within the first five minutes, suffering ninety-one killed in action and sixty-four wounded. Baumgarten landed just after A Company went ashore and was wounded as soon as his landing-craft ramp went down. He made it to the beach after suffering at least three additional wounds and was evacuated the next day.

BELOW: Company E of the 16th RCT and demolitions teams made up of army and navy personnel take refuge from German bullets among a devil's garden of ramps, mined stakes, and hedgehogs east of the Saint Laurent draw. This was one of the few places along Omaha Beach where the three obstacle types were thickly, yet randomly, intermingled. Some soldiers pushed forward in the face of German fire while those that didn't were forced inexorably toward the shore amid a flotsam of wooden obstacle fragments, discarded life belts, Pliofilm wrappings, and corpses.

good my training had been because it was the most automatic thing to bring my rifle to my shoulder—taking the safety off as I brought it up—and squeezing the trigger as calmly as on a firing range.

While similar groups of airborne troops battled in meadows and orchards, ambushed convoys, and held the key crossroads town of Sainte-Mère-Église against determined German counterattacks, other soldiers were fighting bitter battles on the beaches. As British and Canadians stormed ashore on the eastern beaches, men of the 4th Infantry Division led the way on the westernmost beach, Utah, where they completely surprised the Germans. Moving quickly inland, they fought their way across streams and wide marshy areas that had been flooded by the Germans in a failed effort to both discourage the use of parachute and glider troops as well as isolate Utah's smooth shore. By late morning, the 4th Division had linked up with elements of both airborne outfits. Meanwhile, at Omaha Beach in the center, the going was much tougher. Men of the 1st and 29th ("Blue and Gray") divisions moved across underwater obstacles and mines as machine-gun and cannon fire from pillboxes swept the beach, inflicting casualties. The Germans, however, were not able to repulse the landing at Omaha, and by nightfall on D-Day, all five beachheads were secure. Allies were in France to stay.

BOTTOM: E Company soldiers of the 1st Infantry Division's 16th RCT (regimental combat team) huddle behind hedgehog obstacles and a pair of Company A, 741st Tank Battalion's M4 Shermans fitted with wading trunks (*left and center*). The trunks enabled the Shermans' exhausts and air intakes to operate even if the hulls were submerged. Photographer Robert Capa reported that the tank at left was knocked out. Two of the 741st's five surviving DD (Duplex Drive) tanks from its B and C companies are at right, and their close proximity may indicate that they are part of the lucky trio of Shermans brought all the way to shore by the skipper of their LCT landing craft. The lead DD (with a life preserver hanging over its side) is beginning to lower its flotation device, and both still have their wooden, auxiliary steering platform towering above the canvas. This portion of Omaha's Easy Red Beach is being heavily raked by machine-gun fire from a bunker to the right, outside the frame of Robert Capa's photograph, but, thanks to the tanks and the persistence of the infantry, this was the first section of Omaha Beach to be seized. Some infantry in the distant mist already have moved past the shale at the high-tide line. Beyond this image, to the right, is a third Company A tank with wading trunks, and high over the shore is the faint outline of the murderous, 150-foot bluffs.

LEFT: Soldiers trudge toward the shale that marks the hide-tide line in a chilling filmstrip by an army cinematographer. In the final frame (enlarged) the rear-most man is cut down by German bullets, while another has stumbled or perhaps been shot. Although these troops often are reputed to be from the 29th Infantry Division's 116th RCT, the only area of Omaha that had a final obstacle belt of stakes was in the 1st Division's zone.

ABOVE LEFT: Lieutenant General Omar Bradley wore this B-10 jacket during the Normandy Campaign.

ABOVE: On D-Day, Bradley carried ashore a tactical map of the Omaha Beach and adjacent Pointe du Hoc areas.

FIGHTING IN THE HEDGEROWS

After the Allied landings, American soldiers immediately encountered the jumbled *bocage* country of thick, tall hedgerows: berms that were densely packed with tree roots, which Norman farmers used to enclose their fields. German infantry skillfully turned the hedgerow-enclosed fields into death traps by combining well-concealed automatic weapons and mortars with highly effective, portable *Panzerbuchse* and *Panzerfaust* anti-tank weapons. This determined defense by an average of eight under-strength grenadier and parachute divisions held four U.S. corps at bay for week after week, prompting concern among senior Allied commanders that a military stalemate had been reached. This photo was taken less than five miles from the key crossroads town of Saint-Lô on June 18, yet American troops would not enter it for almost a month—and then only with some of the most fierce fighting of World War II, as regiments and divisions independently developed tactics and techniques to isolate and reduce the Germans' mini fortresses in methodical, set-piece assaults.

Bitter field-by-field fighting among the hedgerows had, by mid-July, yielded the Americans a sufficient lodgement for the thousands of tons of supplies needed for Operation Cobra, the breakout and dash across France. The British Second Army in the east around Caen continued to attract the bulk of the German armored forces to its sector, and strained for its own breakout. At the same time, the U.S. First Army inexorably gained as much ground as possible to make room for the Third Army coming in behind it. A variety of recently developed field modifications to American tanks allowed the machines to literally plow through the massive berms of roots and earth. Using this innovation, the First Army planned to punch a hole through the German defenses, then hold the shoulders of the gap while the Third Army stampeded through into the German rear areas.

A massive bombardment by fifteen hundred American heavy bombers preceded the ground attack. The carpet-bombing of a "box" seven thousand yards wide by twenty-five hundred yards deep essentially wiped out the one German armored division in the U.S. sector, Panzer Lehr, on July 25. Tragically, 757 Americans also were killed and wounded in a series of bombing accidents as "shorts" fell into their jump-off positions. An initial wave of three armored divisions streamed through the broken German lines, and Avranches, where the Normandy and Brittany peninsulas meet, was seized on July 30. Lieutenant General George S. Patton rapidly exploited the breakthrough by launching his Third Army divisions at widely separated objectives far to the west, south, and east. The German Army, stretched to the limit by staggering troop losses in Normandy, had nothing left to stand in Patton's way.

RIGHT: *The steel-toothed, berm-busting attachment called a hedge cutter is freshly welded to a M5A1 Stuart light tank. Cutters sometimes varied radically from one to the next because their designs often were determined by what kind of scrap metal or abandoned German obstructions were available. Tanks fitted with some form of the device were called rhinos.*

RIGHT: *On June 14, 1944, American paratroopers from the 101st Airborne Division move warily through a field near Carentan, south of Utah Beach, passing members of their own outfit who fell victim to snipers. The trooper in the foreground apparently died from a single bullet that penetrated his helmet.*

ABOVE: Artist Lawrence Beal Smith's "The Man Without a Gun," depicting the scene in Normandy in 1944, where the army suffered 40,000 casualties in the five weeks of combat it took to capture the key crossroads town of Saint-Lô.

Citation: For conspicuous gallantry and intrepidity at risk of life above and beyond the call of duty, at Rechicourt, France. On September 27, 1944, during a sharp action with the enemy infantry and tank forces, Fields personally led his platoon in a counterattack on the enemy position. Although his platoon had been seriously depleted, the zeal and fervor of his leadership was such as to inspire his small force to accomplish its mission in the face of overwhelming enemy opposition. Seeing that one of the men had been wounded, he left his slit trench (a shallow excavation) and with complete disregard for his personal safety attended the wounded man and administered first aid. While returning to his slit trench, he was seriously wounded by a shell burst, the fragments of which cut through his face and head, tearing his teeth, gums, and nasal passage. Although rendered speechless by his wounds, Fields refused to be evacuated and continued to lead his platoon by the use of hand signals. On one occasion, when two enemy machine guns had a portion of his unit under deadly crossfire, he left his hole, wounded as he was, ran to a light machine gun whose crew had been knocked out, picked up the gun, and fired it from his hip with such deadly accuracy that both enemy gun positions were silenced. His action so impressed his men that they found new courage to take up the fire fight, increase their firepower, and expose themselves more than ever to harass the enemy with additional bazooka and machine-gun fire. Only when Fields' objective had been taken and the enemy scattered did he consent to be evacuated to the battalion command post. At this point he refused to move farther back until he had explained to his battalion commander by drawing on paper the position of his men and the disposition of the enemy forces. Fields' dauntless and gallant heroism were largely responsible for the repulse of the enemy forces and contributed in a large measure to the successful capture of his battalion objective during this action. His eagerness and determination to destroy the enemy was an inspiration to the entire command and are in the highest traditions of the U.S. Armed Forces.

ABOVE: Lieutenant General Courtney H. Hodges was considered a good man and "soldier's soldier." Nevertheless, his First Army was the least aggressive of General Dwight D. Eisenhower's field armies. Hodges and his staff displayed a marked hesitancy in the face of opportunities, and he also was slow to recognize dangerous developments, even though his operations section included some sixteen liaison officers with radio-equipped jeeps.

BELOW: General George S. Patton hangs the Congressional Medal of Honor around the neck of Lieutenant James H. Fields for fighting off a German counterattack despite a face wound.

BREAKOUT AND THE RACE ACROSS FRANCE

No sooner had the Americans moved inland from the beaches than they encountered Normandy's jumbled *bocage* country of hedgerow-enclosed fields that German infantry skillfully turned into death traps for both men and tanks. Saint-Lô was a key to German defenses in this sector. Until it could be taken, now-Lieutenant General Bradley's army group, comprising the U.S. First and Third armies, would not have room to set itself up for an all-out assault on the German defenses and subsequent drive east—perhaps as far as Germany. For more than a month, American forces expanded their perimeter in costly, set-piece engagements against the German's mini fortresses, and Saint-Lô fell to the First Army on July 18 after some of the fiercest fighting of the war. The First Army continued to slice off as much ground as possible in countless small battles in order to allow Patton's Third Army, arriving division by division from England, to deploy behind it. The First Army's seizure of the Carentan Peninsula opened up badly needed ground for airfield development.

More than fifteen hundred American heavy bombers—targeting only a small portion of the German lines—dropped tons of explosives during a concentrated, massed attack on July 25, wiping out in a single stroke the Panzer Lehr Division. Lieutenant General Courtney Hodges' First Army immediately punched a hole through the shattered German defenses, then held the shoulders of the gap while its 2d and 3d Armored divisions and 1st Infantry Division (motorized for the operation) stampeded through into the German rear areas. Under Patton, the Third Army then exploited this breach, with the 6th and 4th Armored divisions going south and west to capture critical ports in the Brittany Peninsula and two corps slashing their way east and southeast into central France.

Hitler now decided a desperate gamble—a counterattack toward Avranches and the sea to cut off the rampaging Third Army from its supply base, now far to the rear, and the First Army. But instead of turning back his spearheads to confront the threat, Bradley decided to let the Third keep going; the First Army would handle the counterattack. German panzer divisions initially surged through and recaptured Mortain, surrounding two battalions of the 30th "Old Hickory" Division (National Guard troops from Georgia, Tennessee, and the Carolinas)—but tanks and men broke though to the "lost battalions" and stopped the attack. Now the Allies caught the Germans, who had unwittingly offered the Allies an opportunity to encircle them, in a pocket between the British and Canadians on the north at Falaise and the Americans on the west and south. Hodges' First Army turned to the northeast, and the lead elements of Patton's eastward drive turned due north toward Argentan.

Parts of three German armies were moving eastward, away from British attacks along the coast and withdrawing from their failed counterattack, unaware that Americans stood between them and the fatherland. Nearly twenty disorganized divisions got caught in the trap as air and ground attacks killed thousands of the enemy and wrecked hundreds of guns, trucks, wagons, and armored vehicles. They lost more than sixty thousand men, including fifty thousand captured. The First Army, along with the British and Canadians, then crossed the Seine River and struck out toward Belgium where, at Mons, the 1st Infantry and 3d Armored divisions caught a confused mass of Germans trying to get back to Germany. The First Army continued eastward entering Luxembourg, taking Leige, and, on September 11, crossing into Germany. Plagued by severe supply shortages, however, the First Army called a halt to its advance.

While this was going on, the Germans had no means of stopping the Third Army drive, and the bulk of Patton's forces continued to fan out to the east in three fast-moving corps, each spearheaded by an armored division. A Free French armored division and the U.S. 4th Infantry Division were directed toward Paris, entering the city on August 25, while tanks and trucks filled with soldiers overran Orleans, Rheims, Châlons, Verdun, Toul, and Nancy. On September 11, the Third met columns of the U.S. Seventh Army that had landed together with French forces on the Riviera of southern France, and then fought its way up the Rhône Valley. But as Patton's lead elements neared Germany, the enemy's defenses began to stiffen along the Moselle River, in the area of Metz and Nancy.

LEFT TOP: VI Corps' audacious commander, Lieutenant General Lucian K. Truscott; Seventh Army commander Lieutenant General Alexander M. Patch; and Sixth Army Group commander Lieutenant General Jacob L. Devers (*left to right*) talk shop at the 3d Division command post near Besançon, France, on September 10, 1944. Patch had experienced the static trench warfare of World War I, while Devers and Truscott had not seen action prior to World War II. Almost obscured by his left arm is a .45-caliber automatic that Devers had slipped into his trouser pocket.

LEFT BOTTOM: Before D-Day, the U.S. Army made few plans for the conduct of operations in the superb defensive terrain beyond the beachheads, because they believed that the British would achieve a quick victory, prompting a general withdrawal of German forces. Said General Dwight D. Eisenhower: "We felt before the invasion that the capture of open ground south of Caen would assist the Americans on the west to get through the difficult *bocage* country following on the capture of Cherbourg." The lack of planning meant that detailed maps were not made of any areas more than a few miles beyond the English Channel until well *after* the landings, further hindering American units in the tangled Norman countryside. In this photo, terrain maps of the 35th Infantry Division's zone are being readied for distribution by the headquarters personnel of the 134th Infantry on July 11, 1944.

FAR LEFT: A 40-mm antiaircraft gun mounted on an M2 carriage is used as a devastating direct-fire weapon in support of the American Infantry fighting along the German border.

LEFT: The M1939 enlisted wool service overcoat was phased out of frontline service because its weight and length impeded movement. However, production shortfalls of the "layered" M1943 combat uniform necessitated that stocks of the overcoat be rushed to the European and Mediterranean theaters for the winter campaign.

BELOW: 90th Infantry Division soldiers of the 358th Infantry's 2d Battalion wait for supporting artillery to soften German positions before pushing beyond Metzervisse, in eastern France. They had fought their way into the town the previous night and it was completely cleared of Germans by the morning of November 17, 1944.

THE SIEGFRIED LINE AND ARDENNES OFFENSIVE

The Siegfried Line, called the *Westwall* by the Germans, was a continuous network of fortifications extending along western Germany from the Dutch border to Switzerland. Its reinforced concrete pillboxes had sides and roofs that were four to eight feet thick, protecting machine guns or medium-field artillery with overlapping fields of fire. Where there was no river or antitank ditch in front of them, the Germans had built rows of concrete "dragon's teeth" as tank obstacles. When an Allied airborne effort failed to get around the *Westwall* at the Dutch town of Arnhem, the First Army began a several-month effort to break through at Aachen, a large German city with a peacetime population of one hundred sixty thousand, to the south of Hürtgen Forest. Although the city fell on October 21 after savage house-to-house fighting, the Hürtgen Forest became the scene of a brutal series of engagements that failed to make worthwhile gains against the Germans.

Further to the south, in an area deemed to be even more unfavorable to offensive operations than the Hürtgen Forest, a virtual rest area stretched for miles along the German border. On the night of December 15, American soldiers bedded

down in the hilly forests of the Ardennes with no more worry than ever in this "quiet sector" of the Western Front. They awoke to the roar of artillery, chatter of machine guns, and the rumble of tanks. Sleepy men in division rear areas looked out through the mist to see German armor and trucks crammed with infantry rolling along nearby roads. Tanks smashed through an advance field for artillery-spotting aircraft before the pilots could fly them to safety, and many units were simply overrun. In all, twenty-four German divisions—including twelve panzer—were attacking through the thinly held Ardennes in Hitler's last great bid to smash the Allies in the west.

But American soldiers fought back. Although most of the 102d Infantry Division was cut off and soon surrendered to the Germans, the tough soldiers of the 28th Infantry Division fought back hard, even though they had been badly mauled by the panzers and had many rookies among their ranks. (The 28th, officially a Pennsylvania Guard division, had suffered so many casualties from Normandy to the Hürtgen Forest before being sent to the Ardennes "rest area" that its front-line regiments had become virtually "nationalized" by its infantry replacements.) The 2d Infantry Division to their north, in one of the great actions of the war, withstood attacks of a German corps for thirty-six hours until others could join it, holding

BELOW: In November 1944, while smoke from the first volley still clings to the ground, field artillerymen fighting in Germany's Hürtgen Forest reload launchers to fire a second round of M8 4½-inch rockets.

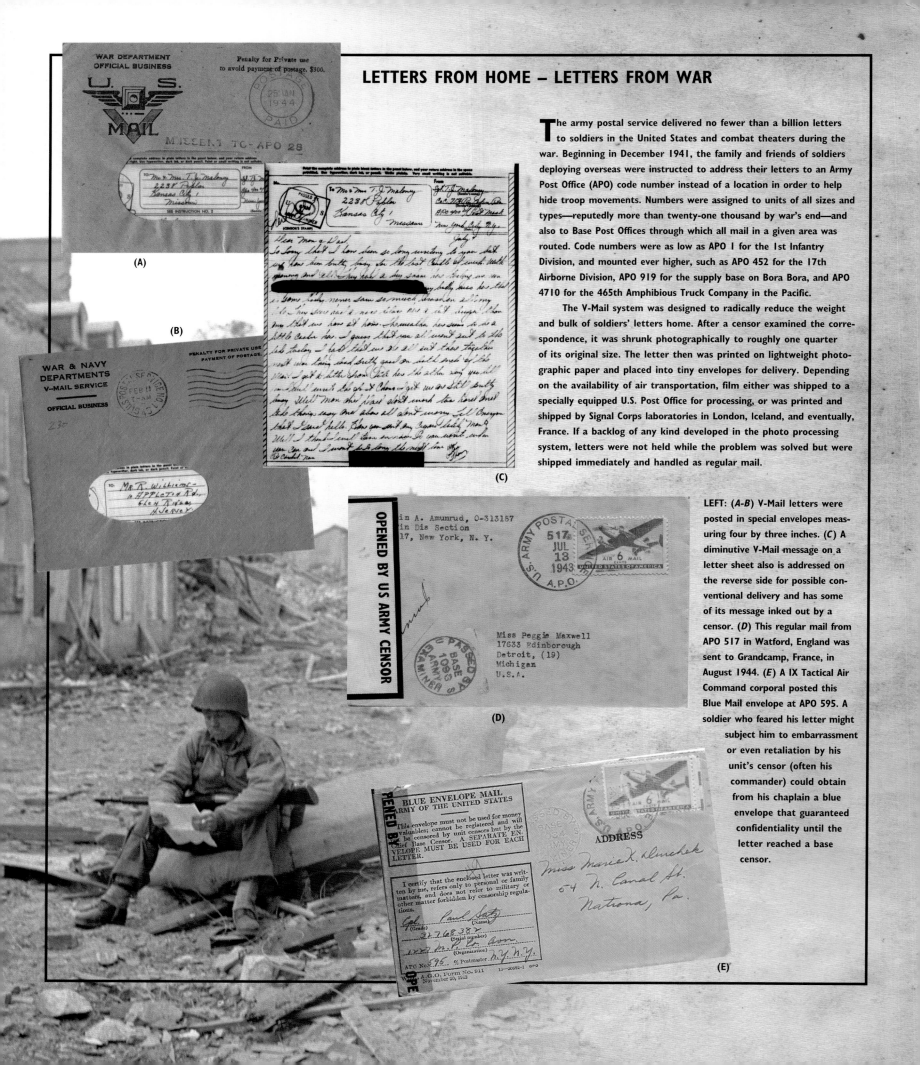

LETTERS FROM HOME – LETTERS FROM WAR

The army postal service delivered no fewer than a billion letters to soldiers in the United States and combat theaters during the war. Beginning in December 1941, the family and friends of soldiers deploying overseas were instructed to address their letters to an Army Post Office (APO) code number instead of a location in order to help hide troop movements. Numbers were assigned to units of all sizes and types—reputedly more than twenty-one thousand by war's end—and also to Base Post Offices through which all mail in a given area was routed. Code numbers were as low as APO 1 for the 1st Infantry Division, and mounted ever higher, such as APO 452 for the 17th Airborne Division, APO 919 for the supply base on Bora Bora, and APO 4710 for the 465th Amphibious Truck Company in the Pacific.

The V-Mail system was designed to radically reduce the weight and bulk of soldiers' letters home. After a censor examined the correspondence, it was shrunk photographically to roughly one quarter of its original size. The letter then was printed on lightweight photographic paper and placed into tiny envelopes for delivery. Depending on the availability of air transportation, film either was shipped to a specially equipped U.S. Post Office for processing, or was printed and shipped by Signal Corps laboratories in London, Iceland, and eventually, France. If a backlog of any kind developed in the photo processing system, letters were not held while the problem was solved but were shipped immediately and handled as regular mail.

LEFT: (*A-B*) V-Mail letters were posted in special envelopes measuring four by three inches. (*C*) A diminutive V-Mail message on a letter sheet also is addressed on the reverse side for possible conventional delivery and has some of its message inked out by a censor. (*D*) This regular mail from APO 517 in Watford, England was sent to Grandcamp, France, in August 1944. (*E*) A IX Tactical Air Command corporal posted this Blue Mail envelope at APO 595. A soldier who feared his letter might subject him to embarrassment or even retaliation by his unit's censor (often his commander) could obtain from his chaplain a blue envelope that guaranteed confidentiality until the letter reached a base censor.

LEFT TOP: 101st Airborne Division senior officers at the drop zone near Zon, Holland: (*left to right*) assistant division commander Brigadier General Anthony C. McAuliffe, Colonel Robert F. Sink of the 506th Parachute Infantry, and Colonel Joseph H. "Bud" Harper of the 327th Glider Infantry. The presence of the jeep indicates that this is either the second or third day of Operation Market Garden; the small number of vehicles assigned to the drop did not start arriving by glider until D+1, September 18, 1944. Several months later, when the 101st was surrounded by German forces at the important Belgium road hub of Bastogne, Harper delivered McAuliffe's response to a demand that the division surrender: "To the German Commander, NUTS! The American Commander."

LEFT BOTTOM: An American soldier examines a German *Sturmgeschutz III Ausf G* knocked out near Luneville, France, on September 29, 1944. Though originally intended to serve as assault guns providing infantry support, the need to counter Allied armor prompted the Germans to up-gun them with higher velocity 75-mm cannons so they could be used as "tank killers" on the Eastern and Western fronts.

BELOW: B Company soldiers of the 114th Infantry Regiment, 44th Infantry Division, squeeze onto the rear deck of an M5A1 light tank in preparation for an attack on Struth, in the Lohr area of France, on November 28, 1944.

RIGHT TOP AND BOTTOM: The battle for Aachen, east of Liege, Belgium, lasted three weeks. It was the first German city to be captured by the Allies. In these pictures, taken on October 19, 1944—two days before the surrender of the German garrison—soldiers of either the 1st or 30th Infantry Division move cautiously around a corner when a sniper in a building they passed cuts one of them down. Most of the men scurried into the building at right for cover, but three risk additional fire as they move the soldier to safety. U.S. and German forces each suffered approximately five thousand casualties during the fighting.

RIGHT: Soldiers from the 1st Infantry Division's 26th Infantry Regiment fighting near the Hotel Quellenhof in the Siegfried Line city of Aachen, Germany, on October 19, 1944.

BELOW: 35th Tank Battalion Shermans of the 4th Armored Division crest a hill near Thal, France, on December 1, 1944, as the division expands its bridgehead over the Saar River. In the foreground, soldiers from the 10th Armored Infantry Battalion watch the proceedings as a white, phosphorus smoke screen in front of the tanks partially masks their movements.

LEFT: On December 23, 1944, paratroopers drag bundles from the first aerial resupply of the 101st Airborne Division holding Bastogne. Some 241 planes dropped 144 tons of supplies to the Bastogne garrison. The following day, 322 more tons of desperately needed food, fuel, ammunition, and medical supplies were dropped. Supplies were dragged to jeeps and trucks, which hauled them to distribution points and sometimes directly to frontline positions.

Though the 101st was a light division, its own medium artillery battalions were supplemented by four more from units that had fallen back into the city. Highly effective fire support during the siege blunted German attacks and forced them to operate at a distance from American lines. Some batteries, however, were down to an average of ten rounds per gun before the air drops, prompting General Anthony C. McAuliffe to tell his artillery commanders not to fire on attacking Germans "until you see the whites of their eyes."

ABOVE: General Bruce C. Clarke as a one-star commanded the 7th Armored Division's Combat Command B. With the 2d and 99th divisions, soon joined by the 1st and 9th divisions, all holding firm along the Elsenborn Ridge against the German's Sixth Panzer Army, possession of the crossroads town of Saint Vith between the heights and Bastogne suddenly assumed great importance. Clarke successfully coordinated the elements—and remnants—of four U.S. divisions centered around his own combat command (essentially a heavily augmented regiment) during his dogged defense of Saint Vith. German plans called for controlling the area on December 17, but Clarke's force held the town until the 21st, then denied the enemy the use of the road system until the 23rd, throwing the offensive far off its timetable and allowing sufficient time for more American troops to reach the battle.

RIGHT: 83d Division Private Frank Vukas, a member of Company C, 331st Infantry, stops to load a clip into his Garand while advancing in the Houffalize sector of Belgium on January 15, 1945. The two dead Germans are wearing camouflage suits.

firm the First Army line in their sector. Throughout the snowy battlefield, many soldiers in "soft" logistical and support units fled before the German onslaught, but many more, in units of all sizes and types, fought to stem the tide.

In the path of the breakthrough, the 2d Armored Division slugged it out with a German panzer division and drove it back with heavy losses. The great fight of the 7th Armored Division at Saint Vith, Belgium, occurred even while German columns rolled far to the west. It disrupted the whole German schedule, making it possible for the buildup of a defense line. South of Saint Vith the 101st Airborne Division and Combat Command B, 10th Armored Division were ordered to hold the important Belgian road center of Bastogne at all costs. Finding that the town was firmly held by the paratroopers, the panzer spearheads continued striking west, leaving it behind to be captured by panzer grenadiers (armored infantry units). When the German commander sent a note stating that the only way the American forces could be saved from total annihilation was to surrender their encircled town, the American commander, Brigadier General Anthony McAuliffe, sent a one-word reply: "Nuts."

COUNTERATTACK INTO "THE BULGE"

While the Germans were attacking the First Army, the U.S. Third Army to its southeast was attacking in the opposite direction against *Westwall* fortifications in the German Saarland. Within two days after receiving orders, the Third Army had pulled back from its attack in the Saar region (the Seventh Army took over there), had hundreds of guns and trucks rolling northward, and three divisions attacking through snow toward Bastogne. Denied vital roads and hampered by an air attack when the weather cleared on Christmas day, the German assault resulted only in a large bulge in the Allied lines, which did not even extend to the Meuse River, the German's first objective. Bastogne was relieved on December 26 and on January 3, Lieutenant General J. Lawton "Lightnin' Joe" Collins' VII Corps opened a First Army counterattack from the north.

German forces fought furiously in an effort to keep from being cut off, but lost large numbers of men and much of their equipment to artillery fire and, now that the number of days with clear flying weather had increased, to American

ABOVE: General Joseph Lawton "Lightning Joe" Collins as a three-star commanding VII Corps. On January 3, 1945, Collins opened a First Army counteroffensive from the north against the right flank of the German penetration. Earlier, he had led the 25th Infantry Division during the fighting on Guadalcanal and played a pivotal role in Operation Cobra, the U.S. breakout from the Normandy hedgerow country after D-Day.

RIGHT: Staff Sergeant George Talbert of the 1st Infantry Division's 18th Infantry keeps watch along a forest firebreak near Sourbrodt, Belgium, on December 19, 1944. During this period, the "Big Red One" destroyed a large number of German tanks and self-propelled guns while defending the main route through the southernmost tip of the Elsenborn Ridge. This forced the enemy columns to use poorer roads farther south, confining their advance to a narrow, vulnerable front. Talbert was part of a detachment sent to protect the division from any German effort to get behind the ridge. He was killed in action near Steinbach on January 16, 1945, when the 1st Infantry and 7th Armored divisions fought their way toward Saint Vith in an effort to cut off retreating German forces.

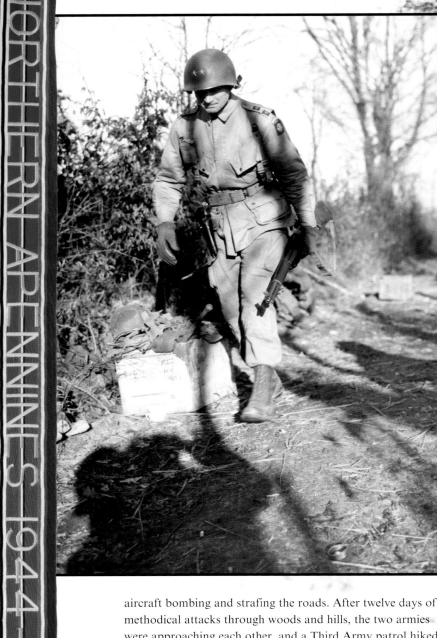

aircraft bombing and strafing the roads. After twelve days of methodical attacks through woods and hills, the two armies were approaching each other, and a Third Army patrol hiked twenty miles in the freezing weather to make first contact with First Army troops near Houffalize.

The fighting, however, was not confined to the Ardennes. In order to keep American troops to the south tied up and unable to throw their support to the north, the Germans launched an offensive in Alsace at the same time that they attacked in the Ardennes. As in the better-known Battle of the Bulge, American soldiers stopped this threat, and again individual and small-unit action played a big part in turning the tide. In one Seventh Army sector, the 15th Infantry—the "Can Do" regiment—held a defensive position that was under heavy pressure. Commanding its Company B was 2d Lieutenant Audie Murphy, a baby-faced young man who entered the army as a private, earned his commission the hard way—on the battlefield—and won the Distinguished Service Cross and the Silver Star.

In early January, six German tanks and waves of infantry attacked Company B, and Murphy ordered his men to withdraw to some nearby woods while he remained at his command post to direct artillery fire. A tank destroyer behind him received a direct hit and started to burn. Large numbers of German infantry were headed straight for him. Murphy climbed to the deck of the smoldering tank destroyer and opened fire with its .50 caliber machine gun. Germans got as close as ten yards, but he mowed them down and was somehow not hit by their return fire. After he killed about fifty infantrymen, the Germans pulled back. Murphy got back to his company and organized a counterattack, which drove out the Germans. His actions that day won him the Medal of Honor, and he ultimately became the most decorated American soldier of World War II.

Counting the large number of prisoners taken by the Germans during their initial thrust, U.S. forces had suffered some seventy-five thousand casualties in the Battle of the Bulge, but the Germans lost eighty thousand to one hundred thousand, leaving the German Army's strength irredeemably impaired. By the end of January 1945, American units had retaken all ground they had lost, and the defeat of Germany was clearly only a matter of time.

ABOVE: Soldiers of the 290th Infantry fight in fresh snowfall near Amonines, Belgium, on January 4, 1945. Detached from the 75th Infantry Division and thrown into the line west of the 82d Airborne at the beginning of the battle, control of the 290th and its sector transitioned through several different division commands, beginning with the 3d Armored, as it beat back attack after attack by German Panzer formations trying to turn north toward the Meuse River. When this photo was taken, the 290th was attached to the 84th Infantry Division.

OPPOSITE TOP: Major General James M. Gavin inspects the Erria, Belgium, area on December 29, 1944. The 82d Airborne Division had just retaken the ground around its Company G, 3d Battalion, 508th Parachute Infantry. Though overrun by the 19th Panzer Grenadier Regiment, the company stayed put and, according to German records, "cut to pieces" the Grenadier's 1st Battalion. Gavin's men found sixty-two Germans dead in front of one of G Company's machine guns. Said Gavin: "As far as the 82d was concerned, that brought the German offensive phase of the Battle of the Bulge to an end."

LEFT: Colonel William L. Roberts, commander of the 10th Armor Division's Combat Command B, receives the Silver Star from Major General Taylor for blunting German attacks toward Bastogne long enough for the 101st Airborne Division to reach the key crossroads town.

MEDAL OF HONOR
Second Lieutenant Audie L. Murphy
15th Infantry Regiment

Citation: Murphy commanded Company B, which was attacked by six tanks and waves of infantry. He ordered his men to withdraw to prepared positions in a woods while he remained forward at his command post and continued to give fire directions to the artillery by telephone. Behind him, to his right, one of our tank destroyers received a direct hit and began to burn. Its crew withdrew to the woods. Murphy continued to direct artillery fire, which killed large numbers of the advancing enemy infantry. With the enemy tanks abreast of his position, Murphy climbed on the burning tank destroyer, which was in danger of blowing up at any moment, and employed its 50-caliber machine gun against the enemy. He was alone and exposed to German fire from three sides, but his deadly fire killed dozens of Germans and caused their infantry attack to waver. The enemy tanks, losing infantry support, began to fall back. For an hour the Germans tried every available weapon to eliminate Murphy, but he continued to hold his position and wiped out a squad that was trying to creep up unnoticed on his right flank. Germans reached as close as ten yards, only to be mowed down by his fire. He received a leg wound but ignored it and continued the single-handed fight until his ammunition was exhausted. He then made his way to his company, refused medical attention, and organized the company in a counterattack that forced the Germans to withdraw. His directing of artillery fire wiped out many of the enemy; he killed or wounded about fifty. Murphy's indomitable courage and his refusal to give an inch of ground saved his company from possible encirclement and destruction, and enabled it to hold the woods that had been the enemy's objective.

BOUNCING THE RHINE

After eliminating the bulge, one great barrier remained before the Western Allies: the Rhine River. German forces by now were thoroughly exhausted from their over-ambitious counter-offensive and were further weakened by transfers of troops to meet the Soviet threat in the east. Germany could no longer effectively defend its territory west of the Rhine, which fell to a new Allied drive that was conducted on a broad front. Bridge after bridge was destroyed by the retreating Germans once they had withdrawn their troops across them—and sometimes before when there was a risk that a bridge might be captured intact by the Americans. Eventually, an old railroad bridge at an out-of-the-way location—the Ludendorff Bridge at Remagen—was the only one standing. On March 7, 1945, elements of the First Army's 9th Armored Division were surprised to find it still intact and seized the unexpected opportunity.

They had to move fast. At 3:15 P.M. they learned from a German prisoner that it was to be blown up at four o'clock sharp. It took thirty-five minutes for the men of Company A, 27th Armored Infantry Battalion, to reach the approaches to the bridge, and tanks went into position nearby to cover the crossing. The Germans set off a charge that blew a crater in the elongated road to the structure, but the Company A soldiers went around it and, at ten minutes till four o'clock, rushed out onto the long span. Another charge, placed over the river, went off, knocking out some supports and flooring—but that was all. A blasting cap went off but inexplicably failed to detonate a massive, five-hundred-pound charge of TNT, and other charges, too, failed to explode. The men raced on. Engineers hurried onto the bridge and began cutting wires and throwing other charges into the river. When they got to the main cable, their small pliers would not cut it, so a sergeant smashed it with three shots from his carbine.

BELOW: 89th Infantry Division troops (probably the 354th Infantry's 2d Battalion) hunker down to avoid German fire while they cross the Rhine near Saint Goar to reinforce the division's foothold on the east bank on March 26, 1945. The U.S. army suffered heavy losses of machine guns and 20-mm antiaircraft guns during the before-dawn assault and throughout the day.

A SNAPSHOT OF BATTLE

Having gained control of a key bridge, a division commander is anxious to move a strong force against a nearby city before its defenses can be solidified. Built-up areas on both sides of the highway leading to the city could, however, spell trouble. The same regiment that had been responsible for seizing the bridge is given the job of expanding the bridgehead and securing the fortified areas. The regimental commander, a lieutenant colonel (or perhaps even a major because of combat attrition and the chronic shortage of officers) assigns a battalion to each side of the main road—but with an easily observed,

raised railroad embankment as the boundary between them. Wary of a counterattack from the city by a force of unknown strength, his third battalion will be pushed across the bridge as quickly as the other two can create room for it.

Companies of the right-flank battalion will simultaneously attack the elongated town in their zone, using the highway that splits through the town as the boundary between the attacking units (see illustration). Tanks standing off, away from the structures, will supply requested fire support. Both infantry companies have engineers attached.

A church with a tall steeple marks the boundary between the two platoons attacking on the right, and one squad, with another in support, is given the job of quickly clearing the structure to both deny its use by German observers and make it available to the battalion. Because it also will be a prominent target of German artillery if the regiment coming across the bridge doesn't immediately storm the city, the company attacking this end of town will establish its command post well away from the structure.

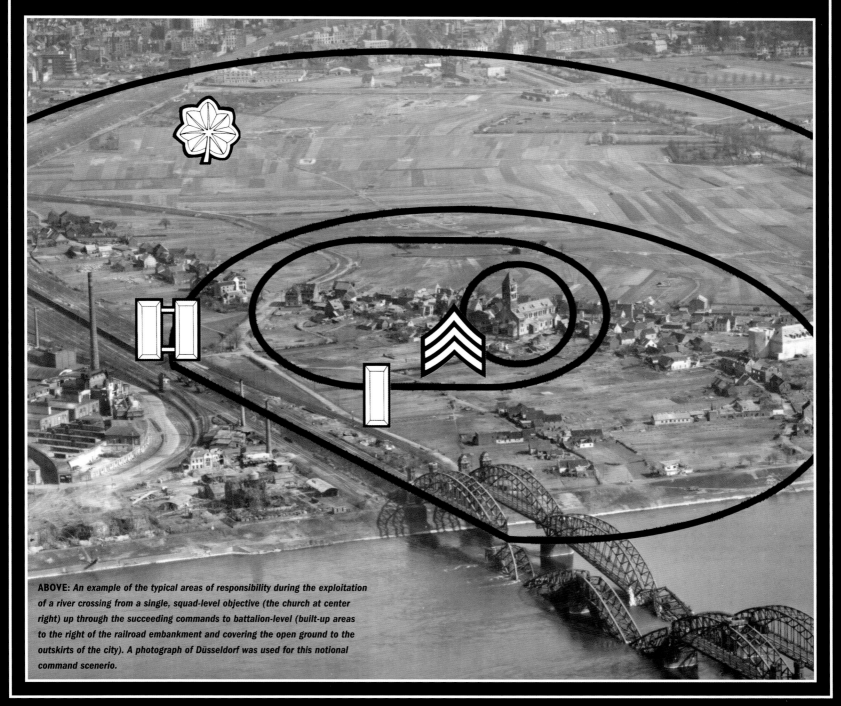

ABOVE: *An example of the typical areas of responsibility during the exploitation of a river crossing from a single, squad-level objective (the church at center right) up through the succeeding commands to battalion-level (built-up areas to the right of the railroad embankment and covering the open ground to the outskirts of the city). A photograph of Düsseldorf was used for this notional command scenerio.*

LEFT: Damaged by German demolitions during its capture and by the cumulative effects of desperate German airstrikes (it also was attacked by Nazi frogmen), the Ludendorff Bridge collapsed on March 17, 1945, killing twenty-eight army engineers who had been laboring to strengthen it. By that time, however, the engineers had laid pontoon bridges both upstream and downstream from the structure, so traffic across the Rhine was barely affected by its loss.

BACKGROUND: A 9th Armored Division soldier looks back on the Ludendorff Bridge at Remagen—the only bridge across the Rhine not blown up by the retreating Germans—after it and the high bluffs on the east bank were secured by the division's 27th Armored Infantry Battalion on March 7, 1945.

LEFT INSET: Sergeant Alexander A. Drabik, the first American to fight his way across the railroad bridge, receives the Distinguished Service Cross from Major General John W. Leonard, the 9th Armored Division's commander.

ABOVE: XII Corps insignia patch

BELOW: Lieutenant General George S. Patton frequently cheered on his Third Army troops saying nothing could stop them and that when they stormed into Germany, he personally would "pee in the Rhine River"—a vow that he also made to General Dwight D. Eisenhower and other senior commanders. Patton fulfilled his pledge with the help of a battalion of XII Corps engineers.

The 5th Infantry Division carried out an assault crossing the river at Oppenheim on March 22, 1945. A trio of pontoon bridges were constructed under fire, including the high-capacity, 1,237-foot bridge that was built within two days by 87th Engineer Battalion (Heavy Pontoon). Patton's command vehicle had almost reached the eastern shore on the 87th's bridge when it abruptly pulled to a stop long enough for the Third Army chief to honor his promise as supply trucks continued to trundle by.

Perhaps after talking it up for so long, the event itself was anticlimactic. In the foreground, Patton's aide-de-camp, Lieutenant Colonel Charley Codman, saunters away after just having memorialized the event for his boss while, to Patton's right, his orderly Master Sergeant George Meeks gazes off in the opposite direction. Hardly a festive occasion. The driver of the passing truck, however, can't take his eyes of the once-in-a lifetime sight.

Characteristically, Patton radioed Eisenhower almost immediately afterwards: "Dear SHAEF [Supreme Headquarters Allied Expeditionary Force], I have just pissed into the Rhine River. For God's sake, send more gasoline." By March 27, five divisions with supporting elements had crossed the three bridges with the entire 6th Armored crossing in less than seventeen hours. More than 60,000 vehicles passed to the east side of the Rhine by the end of the month.

ABOVE: The Combat Infantryman Badge was established in 1943 in recognition of the grim fact that most of the fighting—and more than three-quarters of all army casualties—were suffered by infantrymen of all ranks. Awarded for participation in ground combat, it quickly became a highly prized badge of honor to all who earned it.

RIGHT: Members of a heavy weapons platoon, at least three of whom wear CIBs over their left pockets, pound enemy positions along the German border.

Troops started streaming across the Rhine, and the First Army created a bridgehead. A sign soon appeared: "Cross the Rhine with Dry Feet Courtesy of the 9th Armored Division." Allied forces gained a firm foothold at last on the eastern bank of the Rhine. Two weeks later, troops of the Third Army to the south of Remagen staged a surprise crossing in assault boats. At the same time, in the north, British and American troops crossed the Rhine in a large operation that involved the new 17th Airborne Division and a British airborne division in an assault almost as large as the failed effort the previous September. Having learned the lessons from the Arnhem battle, the gliders and paratroops landed close to their targets and achieved total success. During the last week of March, both the U.S. Seventh and First French armies crossed the Rhine. The stage was set for the final act.

Having successfully "bounced the Rhine," the Allies fanned out with massive columns of armor and motor-borne infantry. Soon, they were making spectacular advances. Resistance was fierce at some points, but Allied strength by this time was overwhelming. When the American Ninth and First armies linked up on April 1 near Lippstadt, they had encircled the industrial Ruhr Valley and bagged more than three hundred twenty-five thousand Germans in what the Army chief of staff, General George C. Marshall, called the biggest pocket in the history of warfare.

Allied armies continued their race across Germany, often against slight opposition since the German Army had completely disorganized. Enemy soldiers surrendered by the thousands and by mid-April the U.S. First, Third, and Ninth armies had reached the Elbe and Mulde rivers within fifty miles of Berlin. While the First and Ninth waited for the approaching Red Army, the Third and Seventh armies drove east and south into Austria and Czechoslovakia. The Nazi regime was done for, and on May 7, 1945, representatives of the German High Command surrendered at General Eisenhower's headquarters at Rheims, France.

LEFT: Flames erupt from a 3d Armored Division M4A3 Sherman that was struck by artillery fire near Bergerhausen, Germany, on the road to Cologne, on March 1, 1945.

BACKGROUND: 3d Armored Division tanks roll through a debris-filled avenue in Cologne on March 6, 1945. Indicative of the German Army in the last days of the Nazi regime, some units put up a lackadaisical defense of their defense zones in the city, while more determined elements fought hard for every block. The factory area along the river proved to be the most difficult part of the city to take; 3d Armored troops encountered massed fire from deadly 88-mm guns and well dug-in infantry supported by self-propelled assault guns. Miraculously, the priceless Renaissance cathedral of Saint Peter and the Blessed Virgin Mary, seen here in the distance, was almost completely untouched during both the seizure of Cologne and the aerial bombardments that preceded it.

Chapter Ten

The Cold War Turns Hot, 1945–1953

The United States fought World War II with an army, including the Army Air Force, that struggled mightily to maintain its congressionally authorized strength of 7,700,00. There was a point in July 1945 when the number of soldiers and airmen briefly spiked at 8,291,366, but this was only because the influx of men from ramped-up draft calls for the planned invasion of Japan coincided with the longest-serving troops—demobilized after the victory in Europe—having not yet been released. In spite of some 12,435,500 men passing through its ranks, the insatiable needs of global war resulted in there never being quite enough human material available. Whole divisions undergoing stateside training were gutted, sometimes repeatedly, to supply new men for the ones already deployed. It was not unusual to find a formation in the midst of training losing nearly the equivalent of its stated strength in a series of "division drafts." One standard-size, 14,253-man infantry division, the 69th, was forced to give up 22,235 enlisted personnel and 1,336 officers before it was finally shipped to France.

Where did all these men go? While the frequently quoted number of U.S. Army and Army Air Force casualties stands at 936,259, this figure does not incorporate 92,656 non-battle deaths, as well as a wide array of administrative separations or other categories, that continually drained the army of manpower and were closely monitored by senior leaders. These included 50,520 disability discharges due to non-battle injuries in combat zones, such as loading accidents; combat-related psychiatric breakdowns accounting for 312,354 discharges; and medical discharges totaling a stunning 862,356 from illnesses contracted in disease-ridden overseas theaters. None of these figures accounted for soldiers who were hospitalized and then returned to their units after recovery.

Fully four-fifths of these casualties were suffered during the final year of the war, the "casualty surge" of June 1944 to June 1945, and no one knows how much higher the numbers would have climbed if Japan had not surrendered. But the army had no illusions that the fighting would be anything but brutal and prolonged. Based on a statistical analysis of the increasingly casualty-intensive battles in the Pacific, the army prepared itself to handle an additional 720,000 "dead and evacuated wounded" through 1946 as America turned all its energies to defeating Japan and getting the boys home as quickly as possible.

ABOVE: A dense column of smoke and fire rises more than sixty thousand feet over the Japanese port of Nagasaki on August 9, 1945. Hiroshima had been destroyed in a nuclear flash on August 6, and the Soviets entered the war, dashing the last hopes of a negotiated settlement. Nevertheless, senior advisors to Emperor Hirohito counseled emphatically against surrender, maintaining that extreme American casualties during the coming U.S. invasion would decide the issue in Japan's favor. But after the Nagasaki blast, a disheartened Prime Minister Kantaro Suzuki announced: "The United States, instead of staging the invasion, will just keep on dropping atomic bombs."

OPPOSITE: An exhausted Major Carroll Cooper of the 17th Infantry Regiment, 7th Infantry Division, breathes deeply during a mission along the gorges of the Yalu River in North Korea, c. November 26–29, 1950. After the division seized Hyesanjin across the river from China, elements of "Task Force Cooper" probed as far as thirty-five miles west along the Yalu in minus twenty-five-degree weather during a futile effort to capture Chinese soldiers for interrogation. A Chinese offensive to the southwest against the 7th's 31st Infantry and the 1st Marine Division at the Chosin Reservoir forced the hasty withdrawal of Cooper's men and all American forces in the area.

CODE NAME DOWNFALL

When the war came to its sudden and unexpected end in 1945 with the dropping of atom bombs on two of Japan's cities, the U.S. First Army and Eighth Air Force were already in the midst of their long journey from Europe to the Pacific. Their task: to reinforce General MacArthur's invasion forces gathering in the Philippines, Marianas, and Okinawa. The invasion of the imperial homeland, code-named DOWNFALL, contained four major components. First, a Connecticut-size area on the southernmost island of Kyushu would be seized by the end of 1945 for the construction of air bases and ship anchorages. Three quarters of a million U.S. soldiers and Marines would be involved in this operation. Next, a similar landing in the spring of 1946, comprising over a million and a quarter assault troops, would land within striking distance of Tokyo itself on the island of Honshu. Third, Tokyo would be surrounded and thus cut off from Japanese reinforcements by summer. Finally, if the Japanese had not yet surrendered, Tokyo would be taken in brutal block-by-block fighting while other U.S. forces seized key portions of the California-size nation. With luck and hard work, Army Chief of Staff George C. Marshall believed,

the deadly business of subjugating Japan might be done by the end of 1946 if much of the remaining country could be induced to surrender.

As early as the summer of 1944, Joint Chiefs of Staff planners had cautiously estimated the cost of this endeavor to be "half a million American lives and many times that number in wounded" because of the willingness of Japanese soldiers to stubbornly fight to the death. A half century after the war, some historians would cherry pick much smaller casualty projections made for specific parts of the opening assault to "prove" that the number of dead and wounded would not have been nearly so dreadful. But the fact of the matter was that casualty numbers were already climbing to record levels as the fighting grew closer to Japan at Iwo Jima and Okinawa, and as the navy fought off Kamikaze suicide aircraft at sea.

Nearly three hundred thousand Japanese civilians had lost their lives and six million had been made homeless even before the atomic bombs were dropped. A July 1945 War Department document grimly predicted: "We shall probably have to kill at least 5 to 10 million Japanese [and] this might cost us between 1.7 and 4 million casualties including four hundred thousand to eight hundred thousand killed." Some

civilian elements in the Japanese government had come to a similar conclusion and were determined to find a way to end the war before the U.S. invasion was launched. Unfortunately, the military was in firm control of the government, and Japanese moderates had to tread gingerly for fear of arrest or assassination. It was the hope of President Harry S. Truman and his senior advisors that the "tremendous shock" of the few nuclear weapons available would stampede the Japanese leadership into a quick capitulation.

In the end, this is precisely what happened, but not before a coup attempt nearly blocked Emperor Hirohito's decree to the Japanese people that they must accept defeat because "the enemy has begun to employ a new and cruel bomb" and warned that continuing the fight would "result in an ultimate collapse and obliteration of the Japanese nation." World War II came to a close when representatives of the Japanese Empire signed the instrument of surrender on the deck of the battleship USS *Missouri* on September 2, 1945, instead of late 1946 or even 1947. Untold lives—Japanese, American, Chinese, and those of a dozen other nations—would be spared, and the U.S. Army found itself in possession of the most wonderful of all war-surplus items: four hundred ninety-five thousand unused Purple Hearts.

ABOVE: Army Chief of Staff General George C. Marshall

BELOW: An Army Service Forces soldier keeps guard over Nazis who surrendered en masse in the Ruhr Pocket on April 25, 1945. The temporary prisoner of war enclosure is near Remagen, Germany, where little more than six weeks earlier the 9th Armored Division seized the first bridgehead across the Rhine River.

ATTRITION AND REPLACEMENTS

Throughout World War II, the army struggled to keep its combat units up to strength. Subsequent to a spate of successful months in early 1943, when the number of men inducted exceeded the draft "calls" (targets), the rest of year and 1944 saw few occasions when quotas were met. The armed services absorbed 4,915,912 draftees during that period, an impressive figure by any standards. However, the calls to fulfill the insatiable demands of global war actually had totaled 5,815,275.

This shortfall of nearly one million men fell heaviest on the draft's biggest customer—the army. It also had an immediate impact on the ground force element that engaged in the heaviest, most prolonged fighting—the infantry. The dearth of young men being sent forward was painfully real and contributed to a total deficit of nearly four hundred thousand soldiers during the countdown to the invasion of France. Without either an upswing in the number of new men wearing khaki or a serious revamping of its force structure, the army would not be able to conduct a two-front war without risking serious reverses and possibly even local defeats that would prolong the fighting and ramp up the nation's cost in "blood and treasure."

The army recognized that it was in a "manpower box" and immediately embarked on myriad initiatives to minimize losses, such as imposing the highest practical hygiene standards on units in the field, while simultaneously fine-tuning and downsizing the composition of combat divisions themselves. For example, the strength of the army's eighty-nine active divisions in April 1945 was only seventy thousand men higher than the three largely paper divisions in December 1942. Still, the huge shortfalls made the formulation of a stable replacement pool virtually impossible. Stateside divisions were gutted, sometimes repeatedly, to supply new men for those already deployed. One standard-size, 14,253-man division, the 69th, was forced to give up 22,235 enlisted personnel and 1,336 officers before it finally was shipped to France.

Said General George C. Marshall in June 1944:

I am sure people do not realize how close we came to catastrophe. Shortages of personnel forced us to strip division after division that we had trained. This drove the division commanders to strenuous protests. Just as those new units were reaching an excellent standard of efficiency, we would rip them to pieces in order to provide men as replacements for the growing battles overseas. We were confronted with a terrible problem for which the armies in the field paid the price.... We had just enough and no more, and it all went in.

ABOVE: AGF Replacement Depot patch

BELOW: Replacements for replacements at Camp Adair, Oregon, c. April 1944. Like nearly two dozen other formations in the United States, the 70th Infantry Division was forced to give up thirty-seven hundred soldiers needed to replace casualties in Europe in the second of two "division drafts" inflicted on it. Restarting its training from scratch, the 70th did not enter combat until late December.

ABOVE: Major General Paul J. Mueller, commander of the 81st Infantry Division on Leyte, informally welcomes replacements sent to his division on June 9, 1945, and hands each a shoulder patch with the Wildcat unit insignia. By the time this photo was taken, his division had lost 2,457 men in combat against the Japanese, including 515 dead, and was scheduled to take part in the invasion of Japan before the year was out.

BELOW: Carbine-armed 7th Infantry Division stretcher bearers on Okinawa carefully move a wounded soldier as Sherman tanks maneuver in the distance.

THE PURPLE HEART

The Purple Heart is awarded to U.S. military personnel wounded in battle and the families of those killed in action. Its history can be traced back to the Badge of Military Merit, established by General George Washington as a way around congressional unwillingness to reward ordinary soldiers for extraordinary deeds. The decoration fell into disuse after the Revolution, and efforts to revive it in the wake of World War I by Army Chief of Staff Charles P. Summerall went nowhere. A decade later, his successor, Douglas MacArthur, had better luck, largely because his campaign coincided with the run-up to the bicentennial of George Washington's birth in 1932. MacArthur changed its name to the Purple Heart and, at the last minute, modified its franchise to include wounds received as a result of enemy action.

After American soldiers entered combat in World War II, the medal became highly prized, as its award criteria was rightly seen as being far less subject to the whims of commanders than other decorations. It proclaimed to all that its recipients had shed blood—or made the ultimate sacrifice—for their country. Approximately 1,531,000 Purple Hearts were made for the war effort, with production reaching its peak as America geared up for the invasion of Japan.

The unexpected ferocity of the Pacific fighting and decision to assault the mainland directly instead of conducting a blockade of unknown duration also led to last-minute scrambling by the U.S. Navy to have awards ready for the invasion. The Navy had believed that its initial 1942 order for the medal would be sufficient of its and the Marines' needs. The army, meanwhile, had long expected to conduct a costly invasion of Japan and functionally soaked up nearly all medals-production capacity in anticipation of the coming inferno. Thus, the Navy's orders could not be fulfilled until late 1946, months after soldiers and Marines were expected to claw their way ashore while sailors battled fresh waves of kamikazes. Seeing the writing on the wall, Navy brass swallowed hard and made arrangements with the army to borrow sixty thousand decorations.

As for the nearly half-million Purple Hearts left over from the cancelled invasion, while all the other implements of war—from bullets to aircraft carriers to tent pegs—had long since been used up or scrapped, medals continued to be distributed, and roughly one hundred twenty thousand still were available at the turn of the century after the Korean and Vietnam wars. Refurbished in the late 1980s and intermingled with small quantities more recently produced, the medals continue to be awarded to American service personnel. Said one veteran who learned that he had received a medal minted for the soldiers' grandfathers: "I will never look at my Purple Heart the same way again."

BELOW INSET: This Soviet 7.62-mm Tokarev automatic pistol—a close copy of the American .45-caliber automatic—was presented to General Omar N. Bradley in April 1945. The inscription on the pistol grip reads, "To General Bradley from Marshall Konev." Ivan Stepanovich Konev commanded one of the two Soviet army groups, called fronts, that seized Berlin and central Germany in the closing days of the war. In 1956 he led the Soviet invasion that suppressed the Hungarian revolt.

RIGHT: 82d Airborne Division soldiers meet troops of the Soviet 49th Army at Grabow, northwest of Berlin, on May 3, 1945. A disarmed but unattended German soldier (*center*, with a bicycle, possibly serving as a translator for one side or the other) watches the proceedings. The American soldier with a cigarette (*center left*) also appears to be keeping a watch on the paratrooper with the bayonet (*lower left*), who appears to be warily eyeing the "Ruskies" in their midst.

LEFT: Some of the generals that "did it" (*seated, left to right*): William H. Simpson, George S. Patton Jr., Carl Spaatz, Dwight D. Eisenhower, Omar Bradley, Courtney H. Hodges, and Leonard T. Gerow; (*standing, left to right*) Ralph F. Stearley, Hoyt S. Vandenberg, Walter Bedell Smith, Otto P. Weyland, and Richard E. Nugent. This photo likely was taken in May 1945 before Spaatz left for Washington and then the Pacific.

OPPOSITE: Huge corrugated drums are used as solitary confinement cells for unruly Nazi officers in a U.S. prisoner of war camp in eastern France on May 30, 1945.

RIGHT: A young Japanese officer, still armed with his samurai sword, rides along with the crew of an M8 Greyhound armored car to act as their interpreter. XXIV Corps' divisions had landed in Korea on September 8, 1945, six days after Japan's formal surrender. Chaos ensued. The abrupt end of the war resulted in almost no preparations for the occupation of the peninsula, and dozens of local political parties were jockeying for position. To make matters worse, the U.S. Military Government had almost no one who spoke Korean, so it turned to the Japanese—for whom it had at least a few interpreters—for administrative help. The Koreans' outcry forced U.S. authorities to abandon their use of Korea's ex-overlords and speeded their reparation back to Japan.

DEMOBILIZATION AND OCCUPATION

Soldiers were anxious to return to their civilian lives and the army was happy to oblige. Within weeks of Japan's surrender, men were being discharged at the rate of 650 per hour—and the pace would swiftly climb to more than twenty-five thousand per day by January 1946. Yet this only seemed to feed Americans' impatience. The army originally had believed that an orderly demobilization would release more than five million men by July 1946. However, political pressure forced an almost helter-skelter acceleration, and by April, nearly seven million, including all postwar draftees, had been discharged by the army together with three million more by the navy and marines. One year later, the army was an all-volunteer body of 306,000 airmen who would soon form the core of an independent U.S. Air Force, and a bare 684,000 ground troops. The army would have been smaller still if international agreements and the need to occupy the defeated Axis nations had not required a substantial troop presence overseas.

The army had appointed military governors to oversee the administration of civilian populations on numerous occasions going as far back as the Mexican-American and Civil wars, and had assumed temporary control of jurisdictions large and small in the United States during times of unrest. For example, Lieutenant General Arthur MacArthur Jr. (father of Douglas MacArthur) had arbitrated dozens of civil disputes while stationed in New Orleans during Reconstruction and in Pennsylvania during the labor violence of 1877. Common sense and military necessity were expected to guide the actions of uniformed administrators. Until World War II, the army had never trained soldiers for such tasks or even produced as much as a field manual to guide soldiers. A higher headquarters would simply appoint an officer when the time came with a cheery, "You are the new military governor. Now get out there and govern!"

The short-lived U.S. occupation of the German Rhineland after World War I clearly demonstrated

RIGHT: A 1st Cavalry Division soldier passes out cigarettes to his counterparts at the Imperial Palace in Tokyo on September 2, 1945. The Japanese guards could carry swords but not small arms.

BELOW: On September 8, 1945, U.S. Military Police stand guard as Japanese soldiers obediently carry surrendered rifles, light machine guns, bayonets, and swords from trucks into a building used as a collecting point by the 382d Headquarters Battalion, XI Corps, in Yokohama, Japan. Although a significant amount of fractious political activity existed in occupied Japan, none of it could be considered a direct threat to American authority, and U.S. occupation forces shrank to just four understrength divisions by 1950.

BELOW: The famous British ocean liner *Queen Mary* arrives in New York Harbor on June 20, 1945, with thousands of U.S. troops from Europe. After their thirty-day leaves, these men—principally medical personnel and engineers—would begin their movement to the Pacific and the planned invasion of Japan. Soldiers returning aboard the biggest liners—*Queen Mary*, *Queen Elizabeth*, *Aquitania*, *Mauretania*, *Nieuw Amsterdam*, and *Ile de France* (collectively known as "The Monsters")—first transited to Britain where the liners were berthed. The Monsters began moving redeployed troops to the Pacific from West Coast ports in fall 1945.

RIGHT: *Queen Mary* docks in New York after bringing home the 82d Airborne Division, which fought all the way from Sicily to central Germany. Paratroopers have poked and torn through a giant banner made by the 505th Parachute Infantry to get a glimpse of the boisterous welcome that awaits them. Not slated for the invasion of Japan, the division became part of the country's strategic reserve.

the deficiencies of such an approach. The army began to examine the need "to train officers in peacetime for civil affairs in wartime," but it wasn't until the Japanese attacked Pearl Harbor that a special school was established to train soldiers of the army's new G-5 staff section. These soldiers often built upon skills developed in their civilian occupations as they prepared to take care of the needs of civilian populations in countries liberated from Nazi Germany and Imperial Japan, and in the Axis powers themselves after hostilities ended.

Called "civil affairs" in liberated territories and "military government" in occupied territories, G-5's mode of operation differed according to Allied directives and local circumstances. To civilians on the receiving end, such differences were of extreme importance. While a heavy hand naturally fell on Nazi Germany, victims like Belgium theoretically were handled with kid gloves unless military operations were in some way jeopardized. In liberated France and French North Africa, however, the fluid political situation did not lend itself to easy answers, and the deadly, three-way cat fight between the Vichyites, Communists, and Gaullists nearly led to the imposition of direct U.S. military rule in some areas.

Much of eastern Germany was ceded to Poland after the war, and what remained of the country was divided into three occupation zones controlled by the United States, Great Britain, and the Soviet Union, with a fourth French zone soon carved from the American and British territories. The city of Berlin, although located deep within the Soviet's eastern zone, was also divided into four sectors, with western Berlin occupied by Allied forces and eastern Berlin occupied by Soviets. The complex, four-power arrangements for governing occupied Germany allowed any party who wanted to engage in mischief to do so with relative impunity. While in the beginning the French were a constant irritation, it soon became apparent that the Soviet occupation authorities were actively working to keep Germany in a state of chaos to delay its recovery.

LEFT TOP: They look perfectly at ease, but these military police—three of whom are armed with Thompson submachine guns—are on their toes as they await whatever might come out of a big Communist rally staged in Berlin on September 14, 1948. The gathering was a reply to an anti-Communist demonstration held a week earlier. People feared trouble, but none materialized because the rally was a flop. Instead of the four hundred thousand people the Soviets expected, only about a quarter of that number turned out, many brought in from outlying areas.

LEFT BOTTOM INSET: Military police commonly wore only the rigid inner helmet liner, made of compressed fiber, during normal duty. They could quickly add the MI "steel pot," as in the photo above, when necessary.

RIGHT: Investigating black-market activities, Tech 3 David Hill and other troopers of the 53d Constabulary Squadron, 2d Constabulary Brigade, search for contraband and check identifications at a displaced persons (DP) camp near Windsheim, Germany, during a May 4, 1948, search and seizure operation.

BELOW: Military police work at Berlin's Potsdamer Platz, where the U.S., British, and Soviet occupation sectors meet. The square was often the scene of confrontations between Communists and supporters of Western democracy. A German Red Cross vehicle is moving down the street at left.

RIGHT INSET: This insignia represents the United States Constabulary, which operated in the U.S. occupation zones of Germany and Austria from 1946 to 1952. The constabulary was made up of mechanized cavalry groups taken from the tactical units and were intended to serve as quick, mobile security reserves. They received special instruction in military government laws and ordinances, and in conducting raids and searches. The special troops wore highly lacquered, black helmet liners with sky blue and yellow bands emanating from the constabulary symbol on the front.

YOU ARE LEAVING
THE AMERICAN SECTOR
ВЫ ВЫЕЗЖАЕТЕ ИЗ
АМЕРИКАНСКОЙ ЗОНЫ
VOUS SORTEZ
SECTEUR AMÉRICAIN

Austria, which had been fully incorporated into Adolf Hitler's Third Reich during the era of appeasement that preceded the war, also was divided into American, British, Soviet, and French occupation zones. The cessation of hostilities found Vienna, like Berlin, deep within a Soviet zone and subdivided into four occupation sectors as well. Unlike Berlin, however, Vienna's city center was administered jointly from the top all the way down to the four-man teams, consisting of soldiers from each of the victorious powers, who were patrolling the streets. The occupation of Austria also required that British and American forces have a secure line of communication to the former Austrian, now Italian, port of Trieste on the Adriatic Sea, which remained under the jurisdiction of the two Allies. Claimed also by communist Yugoslavia, Trieste was a flash point of conflict until the Allied commitment in Austria began to wind down in the 1950s, and a territorial agreement was signed with Yugoslavia.

Throughout this period—and despite Soviet, and for a time French, roadblocks—the shattered German economy made its first steps toward recovery even as the Allies carried out a phased de-Nazification of its government and industry, the Nuremberg trials, as well as the housing and repatriation of millions of displaced persons from across Europe. Genuine recovery, however, did not begin until the three Western powers instituted a desperately needed currency reform in their occupation zones in the face of escalating Soviet resistance and threats. This culminated in June 1948 with the Soviets closing the land routes across their occupation zone to the Western Allies' sectors in Berlin. The Allied governments were unwilling to give in to Soviet intimidation, but—with the United States and other armies all seriously understrength—the United States organized a remarkable airlift of food and fuel to Berlin instead of forcing the issue on the ground. Unwilling to risk general war with the West, the Soviets waited in vain for the airlift to fail. They reopened the land routes the following year when it became clear that it was becoming only more efficient and effective.

On the other side of the globe, the occupation of Imperial Japan at first appears soft when compared with Germany's. Yet, the immense changes imposed on a Japanese society with negligible experience in democratic institutions were no less wrenching than those in Germany, even though they were embraced by a population eager to emulate the victors. General MacArthur—perhaps not too surprisingly—fit quite comfortably into the role of shogun, which further eased the task of administering the alien culture. Changes included democratization of the education system and government, the breaking up of the great industrial and banking trusts, and the institution of genuine land reform for tenant farmers. With the exception of a sizable Australian contingent, the occupation of Japan was predominantly a U.S. Army affair with virtually no Soviet involvement allowed.

Korea presented a completely different set of challenges. Political and economic relations between the United States and the former "Hermit Kingdom" had not existed for decades, and almost no Korean-speaking Americans could be found to assist occupation forces on the peninsula. Consequently, the U.S. Army did essentially the same thing in Korea that it did during its brief occupation of the Czech Sudetenland—turned to the area's original conquerors (in this case, the Japanese) to help administer the U.S. zone. The outcry this raised among Koreans forced a speedy repatriation of their former overlords, but reaching agreements with the Soviets, who occupied the country north of the 38th parallel demarcation line, was not so easy. When efforts to establish a unified Korean provisional government were blocked, the matter was turned over to the United Nations. Communist authorities in the north, with the blessing of the Soviets, refused to participate in Korean elections in 1948, and votes were cast only in the south amid communist agitation, thus setting the stage for future conflict on the peninsula.

LEFT TOP: Lieutenant General Lucius D. Clay, former deputy to General Dwight D. Eisenhower, served as the hands-on deputy military governor in Germany before becoming the U.S. Army's European commander in chief and military governor from 1947–1949. Clay's recommendations were the basis of the Marshall Plan for the reconstruction of Europe, however, he is best known as the man who ordered the Berlin Airlift after the Soviet Union blocked road and rail access between the British and U.S. occupation zones and the city's Western-occupied sectors.

LEFT BOTTOM: These samples of occupation currency for Germany and Japan were produced by the U.S. Bureau of Engraving and Printing in Washington, D.C. The redeemable currency allowed American and Allied soldiers to make purchases in territory they controlled. To varying degrees, the American-styled bank-notes temporarily replaced or supplemented those in Germany, Japan, Austria, Italy, and France.

BERLIN: "EYE OF THE STORM"

Post-war Germany was divided into three occupation zones, with the Soviet Union controlling the east, and the United States and Britain controlling the west and south. The latter two then created a fourth zone by relinquishing parts of their territories to France. The city of Berlin, although located in the eastern Soviet zone, also was divided into four sectors, soon to become known as West Berlin, opposite the Soviet-occupied East Berlin.

Getting the U.S. Army's designated occupation forces into Berlin was not an easy matter. On June 14, 1945, President Harry S. Truman reminded Soviet Premier Joseph Stalin that unhindered access to Berlin "[w]as part of the withdrawal of [U.S.] troops already agreed to." U.S. divisions still controlled 16,400 square miles of the Soviet Zone (the future East Germany), which they had seized from the Nazis at the end of the war. In a *quid pro quo*,

land corridors to Berlin were negotiated in return for a U.S. pullback. Foreshadowing the Communist blockade several years later and the problems that would plague Western access to Berlin for decades, unspecified "technical problems" and suddenly "unsafe bridges" delayed the U.S. and British columns' entry into the city until July 3, 1945.

After three contentious years, the Soviet Union attempted to gain control of all the city's Western sectors in June 1948 by discontinuing surface traffic, cutting off their businesses, and starving out the population. The Truman administration reacted with a round-the-clock airlift that brought desperately needed food and supplies into West Berlin. The Soviet government yielded in May 1949, lifting the blockade when it became clear that the airlift not only was meeting the city's food and fuel needs but was reaching such peaks of efficiency that even its industry was

reviving. Wary of Soviet duplicity, the administration continued the airlift through September of that year to build up large reserve stocks in Berlin in case the blockade was reinstituted.

When the airlift began, Berlin had only two airfields: Tempelhof, with one runway in the U.S. sector, and Gatow, with one runway in the British sector. In 1945, when the Americans arrived, Tempelhof's lone runway was sodded and had been used only for small aircraft and fighters during the latter stages of World War II. Beautifully equipped with hangars and a large terminal building, it unfortunately was surrounded by dangerously high apartment buildings that required a five-hundred-foot ceiling in thick weather.

Before June 1948, army engineers built a twelve-foot-thick rubber base runway and covered it with steel landing mats, an adequate solution for U.S. military needs before the airlift. However,

BELOW: *An American MP and Berlin policeman* (center), *backed up by a 2d Armored Division Sherman named "Destination?" take up position on a Potsdamer Strasse corner near the center of the city on July 4, 1945. The Soviet propaganda placard* (right) *faces an elevated railway station behind the cameraman.*

under the continuous pounding of heavy, loaded aircraft, the steel landing mats started to break. The runway began to form depressions, and soon a force of 225 men was kept busy repairing it between plane landings in an attempt to keep the field operational.

In early July 1948, construction on a new runway at Tempelhof began without interrupting airlift traffic. During the same period the old runway constantly was being repaired. In late 1948, construction began on a third Tempelhof runway, much to the dismay of the Soviets.

RIGHT: *An American sentry from the 1st Military Police Group guards a precious rail shipment of coal that is waiting to be loaded into an aircraft for its flight to Berlin in July 1948.*

BACKGROUND: *C-47 air transport planes, sent from the United States to assist in the transportation of food to Berlin, arrive at Tempelhof Airfield on July 2, 1948, each with a cargo of 190 flour sacks. During clear weather, air traffic controllers and army quartermasters were able to coordinate the landing and unloading of about one aircraft every four minutes.*

ABOVE: U.S. Forces Berlin, 1951

1948 ENLISTED RANK INSIGNIA CHANGES

The Department of the Army Circular No. 202, dated July 7, 1948, discontinues the Sergeant 4th grade and adds Recruit as the 7th grade effective August 1, 1948. The new insignia was smaller (just two inches wide), and the colors changed. Combat personnels' insignia had a gold background with dark blue chevrons, arc, and lozenge, while noncombat personnel's insignia were dark blue with gold chevrons, arcs, and lozenge. The circular also deleted the Technicians effective August 1, 1948.

FIRST SERGEANT COMBAT INSIGNIA

MASTER SERGEANT COMBAT INSIGNIA

TECHNICAL SERGEANT COMBAT INSIGNIA

STAFF SERGEANT COMBAT INSIGNIA

FIRST SERGEANT NON-COMBAT INSIGNIA

MASTER SERGEANT NON-COMBAT INSIGNIA

TECHNICAL SERGEANT NON-COMBAT INSIGNIA

STAFF SERGEANT NON-COMBAT INSIGNIA

OPPOSITE BOTTOM: Soldiers of Battery A, 159th Field Artillery Battalion (105-mm Howitzer, Colored), fire in support of the hard-pressed 25th Infantry Division as it defends the vital supply center and harbor at Pusan.

SOUTH KOREA INVADED

At roughly 4:00 A.M. on Sunday, June 25, 1950, South Korean positions on the far western corner of the country began to receive a light shelling from North Korean artillery across the 38th parallel. Within an hour, heavy artillery fire was reported at locations all along the 38th parallel as seven infantry divisions of the North Korean Peoples Army (NKPA), supported by one hundred fifty Soviet-made T-34 tanks, crossed the border at several points.

The North Koreans had achieved complete surprise. It was a rainy Sunday morning at the start of the monsoon season, and few Republic of Korea (ROK) soldiers were at the frontier when the blow fell. The outnumbered and scantily equipped defenders quickly recovered from the shock of the initial assault, but although they did well in infantry-against-infantry fights, they had no weapons to counter the NKPA's armored spearheads. The South Korean capital, Seoul, fell on the fourth day of the war, and the premature demolition of

bridges over the wide Han River forced the retreating ROK Army to abandon the little equipment it did possess.

On June 25, 1950, the United Nations Security Council passed a resolution calling "for immediate cessation of hostilities" and "upon the authorities of North Korea to withdraw forthwith their armed forces to the thirty-eighth parallel." When the North Koreans failed to comply with these demands, the Security Council passed a second resolution recommending "that the Members of the United Nations furnish such assistance to the Republic of Korea as may be necessary to repel the armed attack and restore the international peace and security in the area." President Truman ordered American air and naval forces to give cover and support to the South Korean troops and, on June 30, further authorized General MacArthur to use all forces available to him to repel the invasion. A Security Council resolution the following week requested the United States to designate a single commander for all the national forces rushing to South Korea's aid. On July 8,

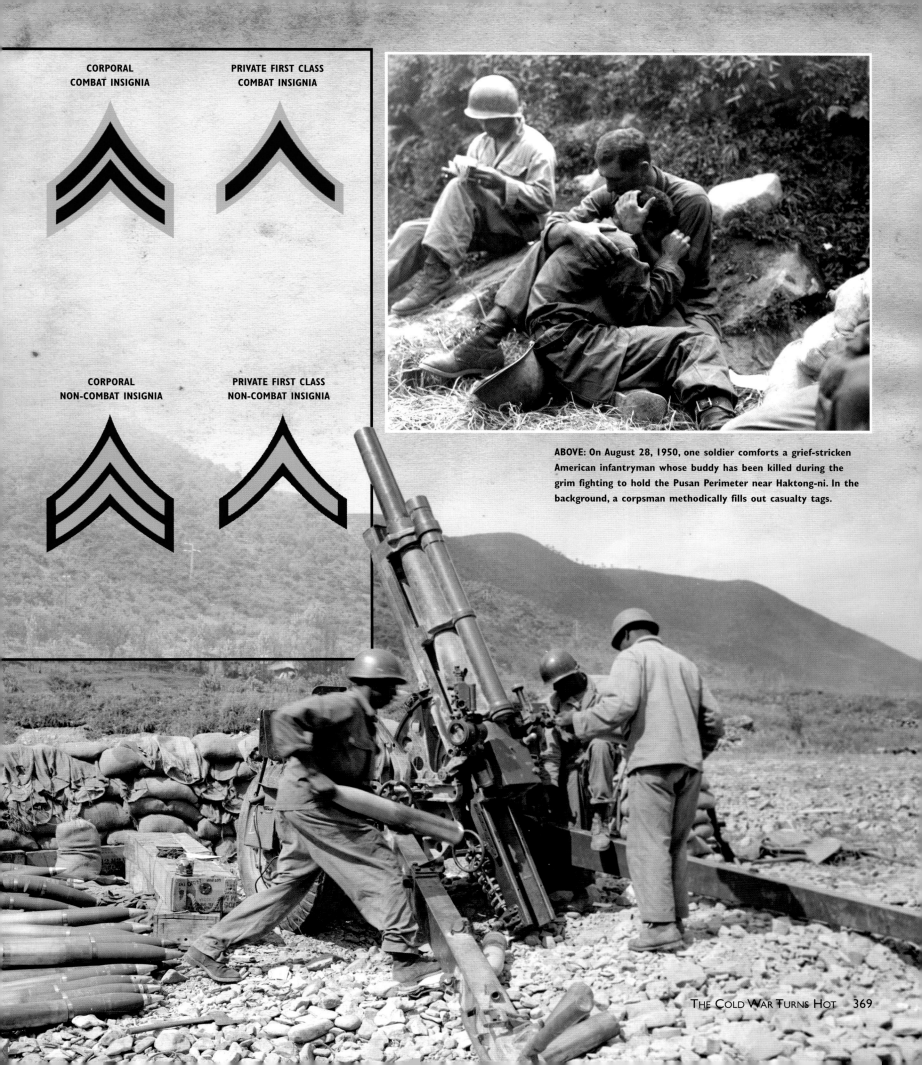

**CORPORAL
COMBAT INSIGNIA**

**PRIVATE FIRST CLASS
COMBAT INSIGNIA**

**CORPORAL
NON-COMBAT INSIGNIA**

**PRIVATE FIRST CLASS
NON-COMBAT INSIGNIA**

ABOVE: On August 28, 1950, one soldier comforts a grief-stricken American infantryman whose buddy has been killed during the grim fighting to hold the Pusan Perimeter near Haktong-ni. In the background, a corpsman methodically fills out casualty tags.

LEFT: An army sniper waves frantically for medics to come assist a fallen comrade who took a mortar blast in the face during fighting in the Pohang front north of Pusan. At left, well-armed NBC television newsreel cameraman Charles Jones does what he can to help, but all efforts were in vain; the wounded soldier died soon after this photo was taken on September 7, 1950.

OPPOSITE: Along the Naktong River, an understrength American squad reinforced by South Korean infantrymen called KATUSAs awaits orders in a roadside ditch as North Korean artillery shells fall in the area on September 19, 1950. KATUSA stands for Korean Augmentation Troops to the United States Army.

M1936 PISTOL BELT

This belt carries an entrenching tool, M1942 first-aid pouch, holster with no weapon, and canteen. The cotton M1936 belt featured a single female snap fastener that was used to attach reciprocal pouches, such as the M1923 and M1 carbine ammunition pockets. Like most pistol belts, it had three rows of eyelets. The lower row was for attaching double-hook fixture equipment, the middle row adjusted the waist size, and the upper row accommodated suspender snaps. Introduced during World War II, the cotton M1942 pouch carried either a field dressing or a compass. It featured a double-hook hanger on the back, and its flap closed with a lift-the-dot fastener.

Truman announced the appointment of MacArthur as commander in chief of the United Nations Command.

By the end of June it was readily apparent that the ROK did not have the means to stop the Communist juggernaut and that American air and naval support were not enough. Combat troops would have to be introduced. The Regular Army had but ten combat divisions spread from Europe to the United States, including what appeared to be a significant portion of its forces—four divisions—in Japan. These formations, however, were not only the most understrength in the entire army but had grown somewhat flabby from years of occupation duty and virtually no rigorous training whatsoever. It fell to these soldiers to repel the NKPA, which was not only well-supplied with Soviet arms (and advisors), but contained many Korean veterans of the long civil war in China.

The state of the U.S. artillery units in Japan was indicative of the kind of shortcomings in units all across the army force structure. When the NKPA swarmed south across the parallel, America's arsenal of artillery was little different than it had been when Germany invaded Poland and was identical to the inventory at the end of World War II. Identical in terms of hardware and doctrine, certainly, but like the rest of the postwar army, the number of combat-ready field artillery battalions had shrunk radically in both number and even weapons per unit. After the war, a variety of reorganizational schemes had been proposed for the field artillery, and the army ultimately decided to increase the number of medium and heavy cannons per division from forty-eight to seventy-two apiece with beefed-up support from corps artillery groups as well.

The actual situation at the outset of the Korean War was somewhat different from this paper organization. Taxpayers and their representatives in Congress had little interest in strengthening America's ten remaining divisions. Although the equipment existed in artillery parks, the additional guns remained unissued since no divisions received enough men to implement the increase. Indeed, many battalions could only field two of their three batteries. This was particularly true for the units on occupation duty in Japan. The table of organization may have called for divisions to employ a robust seventy-two-cannon force of 105 and 155 mm, but the reality was that most contained forty-eight weapons, and those in Korea could not maintain anything above twenty-four in peacetime.

To the newly created South Korean Army, even this amount of artillery looked positively lavish. Their eight divisions contained but fifteen 105-mm howitzers apiece, and their ammunition supply was kept on a very tight leash by MacArthur's Far East Command in Tokyo. By contrast, North Korean divisions were built along Soviet lines and contained twelve 122-mm howitzers and thirty-six 76-mm guns, twelve of which were self-propelled. Both the 122s and 76s out-ranged the South Korean 105s (in the case of the 76-mm gun, by some 2,300 yards). Additionally, each North Korean division contained forty 45-mm antitank guns, which were commonly employed as field artillery, plus one hundred fifty tanks mounting 85-mm guns with their added firepower and maneuverability. With such an overwhelming force at its disposal, the Communists could and did dominate the battlefield—and would for nearly two months.

TASK FORCE SMITH AND THE PUSAN PERIMETER

Elements of the 24th Infantry Division were hastily flown from Japan and thrown into the fight while the rest of the division followed by sea. The first army unit to go into combat was half—two companies—of the division's 1st Battalion, 21st Infantry; reinforced by a battery of artillery and under the command of Lieutenant Colonel Charles Smith. Named simply "Task Force Smith," it arrived in Pusan and was moved to Taejon, where its mission was to buy time for the American buildup by blocking the North Koreans as long as possible. The infantry dug in north of Osan on high ground that had visibility all the way to the next town of Suwon, and the artillery emplaced a mile back. The road on which any NKPA force must advance led right through the little group. Properly manned, it would have been a very strong position, but the task force had no support on its flanks and few antitank weapons, most of which would not penetrate the frontal armor of a T-34 tank.

The position was fully established on the fourth of July 1950, and at 7:30 A.M. the next morning, a column of T-34s rumbled down the road from Suwon. The soldiers of the task force stayed at their posts while thirty-three tanks bore down on them. The artillery, recoilless rifles, and bazooka teams engaged these tanks, but most of them passed straight through the infantry position undamaged and cut communications with the artillery. About an hour after the tanks had passed through, trucks arrived from Suwon containing more than one thousand NKPA infantry that immediately attacked

the Americans. The task force repelled all attempts at frontal assaults, but soon the enemy was moving around the flanks. Without artillery support, low on ammunition, and with more and more enemy infantry moving around his force, Smith decided to withdraw toward Ansong, east of Osan. Most of the one hundred fifty American casualties occurred during this movement in which the task force lost its cohesion, but the whole force might have been lost had they stayed any longer during this first encounter.

The remaining elements of the 24th Infantry Division had reached Korea by this time and were in defensive positions roughly sixty miles south of Osan along the Kum River, north of Taejon, an important communications center. ROK elements, which held positions to the east protecting Taegu, were placed under the control of the U.S. Eighth Army commanded by Lieutenant General Walton H. Walker, and as the ground troops of other United Nations members reached Korea, they also were placed under Walker's command. The U.S. 25th Infantry Division and 1st Cavalry Division arrived from Japan in quick succession, but could do little to stem the North Korean advance as they crossed the Kum River and seized Taejon from the 24th Division on July 20. Its commander, Major General William F. Dean, was separated from his men when North Korean tanks broke through the forward positions, and he was subsequently captured.

The bitter series of delaying actions staged by Dean's division between July 5–20 had traded one hundred miles and nearly four thousand men for enough time to allow the 1st Cavalry and 25th Infantry divisions to join the remnants of the ROK Army, organize themselves, and further delay the

BELOW: 9th Infantry troops, both Americans and KATUSAs, hold on tight while hitching a free ride on a 72d Tank Battalion M26 Pershing and M3E8 Sherman (partially visible behind it) moving into position to counter a North Korean offensive aimed at Yongsan, September 3, 1950. Both the 9th and 72d belong to the 2d Infantry Division. The 72d's unusual composition, mirrored by the 1st Cavalry Division's 70th Tank Battalion, was a product of the army's mad scramble to get units up to strength with anything that was available.

North Koreans. American and ROK troops, under constant pressure, continued to withdraw steadily to the port of Pusan, the main U.S. staging area in the southeastern peninsula. The two-hundred-mile-long defensive perimeter around the port resembled a rectangle, the southwestern side of which was guarded by the 24th and 25th divisions, to prevent a breakthrough to Masan. The 1st Cavalry Division was deployed on the western front along the Naktong River to guard the Taegu railroad approaches, and the newly arrived 1st Provisional Marine Brigade also plugged a dangerously vulnerable sector on the river line, while ROK divisions defended the northern front, extending to a point just south of Yongdok on the east coast.

This entire line became the scene of numerous hard-fought battles and engagements, many of them occuring simultaneously, in the closing days of July as Walter rushed mobile reinforcements from one threatened sector to another. Doggedly trading space for time could not be continued indefinitely, and in early August Walker ordered a final stand along the now one-hundred-forty-mile perimeter around the port. A massive supply and engineering effort had succeeded in turning Pusan into a

well-stocked Eighth Army base, as well as the hub of a rail and road net leading to the battle front. By now the NKPA's lengthened supply lines were under constant air attack, enemy naval opposition had been wiped out, and the blockade of the Korean coast by American and British warships had been clamped tight.

Intense Communist attacks continued almost without letup into the middle of September, yet the North Koreans were clearly reaching the end of their rope. They had expended most of their tanks in earlier fights, and now their troops were literally beginning to starve, as U.S., British, and Australian flyers continued to wreak havoc on their supply lines. Korean veterans of the Chinese Communist Army had, by now, almost all been killed on battlefields from the 38th parallel to the Naktong River and in their place were largely untrained recruits, many of whom had been dragooned from towns and villages in the south. Meanwhile the Eighth Army's strength grew daily. Their own counterattacks were beginning to recover lost ground, and the newly constituted X Corps in Japan readied itself for a blow far behind the Communists' lines at a place called Inch'on.

BOTTOM: On the bridge of the USS *Mt. McKinley*, Major General Edward M. Almond, commander of the X Corps divisions assaulting Inchon, consults with General Douglas MacArthur during the September 15, 1950, pre-invasion bombardment. Others are: (*left foreground*) MacArthur's aide, Brigadier General Courtney Whitney; (*partially obscured behind Whitney*) Vice Admiral Arthur D. Struble, 7th Fleet commander; and (*center rear*) Brigadier General Edwin K. Wright, acting chief of staff for plans and operations.

OPPOSITE BOTTOM: On October 6, 1950, a 24th Infantry Division Sherman barrels past the wreck of a Soviet-made T34/85 tank that was supplied to the North Korean People's Army near Kumchon, the first large city in the north to fall to UN forces.

INVASION AT INCH'ON AND CHINA ENTERS THE WAR

On September 15–16, 1950, the 7th Infantry and 1st Marine divisions conducted a daring landing far behind North Korean lines at the peninsula's largest port, Inch'on, which lay just to the west of the South Korean capital of Seoul. In conjunction with the amphibious assault, the U.N. forces broke out of the Pusan perimeter. The NKPA feared that it might be cut off if it didn't immediately get back to its own territory. It was soon in full retreat with U.N. forces in hot pursuit all the way to—and then beyond—the 38th parallel. On October 26, 1950, the ROK Army's 6th Division reached the Yalu River along the Chinese border and was promptly forced to withdraw fifteen miles south after punishing attacks by Chinese "volunteers" that also badly mauled a regiment of the 1st Cavalry Division that had been sent to restore the situation. This fighting had occurred on the western side of the peninsula, and nearly a month later in the east, the U.S. 7th Infantry Division also moved up to the Yalu.

The People's Republic of China warned the United Nations through intermediaries that it would not allow an approach to the Chinese border, but the U.N. Command ignored these warnings, as well as subsequent evidence of increasing Chinese intervention in Korea. The Eighth Army's advance was halted by the Chinese Fourth Field Army along the Ch'ongch'on River in the west while the X Corps was attacked along both sides of the Changjin (Chosin) Reservoir by the Third Field Army. U.N. forces transitioned to the defense as three hundred thousand Communist Chinese soldiers poured into, around, and through U.N. lines. The United Nations retreated through the fierce winter of 1950–1951 nearly back to their Pusan Perimeter lines of the summer, and the U.S. 2d Infantry Division, recently arrived from the United States, lost most of its artillery during the withdrawal.

The Eighth Army commander, Lieutenant General Walton Walker, was killed in a vehicle accident on an icy road, and the appearance of Lieutenant General Matthew Ridgway as his replacement in December 1950 meant that there would be no more grand, division-size drives up the main roads (which frequently led to American and ROK units being counterattacked and cut off). This general sent foot soldiers into the hills, and in a series of deliberate, limited-objective operations beginning in January 1951, he edged his forces forward, literally battalion by battalion, in set-piece assaults utilizing air strikes, tank support, and *very* heavy artillery preparations. Soldiers regained their confidence and, in a series of methodical advances, stabilized the situation and led to the recapture of Seoul in mid-March.

LEFT: Within days of the Chinese onslaught, it was obvious that they were in Korea not to form a buffer along their border but, instead, to annihilate the UN army. General Douglas MacArthur reported that his men were up against an "overwhelming force," and "consequently, we face an entire new war." Here, army engineers preparing to blow up a railroad bridge near the North Korean capital of Pyongyang on December 1, 1950, place satchel charges on its supports. Note that the engineer in the center found it more convenient to arrange the shoulder holster for his .45-caliber automatic as a pistol belt than to wear it under his heavy coat.

ABOVE: Eighth Army commander Lieutenant General Matthew B. Ridgway arrives at X Corps headquarters in Chongju for a conference with South Korean President Syngman Rhee on February 1, 1951. Ridgway had assumed command of UN ground forces on December 26, 1950, three days after his predecessor, Walton H. Walker, had been killed when his jeep collided with a South Korean Army truck on an icy road.

DECLASSIFIED
E.O. 11652, Sec. 3(E) and 5(D)
WHITE HOUSE PRESS RELEASE
By MLT Nec., NARS Date 3-7-75

PROPOSED ORDER TO LT. GEN. MATTHEW B. RIDGWAY

The President has decided to relieve General MacArthur and appoint you as his successor as Supreme Commander, Allied Powers; Commander in Chief, United Nations Command; Commander in Chief, Far East; and Commanding General, U. S. Army, Far East.

It is realized that your presence in Korea in the immediate future is highly important, but we are sure you can make the proper distribution of your time until you can turn over active command of the Eighth Army to its new commander. For this purpose, Lt. Gen. James A. Van Fleet is enroute to report to you for such duties as you may direct.

ABOVE: This is a draft of the message sent to Ridgway informing him that Douglas MacArthur had been relieved of command and that Ridgway had been appointed his successor. The draft, approved, is initialed by President Harry S. Truman.

RIGHT: Lieutenant General Matthew Ridgway and General Douglas MacArthur, commander in chief of UN forces in Korea, arrive April 3, 1951, at a command post in Yang Yang, approximately fifteen miles north of the 38th parallel separating North and South Korea. MacArthur's chief of staff, Major General Doyle O. Hickey, is seated next to Ridgway in this photo, taken eight days prior to MacArthur being relieved of command.

Ridgway had arrived in the theater to find both his army in Korea and his boss in Tokyo severely shaken by the events of the previous month. A fatigued MacArthur told him, "The Eighth Army is yours, Matt. Do what you think best." Ridgway immediately moved to instill a winning spirit in his demoralized troops. As soon as the momentum of the Communist's offensive slowed in mid-January, he ordered that all units probe north to reestablish contact with the Chinese forces and the partially reconstituted North Korean Army. In a three-month-long series of deliberate, limited-objective operations bearing such names as Thunderbolt, Punch, Roundup, Ripper, and Killer, he edged the Eighth Army north and pushed the Communists back across the 38th parallel.

FAR RIGHT TOP: 1st Cavalry Division Military Police mop up Chinese stragglers in the Chipyang area after Operation Killer on February 27, 1951. The center MP carries an M1D Garand sniper rifle with flash suppressor and M84 scope mounted on a Springfield Armory receiver while the man on his right is armed with a Tommy gun.

ATTACK AND COUNTERATTACK

In the meantime, differences between MacArthur and Truman over national policy and military strategy had been growing, and the general's defiance of his commander in chief finally led to the old soldier's relief on April 11. Ridgway was kicked upstairs to take over all of MacArthur's many command responsibilities, and Lieutenant General James A. Van Fleet, who headed the stateside U.S. Second Army, was appointed to lead the Eighth Army. The newly appointed commander arrived in Korea to find that Chinese Communist Forces (CCF) had been massively reinforced and were looking for trouble.

By the spring of 1951, Chinese tactics had become as predictable to the Eighth Army as the Eighth Army's had been to the Chinese just several months earlier. When it became apparent that the Communists were preparing a

second major offensive in the X Corps' area in May, Van Fleet canceled his own planned drive and prepared to receive the enemy on ground of his own choosing. It was his opinion that, by World War II standards, his army's artillery was short by some seventy battalions. It was equally clear to him that the coming Chinese offensive offered an opportunity to eliminate much of their infantry in Korea, and Van Fleet stated his intent in clear and simple terms. "We must expend steel and fire, not men. . . . I want so many artillery holes that a man can step from one to the other."

Van Fleet had his staff calculate the maximum amount of ammunition that could be fed into the coming battle with the limited available truck transport. It was determined that if transportation of all other supplies was essentially halted, a truly stunning rate of fire could be maintained for approximately seven days—or roughly the amount of time that the CCF could effectively carry on an offensive before their own

strained logistic system, savaged by U.S. air power, would force them to consolidate. Of course, Van Fleet had no intention of letting them consolidate any gains.

The offensive opened on the evening of May 16, but it was not until late the next day, when the exact positions and avenues of approach of all Chinese units were clearly known, that the order was issued for X Corps artillery to open up with their "Van Fleet loads." In spite of considerable success against the South Korean divisions to the east of X Corps, the Chinese abruptly called off the offensive on May 20 and attempted to quickly fall back north in order to get beyond cannon range. The U.S. supply system had been stretched almost to the breaking point but nevertheless had enabled the field artillery to inflict crippling losses to six divisions. The last major Chinese offensive until 1953 was over, and U.N. forces fought their way north some forty miles to a defensible line that nearly approximates the Demilitarized Zone today.

MEDAL OF HONOR
Captain Lewis I. Millett
Company E, 27th Infantry Regiment

Citation: Captain Millett, Company E, distinguished himself by conspicuous gallantry and intrepidity above and beyond the call of duty in action. While personally leading his company in an attack against a strongly held position he noted that the 1st Platoon was pinned down by small-arms, automatic, and antitank fire. Millett ordered the 3d Platoon forward, placed himself at the head of the two platoons, and, with fixed bayonet, led the assault up the fire-swept hill. In the fierce charge Millett bayoneted two enemy soldiers and boldly continued on, throwing grenades, clubbing and bayoneting the enemy, while urging his men forward by shouting encouragement. Despite vicious opposing fire, the whirlwind hand-to-hand assault carried to the crest of the hill. His dauntless leadership and personal courage so inspired his men that they stormed into the hostile position and used their bayonets with such lethal effect that the enemy fled in wild disorder. During this fierce onslaught Millett was wounded by grenade fragments but refused evacuation until the objective was taken and firmly secured. The superb leadership, conspicuous courage, and consummate devotion to duty demonstrated by Millett were directly responsible for the successful accomplishment of a hazardous mission and reflect the highest credit on himself and the heroic traditions of the military service.

RIGHT: As Secretary of Defense George C. Marshall watches from the Rose Garden portico (in the background over Truman's shoulder), President Harry S. Truman congratulates four infantry heroes after presenting them with the Medal of Honor during a July 6, 1951, ceremony at the White House. They were cited for conspicuous gallantry in action. The men are: (*left to right*) Captain Raymond Harvey, 17th Infantry, 7th Infantry Division; Captain Lewis I. Millett, 27th Infantry, 25th Infantry Division; Master Sergeant Stanley T. Adams, 19th Infantry, 24th Infantry Division; and Sergeant Einar H. Ingman, 17th Infantry, 7th Infantry Division.

ABOVE TOP: Lieutenant General Matthew Ridgway (*left*) and 1st Cavalry Division commander Major General Charles D. Palmer talk together during the Greek Independence Day celebration at Chunchon on March 23, 1951. The Greek combat battalion that arrived in Korea in October 1950 was attached to the 1st Cavalry throughout the war.

ABOVE BOTTOM: The original shoulder sleeve insignia (*left*) for the 1st Cavalry Division was designed in 1920 by Colonel and Mrs. Ben H. Dorcy, with the yellow felt taken from Dorcy's cloak and the blue from a pair of dress trousers. Mrs. Dorcy made this first patch on her sewing machine. The second patch (*center*) of satin was made by the 7th Cavalry Regimental tailor and was worn by Dorcy until his death in 1926. The third patch (*right*), the currently approved design, was worn in World War II by an officer of the division and sent to Mrs. Dorcy in 1946.

LEFT: Troops of the 3d Infantry Division's largely Puerto Rican 65th Infantry fight their way down a Chinese trench line east of Yonch'on on June 1, 1951. Note the fragmentation grenade lying ready for use in the foreground to the left of the trench.

LEFT: Private Roman Prauty of the 7th Infantry Division attempts to shield his ears from the blast of an M20 75-mm recoilless rifle. The weapon is being fired in support of infantry fighting across a valley in the Oet'ook-tong area on June 9, 1951.

BACKGROUND: Troops of the 15th RCT, 3rd Infantry Division, advance up the face of the hill, which is their objective in an attack on dug-in Communist positions, near the village of Uijong-bu, Korea, March 23, 1951.

ABOVE: Eighth Army commander General James A. Van Fleet in Seoul, Korea, August 15, 1951. Van Fleet routinely authorized the use of artillery fire far in excess of World War II levels. Great quantities of ammunition were consumed even in limited operations to straighten out portions of the front and particularly to defend the string of outposts designed to keep the Communists out of key positions near the Eighth Army main line of defense.

Later, during congressional hearings into ammunition shortages, Van Fleet's boss in Tokyo, General Matthew Ridgway, went to bat for his aggressive army commander. While not convinced that the artillery was being used in the most efficient manner, he stated in fall 1951 that "whatever may have been the impression of our operations in Korea to date, artillery has been and remains the great killer of Communists. It remains the great saver of soldiers, American and Allied. There is a direct relation between the piles of shells in the ammunition supply points and the piles of corpses in the graves registration collection points. The bigger the former, the smaller the latter, and vice versa."

Citation: His platoon was attacking heavily defended hostile positions on commanding ground when the leader was wounded and evacuated. Sergeant Charlton assumed command, rallied the men, and spearheaded the assault against the hill. Personally eliminating two hostile positions and killing six of the enemy with his rifle fire and grenades, he continued up the slope until the unit suffered heavy casualties and became pinned down. Regrouping the men he led them forward only to be again hurled back by a shower of grenades. Despite a severe chest wound, Sergeant Charlton refused medical attention and led a third daring charge, which carried to the crest of the ridge. Observing that the remaining emplacement that had retarded the advance was situated on the reverse slope, he charged it alone, was again hit by a grenade but raked the position with a devastating fire which eliminated it and routed the defenders. The wounds received during his daring exploits resulted in his death but his indomitable courage, superb leadership, and gallant self-sacrifice reflect the highest credit upon himself, the infantry, and the military service.

FIRST SERGEANT

MASTER SERGEANT

TECHNICAL SERGEANT

STAFF SERGEANT

WAR ALONG THE OUTPOSTS

Artillery use remained high throughout the long, self-imposed stalemate that followed. Great quantities of ammunition were consumed even in limited operations in which forces tried to straighten out portions of the front and defend the string of outposts that were designed to keep the Communists out of key positions near the Eighth Army's main line of resistance, or "MLR." Manned by units of platoon, company, and sometimes battalion size, the tenacity of their defenders—and the use of massive firepower—kept all but a very few of these outposts from falling permanently into CCF hands. During this period, two mobilized National Guard divisions, the 40th from California and 45th from Oklahoma, were sent to Korea. While the United States and South Korea provided the vast majority of the manpower and America provided most of the matériel to fight the war, Great Britain, Australia, New Zealand, Canada, Greece, Turkey, Ethiopia, the Philippines, and other nations also provided combat forces ranging from battalion-size elements up to the Commonwealth Division, which was made up of troops from Britain and her former colonies.

Throughout it all, truce talks that began in July 1951 sputtered on for two years. Both sides had indicated a willingness to end the war roughly along the current front lines, but the fighting was now marked on each side by limited offensives that tried to gain concessions in the negotiations with pressure on the battlefield. Some of the bloodiest actions of the war occurred in these battles that tested the will of the United Nations and the Chinese to continue the war. The main problem at the truce negotiations rested primarily on the issue of the return of prisoners of war (POWs). The Communists wanted all POWs returned without qualification, while the United Nations, recognizing

SERGEANT	CORPORAL	PRIVATE FIRST CLASS

OPPOSITE BOTTOM: South of P'yonggang in the Iron Triangle, a squad-size group of infantry work their way cautiously across the saddle between Hill 717, which had just been captured, and the well-camouflaged Chinese bunkers on the next hill. Back up Hill 717 to the left, a reserve squad observes their progress and gives covering small-arms fire, as does a machine-gun crew in the right foreground. There may be at least one other squad working its way up the hill from another direction.

BELOW: Corporal Sam Ayala of Company L, 7th RCT, 3d Infantry Division, waits for medical evacuation from Hill 717. Ayala was wounded while engaged in a bitter grenade battle with deeply entrenched Chinese troops on July 3, 1951. The fight for this little piece of ridgeline is typical of the thousands of local actions carried out during the seesaw battles of 1951.

M1944 FIELD JACKET
This jacket, worn during the Korean War by Harry Emigh, has his 2d Infantry Division patch on the left shoulder and 7th Army patch on the right. Green tabs on the shoulder loops indicate that Emigh led troops in combat.

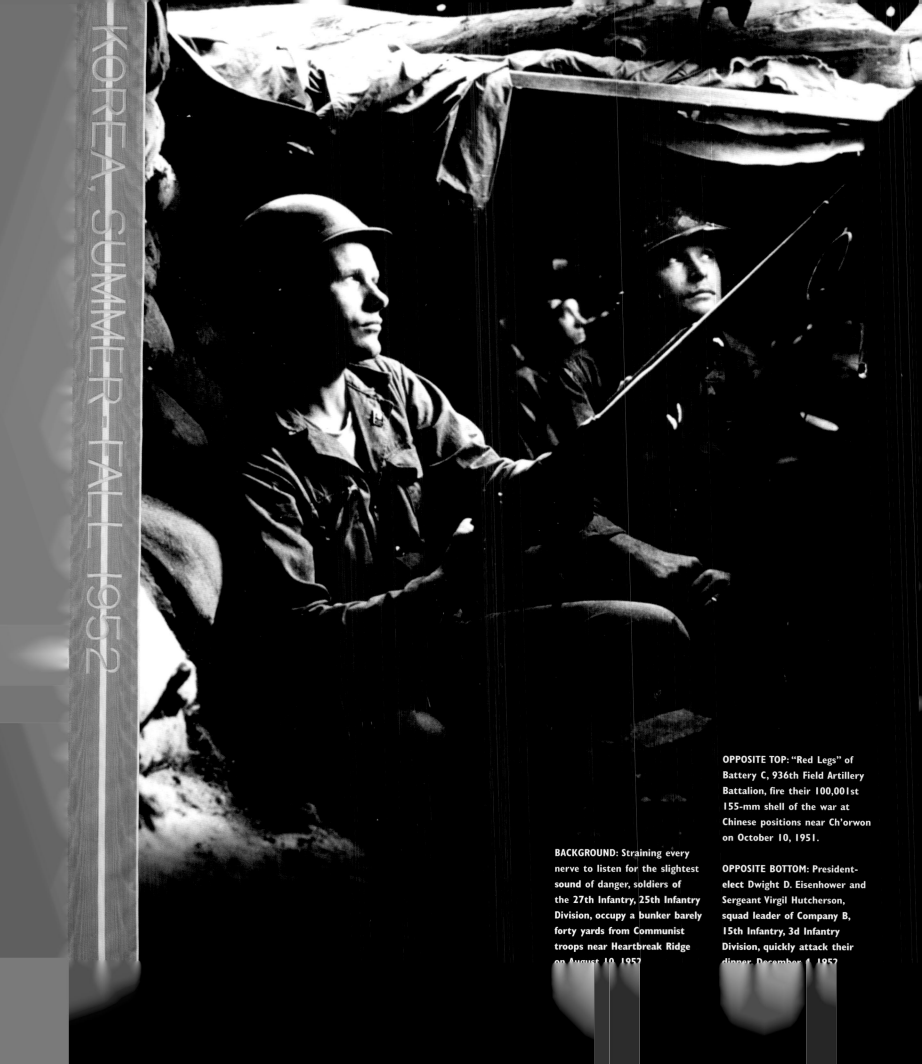

OPPOSITE TOP: "Red Legs" of Battery C, 936th Field Artillery Battalion, fire their 100,001st 155-mm shell of the war at Chinese positions near Ch'orwon on October 10, 1951.

BACKGROUND: Straining every nerve to listen for the slightest sound of danger, soldiers of the 27th Infantry, 25th Infantry Division, occupy a bunker barely forty yards from Communist troops near Heartbreak Ridge on August 10, 1952.

OPPOSITE BOTTOM: President-elect Dwight D. Eisenhower and Sergeant Virgil Hutcherson, squad leader of Company B, 15th Infantry, 3d Infantry Division, quickly attack their dinner, December 4, 1952.

Corporal Ronald E. Rosser
Company L, 38th Infantry Regiment

Citation: Corporal Rosser distinguished himself by conspicuous gallantry above and beyond the call of duty. While assaulting heavily fortified enemy hill positions, Company L, 38th Infantry Regiment, was stopped by fierce automatic-weapons, small-arms, artillery, and mortar fire. Rosser, a forward observer was with the lead platoon of Company L, when it came under fire from two directions. Rosser turned his radio over to his assistant and, disregarding the enemy fire, charged the enemy positions armed with only carbine and a grenade. At the first bunker, he silenced its occupants with a burst from his weapon. Gaining the top of the hill, he killed two enemy soldiers, and then went down the trench, killing five more as he advanced. He then hurled his grenade into a bunker and shot two other soldiers as they emerged. Having exhausted his ammunition, he returned through the enemy fire to obtain more ammunition and grenades and charged the hill once more. Calling on others to follow him, he assaulted two more enemy bunkers. Although those who attempted to join him became casualties, Corporal Rosser once again exhausted his ammunition, obtained a new supply, and returning to the hilltop a third time hurled grenades into the enemy positions. During this heroic action Rosser single-handedly killed at least thirteen of the enemy. After exhausting his ammunition he accompanied the withdrawing platoon, and though himself wounded, made several trips across open terrain still under enemy fire to help remove other men injured more seriously than himself. This outstanding soldier's courageous and selfless devotion to duty is worthy of emulation by all men. He has contributed magnificently to the high traditions of the military service.

KOREA SUMMER 1953

BELOW: A Canadian truck convoy winds its way along a precarious mountain road. Narrow, badly drained, and poorly surfaced Korean roads were inadequate to the Eighth Army's needs, in spite of the Herculean efforts of military engineers.

PORK CHOP HILL

In an effort to effectively screen its front, the 45th Infantry Division, a National Guard formation from Oklahoma, pushed forward its outpost line into an area that would remain hotly contested until the armistice was signed more than a year later. At the southwest end of the June 2, 1952, assault, Old Baldy (Hill 266) and Pork Chop Hill (Hill 255) fell to the Okies after heavy fighting.

Throughout the month, virtually all of the newly won positions were subjected to frequent, determined counterattacks that were well supported by the Chinese's new artillery. As the hills continued to be the scenes of particularly violent actions, the 2d Infantry Division took over the area. In March of the following year, the Chinese seized Old Baldy from the 7th Infantry Division, exposing its defenders on Pork Chop to fire from three sides.

I Corps positions north of the Imjin River were attacked on July 6, 1953, and the Chinese took part of Pork Chop Hill. After several days of vicious fighting in which neither side could dislodge the other, the 7th's soldiers were taken off the hill; the number of likely casualties while retaining Pork Chop was not worth its tactical value, especially since it was slated to be within the four-kilometer-wide Demilitarized Zone between the opposing armies.

ABOVE TOP: A wounded 7th Infantry Division soldier is helped away from Pork Chop Hill on April 17, 1953. Armored vests had started to reach Korea the previous year—and this man's life might have been saved by one. Although they usually couldn't stop a bullet, the vests provided excellent protection from grenade and shell fragments.

ABOVE BOTTOM: The MI helmet worn by Staff Sergeant Randy Jurgenson of the 7th Infantry Division during a March 23, 1953, attack on Pork Chop Hill. Although injured by a Chinese round, Jurgenson recovered from what would have been a fatal wound without the "steel pot."

MEDAL OF HONOR
First Lieutenant Richard Thomas Shea
Company A, 17th Infantry Regiment

Citation: First Lieutenant Shea, executive officer, Company A, distinguished himself by conspicuous gallantry and indomitable courage above and beyond the call of duty in action against the enemy. On the night of July 6, he was supervising the reinforcement of defensive positions when the enemy attacked with great numerical superiority. Voluntarily proceeding to the area most threatened, he organized and led a counter-attack and, in the bitter fighting which ensued, closed with and killed two hostile soldiers with his trench knife. Calmly moving among the men, checking positions, steadying and urging the troops to hold firm, he fought side by side with them throughout the night. Despite heavy losses, the hostile force pressed the assault with determination, and at dawn made an all-out attempt to overrun friendly elements. Charging forward to meet the challenge, Shea and his gallant men drove back the hostile troops. Elements of Company G joined the defense on the afternoon of July 7, having lost key personnel through casualties. Immediately integrating these troops into his unit, Shea rallied a group of twenty men and again charged the enemy. Although wounded in this action, he refused evacuation and continued to lead the counterattack. When the assaulting element was pinned down by heavy machine-gun fire, he personally rushed the emplacement and, firing his carbine and lobbing grenades with deadly accuracy, neutralized the weapon and killed three of the enemy. With forceful leadership and by his heroic example, Shea coordinated and directed a holding action throughout the night and the following morning. On July 8, the enemy attacked again. Despite additional wounds, he launched a determined counterattack and was last seen in close hand-to-hand combat with the enemy. Shea's inspirational leadership and unflinching courage set an illustrious example of valor to the men of his regiment, reflecting lasting glory upon himself and upholding the noble traditions of the military service.

WAR ALONG THE OUTPOSTS

By July of 1951, General James A. Van Fleet was satisfied with the outline of the front and felt that the Eighth Army could repel any assaults on its current position. The terrain was defensible and backed up by an adequate road and rail net, except in the rugged Taebaek Mountains in the east.

By the last week in October, all UN objectives had been met. The capture of the commanding heights above Kumsong by the U.S. 24th, Republic of Korea (ROK) 2d and 6th divisions, brought an end to Korea's war of movement. Though nineteen months of self-imposed stalemate would pass before the front would see any significant realignments, Van Fleet's last push had been enough to convince the Communists to reopen armistice discussions.

On November 12, General Matthew Ridgway ordered Van Fleet to cease offensive operations and limit attacks only to those necessary to strengthen the main line of resistance (MLR). A series of heavily fortified outposts, manned at squad, platoon, and even company strength, were established one to three miles in front of the main trenches. From these highly vulnerable positions, UN forces sent out patrols to capture prisoners and determine enemy dispositions. The outposts were located within range of friendly artillery and would seriously impede any assault aimed at the MLR. It was during this period that the newly arrived 45th Infantry Division captured Old Baldy and Pork Chop Hill (see previous page), while the 1st Marine Division seized and held Bunker Hill.

Northeast of the Marines, the 2d Infantry Division took over the 45th's positions and immediately was thrown off Old Baldy on the night of July 17. The division regained portions of the hill, as weather allowed, on July 23 and August 1, beating off the inevitable, violent counterattacks on each occasion. Old Baldy changed hands for the fourth time on September 18, as Chinese infiltrators fought their way through American trenches on the hill's crest. But two days later, the 2d again became king of the mountain when a tank-supported, two-pronged assault dislodged the Communists.

The negotiations now were proceeding at a breathtaking pace, but, along the I Corps' front, the fighting returned to a familiar, deadly pattern. The last week of March contained some of the most vicious combat of the war. Seesaw battles raged across Old Baldy, Eerie, and Pork Chop Hill (held by the 7th Infantry Division and its Colombian battalion until they were pulled off in July), as well as the Marines' "Nevada Cities" outposts of Carson, Reno, Elko, and Vegas on a series of low hills twenty-five miles to the southwest.

On the night of July 13, 1953, the front erupted in one last convulsion of fighting as the Chinese renewed their effort to secure a final battlefield victory against the South Korean army, a propaganda victory that would only allow them to claim that they had forced the "Yankee imperialists' running dog lackeys" to sue for peace.

FRIENDLY FIRE ON ENEMY POSITIONS

FRIENDLY FLARES

ENEMY ARTILLERY IN VALLEY

ENEMY FIRE ON FRIENDLY LINES

ENEMY ARTILLERY

ENEMY MORTAR POSITIONS

ABOVE: *Flashes in a time-lapse photo show Chinese and friendly positions during a night action at a U.S. outpost. The forces indicated by the first and fifth circles are in direct contact. Note the sandbagged positions along the hilltop trench in the foreground.*

LEFT: *A "quad-50" adds its murderous firepower to a September 21, 1952, counterattack that dislodged Chinese forces from Old Baldy.*

that many enemy soldiers had been forced into service, wanted to allow those who wished to stay in South Korea to do so.

With ground offensive operations curtailed and the Air Force pushed to the fore in the new war of attrition, artillery was literally the only weapon at the army's disposal that could keep pressure on the enemy. Ammunition expenditures were extremely heavy, and Ridgway, Van Fleet's boss in Tokyo, frequently found himself going to bat for his aggressive army commander. He told Congress in the fall of 1951: "Whatever may have been the impression of our operations in Korea to date, artillery has been and remains the great killer of Communists. It remains the great saver of soldiers, American and Allied. There is a direct relation between the piles of shells in the ammunition supply points and the piles of corpses in the graves registration collection points. The bigger the former the smaller the latter and vice versa." Six months later the budget question still raged, and Ridgway was just as adamant. "The only alternative is to effect savings of dollars by expenditure of lives."

In later years, military scholars, safely removed in time from the conflict, would ruminate over whether the army learned the "right" lessons from Korea. But however applicable the self-imposed stalemate and attritional warfare were to later conflicts, it was the best that could be done at that time without risking America's position either in that theater or in Europe, where the Soviet threat was perceived to be growing.

Numerous factors contributed to the Communists' willingness to wrap up the war in 1953: first, the death of Stalin in March and the apparent desire of the new Soviet leadership to let things cool down; second, a worsening Chinese economy largely tied to its war effort; and finally, the discrete warning to China in May that supply bases in its Manchurian sanctuary would be attacked on the heels of the destruction of North Korea's irrigation dams by U.S. air power. The new administration of President Dwight D. Eisenhower was also beginning to rattle the nuclear saber of what would soon be called "massive retaliation." As peace became closer and closer to reality, so, too, did both sides' desire to gain as favorable terrain as possible. This led to a series of vicious battles during the final Chinese offensive in the days before the truce was signed. The Armistice became effective on July 27, 1953.

ABOVE: With the sounds of artillery fire still thundering throughout the surrounding I Corps area, the commander in chief of all UN forces, Lieutenant General Mark W. Clark, countersigns the armistice documents at Munsan, South Korea, on July 27, 1953. While the armistice was negotiated at Panmunjom, it was signed by the United Nations in Munsan and by the North Koreans in Kaesong. The cease-fire agreement went into effect the following day.

Chapter Eleven

Preparing for "The Next War" and Vietnam, 1953–1973

Six large National Guard formations and innumerable smaller units were federalized when the North Koreans crossed the 38th parallel, but American civilian and military leaders could not be sure if the real purpose of the invasion was to tie down America's military strength—if Korea was simply the opening move ahead of a general Communist offensive. For this reason, only two Guard divisions were committed to the Korean fighting, while the 28th (Pennsylvania) and 43d (Rhode Island and Connecticut) Infantry divisions were sent to Germany, and the mobilized Guard regimental combat teams shipped out to bolster defenses at other vulnerable points: the 196th (South Dakota) to Alaska and the 278th (Tennessee) to Iceland. Nearly all of these Guardsmen returned to their civilian lives after two years, replaced by draftees and volunteers who functionally "nationalized" the ranks of these formations.

Almost immediately after the guns stopped firing in Korea, the Eisenhower administration announced that, hence-forth, any further assaults on our interests or Allies would result in massive nuclear retaliation. To many in the army, this widely trumpeted "New Look" in America's military policy bore an uncomfortable similarity to the pre-Korea old look of the Truman administration, when atomic deterrence was the name of the game and the army had very rapidly shrunk to ten understrength divisions. The summer of 1954 saw all of the National Guard formations returned to state control, although the 43d had been reflagged as the 5th Infantry Division while still in Germany. Its colors were returned to Connecticut where the 43d, like the units federalized in 1950, was reconstituted as purely Guard formation again.

Excluding the formations maintaining stateside training bases, the Korean-Cold War mobilization of the early 1950s peaked at twenty divisions. But by the end of the decade, the army indeed found itself down to just eleven active divisions, nearly its pre-war strength. And although the cuts

had come more gradually this time around they—and other policy disagreements—still provoked a rash of senior officer resignations and early retirements that eventually included virtually every surviving general that commanded the Eighth Army in Korea: Matthew Ridgway, James A. Van Fleet, and Maxwell D. Taylor, as well as the army's energetic young chief of research and development, James M. Gavin. The army, meanwhile, grappled with the problems of rapidly changing technologies, the projected nuclear battlefield, and combat divisions reorganized to operate in five widely dispersed battle groups.

The new "pentomic" division structure theoretically provided a semblance of survivability from nuclear attack, yet it stunted the army's ability to engage in offensive operations and effectively prevented any true massing of conventional firepower until it was phased out in the early 1960s. One bright spot in this otherwise depressing period was that the great strides made in the troop-carrying ability of the U.S. Air Force allowed large numbers of men and equipment to be transported across great distances in record time, as in July 1958 when President Eisenhower ordered American forces to intervene in Lebanon. Faced with political turmoil, the pro-Western Lebanese government requested U.S. military inter-vention to prevent a collapse, and, in less than a week, seven-ty-two hundred troops (including three battalions of Marines) were in Beirut, with the army contingent flying in directly from the United States and Europe.

In the early 1960s, the army readied itself for combat during confrontations that erupted over the Communists' building of the Berlin Wall, their successes in Laos, and the Cuban missile crisis. Fearing "a second Cuba" on America's doorstep through a Communist takeover in the Dominican Republic, President Lyndon B. Johnson ordered U.S. forces to the country in April 1965, and some twenty-four thousand soldiers and Marines, centered around the 82d Airborne

OPPOSITE: Privates Lewis Larcesse and Charles Younts of the 27th Infantry "Wolfhounds" wait for a bombardment to lift before storming a hill during a live-fire exercise in Thailand on July 19, 1962. Part of the Hawaii-based 25th Infantry Division at Schofield Barracks, they were rushed to Thailand along with British and ANZAC forces to defend the country after Pathet Lao guerrillas seized control of neighboring Laos with the help of the North Vietnamese. The 27th, along with the rest of the division, returned to Schofield when the threat of invasion subsided, but the 9th Logistical Command remained in Thailand to maintain prepositioned military stocks and provide assistance in civil construction projects.

THE NUCLEAR BATTLEFIELD

In the late 1940s, the army began to study how atomic bombs could be used on the battlefield against the tank-packed spearheads traditionally used by the Soviets and, after the Chinese entered the Korean War, the massed hordes of their infantry as they formed up to attack. In addition to restructuring itself for a mobile defense by ostensibly more nuclear-survivable brigade-sized formations instead of divisions, the army fielded a variety of artillery and rocket systems capable of delivering tactical nuclear weapons. A common problem of the early systems—some used well into the 1970s—was their short ranges, from a maximum of fifteen miles in the M31 Honest John rocket to as little as 1.24 miles in the "light" version of the Davy Crocket recoilless rifle projectile. In all cases, rocket accuracy during this period was highly uncertain, but the development of W33 8-inch nuclear shells for the M110 self-propelled howitzer in 1956 allowed targets nearly ten miles away to be accurately blasted. Over time, missiles with longer ranges and increased accuracy, such as the Lance and Pershings I and II, were fielded, but, thankfully, the "nuclear threshold" was never crossed.

ABOVE: *Artillerymen prepare to load a practice round into the breech of an M65 280-mm "Atomic Cannon" during field-testing at the Aberdeen Proving Grounds, Maryland, on July 25, 1952. Success at developing an atom bomb capable of fitting in to an 11-inch shell—and withstanding the shock of being fired from a cannon—spurred the fielding of the M65, whose variable-yield round could be set to explode with the energy of one to fifteen kilotons of TNT. Although it could fire its atomic round some twenty miles, lack of maneuverability made its use impractical on a nuclear battlefield and it was superseded by the M110 8-inch (203-mm) self-propelled howitzer.*

OPPOSITE BOTTOM: *A paratrooper checks the settings on the M28 (light) launcher for a nuclear M388 Davy Crocket projectile on April 14, 1961. The M28, at 102-mm, was capable of shooting the variable-yield weapon out to 1.25 miles, while the M29 (heavy) launcher of 155-mm doubled the effective range. Davy Crockets not assigned to parachute units were vehicle mounted, and all could be set to provide detonations from ten to 250 tons of TNT.*

BELOW: *The warhead and rocket of an M31 Honest John missile are lowered into position on its launcher during training at Fort Sill, Oklahoma, on September 13, 1956. The Honest John was the centerpiece of the Pentomic Division's nuclear striking power.*

ABOVE: *Some of the three thousand soldiers taking part in the April 25, 1953, nuclear test and field maneuvers, codenamed Simon, crouch down in a slit trench during the detonation near Camp Desert Rock, Nevada. Post-exercise congratulations to the men read: "For the first time in known history, troops successfully attacked directly toward ground zero immediately following the atomic explosion. You can remember, with a sense of pleasure and accomplishment, that you were one of those troops, a real pioneer in experimentation of the most vital importance to the security of the United States." Roughly 225,000 military personnel were present at the 1951–1959 nuclear tests. Many illnesses among them and area residents, nicknamed "downwinders," are believed to have been the results of fallout, and several hundred million dollars were paid out in federal government compensation programs.*

SPECIALIST INSIGNIA

In 1958, specialists were authorized to continue to wear the smaller insignia, and chevrons formerly authorized for E5, E6, and E7 grades were authorized for continued wear until the individual was promoted or demoted. They also continued to use the previous title. In 1965, the Specialist Eight and Specialist Nine grades were discontinued. Black metal insignia were authorized for wear on the collar of work uniforms in December 1967, but though the army was rapidly expanding its forces in Vietnam, the subdued nature of the insignia was not related to combat operations. A new insignia was authorized in May 1968 for Sergeants Majors assigned at the principal NCO of battalion and higher. This insignia was the same as the Sergeant Major insignia except the star was small and a wreath was placed around the star.

SPECIALIST 9

SPECIALIST 8

SPECIALIST 7

OPPOSITE: Private First Class Daniel Fitzpatrick, A Company, 2d Battalion, 16th Infantry, guards Friedrichstrass, a main street in Berlin that the East German soldiers blocked in an effort to stem the flight of Germans to the safety of the city's Western sectors, August 24, 1961. A member of an 81-mm mortar section, he is carrying a teargas grenade and extra ammunition for his M1 Garand. Within a short time, the hastily erected barriers would be strengthened with barbed wire and concrete to become the Berlin Wall—completely encompassing the Western sectors.

Division, restored order and established a climate in which free elections could take place.

The army's role in society also came under increased scrutiny when both regular and Guard elements were called out to restore order during court-ordered racial integration as early as 1957 in Little Rock, Arkansas. They also were used increasingly in the 1960s to quell civil unrest and, eventually, violent antiwar protests.

All of this, however, paled before the extensive—and lengthy—commitment to Vietnam, an undeclared war with no easily defined beginning.

"FLEXIBLE RESPONSE"

Many serving and retired officers as well as political leaders were skeptical of the Eisenhower administration's policy of massive nuclear retaliation. They believed it was irrelevant to the new Communist strategy, which saw the Soviet Union and China turn increasingly to "wars of national liberation." Those two countries learned that a massed invasion across a recognized national border—the confrontation with the U.S. and South Korea—was very costly and, ultimately, futile. Now

they steadily nibbled away at the West through numerous, small, ambiguous wars in an effort to expand their influence while minimizing their own risk.

Generals Taylor, Ridgway, and Gavin all had written books emphasizing the need for the United States to be able to respond effectively to a wider spectrum of conflicts. They pushed for an army that was both larger and more adept at confronting the many challenges of the Cold War. The new administration of President John F. Kennedy agreed and instituted "flexible response" as the strategy best suited to confronting the myriad challenges. With Communist insurgencies seemingly appearing out of nowhere, the man who launched the space race told the 1962 graduating class of the U.S. Military Academy:

In light of this situation, we need to be prepared to fight a different war. This is another type of war, new in its intensity, ancient in its origin, war by guerrillas, subversives, insurgents, assassins; war by ambush instead of combat, by infiltration instead of aggression, seeking victory by eroding

SPECIALIST 6   SPECIALIST 5   SPECIALIST 4

and exhausting the enemy instead of engaging him. It requires, in those situations where we encounter it, a whole new kind of strategy, a wholly different kind of force, and therefore, a new and wholly different kind of military training.

Kennedy strongly backed the expansion of the army's Special Forces. Their activities, centered around counter-insurgency training of foreign armies, were expanded in Africa, Asia, and, much closer to home, Latin America, where many countries were battling guerrillas inspired by Fidel Castro's Cuba and frequently backed by the Soviet Union. Special Forces involvement in Bolivia is particularly well known because they tracked down and captured Communist revolutionary Che Guevara, but in the mid-1960s, some four hundred fifty missions were carried out by the 8th Special Forces Group in other countries, such as Guatemala, Venezuela, and the Dominican Republic. Colombia, strategically located near the Panama Canal, received the highest number of training teams.

M14 7.62-MM RIFLE

The M14 rifle was a direct successor to the highly successful M1 Garand used during World War II and the Korean War. Designed for selective automatic fire, it was also intended to replace the Browning Automatic Rifle, but never fulfilled this role since its pronounced muzzle climb when set on full auto made it suited only for shooting an enemy on stilts after the first round passed down the barrel. At 11 pounds when loaded, the M14 is a heavy weapon of traditional design, and was soon replaced by the 5.56-mm M16 as the standard service rifle. It continued in official use as a ceremonial and training weapon, and in several variations as an extremely effective sniper rifle until brought back into service with line infantry units early in the Afghanistan War.

1958 ENLISTED AND NCO RANK INSIGNIA

The size and color of the chevrons, which had been changed from two inches wide to 3⅛ inches wide for male personnel in 1951, and remaining two inches wide for female personnel, did not change until 1958 when the Department of the Army authorized that all have a dark blue background with olive-drab chevrons, arc, and lozenge.

A LITTLE WAR GETS BIGGER

Not long after World War II, the United States began aiding the French colonial rulers of Indochina in their efforts to suppress a revolt by Communist-dominated guerrillas. Direct American involvement in Vietnam, however, didn't begin until 1957 with the deployment of the 14th Special Forces Operational Detachment, and it was rising steadily well before Kennedy entered the White House. Special Forces soldiers, called Green Berets because of their distinctive headgear, worked hard to deny the Viet Cong ("VC") guerrillas free movement in the countryside by quickly forging the many outlying tribes (which were not ethnically Vietnamese) into competent, anti-Communist forces. Tribesmen formed close bonds with the Green Berets, who scrupulously respected local customs and established medical clinics and schools in regions ignored by the Saigon government. In addition, other U.S. advisers trained the Army of the Republic of Vietnam (ARVN) in both conventional and counterinsurgent tactics.

Under the newly established U.S. Military Assistance Command, Vietnam (MACV), the number of American advisers in the field rose from 746 in January 1962 to more than thirty-four hundred by June. By the end of the year, the entire U.S. commitment was eleven thousand, which encompassed twenty-nine Special Forces detachments. There appeared to be considerable successes in consolidating the population in a series of defended "strategic hamlets" and in establishing local defense forces; however, American efforts could not offset the general unwillingness of many ARVN units—even when accompanied by American advisers—to close with the enemy. Throughout late 1963 and 1964, the South

RIGHT INSET: The more versatile M1951 field jacket replaced versions of the M1943 jacket worn during World War II and the brutal Korean winter of 1950–1951. In both cases the core jacket served as the basic element around which other weather protection, such as hoods and linings, could be added or removed. This jacket was worn by Lieutenant Colonel Dwayne Watson and sports a Military Assistance Command, Vietnam (MACV) patch positioned on the left sleeve to denote his former wartime service with that organization. Although Vietnam is not thought of as having a cold climate, the M1951 was regularly put on at night in the cooler Central Highlands and also used by troops to keep warm during the monsoon rains.

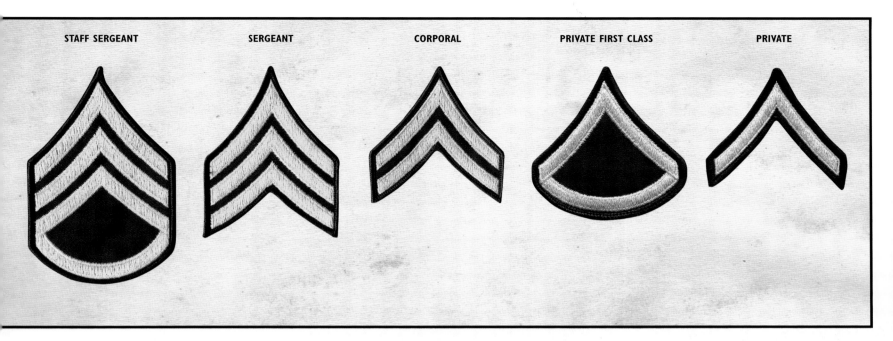

STAFF SERGEANT   SERGEANT   CORPORAL   PRIVATE FIRST CLASS   PRIVATE

BELOW: South Vietnamese paratroopers at Vieng Tau "hurry up and wait" for orders to board UH-I Hueys of the U.S. Army Support Command, Vietnam, on February 27, 1965. Some 137 helicopters airlifted two battalions to landing zones (LZs) in the Mekong Delta area 150 miles southeast of Saigon during offensive operations against Viet Cong guerrillas. Later, in July of that year, the corps-level support command was expanded to become the U.S. Army, Vietnam (USARV), during the rapid buildup of American combat troops in the country.

Captain Roger Hugh Charles Donlon
5th Special Forces Group

Citation: For conspicuous gallantry and intrepidity at the risk of his life above and beyond the call of duty while defending a U.S. military installation against a fierce attack by hostile forces. Captain Donlon was serving as the commanding officer of the U.S. Army Special Forces Detachment A-726 at Camp Nam Dong when a reinforced Viet Cong battalion suddenly launched a full-scale, predawn attack on the camp. During the violent battle that ensued, lasting five hours and resulting in heavy casualties on both sides, Donlon directed the defense operations in the midst of an enemy barrage of mortar shells, falling grenades, and extremely heavy gunfire. Upon the initial onslaught, he swiftly marshaled his forces and ordered the removal of the needed ammunition from a blazing building. He then dashed through a hail of small arms and exploding hand grenades to abort a breach of the main gate. En route to this position he detected an enemy demolition team of three in the proximity of the main gate and quickly annihilated them. Although exposed to the intense grenade attack, he then succeeded in reaching a 60-mm mortar position despite sustaining a severe stomach wound as he was within five yards of the gun pit. When he discovered that most of the men in this gunpit were also wounded, he completely disregarded his own injury, directed their withdrawal to a location thirty meters away, and again risked his life by remaining behind and covering the movement with the utmost effectiveness. Noticing that his team sergeant was unable to evacuate the gun pit he crawled toward him and, while dragging the fallen soldier out of the gun pit, an enemy mortar exploded and inflicted a wound in Donlon's left shoulder. Although suffering from multiple wounds, he carried the abandoned 60-mm mortar weapon to a new location thirty meters away where he found three wounded defenders. After administering first aid and encouragement to these men, he left the weapon with them, headed toward another position, and retrieved a 57-mm recoilless rifle. Then with great courage and coolness under fire, he returned to the abandoned gun pit, evacuated ammunition for the two weapons, and while crawling and dragging the urgently needed ammunition, received a third wound on his leg by an enemy hand grenade. Despite his critical physical condition, he again crawled 175 meters to an 81-mm mortar position and directed firing operations which protected the seriously threatened east sector of the camp. He then moved to an eastern 60-mm mortar position and upon determining that the vicious enemy assault had weakened, crawled back to the gun pit with the 60-mm mortar, set it up for defensive operations, and turned it over to two defenders with minor wounds. Without hesitation, he left this sheltered position, and moved from position to position around the beleaguered perimeter while hurling hand grenades at the enemy and inspiring his men to superhuman effort. As he bravely continued to move around the perimeter, a mortar shell exploded, wounding him in the face and body. As the long awaited daylight brought defeat to the enemy forces and their retreat back to the jungle, leaving behind fifty-four of their dead, many weapons, and grenades, Donlon immediately reorganized his defenses and administered first aid to the wounded. His dynamic leadership, fortitude, and valiant efforts inspired not only the American personnel but the friendly Vietnamese defenders as well and resulted in the successful defense of the camp. Donlon's extraordinary heroism, at the risk of his life above and beyond the call of duty are in the highest traditions of the U.S. Army and reflect great credit upon himself and the Armed Forces of his country.

RIGHT: Shoulder patch of the 173d Airborne Brigade. The "Sky Soldiers" were the first major army combat formation deployed to Vietnam, and one of the very last to leave.

Vietnamese government seemed near collapse as repeated military coups and ongoing Communist infiltration and subversion undermined the regime's stability. In early 1965, guerrillas began to target U.S. air bases critical to the country's defense, and President Johnson began a process of escalation that, by year's end, put 184,000 American troops in South Vietnam, including the 1st Cavalry Division (Airmobile), 173d Airborne Brigade, and elements of the 1st and 25th Infantry divisions, the III Marine Amphibious Corps, a brigade of South Korean marines, and Australian infantry battalion.

During this period, the most effective military deterrent to the Communists, other than the U.S. combat units, came from the Civilian Irregular Defense Group (CIDG) outposts along the border regions. By the late 1960s some forty-five thousand tribesmen had been actively involved in the CIDGs, which were operated by 3,500 Special Forces troops per year in a total of 249 village outposts beyond the easy reach of conventional U.S. and South Vietnamese units. Countless skirmishes and dozens of pitched battles were fought during the nine years of the program. The Green Berets' activities with such tribal allies as the Nungs, Montagnards, and Khmers remained the main focus of Special Forces efforts. But the Ho Chi Minh Trail supply network, running from North Vietnam through Laos and Cambodia to South Vietnam, also saw extensive long-range patrolling, as teams of Green Berets and tribal soldiers often spent weeks at a time in the contested jungles.

Although they were generally far removed from the populous areas targeted for control by the Viet Cong, these village outposts seriously impeded the enemy's resupply of weapons, matériel, and men from communist North Vietnam. To no one's surprise, they increasingly became the scene of large-scale attacks. On October 19, 1965, the North Vietnamese Army (NVA) 32d Regiment attacked a CIDG-Special Forces base at Plei Me, near the entrance to the Ia Drang Valley, as the opening move of a thrust to cut the country in half. With the assistance of massive air strikes, the 1st Cavalry Division thwarted the 32d, then 33d and 66th NVA regiments, in a campaign that lasted nearly a month and included several

BELOW: The PRC-25 voice FM radio was the primary man-portable communication system during the Vietnam War. Frustrated by the short range of the PRC-10 voice FM radio first introduced in 1951, the army began shipping the modular, transistorized, PRC-25 in the summer of 1965. The first 1,500 models to arrive "in country" were immediately distributed to advisors and Special Forces, and it wasn't until May 1967 that the radio was available to all army units.

ABOVE: Within days of its arrival in Vietnam, the 173d Airborne Brigade initiated combat operations. Here, Sp4 Archie L. Gaffee and chief computer Sp4 Robert Crane of the brigade's 3d Battalion 319th Artillery plot a fire mission on May 5, 1965, as fire direction center section leader Sergeant Alfred Bohannon observes their progress.

BOTTOM: American advisor Captain James A. Musselman and Vietnamese soldiers attempt to take cover from small arms fire behind a thin dike dividing rice paddy fields. The September 4, 1965, clash took place on Tan Dinh Island in the Mekong Delta. Vietnamese photographer Huynh Thanh My, who took this photo, was killed the following month. Wounded while on patrol with South Vietnamese Rangers, he was executed along with medics and other wounded when the aid station where he was awaiting evacuation was overrun.

engagements. The Ia Drang Valley battle was the costliest in terms of casualties to date, but the successful defense of the region, including the competent performance of an ARVN task force, visibly improved security in and around the Central Highlands.

Unfortunately, the "1st Cav's" success at forcing the NVA retreat from Plei Me was more the exception than the rule along the border. As the war grew to be more and more a big-unit fight in 1965 with the advance of North Vietnamese formations into the South, the isolated CIDG posts became more and more vulnerable, particularly to artillery, which the North Vietnamese used against them with devastating effect. Camps Due Co and Cai Cai underwent prolonged sieges, and others like Song Be and Bu Dop fell in vicious fighting. Large conventional units could seldom be spared to dash from one beleaguered site to another, and the inability of U.S. and South Vietnamese forces to come to the aid of the CIDG camps led Special Forces to create its own battalion-size mobile reaction units, made up of indigenous troops. Called simply "Mike" forces after the letter M for mobile, these light units were increasingly called upon to

support conventional operations as the war progressed, and they suffered heavy casualties.

Over the next several years, American troop strength in Vietnam rose to five-hundred fifty thousand as the 1st and 25th Infantry divisions' initial brigade deployments were followed by the balance of the formations plus the 4th, 9th, 23d (Americal), and 25th Infantry divisions; 101st Airborne Division (Airmobile); the 11th Armored Cavalry Regiment; numerous separate light brigades; and a vast network of support elements. Barred by policy from invading North Vietnam or Laos to cut off the Ho Chi Minh Trail, the MACV commander, General William C. Westmoreland, adopted a strategy of attrition. It was believed that if enough casualties could be inflicted on the NVA and VC units in the South, the Communists would either enter into serious negotiations or abandon their attempts to reunify Vietnam by force. To this end, American units attempted to locate the elusive enemy and bring him to battle on favorable terms in the mountains of the Central Highlands, the jungles of the coastal lowlands, and the plains near the South Vietnamese capital of Saigon.

LEFT: Platoon Sergeant 1st Class Dilas G. Henningsen and his gunner survey a forward area from the top of their M-48 tank during an October 20–21, 1965, road reconnaissance north of Saigon. The 1st Infantry Division tankers are members of Troop B, 1st Battalion, 4th Cavalry Regiment.

BELOW INSET: Colonel (later Lieutenant General) Harold G. "Hal" Moore

BOTTOM: Colonel Moore, commander of the 1st Cavalry Division's 1st Battalion, 7th Cavalry, during the three-day fight at LZ X-Ray, examines a dead NVA soldier after the Ia Drang battle, November 16, 1965.

LEFT: Clad in "tiger stripe" battle dress, members of the Delta team that reinforced the Plei Me Special Forces camp watch as air strikes pound nearby North Vietnamese Army (NVA) positions with napalm and high explosives. The NVA opened up the Ia Drang Valley campaign with an October 19, 1965, attack at Plei Me, Pleiku, but soldiers from the 1st Cavalry Division (Airmobile) arrived in time to repulse the Communists.

IA DRANG

In the autumn of 1965, the 1st Cavalry Division (Airmobile) locked horns with the North Vietnamese Army (NVA) regulars of the 32d, 33d, and 66th Regiments in fighting that would last for more than a month in the Central Highlands near the major U.S. base at Pleiku. The NVA opened up the campaign on October 19 by attacking Special Forces troops at Plei Me in the Central Highlands' Ia Drang Valley. They melted back into the jungle when units from the 1st Cav lifted the siege of Plei Me, but one of the NVA regiments was detected a few miles to the west.

On October 20, Brigadier General Richard T. Knowles, assistant division commander, sent the 1st Squadron, 9th Cavalry of Colonel Thomas W. Brown's 3d Brigade to pursue the NVA troops. They found them in an area along the valley beneath Chu Pong Mountain along the border with Cambodia, and Knowles ordered the 1st Squadron to Landing Zone (LZ) Mary, where they were landed by UH-1Ds "Hueys," and soon began fighting the enemy. The NVA responded by sending three battalions into the fight in an attempt to annihilate the Americans, but by November 4, the 1st Squadron had inflicted 150 casualties on the North Vietnamese. Brown then sent his men searching in the area south and southeast of Plei Me.

As part of the continuing operation, Lieutenant Colonel Harry G. Moore, 1st Battalion, 7th Cavalry, chose LZ X-Ray for his November 14 air assault near the base of Chu Pong Mountain. Helicopter gunships pounded the position around X-Ray, using up half of their ammunition in a thirty second, blistering barrage. Then Moore's men were lowered to the ground. "Aerial artillery," meanwhile, continued to hover overhead in case they were needed. LZ X-Ray was large enough to hold ten Hueys, a capacity it would need. The landscape at X-Ray was exotic, abounding in 100-feet trees and bristling with neck-high elephant grass and eight-feet-tall anthills—all of which afforded the enemy good cover.

As A, B, C, and D Companies landed, the air became thick with dust and smoke. By mid-afternoon, they were fighting for their lives as the enemy skillfully employed a tactic called "hugging." To avoid the horrendous American aerial and ground artillery fire, NVA soldiers fought the Cav at the closest proximity possible, making it difficult for U.S. fire support to zero in on and destroy them without injuring Americans with "friendly fire."

Incoming supply and reinforcement helicopters were being riddled by enemy fire, and one pilot and his gunner were wounded and a radioman killed. Phosphorus artillery was fired, and by its lurid glare, the killed and wounded were retrieved from the defensive perimeter. Colonel Moore, meanwhile, called for reinforcements, and Company B, 2d Battalion, 7th Cavalry, was sent in. During their landing, two helicopters were hit on the ground, and another, still in the air, spun aimlessly out of control, its main rotor clipping leaves from the treetops before it crashed in a resounding heap. Meanwhile, a platoon from Company B was cut off from the rest of the forces and suffered twenty casualties, leaving it with only seven men.

In the early morning hours, hand-to-hand fighting developed, but by 10 A.M. the enemy had retired in defeat. When U.S. troops emerged from their defenses, they found a dead American in a nearby foxhole surrounded by the remains of five NVA soldiers. Another trooper was found with his hands clasped around the throat of his enemy—both were dead. The area was littered with bodies, and NVA weapons and equipment were strewn wildly. Bloody trails left by the North Vietnamese soldiers led into the jungle. U.S. soldiers dug in for the night, but the battle was over.

ABOVE: *Major Crandall, commanding the 1st Cavalry Division's Company A, 229th Assault Helicopter Battalion, lifts off from a landing zone during the Ia Drang Valley Campaign, October–November 1965. Crandall's call sign during this period was "Ancient Serpent 6."*

RIGHT: *Major (later Lieutenant Colonel) Bruce P. Crandall*

CRANDALL   U.S. ARMY

ABOVE: *Soldiers of the 1st Battalion, 7th Cavalry, answer a flurry of NVA small-arms fire that buzzed through the command post perimeter at LZ X-Ray, November 16, 1965. Intense fighting had surged throughout the area for three days, but trooper J.D. Coleman described this flare-up as "nothing serious." It did, however, provide the "gaggle" of reporters who had recently arrived on the scene with "a good story to tell" said Coleman. United Press International reporter Joe Galloway was the only newsman present throughout the most intense combat—in which he took a direct part. Galloway received a Bronze Star for his actions.*

MEDAL OF HONOR
Major Bruce P. Crandall
229th Assault Helicopter Battalion

Citation: Major Bruce P. Crandall distinguished himself by extraordinary heroism as a Flight Commander in the Republic of Vietnam, while serving with Company A, 229th Assault Helicopter Battalion, 1st Cavalry Division (Airmobile). On November 14, 1965, his flight of sixteen helicopters was lifting troops for a search and destroy mission from Plei Me, Vietnam, to Landing Zone X-Ray in the Ia Drang Valley. On the fourth troop lift, the airlift began to take enemy fire, and by the time the aircraft had refueled and returned for the next troop lift, the enemy had Landing Zone X-Ray targeted. As Crandall and the first eight helicopters landed to discharge troops on his fifth troop lift, his unarmed helicopter came under such intense enemy fire that the ground commander ordered the second flight of eight aircraft to abort their mission. As Crandall flew back to Plei Me, his base of operations, he determined that the ground commander of the besieged infantry battalion desperately needed more ammunition. Major Crandall then decided to adjust his base of operations to Artillery Firebase Falcon in order to shorten the flight distance to deliver ammunition and evacuate wounded soldiers. While medical evacuation was not his mission, he immediately sought volunteers and with complete disregard for his own personal safety, led the two aircraft to Landing Zone X-Ray. Despite the fact that the landing zone was still under relentless enemy fire, Crandall landed and proceeded to supervise the loading of seriously wounded soldiers aboard his aircraft. Crandall's voluntary decision to land under the most extreme fire instilled in the other pilots the will and spirit to continue to land their own aircraft, and in the ground forces the realization that they would be resupplied and that friendly wounded would be promptly evacuated. This greatly enhanced morale and the will to fight at a critical time. After his first medical evacuation, Crandall continued to fly into and out of the landing zone throughout the day and into the evening. That day he completed a total of twenty-two flights, most under intense enemy fire, retiring from the battlefield only after all possible service had been rendered to the Infantry battalion. His actions provided critical resupply of ammunition and evacuation of the wounded. Major Crandall's daring acts of bravery and courage in the face of an overwhelming and determined enemy are in keeping with the highest traditions of the military service and reflect great credit upon himself, his unit, and the United States Army.

TAKING THE OFFENSIVE

After calling the shots for more than a decade in the long conflict, the North Vietnamese and their Viet Cong allies in the south had considerable trouble dealing with the nearly continual American operations, which were essentially three distinct phases of a counteroffensive that extended into 1968. As the North Vietnamese admitted after the war, these operations inflicted significant losses but never forced them to abandon their efforts.

Phase I, December 1965–June 1966: The 1st Cav's victory in the Ia Drang Valley marked the beginning of

LEFT TOP: The APH5 crash helmet of UH-60 Huey pilot Captain Joseph D. Newsome, 118th Assault Helicopter Company. During three one-year tours he earned the Distinguished Flying Cross, Bronze Star, Purple Heart, and the Air Medal with twenty-six oak leaf clusters. The APH5 "brain bucket" was the army's standard aviation headgear at the start of the war, and although it was supposed to have been phased out of combat service in 1965–1966, production shortfalls of the visually similar AFH1 replacement helmets resulted in its use well into the 1970s. Both models featured integral headphones, a boom-type microphone, and a retractable tinted anti-glare visor.

LEFT BOTTOM: The first SPH4 helmets began trickling into Vietnam in late 1969. Though there was some distortion problems in the early visors, the SPH4s were eagerly sought after by air crews because of their significantly improved microphone that picked up and amplified fewer extraneous sounds, plus their greater crash and acoustic protection. This helmet was worn by Captain Ralph E. Barsanti (*below*) who, during earlier service in Vietnam with the 282d Assault Helicopter Company "Black Cats" and 212th Combat Support Aviation Battalion, flew missions throughout the I Corps area, including into Hue during the Communists' 1968 Tet Offensive.

a series of limited operations designed to keep the enemy off balance while the infrastructure necessary for a long war was built. This involved search-and-destroy operations to protect the logistical installations under construction along the coast, as well as the base camps for incoming U.S. units in the provinces near Saigon. The protection of the government and the people of South Vietnam was critical; thus, American efforts were concentrated in the most vital and heavily populated regions. The III Marine Amphibious Force supported the ARVN I Corps in the northern provinces, the I Field Force supported the Vietnamese II Corps in the central region, and the II Field Force supported the III Corps around Saigon. Consequently, the major battles of the year occurred in these areas. The Delta region of IV Corps, which had been the scene of much fighting before, remained primarily an ARVN responsibility.

In late January 1966, the 101st Airborne Division's 1st Brigade, along with Korean and ARVN units, moved to destroy or disrupt the NVA 95th Regiment operating in the coastal rice-producing area of the central region's Phu Yen Province. Though cut short by the annual Lunar New Year (Tet) cease-fire, the North Vietnamese suffered serious losses and were unable to hamper the rice harvest. Afterwards, NVA efforts to infiltrate from Laos and across the Demilitarized

BACKGROUND: A soldier guides in a UH-1D "Dustoff" medevac helicopter to pick up a casualty during Operation Irving, Binh Dinh Province, October 1966. Previous to the arrival of a medevac, messages on a radio net designated the area where the wounded were located plus described the number and condition of the wounded to be extracted. On their approach, smoke was often "popped" to help pilots pinpoint exactly where troops needing evacuation were located.

ABOVE: 1st Cavalry Division medic Private First Class Thomas Cole looks up toward the sound of a medevac helicopter with one uncovered eye as he treats Staff Sergeant Harrison Pell. The Cavalrymen were wounded during Operation Masher, which was launched in the Central Highlands province of Binh Dinh in late January 1966.

Zone (DMZ) into Quang Tri Province were confronted by the 173d Airborne Brigade and 3d Marine Division. On April 12, an American B-52 based on Guam bombed infiltration routes near the Laos border for the first time, forcing the NVA to take refuge in Laos, Cambodia, and North Vietnam. With the regular enemy forces driven away from population centers, the United States and its allies concentrated on curbing local guerrilla activity.

Phase II, July 1966–May 1967: North Vietnam continued to build its own forces inside South Vietnam through continued infiltration by sea, along the Ho Chi Minh Trail, and through the Demilitarized Zone. U.S. air elements received permission to launch air strikes into North Vietnam just north of the border, but ground forces were denied authority to conduct reconnaissance patrols in the northern portion of the DMZ and inside North Vietnam. Confined to South Vietnamese territory, American ground forces continued their war of attrition against the Communists, conducting eighteen major operations in 1966. The most successful of these was Operation Masher, where the 1st Cav, Korean units, and ARVN forces decimated the NVA 3d Division as they cleared the northern half of Binh Dinh Province on the central coast. To the south, some twenty-two thousand South Vietnamese and American troops, centered around the 196th Light Infantry Brigade, were pitted against the VC 9th Division and a NVA regiment northwest of Saigon in the largest weep of the year, Operation Attleboro.

OPPOSITE: 25th Infantry Division soldiers at Hoc Mon in late March 1968.

ABOVE: Soldiers erupt in a roar of approval after a speech by General William Westmoreland, Commander, MACV, commending them on their operations against the Viet Cong in Hau Nghia Province, twenty-five miles northwest of Saigon. Westmoreland (*center*) was at his best in these personal encounters with the troops, in this case the army's 27th Infantry, 25th Infantry Division—the "Wolfhounds."

M60 MACHINE GUN, 7.62-MM

The venerable M2 .50-caliber Browning heavy machine gun, which pumps up to six hundred rounds per minute out to 1,530 yards with great accuracy, formed the cornerstone for the defense of virtually all camps and fire bases in Vietnam. Unfortunately, the .50-caliber in combination with its lightest tripod weighed nearly 100 pounds. However, the crew-served M60 general-purpose machine gun could supply adequate suppressive fire at that same range and, at only two pounds heavier than the Browning Automatic Rifle, was the weapon soldiers carried into the field. Served by a crew of two, the M60, even in the hands of a careful gunner, could use up a considerable amount of bullets in a fire fight, and it was not unusual to see as many as a half-dozen soldiers in a platoon draped in extra belts of the weapon's 7.62-mm (.30-cal.) NATO-standard ammunition.

HELICOPTERS

Rapid, aggressive movement and massive concentration of firepower on the modern battlefield was the dream of forward-thinking World War II and Korean War-era cavalry soldiers—by now colonels and generals—who experimented with heliborne troop movements throughout the late 1950s and early 1960s. However, it was the technological and tactical leap made by the rugged Bell Company UH-1 Huey and Boeing Vertol CH-47 Chinook helicopters that really made airborne tactics possible. Yet even before these "fast movers" arrived in Vietnam, less capable machines were already proving their worth. Ultimately, the war lasted so long that virtually every helicopter type that began the conflict was superceded and replaced by Hueys, Chinooks, and other modern machines by the middle of the conflict.

RIGHT TOP: A UH-1H Huey of the 9th Aviation Battalion prepares to set down on the sixteen-square-foot landing pad of an ATC(H) (armored troop carrier with helipad) during Operation Coronado I, July 26, 1967.

RIGHT BOTTOM: The XM159 19-rocket pod (*A*) in combination with an XM18 7.62-mm minigun pod (*B*) on a Cobra's wing stub, and another minigun (*C*) in the chin turret.

BACKGROUND: The port-door gunner of a UH-1C Seawolf (the Navy Huey) supporting riverine operations pumps M60 machine-gun fire into a VC ambush position in the Mekong Delta, October 1966.

Major Patrick H. Brady
54th Medical Detachment

Citation: For conspicuous gallantry and intrepidity in action at the risk of his life above and beyond the call of duty, Major Brady distinguished himself while serving in the Republic of Vietnam commanding a UH-1H ambulance helicopter, volunteered to rescue wounded men from a site in enemy held territory which was reported to be heavily defended and to be blanketed by fog. To reach the site he descended through heavy fog and smoke and hovered slowly along a valley trail, turning his ship sideward to blow away the fog with the backwash from his rotor blades. Despite the unchallenged, close-range enemy fire, he found the dangerously small site, where he successfully landed and evacuated two badly wounded South Vietnamese soldiers. He was then called to another area completely covered by dense fog where American casualties lay only fifty meters from the enemy. Two aircraft had previously been shot down and others had made unsuccessful attempts to reach this site earlier in the day. With unmatched skill and extraordinary courage, Brady made four flights to this embattled landing zone and successfully rescued all the wounded. On his third mission of the day Brady once again landed at a site surrounded by the enemy. The friendly ground force, pinned down by enemy fire, had been unable to reach and secure the landing zone. Although his aircraft had been badly damaged and his controls partially shot away during his initial entry into this area, he returned minutes later and rescued the remaining injured. Shortly thereafter, obtaining a replacement aircraft, Brady was requested to land in an enemy minefield where a platoon of American soldiers was trapped. A mine detonated near his helicopter, wounding two crewmembers and damaging his ship. In spite of this, he managed to fly six severely injured patients to medical aid. Throughout that day Brady utilized three helicopters to evacuate a total of fifty-one seriously wounded men, many of whom would have perished without prompt medical treatment. Brady's bravery was in the highest traditions of the military service and reflects great credit upon himself and the U.S. Army.

M16 5.56-mm Assault Rifle

Fully five inches shorter and two pounds lighter than the M14, the M16, developed by Armalite and manufactured by Colt, was more easily handled in confined jungle conditions. Moreover, at close range its small, high-velocity, 5.56-mm (.22-caliber) bullets were actually more lethal than larger slower rounds because, as wound ballistics long demonstrated, smaller faster bullets would tumble as they passed through a body instead of tending to pass straight through. A series of early teething troubles centering chiefly around the power used in M16 cartridges had to be rectified before many soldiers and Marines felt comfortable with the weapon. This example also sports the original three-prong "duckbill" flash suppressor detested by troops because it continually snagged on even the lightest foliage when the men moved through underbrush or jungle. Soon after the M16 proved its effectiveness, calls for an even shorter version prompted the design and fielding of the Colt Model 629 Commando assault rifle. Although purchased in quantity for Army Special Forces and other special elements, the Colt Commando was never approved for general use by the army, but nevertheless made its way into the hands of many Infantrymen and vehicle crewmen.

M79 Grenade Launcher

The small, high velocity round of the M16 was not suitable for the family of grenade launchers that were able to be attached to the muzzles of the M1 and M14 rifles. Fortunately, the army had already fielded the M79 grenade launcher (opposite), a shotgun-like, shoulder-fired weapon that fired aerodynamic, exploding projectiles as far as 320 yards from its 40-mm barrel. The M79 filled the need for a weapon that could cover the ground between the reach of a hand-thrown grenade and the shortest range of a mortar—and was loved by the troops. However, any infantrymen issued the M79 had to carry both it and his rifle, and switching from one weapon to the other meant that a target had to be, in effect, disengaged then reacquired before it could be fired upon. A combination rifle/grenade launcher was clearly needed and the M16-mounted XM148 launcher was issued to the 101st Airborne Division and a growing number of other units until the standard M203 rifle-mounted grenade launcher began replacing both the XM148 and beloved M79 on a one-for-one basis in 1969.

OPPOSITE: A "Task Force Oregon" fire team responds to automatic weapons fire from an enemy-held village. The troops are members of Company B, 2d Battalion, 30th Infantry, in the 4th Infantry Division's 3d Brigade, taking part in a September 4–9, 1967, operation in the Duc Pho area of Quang Ngai Province, 320 miles northeast of Saigon.

On January 8, 1967, the U.S. 1st and 25th Infantry divisions, together with the 11th Armored Cavalry Regiment and ARVN troops, launched drives against major VC strongholds in the "Iron Triangle" about twenty-five miles northwest of Saigon. For years this area had been a major logistics base and headquarters controlling enemy activity in and around Saigon. The Allies captured huge caches of rice and other foodstuffs, destroyed what they could find of a mammoth system of tunnels, and seized documents of considerable intelligence value. But, as happened all too often during the war, the area was reoccupied by the VC as soon as the Allied forces left.

In February, the same divisions were committed with other units in the largest allied operation of the war to date, Junction City in Tay Ninh Province bordering Cambodia (War Zone C). Some twenty-two American and four ARVN battalions engaged the enemy, killing 2,728. After clearing this area, the Allies constructed three airfields, erected a bridge, and fortified two camps in which CIDG garrisons remained while the other Allied forces withdrew.

In early 1967, U.S. military personnel in South Vietnam numbered 385,300. NVA and VC forces also increased substantially, so that for the same period, total enemy strength exceeded two-hundred eighty-two thousand, in addition to an estimated eighty thousand Communist political operatives or "cadres." By summer, U.S. troop strength had risen to 448,800, but enemy strength had also increased as traffic down the Ho Chi Minh Trail network grew steadily despite interdiction by U.S. naval and land-based airpower.

Phase III, June 1967–January 1968: At the completion of Operation Junction City, elements of the U.S. and ARVN forces swung back toward Saigon to conduct another clearing operation in the Long Nguyen base area just north of the previously cleared Iron Triangle. Meanwhile, ARVN units were finally becoming more active and capable under American advisers, and Vietnamese Special Forces assumed full responsibility for several Special Forces camps and for the CIDG companies manning them. The South Vietnamese conducted major operations during 1967, and, in spite of strenuous VC attempts to avoid battle, achieved a number of contacts.

ABOVE: In War Zone C, northwest of Saigon, 1st Infantry Division soldiers clean M16 rifles during Operation Junction City, April 1967. As these men and their buddies knew all too well, the M16 needed to be cleaned frequently or it could jam during combat.

THE TET OFFENSIVE

As the Lunar New Year approached, the Allies and Vietnamese population looked forward to the customary thirty-six-hour truce that was called every year during the festive holiday. The enemy had something else in mind—a surprise offensive by roughly eighty-four thousand VC and NVA soldiers. To prepare for this effort, the Viet Cong had for some time been secreting soldiers, supplies, and armaments across the length of Vietnam, and NVA units had been carefully positioned near key population centers. The attack, by design, would be widespread and conceived in such a way as to create panic and confusion in the U.S. and South Vietnamese armed forces and perhaps stir pandemonium in the news media and public. The enemy hoped to undermine American morale and create a major North Vietnamese psychological victory.

By mid-January, teams of specially trained NVA commandos (called sapper units) were infiltrating South Vietnamese cities with their weapons and explosives hidden aboard wagons of farm produce. While the news media had been heralding one U.S. victory in the war after another and seemed oblivious to the growing threat to the Allied war effort, General Westmoreland, by the end of January, had canceled all active military operations and was preparing for

OPPOSITE: The 1st Cavalry Division (Airmobile)'s 3d Brigade operated in support of the 4th Infantry Division from June 24 to July 25, 1967, during Operation Greely in Kontum Province. Here, members of Troop B, 1st Squadron, 9th Cavalry await orders near Binh Dinh on July 21.

ABOVE RIGHT: On the second day of the Tet Offensive, exhausted security forces take up position near the U.S. Embassy in Saigon as battles with VC infiltrators continue to erupt across the city, February 1, 1968. The patch on the M60 gunner's right sleeve indicates previous service in the 173d Airborne Brigade.

BELOW: Troops move out from a landing zone during Operation Junction City. The object of the nearly three-month operation, which began in February 1967, was the destruction of Viet Cong (VC) and NVA bases in War Zone C northwest of Saigon. The VC lost some 1,776 men but, for the most part, cannily refused to fight, abandoning huge amounts of medical supplies, ammunition, and some 800 tons of rice. Within a short time, they again infested the area, which was used to support attacks into Saigon during the Tet Offensive the following year.

a major enemy offensive. He warned that an attack would come around the time of Tet, but no one—the South Vietnamese or the Americans—expected the attack precisely during Tet itself, nor did anyone have good intelligence on exactly where the attacks would occur.

At 3:00 A.M. on January 30, 1968, VC and NVA forces attacked six cities and towns in the center of South Vietnam. All were driven back, and U.S. intelligence immediately recognized these aborted assaults as mistakes. The enemy leadership, it was confirmed later, originally had ordered the offensive to begin at this time, but last-minute problems getting all the units into place

caused the attack time to be pushed back to January 31. Luckily for the Allies, the Communists' poor communication network had failed to inform all the units, and this tipped the enemy's hand, costing the offensive the key element of surprise. After the initial attacks, U.S. units were put on maximum alert and warned of their likely continuation.

The South Vietnamese, meanwhile, began their Tet festivities and fireworks, disregarding the early fighting. The Americans dug in, expecting a battle. The next day, January 31, NVA and VC soldiers and cadre launched their countrywide offensive on forty cities and towns. In one of the largest attacks thus far in the war, the Communists attacked Saigon, Quang Tri, Hue, Da Nang, Nha Trang, Qui Nhon, Kontum City, Ban Me Thuot, My Tho, Can Tho, and Ben Tre. Most of the attacks were hastily beaten

LEFT INSET: An M1 helmet with helmet cover. The elastic camouflage band rarely held foliage to blend its hard edges into the background, securing instead all manner of small items important to their wearer, most frequently weapons oil, cigarettes, and here, matches and bug repellant.

BELOW: Specialist 4 Roger Floyd of Company D, 3d Battalion, 187th Infantry, 101st Airborne Division, listens to a February 11, 1968, ball game on his radio at Tan Son Nhut Air Base outside Saigon.

LEFT: Artillerymen of B Battery's No. 6 Gun, 2d Howitzer Battalion, 320th Artillery, clear the area in front of their 105-mm howitzer after retaking it a second time from 24th NVA Regiment troops. The North Vietnamese had broken into the position during their June 7, 1968, attempt to overrun the battery. Other artillerymen swept the site with beehive rounds at point blank range, greatly facilitating the retaking of the gun, and the 101st Airborne Division's A Company, 2d Battalion, 502d Infantry, provided security that beat back persistent attacks at other points along the perimeter. Continued attacks that night were unsuccessful and the NVA withdrew before dawn leaving behind eighty-six dead, including thirteen inside No. 6 Gun's position. The impromptu fire support base near the Laotian border was part of Operation Hawthorne, the 101st's effort to prevent the NVA from seizing the Special Forces outpost at Toumorong and blunt its drive on Dak To and Kontum in the Central Highlands.

back, but fighting continued for the next two weeks in some areas and for up to a month at the old imperial city of Hue. The offensive had also dealt a severe setback to the pacification program because of the intense fighting needed to root out VC elements that clung to fortified positions inside the towns. For example, the densely populated Mekong Delta had approximately fourteen thousand refugees in January. After Tet some one-hundred seventy thousand were homeless. The requirement to assist them seriously inhibited national recovery efforts.

For the Viet Cong, however, the Tet Offensive had been disastrous. During the various assaults, the VC suffered appalling casualties among their regular soldiers and especially their political cadre, which saw as many as forty thousand dead. The Communists had expected a great uprising by the South Vietnamese people against their government, but this failed to materialize, and the principal value of the offensive came in the political arena. For example, one of the failed—but most heavily publicized—attacks was on the U.S. Embassy in Saigon. Although polls showed that the surprise offensive had little effect on America's determination to prosecute the war and that it, in fact, had rallied public opinion, the way it was reported in the press and on television in the United States had an immense impact on U.S. leaders and opinion-makers, resulting in a major North Vietnamese psychological victory that affected the war's outcome.

ABOVE LEFT: M18 smoke grenade, violet (also available in red, yellow, and green).

ABOVE RIGHT: An M26 fragmentation grenade or M26A1 with internal fragmentation serrations. Because of accidental detonations due to the pin being pulled out in heavy underbrush, an additional safety clip, or "jungle clip," was added around the lever on the grenade's M61 variant.

Citation: For conspicuous gallantry and intrepidity in action at the risk of his life above and beyond the call of duty. Staff Sergeant Bacon distinguished himself while serving as a squad leader with the 1st Platoon, Company B, during an operation west of Tam Ky. When Company B came under fire from an enemy bunker line to the front, Bacon quickly organized his men and led them forward in an assault. He advanced on a hostile bunker and destroyed it with grenades. As he did so, several fellow soldiers including the 1st Platoon leader, were struck by machine gun fire and fell wounded in an exposed position forward of the rest of the platoon. Bacon immediately assumed command of the platoon and assaulted the hostile gun position, finally killing the enemy gun crew in a single-handed effort. When the 3d Platoon moved to Bacon's location, its leader was also wounded. Without hesitation Bacon took charge of the additional platoon and continued the fight. In the ensuing action he personally killed four more enemy soldiers and silenced an antitank weapon. Under his leadership and example, the members of both platoons accepted his authority without question. Continuing to ignore the intense hostile fire, he climbed up on the exposed deck of a tank and directed fire into the enemy position while several wounded men were evacuated. As a result of Bacon's extraordinary efforts, his company was able to move forward, eliminate the enemy positions, and rescue the men trapped to the front. Bacon's bravery at the risk of his life was in the highest traditions of the military service and reflects great credit upon himself, his unit, and the U.S. Army.

RIGHT AND OPPOSITE: U.S. advisors attached to ARVN units were authorized to wear their Vietnamese units' camouflage uniforms with U.S. insignia, and soon all SF troops were also permitted to wear them as well. Early on, the older "lizard pattern" French uniforms (*right*) and a French pattern (*opposite center*) similar to the American 1948 ERDL four-color camouflage were available in both Vietnamese and Western sizes. However, the expanding number of ARVN tiger-stripe patterns (*opposite bottom and page 400*) kept Saigon tailors busy making fatigues for the Americans. Varieties of woodland (*opposite right*) and dapple patterns also existed but were far less common—and popular—than the tiger-stripes which the 5th Special Forces Group contracted Vietnamese firms to manufacture starting in 1969. A year earlier, reconnaissance units and advisory personnel were authorized to receive the new ERDL-pattern jungle fatigues, and additional stocks were made available to other special units as they became available. The uniforms pictured at right all belonged to U.S. advisors serving with the Vietnamese Airborne Division.

ABOVE: A parachutists jump smock (former French Army) used by a Colonel Dickson when attached to the Vietnamese Airborne Division. The mixed insignia include an ARVN jump badge over the right pocket, the division shoulder patch, U.S. colonel's eagles, name, Combat Infantry Badge, Master Parachutist Badge, and "US ARMY" embroidered in black. The gold bar and three white cherry blossoms is the rank insignia of an ARVN colonel.

LEFT: The tropical combat uniform coat worn by General Westmoreland in Vietnam. Climate and terrain conditions in Vietnam necessitated that the army design combat clothing that sustained a reasonable degree of comfort and utility in spite of the country's high temperature and humidity. The tropical combat uniform approved in 1963 was based on the paratrooper jumper of World War II and consisted of loose-fitting 5.5-ounce cotton poplin coat and trousers with large pockets. The design was constantly evaluated. Perhaps the most visible modifications were a 1965 change to pocket flaps extending over the coat's pocket buttons in order to prevent snagging, and the limited distribution of the uniform with the ERDL camouflage pattern—a design that would later serve as the basis of the army's widely used "woodland" pattern.

ABOVE: A former French Army jacket used by Captain Peter J. Long Jr. when attached to the Vietnamese Airborne Division. The mixed insignia include an ARVN jump badge over the right pocket, plus winged sword airborne insignia on left pocket, the division shoulder patch, U.S. Infantry and captain's insignias on collars, name, Combat Infantry Badge, and Senior Parachutist Badge. The three cherry blossoms sans bar is the rank insignia of an ARVN captain.

ABOVE: An ARVN paratroopers coat used by Major Robert Hattler when attached to the Vietnamese Airborne Division. The mixed insignia include an ARVN jump badge over the right pocket, plus winged sword airborne insignia on left pocket, the division shoulder patch, U.S. Armor and major's insignias on collars, name, and Parachutist Badge. The black bar and one cherry blossom is the rank insignia of an ARVN major.

BELOW: A Special Forces soldier and Vietnamese troops fighting in the Central Highlands during the NVA's two-month monsoon offensive to roll up the border outposts near Laos in 1969. Moments after this June 18 photo was taken the SF trooper was hit.

RIGHT: 1st Cavalry Division private Ronald Benner loads up on ammunition for his M60 machine gun prior to moving out on patrol in Vietnam's National Forest Reserve, south of Quang Tri during Operation Jeb Stuart III, August 14–15, 1968. Private Benner is a member of Company A, 1st Battalion, 12th Cavalry, in the division's 1st Brigade.

OPPOSITE TOP: A Huey brings additional 1st Cavalry Division troops to Landing Zone Cecile during Operation Delaware in the A Shau Valley west of Hue and along the border with Laos on April 25, 1968. The men are members of the division's Company B, 2d Battalion, 8th Cavalry.

FIGHTING BACK AND VIETNAMIZATION

A countrywide effort began to restore government control of territory lost during the Tet Offensive. A second Communist offensive on August 17–18 (sometimes called the "Mini-Tet") was feeble in comparison and quickly overwhelmed by Allied forces. After careful preparation, the South Vietnamese government—with extensive American support—launched an "accelerated pacification program" in the fall of 1968. In these intensified operations, friendly units first secured a target area, then Vietnamese government units, regional forces/popular forces, and police and civil authorities screened the inhabitants, seeking members of the Viet Cong infrastructure. This technique was so successful against the political apparatus that it became the basis for subsequent operations. Government influence expanded so well into areas of the countryside previously dominated by the Viet Cong that, two years later, some measure of government control was evident in all but a few remote regions.

Meanwhile, Special Forces began the slow process of turning its CIDG camps over to the Vietnamese Army. This was part of President Richard M. Nixon's "Vietnamization" policy, which was designed to enhance the South Vietnamese military to such a degree that they eventually would be able to prosecute the war with little reliance on American ground units. By now, the threat from the

Viet Cong's revolutionary cadres was steadily diminishing, thanks to a highly successful effort to keep the insurgents from rebuilding their ranks after the terrible losses they suffered during the Tet Offensive. The well-trained CIDG tribesmen were given the option of either reverting to civilian life or becoming members of the army of the Republic of Vietnam, and more than fourteen thousand stayed on to form light-infantry Ranger battalions.

Building up the strength of the South Vietnamese armed forces and re-equipping it with modern weapons would, by necessity, be a gradual process. U.S. efforts now centered on buying time for the Vietnamization to develop. Although the new MACV commander General Creighton W. Abrams favored small-scale operations aimed principally

XM-21 SNIPER RIFLE

Soldiers and marines began using scoped M14s as sniper rifles almost as soon as they made their appearance in Vietnam. The weapon was standardized as the XM-21 sniper rifle in 1969 and came with a Redfield 3x9-power daylight scope sight and the then-state-of-the-art automatic ranging telescope (ART) mount, Sionics silencer, and an ANPVS-2 night vision device. Skilled trigger-pullers regularly achieved pinpoint accuracy on two-round shoots at 750 yards and single rounds out to as much as 930 yards (theoretically, the optics would allow such shots to 985 yards). After the war, the weapon was issued as the M21 with a fiberglass stock and served as the army's standard sniper rifle until 1988. It continues on in highly accurized form as a special purpose weapon by the 1st Special Forces Operational Detachment, Delta, and other units. To fill the continuing need for a light sniper rifle, a joint Special Forces–Navy SEALs project adopted a further upgraded version of the weapon developed by the 10th Special Forces Group as the M25 Sniper Weapon System.

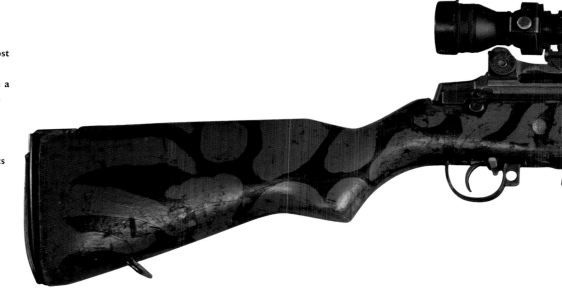

FUTURE LEADERS

Gordon R. Sullivan

Deployed to Vietnam in 1962, serving as an ARVN adviser and then as MACV Intelligence assistant chief of staff in 1963–1964, then returned as a staff officer in Headquarters, I Field Force, during 1969–1970.

Post Vietnam: Served as Assistant Commandant of the Armor School and Deputy Commandant at the Command and General Staff College. Commanded the 3d Armored Division's 1st Brigade, the 1st Infantry Division then served as Army Chief of Staff in 1991–1995.

Colin L. Powell

Deployed to Vietnam in 1962, serving as an ARVN adviser when he was wounded in action. He returned to Vietnam in 1968, serving as the American Division's assistant chief of staff for operations.

Post Vietnam: Powell served in Korea and as the senior military assistant to Secretary of Defense Caspar Weinberger. In 1986 he took command of V Corps in Germany and was selected as the Chairman of the Joint Chiefs of Staff in 1993.

Carl E. "The Godfather" Vuono

Served as an artillery battalion executive officer with the 1st Infantry Division in 1966–1967 and returned in 1970–1971 as Division Artillery executive officer of 1st Cavalry Division, then commander, 1st Battalion, 77th Artillery.

Post Vietnam: Served in Korea and Europe, appointed in 1986 to head the Training and Doctrine Command, then to Army Chief of Staff in 1987–1991, where he lead the force during operations Just Cause, Desert Shield, and Desert Storm.

H. Norman "Stormin' Norman" Schwarzkopf Jr.

Deployed to Vietnam in 1965 as a task force adviser to the South Vietnamese Airborne Division, and returned in 1969 to command the 1st Battalion, 6th Infantry, in the American Division, where he was twice wounded.

Post Vietnam: Commanded the 9th Infantry Division's 1st Brigade, the 24th Infantry Division (Mechanized), I Corps, and the U.S. Central Command (including all Coalition forces) during operations Desert Shield and Desert Storm in 1990–1991.

William E. Depuy

Deployed to Vietnam in 1964, serving as Chief of Staff of Operations for Military Assistance Command, Vietnam, and then Commanding General of the 1st Infantry Division, in 1966.

Post Vietnam: As the commander of the Training and Doctrine Command in 1973, he created the mechanisms to restore the army's self-image as a force trained and configured for continental warfare. Depuy virtually rewrote the army's field manual and prompted a rethinking on how to conduct battles.

General Roscoe Robinson Jr.

In 1965 Robinson led the 2d Battalion, 7th Cavalry, 1st Cavalry Division, during the Ia Drang Valley fighting in 1965, then served on the division staff, receiving the Distinguished Flying Cross, eleven Air Medals, and two Silver Stars.

Post Vietnam: Commanding General of the 82d Airborne Division, Deputy Chief of Staff for Operations for U.S. Army Europe, Commander of U.S. Army Japan and IX Corps, and U.S. Representative to NATO Military Committee.

Frederick M. Franks

Deployed to Vietnam in 1969, serving as the 2nd Squadron, 11th Armored Cavalry Regiment operations officer until critically wounded during the invasion of Cambodia in May 1970.

Post Vietnam: Served as Deputy Commandant at the Command and General Staff College in 1985–1987, commanded the 1st Armored Division in Germany in 1988–1989, VII Corps during operations Desert Shield and Desert Storm in 1990–1991, and then the Training and Doctrine Command from 1991–1994.

Maxwell R. "Mad Max" Thurman

Served from 1961–1963 as an Intelligence Officer for the ARVN's I Corps. He returned in 1968–1969 as commander of the 2d Battalion, 35th Field Artillery, coming aboard in time for the Tet Offensive.

Post Vietnam: When in charge of army recruiting in 1979, he instituted the highly successful "Be All You Can Be" recruiting campaign. As Commander-in-Chief, U.S. Southern Command he planned and executed the 1989 invasion of Panama.

BELOW: A column of Vietnamese Airborne Division troops, including U.S. advisor Major Norman Schwarzkopf, march past an ARVN M41 Walker "Bulldog" light tank and on to Pleiku after clearing Highway 19 from Duc Co of Viet Cong forces. The Vietnamese joined up with American forces the day before, August 17, 1965, after having relieved the weeklong siege of the Duc Co Special Forces Camp.

Citation: For conspicuous gallantry and intrepidity in action at the risk of his life above and beyond the call of duty. First Lieutenant Howard (then Sergeant First Class), distinguished himself while serving as platoon sergeant of an American-Vietnamese platoon which was on a mission to rescue a missing American soldier in enemy controlled territory in the Republic of Vietnam. The platoon had left its helicopter landing zone and was moving out on its mission when it was attacked by an estimated two-company force. During the initial engagement, Howard was wounded and his weapon destroyed by a grenade explosion. Howard saw his platoon leader had been wounded seriously and was exposed to fire. Although unable to walk, and weaponless, Howard unhesitatingly crawled through a hail of fire to retrieve his wounded leader. As Howard was administering first aid and removing the officer's equipment, an enemy bullet struck one of the ammunition pouches on the lieutenant's belt, detonating several magazines of ammunition. Howard momentarily sought cover and then realizing that he must rejoin the platoon, which had been disorganized by the enemy attack, he again began dragging the seriously wounded officer toward the platoon area. Through his outstanding example of indomitable courage and bravery, Howard was able to rally the platoon into an organized defense force. With complete disregard for his safety, Howard crawled from position to position, administering first aid to the wounded, giving encouragement to the defenders and directing their fire on the encircling enemy. For more than three hours Howard's small force and supporting aircraft successfully repulsed enemy attacks and finally were in sufficient control to permit the landing of rescue helicopters. Howard personally supervised the loading of his men and did not leave the bullet-swept landing zone until all were aboard safely. First Lieutenant Howard's gallantry in action, his complete devotion to the welfare of his men at the risk of his life were in keeping with the highest traditions of the military service and reflect great credit on himself, his unit, and the U.S. Army.

at NVA–VC logistics—starving the Communist forces of badly needed supplies instead of performing the grand search-and-destroy missions of the mid-1960s—aggressive operations still proved to be necessary. Even though U.S. troop strength continued climbing (it would reach a peak of 543,400 personnel in April 1969), plans were in the works to begin a steady drawdown. From November 1968 through February of the following year, forty-seven ground combat operations were conducted, virtually all of which were designed in some way to support the accelerated pacification program of the South Vietnamese.

The continual pressure on the Communists during this period thwarted their attempt to restage another Tet in 1969, and great success was made in disrupting enemy infiltration of materials from the Parrots Beak area of Cambodia, which jutted into South Vietnam dangerously close to Saigon. Heavy enemy losses occurred throughout the country as sustained operations forced the continual movement of NVA units that were trying to avoid Allied forces or to search for food and supplies. Consequently, enemy-initiated ground attacks decreased markedly, and those that did occur, such as a widespread series of attacks in late February, were easily rebuffed. During the summer and fall of 1969, operations were increasingly turned over to Vietnamese. Nixon reaffirmed America's support for the Republic of South Vietnam while announcing the reduction of the U.S. military presence with the first withdrawal of twenty-five thousand troops by August 31, 1969.

BELOW: Officially an army "beret, man's wool," this "Green Beret" is identified to Sergeant Richard A. Thomas of the 5th Special Forces Group who was killed in action on January 9, 1970, in Cambodia while serving with the Special Operations Augmentation, Command and Control South. Several months later, U.S. and ARVN ground forces entered Cambodia in a campaign aimed at destroying the extensive NVA base areas located there.

ABOVE: The foldable, full-brimmed tropical—or "boonie"—hat authorized in 1967 was extremely popular with the troops because of its practicality, and thoroughly detested by MACV commander General Creighton Abrams because of its "slovenly" and "unmilitary" appearance. Efforts by Abrams over a period of several years to quash its use were unsuccessful and even met with firm "push back" from senior officers in field units. This example is one of the countless Vietnamese-produced models and lacks the band for holding local foliage for camouflage that came with the American-made hats. Its owner, D. Martin, decorated his headgear with a YMCA button and another from the rock band "Big Brother and the Holding Company." A "Burn Pot Not People" button is affixed to the inside.

BUYING TIME: LAOS AND CAMBODIA

The number of Communist attacks continued to fall, particularly in heavily populated areas, and their strongest efforts were launched in the Central Highlands against strategically located CIDG camps near the Laotian border. The NVA also conducted numerous bombardments on U.S. fire support artillery bases with their own long-range artillery in "neutral" Laos, and they also staged direct assaults on these positions. Allied forces concentrated on finding and destroying NVA and VC units, penetrating enemy "base camp" staging areas and installations along the border regions, and seizing enemy supplies and matériel. These operations sought to deny the enemy the initiative and to inflict heavy losses in men and equipment.

Meanwhile, enough progress was achieved in Vietnamization by improving the Republic of Vietnam's armed forces that the U.S. 1st Infantry Division and several major Marine units were withdrawn from Vietnam. The NVA made several efforts to take the offensive against the Dak Seang and Quang Duc CIDG camps, but the sieges were broken by ARVN forces acting with little U.S. support. The South Vietnamese also launched an April 1970 offensive in a bold, three-day operation in the Angel's Wing area along the Cambodian border. They completed this mission in an aggressive, professional manner without any reliance on American ground units.

The emergence of an anti-Communist government in Cambodia now prompted a relaxation in the restrictions on

BELOW: The M1952 body armor was developed out of the experience of World War II and Korea, where most casualties were the result of fragmentation wounds. Although completely inadequate against the new high-velocity rounds, they nevertheless saved many lives, particularly among helicopter crews. Although Infantry very rarely wore body armor because its weight quickly fatigued men in the sweltering climate, it would frequently be seen on any soldier that didn't have to do much walking such as truck drivers, mechanized troops, and the aforementioned helo crews.

BELOW: A helicopter crew dives for cover under the insubstantial protection provided by their Huey as NVA rocket fire perks up before an assault on the besieged Bu Prang Special Forces camp, November 24, 1969. Bu Prang came under siege during the last months of the year, and the battle spilled over to the Duc Lap camp and saw the loss of several nearby firebases. Major fights occurred at four Special Forces camps during this period, but despite the NVA's use of tanks, none fell, thanks largely to U.S. airpower.

RIGHT: An ARVN soldier leaps into a roadside ditch as an ammunition truck struck by guerrilla-fired mortar rounds explodes behind him. One government soldier was killed and two wounded in the August 25, 1972, action near Cai Lay, some forty-five miles southwest of Saigon.

ABOVE: An M72 light anti-tank weapon (LAW), c. 1970. Introduced in 1963, the LAW was a disposable anti-armor shoulder-fired rocket that was capable of penetrating up to twelve-inch plate steel. In April 1972, LAW-armed ARVN soldiers wiped out a column of Soviet-made T54/55 tanks that had attacked across the Cambodian border. Unprotected by NVA infantry as they moved through the streets of An Loc, the armored unit was easy prey for teams of tank-hunting South Vietnamese. Although retained in the inventory and optimized for blast effect (instead of penetration) for use by special units, the M72 was largely a forgotten weapon for the next three decades until troops in Iraq discovered its value at blowing through walls. Soldiers in Afghanistan found the eight-pound weight of the improved M72A7 perfect for extended mountain patrols and that it provided accurate, lethal suppressive fire.

moving against the long-established logistical bases inside Cambodia. When NVA forces began to move against the Cambodian capital of Phnom Penh, the new government appealed to the United States and South Vietnam for help. This prompted South Vietnamese assistance near the capital, plus eight major cross-border operations by U.S. and ARVN forces in May and June 1970 against the sanctuary areas dangerously close to Saigon. Through these, Abrams intended to cut enemy communication lines and seize the sanctuary areas. He also hoped to capture, if possible, the shadowy Central Office for South Vietnam, which directed Communist military and political activities in the Saigon area and the wide swath of South Vietnam generally corresponding with the III Corps and IV Corps Tactical Zones.

Though limited to shallow penetrations no more than eighteen miles deep, the 1st Cavalry Division and 11th Armored Cavalry Regiment, supported by elements of the U.S. 4th, 5th, 9th, 25th, and 101st Airborne divisions and roughly twenty ARVN battalions, seized stunning quantities of war materials, food, and communications equipment, plus multiple base facilities that included truck repair shops, hospitals, a lumber yard, eighteen mess halls, and even a swimming pool. North Vietnamese officials later admitted that the lengthy, multidivision operation

and continuing South Vietnamese efforts in Cambodia effectively forestalled a huge, planned assault on the Saigon area, setting back Hanoi's timetable by more than a year. Indeed, the fighting throughout the entire country fell off sharply in 1970 as special ARVN counterinsurgency teams continued to roll up the Communist political cadres.

The following year, South Vietnamese forces conducted a spoiling attack, Lam Son 719, against the NVA's long-established logistical system in southern Laos which had been built up around the Ho Chi Minh Trail. The main supply route extending through southern Laos had by now grown to include a complex series of branches into three of Vietnam's northwest provinces. The objective of the four-phase offensive—which was launched out of I Corps Tactical Zone by Vietnamese troops with American artillery and air support—was to cut the Trail and to destroy enemy bases at Tchepone, Laos.

In Phase I, called Operation Dewey Canyon II, the U.S. 5th Infantry Division's 1st Brigade occupied the Khe Sanh area and cleared Route No. 9 up to the border during the first week of February 1971. Simultaneously, the 101st Airborne Division conducted diversionary operations in the A Shau Valley that, like Khe Sanh, had been the scene of a furious battle early in 1968. In Phase II, American forces continued to provide fire support, helicopter, and air support for ARVN units during the rest of the month. Phase III ran through March 16, 1971, and was followed by Phase IV: the withdrawal. Stiff NVA resistance and mounting losses forced the early termination of Lam Son 719. Although ARVN had not performed well, the operation nevertheless forestalled the Communists' planned spring offensive.

CONSOLIDATION AND EXIT

ARVN forces assumed full defensive control of the area immediately below the DMZ in July, and American battle deaths for that month were sixty-six, the lowest monthly figure since May 1967. The United States relinquished all ground combat responsibilities to the Republic of Vietnam on August 11, 1971, although U.S. maneuver battalions were still conducting missions in conjunction with ARVN units. The last major combat operation in Vietnam involving American troops—the 101st Airborne Division—took place in Thua Thien Province in October 1971. Following the close of Operation Jefferson Glen, the 101st began stand-down procedures and was the last U.S. division to leave Vietnam.

Early November saw U.S. troop totals drop to one-hundred ninety-one thousand, the lowest level since December 1965. That same month Nixon announced that American forces had reverted to a defensive role in Vietnam. By year's end, the American military presence had decreased to one-hundred fifty-seven thousand. By the following December, it was just twenty-four thousand. In the intervening year, however, army advisers played a key role in defeating the NVA's 1972 Easter offensive, an all-out conventional attack that laid Communist forces open to a series of massive U.S. air strikes.

The Paris Peace Accords of 1973, ostensibly ending the war and American involvement in Vietnam, were signed on January 27, 1973. Saigon, and, with it, the government of South Vietnam, fell in April 1975 after ARVN forces were finally overwhelmed by an armor-heavy North Vietnamese invasion launched in 1975.

COLT MODEL 629 COMMANDO

The Colt Model 629 Commando, or CAR-15, assault rifle was nearly ten inches shorter than the M16. The weapon was purchased in quantity for Special Forces troops involved in strategic reconnaissance missions, but never approved for general use by the army. Nevertheless, the CAR-15 made its way into the hands of many "conventional" soldiers like this 1st Infantry Division point man at right, near Tan Hiep, who, lacking web gear, could travel much more lightly than the other 1st Division infantrymen in the picture. The point man has also dyed his jungle fatigues black so that at a distance it will resemble Vietnamese peasant garb.

Chapter Twelve
The Volunteer Army, Panama, and the Persian Gulf, 1972–1991

The Vietnam War was the last great conflict to see hundreds of thousands of young American conscripts sent halfway around the world to an alien land. Despite this, however, the popular image of the draftee army during the 1960s is less true than it seems. Of the 2,594,000 personnel who served within the Republic of Vietnam's (South Vietnam's) borders, fewer than 25 percent were draftees; a figure far below the 66 percent of World War II. In all, some 3,403,100 Americans served in the Southeast Asia theater of operations, from the air bases and intelligence facilities in Thailand to the Seventh Fleet ships on "Yankee Station" in the South China Sea, between 1965 and 1975.

Much of the raw data from the war is not surprising, such as 10 percent of the 47,400 combat and 10,800 noncombat deaths in Vietnam coming from helicopter crews. Other data defies the common media myths or is, at least, counterintuitive. For example, 23 percent of the soldiers in Vietnam came from "privileged" families where the fathers held professional, managerial, or technical occupations. Of the men who actually served in Vietnam, 88.4 percent were Caucasian, 1 percent "other," and 10.6 percent African American—even though black Americans of military age were 13.5 percent of the population. Black soldiers, nevertheless, represented 12.1 percent of those killed in action because of their higher representation in infantry units. It also turns out that 79 percent of the service-men sent to Vietnam had completed high school or some college—16 percent more than those who fought in Korea.

The army of the early 1970s was undeniably at a low ebb of morale and discipline, and its military effectiveness suffered accordingly. Complicating matters was the fact that the draft—in place almost continuously for more than three decades—would end on July 1, 1973. Large numbers of young men had volunteered for service even as public support for the war in Vietnam fell, but army studies indicated that by the later war years roughly half of them were joining in order to avoid being arbitrarily placed in infantry units. With no draft—or the threat of a draft—many army leaders wondered aloud how its ranks could be filled and the nation's obligations met. The army, which had never put much thought or effort into recruiting soldiers because of the guaranties that the draft provided, now had to come to grips with manning an all-volunteer force.

As early as 1967, President Nixon had proposed an end to the draft. Immediately after his inauguration as president in January 1969, he ordered the Defense Department to create an all-volunteer force. A commission, which included economists Milton Friedman and Alan Greenspan, was formed under Thomas S. Gates Jr., a former secretary of defense in the Eisenhower administration, to examine how adequate military strength could be maintained without the crutch of national conscription.

IF YOU'RE GOOD ENOUGH

JOIN THE NEW U S A Action ARMY

A PROUD FUTURE CAN BE YOURS

ABOVE: A metal, double-sided, 25-inch by 38-inch "New Action Army" sign produced for use outside recruiting offices, dated August 1965.

OPPOSITE: A 10th Mountain Division (Light Infantry) soldier practicing squad battle drills at Fort Drum, New York, in 1989. Like the other three divisions that were reactivated or redesignated as light divisions in the mid-1980s (the 6th, 7th, and 25th), the 10th Mountain had a greatly reduced complement of vehicles, artillery, and support elements in order to make it more quickly deployable. Said one wide-eyed, young "7th Light" captain to this author after his division had been stripped of much of its firepower and equipment: "They've got us down to shields and spears!"

The idea was strongly opposed by most senior military leaders and influential members of Congress, plus Nixon's own national security advisor, Henry Kissinger, and Secretary of Defense Melvin Laird. Illinois Congressman Donald Rumsfeld enthusiastically introduced legislation supporting the proposal, and Senate and House hearings were held on the bill. It was not successfully pressed, though, until after Nixon's landslide reelection in 1972 and the many key obstacles to its effective implementation had been thrashed out.

Even though the army needed far fewer men due to the post-Vietnam downsizing that reduced the force from 1,124,000 in 1971 to 781,000 by 1974 (the Nixon Administration had already managed substantial reductions from its mid-war peak of 1,570,000), the number of volunteers still fell short during the first year after the draft was eliminated. Yet with more funding for army recruitment, a general increase in pay approved by Congress, plus enlistment bonuses for a wide

LEFT: The steady and pronounced buildup of Soviet and Warsaw Pact armored divisions in Eastern Europe while Americans were fighting in Vietnam forced an increased U.S. reliance on nuclear deterrence to bolster the 180,000-man Seventh Army in West Germany. A U.S. soldier in West Germany prepares to attach a tail fin to a Lance short-range ballistic missile.

BELOW: Artillerymen are put through their paces during a test firing of eight Pershing IA missiles in September 1972. The medium range ballistic missile was highly mobile and capable of striking targets as far as four hundred miles from launch.

range of specialist categories, yearly quotas were easily met from that point forward. A misplaced (and unevenly applied) effort to entice more young men to join up by loosening "grooming standards" and discipline was jettisoned in favor of a less permissive atmosphere—plus more and better training—which instilled in the soldiers a stronger sense of professionalism and encouraged the building of greater individual and unit pride. The civilianization of "Mickey Mouse" details, such as grounds maintenance and the infamous KP duty, also improved morale and freed up more time for military training.

A NEW DOCTRINE AND FOCUS ON EUROPE

Throughout the Vietnam War, NATO members had expressed, both privately and publicly, their dissatisfaction at the perceived lack of attention that the United States was giving to their defense. No fewer than five new Soviet armored divisions had been added to their forces in Eastern Europe, and many existing formations had been repositioned closer to West Germany. The Soviets were also engaged in a rapid modernization of the complete range of weapons systems, from Frog-7 artillery rockets to the new T-64 main battle tank (which was supplied exclusively to elite Soviet forces in East Germany). Their T-72 steadily replaced older-model tanks and were even distributed on a limited basis to Communist Warsaw Pact nations facing NATO, as well as client states in the Middle East.

During this period, the U.S. Army was painfully aware of its shortcomings. Although it possessed a fine and easily upgraded main battle tank in the M-60, overall modernization had taken a backseat to the demands of Vietnam. This left the Warsaw Pact's qualitative and numerical superiority plainly visible to friend and foe alike. The October 1973 Yom Kippur War between the Israeli Defense Force and the combined armies of Egypt, Syria, and Iraq further intensified concerns about the state of the army, since more Israeli tanks were destroyed or temporarily put out of commission in the three weeks of intensive fighting than the U.S. forces possessed in all of Europe. Even more disturbing was that roughly half of these losses were inflicted by Egyptian infantry armed with portable antitank guided missiles.

If a war in Europe followed the same pattern—and there was every indication that it could—men and matériel would be consumed at a shocking rate. No longer could largely dispersed American formations count on standing off while nuclear strikes decimated Soviet spearheads; the increasingly lethal conventional weapons allowed even severely mauled enemy units to overwhelm the defenders and win an early victory. It was imperative that the army rethink its tactics in light of the newly revealed lethality of the modern battlefield, and that it devise a way to win any future war quickly. What emerged was the concept of "active defense." This entailed moving the bulk of U.S. and Allied forces right up to the front line with the intent of concentrating their conventional

ABOVE: A shoulder patch of the U.S. Seventh Army in Germany. Though numbering more than 180,000 men, it was a neglected force that was progressively weakened throughout the latter half of the 1960s.

BELOW: Under a sign warning "Halt! This is the Frontier," members of the 2d Armored Cavalry Regiment monitor activity along the inner-German border—and are themselves watched by East German troops in the watchtower beyond the border barricades, c. 1972.

ABOVE: Army Reservists use the newly developed simulation network (SIMNET) to complement the annual Brigade Battle Simulation training at Fort Knox, Kentucky, in 1986. Large-scale maneuvers and live-fire exercises in the heavily urbanized landscape of West Germany came under increasing pressure from the country's environmentalists during the 1980s. This and the need for more efficient training speeded the army's adoption of a wide variety of simulation systems—from the use of low-intensity lasers instead of bullets at the tactical level to electronic battles involving whole armies—that greatly enhanced training even as the new AirLand Battle doctrine was adopted and refined.

firepower at the onset of a Soviet invasion. They wanted to "kill" the maximum possible number of tanks before they could break out into West Germany, and they hoped to force the Warsaw Pact formations behind them to remain "stacked" and vulnerable to NATO airpower.

While certainly a step in the right direction, it was immediately recognized that the change to a "forward defense," no matter how ruthlessly it was carried out, could well push the war to such a speedy—and not necessarily favorable—conclusion that American reinforcements from across the Atlantic would play only a minor role. United States and NATO forces might win an exceedingly costly opening battle in a "come as you are" war, but the Soviets, with their large army, could almost certainly gather additional forces from farther in the rear and launch a second offensive before significant U.S. and NATO reinforcements could arrive.

To help rectify this dangerous situation, the army, supported by the Military Airlift Command, Military Sealift Command, and later the Civil Reserve Air Fleet, increased the size and scope of its annual Reforger (Return of Forces to Germany) exercises, where major elements of U.S.-based combat divisions and support units were shipped to Europe

to take part in NATO maneuvers. An emphasis was also made to speed up and simplify the transatlantic movements by pre-positioning huge stocks of equipment and supplies. This freed more space on the planes and ships for the transportation of troops that would then "marry up" with the waiting implements of war.

Improvements such as these, though important, did not get to the heart of the problem: The best that could be hoped for under the active defense was a stalemate on the ravaged soil of West Germany. Said Lieutenant Colonel (later Brigadier General) Huba Wass de Czege:

> Once political authorities commit military forces in pursuit of political aims, military forces must win something—else there will be no basis from which political authorities can bargain to win politically. Therefore, the purpose of military operations can not be simply to avert defeat—but rather it must be to win.

General Donn Starry of the U.S. Army's Training and Doctrine Command believed that the surest way to victory was to extend the battlefield deep into the Warsaw Pact rear areas in order to thoroughly disrupt—and defeat—any invasion led by the numerically superior Soviets. Starry's initiative spurred considerable study and spirited debate on the need to see deep into the enemy's rear and how best to delay, disrupt, nd destroy enemy second-echelon forces while simultaneously fighting the assaulting forces. By the early 1980s, the comprehensive yet flexible "AirLand Battle" concept had been hammered out and made army doctrine. In 1984 it was accepted as the battle plan for all NATO forces.

AirLand Battle emphasized close coordination between land forces acting as an aggressively maneuvering defense and air forces attacking rear-echelon forces feeding those frontline enemy forces. The battlefield was viewed as having a deeper physical dimension than had previously been considered, and it focused not only on the linear dimension but also the time dimension in combat operations. Once accepted, this war-fighting doctrine became the dominant influence on the modernization of the 1980s that brought the army the principal weapons systems in use today. Although an AirLand battle was never fought with the Soviet Union, these systems have effectively been employed twice against a former client state of the now defunct superpower.

ABOVE: 7th Infantry Division (Light) soldiers supply a base of fire while others maneuver toward an objective during a 1986 exercise.

ABOVE: 25th Infantry Division (Light) snipers peer down range at a potential target during a combined arms, live-fire exercise.

BELOW: 3d Infantry Division armor at the 1984 Reforger exercise experiment with AirLand Battle techniques even though its new, fast—and deadly—M1 Abrams tanks must maneuver with the slower and less capable M113 troop carriers instead of the M2 Bradley Infantry fighting vehicles, which had yet to be delivered.

EAGLE CLAW AND URGENT FURY

Threats to the United States and its interests were not confined to the Soviet armored divisions massed along the German border. Quickly deployable "light divisions"—somewhat smaller, and considerably less heavily armed, than the standard infantry division of the day—were organized for use in short-notice contingencies and limited wars. These formations could be speedily inserted into airfields first seized by airborne elements or Rangers, but they lacked the heft to slug it out with the forces of many Soviet client states (let alone the "ten-foot-tall" Russians) without considerable augmentation. Then there was the plain fact that they were too large and unwieldy for a wide array of threats, which required the finesse of Army Special Forces.

The holding of fifty-two American hostages by Iranian militants after the November 1979 seizure of the U.S. Embassy in Tehran required firm U.S. action. Inspired by a successful Israeli raid at an airport at Entebbe, Uganda, where more than a hundred hostages were freed, the U.S. military planned a rescue operation made far more complex and difficult because of the captives' location. The 1st Ranger Battalion and the counterterrorist unit 1st Special Forces Operational

Detachment, Delta (popularly known as Delta Force) coordinated their roles in the rescue mission with navy, marine, and air force elements, some of which lacked the proper training and equipment for the mission.

Operation Eagle Claw was launched on April 24, 1980, but by the time the rescue helicopters and tanker aircraft reached a secret refueling site halfway to Tehran, dust storms and multiple systems failures had caused so many problems for the marine helos that the mission had to be scrubbed. Tragically, a collision during refueling operations caused an explosion that killed eight personnel and destroyed a helicopter and tanker. The remaining helicopters were also abandoned, and the hostages would not be freed until January 1981. The debacle at the Desert One refuel site led directly to the establishment of U.S. Special Operations Command. The command was to supervise the coordination and training of each services' special operations elements, as well as the formation of 160th Special Operations Aviation Regiment (SOAR), which was specifically equipped for such challenging missions.

With the memory of the lengthy Iranian hostage crisis still fresh in Americans' minds, another foreign threat suddenly seemed to appear out of nowhere. The small Caribbean nation of Grenada boasted a medical school attended by some eight hundred students from the United

BELOW: Airborne artillerymen of Battery C, 319th Field Artillery, fire their M102 105-mm howitzer in support of an attack on the Grenadan troops holding the government radio station on the second day of the invasion, October 26, 1983. The Grenadans attempted to hold the facility, even though it had been rendered inoperative the day before by a Navy Sea Air Land (SEAL) team.

RIGHT: 82d Airborne troopers hitch a ride on a commandeered Cuban dump truck used in the absence of U.S. vehicles. These men are some of the lucky ones, as many had to hoof it with packs that exceeded 100 pounds because of the gear that they were directed to carry. Subsequent examination resulted in reduced loads, which, not unexpectedly, soon began to creep up again.

ABOVE: Shoulder patch of the 82d Airborne Division

LEFT: Army Rangers deploying from the Point Salines area on October 26, 1983, the day after the two battalions of the 75th Infantry Regiment (Ranger) seized Grenada's international airport. A third Ranger battalion was created in 1984 and the formation was redesignated the 75th Ranger Regiment in 1986.

BELOW: A member of the 82d Airborne Division guards stacks of Soviet-made 7.62-mm ammunition seized during Operation Urgent Fury. The Grenadan People's Liberation Army and People's Liberation Militia fielded both obsolescent and current Soviet armored vehicles, 130-mm towed artillery, plus robust antiaircraft defenses that had trained to counter U.S. tactics, and indeed succeeded in shooting down three helos during the initial assaults. In addition to the Cuban Revolutionary Armed Forces engineer battalion and attached construction workers, the nine Grenadan battalions all had Cuban advisers or, in several cases, commanders.

States. The overthrow of a British-style democracy on the island in 1979 by the Communist New Joint Endeavor for Welfare, Education, and Liberation (New Jewel Movement or NJM) at first was not viewed as a direct threat to the students. But a close eye was kept on the new government's expanding ties with the Soviet Union and numerous client states, including Cuba. Increased arms shipments from these countries and the construction of a mammoth ten-thousand-foot runway capable of handling fighter aircraft and jumbo transports aroused suspicion that the effort was part of a Soviet expansion in the Caribbean. It did not escape notice that what was being dubbed an "international airport" meant to encourage a "tourist industry" had no corresponding hotel construction in the works.

A dispute within the NJM led to the ouster of the prime minister by a rival Marxist faction on October 13, 1983. Mass demonstrations and killings followed as the prime minister was freed, recaptured, and executed along with numerous other party leaders, one of whom was pregnant. The even more radical People's Revolutionary Army seized control of the government on October 19 and issued a curfew with shoot-on-sight orders to prevent demonstrations. The breakdown in civil order and the murders were observed with alarm in Washington and neighboring Caribbean nations. President Ronald Reagan soon issued orders to secure and evacuate the American students and remove "the brutal group of Leftist thugs." Operation Urgent Fury was hastily thrown together. The following week,

LEFT: A close-up of the contents inside one of the innocuous, rope-handled wooden boxes labeled "*Oficina Economica Cubana*" ("Cuban Economics Office")—7.62-mm rounds manufactured in the Soviet Union.

on October 25, 75th Infantry Regiment (Ranger) and the 82d Airborne Division, as well as marines and both army and navy special operations forces, seized key locations on the island in the first major U.S. combat operation in more than a decade.

Though successful, Urgent Fury revealed many problems that would have to be addressed such as better coordination and interoperability between the armed services in the areas of communications and command and control. Soldiers from numerous Caribbean nations also served as useful liaisons between U.S. forces and Grenada citizens, and the country soon was able to return to a representative form of government. Eighteen U.S. soldiers, sailors, and marines were killed in action during the operation, but all of the students got out with nary a casualty. The safe return of the medical students deeply affected Reagan, who later wrote:

I was among many in our country whose eyes got a little misty when I watched their arrival in the United States on television and saw some of them lean down and kiss American soil the moment that they stepped off the airplanes that brought them home. When some of the students later came to the White House and embraced the soldiers who had rescued them, it was quite a sight for a former governor who had once seen college students spit on anyone wearing a military uniform.

LEFT: Some of the eight hundred medical students rescued as Grenada's government was seized by a succession of ever more radical factions, pose with an equally young para-trooper at Point Salines, on October 25, 1983.

LEFT: A soldier attaches hoisting straps and chains to a Cuban (Czechoslovakian-made) M-53 quad 12.7-mm antiaircraft machine gun seized at Point Salines airport. Despite complete U.S. air superiority, Grenadan antiaircraft defenses downed three helicopters.

ABOVE: General Maxwell Thurman observing a live-fire exercise at the National Training Center, Fort Irwin, California. The appointment of "Mad Max" Thurman to lead the U.S. Southern Command greatly accelerated planning for the upcoming invasion of Panama. Said a colleague: "He is mobilized when he gets up in the morning, which is in the middle of the night."

RIGHT: As part of the largest combat jump since World War II, soldiers of the 82d Airborne Division's 1st Battalion, 509th Infantry, parachute into a drop zone outside Panama City to set up blocking positions and prevent Panama Defense Force elements from entering the capital.

OUSTING NORIEGA AND DEFEATING THE DIGBATS

Relations had for years been rocky between the United States and Panamanian strongman General Manuel Noriega. Corruption in the government became widespread, and eventually Noriega threatened the security of the United States by cooperating with Colombian drug producers. Still, it wasn't until the steep rise in political unrest and a stolen Panamanian presidential election in May 1989 that events came to a head. Noriega's attempt to rig the ballots failed; his candidate lost badly. Rather than allow the results to be released, however, he declared them void because of "foreign interference," prompting former U.S. President Jimmy Carter, in Panama as an official observer, to declare that the election had been stolen. Noriega named his own man as president. The United States imposed economic sanctions, and a tense, months-long standoff ensued between the U.S. Army, tasked with safeguarding the Panama Canal, and the forces aligned with Noriega. Although he was the head of the Panamanian Defense Force (PDF), Noriega's faltering control over the organization had caused him to create Dignity Battalions (DIGBATs), essentially street-thug militia units, as a surer way to enforce his will.

The DIGBATs and PDF elements loyal to the "maximum leader" stepped up their harassment of U.S. military personnel, American civilians, and Panamanians opposed to the dictator. Leaders of the opposition were viciously assaulted in the streets in full view of the news media, and a U.S. Marine was fatally shot when "resisting arrest." The Panama-based—and heavily augmented—193d Infantry Brigade began conducting regular "freedom of movement" maneuvers between sections of the old American-administered Canal Zone, but while the army contended that these exercises were justified by the Panama Canal, or Torrijos-Carter, Treaty of 1980—which guaranteed the U.S. forces freedom of movement in the country in defense of the canal—the legislature, dominated by Panama loyalists, considered them acts of "American aggression." On December 15, 1989, they declared that a state of war existed with the United States.

Although Noriega later claimed that this statement referred to American actions and did not represent a declaration of hostilities by Panama, measures subsequently adopted to confront the movements belied this. Two days later, U.S. President George H.W. Bush authorized Operation Just Cause, a 26,000-man assault under the U.S. Southern Command to commence at 1:00 A.M. on Wednesday, December 20. The 75th Ranger Regiment and 82d Airborne Division were called upon

BELOW: A Black Hawk gunner keeps an eye out for trouble during one of the "freedom of movement" exercises conducted in Panama City during the summer of 1989.

ABOVE: A 193d Infantry Brigade M113 armored personnel carrier controls movement along a street near the destroyed Panamanian Defense Force headquarters building during the second day of Operation Just Cause, December 21, 1989.

RIGHT: Members of a 7th Infantry Division patrol keep alert during a break.

OPPOSITE: Rangers attached to the 193d Infantry Brigade searching for snipers near the Comandancia.

again to lead the way (for the 82d, their first combat jump since World War II). They were divided into four task forces: Pacific, Bayonet, Atlantic, and Semper Fi.

Contingency planning for the invasion and removal of Noriega had been studied since 1987, and Panama-based units had been training for it for several months as part of the "freedom of movement" exercises. Planners knew the operation had to be carried out at great speed, and it was to be preceded by special operations missions, such as the Task Force Pacific insertion of a Special Forces team onto the Pacora River Bridge east of Panama City. Arriving at fifteen minutes before H-Hour, Special Forces took up positions just as a large convoy of PDF vehicles was seen coming their way. Assisted by an AC-130H Spectre gunship, the team prevented the convoy from crossing the bridge. Task Force Pacific also had responsibility for seizing Omar Torrijos International Airport and the adjacent Tocumen military airfield to prevent Noriega from using them to flee the country. This mission fell to four Ranger companies that were quickly joined by three battalions of the 82d Airborne Division.

Multiple missions supported by tanks, Spectre gunships, and artillery operating in the direct-fire mode were carried

out nearly simultaneously across the country. In addition to the PDF's La Comandancia headquarters in the heart of Panama City, other military bases and key infrastructure were secured, sometimes with considerable fighting. Fort Escobar, for example, was seized by a battalion from the 7th Infantry Division (Light)'s 17th Infantry, and its large PDF base fell to the Rangers. At Fort Cimarron, stubborn resistance (and a decision to not inflict too many casualties on the PDF hold-outs) delayed its capture by the 82d's 325th Infantry until after midnight on December 21. A Delta-160th SOAR team pulled off a dangerous rescue of an American CIA agent, who was being held at a prison adjacent to the La Comandancia, during an attack on the headquarters by Spectre gunships and elements of the 5th Infantry Division. Noriega, who had taken refuge in the Vatican Embassy, surrendered on January 3, 1990, and was later convicted on eight counts of racketeering, drug trafficking, and money laundering. Meanwhile, the U.S. Army in Panama quickly shifted from a military to peacekeeping operation and, after a decidedly rocky start, was able to help the Panamanians return to prosperity and allow a normal political process to resume without fear of reprisals.

A vague Army Public Affairs release on Operation Just Cause stated simply that all units from the "special operations command participated" in the invasion, but the rescue of an American businessman held in Panama's notorious Modelo Prison nevertheless became the most widely known "Delta Force" operation since the disaster at Desert I in Iran.

Kurt Muse was a resident of Panama and, in concert with fellow Panamanian businessmen, had been part of a self-started psychological operations mission against Panama's strongman, Manuel Noriega. The group had gotten together after Noriega's goons had burned a print shop owned by Muse and murdered a good friend. Dubbed the "Rotarians from Hell" by *Soldier of Fortune* magazine, the businessmen caused Noriega a great deal of trouble by operating a clandestine radio station that filled the air waves with exhortations to vote him out of office: "Together we can bury General Noriega's dictatorship under a mountain of ballots!" In some instances, the conspirators reported misleading or confusing instructions to the PDF on military radio frequencies.

Muse, who'd earlier served in the U.S. Army, joining through the ROTC, was able to keep his activities secret for many months before being turned in by the wife of a former co-conspirator. He was arrested upon his return to Panama from a routine trip to Miami and jailed at Modelo, located a stone's throw from General Noriega's Comandancia command post/headquarters turned fortress.

ABOVE: *The battered Comandancia across from Muse's prison cell. The close patterns of hits from the orbiting AC-130 gunships is testament to the accuracy of their targeting and weapons systems.*

RIGHT: *The MH-6 Little Bird that lifted Kurt Muse to freedom is moved out of the street by mechanized troops after they secured the area around General Manuel Noriega's headquarters. Note the three-man troop seats along each side and the large crane-like appendage for fast-roping from the chopper. It folds forward against the side of the bird when not in use and, in this early configuration, inadvertently prevented troopers from easily exiting the interior from the starboard side. A fire-support MH-6 was also shot down, crashing inside the Comandancia compound across the street. Fearing friendly fire from the AC-130s as much as the PDF, the crew made their escape by throwing their flack vests on top of the barbed wire fence, climbing over, and quickly getting away.*

In the early morning hours of December 19, 1989, Muse was rescued by members of the 1st Special Forces Operational Detachment–Delta in a classic CT (counterterrorist) operation. Transported to the rooftop of the prison by specially configured MH-6 "Little Bird" helicopters, the assault teams, backed up by a man on the inside who disabled the facility's emergency generator, cleared the upper floors from the top down and fought their way to the cell holding area where Muse was imprisoned. Armed with MP5 9-mm submachineguns of various configurations, the troopers took out the armed guards who resisted with lethal shock and firepower and cuffed the hands and feet of those who surrendered. Just enough explosives to open the door without harming Muse blasted the lock.

White beams of light from the troopers' weapon-mounted pointers pierced the smoke-filled cell after its door was blown, and Muse was whisked to the roof up a darkened stairwell as a pair of AC-130 Specter gunships pummeled the Comandancia across the street. The waiting MH-6 was piloted by soldiers of the 160th Special Operations Aviation Regiment. Two troopers fought their way to Muse's cell, others provided security on the stairwell, and more were on the roof, exchanging fire with prison guards in the barracks beyond a small walled prison yard. The operation, so far, had unfolded with the clockwork precision of a training exercise. As the security and rescue teams loaded into the helos and along their outside-mounted seats, the heavily laden Little Birds lifted into the night sky six minutes after the first Delta troopers set foot on the roof.

What Muse saw was as close to a living hell as Wagnerian opera. AC-130s firing over the top of his head were tearing great chunks out of the Comandancia's defenses, while tracers streamed upward at buzzing Blackhawks and Little Birds—shooting down one behind Muse—while in the streets below, conventional mechanized infantry and Rangers brought maximum pressure to bear on the PDF. In this deadly symphony, the overloaded chopper, unlike a *Valkyrie* of lore, did not bear the men off to *Valhalla*, but was also hit by ground fire and landed with an unceremonious thud on the street below.

The iron-nerved SF aviator maneuvered it down the street like a taxi and pulled into a vacant lot. Using several tall apartment buildings as a shield, the pilot again tried to make his getaway but the Little Bird was knocked down again, this time for good, and the men formed a defensive perimeter nearby. Seconds after a Delta trooper held up an infrared strobe light, they were spotted by a Blackhawk, and the cavalry came to the rescue in the form of three M113 armored personnel carriers of the 4th Battalion, 6th Infantry crashing through parked cars to reach them. Four Delta troopers were hurt, one seriously, but unlike the events some nine years earlier in Iran, this rescue was carried out and with the intended results.

CENTRAL AMERICA

Operations in Grenada and Panama occurred against the backdrop of turmoil and insurgency in Central America. During the Vietnam War, the U.S. Army quickly discovered that the dirty work of fighting guerrillas must be accompanied by genuine reforms if an insurgency was to be defeated rather than temporarily checked. The army also learned that if another nation's people lack the will to persevere, you cannot expect to win a war for them. Consequently, the lessons of Vietnam led to now-almost-forgotten successes in El Salvador, Nicaragua, and Honduras in the 1980s and early 1990s.

Right from the beginning of the decadelong U.S. effort to help El Salvador fight its Communist insurgency, both governments made—and stuck with—a decision not to encourage a "gringoization" of the war, and army involvement was principally in the form of trainer-advisers and a limited number of Special Forces personnel. Instead of acting solely on the defensive, counterpressure was applied against the leftist Sandinista government in Nicaragua (which directly assisted the insurgency) by supporting anti-Sandinista guerrillas operating out of neighboring Honduras. The only large-scale infusion of army troops during this period came in the March 1988 deployment of 7th Infantry Division (Light) and 82d Airborne Division regiments. They were rushed to the Honduras border with Nicaragua for a "training exercise" in response to Sandanista incursions aimed at the guerrilla base camps. Sandanista forces withdrew as U.S. troops engaged in live-fire exercises in the border region.

BELOW: Members of the 504th Parachute Infantry, 82d Airborne Division, land at Palmerola Air base, Honduras, on March 17 and 18, 1988, for a hastily executed live-fire exercise. Dubbed Golden Pheasant, it included the 7th Infantry Division (Light) and was intended to discourage Nicaraguan forces from attacking the bases of U.S.-backed, anti-Communist guerrillas in Honduras.

IRAQ INVADES KUWAIT

With the precipitous withdrawal of Soviet forces from Eastern Europe came the collapse of the Soviet Union into more than a dozen states. Victory in the Cold War saw the fall of the Iron Curtain, dissolution of the Warsaw Pact, and the decades-delayed unification of Germany. NATO's member nations looked forward to a "peace dividend" as costly military forces were quickly slashed, but the United States moved more cautiously.

Plans were put in place to slowly reduce the army from its 1989 strength of 780,000, with an emphasis on not creating the kind of "hollow" force that had resulted in the early debacles on the Korean Peninsula. The downsizing was delayed, however, by events in the Middle East.

On the morning of August 2, 1990, three Iraqi armored divisions of Saddam Hussein's elite Republican Guards stabbed across the desert frontier separating Iraq and Kuwait east of the disputed Rumalia oil field. Iraqi forces had been massing steadily across the border for almost

two weeks before the invasion, but both Western and Arab governments believed this to be nothing more than a show of force to bolster Saddam's financial claims against the oil-rich kingdom. By midday, all meaningful resistance by Kuwait's tiny army had been crushed, and its royal family had fled to a sumptuous exile in Saudi Arabia. The Baathist government in Baghdad rejoiced over its seemingly decisive, quick victory. Saddam expected a toothless condemnation from the United Nations and perhaps even a half-hearted economic embargo

LEFT: A 5th Special Forces Group soldier instructs Qatari troops in MOUT (Military Operations on Urban Terrain) techniques. During the failed January 29–February 1, 1991, Iraqi offensive at Khafji, Saudi Arabia, Qatari and Saudi troops performed well and, together with U.S. Marines and Army Special Forces elements, blunted the attack.

BELOW: A soldier from the 3d Battalion, 73d Airborne Armor Regiment, lays out equipment for his M551 Sheridan armored assault vehicle prior to an 82d Airborne Division live-fire exercise during the build-up in Saudi Arabia. For two weeks before the arrival of the M1 Abrams tanks of the 24th Infantry Division (Mechanized) at the end of August 1990, the 82d's eighteen Sheridans and 7th Marine Expeditionary Brigade's M60 tanks were the only U.S. armored force opposing Iraq's Republican Guard.

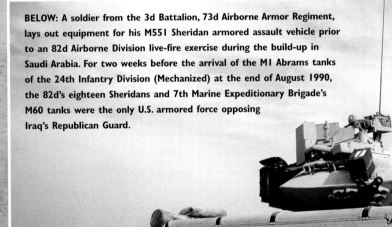

ABOVE: Dressed in rain suits, gloves, and M17A1 protective masks, paratroopers walk around their camp to acclimate their bodies to the heat of the Saudi summer. Extensive testing in protective gear several months later confirmed that all combat and combat support tasks were severely degraded even when the temperature was comparatively moderate. This reinforced the conviction that Saddam Hussein should not be allowed to drag out negotiations, thus forcing the invasion to be launched in the summer of 1991.

BELOW: One of the nine AH-64
Apache attack helicopters that
destroyed a pair of Iraqi radar
stations arrives back at its Saudi
base on the morning of January
17, 1991. The successful strike
by the 101st Airborne Division
(Air Assault) opened the door to
low-flying cruise missiles and
conventional aircraft heading for
targets in Iraq.

INSET: A target at one of the
Iraqi surveillance radar sites
is locked on and destroyed
by an army Apache in Desert
Storm's opening strike. The
chopper's Hellfire missile can be
seen falling toward the target
in the first two frames.

that would soon fade away. Even before Iraqi divisions began to belly up threateningly against the Saudi border, President Bush and British Prime Minister Margaret Thatcher immediately resolved that the rest of the Middle East's oil resources must be kept out of Saddam's hands at all costs.

Iraq had emerged from its 1980–1988 war with Iran with a large, battle-hardened army that was left completely intact after the fighting, and thus, "all dressed up with no place to go." The U.S. Army began formulating contingency plans in case the bellicose leader made a grab for his neighbor's oil fields. Ironically, the same month—February 1990— that a war-game structured around such a scenario was run in California's Mojave Desert, Saddam demanded that U.S. warships leave the Gulf. The exercise provided planners with a clear idea of the size and type of forces that would be needed to protect the fields, but there was no way of knowing if they could arrive in time to deter the Iraqis. The most dangerous period for the West and Saudi Arabia was the first weeks after Kuwait fell, when there was little military strength available in the region to prevent an Iraqi attack along the Persian Gulf coast. The main ports 125 miles to the southeast were needed

by the Americans to bring in their heavy forces. Thankfully, the armor-heavy Iraqi Army was not equipped for operations far from their supply bases, and even though they soon massed along the Saudi border, the short strike into Kuwait had temporarily exhausted their supplies.

Operation Desert Shield was set in motion as military forces with a tactical wing were rushed to Saudi Arabia on August 7. The lead elements of the 82d Airborne Division followed two days later. The paratroopers, who referred to themselves as mere "speed bumps" at this stage of the buildup, would soon be followed by the101st Airborne Division (Air Assault) and the 24th Infantry Division (Mechanized) under the XVIII Airborne Corps and the 1st Marine Division. The 1st Cavalry Division, the 3d Armored Cavalry Regiment, and elements of the 2d Armored Division were told to expect orders to deploy as well, and other nations in the coalition opposing the Iraqis were in the process of gathering their own forces. By the time the 24th Infantry Division began to deploy along the Kuwaiti border in mid-September, any chance that the Iraqis could actually succeed in capturing the ports was gone. Sufficient coalition

LEFT: An M270 Multiple-Launch Rocket System (MLRS), armed with two "six-packs" capable of firing a wide variety of guided and unguided 8.227-mm rockets, moves into position for one of many "artillery raids" before the ground offensive. The MLRS fire of small M77 submunitions, called "steel rain" by Iraqis, contributed to the surrender of many front-line soldiers.

BELOW: An MLRS fires a guided 24-inch ATACMS missile at a target far behind Iraqi lines. The system could be set up to fire as many as two deep strike missiles of this type.

DEFENSE OF SAUDI ARABIA 1990-1991

RIGHT: Although VII Corps' assault into Iraq was conducted much farther to the west than the Iraqis thought possible, the thrust's eastern flank overlapped a portion of the Iraqi defense line. The 1st Infantry Division was given the task of conducting a frontal assault and breaching operation to make a corridor for itself, the follow-on British 1st Armored Division, and U.S. 1st Cavalry Division. Pictured here at a January 18, 1991, breach rehearsal in Saudi Arabia are (*left to right*), Task Force 2-34 Armor (2d Battalion, 34th Armor Regiment) commander Lieutenant Colonel Gregory Fontenot, 1st Infantry Division commander Major General Thomas Rhame, VII Corps commander Lieutenant General Frederick M. Franks Jr, 1st Brigade commander Colonel Lon E. Maggart, and the 1st's Assistant Division Commander (Maneuver) Brigadier General William E. Carter.

airpower had arrived in the theater to wreak terrible losses on any Iraqi divisions attempting to make a long, long punch toward the Ad Dammam-Dhadran area on the coast.

Ignoring UN mandates to vacate Kuwait, which now had been declared Iraq's 19th province, Saddam's generals built an elaborate, deeply layered defense across his new prize, extending partially into Iraq's desert wastes to the west. Meanwhile, the wide variety of nations opposing him—though they had many and varied interests and limitations, both politically and in military power—all agreed that the Iraqis must be ousted from little Kuwait and its sovereignty restored. To this end,

Bush announced in early November that the United States would deploy an additional two hundred thousand ground troops to the theater, including VII Corps in Germany. With the addition of another Marine division and First Marine Expeditionary Force (I MEF) headquarters and support elements in December (augmented by one of the 2d Armored Division's brigades), the United States now had the offensive power of three corps on the ground under the General H. Norman Schwarzkopf, commander in chief of U.S. Central Command. In addition, Great Britain fielded their powerful 1st Armored Division as part of VII Corps. The France 6th Light

ABOVE: Two MRE packs and the contents of a chicken with salsa meal.

MEALS READY TO EAT (MRE)

Although the self-contained field ration had been standard issue in the army since 1986, it was the Gulf War that provided most soldiers, and large numbers of personnel from the other services, their first taste of the MRE. Released on the heels of numerous well-publicized famines in Africa, including the army's deployment to Somalia, the ration quickly gained the appellation "Meals Rejected by Ethiopians" but, in truth, the assortment of twelve different meals (today sixteen) contained in the thick plastic pouches were a great improvement over the canned "C" rations and nearly identical MCI rations. MREs were much lighter, contained a main course, side dishes, dessert, snacks, chewing gum, a flameless ration heater, seasonings, beverage mixing bag (just add water!), and large stiff crackers that a soldier who fought in the American Civil War, surviving for days on "hardtack," might find comfortingly familiar.

ABOVE: A Special Forces long-range reconnaissance patrol deep inside Iraq. The sand-colored M998 HMMWVs that the men parked down in a wadi (dry river bed) for cover have had red-brown squiggles hastily applied by spray cans to provide a modicum of camouflage. Taken with one of the troopers' own cameras, there could well have been pictures of his kid's birthday party on the same roll of film.

A large number of Middle Eastern nations joined the coalition forces arrayed against Iraq. The Egyptian Army had been conducting extensive exercises with its U.S. counterpart for nearly a decade, but most Arab armies knew little of American military procedures, and language problems were as vexing as ever. Because of this, virtually every available Green Beret was committed to serving as a liaison with the Saudi and Qatari units, training Kuwaiti resistance forces, or conducting reconnaissance missions.

Manpower was in such short supply that even Delta soldiers were pulled into the show to perform standard Special Forces missions after Saddam Hussein's release of Iraq's Western "guest workers" made it clear that they would not be needed for hostage rescues. The Delta counterterrorists were principally given the impossible task of finding and destroying the mobile Scud missile launchers targeting Israeli and Saudi population centers.

Saddam Hussein believed that targeting Israeli cities would push Israel into an assault against his country, almost certainly driving a wedge between the United States and its Muslim allies. The deployment of the army's Patriot surface-to-air missile batteries to Israel, a lavish (and usually frustrating) "Scud hunt" by U.S. Air Force F-15s, and Special Forces' efforts deep in the Iraqi desert all persuaded the Israelis to cancel two planned operations.

ABOVE: A border berm erected years before to prevent smuggler vehicles from crossing into the Saudi Kingdom is bulldozed open before the commencement of ground operations by an M9 ACE (armored combat earthmover) of Company A, 299th Engineer Battalion, attached to the 3d Engineer Battalion, 24th Infantry Division (Mechanized). Engineer earthmovers also covered the above-ground Trans-Arabia Pipeline at fifty locations to allow safe movement over it.

BELOW: M998 High-Mobility Multipurpose Wheeled Vehicles (HMMWVs), an M577 command post, and a plethora of other armored and soft vehicles crest a low ridge and surge across the desert near Iraq as they move into position for the attack north. The vehicles in the foreground belong to the 1st Armored Division's 3d Battalion, 1st Field Artillery.

Armored Division, a formation comparable in offensive capability and flexibility to a U.S. armored cavalry regiment, was folded into the XVIII Airborne Corps. An Arab-Islamic Joint Forces command of two light, mixed corps, plus the somewhat more powerful Egyptian II Corps made up of armor and mechanized divisions, rounded out the coalition.

Displaying the bravado he was already well known for, Saddam scoffed at the international army arrayed against him and singled out America as "a nation that cannot afford to take ten thousand casualties in a single day." He was convinced that he could make the cost of liberating Kuwait higher than the coalition would be willing to pay. The U.S. Army was indeed prepared to pay a heavy price if that became necessary. National Guard brigades originally intended to round out some of the regular divisions had not been deployed with their formations so that they could receive additional training. But they were in the reinforcement pipeline along with additional regular formations, because heavy losses among the assault divisions would inevitably force them to pull back and be reconstituted. Thus if the assault divisions became bogged down in a protracted battle—"caught up in the wire"—the follow-on divisions and brigades would, in effect, be the cavalry coming to the rescue.

The army had girded itself for a brutal battle with the veterans of the long Iran-Iraq War when, suddenly, the situation began to look a whole lot better. The air war against Iraq, Desert Storm, had commenced on January 17, and, in the last days of the month, Iraqi forces launched a corps-size spoiling attack against a force of Saudi Arabian and Qatari troops at the Saudi coastal town of Khafji and against U.S. Marines farther inland. The attacking Iraqi armored force was soundly defeated, and the two supporting divisions behind them were so badly mauled by marine and other coalition airpower that they were unable to even reach the battlefield. Army combat commanders and planners reviewing the course of the battle came to the same cautious conclusion: "Hey, we may be able to roll these guys."

Approximately 545,000 Iraqi troops were in the Kuwait theater of operations when the coalition ground assault, Desert Sabre, was launched on February 24, 1991. Entrenched behind protective barriers along the Kuwaiti border and extending a relatively short distance into Iraq to the west, a long string of infantry divisions was backed up by a mix of infantry and standard armored divisions. This force, whose job was to soak up and blunt the initial blows of a coalition invasion, was made up of roughly

ABOVE: Lieutenant General Gary E. Luck, commander of the XVIII Airborne Corps during Operations Desert Shield and Desert Storm.

BELOW: After a brief winter downpour, a squad from the 14th Military Police Brigade moves out on a patrol of a Tactical Assembly Area south of the Tapline Road in mid-January 1991. The road, codenamed Main Supply Route (MSR) Dodge, paralleled the Saudi's Trans-Arabia Pipeline roughly twenty miles south of the Iraqi border. Thanks to deception operations and air supremacy, the Iraqis were completely unaware of the gigantic movement and buildup hundreds of miles from support bases along the coast.

RIGHT: Having punched through the Iraqi bunker and trench system, then expanded the breach in the early morning of February 25, 1991, the Task Force 2-34 Armor operations group prepares to strike other Iraq positions close enough to interfere with movement through the corridor. The shiny domed soldier at center is its commander, Lieutenant Colonel Gregory Fontenot. Later interrogations of prisoners revealed that many Iraqi soldiers were fearful of American troops wearing green battle dress uniforms, surmising that they were elite troops from Europe who had trained to fight Soviet armies.

ABOVE: A VII Corps mailed fist plunges northeast across the Iraqi desert to strike Republican Guard divisions still not fully aware of the threat to their rear area. Note that the outer protective columns of M1 Abrams tanks have their turrets turned to the flanks so that they can respond instantly at the appearance of "hostiles" along their line of march.

ABOVE: Bradley infantry fighting vehicles and Abrams tanks reach the Kuwaiti oil fields systematically set alight by vengeful Iraqis even as tank battles continued to erupt all along the front, February 27, 1991.

LEFT: A VII Corps Bradley with add-on protection is topped off just before the opening of the ground offensive. Refueling the thousands of VII and XVIII vehicles plunging to their rendezvous with the Republican Guard—and in later stages, inside the zone of contact—required an extraordinary effort and complex planning. Each U.S. combat division operated from 6,000 to 8,000 vehicles, with VII Corps topping some 55,000, and were supplied by more than 3,500 convoys during Desert Shield and Desert Storm.

VII CORPS AND THE DEATH OF THE IRAQI ARMORED FORCE

"The fight that's going on with the Republican Guard right now is a classic tank battle. You've got fire and maneuver, they are continuing to fight and shoot at us as our forces move forward, and our forces are in the business of outflanking them, taking them in the rear, using our attack helicopters, using our advanced technology. I would tell you that one of the things that has prevailed, particularly in this battle out here, is our technology.

"We had great weather for the air war, but right now, and for the last three days, it's been raining out there, it's been dusty out there, there's black smoke and haze in the air. It's an infantryman's weather — God loves the infantryman and that's just the kind of weather the infantryman likes to fight in. But I would also tell you that our sights have worked fantastically well in their ability to acquire, through that kind of dust and haze, the enemy targets. The enemy sights have not worked that well. As a matter of fact, we've had several anecdotal reports today of enemy who were saying to us that they couldn't see anything through their sights and all of a sudden, their tank exploded when their tank was hit by our sights."

—General H. Norman Schwarzkopf,
U.S. Central Command press briefing
of February 27, 1991

"When the war started I had 39 T-72s; after 38 days of air attack I was down to 32. After 20 minutes with the 2d Armored Cavalry Regiment, I was down to zero."
—From Iraqi battalion commander interrogation
in March 1991

The main attack of the coalition forces arrayed against Iraq was that of the heavily armored VII Corps. This massive steel fist boasted over 146,000 soldiers and almost 50,000 vehicles. Its divisions advanced along frontages twenty-four kilometers wide by forty-eight kilometers deep. Never before had so much firepower been concentrated into such an organization, and never before had such an organization featured such extraordinary tactical mobility. Generally, a main attack seeks to crush an enemy's center of gravity, that asset or attribute most essential to his prospects for success. The Iraqi center of gravity was adjudged to be the Republican Guard, three heavy and five motorized divisions equipped and trained to Iraq's highest standards. As formidable as the Republican Guard was, the even more superbly equipped and far more highly trained VII Corps seemed the right force to defeat it.

The VII Corps' 1st Infantry Division breach was as methodical as that of the marines farther east. Tightly synchronized teams of M1A1 bulldozer tanks, M1A1 mine plow tanks, combat engineer vehicles, and accompanying engineers in M113 armored personnel carriers bored through sand berms, minefields, and other obstacles. The teams were guarded by sniper tanks and supported by the preparatory fires of fourteen battalions of field artillery. A carefully derived intelligence picture hopelessly compromised the Iraqi defenders, who found their crew-served weapons destroyed even before the first American target offered itself. In a few hours the "Big Red 1" had cut twenty-four lanes across a ten-mile front without the loss of a single soldier. In short order the division pulled its own units through the breach and passed the British 1st Armored Division through as well.

Meanwhile, the 2d Armored Cavalry Regiment (ACR) and 1st and 3d Armored Divisions had swept around the western margin of the obstacle belt and had swung east to envelop the Iraqi defenses. Finding little opposition short of Al Busayyah, the 1st Armored Division hammered that town with preparatory artillery and then swept through it, overrunning an Iraqi division and a corps headquarters en route. Farther east, the 3d Armored Division had made contact with the Republican Guard's Tawakalna Division, as had the 2d ACR screening to the east of the two armored divisions. Outnumbered but engaging accurately at extended ranges, the cavalrymen soon identified the basic contours of the Republican Guard defenses, including several regular army heavy divisions that augmented its force structure. Within hours the 1st and 3d Armored Divisions rolling in from the west and the 1st Infantry Division and British 1st Armored Division emerging from the breach were on line facing the east to deliver the decisive blow.

The VII Corps attack on the Republican Guard was a massive and well-coordinated armored assault. The M1A1 Abrams tanks moved forward on line, closely supported by M2 Bradley infantry fighting vehicles as a series of massive tank battles erupted at places called Objective Norfolk, Medina Ridge, and 73 Easting. The tanks destroyed major enemy armored vehicles with their main guns while the infantry vehicles used their machine guns on thinner-skinned targets. Infantry dismounted from the Bradleys as needed to clear positions or collect prisoners. Farther to the rear, M113s sped along with communicators, engineers, mortarmen, mechanics, and other supporting troops, accompanied by the occasional recovery vehicle. Even farther to the rear, howitzers kept the advance in range of their supporting fires. Potential targets were destroyed by the tankers or surrendered to the infantrymen so quickly that the artillerymen seldom had an opportunity to fire; but when they did, the effects were devastating. In the end, the Iraqi Army lost a total of 3,847 tanks and 1,450 armored troop carriers to all U.S. and coalition elements combined—as many as 1,350 and 1,223 respectively were destroyed during its 89 hours of combat with VII Corps.

The Americans, equipped with night-vision sights and devices, relentlessly pressed the attacks in daylight and darkness with equal ferocity. The elite Republican Guard—outflanked, surprised, outranged, and in any given exchange outgunned—had no chance. The decisive attack achieved decisive results; in little more than a day VII Corps smashed the Republican Guard in its path as well as those regular army units chosen to fight alongside it and then swept on across northern Kuwait.

ABOVE: *Colonel Daniel R. Zanini of the 3d Brigade, 2d Armored Division (attached to the 1st Infantry Division) briefs his soldiers on the plan of attack.*

LEFT: *A snapshot of 2d Armored Cavalry Regiment (ACR) vehicles taken at 4:30 PM during the February 26, 1991, battle at 73 Easting. The 2d Squadron's operations officer is in the Abrams at left and the forward command post Bradley is at right. The Abrams of E Troop's company commander Captain Herbert R. McMaster is partially visible beyond the Bradley.*

BELOW: *Flanked by a protective screen of Abrams tanks, 3d Armored Division M109 155-mm howitzers move through the Iraqi desert on February 25, 1991. Because of the fluid nature of the combat, the self-propelled artillery had to—and did—respond quickly to calls for fire support and likely saved 2d ACR's G Troop from being overwhelmed. Not surprisingly, though, and despite the best efforts of all involved, no useful way was found to utilize the howitzers during close-in night fights.*

BELOW: A 1st Armored Division M978 fuel servicing truck gets bogged down in soft sand on February 26, 1991. The drivers ultimately were able to free it using shovels and it did not require a tow. The depressions made when freeing the vehicle were speedily filled in and the 3rd Infantry Division M933 tractor truck hauling fuel behind it rolled through unhindered. The 3rd Infantry Division's 26th Support Battalion was assigned to the 1st Armored Division throughout the operation.

Bigger potential problems than soft sands were the *sabkhats*, which, even though they were clearly marked on maps, were nevertheless driven over by heavy vehicles that became thoroughly bogged down when they broke through the hardened sand crust on the surface.

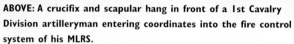

ABOVE: A crucifix and scapular hang in front of a 1st Cavalry Division artilleryman entering coordinates into the fire control system of his MLRS.

ABOVE: During the pre-invasion fighting near Wadi Al-Batin, Private First Class Anthony Gibson of the 1st Cavalry Division pushes a 155-mm round down the slide from the ammo carrier to his howitzer, February 20, 1991. The private is wearing chemical protective clothing in the event that the Iraqis respond with a chemical attack.

LEFT: An exhausted Captain Scott Bickell, commander of B Company, 9th Combat Engineer Battalion, 7th Engineer Brigade, checks on the progress of a platoon blowing enemy equipment and marking mine fields.

LEFT: A DH-132 combat vehicle crew helmet used in the Gulf War.

ABOVE: An M1A1 Abrams main battle tank of the 3d Brigade, 1st Armored Division, moves across the desert in northern Kuwait in the final stages of Operation Desert Storm. Nearly all of the 1,848 Abrams tanks shipped to the Gulf were employed in the February offensive. Iraqi tanks, which could not acquire targets at ranges more than 1,500 meters (1,640 yards) were at an extreme disadvantage when confronted by the Abrams. Able to see and engage targets at up to 2,500 meters (2,870 yards) because of their thermal sights, which were little-affected by adverse weather and sand storms, U.S. tankers were able to destroy many Iraqi tanks before they were even seen by their opponents. Numerous fights, however, were conducted at less than 1,000 meters.

LEFT: A Personnel Armor System Ground Troops Helmet, popularly known as a "Kevlar helmet," with "Chocolate Chip" pattern helmet cover that was worn in the Gulf War. Kevlar helmets made from bullet-resistant synthetic fibers offer a much higher degree of ballistic protection than the M1 helmet of old but, unlike the legendary "steel pot," it can't be used over a cooking fire.

ABOVE: A war party of Apaches and Kiowas are arrayed for quick action at a forward refueling and rearming point (FARP) deep in Iraq.

BELOW: An Iraqi T-72, destroyed in its dug-in position, rests within a ring of Apaches at a 1st Infantry Division FARP, February 27, 1991.

ABOVE: Corps, division, and regimental commanders coordinating plans to envelop the remaining Iraqi forces in their zone of attack, 10:30 PM, February 27, 1991. Clockwise from VII Corps commander Franks (with pointer) is VII Corps JUMP TAC operations officer Major Ronald McConnell, 1st Cavalry Division operations officer Lieutenant Colonel Jim Gunlicks, 2d Armored Cavalry Regiment commander Colonel Don Holder, and 1st Cavalry Division Commander Major General John Tilelli Jr. Plans were cancelled just before midnight when orders were received to halt offensive operations.

LEFT: The artificial leg worn by Lieutenant General Franks during the Gulf War. Severely wounded in Cambodia during the Vietnam War, he lost his left leg but was successful in his effort to continue to serve in combat units.

435,000 soldiers whose training ran from mediocre to fairly extensive. By the time the ground war started, many of these units had been nearly cut off from regular supply bases for more than a month because of the intensity of the air offensive, and they were in rather sad shape (a turn of events that encouraged a high degree of surrenders among frontline units). Backing up the cannon fodder units along the front were eight formidable Republican Guard armored and mechanized divisions generally concentrated in the vicinity of Kuwait's northern border with Iraq as a massive, 110,000-man counterattack element. These Republican Guard formations—which the Iraqis believed to be far to the rear—were in fact the main target of the attack.

Saddam and his generals had anticipated that the main American effort would be well inland from the Gulf: a left hook to circumvent the mass of troops along the front by instead striking up the long Wadi Al-Batin, that made up Kuwait's western border with Iraq. A series of probing attacks by the U.S. 1st Cavalry Division in this very area seemed to confirm the Iraqis' suspicions, and the Republican Guard divisions were deeply arrayed on both sides of the wadi in the joyful expectation of destroying large numbers of American tanks in a coordinated series of flank attacks.

The Iraqis were, indeed, right about the Americans making a flanking attack far to the west. What they didn't anticipate was just how far to the west that U.S. armored formations could effectively operate, nor how deep and swiftly they could strike into Iraq itself. The 1st Cav's attacks were nothing more than a feint, and blinded by the coalition air effort, which had long since destroyed the Iraqi air force, Saddam's forces were completely unaware that VII Corps, the mailed fist of Central Command under Lieutenant General Frederick M. Franks Jr., had charged north into Iraq from jump-off spots as far as two hundred miles inland. Remarkably, XVIII Corps was even farther west, protecting VII Corps' flank in a drive that carried it all the way to the Euphrates River on February 25–26.

The easternmost division of VII Corps had to punch through fixed defenses stretching out beyond the wadi, and the corps performed a giant turning movement to the east, literally catching unawares the Republican Guard divisions—still oriented toward the wadi—in the flank or rear. A series of large-scale tank battles occurred as VII Corps burned its way east through formation after formation. Arrayed south-to-north on this remarkable drive was the British 1st Armored Division, the U.S. 2d Armored Cavalry Regiment, 1st Infantry Division (Mechanized), 3d Armored Division, 1st Armored Division, and beyond the corps boundary (which had been bent horizontal), XVIII Corps' 3d Armored Cavalry Regiment and the 24th Infantry Division (Mechanized). To the southeast, the I MEF's 1st and 2d Marine divisions and their attached brigade of the 2d Armored Division had breached the vaunted Iraqi defenses and were striking for the capital, Kuwait City, with the Arab-Islamic corps coming up on I MEF's flanks.

The Iraqi front had collapsed. The remaining units, many in a high state of disorganization, attempted to flee north with varying degrees of success. The main road to Iraq became a scene of terrible destruction and was fittingly labeled the "highway of death" even before the last major tank battles took place on February 27, 1991.

ABOVE: General H. Norman Schwarzkopf, U.S. Central Command commander-in-chief, during the Gulf War.

BELOW: A Bradley from the 1st Battalion, 34th Armor, destroyed in the middle of an Iraqi defense position during the "Fright Night" battle for Objective Norfolk, February 26–27, 1991. Mistaken for an Iraqi vehicle, it was targeted by a follow-on U.S. unit. Nearby, a Bradley belonging to the 2d Armored Cavalry was disabled by enemy fire, evacuated, and subsequently struck by U.S. rounds.

OPPOSITE INSET: The Saudi Arabian version of the Kuwait Liberation Medal awarded to members of U.S. and coalition forces who participated in Operation Desert Storm.

OPPOSITE BOTTOM: The remains of an Iraqi armored brigade that made the mistake of firing on the 24th Infantry Division (Mechanized) on March 2, 1991, days after the "suspension of offensive action." Some 200 vehicles were destroyed.

ABOVE: 1st Brigade, 2d Armored Division soldiers guard Iraqi prisoners early in the ground offensive. The prisoners came from units defending the area northwest of the point where Saudi Arabia, Iraq, and Kuwait meet. The brigade was attached to the First Marine Expeditionary Force.

MAKING A SOLDIER

ABOVE: A drill instructor and trainees encourage another young trainee to "be all that he can be" during basic training. Emphasis is placed not only on physical training but also on helping recruits make a quick psychological adjustment to an unfamiliar way of life.

ABOVE RIGHT: Recruits assigned to the 50th Infantry Regiment recover after leaving the gas chamber at Fort Benning, Georgia. After entering the chamber with their gas masks on, they are told to remove them and recite their name and the last four digits of their social security number. They are released after approximately one minute.

OPPOSITE BOTTOM: Gas, mud, barbed wire, and live ammunition—later stages of basic training such as this exercise at Fort Hood, Texas, stress teamwork. Advanced individual training (AIT) is geared to making the new soldiers experts in their chosen field and can last as long as a year as the trainees are sent to specialized schools such as the Army Medical Department School at Fort Sam Houston, Texas, for medics, or the Intelligence School at Fort Huachuca, Arizona, for intelligence collectors.

BACKGROUND: The campaign-hatted drill sergeant, symbol of the army's tough Basic Combat Training program, skillfully transforms new recruits into trained soldiers capable of performing effectively in wartime.

Chapter Thirteen
A "New" Enemy, 1991–2011

The eviction of Iraq's army from Kuwait prevented Saddam Hussein's domination of the world's volatile oil markets through seizure of much of the Middle East's oil supplies, and put on hold the dictator's quest for nuclear weapons. Saddam's large, modern air force was destroyed, the Soviet-supplied air defense system degraded to the point of near impotence, and, finally, forty-two of the country's fifty-six combat divisions were either wiped out or "rendered ineffective" during Operation Desert Storm's crushing ground assault.

Fully 3,847 of Iraq's 4,280 tanks, 1,450 other armored vehicles, and 2,917 artillery pieces were destroyed or captured. In all, roughly 20,000 Iraqi troops had been killed, reportedly the same number missing, and more than 70,000 wounded. Some 71,000 Iraqi soldiers who were captured by U.S. forces were sent to POW camps in Saudi Arabia. Tens of thousands more melted away from the front during the confusion, most ending up in the southern Iraqi city of Basra. Political constraints imposed by the fragility of the anti-Saddam coalition resulted in several elite Republican Guard divisions trapped south of the Euphrates River in the Basra area from being destroyed by the VII and XVIII Corps. However, a withdrawing Iraqi armored brigade made the mistake of firing on the U.S. 24th Infantry Division several days after the March 3, 1992, cease-fire agreement, and a coordinated air-ground reaction destroyed 140 assorted armored vehicles and dozens of trucks in exchange for the loss of one Abrams tank (whose crew survived).

The number of Americans in the theater of operations peaked at 553,000, and the U.S. Third Army launched the Desert Saber ground offensive with 333,000 troops, including 45,000 British and French men. America lost 148 battle (ninety-eight army) and 145 non-battle personnel, and another 467 were wounded in action. Excluding Kuwaiti military casualties during the initial Iraqi invasion, coalition forces lost an additional forty-two troops and had 242 wounded in action. Despite the poor performance of Iraqi formations during their cross-border strike into Saudi Arabia, the vast disparity in friendly and enemy losses still came as a surprise to civilian and military leaders alike. Brigadier General Robert H. Scales Jr., tasked with analyzing the army's performance during the war, later wrote:

"The rapid pace and low casualties [during the offensive] stemmed directly from effective planning and violent execution of both direct and indirect fires....In countless past wars, a dispirited soldier's reaction to disciplined troops wielding superior firepower has always been the same. He either cowers before the firepower or runs away. The Iraqis were no exception."

Despite its drubbing and massive loss of equipment, Iraq's army remained one of the largest in the world, and Saddam's regime quickly—and savagely—employed it to suppress uprisings against the regime by the largely Shiite Muslims in southern Iraq and in the Kurdish region bordering Turkey and Iran in the north. The U.S. Army did not become involved in the Shiite uprising beyond providing a safe haven, food, and medical care for more than 50,000 refugees before placing them under Saudi care or letting them leave on their own. In the Kurdish areas, a well-organized guerrilla organization was working in conjunction with the 179th Airborne Brigade

ABOVE: The War on Terrorism Service Medal awarded to those who have served in antiterrorism operations, including airport security and domestic support, from September 11, 2001, to date. As operations expanded, many recipients became eligible for the Global War on Terrorism Expeditionary Medal (*see page 475*).

OPPOSITE: A tank commander at a checkpoint outside Baqaba, Iraq, keeps a sharp eye out for trouble on Christmas Eve, December 24, 2003.

and Special Forces personnel, but the Americans' operational area was necessarily limited. When Kurdish groups, fighting on their own and far from U.S. troops, captured numerous towns, the Iraqis struck back.

Fearful of Saddam's retribution and a repeat of the poison gas attacks that had slaughtered 3,200 to 5,000 Kurdish residents of Halabja in 1988 (with an additional 7,000 to 10,000 grievously injured), more than two million fled into the barren mountains. The Iraqis were purposely driving the Kurds ahead of them like cattle in the hopes that as many as possible would die. Among the pockets along the Turkish border that held 700,000 men, women, and children, no fewer than one thousand were dying each day by early April 1992, when U.S. President George H.W. Bush ordered a massive intervention and relief effort centered around three battalions of the 10th Special Forces Group and elements of the 3d Infantry Division. American commanders meeting

with their Iraqi counterparts let it be known that they would brook no interference, and meetings were punctuated with the low over-flights of menacing A-10 ground attack aircraft and F-16 fighter bombers.

A no-fly zone to protect relief activities was declared across the northern border region extending south from Turkey, and coalition aircraft shot down several hostile jets that had survived the war, convincing the Iraqis to keep clear of the area. (A no-fly zone was later established across the southern region as well.) Nearly 12,000 U.S. and 8,700 other NATO personnel took part in Operation Provide Comfort and narrowly prevented a humanitarian disaster of terrible proportions. With NATO airpower above and American combat boots on the ground, the refugees felt secure enough to return to their homes, and the Kurdish area remained free of Saddam's depredations.

SMALLER FORCE, INCREASED DEPLOYMENTS

The post-Cold War reductions in the army's manpower were already well under way when Saddam's tanks stormed into Kuwait. Active and Reserve components had shed more than 100,000 men during the previous year. From Desert Storm through the end of 1994, the active duty strength shrank by nearly 200,000 more to 529,000, while the National Guard dropped from 458,000 to 397,000, and the number of Reservists from 335,000 to 260,000. Yet in the midst of these rapid reductions—and all the dislocations they entailed—the breakup of the Soviet superpower and extreme violence in numerous third world states led to a largely unanticipated level of chaos. The result was a steep increase in the number of army deployments, large and small, to trouble spots in Africa, Europe, South America, the Caribbean, and southwest Asia.

OPPOSITE TOP: American and Iraqi officers in Kuwait discuss the exchange of their prisoners after Iraq was defeated in the Gulf War, March 1991.

OPPOSITE BOTTOM: Soldiers recently returned from Iraq march proudly in the July 8, 1991, victory parade in Washington, D.C.

BELOW LEFT: Class A officers' service coat. This example was worn by Colonel Schuhle. On the right shoulder sleeve is the insignia of the 101st Airborne Division, indicating the formation he was with during his first combat action. The 1st Armored Division patch of his final posting is on the left shoulder sleeve.

BELOW RIGHT: Class A enlisted service coat. Like the Class A officers' service coat, the enlisted man's coat came into service in 1957. This example was worn by Specialist Ives who served with the 32d Signal Battalion.

Sergeant First Class Randall David Shughart
1st Special Forces Detachment

Citation: Sergeant First Class Shughart, United States Army, distinguished himself by actions above and beyond the call of duty on October 3, 1993, while serving as a Sniper Team Member, United States Army Special Operations Command with Task Force Ranger in Mogadishu, Somalia. Sergeant First Class Shughart provided precision sniper fires from the lead helicopter during an assault on a building and at two helicopter crash sites, while subjected to intense automatic weapons and rocket propelled grenade fires. While providing critical suppressive fires at the second crash site, Shughart and his team leader learned that ground forces were not immediately available to secure the site. Shughart and his team leader unhesitatingly volunteered to be inserted to protect the four critically wounded personnel, despite being well aware of the growing number of enemy personnel closing in on the site. After their third request to be inserted, Shughart and his team leader received permission to perform this volunteer mission. When debris and enemy ground fires at the site caused them to abort the first attempt, Shughart and his team leader were inserted one hundred meters south of the crash site. Equipped with only his sniper rifle and a pistol, Shughart and his team leader, while under intense small arms fire from the enemy, fought their way through a dense maze of shanties and shacks to reach the critically injured crew members. Shughart pulled the pilot and the other crew members from the aircraft, establishing a perimeter which placed him and his fellow sniper in the most vulnerable position. Shughart used his long range rifle and side arm to kill an undetermined number of attackers while traveling the perimeter, protecting the downed crew. Shughart continued his protective fire until he depleted his ammunition and was fatally wounded. His actions saved the pilot's life. Sergeant First Class Shughart's extraordinary heroism and devotion to duty were in keeping with the highest standards of military service and reflect great credit upon him, his unit, and the United States Army.

BELOW: Sergeant First Class Randall Shughart (*left*) and Master Sergeant Gary Gordon were awarded with the Medal of Honor posthumously for their actions in Mogadishu on October 3, 1993.

SOMALIA

On the heels of a long series of bloody wars in the Horn of Africa and several years of little rain, Somalia was hit by the worst drought in more than a century during the early 1990s. With the death toll reaching horrific proportions and desperately needed humanitarian aid operations repeatedly interrupted by greedy, warring clans, the United Nations in December 1992 authorized a U.S.-led operation called Restore Hope to protect relief workers and food shipments. In a massive show of force, more than 13,000 troops centered around the 10th Mountain Division and 1st Marine Division and supported by special operations forces conducted assault landings and seized airfields. Other UN troops followed. Needed supplies finally began to reach starving Somalis as the U.S. commitment climbed to 25,000 of the 37,000 UN personnel deployed. More than five thousand weapons, including mortars, rocket launchers, and heavy machine guns, were seized.

In May 1993, the situation appeared to be stable enough for the humanitarian effort to be turned over to a UN peacekeeping force backed up by a much smaller number of U.S. combat troops. Still, rival clans continued to jockey for control of the port area of Mogadishu, the Somali capital. By October, the number of Americans had dwindled to just three thousand logistics personnel and one thousand combat troops, including a rapid-reaction force made up principally of army Rangers and special operations elements. An ambush by one of the clans and a bomb detonation killed twenty-five Pakistani peacekeepers and four American solders, prompting retaliation by U.S. and UN troops. But the dual nature of the command structure and general lack of effort to coordinate their efforts hampered operations. Ominously, the special operations commander's request for more firepower to back up the missions was turned down as sending the "wrong signal," because senior advisors to the newly elected president, William Jefferson Clinton, did not want it to appear that the United States was increasing its military presence.

The under-resourced Americans were, in effect, taking a knife to a gunfight, and the October 3 capture of the warlord "General" Mohamed Farrah Aidid's senior henchmen turned into a near disaster. Two Black Hawk helicopters were shot down midway through the operation, forcing the individually well-armed but badly outnumbered Rangers and Special Forces soldiers to fight in a brutal, close-in slugfest among the streets and alleys of Mogadishu. Meanwhile, two ad hoc relief columns were formed from other 10th Mountain Division and Ranger elements. Together, with the assistance of Malaysian armored personnel carriers and a Pakistani tank platoon, they broke through to the cut-off Americans after hours of street-by-street, house-by-house fighting, and brought them to safety. Armor-heavy elements of the 24th Infantry and 10th Mountain divisions as well as the previously requested AC-130 gunships subsequently were rushed to Somalia to bolster the UN presence.

ABOVE: A UH-60 Black Hawk lands soldiers of the 10th Mountain Division's 2d Brigade north of Mogadishu at Belet Uen.

LEFT: A quick reaction force of 2d Battalion, 14th Infantry, hugs the walls along a Mogadishu street during a lull in the hail of Somali small arms and rocket propelled grenade fire. These 10th Mountain Division soldiers were attempting to reach the besieged assault group of 3d Battalion Rangers and Delta troopers at the site of one of the special operations Black Hawks downed on the afternoon of October 3, 1993.

U.S.-UN casualties amounted to eighteen Americans and two Malaysians dead, with eighty-four Americans, seven Malaysians, and two Pakistanis wounded. Estimated Somali casualties range from 700 to 1,500, with at least 300 dead. Losses to Aidid's forces were so severe that he was never able to extend his control beyond southern Mogadishu. Aidid was wounded during fighting with another faction and died of gunshot wounds in 1995, even as the country moved toward a degree of normalcy in the vast areas beyond its capital. U.S. and UN military forces withdrew from Mogadishu by the end of March 1994 and from the rest of Somalia the following year. And although army campaign streamers were approved for such things as the "Kosovo Air Campaign," the operations in Somalia, like the three-year fight to keep open the Bozeman trail (see Chapter 4), have received no similar recognition.

HAITI

In the early 1990s, the Caribbean island of Hispaniola became a focal point of violence. A military junta ousted Haiti's first freely elected president, Jean-Bertrand Aristide, and, together with remnants of the Tonton Macoutes secret police, suppressed Aristide's supporters, prompting a UN embargo of Haiti. A UN-sponsored agreement declared that the junta would relinquish power, but a U.S. Navy ship carrying the initial elements of Joint Task Force Haiti Assistance Group was threatened by the junta and withdrew from the Haitian capital, Port-au-Prince, in October 1993.

Protected by a strong Special Forces security detail and other immediately available assets, several high-ranking Americans, including Secretary of State Colin Powell, former president Jimmy Carter, and United Nations officials, went to Haiti in late 1994 to negotiate for the peaceful entry of a U.S. stabilization force and to assess election preparations. If negotiations failed, the 82d Airborne and 10th Mountain divisions were prepared to make a forced entry. On September 19, 1994, as an agreement was reached, the lead elements of the 82d that were already in the air turned around midflight and returned the paratroopers to Fort Bragg in North Carolina, while waves of army helicopters, staged from Navy carriers offshore, set down 10th's troops at key points. No longer part of a combat mission, the Mountain Division—augmented by more than one thousand military police—turned to peacekeeping and nation-building operations, while the twelve-hundred-man 3d Special Forces Group fanned out across the country to establish order and humanitarian services.

Other Caribbean nations also were involved in the effort, and in January 1995, the 25th Infantry Division took over from the 10th. In addition to returning the previously elected Aristide regime to power, the U.S.-led multinational force ensured security, assisted with the rehabilitation of civil administration (including retraining the police force), and helped prepare for elections. Operation Uphold Democracy succeeded both in restoring the democratically elected government of Haiti and in stemming the emigration of Haitian "boat people" desperately trying to reach American shores. In March 1995 the United States transferred peacekeeping responsibilities to the United Nations.

BELOW: Behind a safety line of USS *Eisenhower* flight deck personnel, elements of the 10th Mountain Division's 1st Brigade ride up an elevator to board helicopters from the division's aviation brigade for a "forced entry" into Port-Au-Prince, Haiti. The September 13, 1994, operation restored the elected government of Haiti and led the way for the entry of a UN peacekeeping force.

LEFT TOP: While other Haitians wisely keep their distance, one of their number (center) ventures forward to take a look at the 10th Mountain soldiers establishing a perimeter around the airport at Port-Au-Prince.

LEFT BOTTOM: Corporal Alex Cadet of the 511th Military Police Company (Multirole Bridge), 10th Mountain Division, talks to a Haitian man while on patrol at Cap Haitien, Haiti. The first order of business when moving into an area in Haiti was to restore the rule of law and ensure that retribution was not exacted on either supporters of the military coup that overthrew Haitian president Jean Bertrand Aristide or the Haitians that opposed them.

RIGHT: With the sabotaged Sava River bridge beyond repair, soldiers of the 502d Engineer Company, 130th Engineer Brigade, connect segments of a pontoon bridge near the town of Zupanja, 174 miles east of Zagreb, on Saturday, December 23, 1995. Here, the 502d is assembling the first seven segments on the flooded Sava as a test, and the rest were added as they were brought forward from the Slavonski Brod train station.

Throughout the operation, the engineers were ably assisted by A Company, 5th Battalion, 159th Aviation Regiment, which lifted bridge bays and dropped them into the river to help speed construction of the bridge. When the Sava overflowed its banks, washing away the 502's camp, the aviators quickly resupplied the engineers on December 29–30 so they could continue their mission.

BELOW: The 1st Armored Division crosses the Sava River on January 3, 1996. Because of severe flooding which disrupted bridging operations and dramatically widened the river, the engineers had to double the length of the planned structure to nearly 2,000 feet—longer than the center span of the Brooklyn Bridge.

BOSNIA

The breakup of the Soviet Union in the late 1980s encouraged nationalist and ethnic groups in Communist Yugoslavia to go their own way and establish their own states. The country had been cobbled together in the wake of World War II and held together under the leadership of Josip Broz Tito, a former Bolshevik revolutionary and member of the Soviet secret police, who unified and led anti-Nazi partisans during the war. After his death, the largest of the Yugoslav republics, Serbia (under Slobodan Milošević), attempted to prevent any group from gaining autonomy from the Serbian central government. In 1991, Slovenia and Croatia in the western part of the country and Macedonia in the south succeeded in breaking away and gaining international recognition. But Bosnia-Herzegovina, which shared a long border with Serbia and its ally Montenegro, was not so fortunate.

Bosnia-Herzegovina, usually referred to simply as Bosnia, is nearly half Muslim and a third Serbian, with Croatians making up most of the rest of the population. When Bosnia declared its independence in April 1992, nationalist Serb paramilitary

forces immediately went on the offensive against the country's Croatian and Muslim regions. Backed by the Serbian-controlled Yugoslav army, they quickly gained the upper hand in a brutal campaign of "ethnic cleansing" that forced terrorized civilians away from lands coveted by the Serbs. A large UN protective force was sent to facilitate humanitarian relief and enforce the periodic cease-fires, but it was outnumbered and outgunned by the Serbians. Though fielding nearly forty thousand troops from three dozen countries, the UN force proved to be remarkably ineffectual. With the almost sole

LEFT: In a scene reminiscent of the link-up of US and Soviet forces along Germany's Elbe River in 1945, soldiers prepare for the two militaries' first combined patrol in a hostile environment since World War II on February 14, 1996. US Major Thomas Wilhelm (foreground with Russian headgear) and Lieutenant Aleksei Terebov, a Russian platoon leader from their 76th Airborne Division, examine a map showing the location of minefields in the Zone of Separation (ZOS) near Delici on the Bosnian Serbian border before moving out in Terebov's BTR-80 armored personnel carrier.

BELOW: 1st Armored Division Bradley fighting vehicles of the 3d Battalion 5th Cavalry and an attached M113A2/A3 Armored Ambulance manning checkpoint 7 on "Desolation Boulevard" in January 1996. "Desolation Boulevard" ran through a destroyed Croatian Village near Brcko in northeast Bosnia.

exception of a pair of aggressively handled, heavy mechanized Canadian battalions that had both the means and, more important, the will to impose order, UN elements were regularly intimidated by aggressive Serb units, which even took entire companies and platoons of the multinational force hostage.

In July 1995, the Serbs continuing pillaging and committing mass murders in two designated UN safe areas near the Serbian border. Those actions, plus continued mortar and artillery attacks on civilians in the nearly surrounded capital of Sarajevo, finally prompted the U.S. and NATO to act. They launched a sustained air campaign in support of the beleaguered UN troops, and the Croatian army (assisted by civilian American advisors who recently had left the U.S. Army) intervened in support of the Bosnian Muslims and Croats. Serb forces were ejected from much of the territory they had seized. In October, the Serbs agreed to enter into negotiations to be held at a U.S. Air Force base outside Dayton, Ohio, and the resultant Dayton Accords called for a yearlong deployment of a NATO-led implementation force (IFOR). This force was responsible for separating the warring parties, securing heavy weapons such as artillery, and safely withdrawing both the UN forces from Bosnia and various combatants into their respective territories.

The U.S. 1st Armored Division moved overland from its bases in Germany across former Warsaw Pact countries, while French and British forces entered Bosnia through overtaxed ports along the Adriatic coast. A battalion task force from the 82d Airborne Division parachuted into Tuzla, the principal city in the American Zone, and, in the midst of the winter weather, the 1st Armored's engineer brigade succeeded in constructing a temporary, heavy-capacity, floating bridge across the flooded Sava River near Županja, Croatia. The warring factions quickly discovered that the U.S. and other NATO elements meant business, as early efforts to circumvent the Dayton Accords, principally by the Serbs, were firmly dealt with. Challenges to IFOR's authority—both direct and indirect—gradually fell off, but various parties were biding their time until the heavy forces left in December 1996. Instead, the U.S. and NATO girded themselves for a lengthy occupation of Bosnia and, with UN concurrence, continued the mission as a stabilization force (SFOR).

ABOVE: A Russian soldier watches as 1st Armored Division engineers prepare to destroy a defunct Serbian T34/76 tank abandoned in the Zone of Separation north of Tuzla, Bosnia. Thermite explosives are used to seal its gun and fuse its moving parts so that it cannot be repaired.

MACEDONIA AND KOSOVO

Throughout this period, an American battalion operating under the UN flag patrolled Macedonia's long border with the shrunken but aggressive Yugoslav state to ensure that the fighting did not spread south. The battalion's infantry, engineer, military police, and other elements of the Berlin Brigade combined as Task Force Able Sentry and headed to a zone across the border from the rebellious Serb province of Kosovo in July 1993. Numerous active-duty, National Guard, and Reserve units rotated through a series of uneventful deployments until early 1997, when a 1st Armored Division battalion was rushed to Macedonia to deal with chaos in Albania and increasing strife in Kosovo.

Escalating repression led to civil war and a new round of ethnic cleansing. A fourteen-thousand-man Yugoslav Army and Serbian paramilitary units burned and pillaged their way through Kosovo in March 1999. A NATO air campaign tried for months to push Serb strongman Milošević to the negotiating table until June when Serbian forces withdrew to make way for Kosovo Force (KFOR) peacekeepers. This had only been accomplished, however, after 78 days of unrelenting bombardment, increasingly effective attacks by the Kosovo Liberation Army on the ground, and the establishment in

Albania of Task Force Hawk built around the U.S. 12th Aviation Brigade, the 11th Helicopter Regiment, and an artillery-heavy ground component. This dangerous threat to Serb forces also included a brigade combat team from the 1st Armored Division as well as individual battalions from the 1st Infantry, 10th Mountain, and 82d Airborne Divisions. Task Force Hawk then provided troops to KFOR's American-led multinational brigade.

Thousands of civilian lives were saved in both Bosnia and Kosovo. In each operation, American forces maintained a fragile peace and found themselves time and time again having to firmly enforce freedom of movement when members of one ethnicity would attempt to block the transit

RIGHT INSET: Shoulder patch of the Berlin Brigade

RIGHT: A rapid response team from Company C, 6th Battalion, 502d Infantry responds to a simulated sniper attack and the wounding of two people during a July 1993 drill in Skopje, Macedonia. These and other Berlin Brigade troops manned checkpoints, observed military activities, and reported violations to the United Nations as part of Task Force Able Sentry.

BELOW: Members of Company C standing in review at Camp Able Sentry outside Skopje.

army could be reduced even further and deployed faster with lighter, more easily maintained equipment that, coincidentally, cost less money and freed up funds for technological innovations.

Eventually, the army saw the political writing on the wall; it had been severely stung by press and congressional criticism that Task Force Hawk's helicopters had taken nearly four weeks to reach their Albanian base—and still were not fully operational. It seemed clear that, with the sole exception of the light and tactically immobile 82d Airborne Division, the army would not be a factor in the fast-breaking situations that were anticipated as the norm in the post Cold War world of the 21st century. The army was in danger of being viewed as largely unnecessary.

The apparent answer was to convert much of the force into smaller, lighter, wheeled units that would police up what was left of the battlefield after the Air Force had soundly pasted it—then hand out humanitarian aid. Tanks were deemed "legacy" weapons, as were armored personnel carriers and artillery. Everyone understood that the army would have to maintain some number of heavy formations for the time being, but many military and civilian leaders firmly believed that tanks eventually would go the way of the horse cavalry. Technology was expected to provide complete knowledge of the battlefield, and enemy tanks and artillery no doubt would be completely destroyed from the air long before the U.S. Army reached a trouble spot. What arrived would not be a light infantry, or airborne or air assault, or armored or mechanized division tailored for a specific combat setting and enemy. All forces would be reorganized into identical, modular brigades of either a light or slightly heavier configuration—smaller structures judged capable of fulfilling the missions most likely to be encountered in the 21st century.

The service was busily engaged in its "Army Transformation" to a force suited for the coming brave new "Information Age" of near-perfect battlefield intelligence right up until—and even after—the hijacked aircraft slammed into New York City's twin towers and the Pentagon in Washington, D.C.

ABOVE: 1st Infantry Division soldiers, including (third from left) Staff Sergeant Andrew A. Ramirez of the 1st Squadron, 4th Cavalry, coordinate their activities with British paratroopers as they monitor the unmarked border between Macedonia and Kosovo on March 30, 1999. During a reconnaissance mission the next day along the forested trails winding through the hills, Ramirez's HMMWV became separated from others on the patrol and came under heavy small arms fire from Serbian troops. While turning to maneuver away, the vehicle got stuck in a ditch. Ramirez and two other soldiers were taken prisoner, undergoing rough interrogations and a mock execution before being released on May 2.

across their territory of another group that was trying to visit family, grave sites, or property. Serbs who stayed behind in Kosovo after the Yugoslav army withdrew also became the subject of reprisals until more KFOR troops arrived. An uneasy peace eventually settled over both areas, and U.S. rotations, which included National Guard components such as 49th Armored Division elements from Texas, slowly but steadily drew down in size. In 2010, American task forces of 1,450 soldiers each remained in both Bosnia and Kosovo as an important guarantors of peace and stability.

The defense establishment and the U.S. Army's senior leadership learned a variety of lessons from the deployments of the 1990s (frequently referred to as "meals on wheels" operations by enlisted and officers alike) that remain controversial today.

The Defense Department had resurrected the seductive airpower theories advanced in the 1920s by Giulio Douhet, who maintained that the will of a people to wage war could be shattered if their industries and cities' infrastructure were destroyed. Though actual results repeatedly had discredited the notion, it became a matter of common "wisdom" that the advent of mass produced, comparatively inexpensive precision-guided munitions ("smart bombs") could do the job while keeping civilian casualties down to a politically acceptable minimum. In such a scenario, and with the massive Soviet armies a thing of the past, the size of an

AFGHANISTAN

On October 8, 2001, U.S. President George W. Bush told the American people: "On my orders the United States military has begun strikes against al Qaeda terrorist training camps and military installations of the Taliban regime in Afghanistan." These camps were where nomadic terrorist Osama bin Laden and his partners in terror trained their recruits, including those involved in the 9/11 hijackings. When it became clear that no cooperation would be forthcoming from the Taliban, a pathologically fundamentalist Islamic movement with no per-manent base of operations, it was clear that the United States knew it had its work cut out for it in Afghanistan.

Secretary of Defense Donald L. Rumsfeld, the leading advocate of future high-tech war, had just come into office determined to reduce the army by two or three divisions to pay for the new technology. After the 9/11 tragedy, he was convinced that with the advent of precision guided munitions, Giulio Douhet's airpower theory

would hold and that the United States would not have to commit large numbers of troops, only special operations elements, which would work closely with anti-Taliban groups by calling in precisely targeted air strikes. The Northern Alliance of ethnic Tajiks, Uzbeks, Hazara, and some Pashtuns already held part of the country and were facing a force of roughly thirty thousand Taliban (Pashtuns from both sides of the Afghanistan-Pakistan border) plus three thousand multinational Al Qaeda terrorists. U.S. Army Special Forces already were conducting training missions in several neighboring countries, and within a week of 9/11, twelve-man Special Forces teams, and then CIA agents, were infiltrating into Afghanistan through Uzbekistan to link up with the Northern Alliance.

Carrier aircraft and massive B-52 bombers, guided by the Special Forces teams, began to strike the Taliban and al Qaeda. Their deadly work was made much easier than originally anticipated because the enemy did not operate as guerrillas, but as easy-to-target, conven-tional forces. Mounted on Toyota pickup trucks

BELOW: At Qala Jangi prison west of Mazar-e-Sharif, a mixed force of U.S. soldiers crouch behind a low wall as a laser-guided bomb finds its mark. The men are fighting several hundred prisoners who revolted against their Afghani guards and gained access to Northern Alliance weapons, November 26, 2001. The prisoners, which included an American, were mostly Pakistanis and other foreigners fighting for the Taliban.

LEFT INSET: The Global War on Terrorism Expeditionary Medal awarded to military service personnel who have deployed overseas for operations conducted since September 11, 2001 (*see also page 462*).

BELOW: A June 19, 2004, search
of a village on the Afghan-
Pakistan border near Khost
turns up a cache of weapons,
ammunition, and cassette tapes
used by the Taliban to promote
recruitment and cooperation
among the border tribes.

and leftover Soviet vehicles, they fought as light cavalry and usually were deployed in lines against the Northern Alliance, allowing the Special Forces teams to coordinate devastating air strikes against the linear, easily detected units. Taliban and al Qaeda forces dissolved under the weight of the coordinated air assault and Northern Alliance offensive, which pushed quickly into the cities in early November.

It seemed that the vision of "future war" was justified, but as the British and Soviets had earlier learned the hard way, possession of Afghanistan's cities did not mean control of the country. Scattered remnants of the Taliban did their best to keep out of sight, but an organized body of approximately one thousand al Qaeda still holed up near the Pakistani border in prepared mountain defenses above the Sharikot valley. They could not be defeated by airpower and local forces alone, so conventional army units had to dig them out in Operation Anaconda. The 101st Air Assault Division's 3d Brigade head-quarters directed the assault of the division's 1st Battalion, 187th Infantry and the 1st Battalion, 87th Infantry from the

10th Mountain Division. The thirteen-day battle in March 2002 eventually involved additional soldiers from the 187th Infantry's 2d Battalion; the 10th Mountain's 4th Battalion, 31st Infantry; the 75th Ranger Regiment; Special Forces and Navy SEAL elements; the Canadian 3d Battalion Princess Patricia's Canadian Light Infantry; and numerous helicopter units.

It was all over by March 16, with fifteen Americans killed and eighty-two wounded. Bin Laden proved an elusive quarry, but many of his lieutenants were successfully caught. They provided vital information about future terrorist attacks that were quashed. As for al Qaeda, it no longer existed as a coherent conventional force; it was shattered and discredited, while the U.S. Army's light infantry and air assault forces proved that they remained essential elements of modern combat. U.S. forces now prepared for the next phase of the war, and as the nation's focus turned from Afghanistan to Iraq, the Taliban began its slow revival—this time as a guerrilla force. It wasn't a very good guerrilla force, but one that would improve over time.

BELOW: A June 19, 2004, search of a village on the Afghan-Pakistan border near Khost turns up a cache of weapons, ammunition, and cassette tapes used by the Taliban to promote recruitment and cooperation among the border tribes.

LEFT: Sergeant 1st Class Matthew Kahler (*left*) supervises and provides security for privates Jonathan Ayers and Adam Hamby while they emplace an M240 machine gun during fighting in Afghanistan's mountainous Kunar Province, October 23, 2007. The soldiers are all from the 101st Airborne Division (Air Assault)'s 2d Battalion, 503rd Parachute Infantry. Sergant Kahler was killed by an Afghan soldier in a friendly-fire incident three months later on January 26, 2008.

BELOW: U.S. soldiers prepare to enter a building as they "mop up" in the Shahi Khot Valley near Gardez, Afghanistan, during Operation Anaconda, March 11, 2002. Nearby al Qaeda and Taliban strongholds came under intense bombing and were the scene of numerous fire-fights as U.S. and coalition forces battled to root them out.

THE IRAQ WAR

Despite his bloody suppression of the Kurds and Shiites in the aftermath of the Gulf War, Iraqi dictator Saddam Hussein at first appeared to be in general compliance with the 1991 cease-fire agreement that ended the fighting. It wasn't long, however, before he began to fire on United Nations jets enforcing the no-fly zones. In 1998 he defied disarmament obligations by kicking UN weapons inspectors out of the country. Based on U.S. intelligence, President Clinton's administration was convinced that Iraq was continuing to work on its ballistic missile program and still possessed hidden stockpiles of "WMDs"—weapons of mass destruction. British intelligence corroborated that information.

The U.S. Congress passed the Iraq Liberation Act of 1998, which called for assistance to the exiled Iraqi opposition as well as presidential pressure on the UN to create a war crimes tribunal to prosecute Saddam and his Baath Party henchmen. The act, however, was largely rhetorical and pointedly excluded any direct military action

BELOW: 3d Infantry Division soldiers at Objective Rams take up firing positions at the approach of enemy troops. The Saddan Fedayeen paramilitary troops and regular army units were surprised at the sudden appearance of the Americans and counterattacked in a steady but disorganized stream from nearby Najaf on March 23, 2003.

against the regime. This policy, continued by the incoming Bush administration, was reevaluated in the wake of the devastating 9/11 attacks.

Under Saddam, Iraq had launched ballistic missiles at Saudi Arabia and Israel, murdered tens of thousands of political opponents, invaded Iran and Kuwait, defied multiple UN resolutions, used poison gas against its Kurdish citizens, and openly funded suicide bombers in Israel. Meanwhile, several parties uncovered in Afghanistan documentation al Qaeda's interest in all forms of WMDs— nuclear materials, poison gasses, and biological agents. This immediately raised red flags in the Bush administration. Just as the Soviet Union had sponsored Third World insurgents during the Cold War, Saddam gave every indication of being willing to unleash his own proxies, be they al Qaeda or other international terrorists. The rapidly approaching danger point would come once the West grew tired of maintaining sanctions on Iraq and Saddam was able to restart his WMD programs. Bush emphatically stated that a rogue Iraq possessing WMDs "could enable (Saddam) to dominate the Middle East and intimidate the civilized world."

Under the threat of U.S. action, Iraqi officials agreed to allow inspectors back into their country, but it soon became obvious that a variety of evasions were being perpetrated. U.S. Secretary of State Colin Powell addressed the UN Security Council early in February 2003 and insisted that Iraq was not complying with previous UN resolutions.

ABOVE LEFT: A soldier with the 82d Airborne Division's 1st Battalion, 505th Parachute Infantry, sights potential enemy targets moving along the rooftop of a nearby building during a March 4, 2004, cordon and search operation in Fallujah, Iraq.

ABOVE RIGHT: During a gun battle between Saddam Hussein's brutal sons Qusay and Uday—the second and third "most wanted" Baath Party officials—and 101st Airborne Division troops, flames erupt when their safehouse in Mosul is hit by a TOW missile, July 21, 2003.

BELOW: A 3d Infantry Division Bradley and line of Abrams tanks prepares to cross the Euphrates River as hundreds of armored vehicles push toward the southern outskirts of Baghdad on April 6, 2003.

ABOVE: 82d Airborne Division soldiers conduct a dawn raid to search for weapons in the town of Khaldiya, 45 miles west of Baghdad. A strike force of roughly 100 airborne infantry, military police, and scouts swooped on six houses in the early hours of Monday morning of June 16, 2003, following a tip-off. In the highly choreographed assault, designated paratroopers cover a potentially dangerous site adjacent to one of their targets. Note that the soldier at far left is armed with a Mossberg 500 with a special-purpose barrel.

France and Russia, who were allies of Iraq, refused to take any action beyond the inspections. With no UN-sanctioned support and very little support from other countries, the United States and Great Britain decided to take joint military action. UN inspectors left Iraq on March 18, and the following day, the invasion of Iraq began.

With less than two hundred thousand ground troops, the force invading Iraq in 2003 was almost half that of the total Desert Storm attack force. It was made even smaller when Turkey, at the last moment, withheld permission for the 4th Infantry Division (Mechanized) to move through its territory and establish a northern front in the Kurdish region, which lay close to Baghdad. Despite the monkey wrench that Turkey's decision threw into the U.S. plans, theater commander General Tommy R. Franks was mindful of the huge destruction that the vengeful Saddam had inflicted on Kuwait's oil fields when his forces withdrew during the Gulf War. A lengthy delay waiting for the 4th Infantry and its equipment would allow time for the Iraqis to reposition more units in the south, possi-

bly forcing the coalition to conduct its battles in the oppressive desert heat while encumbered by nonporous gear designed to protect against poisoned gas.

Franks was convinced that he should start the ground war with the forces on hand and feed in reinforcements as they became available. Thus began a "rolling start" for Operation Iraqi Freedom. Only one heavy American formation, the 3d Infantry Division (Mechanized), was available at the beginning of the offensive. Supporting the V Corps' drive to the west of the Euphrates River—as they became available— would be the 11th Attack Helicopter Regiment, 101st Airborne (Air Assault), and 82d Airborne divisions. To V Corp's right, the 1st Marine Division would capture the Rumaylah oil fields before starting their own drive north and Britain's 1st Armored Division secured the large port of Basra.

The Air Force, meanwhile, conducted a much heralded "shock and awe" campaign (that fell flat in terms of its effect on the Iraqi morale), and also made a concerted, but unsuccessful, effort to "decapitate" the Iraqi leadership by targeting Saddam and senior leaders. The tactical air support for ground operations proved very effective in the V Corps and Marine drives, and it was invaluable in operations in the western desert where Special Forces foiled all Iraqi efforts to launch Scud ballistic missiles. In the north, a reinforced battalion of the 173d Airborne Brigade parachuted into Kurdish territory, and anM1A1 tank company air landed to help Peshmerga guerrillas and Special Forces establish a presence near the vital Mosul oil field.

The speed of the ground offensive did indeed take the Iraqis by surprise, severely dislocating the conventional Iraqi units, which were much fewer in number than during the Gulf War. Baghdad was seized on April 7–8 after the 3d Infantry Division had twice sent armored columns at will through western portions of the capital, one of which captured the international airport. However, because of the extremely thin American presence, combined with the virtual disappearance of the capital's police, only a relatively small number of important sites were secured adequately. Wide-scale looting and a general lawlessness prevailed across Baghdad for nearly a week, giving the coalition victory a very public black eye.

The White House and many Americans were surprised that U.S. troops were more tolerated than treated as the liberators, as they had been in Kuwait. But with the Baathists— Saddam loyalists all—spread thickly throughout the Sunni population, and the quick withdrawal of U.S. forces in the last war still fresh in the minds of southern Iraq's Shiites, the only place troops were greeted with cheers and flowers was in the northern front in the Kurdish region, where the absence of Baathists and presence of the Peshmerga freed the populace from fear of reprisals.

ABOVE: An Army M1070 Heavy Equipment Transport (HET) pulls a Soviet-built MiG-25R Foxbat-B from beneath the sands at Al Taqadum Air Base (today Camp Ridgeway) on July 6, 2003. The joint-service search team also discovered several other MiG-25s and Su-25 ground attack jets at the airbase west of Baghdad, and prompted the question: "What else might be buried around here?"

M249 SAW (Squad Automatic Weapon)

The 5.56-mm M249 Squad Automatic Weapon is a light machine gun that can be carried and fired by one soldier or mounted on a vehicle. At 16.5 pounds, it is considerably lighter than the 21-pound M60 machine gun formerly carried. It delivers a large volume of effective fire to more than 850 yards and area fire to 1,100 yards. Each squad carries two SAWs, allowing one per fire team. The troops love their SAWs—until they jam in the middle of a fire fight.

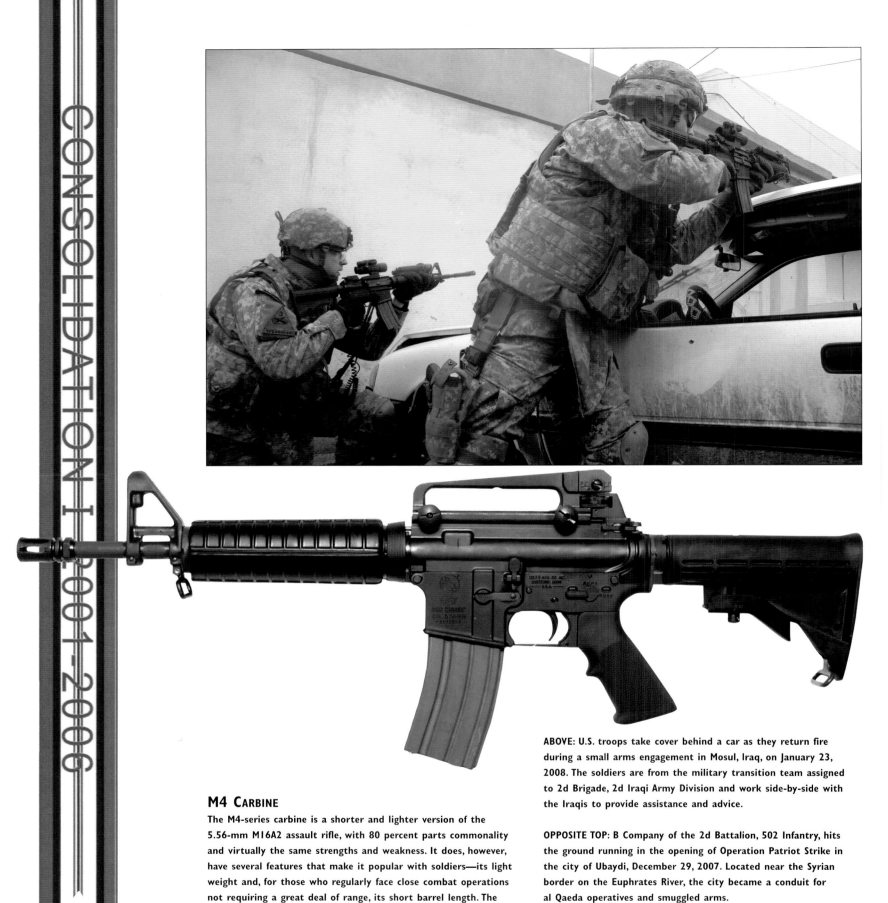

M4 CARBINE

The M4-series carbine is a shorter and lighter version of the 5.56-mm M16A2 assault rifle, with 80 percent parts commonality and virtually the same strengths and weakness. It does, however, have several features that make it popular with soldiers—its light weight and, for those who regularly face close combat operations not requiring a great deal of range, its short barrel length. The M4-series carbine buttstock has four positions: closed, 1/2 open, 3/4 open, and fully open. It is designed to fire either semiautomatic or a three-round burst through the use of a selector lever, and the M4A1 variant is fully automatic. The carbine becomes the M4 MWS when its rail adapter system is installed.

ABOVE: U.S. troops take cover behind a car as they return fire during a small arms engagement in Mosul, Iraq, on January 23, 2008. The soldiers are from the military transition team assigned to 2d Brigade, 2d Iraqi Army Division and work side-by-side with the Iraqis to provide assistance and advice.

OPPOSITE TOP: B Company of the 2d Battalion, 502 Infantry, hits the ground running in the opening of Operation Patriot Strike in the city of Ubaydi, December 29, 2007. Located near the Syrian border on the Euphrates River, the city became a conduit for al Qaeda operatives and smuggled arms.

OPPOSITE BOTTOM: While attached to the 82d Airborne Division, 8th Cavalry troopers wait for orders to conduct a house search for weapons caches near Contingency Operating Base Speicher, Iraq, on February 10, 2007.

CLOSE COMBAT BADGE

COMBAT MEDICAL BADGE

Leigh Ann Hester
Sergeant, 617th Military Police Company

Note: Hester is the first woman since World War II awarded the Silver Star and the first ever to receive the medal for direct actions against an enemy force.

Citation: Sergeant Leigh Ann Hester, 617th Military Police Company, Kentucky National Guard. Hester, along with others, distinguished herself in action on March 20, 2005. A three-vehicle, squad-sized element of her company was escorting a convoy of 30 trucks driven by civilian contractors along Alternate Supply Route Detroit, Iraq. The convoy was attacked by 50 enemy fighters, using rocket-propelled grenades, heavy machine guns, and small arms. Most of the enemy was concealed in an irrigation ditch and orchard, making them difficult to engage. The initial attack disabled the lead truck of the convoy, blocking the rest in the kill zone. Staff Sergeant Timothy F. Nein had members of his squad move forward to outflank them on the right side. Hester ordered her HUMVEE gunner to place covering fire on the enemy positions. Hester then moved her vehicle to a flanking position and dismounted, ordering her gunner to continue his fire into the orchard, adding hers to the battle. Using her M4 carbine with an attached grenade launcher, she fired grenades into the field. While this was happening, Nein, noting an insurgent behind a 10-foot embankment, threw a grenade, killing him. He then moved forward to the right side of the berm, followed by Hester. Nein quickly engaged and eliminated five enemy fighters. As they proceeded along the embankment, they both continued to take out insurgents, with Hester killing three. Once they reached the end of the trench, Nein called a cease fire. In total, this action resulted in 27 enemy fighters killed and seven captured (six of them wounded). While the squad suffered at least four serious casualties, none died from their wounds.

THE INSURGENCY

The first and foremost mission of the coalition forces in Operation Iraqi Freedom was to end the reign of Saddam Hussein and his Baath Party. It was believed that achieving this key goal would open the door to success on a series of other vital objectives, including eliminating Iraq's weapons of mass destruction; capturing or driving out terrorists who had found a safe haven in Iraq; collecting intelligence related to terrorist networks in Iraq and beyond; securing the country's oil fields and resources for the Iraqi people; and helping them create the conditions necessary for a rapid transition to representative self-government.

Even before Baghdad and Basra fell, tough fighting against the Iraqi Republican Guard and irregular forces prompted a question that would be repeated in the days, months, and years ahead: does the United States have enough troops in Iraq? Secretary of Defense Rumsfeld maintained throughout that yes, there were enough "boots on the ground."

A Coalition Provisional Authority was established with executive, legislative, and judicial authority over the Iraqi people until a democratic government was formed. A week later, on May 1, 2003, the Pentagon announced that major combat operations were over but attacks on U.S. checkpoints and along the highways were actually on the increase. Fully aware of the weakness of his army, Hussein had organized a large, Sunni Muslim paramilitary force called the *Fedayeen* (quickly dubbed the "*Saddam Fedayeen*") to conduct irregular warfare behind American lines if the country was invaded. Many of its members expended themselves in suicidal attacks against U.S. columns during the invasion, but thousands more remained armed and organized after the Baathist government fell. Complicating matters even further, the Baathists released 30,000 criminals into the population shortly before the invasion and U.S. authorities ordered the Iraqi Army disbanded; throwing nearly 280,000 combat-trained young men into unemployment in a country whose economy had been plundered by its leaders.

Although Shiite-dominated southern Iraq, part of which was garrisoned by the British and other coalition troops, often seemed on the verge of insurrection due to the influence of the Shiite fundamentalists who controlled neighboring Iran, it was the Baathist strongholds to the north and west of Baghdad—the "Sunni Triangle"—which would prove to be the most hotly contested areas over the coming years. The army, which had originally planned to quickly draw down to 30,000 troops on 12-month deployments by the end of the summer suddenly found itself maintaining 127,000 to 138,000 troops in Iraq, and even more as the necessary overlap of combat deployments and the need to provide extra security during elections regularly bumped the numbers up by tens of thousands.

Significant violence began to erupt in April, even before the announcement that major combat operations had ended. Forty miles west of Baghdad, in Fallujah, elements of

OPPOSITE LEFT: After being struck by a vehicle-borne improvised explosive device (IED) in Baqubah, Iraq, thirty miles northeast of Baghdad, a 2d Infantry Division Bradley Infantry Fighting Vehicle immediately caught fire with its occupants still inside. Specialist Christopher Waiters, a senior medic assigned to the division's 5th Battalion, 20th Infantry, 3d Stryker Brigade, makes his first attempt to climb into the flaming Bradley to rescue a third soldier trapped in the vehicle after he had moved two other casualties back to his Stryker Medical Evacuation Vehicle and treated them.

OPPOSITE RIGHT: Specialist Waiters tries a second time to reach the third crewman— his fourth time entering the burning vehicle.

LEFT: Sergeant Daniel Kear of B Company, 1st Battalion, 6th Infantry, makes his way down a road after canal vegetation is set ablaze near Tahwilla, Iraq, July 30, 2008. Insurgents frequently used the concealment provided by the canal system to place improvised explosive devices (IEDs) under the cover of night. The 6th Infantry, was assigned to Task Force 1-35 Armor, 2d Brigade Combat Team, 1st Armored Division.

LEFT: Sergeant Robert S. Pugh, Company A, 1st Battalion, 155th Infantry, Mississippi National Guard. On March 2, 2005, Pugh and another soldier were severely wounded by an IED in Iraq. Pugh, an A Company medic, directed the treatment for his comrade, saving his life while Pugh died of his injuries.

INSET: Shrapnel from the IED which mortally wounded Sergeant Pugh.

Official Citation: The President of the United States of America, authorized by Act of Congress, July 9, 1918 (amended by act of July 25, 1963), takes pleasure in presenting the Distinguished Service Cross to Staff Sergeant Christopher Bernard Waiters, United States Army, for extraordinary heroism in action while serving with Company A, 5th Battalion, 20th Infantry Regiment, 3d Brigade Combat Team, 2d Infantry Division, Multi-National Division-North, on April 5, 2007. Specialist Waiters distinguished himself by exceptionally valorous conduct in support of Operation Iraqi Freedom. During a clearance mission, a Bradley Fighting Vehicle was struck by an improvised explosive device and began to burn with its occupants inside. Specialist Waiters, the company's senior medic, quickly parked his Medical Evaluation Stryker in a security position and engaged two armed enemy personnel. He then dismounted alone from his vehicle and ran 80 meters through fierce small arms fire toward the flaming Bradley. Specialist Waiters then pulled out the driver and the vehicle commander, treated both, and safeguarded the casualties back to his Stryker for further treatment. At this point, Specialist Waiters learned that another soldier was trapped inside the Bradley. Without hesitation, he sprinted back and climbed into the troop compartment. While inside, the Bradley's 25-mm ammunition began exploding, forcing his exit. Again, he re-entered the vehicle and found a deceased American soldier. He sprinted back to his Stryker to secure a body bag. Upon his return, another medic had taken charge of the scene, allowing Specialist Waiters to evacuate the two casualties in his Stryker. Specialist Waiters' personal courage, uncommon valor, and selfless service directly contributed to the safety and evacuation of two wounded and the recovery of one fallen soldier. His actions reflect great credit upon himself, the 20th Infantry Regiment, Multi-National Division-North, and the United States Army.

Staff Sergeant
Christopher B. Waiters

SNAPSHOT OF A ROTATION

During the World Wars and Korea, soldiers knew that they served "for the duration" of the fighting unless they were either killed or invalided home because of wounds, disease, or psychiatric break-downs. The only major exception to this occurred after the 1945 victory in Europe when over a half-million men—some of whom had been drafted more than a year before Pearl Harbor—were released under the precise calculations of the Points Discharge System, which factored in a soldier's length of service with the amount of combat that he had survived. A similar system was established during the Korean War after the front stabilized in mid-1951.

In Vietnam, tours of duty were finite and each soldier deployed with a DEROS (date of expected return from overseas) of one year. It was believed that this enforced limitation in the soldiers' exposure to intense combat would lessen the number of men lost to combat-related psychiatric breakdowns, which in World War II had added a stunning 312,354 discharges on top of the army's 936,259 battle casualties. In this narrow respect, the one-year tours of the Vietnam period were a complete success, but it did not take long for the destructive aspects of the policy to become painfully apparent.

Combat formations deployed to Vietnam as cohesive, well-trained organizations during the war's first few years. Nearly all stayed "in country" as men rotated out but, for a time, the number of soldiers signing up for additional tours of duty helped ensure a degree of continuity. However, even in the best units, integrity and cohesion became compromised. In some, it was almost completely shattered by the constant and irregular turnover combined with the inevitable casualties. Time and the pace of operations seldom allowed commanders (who were sent to Vietnam for absurdly brief "ticket punch" six-month tours to gain combat experience) to pull formations out of the field to train and integrate the waves of FNGs ("f---ing new guys").

Another difference between Vietnam and World War II had to do with how the men closed out their wartime service. When the fighting ended in Europe, nearly every soldier—whether on his way home, staying for the occupation, or redeploying for the invasion of Japan—spent months in camp, then at sea, with either members of his own unit or men who had shared war-time experiences similar to his own. This level of emotional support and ability to "decompress" was not available to a young soldier who boarded a Pan Am jet "back to the world" within days, or even hours, of his DEROS.

Combat operations throughout the rest of the century, even the massive commitment to the Persian Gulf War, were relatively short, allowing soldiers to deploy, fight, and return as units. Yet the possibility of a long war always existed and, with Vietnam still fresh in its institutional memory, the army was determined that nothing similar to the highly destructive individual rotations would be reinstituted. When

it became clear early in the 2003–2010 Iraq War that forces in Iraq would have to be increased, rather than drawn down, after the toppling of the Baathist regime, the planned deployments of units in the country were lengthened as a complex rotation plan was worked out for continuing operations involving the army's new brigade-centered structure.

Instead of maintaining the same divisions over an unknown number of years as their personnel remained in nearly continuous flux, division head-quarters and brigades—many of them, unlike in Vietnam, National Guard formations—rotated through Iraq, and Afghanistan as well. What follows is a snapshot of the units rotating into Iraq near the center point of the war, mid-2005 through mid-2006, replacing others that had been in the country for twelve to an extended fifteen months:

- V Corps, Heidelberg, Germany, and its major subordinate units including 3d Corps Support Command, V Corps Artillery, 205th Military Intelligence Brigade, 130th Engineer Brigade, 22nd Signal Brigade, and 30th Medical Brigade.
- 4th Infantry Division (division headquarters, 4 brigades, and subordinate units), Ft. Hood, Texas
- 101st Airborne Division, Air Assault (division headquarters, 4 brigades, and subordinate units), Fort Campbell, Kentucky
- 1st Brigade 1st Armored Division, Wiesbaden, Germany
- 2d Brigade 1st Armored Division, Wiesbaden, Germany
- 48th Infantry Brigade (Separate), Georgia Army National Guard
- 172d Stryker Brigade Combat Team, Fort Wainwright, Alaska
- 1st Brigade, 10th Mountain Division, Fort Drum, New York
- 2d Brigade Combat Team, 28th Infantry Division, Pennsylvania Army National Guard
- 1st Brigade, 1st Infantry Division, Fort Riley, Kansas

Rotating into Afghanistan during the same period were:
- 10th Mountain Division (division headquarters, 2 brigades, and subordinate units), Fort Drum, New York
- 53d Infantry Brigade, Florida Army National Guard

This rotation—as all others until near the close of the campaign in Iraq—displays the army's brigade-centered structure of the twenty-first century. Prior to operations in Afghanistan and Iraq, the army had decided that in future conflicts, the brigade would be the primary, and probably largest, unit deployed. Divisions were supposed to eventually disappear. The fighting in these two theaters quickly demonstrated, however, that brigade staffs lacked the redundancy, experience, and clout provided by senior officers and staffs, as well as the unity of effort and intelligence provided by higher level staffs and organizations.

One of the primary tasks of senior staffs is to filter information and protect their subordinate

V Corps

BELOW: *Soldiers watch a taxiing C-130 Hercules from Dyess AFB, Texas, as they wait to board a C-17 Globemaster III aircraft at Sather Air Base, Iraq, on April 19, 2008. Approximately 32,000 service members per month processed through the base's passenger terminal.*

elements from the excessive demands and never-ending flood of communications that relentlessly chew up the time needed to plan and conduct combat operations. The first six months in Afghanistan proved the necessity of division and corps organizations and, almost begrudgingly, such formations became common-place in the theaters. Divisions, though, remained out of favor, were sparingly deployed, and consequently (and particularly in Iraq), sometimes found themselves with as many as double the number of brigades that they

1st Infantry Division

3d Infantry Division

1st Armored Division

4th Infantry Division

101st Airborne Division

were designed to control and protect. It wasn't until the campaign in Iraq was drawing to a close that a more effective balance became commonplace again. As for the brigades themselves, a cavalryman of the nineteenth century might describe them as being "rode hard and put away wet" by the decade-long cycle of deploy, refit, retrain, and redeploy.

During Vietnam, professional soldiers rotated back into combat after a year's stateside duty. In Iraq and Afghanistan, regular army units serve twelve-to fifteen-month combat tours, come home and return to combat in twelve months—essentially an interrupted variant of the "for the duration" of World War II. Psychiatric casualties still occur from these multiple unit deployments, but the results are nevertheless far and away better than the painful Vietnam experience of individual replacements, which was so damaging to both the army and the nation as a whole. Further, tours for officers, depending on the level of command, now run as long as eighteen months. In combination with the rotation of complete units, this has resulted in better-led formations with greater unit coherence and integrity; a Volunteer Army that has not only held together, but has performed superbly during the longest sustained campaigns in America's history.

BACKGROUND: Soldiers from the 3d Infantry Division's 15th Infantry Regiment, 3d Brigade Combat Team, being briefed on a joint search operation in Jisr Diyala, Iraq, April 23, 2007. Together with Iraqi police they will try to locate a clandestine hospital for Jeish al-Mahdi activists engaging in sectarian violence. By the end of 2006, Jeish al-Mahdi, also known as the "Mahdi Army" under the control of the radical Shiite cleric Muqtada al-Sadr, had replaced al Qaeda in Iraq as the biggest threat to the security of the country.

BELOW: U.S. soldiers of "The Old Guard" and Iraqi soldiers take a break while pulling security during a building clearing mission in Rashid, Iraq, on June 2, 2007. The U.S. soldiers are members of A Company, 2d Battalion, 3d Infantry Regiment.

OPPOSITE: Iraqi Army soldier Zatar Jeba (*left*) and Private First Class Yasuo Albert of the 66th Armor, 4th Infantry Division, share a rooftop security position on a coalition forces building during counter-insurgency operations in Tarmiya, Iraq, March 25, 2006. An Iraqi Army M113A2/A3 Armored Ambulance stands on call within the compound gates while a trio of Soviet-made BMP1s are flanked by American HUMVEEs beyond the wall. Across the street is an elderly Soviet-made MTBL that, presumably, is still in running condition.

82d Airborne Division and 3d Armored Cavalry Regiment (ACR) were involved in deadly confrontations with Sunni Muslim townspeople, many with ties to the Baath Party. In Baghdad itself, the "Sadr City" slums, named after the deceased Shiite Muslim grand ayatollah Mohammad Mohammad Sadeq al-Sadr, saw clashes between followers of his son, Muqtada al-Sadr, and the 2d Battalion 37th Armor and attached MP units. Quickly learning that direct assaults against U.S. forces were futile, insurgents turned increasingly to guerrilla tactics including sniping, hit-and-run mortar and rocket propelled grenade attacks, car and suicide bombs, as well as use of improvised explosive devices (IEDs) along the roads.

Attacks soon expanded to include the petroleum, water, and electrical infrastructure in an effort to make the country ungovernable as coalition forces stepped up efforts to round up former regime leaders; some three hundred of whom were killed or captured, as well as large numbers of lesser functionaries and military personnel. On July 22, 2003, a raid by the 101st Airborne Division and a special operations task force killed Hussein's brutal sons Uday and Qusay in Mosul. Saddam Hussein himself was captured on December 13, 2003, on a farm near Tikrit by 4th Infantry Division and the special operators. Meanwhile, the new Iraqi interim government began taking its first shaky steps in leading the fragile nation as Shiites, Sunnis, and the northern Kurdish minority maneuvered to establish their roles in the country's future.

A relative lull in violence in the opening months of 2004 ended as Iraq became a magnet for Islamist fighters, principally Sunni, from across the Middle East who formed the core of al Qaeda in Iraq while attacks from Shia militias also increased in both Baghdad and southern Iraq. The new Iraqi Security Forces were increasingly targeted by both religious sects while al Qaeda operatives concentrated more on attacking Shia civilians than government soldiers and police in order to whip up destabilizing sectarian violence. In the midst of this near chaos, four armed contractors conducting a food delivery in Fallujah were killed and their burned bodies hung from a bridge.

The marines, who had recently taken over operations in the area, suspended their strategy of foot patrols, less aggressive raids, humanitarian aid, and close cooperation with local leaders to instead launch a combat operation in April to clear guerrillas from Fallujah. With little time to prepare and gather intelligence, the attack failed. Renewed again in November,

RIGHT: Close combat uniform top worn by Specialist Alex Aguliar, A Company A, 1st Battalion, 155th Infantry, of the Mississippi National Guard 155 Heavy Brigade Combat Team during Operation Iraqi Freedom.

BACKGROUND: Soldiers with 2d Stryker Cavalry Regiment move to their next objective during an October 7, 2007, search operation in Baghdad.

BELOW: A uniform over-garment chemical protection suit worn by Specialist Paul Chrismer of the 3d Infantry Division during the invasion of Iraq.

LEFT: A close combat uniform issued to the 3d Stryker Brigade Combat Team in December of 2003, worn by Sergeant Justin White, medical squad leader for A Company, 2d Battalion, 3d Infantry Regiment, 2d Infantry Division.

RIGHT: A Universal Camouflage Pattern (UCP) army combat uniform worn by Specialist Amanda Kistler, 34th Brigade Combat Team of the Minnesota National Guard during Operation Iraqi Freedom. Kistler deployed as a medic in March 2006.

LEFT: Specialist Jesus B. Fernandez, an assistant team leader with 3d Platoon, C Company, 2d Battalion, 12th Infantry, 4th Brigade Combat Team, crosses a stream during a unit visit to meet with Angla Kala village elders in Kunar province, Afghanistan, on February 6, 2010. The Army quickly found (and should have realized beforehand) that the Universal Camouflage Pattern issued in 2005 was completely unsuited to the terrain in Afghanistan. A search for a new pattern was initiated in 2008. Fernandez wears the MultiCam uniform during field tests by his battalions in 2010 while another battalion wore uniforms with the UCP-Delta pattern. The fire-resistant MultiCam pattern already used by Special Forces units was chosen for use in Afghanistan.

MultiCam Camouflage Pattern

UCP-Delta Camouflage Pattern

Marine regimental combat teams were backed up by the Army's 2d Battalion, 7th Cavalry, and 2d Battalion, 2d Infantry (Mechanized), all supported by numerous army combat, support, Special Forces elements, and the well trained Iraqi 36th Commando Battalion (and somewhat less reliable elements of the Iraqi Army).

The 46-day battle—the heaviest urban combat that U.S. troops had been involved in since the battle of Hue in 1968—resulted in a victory, with approximately 1,350 insurgents killed for a loss of 95 Americans. Fallujah, however, was left totally devastated and the Iraqi troops which took over after U.S. forces left ultimately abandoned the city to the enemy. Coming at the same time as revelations of widespread prisoner abuse at the Abu Ghraib detention facility in April 2004, and charges—later found to be false—of American atrocities in Fallujah, the failure to achieve a lasting victory in the city contributed to growing doubts about the wisdom of the war. The battle also undermined the U.S. moral authority in the eyes of many Sunnis who boycotted the January 31, 2005, elections for the Iraqi Transitional Government that would draft a permanent constitution. Most of the eligible Kurd and Shia populace participated.

Shia militias had also risen up in Sadr City and Najaf during 2004, but not having broad-based support, were unable to make much headway against U.S. forces. Instead, they increased their efforts against their fellow Iraqis. Several months of relative quiet followed the elections, raising hopes that the insurgency was winding down, but May 2005 brought Iraq's bloodiest month since the invasion. Suicide bombers, mainly Syrians, Saudis, and disheartened Iraqi Sunnis under the direction of al Qaeda, tore through the country in an effort

ABOVE: Staff Sergeant Hank Moreno, a sniper with 4th Battalion, 9th Infantry, pulls security in front of an M1126 Stryker Infantry Carrier Vehicle (ICV) during a 4th Stryker Brigade infiltration into Rawad, Iraq, October 1, 2007.

RIGHT: The subdued shoulder patch of the 2d Infantry Division.

BELOW: Modern-day dragoons of C Troop, 8th Squadron, 1st Cavalry Regiment prepare Stryker armored vehicles to convoy General Stanley McChrystal, commander of the International Security Assistance Force, and his staff to the Wesh border crossing in Afghanistan on March 4, 2010.

to derail the political process. Their targets were often Shia religious gatherings or other concentrations of Shia civilians, 700 of whom died along with 79 Americans and roughly twice as many Iraqi police and soldiers of both sects.

To stem the flow of arms and insurgents infiltrating into the country, a series of operations were carried out in north-western Iraq to seal off the Syrian border. One in particular, the seizure and pacification of Tel Afar by the 3d ACR, would later serve as a model for similar efforts and was greatly aided by the fact that the Americans were supported by a much larger number of well-trained and reliable Iraqi troops than had been available the year before at Fallujah. A similar effort to "clear, hold, and build" spearheaded by the 325th Airborne Infantry, 82d Airborne Division, in Sadr City also showed much promise, but all gains withered away after the regiment turned the hard-won area over to Iraqi security forces who were not yet up to the task of holding the area, let alone furthering the gains. However, Tel Afar, which had been cleared twice before by U.S. soldiers, stayed in friendly hands.

A costly stalemate appeared to be in the offing as U.S. and coalition forces continued their effort to train the Iraqi army and police, and a referendum was held on October 15, 2005, in which the new Iraqi constitution was ratified. An Iraqi national assembly was elected in December, with participation from the Sunnis as well as the Kurds and Shia. For the enemies of a democratic Iraq, these advances could not be allowed to stand. On February 22, 2006, a bomb planted by al Qaeda blew up the golden dome of the al Askari Mosque in Samarra, one of the holiest shrines in Shi'a Islam, setting off sectarian violence in cities and towns across Iraq as protesting mobs took to the streets to chant for revenge and set fire to dozens of Sunni mosques. In Baghdad alone, the numbers of murders tripled to an average of thirty-three a day as counter reprisals followed reprisal and the country teetered for months on the verge of civil war.

The U.S. military response to the chaos was largely reactive. Senior commanders believed that an active American presence was more of an irritant than a help and maintained that increased U.S. counterinsurgency operations would only encourage the Iraqi Army to lay back while the Americans took the lead. They wanted U.S. troops to be withdrawn as soon as possible. However, Lieutenant General Raymond Odierno, commanding Multi–National Corp-Iraq in the Baghdad region was convinced that if U.S. and Iraqi forces secured the safety of the civilian populations at risk, these safe areas could be expanded and ultimately force out the insurgents. This, however, was a very "soldier-intensive" solution and the U.S. Army in Iraq simply did not have the manpower.

The deteriorating situation in Iraq led to the exit of Secretary of Defense Rumsfeld. President Bush and his security advisers, meanwhile, came to the conclusion that the largely Shiite leadership of Iraq was capable of—and most important, willing to—confront insurgents that were co-religionists, and also that the Sunni population was showing signs that it would be more willing to seek American protection. Neither of these two things would happen, however, unless it was clear that

BELOW: Specialist Lonnie Kirk moves ahead of a Mine Resistant Ambush Protected (MRAP) vehicle from 1st Battalion, 2d Infantry Regiment, attached to 1st Stryker Brigade Combat Team, 25th Infantry Division. The unit was patrolling between Iraqi army checkpoints in the village of Tawilla in the Diyala province of Iraq on February 27, 2009. The army began fielding a family of MRAP vehicles, with V-shaped hull design to deflect blasts away from crewmen, in 2007, as a response to increasing losses to IEDs in Iraq.

ABOVE: General Raymond T. Odierno. From 2003 to 2010, General Odierno served in Iraq as the 4th Infantry Division (Mechanized) commander, the III Corps and Multi-National Corps commander, then Multi-National Force commander, and as Commander, United States Forces–Iraq. Odierno became the U.S. Army's 38th Chief of Staff in September 2011.

America was not going to abandon Iraq. In the midst of loud calls from a wide cross section of American opinion makers at home and opponents abroad for the United States to withdraw its troops and let the Iraqis fight it out among themselves, President Bush announced in early January 2007 that he was ordering a "surge" of five combat brigades—some 21,000 troops—to bolster the twenty combat brigades already there. Lieutenant General David H. Petraeus, who had formerly commanded the 101st Airborne Division in the country, was also named commander of Multi-National Forces–Iraq.

Bush and Petraeus maintained that the additional military strength would quell the growing sectarian violence and provide the time and conditions conducive to reconciliation among political and ethnic factions. This move pleased many Americans, but opponents reacted bitterly to the decision; the Senate majority leader famously declaring "this war is lost" and "the surge is not accomplishing anything" even before many of the troops had arrived in the country.

Petraeus accepted Odierno's suggestion to divide the surge forces between Baghdad and surrounding areas so that insurgents would have no "safe havens" where they could rebuild their forces and infiltrate back into the city. With increased troops, U.S. forces made their presence permanent in joint American–Iraqi neighborhood command posts, and trust developed between them and local civilians who no longer had to fear that they would be at the mercy of insurgents when the

American and government soldiers left. More tips on where to find enemy hideouts and roadside bombs were received by the U.S. and Iraqi militaries. Tribal sheiks also took more leadership, and the people, who had grown weary of the growing savagery of the largely foreign and fundamentalist al Qaeda cells and the constant upheaval caused by violence, followed their lead. Once the areas were secured, day-to-day activities quickly revived.

On the war's fifth anniversary in March 2008, President Bush spoke about the fight in Iraq: "Five years into this battle, there is an understandable debate about whether the war was worth fighting, whether the war was worth winning, and whether we can win it. The answers are clear to me. Removing Saddam Hussein from power was the right decision, and this is a fight that America can and must win." A few days later, a roadside bomb killed four American soldiers, bringing the death total to 4,000. Yet, the month of June saw the lowest American casualties thus far in the war—19 deaths.

The U.S.–Iraq Status of Forces Agreement, in negotiation for nearly a year, was approved by the Iraqi government on December 4, 2008. It established that U.S. combat forces would withdraw from Iraqi cities by June 30, 2009, and that all U.S. forces would be completely out of Iraq by December 31, 2011, subject to possible further negotiations which could either delay or otherwise modify the withdrawal.

Throughout 2009 the Iraqis took responsibility for security in large swaths of territory and U.S. forces ceased independent

RIGHT: 1st Lieutenant Steven Rose launches an RQ-11 Raven unmanned aerial vehicle near a new highway bridge project along the Euphrates River north of al Taqqadum, Iraq, on October 9, 2009. Rose served in the 1st Battalion, 504th Parachute Infantry, 1st Brigade Combat Team, 82d Airborne Division which is assisting Iraqi police in providing security for the work site.

LEFT: Specialist Bruce Nemeth, assigned to the 1st Battalion Special Troops Brigade, 10th Mountain Division, assists Iraqi police in providing security at recruiting station Albu al Katab, Iraq, July 26, 2008. The applicants are receiving an initial screening for the Sons of Iraq program, part of the "Sunni Awakening," in which groups of primarily Sunni citizens have been joining with U.S. military forces to fight against Shiite militias, as well as the Sunni terrorist group al Qaeda in Iraq.

LEFT: Captain Chad Klascius leads Lieutenant General Ray Odierno, commander of Multi-National Corps–Iraq, and Sheikh Ali Majeed Imseer al-Dulaimi, president of the Hawr Rajab Awakening Council, on a tour of the city on November 9, 2007. Local leaders in Hawr Rajab have organized more than 400 concerned citizens who are helping provide security at various sites around the city. Captain Klascius commands Troop A, 1st Squadron, 40th Cavalry, in the 25th Infantry Division's 4th Brigade.

A "NEW ENEMY" 495

ABOVE: From 2003 to date, General Petraeus has held numerous commands in the Middle East: the 101st Airborne Division (Air Assault), Multi-National Security Transition Command Iraq, Multi-National Force–Iraq, U.S. Central Command, United States Forces–Afghanistan, and International Security Assistance Force (Afghanistan). Petraeus took over as Director of the Central Intelligence Agency in September 2011.

FAMILY TIES . . . AND TIES, AND TIES.
The father-in-law of General Petraeus was General William A. Knowlton, who managed a civil-military campaign in Vietnam much like what Petraeus instituted in Iraq, the Civil Operations and Revolutionary Development Support (CORDS) project. Knowlton himself was the adopted son of Colonel Richard C. Burleson, a cantankerous yet witty master of artillery who prefaced both praise and scorn with the words "By God!" Burleson mentored a young artillery captain named Harry Truman and was subsequently his colleague during the long, between-wars years. He was also an early and vocal advocate of what would later be called "combined arms operations." Burleson came from a military family and an uncle, Edward Burleson, commanded the center of the Texan line during its assault at the Battle of San Jacinto.

foot patrols in Baghdad. By the end of August 2010, more than 90,000 U.S. troops, 40,000 vehicles, and 1.5 million items, from radios to generators, had left Iraq. With the withdrawal of the last combat troops, that month Operation Iraqi Freedom transitioned to Operation New Dawn with the new U.S. Forces–Iraq coordinating the activities of 49,700 soldiers in seven brigade combat teams that had been redesignated Advise and Assist Brigades (AABs) after receiving specialized training, as well as two security brigades, and two aviation brigades.

The AABs trained Iraqi Security Forces and, when requested, assisted with security and stability missions as the Iraqis' competence and pride that they were now the defenders of their country soared. The phased drawdown of U.S. forces continued and in January of 2011 U.S. forces in Iraq consisted of only five AABs and an aviation brigade operating under three division headquarters: the 4th Infantry Division in the north, 1st Infantry Division in the south, and the 25th Infantry Division, stationed at the Victory Base Complex outside Baghdad. Any American presence in Iraq beyond 2011 would be in accordance with agreements negotiated between the two governments, as is done wherever there are U.S. bases or training personnel.

THE LONGEST WAR

Even as the surge and rejection of al Qaeda by tribal leaders—the "Sunni Awakening"—was bringing victory in Iraq, violence in Afghanistan increased in June 2008 when 22 American plus 23 NATO and Afghani troops were killed, the highest monthly total since the invasion of 2001. The situation had been

OPPOSITE: After a 20-minute gun battle, a 4th Infantry Division soldier watches as U.S. Air Force F-15s strike fleeing insurgents in Afghanistan's Korengal Valley on August 13, 2009. The men of Company B, 2nd Battalion, 12th Infantry, part of the 4th Infantry Division's 4th Brigade Combat Team, routinely engaged insurgents in the volatile Kunar province valley. International Security Assistance Forces across Afghanistan increased operations during the spring and summer of 2009 in order to ensure safety and security during Afghanistan's second national election in August of that year.

BACKGROUND: 1st Sergeant Eric Davis exits an abandoned home after clearing the upper floors, December 16, 2007. Davis and his fellow soldiers from the 3d Battalion, 187th Infantry, in the 101st Airborne Division's 3d Brigade Combat Team, were searching for al Qaeda remnants in Fair al Jair, Iraq.

MEDAL OF HONOR
Specialist Salvatore A. Giunta
173d Airborne Brigade

Specialist Salvatore A. Giunta distinguished himself conspicuously by gallantry and intrepidity at the risk of his life above and beyond the call of duty in action with an armed enemy in the Korengal Valley, Afghanistan, on October 25, 2007. While conducting a patrol as team leader with Company B, 2d Battalion (Airborne), 503d Infantry Regiment, Giunta and his team were navigating through harsh terrain when they were ambushed by a well-armed and well-coordinated insurgent force. While under heavy enemy fire, Giunta immediately sprinted towards cover and engaged the enemy. Seeing that his squad leader had fallen and believing that he had been injured, Giunta exposed himself to withering enemy fire and raced towards his squad leader, helped him to cover, and administered medical aid. While administering first aid, enemy fire struck Giunta's body armor and his secondary weapon. Without regard to the ongoing fire, Giunta engaged the enemy before prepping and throwing grenades, using the explosions for cover in order to conceal his position. Attempting to reach additional wounded fellow soldiers who were separated from the squad, Giunta and his team encountered a barrage of enemy fire that forced them to the ground. The team continued forward and upon reaching the wounded soldiers, Giunta realized that another soldier was still separated from the element. Giunta then advanced forward on his own initiative. As he crested the top of a hill, he observed two insurgents carrying away an American soldier. He immediately engaged the enemy, killing one and wounding the other. Upon reaching the wounded soldier, he began to provide medical aid, as his squad caught up and provided security. Giunta's unwavering courage, selflessness, and decisive leadership while under extreme enemy fire were integral to his platoon's ability to defeat an enemy ambush and recover a fellow American soldier from the enemy. Specialist Salvatore A. Giunta's extraordinary heroism and selflessness above and beyond the call of duty are in keeping with the highest traditions of military service and reflect great credit upon himself, Company B, 2d Battalion (Airborne), 503d Infantry Regiment, and the United States Army.

Citation: Staff Sergeant Robert J. Miller distinguished himself by extraordinary acts of heroism while serving as the Weapons Sergeant in Special Forces Operational Detachment Alpha 3312, Special Operations Task Force-33, Combined Joint Special Operations Task Force-Afghanistan during combat operations against an armed enemy in Konar Province, Afghanistan on January 25, 2008. While conducting a combat reconnaissance patrol through the Gowardesh Valley, Miller and his small element of U.S. and Afghan National Army soldiers engaged a force of fifteen to twenty insurgents occupying prepared fighting positions. Miller initiated the assault by engaging the enemy positions with his vehicle's turret-mounted Mark-19 40-millimeter automatic grenade launcher while simultaneously providing detailed descriptions of the enemy positions to his command, enabling effective, accurate close air support. Following the engagement, Miller led a small squad forward to conduct a battle damage assessment. As the group neared the small, steep, narrow valley that the enemy had inhabited, a large, well-coordinated insurgent force initiated a near ambush, assaulting from elevated positions with ample cover. Exposed and with little available cover, the patrol was totally vulnerable to enemy rocket propelled grenades and automatic weapon fire. As point man, Miller was at the front of the patrol, cut off from supporting elements, and less than 20 meters from enemy forces. Nonetheless, with total disregard for his own safety, he called for his men to quickly move back to covered positions as he charged the enemy over exposed ground and under overwhelming enemy fire in order to provide protective fire for his team. While maneuvering to engage the enemy, Miller was shot in his upper torso. Ignoring the wound, he continued to push the fight, moving to draw fire from over one hundred enemy fighters upon himself. He then again charged forward through an open area in order to allow his teammates to safely reach cover. After killing at least ten insurgents, wounding dozens more, and repeatedly exposing himself to withering enemy fire while moving from position to position, Miller was mortally wounded by enemy fire. His extraordinary valor ultimately saved the lives of seven members of his own team and fifteen Afghanistan National Army soldiers. Staff Sergeant Miller's heroism and selflessness above and beyond the call of duty, and at the cost of his own life, are in keeping with the highest traditions of military service and reflect great credit upon himself and the United States Army.

growing steadily worse ever since 2006 when the Pakistani government cut a deal with the Taliban insurgents that effectively granted them a sanctuary in the "tribal areas" bordering Afghanistan. U.S. forces, already heavily committed to Iraq, responded by conducting targeted air attacks on insurgent leaders in Pakistan. Though these attacks were very effective, it was clear to Bush and his new Defense Secretary, Robert Gates, that such measures could only delay, not prevent, Taliban inroads into southern Afghanistan. Based on the broad consensus among both Democrats and Republicans in Congress, and each party's presidential candidates, that American combat strength in Afghanistan must be increased, Bush and Gates pledged to the Afghani government and NATO that the United States would raise its troop levels in 2009.

A brigade from the 1st Infantry Division and marine units were already fighting the Taliban, and to this was added a marine air-ground task force and brigade from the 10th Mountain Division between November 2008 and January 2009. The 82d Airborne Division's aviation brigade was also ordered to join them, adding badly need airlift and fire support to operations in the mountainous country. Meanwhile, Secretary Gates, who had been asked to stay on by the incoming president, Barak Obama, expressed his hope that two to three more combat brigades would be added by the following summer.

Within days of taking office, the new president added a marine brigade, brigade combat teams from the 2d and 4th divisions, and the 82d Airborne Division's headquarters and support elements. By the end of 2009, some 68,000 troops were in Afghanistan, but only a third of them were in combat formations. For example, the National Guard brigade combat teams, the 33d (Illinois), 48th (Florida), and 53d (Georgia), were all involved in the critically important role of training the Afghan National Security Forces. A further increase of 30,000 troops, dubbed the "Afghanistan Surge" was announced at West Point on December 1, 2009, and the president promised to begin withdrawals of some U.S. forces in the summer of 2011.

Despite adding the qualifier that this would only be done after "taking into account conditions on the ground," the specter of decreased support of the war effort by Afghanis if they believed that the Americans were going to "abandon" them was immediately raised. Why put one's life on the line if the Americans are going to go home? Better to cut deals with the Taliban who, now that the United States has a perceived withdrawal date, can simply wait for the Americans to leave. In an effort to bring badly needed clarity to U.S. intensions, a target date of 2014 was released as the time when it was hoped that Afghan soldiers and policemen would be ready to take the lead in securing the nation. NATO leaders endorsed the plan in November 2010, but conceded that 2015 was a more realistic date. As for General Petraeus, he carefully stated: "I don't think there are any sure things in this kind of endeavor."

Petraeus had suddenly found himself in the position of being the third commander in Afghanistan in little more than a year when General Stanley McChrystal, who'd done yeoman work as the head of the Joint Special Operations Command, was forced to resign after making critical comments about the administration in Washington and its policies in Afghanistan. To help dampen the firestorm of criticism already erupting from across the political spectrum, the widely respected Petraeus was asked to take over, even though, as commander of U.S. Central Command, the new job would technically be a demotion. A good soldier to the end, Petraeus saluted smartly and took over command of both the International Security Assistance Force (ISAF), which is the NATO contingent in Afghanistan, as well as the U.S. Forces Afghanistan (USFOR–A).

British and U.S. Marine operations in Helmand Valley during 2009 secured numerous canal and river crossings in the Taliban's southern stronghold and, for the first time, established a permanent ISAF presence in the area. In the following year, further hard-won progress was made in Helmand as well as Kandahar province. Notably, a much higher degree of security was attained in Kabul province around the capital, where fully one in five of all Afghanis live. Numerous areas that had been considered safe havens by the Taliban were seized and secured by NATO, U.S., and Afghan forces, while the mid-level insurgent leadership suffered extensive losses during combat.

Going on the offensive has its costs and 2010 saw 499 Americans killed in action or died of wounds. A further 103 British and 109 NATO troops, 16 of them Canadian, were also killed. Looking back on the gains of recent years, General Petraeus reminded the troops that:

Our core objective here is to ensure that Afghanistan never again becomes a sanctuary for al Qaeda or other

BELOW: At Firebase Lindstrom, soldiers fire mortars on mountainside Taliban positions near the Nuristan province town of Barg-e Matal, Afghanistan. In 2009, Company C, 1st Battalion, 32d Infantry, of the 10th Mountain Division's 3d Brigade Combat Team regularly received small arms and RPG fire at dawn and again at dusk.

THE 7.62-MM M14 ENHANCED BATTLE RIFLE (EBR)

Not your grandfather's M14! Units in Afghanistan quickly found that half of their engagements occurred beyond the 200- to 300-yard effective range that the average rifleman can accurately target and bring down an enemy with the M16/M4's light bullet. Soon, each deploying squad was assigned an M14 for long range suppressive fire which makes even an ordinary marksman capable of taking out an enemy at up to (without optics) 750 yards with the weapon's heavy 7.62-mm round. Existing stocks of M14s were used—and received a wide variety of personal and unit modifications. By 2008, the Army began issuing the standardized M14EBR featuring an aluminum stock with upper, lower, and side accessory rails, adjustable comb, and adjustable buttstock length; a Harris bipod; vertical pistol grip; and a Leupold variable power scope. In 2010, the number of M14EBR-armed marksmen per squad was doubled, which, counting the two SAWs, gave each unit the power and flexibility of four long-range weapons.

BELOW: Task Force No Slack soldiers at Combat Outpost Badel in eastern Afghanistan's Kunar province prepare to return fire during an August 26, 2010, insurgent attack. No American or Afghan National Security Forces personnel were wounded. The men are members of the 101st Airborne Division's 2d Battalion, 327th Infantry.

transnational extremists. . . . Achieving that objective requires that we help Afghanistan develop the ability to secure and govern itself. This, in turn, requires the conduct of a comprehensive civil-military campaign, carried out in full partnership with our Afghan counterparts, to improve security, develop Afghan security forces, and support the establishment of good governance and economic development.

Many who have served in Afghanistan can't help but wonder, however, if their war, like Korea, might be on its way to becoming yet another "forgotten war." It was a commonly held assumption among soldiers that when the "anti-war" candidate won the 2008 presidential election, articles and casualty reporting would all but disappear from the front pages of newspapers unless they were tied to some spectacular event. The press did not disappoint them.

Lacking the screaming headlines of the long campaign in Iraq or the terrible cost of the Soviet's decade-long struggle in which 14,453 of their own troops, 18,000 Afghan Government soldiers, roughly 75,000 guerrillas, and upward of 600,000 civilians were killed, the hard fighting in Afghanistan has been largely invisible. Already it is America's longest war, but it remains to be seen if, as some soldiers and marines maintain, it is already a forgotten war. Perhaps their fellow Americans will prove them wrong.

ABOVE: Specialist Michael Scarsbrook, a Minnesota Guardsman with the 133rd Infantry, Task Force Ironman, looks down on a spot in Tupac, Afghanistan, where his unit was struck by an IED two days earlier on January 19, 2011. Task Force Ironman is a part of the 2d Brigade Combat Team, 34th Infantry Division, the "Red Bulls."

LEFT: As an Afghan soldier looks on at left, a local man from Nawbor Village in Baghdis Province talks through an interpreter to 4th Infantry Division Staff Sergeant Nicholas Lewis, a scout with White Platoon, Bulldog Troop, 7th Squadron, 10th Cavalry, on January 16, 2011. The man thanked the Afghan National Army and U.S. scouts for ridding his village of insurgents and bringing a better life to the Nawbor children, who gathered on the hill.

Epilogue

It wasn't supposed to work out this way. The idealistic vision of how wars would be conducted in the twenty-first century—where precision munitions, speed, and near perfect intelligence enabled the U.S. military to dominate every battlefield—was held fast by the army's leadership long after it was exposed as utterly false along the dusty roads and villages of Iraq and Afghanistan.

The main problem was that the enemy refused to cooperate. Instead of fighting in easily targeted formations as they were projected to in the computer simulations, insurgents took great care to reap the fullest advantage of the complex urban areas and natural terrain, which frequently rendered them beyond the reach of the U.S. military's most sophisticated technologies. The planned "Army Transformation" from a heavy Cold War force to a lighter structure was based on assumptions that ignored even the possibility that manpower-intensive—and *protracted*—campaigns would be the norm in the century's opening decade. This affected everything from the number of American "boots on the ground," to the quantity and types of vehicles available, to the tactics that insufficiently manned and resourced units were, by necessity, forced to employ.

Lacking enough troops to hold territory, U.S. forces in Iraq used technical intelligence and surveillance capabilities to locate and raid insurgent leaders and networks. Although these operations were often successful, the inevitable withdrawal after a mission left civilian populations vulnerable to coercion. Meanwhile, this same lack of troops necessitated that units be constantly on the road, increasing their vulnerability and losses to improvised explosive devices (IEDs) and ambushes. It wasn't until the number of U.S. troops was ramped up in order to maintain a presence in targeted civilian areas; Iraqi security forces had been trained in sufficient numbers to secure contested territory; and the population itself had turned against the cruel, fundamentalist insurgents, that victory was achieved.

Since the attacks of September 11, 2001, the ceiling on the number of volunteers to enter the army had slowly been raised, allowing the service to grow by roughly 90,000 soldiers. Though this has greatly relieved the strain on the force, the leadership, in and out of the army, was for years reluctant to begin this process even though it was also clear that the theoretical concepts of Transformation were delaying rather than hastening a successful conclusion to the campaign in Iraq. This modest expansion, together with the end of combat operations in Iraq, allowed a welcome—and needed—increase in the amount of "dwell time" that formations can retrain and refit at home, despite increased commitments to the campaign in Afghanistan. Meanwhile, the army continued to grapple with much the same dilemma as it has throughout America's brief nationhood. How should it structure itself? How should it fight future wars, be they large-scale confrontations between great powers, or murky counter-insurgencies? What is the most sensible balance of the science of war with the art of war?

In a move to "rebalance" the army away from its Cold War force structure, it has stood down about two hundred artillery batteries, tank companies, and air defense batteries, while standing up a corresponding number of Special Forces, civil affairs, and military police companies. This occurred throughout the same period that units were rotating in and out of Iraq, with little time for proper training between deployments, which has raised fears that another "hollow army" was in the making. Victory in Iraq and the increases in manpower, however, have helped open enough space between missions that instead of having only enough time to train in counterinsurgency operations before shipping out, soldiers can now polish up on the core tasks that make them the finest war-fighting team in the world.

The campaigns in Iraq and Afghanistan also brought home to the army that the countermeasures of a thinking enemy can place his intentions and the situation on the battlefield beyond the reach of technology. But while many aspects of the army's excursion into Transformation fell short of expectations, others have greatly enhanced its ability to fight and win. In spite of the fact that perfect situational awareness can never be fully achieved, rapid adaption to the unexpected, a large enough army to successfully carry out its missions, and appropriate training will enable the soldiers to serve their country well when the deadly business of war falls squarely on their shoulders. And it will, again and again, whatever advances technology might bring. Six decades after he fought among Korea's bloody hills, the words of a young officer, T.R. Fehrenbach, remain just as true today:

Americans in 1950 rediscovered something that since Hiroshima they had forgotten: you may fly over a land forever, you may bomb it, atomize it, pulverize it, and wipe it clean of life—but if you desire to defend it, protect it, and keep it for civilization, you must do this on the ground, the way the Roman legions did, by putting your young men in the mud.

LEFT: Members of the Honor Guard practice their moves prior to the start of the U.S. Army Chief of Staff change of responsibility ceremony at Fort Myer, Virginia, April 10, 2007. General George W. Casey took over as chief of staff from General Peter J. Schoomaker.

Appendix A
Medals and Decorations

Listed in order of precedence are medals for valor in combat and service and campaign awards. For those that are both heroic and meritorious, a small gold "V" device is added to indicate a medal awarded for combat. The Purple Heart is awarded for each wound sustained in combat. Small silver and bronze stars denote multiple awards.

Medal of Honor
Established: March 3, 1863

Army Distinguished Service Cross
Effective: January 2, 1918

Defense Distinguished Service Medal
Established: July 9, 1970

Army Distinguished Service Medal
Effective: January 2, 1918

Silver Star
Approved: August 7, 1942

Defense Superior Service Medal
Effective: February 6, 1976

Legion of Merit
Effective: September 8, 1939

Distinguished Flying Cross
Established: July 2, 1926

Soldier's Medal
Effective: July 2, 1926

Bronze Star
Effective: December 7, 1941

Purple Heart
Effective: April 5, 1917

Defense Meritorious Service Medal
Effective: November 3, 1977

Meritorious Service Medal
Effective: January 16, 1969

Air Medal
Effective: September 8, 1939

Joint Service Commendation Medal
Effective: January 1, 1963

**Army
Commendation Medal**
Effective: March 31, 1960

**Joint Service
Achievement Medal**
Effective: August 3, 1983

**Army
Achievement Medal**
Effective: April 13, 1981

**Prisoner of War
Medal**
Effective: April 5, 1917

**Army
Good Conduct Medal**
Established: June 28, 1941

**USAR National Guard
Achievement Medal**
Effective: August 11, 1969

**Women's Army Corps
Service Medal**
Effective: September 1, 1943–
September 2, 1945

**American Defense
Service Medal**
Effective: September 8, 1939–
December 7, 1941

**American Campaign
Medal**
Effective: December 7, 1941–
March 2, 1946

**European-African-
Middle Eastern
Campaign Medal**
Effective: December 7, 1941–
March 2, 1946

**Asiatic-Pacific
Campaign Medal**
Effective: December 7, 1941–
March 2, 1946

**World War II
Victory Medal**
Effective: December 7, 1941–
December 31, 1946

**Army Occupation
Service Medal**
Effective: April 5, 1946

**Medal for
Humane Action**
Effective: June 26, 1948–
September 30, 1949

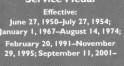

**National Defense
Service Medal**
Effective:
June 27, 1950–July 27, 1954;
January 1, 1967–August 14, 1974;
February 20, 1991–November
29, 1995; September 11, 2001–

**Korean Service
Medal**
Effective: June 27, 1950–
July 27, 1954

**Antarctica Service
Medal**
Effective: January 2, 1946

**Armed Forces
Expeditionary Medal**
Effective: July 1, 1958

Vietnam Service Medal
Effective: July 4, 1965–
March 28, 1973

Southwest Asia Service Medal
Effective: August 2, 1990–
November 30, 1995

Kosovo Campaign Medal
Effective: March 24, 1999

Afghanistan Campaign Medal
Effective: October 24, 2001

Iraq Campaign Medal
Effective: March 19, 2003

Global War on Terrorism Expeditionary Medal
Effective: September 11, 2001

Global War on Terrorism Service Medal
Effective: September 11, 2001

Korea Defense Service Medal
Effective: July 28, 1954

Armed Forces Service Medal
Effective: June 1, 1992

Humanitarian Service Medal
Effective: April 1, 1975

Outstanding Volunteer Service Medal
Effective: December 31, 1992

Armed Forces Reserve Medal
Effective: August 1, 1990

French Croix de Guerre Medal (World War I)
Authorized: April 8, 1915

Republic of Vietnam Gallantry Cross with Palm
Effective: March 1, 1961–
March 28, 1974

Philippine Defense Medal
Effective: December 8, 1941–
June 15, 1942

Philippine Liberation Medal
Effective: October 17, 1944–
September 3, 1945

Philippine Independence Medal
Effective: December 8, 1941–
September 3, 1945

United Nations Service Medal (Korean Service)
Effective: June 27, 1950–
July 27, 1954

Ribbon-Only Awards

United Nations Medal
Authorized: July 20, 1959

NATO Medal (For Service in the Former Yugoslavia)
Effective: July 1, 1992

NATO Kosovo Medal
Effective: October 13, 1998

Army Sea Duty Ribbon
Effective: 2006

Army NCO Professional Development Ribbon
Effective: 1981

Army Service Ribbon
Effective: 1981

Army Overseas Service Ribbon
Effective: 1981

Army Reserve Component Overseas Training Ribbon
Effective: 1984

Multinational Force & Observers Medal
Effective: August 3, 1981

Republic of Vietnam Campaign Medal
Effective: March 1, 1961–March 28, 1973

Kuwait Liberation Medal (Saudi Arabia)
Effective: January 17–February 28, 1991

Unit Commendations and Foreign Citations

When medals are worn on the left breast, these ribbons are worn on the right; otherwise they are integrated into all others according to seniority.

Army Presidential Unit Citation
Effective: 1942

Joint Meritorious Unit Award
Authorized: July 22, 1982

Army Valorous Unit Citation
Effective: 1963

Army Meritorious Unit Citation
Effective: 1944

Army Superior Unit Award
Effective: 1983

Kuwait Liberation Medal (Emirate of Kuwait)
Effective: August 2, 1990–August 31, 1993

Republic of Korea War Service Medal
Effective: June 25, 1950–July 27, 1955

Philippine Presidential Unit Citation
Effective: September 14, 1946

Korean Presidential Unit Citation
Effective: June 27, 1950–July 27, 1953

Vietnam Presidential Unit Citation
Effective: March 1, 1961–March 28, 1974

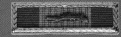

Republic of Vietnam Unit Citation Gallantry Cross
Effective: March 1, 1961–March 28, 1974

Republic of Vietnam Unit Citation Civil Actions
Effective: January 20, 1968–March 28, 1974

Appendix B
Campaign Streamers

The campaign streamers attached to the staff of a unit's national flag denote campaigns fought by the unit or its predecessor units throughout our nation's history. Each streamer (2¾ inches wide and 4 feet long) is embroidered with the designation of a campaign and the year(s) in which it occurred. The colors derive from the campaign ribbon authorized for service in that particular war. The concept of campaign streamers came to prominence in the Civil War when army organizations embroidered the names of battles on their regimental colors. This was discontinued in 1890, when units were authorized to place silver bands, engraved with the names of battles, around the staffs. When AEF units in World War I were unable to obtain silver bands, General John J. Pershing authorized the use of small ribbons bearing the names of the World War I operations. In 1921 all color-bearing army organizations were authorized to use the large campaign streamers.

REVOLUTIONARY WAR

Lexington
Ticonderoga
Boston
Quebec
Charleston
Long Island
Trenton
Princeton
Saratoga
Brandywine
Germantown
Monmouth
Savannah
Cowpens
Guilford Court House
Yorktown

WAR of 1812

Canada
Chippewa
Lundy's Lane
Bladensburg
McHenry
New Orleans

MEXICAN WAR

Palo Alto
Resaca de la Palma
Monterey
Buena Vista
Vera Cruz
Cerro Gordo
Contreras
Churubusco
Molino del Rey
Chapultepec

CIVIL WAR

Sumter
Bull Run
Henry and Donelson
Mississippi River
Peninsula
Shiloh
Valley
Manassas
Antietam
Fredericksburg
Murfreesboro
Chancellorsville
Gettysburg
Vicksburg
Chickamauga
Chattanooga
Wilderness
Atlanta
Spotsylvania
Cold Harbor
Petersburg
Shenandoah
Franklin
Nashville
Appomattox

INDIAN WARS

Miami
Tippecanoe
Creeks
Seminoles
Black Hawk
Comanches
Modocs
Apaches
Little Big Horn
Nez Perces
Bannocks
Cheyennes
Utes
Pine Ridge

WAR WITH SPAIN

Santiago
Puerto Rico
Manila

PHILIPPINE INSURRECTION

Tientsin
Yang-tsun
Peking

MEXICAN EXPEDITION

Mexico 1916–1917

WORLD WAR I

Cambrai
Somme Defensive
Lys
Aisne
Montdidier-Noyon
Champagne-Marne
Aisne-Marne
Somme Offensive
Oise-Aisne
Ypres-Lys
St. Mihiel
Meuse-Argonne
Vittorio Veneto

WWII — AMERICAN THEATER

Antisubmarine

WWII — ASIATIC-PACIFIC THEATER

Philippine Islands
Burma, 1942
Central Pacific
East Indies
India-Burma

ABOVE: Streamers are put on the Fort Sill army flag during the army birthday ceremony June 13, 2008.

Air Offensive, Japan
Aleutian Islands
China Defensive
Papua
Guadalcanal
New Guinea
Northern Solomons
Eastern Mandates
Bismarck Archipelago
Western Pacific
Leyte
Luzon
Central Burma
Southern Philippines
Ryukyus
China Offensive

WWII — EUROPEAN-AFRICAN-MIDDLE EASTERN THEATER

Egypt-Libya
Air Offensive, Europe
Algeria-French Morocco
Tunisia
Sicily
Naples-Foggia
Anzio
Rome-Arno
Normandy
Northern France
Southern France
North Apennines
Rhineland
Ardennes-Alsace
Central Europe
Po Valley

KOREAN WAR

UN Defensive
UN Offensive
CCF Intervention
First UN Counteroffensive
UN Summer-Fall Offensive
Second Korean Winter
Korea, Summer-Fall 1952
Third Korean Winter
Korea, Summer 1953

VIETNAM

Advisory
Defense
Counteroffensive
Counteroffensive, Phase II
Counteroffensive, Phase III
Tet Counteroffensive
Counteroffensive, Phase IV
Counteroffensive, Phase V
Counteroffensive, Phase VI
Tet 69/Counteroffensive
Summer-Fall 1969
Winter-Spring 1970
Sanctuary Counteroffensive
Counteroffensive, Phase VII
Consolidation I
Consolidation II
Cease-Fire

ARMED FORCES EXPEDITIONARY

Grenada 1983
Panama 1989–1990

SOUTHWEST ASIA SERVICE

Defense of Saudi Arabia
1990–1991
Liberation and Defense of
Kuwait 1991
Cease-Fire 1991–1995

KOSOVO CAMPAIGN

Kosovo Air Campaign 1999
Kosovo Defense Campaign

AFGHANISTAN CAMPAIGN

Liberation of Afgahnistan 2001
Consolidation I 2001–2006

GLOBAL WAR ON TERRORISM EXPEDITIONARY CAMPAIGN

Global War on Terrorism

IRAQ CAMPAIGN

Liberation of Iraq 2003
Transistion of Iraq
2003–2004
Iraqi Governance
2004–2005
Iraqi Governance
2004–2005
National Resolution
2005–2007
Iraqi Surge 2007–2008

Chiefs of Staff of the U.S. Army

ABOVE: A sea of "Firsties" march across the plain during the Graduation Parade, May 21, 2010, at West Point Military Academy. They are in the process of separating themselves from the rest of the Corps of Cadets prior to graduation. Of the thirty-seven generals who have held the post of Chief of Staff of the Army, all but ten are graduates from the Academy and one of those, George Marshall, graduated from the Virginia Military Institute (VMI).

NAME	SERVICE	FINAL RANK
Samuel B.M. Young	August 15, 1903–January 8, 1904	Lieutenant General
Adna Chaffee	August 19, 1904–January 14, 1906	Lieutenant General
John C. Bates	January 15, 1906–April 13, 1906	Lieutenant General
J. Franklin Bell	April 14, 1906–April 21, 1910	Major General
Leonard Wood	April 22, 1910–April 21, 1914	Major General
William Wallace Wotherspoon	April 22, 1914–November 16, 1914	Major General
Hugh L. Scott	November 17, 1914–September 22, 1917	Major General
Tasker H. Bliss	September 23, 1917–May 19, 1918	General
Peyton C. March	May 20, 1918–June 30, 1921	General
John J. Pershing	July 1, 1921–September 13, 1924	General of the Army
John L. Hines	September 14, 1924–November 20, 1926	Major General
Charles Pelot Summerall	November 21, 1926–November 20, 1930	General
Douglas MacArthur	November 21, 1930–October 1, 1935	General
Malin Craig	October 2, 1935–August 31, 1939	General
George Marshall	September 1, 1939–November 18, 1945	General of the Army
Dwight D. Eisenhower	November 19, 1945–February 6, 1948	General of the Army
Omar Bradley	February 7, 1948–August 15, 1949	General
J. Lawton Collins	August 16, 1949–August 14, 1953	General
Matthew B. Ridgway	August 15, 1953–June 29, 1955	General
Maxwell D. Taylor	June 30, 1955–June 30, 1959	General
Lyman L. Lemnitzer	July 1, 1959–September 30, 1960	General
George H. Decker	October 1, 1960–September 30, 1962	General
Earle G. Wheeler	October 1, 1962–July 2, 1964	General
Harold K. Johnson	July 3, 1964–July 2, 1968	General
William C. Westmoreland	July 3, 1968–June 30, 1972	General
Bruce Palmer Jr. (acting)	July 1, 1972–October 11, 1972	General
Creighton W. Abrams	October 12, 1972–September 4, 1974	General
Frederick C. Weyand	October 3, 1974–September 30, 1976	General
Bernard W. Rogers	October 1, 1976–June 21, 1979	General
Edward C. Meyer	June 22, 1979–June 21, 1983	General
John A. Wickham Jr.	July 23, 1983–June 23, 1987	General
Carl E. Vuono	June 23, 1987–June 21, 1991	General
Gordon R. Sullivan	June 21, 1991–June 20, 1995	General
Dennis J Reimer	June 20, 1995–June 21, 1999	General
Erik K. Shinseki	June 21, 1999–June 11, 2003	General
Peter J. Schoomaker	August 1, 2003–April 10, 2007	General
George W. Casey Jr.	April 10, 2007–	General

JOINT CHIEFS IDENTIFICATION BADGE

Appendix C
Branches of the U.S. Army

Enlisted, Infantry

LEFT: U.S. Military Academy First Captain Tyler Gordy (*foreground*) leads the brigade staff during the Acceptance Day Parade, August 15, 2010, at West Point, New York. Left to right behind their first captain are brigade staff cadets Edwin Mobley, Eric Bernau, and Ali Ihusaan. Gordy's road to West Point began as an infantry-man with the 101st Airborne Division (Air Assault). During a 2003 grenade attack on his two-vehicle patrol in Mosul, then-Sergeant Gordy, though wounded in the legs, one arm, and face, rushed with another soldier back into the kill zone to form a perimeter around another ser-geant whose legs had been shred-ded. They returned fire from the exposed position while other sol-diers put a tourniquet on the injured soldier and removed him from further danger. For his actions that day, Gordy received the Purple Heart and the Army Commendation Medal with Valor device.

BELOW: U.S. Military Academy Corps of Cadets pass in review during the 1992 Homecoming Parade of Cadets at West Point, New York. Above them is the Cadet Chapel, dedicated in 1910. Cadets make their choices for which branch of the army they would like to enter during Branch Selection Night, which is held in the fall of their senior year. They indicate their top three preferences and the army then assigns branches to each cadet based upon their class rank.

ENLISTED, NON-COMISSIONED OFFICER
Infantry

Enlisted, Engineer

Enlisted, Artillery

Enlisted, Air Defense

Enlisted, Armor

Enlisted, Cavalry

**Enlisted,
Military Intelligence**

LEFT: Paratroopers from Scout Platoon, 1st Battalion, 501st Parachute Infantry Regiment, get accustomed to water-borne operations during training on the Euphrates River in Iraq on February 5, 2007. The men are part of the 25th Infantry Division's 4th Brigade Combat Team (Airborne). Part of the 172d Infantry Brigade (Separate) during 2003–2004 operations in Afghanistan, the 501st was inactivated as part of the transformation of the 172d to a Stryker Brigade Combat Team. It was subsequently reorganized and redesignated as the 1st Battalion (Airborne), 501st Parachute Infantry Regiment and reassigned to the 4th Brigade Combat Team (Airborne).

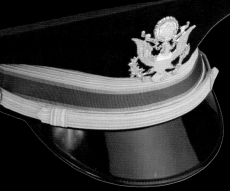
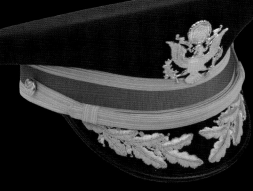

COMPANY GRADE OFFICER
Military Intelligence

FIELD GRADE OFFICER
Artillery

GENERAL OFFICER

Enlisted, Aviation

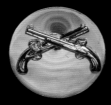
Enlisted, Military Police

Enlisted, Medical Corps

Enlisted, Ordnance

Enlisted, Adjudant General

Enlisted, Quartermaster

BELOW: Paratroopers from the 782d Brigade Support Battalion, 4th Brigade Combat Team, 82d Airborne Division watch as combat delivery system bundles carrying food and water float to the ground in the Paktika province of Afghanistan, October 11, 2007.

RIGHT: Combat vehicle crew helmet worn by Specialist Geoffrey Ives 1st Cavalry, Headquarters and Supply Company, 615 Aviation Support Battalion. Ives drove a fuel truck to support aviation missions during Operation Iraqi Freedom.

OPPOSITE LEFT: Flight helmet worn during Operation Iraqi Freedom by Chief Warrant Officer Joseph Luciano, 104th Attack Reconnaissance Battalion, 28th Infantry Division, Pennsylvania National Guard. Luciano used the call sign "Godfather" when operating out of the Special Forces camp at Ban Me Tuot, Vietnam, and again in Iraq.

Enlisted, Special Forces

Enlisted, Chemical

Enlisted, Finance

Enlisted, Chaplain Assistant

Enlisted, JAG Corps

Enlisted, Transportation

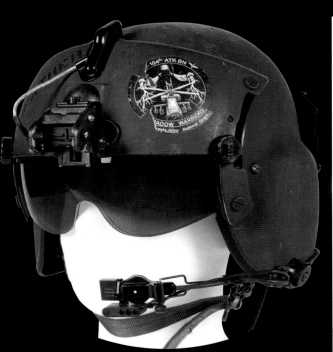

Enlisted, Signal

LEFT: A UH-60 Black Hawk crew chief in Iraq wearing a Gentex HGU-56/P rotary wing helmet, selected by the army in 2008 as standard issue for helicopter crews, on January 1, 2010.

BELOW: A UH-60 Black Hawk with lit cockpit under a full moon at Salah ad Din, Iraq. The airfield formerly served Saddam Hussein's massive palace complex in Tikrit.

Distinctive Unit Insignia (DUI) Pins

On these pages are a tiny fraction of the more than 3,100 Distinctive Unit Insignias recognized by the U.S. Army, and includes currently serving units as well as some that either no longer exist or whose heritage has become a part of those making up today's Active, National Guard, and Reserve.

5th Infantry Regiment

8th Infantry Regiment

9th Infantry Regiment

13th Infantry Regiment

14th Infantry Regiment

38th Infantry Regiment

503d Infantry Regiment

506th Infantry Regiment

187th Field Artillery Battalion

75th Ranger Regiment

25th Transportation Battalion

JFK Special Warfare Center

1st Special Forces

34th Armored Regiment

78th Signal Batallion

963d Field Artillery Battalion

955th Field Artillery Battalion

941st Field Artillery Battalion

880th Field Artillery Battalion

884th Field Artillery Battalion

806th Field Artillery Batallion

165th Infantry Regiment

181st Infantry Regiment

167th Infantry Regiment

137th Infantry Regiment

501st Aviation Brigade

317th Infantry Regiment

**313th Infantry
Regiment**

**306th Infantry
Regiment**

**7th Cavalry
Regiment**

**150th Cavalry
Regiment**

**160th
Special Operations
Aviation Regiment**

**2d Cavalry
Regiment**

**6th Cavalry
Regiment**

**3d Cavalry
Regiment**

**399th Infantry
Regiment**

**501st Infantry
Regiment**

**442d Infantry
Regiment**

**390th Infantry
Regiment**

**130th Engineer
Brigade**

**6th Infantry
Regiment**

**1st Engineer
Battalion**

**11th Armored
Cavalry Regiment**

**52d Air Defense
Artillery Regiment**

**310th Military Police
Battalion**

**382d Infantry
Regiment**

**406th Infantry
Regiment**

**415th Infantry
Regiment**

**2d Field Artillery
Battalion**

**10th Field Artillery
Battalion**

**26th Field Artillery
Battalion**

**4th Field Artillery
Battalion**

32d Signal Battalion

**31st Infantry
Regiment**

**40th Armored
Regiment**

**2d Engineer
Battalion**

**214th Aviation
Battalion**

Appendix D

Rank Structure of the U.S. Army

SPECIAL General of the Army (GA)

0-10 General (GEN)

0-9 Lieutenant General (GA)

0-8 Major General (MG)

0-7 Brigadier General (BG)

0-6 Colonel (COL)

0-5 Lieutenant Colonel (LTC)

0-4 Major (MAJ)

0-3 Captain (CPT)

0-1 Second Lieutenant (2LT)

0-2 First Lieutenant (1LT)

WARRANT OFFICER

Warrant Officer (WO1)

Chief Warrant Officer (CW2)

Chief Warrant Officer (CW3)

Chief Warrant Officer (CW4)

Chief Warrant Officer (CW5)

ENLISTED

E-1 Private (PV1)

E-2 Private (PV2)

E-3 Private First Class (PFC)

E-4 Specialist 4 (SPC)

E-4 Corporal (CPL)

E-5 Sergeant (SGT)

E-6 Staff Sergeant (SSG)

E-7 Sergeant First Class (SFC)

E-8 Master Sergeant (MSG)

E-8 First Sergeant (1SG)

E-9 Sergeant Major (SGM)

E-9 Command Sergeant Major (CSM)

Sergeant Major of the Army (SMA)

Photography Credits

Courtesy of the 812th Military Police Company
446 (MRE packs)

The Abell-Hanger Foundation and the Permian Basin Petroleum Museum
86–87

© AP Images
397 bottom; 474 top, Timothy Baker; 470 top, Zoran Bozicevic; 371, Gene Herrick; 405, Henri Huet; 399 bottom, Huynh Thanh My

Art Resource
44–45, 64, 84 (Grant), 85 (Jackson)

Barsanti Collection
404 (SPH4 helmet, inset bottom photo)

The Bridgeman Art Library
16, 17, 20 top, 27 inset, 35 (bed), 38 top, 40, 47, 59 top, 151 bottom

Brigham Young University, Lee Library, L. Tom Perry Special Collections
144–145 (MSS P Item 172), 145 top (MSS P Item 1), 152 (Godfrey, MSS P Item 50), 158 (MSS P Item 51), 159 top left (MSS P Item 56)

Amon Carter Museum
78 bottom, 78–79, 79 top right, 80–81

The Chapman Museum
19 bottom

Colorado Historical Society
144 inset

Congressional Medal of Honor Society
284 bottom, 316 left, 345 right, 381 top right, 385 top right, 387 bottom right, 416 left

Corbis
136, 152 top, 168 top left, 211 top left, 231 top, 238 top, 239, 256 inset, 261 inset left, 272 top left, 272–273, 287 top, 293 inset, 303 inset, 308 left, 316–317, 317, 318 bottom, 319, 320 left, 332 bottom, 336 inset, 342 top left, 362 inset, 363 inset top, 367 inset top, 370 top, 373 right, 387 left, 411 top, 413 inset top, 417 bottom, 421, 423 bottom, 424, 458 bottom; 433 top © Jean Louis Atlan/Sygma; 476, 499 © David Bathgate; 480 © Chris Helgren/Reuters; 479 bottom © David

Leeson/*Dallas Morning News*; 281 © The Mariner's Museum; 129 top © Minnesota Historical Society; 477 bottom © Joe Raedle/epa; 472 © Leif Skoogfors; 510 bottom © Joseph Sohm/Visions of America; 513 left and bottom © Stocktrek Images; 464 top, 469 top © Peter Turnley; 463 © Shamil Zhumatov/Reuters

Denver Public Library, Western History Collection
156 left (X-31744), 159 bottom (X-31538), 160–161 bottom (B-837)

© James Dietz
322 bottom, 327 bottom

Courtesy of General Wayne Downing
447

Mary Evans Picture Library
33

Courtesy of Colonel Gregory Fontenot
446 top, 450 top, 471 bottom

Fort Meade Museum
254

Fort Ticonderoga Museum
25

Getty Images
389; 464 bottom © Terry Ashe/Time Life Pictures; 475 © Oleg Nikishin; 516 © Joe Raedle; 286, 288 © George Strock/Time Life Pictures; 353 © Hank Walker/Time Life Pictures

D. M. Giangreco Collection
77 bottom, 85 top, 87 inset top and bottom, 120 bottom, 130, 160 top, 161 top, 175 top, 189 (belt), 203 inset bottom, 204 top, 213 top, 214 inset, 215 top, 218, 220 top, 221 top, 221 bottom left, 222, 229 (both), 230 bottom, 232 top, 235, 237 bottom, 245 top, 246–247, 248 (correspondence), 248–249, 252 (Eisenhower), 253 (MacArthur, Patton), 255 top, 258 top, 259 inset, 262 top, 262–263 bottom, 263 top, 265 (both), 267 (both), 268 (patch), 274 bottom, 276–277, 283, 284–285, 289 (both), 291 top, 293 bottom, 295, 299 (both), 301, 304, 307 (Soldier's Guide), 309 top and bottom, 312, 312–313 bottom, 314, 315 bottom, 318 top, 320 right, 333 top, 334 top and bottom, 335, 336 (correspondence), 337 bottom, 338–339, 340 top, 340–341 bottom, 342 right, 343 right, 347, 348 top and middle insets, 349 (patch, photograph), 351 inset, 354–355 bot-

tom, 356, 358 top and bottom, 359 bottom, 360, 361 (both), 363 (helmet), 364 top and bottom, 365 (all), 366, 367 bottom, 375 (all), 376–377, 378–379 (photographs), 380–381, 381 top left, 382 bottom, 385 left top and bottom, 386, 388 bottom, 388–389, 391, 392 (both), 393 (both), 395 right, 402–403, 406 top, 407, 408 top and bottom, 409 left, 410, 422 ("boonie" hat), 425, 426, 427, 428 (both), 429 (both), 430, 431 (all), 437, 439, 440 (both), 442 inset top, 443 top, 444 (both), 445 (both), 447, 449 bottom, 450 bottom, 451 (both), 452–453, 453 inset top, 454 (all), 455 top left, 456 bottom, 457 top, 459 top left and bottom, 460 bottom, 461, 467 top, 468, 470 bottom, 473 top and bottom

The Granger Collection
34, 77 inset

Harvard College Library, Theodore Roosevelt Collection
174–175 (R560.3.Scr 7-037), 179 top left (560.3-031)

The Historical Museum of Southern Florida
69 top

Courtesy of David Jolley
206

John Henry Kurtz Collection
88, 91 bottom, 95 (headgear), 96 (coat), 98–99 (rifle musket), 104 (enlisted and officer's kepis, coat), 105 (headgear), 106 (coat and bottom right), 109 (sword), 116 bottom, 125 (5th Corps insignia), 136–137 (rifle); 125 (II Corps insignia, 14th Corps insignia) © Don Troiani

Library of Congress
2, 5, 6–7, 8, 10, 19 top, 22, 24, 26–27, 30–31 top, 39 (both), 44–45 bottom, 51, 52 top, 54–55 (map), 65, 66 (both), 71 top, 78 top, 80 top, 83 bottom, 89, 90, 92–93 bottom, 94–95, 96–97, 98–99, 100 top left and bottom, 101 (both), 102–103 (both), 106–107, 108, 109 top left and background, 110 top, 111 top, 112–113 (all except drum), 114 (both), 115 top right, 117, 119, 120 top, 121 (all), 122 top, 123, 124–125, 125 portrait, 128, 129 top left and bottom, 131 top and bottom, 132 bottom, 138–139, 140 top, 141, 142, 144 top, 147 top left and right, 150 top, 151 (Crook, MacKenzie), 153 right, 154 bottom, 155 top right, 156 right, 170–171 bottom, 171 inset, 173 top and bottom, 174 inset, 178 right, 179 bottom, 180 top, 181 inset, 182

(portraits at left), 186–187 (both), 193 (poster), 194–195 (posters), 196 bottom, 202 (both), 203 (map), 207 (posters), 211 (poster), 212, 224 (poster), 226 top left and bottom, 240–241, 241 portrait and bottom, 244 (poster), 244–245 bottom, 246 top left, 249 inset, 250–251 bottom, 256–257 bottom, 257 top, 261 poster and bottom, 263 (poster), 264 bottom and right, 271, 272 bottom right, 278 bottom, 279 (all), 280, 282 left and right, 290, 355 top, 522–523

The Life and Art of Charles Schreyvogel
146 top and bottom

© Gary Lucy Gallery
55 top

Maryland State Archives
21 bottom

Massachusetts Historical Society
12

Courtesy of Michael McAfee
1, 96 left, 97 inset, 124 bottom left, 126 top

Minnesota Historical Society
118, 302 (master sergeant's jacket)

James C. Nannos Collection
16 (halberd), 20 (powder horn), 21 (powder horn), 22–23 (musket), 26 (drum), 31 (fife), 36 (cap), 41 (holsters and pistol), 42–43 (dragoon sword, harness), 48 (polearm), 56–57 (muskets), 58 (jacket), 59 (canteen, backpack), 67 (all artifacts), 68 (yeoman pattern shako, 1813 pattern shako), 69 (shakos), 70 (sergeant's sword), 75 (drums), 83 (bugle), 112 (drum)

National Archives
90 (telegram), 135, 147 bottom, 151 (Adams), 163, 169 top, 176–177, 181 top, 182 right, 182–183, 184 bottom, 185 left, 188–189, 190–191, 191 inset top, 192 top, 192–193 bottom, 193 top and middle, 194 bottom left and right, 195 bottom, 196 top, 197, 198 (both), 199 top (both), 207 bottom, 208 bottom, 209 bottom, 210–211 bottom, 216 bottom, 217 bottom, 220 bottom, 225 bottom, 226 top right, 230 top right, 232 bottom, 234, 236, 243, 246 inset top right, 247 inset top, 251 top, 253 top, 255 bottom, 259 bottom, 272 (poster), 276 top, 277 top, 287 bottom, 298 bottom, 300 bottom, 306, 315 top, 323 left, 324–325, 326 bottom left, 344–345, 346, 350 top, 350–351, 352, 354

(both), 359 top, 362–363, 369 (both), 372, 374, 376 bottom, 384, 398 top, 400–401, 401 top and inset right, 404–405, 412, 413 bottom, 414, 415, 418 top, 419 top, 520–521, 527

The National Cowboy Museum
148–149

National Guard Bureau
238, H. Charles McBarron; 12–13, 14–15, 42, 62–63, 227 © Don Troiani

The National Museum of the U.S. Navy
455 (Personnel Armor System Ground Troops Helmet)

The Naval Historical Foundation
273 inset, 313 top

The Neville Public Museum
46

The New York Public Library
76 bottom

The New York State Military Museum
92 top (flag)

New York State, Office of Parks, Recreation and Historic Preservation: New Windsor Cantonment State Historic Site
48 (Badge of Military Merit)

Ohio Historical Society
52 bottom

Private Collection
84 (Sheridan, Crook, Nugen, Thomas, Lee), 143 (both), 152 (Benteen, Custer, Calhoun), 157 bottom, 167 inset, 176 (Welborn), 189 (clip), 230 (Pierce), 233 (Bronson), 239 (Whittlesey, McMurtry, Holderman), 240 left, 241 (medal), 248 (insignia), 264 middle, 267 (patch), 268–269 (rank insignia), 274 (Bianchi, Wermuth, Ninnger), 275 top, 277 (leggings), 290 (mortar rounds), 297 (belt), 310 (patch), 323 right, 324, 327 (Ray, Lomell, Baumgarten), 328 left and inset, 328–329, 330–331, 331 left, 332 top, 333 bottom, 339 (both), 343 top left, 348–349, 350 (badge), 357 (medal), 364 (insignia), 398 (patch), 433 (patch), 458 (medal), 462 (medal), 475 (medal), 483 (badges),

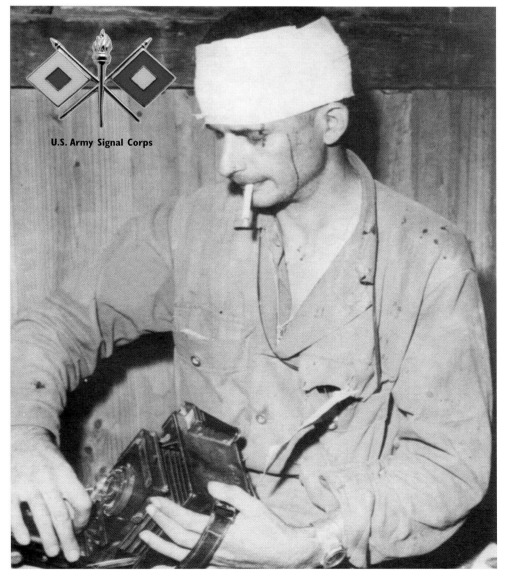

U.S. Army Signal Corps

LEFT: An army photographer on Okinawa prepares to return to the front after having a mortar wound bandaged, c. May 1945.

Index

Note: Page numbers in *italics* indicate illustrations.

BACKGROUND: Troop I, 8th U.S. Cavalry, 1889

BELOW: Japanese naval hero Admiral Togo Heihachiro with Major General Thomas Henry Barry, superintendent of the U.S. Military Academy, review cadets at West Point, New York, in August 1911.

BELOW: U.S. artillery dress helmet, M1872

Maggart, Lon E., *446*

Main Line of Resistance (Korea), 382, 388

Makin Atoll, 288

Manassas Junction, 98

Mangas Coloradas, 150

map cases, *230*

maps: Argonne Forest, 1918, *202–3;* Battle of Bladensburg, *65;* Battle of Chancellorsville, *108–9;* Battle of New Orleans, *66;* Boston (1775), *24;* Bunker Hill and Breed's Hill, *22;* Gettysburg, day 2, *112;* Mexico City, *83;* Mississippi River, *54;* Omaha Beach vicinity, *329;* route of Rochambeau's French Army, 1782, *44–45;* Saratoga, *30–31*

Mariana Islands, 285, 294, 354

Marines in Iraq, 489, 492

Marion, "The Swamp Fox" Francis, 40

Marjoram, Ernest, *287*

Mars Task Force, 292

Marshall, George C., *253, 318,* 351, *354, 355,* 356, *378*

Marshall Islands, 288

Maryland Militia, *62, 64*

Masland, Matthew Henry, *80*

Massachusetts Bay Colonial Militia, 12, *14–15*

Massaponax Church, Virginia, council of war, *122–23*

Maxim, Hiram, *186–87*

Maximilian, Archduke, 136, 137

McAuliffe, Anthony C., *337, 341,* 342

McCall, George Archibald, *85*

McCall, William H.H., *145*

McChrystal, Stanley, *499*

McClellan, George B., 84, 91, *92,* 94, 98, 102, 103, *103*

McColm, George, *269*

McColm, J. Edwin, *269*

McConnell, Ronald, *457*

McCoy, Frank R., *182, 182*

McDowell, Irvin A., 90, *90*

McElfish, Roy E., *276*

McFeaters, Charles Paul, *281*

McGrath, Hugh J., 183

McIver, George W., *167*

McKenzie, Edmund, *164*

McKinley, William, 180

McLane, Allan, 38

McMaster, Herbert R., *453*

McMurtry, George G., 239, *239*

McNair, Lesley J., *279*

Meade, G.W., *312*

Meade, George G., 109, *109,* 112, *114,* 114–15, *122*

Meals Ready to Eat (MRE), *446–47*

mechanization of the army, 192–93

medals and decorations, *504–7;* "Badge of Military Distinction" (Continental Army), 35, 48; "Badge of Military Merit" (Continental Army), 48, *48;* Close Combat Badge, *483;*

Combat Infantryman Badge, *350;* Combat Medical Badge, *483;* Distinguished Service Medal, *241;* Gettysburg's Medal of Honor recipients, *118–19;* Global War on Terrorism Expeditionary Medal, *475;* Indian Campaign Medal of 1907, *159;* Kuwait Liberation Medal, *458–59;* Medal of Honor, *158–59;* Medal of Honor, 1904, *179;* Medal of Honor, 1944, *284;* Purple Heart, 49, *357;* Silver Star, *484;* War on Terrorism Service Medal, *462;* World War I Victor Medal, *240*

Meeks, George, 349

Meredith, Solomon, 111

Merrill, Frank D., *291, 293*

Merrill's Marauders, 291–93, *293*

Merritt, Wesley, *141, 159, 176–77*

Meuse-Argonne Campaign, 233–41, 254

Mexican border, fighting along, 136–37, 250

Mexican Expedition, *189,* 190–99, 200

Mexican-American War, 76–85

Mexico City, Battle for, 82, 85

Miles, John, *57,* 165, 168

Miles, Nelson A., *143, 150,* 156

Military Assistance Command, Vietnam (MACV), 396

military police, *363*

Miller, James, 60–61

Miller, Robert J., 498, *498*

Millett, Lewis L., *378, 378*

Mills, Albert L., *179*

Mills, John, *10*

Milošević, Slobodan, 471, 473

Milton, John S., *113*

Mine Resistant Ambush Protected (MRAP) Vehicle, *493*

Minuteman, 12, 20, 24

missiles: Patriot missiles, *447;* Pershing IA missiles, *428*

Missionary Ridge, Battle of, 119

Mississippi Rifles, 82

modernization of the army, 258–59

Modoc uprising, *147,* 150

Mole, Arthur, *255*

Monmouth, Battle of, 40

Monongahela, Battle of, 15, *17*

Monroe, James, 28

Monroe Doctrine, 136, 137

Monte Cassino, 320

Monterey, Battle of, 77, 80

Montgomery, Bernard L., 310

Montgomery, Robert, 314

Moore, Elliott, *282*

Moore, Harold G., *401,* 402

Moreno, Hank, *492*

Morgan, Daniel, *30,* 31, 43, 60

Morgan, George H., *169*

Morgan's Rifles, *30,* 31

Mormons, 88

Moros, 177–79, *182–85*

Morristown, New Jersey, 48

Mosby, John S., *138–39*

Mott, T. Bentley, *167*

Mounted Rifles, U.S., 88

MOUT techniques, *443*

Mueller, Harry S., *4,* 8

Mueller, Paul J., *296, 357*

mules, *315*

Multiple-Launch Rocket System (MLRS), *445*

Mumbler, M., *31*

Munro, Nathaniel, *31*

Murphy, Audie, 344–45

Muse, Kurt, 440–41

musette bag, *323*

musicians, army, *31, 49, 137, 180, 225*

muskets. See firearms

Musselman, James A., *399*

Mussolini, Benito, 316

Nagasaki, *352*

Napoleon III, 136, 137

Nashville, Battle of, *129*

National Defense Act of 1916, *207*

National Defense Act of 1920, 256–57

National Guard, 202, 203, 256–57, 259, *260–61,* 382, 390, 498. See also specific divisions

NATO, 429–30

Neibaur, Thomas C., 240

Nemeth, Bruce, *495*

New Britain, 285

New Guinea, 280, 286–87, 288–89

New Mexico Volunteers, 145

New Orleans, Battle of, 65, 66–67, 67

Newsome, Joseph D., *404*

Nez Perce Indians, 158

Niagara Campaign, *60*

Nicaragua, 441

Nimitz, Chester A., 285, 288, 294

Nininger, Alexander R., Jr., *274*

Ninth Army, 351

Nixon, Richard M., 418, 425, 428

Noailles, Louis-Marie, *47*

Noriega, Manuel, 436–39, 440

Normandy, invasion of, 324–29

North Korea, 368–89

Northwest Indian War, 52–53

Northwest Territory, 50

nuclear battlefield, 392–93

Nugen, John, *84–85*

Nugent, Richard E., *359*

nurses, army, *317*

Obama, Barack, 498

Odierno, Raymond, 493, *494, 495*

Okinawa, 304–9, 354

Old Baldy, 387, 388

Operation Anaconda, 476, *477*

Operation Cobra, 330

Operation Desert Saber, 462

Operation Desert Shield, *442,* 444–49

Operation Desert Storm, 449–61, 462, 480

Operation Dewey Canyon II, 424

Operation Eagle Claw, 432

Operation Iceberg, 306

Operation Iraqi Freedom, 480, 484–85, 496

Operation Irving, *405*

Operation Jefferson Glen, 425

Operation Junction City, *411*

Operation Just Cause, 437–40

Operation Masher, *405, 406*

Operation New Dawn, 496

Operation Overlord, 324–29

Operation Provide Comfort, 465

Operation Restore Hope, 466

Operation Torch, 310

Operation Urgent Fury, *434,* 434–35

Ord, Jules G., 173

Organized Reserves, 256, 259

Osceola, 68, *69*

Otani, Kikuzo, *246–47*

"other duties," 260–63

Otis, Elwell S., 178

Otto, Bodo, compass of, *38*

outpost life, 160–61

Pakenham, Edward, 65

Pala, Datu, 183

Palmer, Charles D., *379*

Palo Alto, Battle of, *76,* 77

Panama, 436–39

Panama Canal, 395

Panama Canal Treaty, 437

Panzer Army (Germany), *342*

paratroopers, *322–23, 341,* 397, *436, 443, 511, 512*

Paris, Treaty of (1783), 50, 58

Paris, Treaty of (1898), 178

Paris Peace Accords (1973), 425

Parker, Quanah, 150

Parker, Samuel I., 228

Patch, Alexander M., *333*

Patton, George S. Jr., *242–43, 253, 254, 256,* 258, *278,* 310, 312, 315, *315,* 330, *332,* 333, *349, 359*

Paul, François Joseph, *44–45*

Pearl Harbor, 270, 272, *272–73*

Peglow, Art, *248*

Peleliu, 306

Pell, Harrison, *405*

Pemberton, John C., 96

Peninsula Campaign, *92–93, 94,* 98, *131*

Pequot Indians, 12

Percival, Arthur E., *354*

Perry, Oliver Hazard, 59

Pershing, John J., *173,* 177, *189,* 190, *190–91,* 192, 200, *202–3,* 203, 205, *212, 212,* 231, 233, 238, *240, 240–41,* 244, *245,* 252

Persian Gulf Command, *310*

Peterman, Jonas P., *225*

Petraeus, David H., *494,* 496, 498–99

Phelps, Noah A., *36*

Philippine Division, 272

Philippine Scouts, *264, 266, 269*

Philippines, the: Spanish-American

War, 170, 176–79, 182–85, 200; World War II, 270–77, 294, 298–303, 354

photography, first military, *78–79, 94–95*

Pickens, Andrew, 40

Pickett, George E., 115–17, 132–33

Pickett's Charge, *113, 116,* 116–17

Pierce, Palmer E., *230*

Pigut, Stanley, *248*

Pike, Zebulon, 54

Pisa-Rimini Line, *320*

pistols. See firearms

Plattsburgh, New York, military training camp, *186–87*

Plunkett, Thomas, *124*

pommel holsters, *41*

Pope, John, 98

Pope, Percy, 52

Pork Chop Hill, 387, 388

Porter, David Dixon, *87,* 96

Porter, Horace, 136

Posse Comitatus Act of 1878, 165

powder horns, eighteenth-century, *20–21*

Powder River War, 142

Powell, Colin L., *420,* 468

Prauty, Roman, *380*

Prescott, William, 22

Presentation Regimental Color (1821), *71*

presidential inauguration ceremony, *9*

Pressman, Aaron A., *276*

Price, Herbert H., *209*

Price, Sterling, 132

Prinas, H.D., *240–41*

Princeton, Battle of, *28*

prisoner rescue, 440–41

PT boats, 286

Pugh, Robert S., *485*

Pulaski, Casimir, 38

Pullman Strike of 1894, 168

Pusan Perimeter, 372–73

Putnam, Israel, 21, 22

Queen Mary, 362

Quitman, John, 85

Rabaul, 285, 286, 288

radio communications, *399*

railroad, U.S. military, 120, *120–21*

Ramirez, Andrew A., *474*

rank structure of the U.S. Army, *516–17*

Rawlins, John A., *122*

Ray, John, *327*

Reagan, Ronald, 434

Reconstruction, 137, 139, 162

recruiting posters: National Guard, *260–61;* post-World War I, *244;* pre-World War I, *194–95;* Vietnam-era, *426;* World War I, *2, 4,* 202, 207, *211;* World War II, *4, 6–8*

Red Cloud, 142

BELOW: 25th Infantry Division members of Headquarters Platoon, Company B, 1st Battalion, 27th Infantry, wade across a deep canal with weapons held high over their heads, May 13, 1968, in Vietnam.

BELOW: A 3d Armored Cavalry Regiment soldier scans the immediate area from behind a dried mud wall as he provides security during a patrol in an area outside of Mosul, Iraq, on January 4, 2008.